The State of Economics, the State of the World

The State of Economics, the State of the World

Edited by Kaushik Basu, David Rosenblatt, and Claudia Sepúlveda

The MIT Press
Cambridge, Massachusetts
London, England

This book was set in Stone Serif and Stone Sans by Westchester Publishing Services. Printed and bound in the United States of America.

Library of Congress Cataloging-in-Publication Data

Names: Basu, Kaushik, editor. | Sepúlveda, Claudia Paz, 1969– editor. | Rosenblatt, David, editor.
Title: The state of economics, the state of the world / edited by Kaushik Basu, Claudia Sepulveda, and David Rosenblatt.
Description: Cambridge, MA : MIT Press, [2019] | Includes bibliographical references and index.
Identifiers: LCCN 2018046336 | ISBN 9780262039994 (hardcover : alk. paper)
Subjects: LCSH: Economic development. | Information technology--Economic aspects. | Monetary policy. | Social change.
Classification: LCC HD82 .S8223 2019 | DDC 330.1--dc23
LC record available at https://lccn.loc.gov/2018046336

10   9   8   7   6   5   4   3   2   1

Contents

Preface

Kaushik Basu, David Rosenblatt, and Claudia Sepúlveda

Origin

We live in troubled times. Over the past decade, the world economy has been wracked by financial crises, sovereign debt problems, backlash from political conflict and migrant crises, and, recently, a rise in xenophobia and protectionism. These issues raise major questions about the state of the world and also about the ability of economics to take on such challenges. Are these many economic and political crises and flare-ups symptoms of some deeper, underlying issues? Is economics as a discipline failing us at this time of soul searching? These are the questions that many are asking and that prompted the conference at the World Bank on which this book is based. We decided to bring in some of the finest minds in the profession—economists who have shaped modern economics—to ponder the state of the field and the state of the world in a series of papers. The conference consisted of 2 days of deliberation: The papers were presented, a distinguished group of economists commented on the presentations, and a large audience engaged with them in conversation and debate. This book is the outcome of these 2 days of deliberation.

In the 1950s through the 1970s, neoclassical economics reached a reasonable consensus in the economics profession, at least in the "West." The United States and Western Europe experienced postwar rapid economic growth. Asia was still a sleeping giant in economic terms, the Soviet Union—with its particular economic system—was very much intact, and African countries were only beginning a wave of independence from colonial rule. Development economics focused on structural transformation along the lines laid out by Sir Arthur Lewis, and dependency theories also emerged that asserted that the global capitalist system was essentially rigged against the developing world. Despite the neoclassical consensus, some economists believed that advanced mathematical and engineering techniques could allow social planners to optimally set the path of economic growth and development.

Fast forward in history and one sees a very different evolution of the global economy over the past 25 years. The latest wave of globalization has led to the intensification of global value chains. Asia is now home to some of the most advanced economies on earth. It began with Japan, which was soon followed by Singapore, South Korea, Taiwan, and Hong Kong. By the mid-1980s, China was a growth leader, and in recent times, India and Vietnam are growing at exemplary rates. The Soviet Union no longer exists. Many middle-income countries—including those in Latin America—have achieved social progress, but dramatic income inequality persists, as do challenges to compete in the new global context. Africa has emerged from debt relief to achieve growth and reduced poverty rates, albeit at a variable and erratic pace. Rapid technological change provides both opportunities for technological leapfrogging as well as challenges to adapt.

As we see in this volume, the economics profession has adapted to the changing state of the world by learning from practical experience, challenging traditional assumptions, and developing new techniques and the use of big data. A predominant view in Western universities in the 1980s was that all economies were alike and that all developing countries needed to do was to "get prices right." Development economics languished as a field of study. Since then, as developing economies have gained more prominence on the global stage, development economics has become one of the most dynamic fields in economics—particularly in terms of new statistical techniques and the ability to blend economic theory with empirical methods.

Despite all these changes and adaptations, the financial crisis that started in 2008 and caused a protracted recession has left scars on the world economy that linger even today. These scars show that the economics profession still faces major intellectual and research challenges. Addressing such challenges was one of the motivations for our conference.

With time, the societal goals of economics and the normative presumptions underlying the profession have also shifted. From a narrow focus on gross domestic product, economists have come to recognize the need for a broader conception of human welfare and capability. Even the World Bank decided to broaden its mission goals from development and poverty reduction to a more direct targeting of inequality mitigation, which it refers to as the promotion of "shared prosperity." This book is an assessment of our discipline at the crossroad of all these changes.

We regret that Kenneth Arrow did not live to see the publication of this book. Kenneth Arrow was one of the greatest minds of our time, an economist who straddled like a colossus the second half of the past century and the opening years of this one, and who opened the conference with a presentation of enormous sweep. Ken Arrow passed away at the age of 95 on February 21, 2017, while he was working on completing his paper for this volume. He was in touch with us in our capacity as the volume editors until the last weeks of his life. After some deliberation, we decided to include his paper, despite it being an unfinished work. We did not want to put words into his mouth, nor leave out this final statement from him. We are grateful to Larry Summers for helping us edit the paper lightly; we also worked on it to make obvious corrections but took care not to change any of the original meanings. As a result, some parts of the paper are obviously incomplete. We hope that this chapter from an economist who helped shape so much of modern economics will be of value to all readers. Indeed, we believe that part I of this book—the three sweeping essays by Kenneth Arrow, Amartya Sen, and Joseph Stiglitz—will be viewed as a short summary of the theoretical foundations of modern economics.

Road Map

The Introduction that follows this Preface recounts the intellectual underpinnings that preceded the neoclassical consensus of the mid-twentieth century. This historical perspective reminds us of the role of theory and intuition in guiding our understanding of economics—even in the current age of more abundant data and more evolved statistical analysis. The Introduction makes the case that both theory and empirics are essential to closing key knowledge gaps and crafting policy that can enhance human well-being.

Thereafter, the book is organized in three parts. Part I deals with Foundations. Twentieth-century economic theory—or neoclassical economics—reached a pinnacle in the middle of the past century based on two pillars:

general equilibrium theory and welfare economics. Part I includes chapters by three Nobel laureates. Ken Arrow and Amartya Sen each provide a recounting of the two pillars of equilibrium and welfare. Chapter 1, Professor Arrow's contribution, is poignant, being published posthumously. It takes us through the origins of some of the key ideas of economic theory, going back to John Stuart Mill and Augustin Cournot and to the birth of the "demand curve," which would be such a central idea for so much of economics. Professor Arrow tells the history of economic thought that led to the formal characterization of general equilibrium and to a proof of existence and its optimality properties, which are enshrined in the two fundamental theorems of welfare economics. It was a monumental breakthrough for economics when he and Gerard Debreu published their 1954 paper in *Econometrica*.[1] In chapter 1 in this book, Ken Arrow points out how we need to be careful when jumping from these abstract ideas to policy decisions. He reminds us that economics is different from a science like astronomy: In economics, we are ourselves participants in the system that we are trying to understand. Thus, we are too close to the subject of our analysis. As a consequence, we might not see the whole picture, or our views might be biased.

Amartya Sen has done pioneering work on individual choice and social welfare, with fundamental research that lies at the intersection of economics and philosophy, a pointed example being his celebrated "liberty paradox," which has spawned a large literature in both disciplines. In chapter 2 of this book, Sen provides a history of the theory of rational decision-making and social welfare. He notes that the early theorists of the late eighteenth century were preoccupied with two concerns: avoiding authoritarianism and avoiding arbitrariness. Sen's chapter is a natural sequel to chapter 1 by Arrow. Just as Professor Arrow was a key figure in general equilibrium theory, he also provided the initial impetus for social choice theory, with his famous "impossibility theorem." Professor Sen, arguably the leading social choice theorist in the world, relates the work of Arrow to research going back to the work of John Stuart Mill in the nineteenth century. Turning to welfare economics, Sen starts with Pigou's classic 1920 book on the subject.[2] Unlike social choice theory, welfare economics' philosophical ori-

---

1. Arrow and Debreu (1954).
2. Pigou (1920).

gin lies in Bentham's utilitarian approach, and consequently, it focuses on the sum of the utilities of the individuals in the community. Sen notes that the disregard for the distribution of those utilities reflects "a partial blindness of considerable ethical and political import" and goes on to elaborate on how this neglect can be remedied. This major recounting of rational choice and welfare economics will be useful both for students of economics and philosophy, and for researchers trying to break new ground.

In chapter 3, Joseph Stiglitz summarizes the evolution of the economics of information and the role of information asymmetry in market failures, fields in which he himself has made seminal contributions. Much of early economics was based on the assumption of perfect information. The consumer knew what kind of good she was buying, the creditor knew exactly what the risks of lending to a person or a firm were, and the employer knew how good a worker he was hiring and also had full information on what the worker was doing when on the job. All these assumptions are of course wrong. But economists persisted with them, often in the belief that they were innocuous assumptions that made it easier to build models and make progress, but at times out of cussedness. In a series of papers, Joe Stiglitz showed that, first, the assumptions were not innocuous—they led to serious policy mistakes—and second, with patience and ingenuity, we could make room for imperfect and asymmetric information and still build formal models of analysis.

Some critical features of traditional economics (such as wage rigidities, excess supply of labor, and excess demand for credit), which in the works of Keynes and Arthur Lewis were assumptions, could now be explained endogenously. Thanks to Professor Stiglitz's early publications, this work is now part of the mainstream, and chapter 3 of this book provides a bird's-eye view of the background for this field.

Part II of the book consists of three chapters that deal with macroeconomic stabilization and growth. Developing countries have suffered multiple macroeconomic crises over the past three-quarters of a century. But the 2008–2009 global financial crisis that started in the United States, pummeled many rich countries, and then swept through developing economies has resulted in some deep soul searching in the profession of economics. One issue that has become clear to the economics profession, based on experience, is the close link between macroeconomic policies and the regulation and evolution of the financial system. In part II, Guillermo Calvo (chapter 4) and Hyun Song Shin (chapter 5) discuss new thinking on inflation and financial stability, respectively. Moving from short-run stabilization to long-run growth, theory has evolved beyond the original Solow model to endogenize Solow's careful accounting of the role of total factor productivity. Part II closes with chapter 6 by Philippe Aghion, which brings the reader up on the latest thinking on endogenous growth theory.

Guillermo Calvo's focus in chapter 4 is on more chronic but equally compelling matters. His concern is with two key macroeconomic phenomena that have occurred since the middle of the past century: chronic inflation and more recently, chronic deflation. From the perspective of the history of economic thought, Calvo draws on the role of rational expectations in macroeconomic theory and its role in helping us understand these phenomena. Although some rich countries experienced unusually high inflation in the 1970s, emerging markets suffered much more severe inflationary episodes, accompanied by debt crises. Macroeconomists initially attributed the emerging market crises purely to policy mistakes that affected the fundamentals for investing in those markets. However, the persistence and systemic nature of these crises led economists to think about the role of expectations in generating "sudden stops" of access to foreign capital. Guillermo Calvo, who pioneered this literature, is clearly in a special position to review it. In keeping with a recurring theme of this book, Calvo points to "intellectual inertia," triggered by traditional models working well to explain macroeconomic performance in high-income countries, as a probable cause of some our discipline's failings.

More than ever, financial market developments—including exchange rate movements—are impacting the real economy. As Hyun Song Shin puts it in "Global Liquidity and Procyclicality" (chapter 5), "the financial tail appears to be wagging the real economy dog." More specifically, exchange rates do not seem to adjust in the required direction to help eliminate external imbalances in key economies. Global financial markets have become highly integrated, implying that policy makers everywhere are focused on the next move of the US Federal Reserve Board. Anomalies in interest rates across currencies, the rise of the dollar in global transactions, and cyclical instabilities have been a focus of a lot of our attention, especially since the 2008–2009 financial crisis. Shin, a world authority on international finance, dissects and analyzes these concerns in a chapter that is of special interest in today's world, especially since the financial sector crisis of a decade ago.

Philippe Aghion has contributed to many areas of economic theory. One of his works that attracted an enormous amount of attention with an abundance of follow-up research is the "Schumpeterian theory of economic growth." Although nations strive to fulfill many different objectives, growth is a central concern of development economics, if for no other reason than as an enabler of some of our other aims and objectives. In chapter 6, Aghion starts from the Solow model, "the true template in growth economics," and goes on to use the Schumpeterian growth paradigm to shed light on a host of topics of contemporary interest. Thus, his chapter analyzes the relationship between competition and innovation-led growth; the possible causes of secular stagnation; and the recent rise in inequality, especially the gap between the super-rich and the rest.

Part III of the book is a set of four chapters brought together under the heading "New Areas of Research and Inquiry." These four chapters represent branches of economics that are relatively new. They are based largely on challenging the traditional assumptions of neoclassical economic theory and traditional approaches to empirical economics, as well as on the application of economics to emerging global concerns.

Chapter 7 is based on the lecture at the conference given by Nick Stern, the world's leading authority on environmental economics and the economics of climate change. The chapter provides an overview of the economics of climate change—perhaps the most pressing—and the most fractious—issue of our times, concerning all nations. Written jointly with Sam Fankhauser, chapter 7 provides a thorough overview of the unique threat to global prosperity that is posed by climate change. The authors review the history of environmental and natural resource economics. They then make the case for a "radical deepening of economics analysis" to accommodate sustainability concerns and guide the policy response to climate change. It is unfortunate that development policy traditionally did not focus on environmental issues, despite work on environment and natural resources dating back to the eighteenth and nineteenth centuries. The risks posed by climate change are staggering, and the options that we have are laid out with care in this chapter.

No stocktaking of modern economics is complete without an account of behavioral economics. Cass Sunstein is a leading authority on law and economics and on behavioral economics, with original works in both these fields. In chapter 8, Professor Sunstein provides an overview of behavioral economics, where the traditional approach of a rational *Homo economicus* is challenged by our understanding of human psychology and human behavior in the real world. It seems natural to presume that a nation's economic well-being depends on economic policy. It therefore took time for us to realize that many drivers of an economy lie outside economics, in social norms, cultural mores, and psychology. Behavioral economics, the subject of a recent *World Development Report* of the World Bank,[3] sensitized economists to these important influences that lie outside the discipline but are key determinants of development. Behavioral economics, including important contributions by Cass Sunstein, alert us to the fact that human beings are often irrational, and more importantly, that these irrationalities are often systematic. Understanding them can enable us to promote development more effectively.

Professor Sunstein's chapter is followed by another one dealing with a relatively new field of inquiry, the evolutionary prospects of economies and societies. Although the origins of evolutionary game theory go back to the early 1970s, the entry of this discipline into mainstream economics is more recent. One of the most prominent contributors to this field of research is Jorgen Weibull. In chapter 9, he and Ingela Alger discuss the role of morality and the evolutionary foundations of human motivation, showing that unqualified selfishness may be good for the individual in an immediate sense, but if acquired by all in a society, it sets that society on a course toward extinction. Morality, in the sense of Kant, is evolutionarily stable. That is, if all of us are prepared to forgo a little bit of our self-interest to uphold some of our collective interests in the Kantian sense, our society will be more robust in terms of surviving natural selection. Even apart from this reasoning, the ideas of evolution, once a preserve of biology, have now come into economics in a big way. Chapter 9 summarizes some of the most important ideas in this discipline for the wider community of economists and students of social science.

One of the most important advances in modern development economics is the use of randomized control trials (RCTs) to get at causal explanations of various policy interventions and alternative economic outcomes. Did the election of women as leaders of village councils play a role in the

---

3. World Bank (2015).

better provision of local public goods in India? Did deworming help school-children in Kenya attend school more regularly and do better in their studies? By bringing the method of RCTs from epidemiology to development economics, we can now hope to answer such questions with a clarity that we did not have earlier. The RCT has been a source of celebration, criticism, and controversy, but as a method in the toolkit of development economics, its value is undeniable. Chapter 10, which closes the book, is by Esther Duflo, written jointly with Abhijit Banerjee and Michael Kremer. Duflo's own research and publications played a critical role in the development of this field of research. She gives a detailed account of the rise of the field, its achievements, and some of its pitfalls.

Acknowledgments

We as editors thank a large group of individuals who helped carry out this megaproject, including the organization of the conference on June 8–9, 2016, at World Bank headquarters. Over and above the authors of the chapters, who presented papers at the conference and whose work we commented on above, there was a stellar cast of discussants, who read and commented on those papers and whose comments are included in this volume. Here is the list of discussants, in alphabetical order (to minimize discontent) to whom we are extremely grateful: Larry Blume, Francesco Caselli, Shanta Devarajan, James Foster, Varun Gauri, Xavier Gine, Gäel Giraud, Gita Gopinath, Robert Hockett, Karla Hoff, Ravi Kanbur, Aart Kraay, Aslı Demirgüç-Kunt, David McKenzie, Célestin Monga, Maurice Obstfeld, Hamid Rashid, Martin Ravallion, Luis Servén, and Mike Toman.

The chairs of the conference sessions were Augusto Lopez Claros, Makhtar Diop, Felipe Jaramillo, Ayhan Kose, Bill Maloney, Kyle Peters, Martin Rama, Ana Revenga, and Augusto de la Torre. We are grateful to them for conducting the sessions and also for their comments and ideas during the session.

We also thank Gabriela Calderón for her help in organizing a superb conference and the Development Economics Communication team for their help with disseminating information about the conference. We are also grateful to Gabriela Calderón and Trang Huyen Hoang for preparing the manuscript for submission to the MIT Press, as well as our references "police," Woori Lee and Ruth Llovet Montañes.

Finally, we take this opportunity to express our gratitude to our editor at the MIT Press, Emily Taber, for her help and cooperation at every stage and also her patience, as we crossed over some of our own deadlines in bringing this large project to a close.

References

Arrow, Kenneth J., and Gerard Debreu. 1954. "Existence of an Equilibrium for a Competitive Economy." *Econometrica* 22 (3): 265–290.

Pigou, Arthur C. 1920. *The Economics of Welfare*. London: MacMillan.

World Bank. 2015. *World Development Report 2015: Mind, Society, and Behavior*. Washington DC: World Bank.

Introduction: The State of Economics, the State of the World

Kaushik Basu

1776 and 1860

For the discipline of economics, and for the world at large, these are unusual times. The shock and awe of the financial crisis that began in the United States in 2008 and the series of economic fault lines it ripped open—from the sovereign debt crisis in the European Union to the massive slowdown in several emerging economies that we are currently witnessing—have led to much soul searching.

The past nearly two and a half centuries, from Adam Smith's *The Wealth of Nations* (1776) to the flourishing of empirical research and big data in current times, mark the astonishing rise of a discipline. From a broad, descriptive, and speculative subject, economics has come to acquire a common methodological foundation, mathematical structure, and a growing database. It has vastly enhanced our understanding of markets, exchange, money, finance, and the drivers of economic development.

How did this come to be? Where is economics headed? Will it be up to the diverse challenges of our times? Will global poverty be eradicated, or will it be exacerbated under the strain of a deteriorating environment? These are the questions we grappled with over the 2 days of the conference that is the basis of this book. The conference brought together some of the most prominent individuals who have, for better or for for worse (depending on your love or distaste for economics), played a role in making economics what it is today.

This essay is based on the opening remarks made on June 8, 2016, at the conference titled "The State of Economics, The State of the World," at the World Bank, Washington, DC. I am grateful to Alaka Basu, Oliver Masetti, Claudia Paz Sepulveda, and David Rosenblatt for comments and discussion.

There have been achievements in economics from well before 1776 to now. But for me, the transformational period of the discipline was the 100-odd years, starting from the second half of the nineteenth century. If you like birthdays, I have a date to propose to mark the birth of modern economics: February 19, 1860.

Stanley Jevons wrote a celebrated letter to his brother on June 1, 1860, saying that he had made a stunning discovery in the past few months that explained the "value" of different goods and gave him insights into "the true theory of Economy." He told his brother that so thoroughgoing and consistent was his theory that "I cannot now read other books on the subject without indignation" (Collison Black 1973, 410).

When exactly did he hit upon the idea? Historians of economic thought have drawn our attention[1] to a special entry in Jevons's diary, on February 19, 1860: "At home all day and working chiefly at Economy, arriving I suppose at a true comprehension of Value." Birthdays for scientific breakthroughs are always questionable. But if we can have Mother's Day, Valentine's Day, Administrative Professional's Day, I see no reason we cannot have Modern Economics Day, and February 19 would be my pick.

Of course, thinkers were already laying the foundations for Jevons's breakthrough. Gossen had worked out quite a lot of this a good one or two decades before Jevons. Cournot laid some of the substructure in 1838. And the law of diminishing marginal utility and its significance were described by Daniel Bernoulli as early as 1738, to solve the St. Petersburg paradox, which had been discovered in 1713 by Nicolaus Bernoulli. (And, yes, it was all in the family, Nicolaus being Daniel's brother.)

It is also important to note that although Stanley Jevons (1871) was clearly on to the main ideas of general equilibrium and value, he never quite got all the way there. We needed Léon Walras (1877) to put up the main structure. And for the full general equilibrium project to be completed, with the existence of equilibrium proved and its welfare properties spelled out, we needed to wait another 75 years for the seminal contributions of Kenneth Arrow.

By the time John Hicks, Paul Samuelson, Ken Arrow, Gerard Debreu, Lionel McKenzie, and others were doing their work,[2] modern game theory had been born. Over the next decades, the combination of a fully worked-out

---

1. See La Nauze (1953).
2. See Hicks (1939), Samuelson (1947), Arrow and Debreu (1954), and McKenzie (1959).

general equilibrium system, game theory, and a little later, social choice, ideas of asymmetric information and adverse selection, endogenous price rigidities, theories of economic growth and development economics, and the first understandings of the rudiments of monetary policy would transform the landscape of economics.

Few activities in life are as innately joyous as the pursuit (and if one is lucky, the discovery) of new ideas, the unearthing of patterns in the abstract space of concepts and numbers or in the world of data and statistics. Frontline researchers must have the space, like artists and composers, to do what they do as an end in itself. The greatest benefits of research are usually a by-product of this freedom. But here at the World Bank, our preoccupation is much more down to earth and is driven by policy needs. Hence, what we wanted to take away from the conference was how we can draw on the best of economics to promote development and sustained, inclusive growth, and contribute to making the world a better place. The World Bank's research and data analyses have been enormously influential, reaching the desktops of finance ministers and policymakers all over the world; indeed, a special responsibility comes with this influence.

At the time of this writing, I have been chief economist of the World Bank for nearly 4 years. This conference and the book are an opportunity to share some of my concerns and questions with the distinguished gathering at the conference and also with a wider readership. The hope is that the conference and its proceedings (to wit, the present book) will strengthen the World Bank's mission of promoting development.

Because the World Bank's engagement is primarily with development economics, it may be worthwhile to point out that development economics, like economic theory, has had its moments of epiphany. Arthur Lewis had been troubled by two problems. First, there was the age-old question of why industrial products, such as steel, were so much more expensive than agricultural products. Second, why were some countries persistently poor, while others were so rich?

In an autobiographical essay, Lewis (1980, 4) writes about his eureka moment in 1952: "Walking down the road in Bangkok, it came to me suddenly that both problems have the same solution. Throw away the neoclassical assumption that the quantity of labor is fixed. An unlimited supply of labor will keep wages down, producing cheap coffee in the first case and high profits in the second. The result is a dual national or world economy." This epiphany was the genesis of his classic paper on dual economies in the

Manchester School (Lewis 1954), which would play a major role in his being awarded the Nobel Prize in 1979[3] and in triggering research on development economics.

Intuition and Causality

I turn now, more specifically, to the subject of development policy. For the project of converting research to good policy, we need three ingredients: data (and evidence), theory (and deductive reasoning), and intuition (and common sense).

One of the great achievements of economics in recent decades has been in the area of empirical analysis. We have good reason to celebrate the rise of data and our ability to analyze data using different methods: from intelligent bar charts, through simple regression analysis and structural models, to randomized control trials. This recent success raises the hope of economics becoming a truly useful science (see Duflo and Kremer 2005; Banerjee and Duflo 2011).

There is, however, a propensity among some economists to dismiss all theory as esoteric.[4] Among other dangers, we run the risk of making our discipline inefficient. Suppose we insisted that Pythagoras could only use empirical methods. Would he ever have gotten to his famous theorem? The answer is: He might have. If he had collected a large number of right-angled triangles and measured the squares on their sides, he might have hit on the conjecture of the two smaller squares adding up to the one on the hypotenuse. But this approach would be extremely inefficient. Moreover, there would be a lot of debating and dissent. Some would charge him with using a biased sample of right-angled triangles, all from the Mediterranean region. "Would it work in the Arctic, in the Southern Hemisphere?" they would query.

We must acknowledge that many truths can be discovered more efficiently and more compellingly using pure reason. Further, there is a great

---

3. This idea, combined with the rise of modern growth theory (see Arrow 1962; Lucas 1988; Romer 1994; Ray 1988; Aghion and Howitt 2009), has given us insights into the development process and development policy that were unthinkable even a few decades ago.

4. For one of the best discourses on the strengths and vulnerabilities of economic theory, see Rubinstein (2006).

deal of sloppiness in the way we reason about the use of evidence. For instance, hard-headed practitioners will often tell you the following: "If we do not have any evidence about whether some policy X works, we must not implement X." (I was told exactly this fairly recently, in response to a suggestion I made.)

Let me call this rule in quotes an "axiom." To see that it is an unreasonable axiom, observe that if we do not have any evidence about whether X works, then we also do not have any evidence about whether not-X works. But because we have to do either X or not-X, the original axiom has to be flawed.

For good policy, we need facts and evidence, but we also need deduction and reasoning. We can go a step further and make a case for using mathematics. Although the use of mathematics can be overdone (as has happened in economics), the immense achievements of Cournot (1838) and Walras (1877), and of modern economics, would not have happened without it. This is because mathematics is a disciplining device, even though it is demanding and clearly not something that is applicable in all situations. As Krugman (2016, 23), not being able to make up his mind whether a particular argument of Mervyn King (2016) was right, observes, "words alone can create an illusion of logical coherence that dissipates when you try to do the math."

The power of doing a model right, even if it is abstract and uses assumptions that may not be real, can be seen from general equilibrium. Take Gerard Debreu's (1959) classic *The Theory of Value*. This book is of great beauty, as spare as poetry. In some ways, it is comparable to the work of Euclid, for it brings together in a systematic way an amazing range of ideas. Euclid may not have been as original as Pythagoras or Archimedes, but in bringing intellectual order to a scattered discipline, he had few peers, and he served an enormous role in the progress of knowledge. Likewise for Debreu's slim book.

The pathbreaking general equilibrium model of Walras, Arrow, and Debreu provided a template that sparked off some of the most original works in microeconomic theory—notably those by Akerlof and Stiglitz—which have to do with modeling the functioning of markets under imperfect information.[5] These works have greatly enhanced our understanding of micromarkets; why markets fail; and why prices are often endogenously rigid, resulting in credit markets with excess demand and labor markets

---

5. See Arrow (1963), Akerlof (1970), Stiglitz (1975), and Stiglitz and Weiss (1981).

with excess supply. This research also has hopes of improving our macro-economic analysis, because, as we know, Keynesian macroeconomic analysis, like Arthur Lewis's dual economy model, makes extensive use of price rigidities, and neither Keynes nor Lewis had an explanation for these rigidities. Thanks to the work of Stiglitz and a few others, we now have a formal understanding of open unemployment and credit markets that do not clear despite the absence of exogenous restrictions on interest rate movements.

Along with these positive theories, we have seen the rise of normative economics. Perched between analytical philosophy, mathematical logic, and the social sciences, this achievement was remarkable. Major contributions were also made by Samuelson (1947), Bergson (1938), and others, but the truly astonishing breakthrough was Ken Arrow's (1951) slim book: *Social Choice and Individual Values*. Arrow's impossibility theorem became the bedrock of an enormous research agenda. The leading figure here was Amartya Sen, whose work, straddling philosophy and economics, demonstrated that it is possible to bring the finest traditions of theory and mathematical logic to bear on age-old questions of ethics and normative principles (Sen 1970; see also Suzumura 1983). This work brought into the mainstream of rigorous analysis such concepts as rights, which were widely talked about but seldom subjected to careful scrutiny (Sen 1996). This body of work has been important for the World Bank, because its mission goals have foundations in such concepts (World Bank 2015b) and also in related country-specific research (Subramanian and Jayaraj 2016).

It is worth digressing for a moment to note that data and statistics belong to a larger domain of inquiry, which has to do with description. The term "descriptive social science" is often treated as a pejorative, which is unfortunate. As Amartya Sen (1980) points out in a powerful essay, developing a good description is not easy, and a huge amount of the progress of science depends on description. Description, be it in words or data, entails choice. Description is not regurgitating everything we see around us. We have to pick what is vital and make that available to others. How we describe and what we describe shape our understanding of the world. The "describer" is therefore a pivotal agent.

It is important to be aware that description can take many forms. What the anthropologist describes often does not take the form of numbers and data. But the description of what he or she has seen and, more importantly, experienced is vital for our understanding of the world. The concept of "thick description"—which we owe to Gilbert Ryle (1968) and Clifford Geertz (1973) and used by umpteen anthropologists—has vastly enhanced our understanding of traditional and remote societies. It has enabled us to intervene more effectively. At times this intervention has been for the wrong reasons (for instance, to enable colonial domination), but it has also helped carry the development agenda further by extending the reach of modern medicine and education.

Historically, we have learned of the motivation and purpose of other lives, which are distant from ours, by the ardor and work of anthropologists. These topics are very difficult to learn and comprehend by data and statistics alone. Living with the subject and acquiring an intuitive understanding are often necessities. This knowledge has been put to good and bad uses, to help the poor living in distant lands and in traditional societies, and also to exploit people and spread imperialism and colonial control. For good or for bad, the knowledge has been useful.

The absence of such knowledge can create major handicaps. Consider terrorism. Because of the dangers associated with observers interacting with terrorist groups, we do not have studies of the kind anthropologists have provided for remote societies, resulting in an insurmountable knowledge gap.

The skeptics, from Pyrrho to David Hume and Bertrand Russell, were right: Neither fact nor deduction can take you all the way to the best policy to implement. The reason is that causality, regardless of whether it is present, can never be demonstrated. In the end, causality lies in the eyes of the beholder. For me, the most thought-provoking observation on this comes from a tribesman from Nepal. The famous National Geographic photographer, Eric Valli, seeing the tall trees these tribesmen climbed to gather honey, asked one of them whether they ever fell out of those trees. The answer he received was: "Yes, you fall when your life is over."[6]

Given the impossibility of discovering causality, for good policy, it is not enough to have the facts; it is not enough to combine facts with theory. I am convinced we need one more ingredient: common sense and what I have elsewhere called "reasoned intuition" (Basu 2014).

Researchers refuse to admit it, but it is true that there is no escape from the use of intuition, and the bulk of what we call "knowledge" that we

---

6. This quote, as well as the argument on causality, which is more intricate than may appear from these brief remarks, are taken from Basu (2014, 458).

acquire through life occurs casually, mainly by using common sense. It would be a mistake to insist that all knowledge has to be rooted in scientific method, such as controlled experiments. It is quite staggering to consider the number of things a child learns through nonscientific methods.

As to why such knowledge, acquired through intuition and common sense, may have value, we have to recognize that our intuitions are what they are because of evolution. These methods have survived natural selection, and so their power must not be dismissed out of hand. Evolution has shaped a lot of what we see in our economic life; this is widely acknowledged, but our understanding of the interface between evolution and economics, for which some foundations were laid by Maynard Smith and Price quite some time ago (see Maynard Smith and Price 1973; Weibull 1995) remains rudimentary. There is a foray into this topic in this book (see chapter 9) in the context of morality and its origins (see also Alger and Weibull 2013). But it is arguable that such innate knowledge acquision applies to many other domains. The way people commonly acquire knowledge may not meet the test of scientific standards, but it cannot be dismissed out of hand. At the same time, casual empiricism can lead to superstitions, which we have to guard against. I have argued elsewhere (Basu 2014) that what we need is "reasoned intuition," that is, the use of intuition vetted by reasoning. This is not a surefire method, but it is the best we can do.

Data, theory, and intuition are the three ingredients for human knowledge and progress. But even with all three in place, skepticism, as philosophers through the ages have reminded us and as Keynes (1936) did in chapter 12 of *General Theory*, must be a part of the thinking person's mindset. One problem with scientists who lash out against superstition but do not question scientific knowledge is the double standard. They fail to recognize that, when it comes to certainty about the future, scientific wisdom is as much open to question as many other forms of knowledge.

Knowledge and Caveats

We are heading into uncharted territory and struggling with the world's economic problems. Recent problems include United Kingdom's vote in favor of exiting the European Union (I suspect this important issue will persist for some time) and the decline in commodity prices (especially that of oil), which is creating a lot of stress in commodity exporting nations and in corporations that have invested in this sector. Questions are being raised about the readiness of the discipline of economics to address such issues. The first thing to recognize, however, is not that economists misread or underestimated these crises, but how these problems show that there is still a lot about the economy that we do not know.

Experts in any discipline suffer from the disadvantage of not knowing exactly what it is they do not know. Take, for instance, medicine. Given how little we know about the human body and brain, when we consult a doctor with health problems, in most cases the right answer for the doctor to give is: "I have no idea." But we seldom hear this. Doctors almost invariably tell you what your problem is. What should warn you that when doctors say they know what your ailment is, they in fact often do not is that, even in the eighteenth century, well before the arrival of modern medicine, doctors seldom said they had no idea what ailed the patient. This is because doctors in the eighteenth century did not know—and doctors now do not know—what they did not and do not know. It is much the same with economists.

Among the areas of darkness that hamper development policy is our inability to link the micro and the macro. Suppose a government undertakes some intervention X in a thousand villages. X can be a conditional cash transfer, an employment creation program, or provision of a fertilizer subsidy. How do we evaluate the success of the program in reducing poverty? Typically, we do this by collecting data on the well-being of the people in these villages. If we are fussy, we may use all kinds of controls, including proper randomization. Suppose, through such a study, it is found that poverty has indeed gone down in the villages where X was implemented. Does this mean X is a good intervention? Not necessarily. Suppose the intervention X in a village has the following effect. It raises food prices a little and raises wages more. This will indeed lead to lower poverty in the village. But because a rise in food prices typically cascades across the whole economy, this intervention could mean that in other villages, which will only feel the full rise in food prices and a negligible effect on wages, poverty will rise. So it is entirely possible that the nationwide effect of the intervention will be no effect on poverty or even an increase in poverty, though poverty falls in the villages in which the interventions occurs.

These links between micro interventions and macro effects are poorly understood. We need to invest much more in this kind of research if we are to succeed in battling nationwide and even global poverty and to combat inequality.

In other micro-theoretic areas, such as finance and the psychological foundations of human behavior, economics has made great strides, as discussed in this book.[7] But open questions still exist. In finance, it is increasingly recognized that there is no such thing as an ideal regulation. This is because financial products are amenable to endless innovation. Banks and financial organizations will keep developing new products, just as the pharmaceutical industry keeps discovering new drugs. And with each such financial innovation, we may need to modify and make our regulatory regime more sophisticated. Hence, this is one area where we have to reject the language of optimal regulation, which has a static connotation, and to create regulatory bodies that are flexible and ready themselves to innovate. This effort is complicated by the fact that when selecting financial products, people are often not rational and instead give into emotions, hyperbolic discounting, and framing delusions, as pointed out repeatedly in the recent behavioral economics literature.

One possibility is to label certain financial products as "prescription goods" and create the equivalent of doctors in finance, who have to sign off before a person is allowed to buy a financial product. We could, for instance, decide to allow balloon mortgages, but before a consumer can commit to one, he or she has to get a "finance doctor" to sign off on the financial viability of taking on such a contract. This cannot be done by mechanically following practices in medicine, but a case can be made for giving serious thought to such an architecture.

The interface between economics and psychology, and, more specifically, behavioral economics, has witnessed great strides; and we at the World Bank have tried recently to bring this progress to bear on the agenda of development policy with our *World Development Report on Mind, Society, and Behavior* (see World Bank 2015a). By drawing on evidence from laboratory experiments and field observations from around the world, behavioral

---

7. For an elegant example of how economic theory can be brought to bear on a compelling idea in finance and financial crisis (namely, the phenomenon of infection, which has been widely noted, whereby one economy, seemingly unconnected to another, infects it with financial panic), see Morris and Shin (1998).

economics teaches us a lot about how and where we should intervene.[8] However, this discipline might risk becoming a catalog of findings. I call this a risk because of a propensity to think of the findings as set in stone, not realizing that they may be true in some societies at certain stages of development and might differ with place and time.

What is also needed is an effort to marry these findings more effectively with the concept of equilibrium (Akerlof and Shiller 2015). Then we would be able to leverage these findings to get much more out of them and also be able to predict better how the findings are likely to change from one society to another and to evolve over time. To my mind, one of the great contributions of traditional economics is the idea of equilibrium, which has many manifestations, from the general competitive equilibrium to Nash. We need to broaden the description of individuals from the narrow *Homo economicus* to that of more realistic individuals (with quirks, irrationalities, and social norms) and to use the idea of equilibrium in conjunction with this more realistic description.[9] What makes this effort intellectually challenging is that for most real phenomena, which seemingly rely on human irrationality or adherence to social norms, it is possible, with analytical ingenuity, to accurately model the same behavior using perfectly rational individuals.[10] In the end, better modeling calls for the use of judgement and intuition when deciding what assumptions we should rely on.

The World Bank has been increasingly engaged in this difficult area. Given the current drift of global concerns, we do not have a choice. These concerns naturally lead to another related field beyond the narrow confines of economics, that is, institutions and governance.[11] Our *World Development Report on Governance and the Law* (see World Bank 2017) takes on this

---

8. See Kahneman (2000), Thaler and Sunstein (2008), and Hoff and Stiglitz (2016).

9. For a very interesting paper that that attempts this, see Hoff and Stiglitz (2016). Earlier, Gintis (2009, chapter 10) provided an elegant model of bringing together the idea of human sociality and economic equilibrium in a unified game-theoretic discourse.

10. For an ingenuous exercise in this type of modeling, see Myerson (2004). Behavior, which at first sight seems so obviously driven by an irrational adherence to norms, can be explained as rational behavior in a more complex setting.

11. The importance of this field is stressed by Bourguignon (2015) in analyzing the African experience. As he stresses, this analysis is much more than an academic exercise. It is germane to the design of successful policy interventions.

challenging task.[12] One important area of policy making is the control of corruption, a big task faced by those at the helm of policy. Traditional economics treated an act of corruption (e.g., whether to pay a bribe to get an illegal electricity connection) on par with any other purchasing decision (e.g., whether to buy an apple)—that is, as an exercise in narrow cost-benefit analysis (see Bardhan 1997; Mishra 2006). It is not surprising that we have been so singularly unsuccessful in controlling corruption. To understand this phenomenon, it is important to bring in psychology and political institutions. Development policy cannot be built on economics alone.[13]

Finally, one area in which we have knowledge gaps but not as much as conservative commentators make out, is the connection between climate change and development. If we proceed the way we have done thus far, it is a journey headlong into disaster. This is unfortunate, because awareness of the connection between environmental resources and economic development came early, as evidenced in the works of Thomas Malthus, David Ricardo, Knut Wicksell, and others, even though we have been tardy in terms of action and policy. In recent times, the importance of this connection has been stressed by several authors, notably by Stern (2007, 2015).

---

12. The challenge of this task is captured well in the short essay by Green (2016), which points to the necessity of delving into this arena if we want to do economic policy right, and to how hard it is to do, because it ruffles feathers and is intellectually such treacherous terrain. Academic research that addresses governance and political institutions with the sharp scalpel of analysis is still relatively rare, but see Dixit (2009) and Acemoglu and Robinson (2012).

13. Here I give the example of corruption to illustrate the need for multiple disciplines, but the need is quite ubiquitous in today's world of strife and conflict. An excellent example is the Middle East. It is difficult to explain what is happening there purely in terms of economic indices, from gross domestic product through poverty to various measures of inequality and polarization. As Devarajan and Mottaghi (2015) argue, what is happening, in essence, is a breakdown of a social contract, which, like plumbing, goes unnoticed when it functions well but is always important. One can go further and look at areas that seem squarely situated in the domain of economic problems, such as the subject of poverty and inequality mitigation, which is central to the World Bank's work. Is it enough to rely on market forces and natural economic growth? Careful econometric studies of countries that have been most successful in this, such as Brazil, show that we have to go beyond these phenomena. Ferreira, Ravallion, and Leite (2010), for instance, find hard evidence that changing social security practices and increasing social assistance expenditure by the federal government was critical, and in fact happened because of the 1988 Constitution.

Now with the Paris Agreement of 2015, there is a platform to relate what we know on the subject with action on the ground, which is not easy, because it entails some cross-country coordination. It is worth stressing here that this engagement should be viewed very much as part of shared prosperity, because it entails intergenerational sharing of resources and well-being.

Money and the Person of Influence

The previous section discussed some gaps in our knowledge. One big gap is in the area of monetary policy. Although economics has made some dramatic breakthroughs in some practical areas (such as how to design auctions and how to micromanage demand and supply in sectors), its grasp of the impact of macroeconomic and especially monetary policy interventions is rudimentary. It is true that we have learned to manage hyperinflation, and we can hope never to see again, at least in advanced economies with sophisticated central banks, the kind of runaway inflation seen in, for instance, Hungary in 1946 and Germany in 1923. But as the global financial and growth crisis that began in 2008 continues unabated, and governments and central banks flail at this with different policies, it is evident that large gaps exist in our understanding of the impact of macroeconomic policies, and the linkage between the financial and real worlds (Stiglitz 2011). This is something I learned by fire, during my nearly 3 years as a policy maker in India (from 2009 to 2012). Although monetary policy was not my charge, it became clear during this time that much of our interventions were based on imitating policies followed by central banks in advanced economies, unmindful of the fact that their contexts differed.[14]

One reason for this deficiency is that we do not understand the functioning and role of money in a market economy the way we understand, for instance, the Walrasian general equilibrium system for real goods and services. Money in general equilibrium was part of a big research agenda in the 1980s, but that agenda has remained incomplete. One reason is that it

---

14. I discuss this in my recent book (Basu 2015), where I also argue for the need to make more experimental policy interventions in emerging economies, which would allow them to collect their own data and use these to develop their own, more context-specific policies.

is mathematically a very hard problem. But it must not be abandoned for that reason. In the rush to solve the next morning's problem, often these deep questions take a back seat. But as the world struggles to cope with the slowdown, and the widespread use of negative interest rates does not seem to work (and in fact has a negative backlash from which no country is able to individually break out of), it is important for economists to keep working on some of this fundamental research.[15] If the full general equilibrium model took some 75 years—from Jevons and Walras to Arrow and Debreu—and the study of money in equilibrium started in earnest in the 1970s and 1980s, we have little reason to abandon the problem as unsolvable.

To see the mystifying nature of money, one can look at a very different problem—the power of peddlers of influence. With the US presidential election in the offing, there was a lot of writing about lobbying, influence peddling, and corruption. In my youth in India, I remember talk about "persons of influence," referred to those days as "men of influence." I recall being baffled by one particular person and wondered why he was so well off. He had no special skill, no resources. He was just the man of influence (let me call him "M"). In those days, it took a wait of 6 years to get a phone connection. If you needed it sooner, you could try calling M and requesting his help. He would call up the relevant person in government; and more often than not, the favor would be done. If someone needed to get a child into a good school, she could ask M, and if M agreed, he would request the school principal to make an exception and take in this kid out of turn. It struck me much later what he was doing and I wrote it up as a model of the man of influence (Basu 1986). M was a person with a mental ledger of favors done. If i needed something from j, whom she did not know, she could ask M to ask j. Then j would do the favor, not because j cared for i or ever expected to need a special favor from i, but because j knew that someday he would need a favor from k and would need M to make a request of k. It is M that no one wanted to offend, because M was a clearinghouse with a memory. This is what made M a man of influence. In some sense, a person of influence is like money or a blockchain. It is a record of information and works only because everybody thinks it will work.

This description and even the model is straightforward enough. But its integration into a full general equilibrium model is extremely hard and

---

15. Some of the fundamental questions in this area are raised in Calvo (1996).

remains an open agenda, thereby handicapping policy makers greatly and forcing them to rely more on intuition and guesswork than hopefully will be necessary in the future.

Politics and Economics

When discussing development policy, I have been stressing the role of economic theory and empirical economics—in brief, input from professional, scientific analysis. The lack of this input dooms many a developing economy. But it is not always easy to marry scientific analysis with the ground realities of politics. Maybe because I moved so abruptly from academe to policy making, I cannot be unmindful of the importance of the role of how one engages with politics and politicians. When I moved from Cornell University to the Indian government at the end of 2009, I quickly became aware of the potential conflict between the prescription coming from theoretical economics and political compulsions. One quickly learned that when a politician tells an economist, "You are so good at theory," it is meant to be a devastating criticism.

I have recounted in Basu (2015) how, at one of my first meetings in my new job with the prime minister and some of his advisers, I was discussing how to control food inflation, which was then at double digits. I spoke at some length on changing the manner in which food reserves are released in India to get the maximum dampening effect on prices. I basically drew some policy lessons from the logic of Cournot equilibrium. I was delighted that my suggestion was accepted, which, I now believe, owes as much to my not uttering the words "Cournot" or "equilibrium" as to Cournot's excellent theorizing.

One gets a fascinating glimpse of the interface between the world of economic ideas and political compulsions in developing countries from Arthur Lewis's experience as chief economic adviser to the Ghanaian government. He was invited to take this position by Kwame Nkrumah, the country's first prime minister and president. The United Nations and the United States tried to block this appointment on the grounds that Lewis was "not very sympathetic to the Bank [the International Bank for Reconstruction and Development, commonly referred to as the World Bank]" (Tignor 2006, 147). There were also concerns, such as the one expressed by A. W. Snelling, an official in the British government, that "Lewis is a socialist, but a moderate one" (Tignor 2006, 148).

Lewis's tenure began extremely well, with Nkrumah personally excited at the prospect of Lewis steering the Ghanaian economy to a takeoff. On taking office, Lewis plunged into work, especially related to the second Five-Year Plan, with widespread support from others in government. But soon Lewis's idea of what constitutes good economics and Nkrumah's insistence on political compulsions came into conflict. Seemingly small differences of opinion— for instance, whether to spray cocoa trees that had been attacked by capsid beetles (pardon me for having forgotten who took which side)—became the cover for deeper conflict: the professional economist's insistence on good economics and the politician's stubbornness about what is politically good.

Lewis left office at the end of 1958, with Nkrumah's letter, gracious but recognizing that they could not work together, in his pocket: "The advice you have given me, sound though it may be, is essentially from the economic point of view, and I have told you on many occasions, that I cannot always follow this advice as I am a politician and must gamble on the future."[16]

Interests and Ideas

Some months after I moved from academe to the Indian government, a reporter asked me: What was the one thing that I had learned in this transition? Unusually for a question of this kind, I had an answer. The reader may recall Keynes's beautiful observation on the power of ideas, which ended with the following: "I am sure that the power of vested interests is vastly exaggerated compared with the gradual encroachment of ideas" (Keynes 1936, 283–284).

As an academic, I loved the observation but did not believe in it, viewing it as the self-serving remark of a professor. It was only after I joined the Indian government and sat in interminable meetings with ministers and bureaucrats that I came to believe in Keynes's observation.

Ideas play an unbelievably important role, and so those in the business of ideas have a special responsibility. As a consequence, I view this conference and this book not just as an intellectual contribution but as a critical ingredient for the work that is meant to be done in an organization such as the World Bank.

---

16. Nkrumah to Lewis, December 18, 1958, quoted in Tignor (2006, 173).

References

Acemoglu, Daron, and James A. Robinson. 2012. *Why Nations Fail: The Origins of Power, Prosperity, and Poverty*. New York: Crown Publishing.

Aghion, Philippe, and Peter W. Howitt. 2009. *The Economics of Growth*. Cambridge, MA: MIT Press.

Akerlof, George A. 1970. "The Market for Lemons: Quality Uncertainty and the Market Mechanism." *Quarterly Journal of Economics* 84 (3): 488–500.

Akerlof, George A., and Robert J. Shiller. 2015. *Phishing for Phools: The Economics of Manipulation and Deception*. Princeton, NJ: Princeton University Press.

Alger, Ingela, and Jörgen W. Weibull. 2013. "Homo Moralis—Preference Evolution under Incomplete Information and Assortative Matching." *Econometrica* 81 (6): 2269–2302.

Arrow, Kenneth J. 1951. *Social Choice and Individual Values*. New York: Wiley.

Arrow, Kenneth J. 1962. "The Economic Implications of Learning by Doing." *Review of Economic Studies* 29 (3): 155–173.

Arrow, Kenneth J. 1963. "Uncertainty and the Welfare Economics of Medical Care." *American Economic Review* 53 (5): 941–973.

Arrow, Kenneth J., and Gerard Debreu. 1954. "Existence of an Equilibrium for a Competitive Economy." *Econometrica* 22 (3): 265–290.

Banerjee, Abhijit V., and Esther Duflo. 2011. *Poor Economics: A Radical Rethinking of the Way to Fight Global Poverty*. New York: Public Affairs.

Bardhan, Pranab. 1997. "Corruption and Development: A Review of Issues." *Journal of Economic Literature* 35 (3): 1320–1346.

Basu, Kaushik. 1986. "One Kind of Power." *Oxford Economic Papers* 38 (2): 259–282.

Basu, Kaushik. 2014. "Randomisation, Causality and the Role of Reasoned Intuition." *Oxford Development Studies* 42 (4): 455–472.

Basu, Kaushik. 2015. *An Economist in the Real World: The Art of Policymaking in India*. Cambridge: MIT Press.

Bergson, Abram. 1938. "A Reformulation of Certain Aspects of Welfare Economics." *Quarterly Journal of Economics* 52 (2): 310–334.

Bourguignon, François. 2015. "Thoughts on Development: The African Experience." In *The Oxford Handbook of Africa and Economics: Volume I, Context and Concepts*, edited by Célestin Monga and Justin Yifu Lin, 247–270. Oxford: Oxford University Press.

Calvo, Guillermo A. 1996. *Money, Exchange Rates, and Output*. Cambridge, MA: MIT Press.

Collison Black, R. D. 1973. *Papers and Correspondence of William Stanley Jevons, Volume II*. London: Macmillan.

Cournot, Antoine. 1838. *Recherches sur les Principes Mathématiques de la Théorie des Richesses*. Paris: L. Hachette.

Debreu, Gerard. 1959. *The Theory of Value: An Axiomatic Analysis of Economic Equilibrium*. New Haven, CT: Yale University Press.

Devarajan, Shantayanan, and Lili Mottaghi. 2015. "Towards a New Social Contract." *Middle East and North Africa Monitor*, April. Washington, DC: World Bank.

Dixit, Avinash K. 2009. "Governance Institutions and Economic Activity." *American Economic Review* 99 (1): 5–24.

Duflo, Esther, and Michael Kremer. 2005. "Use of Randomization in the Evaluation of Development Effectiveness." In *Evaluating Development Effectiveness*, edited by George K. Pitman, Osvaldo N. Feinstein, and Gregory K. Ingram, 205–231. New Brunswick, NJ: Transaction Publishers.

Ferreira, Francisco H. G., Martin Ravallion, and Phillipe G. Leite. 2010. "Poverty Reduction without Economic Growth? Explaining Brazil's Poverty Dynamics, 1985–2004." *Journal of Development Economics* 93 (1): 20–36.

Geertz, Clifford. 1973. *The Interpretation of Cultures*. New York: Basic Books.

Gintis, Herbert. 2009. *The Bounds of Reason: Game Theory and the Unification of the Behavioral Sciences*. Princeton, NJ: Princeton University Press.

Green, Duncan. 2016. "The World Bank Is Having a Big Internal Debate about Power and Governance. Here's Why It Matters." *Oxfam Blogs*, July 26. https://oxfam blogs.org/fp2p/the-world-bank-is-having-a-big-internal-debate-about-power-and -governance-heres-why-it-matters/.

Hicks, John R. 1939. *Value and Capital: An Inquiry into Some Fundamentals and Principles of Economics*. Oxford: Oxford University Press.

Hoff, Karla, and Joseph E. Stiglitz. 2016. "Striving for Balance in Economics: Toward a Theory of Social Determination of Behavior." *Journal of Economic Behavior and Organization* 126 (June): 25–57.

Jevons, William S. 1871. *The Theory of Political Economy*. London: Macmillan.

Kahneman, Daniel. 2000. *Choices, Values, and Frames*. Cambridge: Cambridge University Press.

Keynes, John Maynard. 1936. *The General Theory of Employment, Interest, and Money*. London: Macmillan.

King, Mervyn. 2016. *The End of Alchemy: Money, Banking, and the Future of the Global Economy*. New York: W. W. Norton & Company.

Krugman, Paul. 2016. "Money: The Brave New Uncertainty of Mervyn King." Review of *The End of Alchemy: Money, Banking, and the Future of the Global Economy*, by Mervyn King, *New York Review of Books*, July 14, 21–23.

La Nauze, John A. 1953. "The Conception of Jevon's Utility Theory." *Economica* 20 (80): 356–358.

Lewis, Arthur W. 1954. "Economic Development with Unlimited Supplies of Labour." *The Manchester School* 22 (2): 139–191.

Lewis, Arthur W. 1980. "Biographical Note." *Social and Economic Studies* 29 (4): 1–4.

Lucas, Robert E. 1988. "On the Mechanics of Economic Development." *Journal of Monetary Economics* 22 (1): 3–42.

Maynard Smith, J., and George R. Price. 1973. "The Logic of Animal Conflict." *Nature* 246 (5427): 15–18.

McKenzie, Lionel W. 1959. "On the Existence of General Equilibrium for a Competitive Market." *Econometrica* 27 (1): 54–71.

Mishra, Ajit. 2006. "Corruption, Hierarchies and Bureaucratic Structures." In *International Handbook on the Economics of Corruption*, edited by Susan Rose-Ackerman, 189–215. Cheltenham, UK: Edward Elgar.

Morris, Stephen, and Hyun Song Shin. 1998. "Unique Equilibrium in a Model of Self-Fulfilling Currency Attacks." *American Economic Review* 88 (3): 587–597.

Myerson, Roger B. 2004. "Justice, Institutions, and Multiple Equilibria." *Chicago Journal of International Law* 5 (1): 91–107.

Ray, Debraj. 1988. *Development Economics*. Princeton, NJ: Princeton University Press.

Romer, Paul M. 1994. "The Origins of Endogenous Growth." *Journal of Economic Perspectives* 8 (1): 3–22.

Rubinstein, Ariel. 2006. "Dilemmas of an Economist Theorist." *Econometrica* 74 (4): 865–883.

Ryle, Gilbert. 1968. *The Thinking of Thoughts*. Saskatoon: University of Saskatchewan.

Samuelson, Paul A. 1947. *Foundations of Economic Analysis*. Cambridge, MA: Harvard University Press.

Sen, Amartya K. 1970. *Collective Choice and Social Welfare*. San Francisco: Holden Day.

Sen, Amartya K. 1980. "Description as Choice." *Oxford Economic Papers* 32 (3): 353–369.

Sen, Amartya K. 1996. "Rights: Formulation and Consequences." *Analyse & Kritik* 18 (1): 153–170.

Smith, Adam. 1776. *An Inquiry into the Wealth of Nations*. London: Strahan and Cadell.

Stern, Nicholas H. 2007. *The Economics of Climate Change: The Stern Review*. Cambridge: Cambridge University Press.

Stern, Nicholas H. 2015. *Why Are We Waiting? The Logic, Urgency, and Promise of Tackling Climate Change*. Cambridge, MA: MIT Press.

Stiglitz, Joseph E. 1975. "The Theory of 'Screening,' Education, and the Distribution of Income." *American Economic Review* 65 (3): 283–300.

Stiglitz, Joseph E. 2011. "Rethinking Macroeconomics: What Failed, and How to Repair It." *Journal of the European Economic Association* 9 (4): 591–645.

Stiglitz, Joseph E., and Andrew Weiss. 1981. "Credit Rationing in Markets with Imperfect Information." *American Economic Review* 71 (3): 393–410.

Subramanian, Sreenivasan, and Dhairiyarayar Jayaraj. 2016. "The Quintile Income Statistic, Money-metric Poverty, and Disequalising Growth in India: 1983 to 2011–12." *Economic & Political Weekly* 51 (5): 73.

Suzumura, Kotaro. 1983. *Rational Choice, Collective Decisions, and Social Welfare*. Cambridge: Cambridge University Press.

Thaler, Richard H., and Cass R. Sunstein. 2008. *Nudge: Improving Decisions about Health, Wealth, and Happiness*. New Haven, CT: Yale University Press.

Tignor, Robert L. 2006. *W. Arthur Lewis and the Birth of Development Economics*. Princeton, NJ: Princeton University Press.

Walras, Léon. 1877. *Éléments d'économie Politique Pure ou Théorie de la Richesse Sociale*. Lausanne: Corbaz.

Weibull, Jörgen W. 1995. *Evolutionary Game Theory*. Cambridge: MIT Press.

World Bank. 2015a. *World Development Report 2015: Mind, Society, and Behavior*. Washington, DC: World Bank.

World Bank. 2015b. *A Measured Approach to Ending Poverty and Boosting Shared Prosperity: Concepts, Data and the Twin Goals*. Policy Research Report. Washington, DC: World Bank.

World Bank. 2017. *World Development Report 2017: Governance and the Law*. Washington, DC: World Bank.

I   Foundations

1 Equilibrium, Welfare, and Information

Kenneth Arrow

Kenneth Arrow passed away on February 21, 2017, before he could complete this paper, which is based on his lecture at the World Bank conference. In a phone conversation on February 17 with one of us, he said he expected to complete the manuscript within a month, but that was not to be. We are immensely grateful to Larry Summers, who worked on the transcript of Ken Arrow's lecture, editing it lightly, and made this publication possible. We, as editors of the volume, have subsequently added some minor edits. It was our conscious decision to do minimal work on Ken Arrow's transcript, even at the risk of the text reading somewhat colloquially. As a last statement from him, we expect this paper to be an important document and were keen to maintain the texture of his voice. It is also clear that during the lecture, he ran out of time and so in some sense, this paper is not complete. That must have been the reason that Ken Arrow was keen to work on it before submitting it for publication. We do not have that choice now. But, as editors, we expect that his fascinating reflections on how modern economics came to be what it is, and his assessment of the weaknesses and strengths of modern economics, as well as his views on various historical figures in economics, will be of wide interest.

—Editors

I was asked to talk today about equilibrium and welfare. The word "information" was not in my suggested title, but as I shall argue, issues regarding information are fundamental to understanding the problem. I won't go into technical questions of existence theorems. What I really want to do is to remark on what exactly the point of equilibrium theory is. What question are we asking? How does it contribute to our economic knowledge, to our understanding of the economy? Inevitably, given the many aspects of these questions, my remarks will be a bit scattershot.

One of the questions is: Why do people talk in equilibrium terms? What is the purpose of relying on the notion of equilibrium? Well, knowing about the economy is a little different from knowing about astronomy, because it's part of our daily life. Astronomy is something you have to study. You have to stop and look at the stars. You have to watch what's going on. Whereas we are part of the economy.

It reminds me of the story of an astronomer who used to take summer vacations hiking. He went to the Pyrenees, France, and ran across a shepherd. They decided to walk together for a while and have dinner together. The astronomer was trying to explain what it was he did. He pointed at the stars and said, "Well tomorrow they're going to be in this different position." The shepherd listened. "Marvelous," he said, "I see the point. Since I follow my sheep and I know where they are, I know if I'm missing one, he probably went down that valley. So, I can see if you spend enough time, you'll begin to know where the stars are. But the one thing I can't understand is how do you know their names?" The story captures some of what we think about when we think of the difference in the positions of astronomers and economists.

We are part of the economy. For us, the economy is not like the stars are to the astronomer. The economy is a part of our everyday life; we observe it from the perspective of a participant. This creates advantages of proximity. But there is the disadvantage that we are too close in many ways. So, we are likely to see only one aspect, and even that aspect we do not see in a very unbiased fashion.

One thing, however, every day observation tells you is that somehow, I'm provided goods; I don't really worry that they won't be there. They're usually there when I want to buy them. My house is there, rented or whatever. When I go to the store, there's butter. Or, if you're up to date, there is some healthier kind of spread for you. But whatever it is, it's there.

Early History

Goods and services are available in a straightforward way. I may look at the price I have to pay, but that's all I ever have to know. I don't know how they make this stuff. I don't know where it comes from. This aspect of economic life goes back a long time. In the great days of Athens, the most traveled and most knowledgeable person about the world was Herodotus. And when he was writing his history of the Persian wars, he actually went all around the known world or the eastern Mediterranean, as we'd look at it today. He writes on the subject of bronze. You make bronze by mixing copper and tin. Well, copper comes from a lot of places, but tin comes from very few. In fact, if you look at what we know about the ancient world, tin either came from Iran or it came from Cornwall. Cornwall is a long way from the eastern Mediterranean.

Tin from Cornwall, as we now know, was brought to what we now call Marseille. The Gaelic merchants rafted it down to Rome and sold it. The Greeks had no idea where it came from. They didn't even know—at least at the time of Herodotus—they didn't even know there was an island now called "Britain." They didn't know it existed. All they knew was they paid their price to the Gaelic merchants and bought their tin, and that was the tin that was used for making bronzeware. And of course, the modern world has these transactions multiplied n-fold.

So, we see a relatively smooth operating mechanism. We see it's regulated by prices, and prices, for the most part, aren't arbitrary. Firms, when they sell things, don't make 500% profit. They make—most of the time—some normal level of profit. So there seem to be some rules, and it's these observations that motivate the development of economic theory dating from the time of Adam Smith or even earlier. In fact, some people ascribe quite a bit of the development of economic theory to the medieval commentators who were concerned with the concept of profit and worried about excessive profit. A vast literature seeks to interpret Smith, but it was this mechanism and the "normal" level of prices that he had in mind when he famously spoke of the invisible hand.

This leads naturally to the question of how prices affect behavior, a topic that really did not come up at the time of Adam Smith or immediately after. But one thing that was already stressed in Smith, and I suppose, some of his predecessors, was the importance of competition. The idea that you really cannot make supernormal profits because somebody will see a profit opportunity. Now they didn't spell out how this works. Presumably, if you have high profits, other people enter, and of course, other people can cut the price a little bit to take the trade. The implication in Smith is that it's more about entry than about firms explicitly moving prices. So, a demand function must be implicit in the story. Yet you have no explicit notion of a demand function in Smith, his immediate successors, or Ricardo.

It was implicit and became explicit in the post-Jevons era that there's a circular flow element. Somehow, there are primary factors that enter into production. Production then goes on, and the goods are delivered, and they are bought by other producers or consumers. So the prices paid for the primary factors are the purchasing power. They ultimately determine the demand functions.

Now, it was the production side rather than the consumption side that was most emphasized in the Classical period. Returns to scale played and continue to play a major role in equilibrium theory. One natural assumption is that returns to scale are constant, and so firms can enter an industry at any scale with equal efficiency. But that poses a constraint, because if the price of the product is a little too high compared to the prices of the inputs, then with constant returns to scale, it pays to increase your scale of operations indefinitely. The question is then: What is it that restricts prices and the levels of output?

And so the demand function was invented. Cournot certainly uses it and indeed was an inventor of it. As an observation about how economic science developed, it is noteworthy that Cournot published his book in 1838, yet the first known review is somewhere around 1877. It was completely ignored, and it was reviewed because Walras's book came out, and people began to go back. And Walras does pay some credit to Cournot, but Cournot, by this time a rather old man, going blind, was very bitter that he did not get the credit he deserved. And there was a very famous review by an astronomer named Bertrand, which is where the concept of Bertrand Competition is introduced.

But there was another introduction of demand functions besides in Cournot, and that is in John Stuart Mill. One of Ricardo's greatest innovations was the idea of comparative advantage as a determining factor in foreign trade. But without demand functions, you don't really have an explanation of quantities, you have theories about prices. So, Ricardo was taking the prices as cost driven and therefore given. There are a lot of ambiguities in that, which I won't go into now, but that's the way he saw it. Mill wanted to know something about quantities. So, he produced the idea of demand curves. For example, Germany had a demand curve for English cotton. And England had a demand curve for German linen. I think that was the example he gave. This was Mills's first paper and probably one of the most brilliant things he wrote.

The next step in the development of equilibrium theory was the attempt to provide foundations for thinking about the idea of profit. One of the questions you get into is: Why are there profits at all? Why aren't there zero profits? Presumably, it's a cost-driven thing, but in the simplest economic model, there is just one primary factor, labor, and then everything essentially is priced based on how much labor is embodied in it. That doesn't give you any profits at all. This is what Marx, of course, took up. The rates of profit are equal, but why do they have to equal zero? Nassau Senior, who was a professor of political economy at Oxford at the time, said, "well, there's a cost to waiting." That's a subjective cost. That's not a cost in any literal sense. If goods are produced, they take time. I'm going to come back to that as one of my main themes. There were also important contributions by Gossen, Jevons, and Menger that clarified these matters further.

Externalities

So general equilibrium theory seems to have something to say about a good part of the economy. Does it say everything? Well, no. We're now accustomed, I'm sure the World Bank especially, to talk about externalities. We find that the markets somehow don't work properly.

And that realization took quite a while. Although you see it recognized: Walras, for example, has some statements that are pretty clear, not in his book but in some of his essays, on the subject. Jules Dupuit in 1844 was concerned with some ideas along these lines: Why the criteria for public works? When should you build a road? When should you build a railroad? How do you price railroads? And so forth. He was an inspector of bridges and highways for the French government.

It was really quite a bit later that Pigou gave us a really clear statement on externalities. But Pigou's original formulation was pretty faulty, and it was reviewed by an economist—I don't know how many have heard of him—Allyn Young. Allyn Young wrote a book review of the first edition of Pigou's famous work—first called *Wealth and Welfare*, and the later editions called *The Economics of Welfare*. Pigou didn't get it quite right, but in the review, Young explained very clearly and correctly what an externality was. And later there was, in the 1930s (the one I learned it from) a paper by Jacob Viner, distinguishing pecuniary from technological externalities. Technological externalities are the ones we think of as the welfare implications. I don't want to go into that, because there's hardly any advanced country with less than 30 percent of its national income going through the government. Those are the externalities we attempt to take care of, but they are not the only ones. Externalities, public goods, whatever you want to call it. I didn't want to elaborate, except to mention it now; I'll come back to it later.

General equilibrium is useful here. It doesn't explain the externalities, it doesn't explain what's done to meet the externalities, but it does essentially, at least for many economists, have some effect on real life. When analyzing policies, we ask: What would general equilibrium say if it were operative? And that's the criterion we have. In almost all our analysis, policy analysis, in situations where externalities govern, we ask: What would general equilibrium say, if it even were applicable? And that is in a way the main theme I want to present in the end. Of course, there's another aspect, namely, the failure of effective demand. When I was a graduate student, an infinite period of time ago, we'd talk about business cycles. That was the big macro issue—at least around places like the National Bureau of Economic Research. I personally took macro from Arthur Frank Burns in the 1940s.

The Influence on Early Econometric Models

The idea of pursuing systematic empirical work (not just collecting numbers but putting them into models—the econometric movement) is the product of the creation of the Econometric Society around 1932. It was kind of a movement, perhaps a little more European than American, but international. One of its first examples in practice was a business cycle model of the Netherlands by Jan Tinbergen, who subsequently led a much bigger study sponsored by the League of Nations in Geneva. One thing that Tinbergen picked up from general equilibrium theory is the idea of a complete system. If you're going to forecast the future, you've got to have a complete system. Or if you're going to ask what the effect is of a policy, you have to have a complete system. And we see today at least one tendency is to essentially take a general equilibrium system, say, the prices don't immediately move in a right direction (they're sticky).

So now we have I guess what you would call the "New Keynesian" models. I don't know if they do any better, but anyway, they're complete systems. And they deal with motivation as to individual relations from the same basis but put in layers trying to say it's costly to change your prices all the time, or something along these lines.

Goods as Complements and Substitutes

A lot of the early literature on the production side assumed fixed coefficients. In other words, to produce good A, you just need so much of good B. So you can have intermediate goods, but ultimately, directly or indirectly, you're drawing on the primary factors. And the idea that you're going to have substitution in alternative kinds of production was elaborated by John Bates Clark in the late nineteenth century. Walras in his work—not in his first edition but in his later editions—has production functions. What Walras introduced really was the idea that (and he did this more elaborately, I think, than Jevons did) the demand for one commodity might depend not only on the price of that commodity but also on the prices of other commodities. Now once you say it's an allocation problem (and this is certainly there in Jevons), the idea of demand then becomes more complex, and we have the standard notion that these commodities are in some sense substitutes for each other. The fact that they are all competing for a limited purchasing power means that, in some sense, substitution is bigger than complementarity. But complementarity is still there: The price of butter may affect the demand for bread. Once you bring in production functions, you have a similar idea in production. So the idea that something that happens in one part of the system can then work its way through and affect seemingly remote parts of the system is the big lesson to be learned from general equilibrium. If you think of someone like Alfred Marshall, he clearly saw this. In fact, his initial review of Jevons wasn't terribly friendly. He was angry at Jevons (as he himself said in his memoirs), because Jevons was so contemptuous of Ricardo. Marshall said in his memoirs that he would write very angry comments, then cut them out, but they would "reappear" again. This was a very interesting discussion of the subconscious!

"Complementary Slackness"

Let me make two additional points. The first is an issue that sounds a little technical, but it really is not. This is what mainly drove the discussion on existence, which began in the 1930s and was completed in the 1960s. It's what the people who have a linear programming background would say: "complementary slackness." Menger made this observation. There are some goods that are free, but they are free only because they are very abundant.

In other words, if they were not so abundant, they wouldn't be free. What are the examples? Air is free. In many parts of the world, water is free. In a region with a lot of rain, water is free: I mean rainwater for agriculture. Of course, water for drinking has got to be processed. It's not the water that is scarce, it is the processing. So the idea that a good is free or not depends on economic circumstances. Well, this means that supply is not necessarily equal to demand. Of course, supply can't be less than demand in equilibrium. You can't meet the demand then. But supply could be greater than demand, and then the price would be zero. That's recognized by Menger.

What happened was that several German authors (and two in particular, Hans Neisser and Heinrich von Stackelberg) in the 1930s had different arguments—I won't try to reproduce them now—as to why the equations of general equilibrium could be inconsistent. Actually, even though the arguments were very easy, it would still take a few minutes, and I'm told I have less than that! A private banker named Karl Schlesinger fled Hungary, which was then under a communist threat, to Vienna and set himself up as a private banker there, but he kept his interest in economics as an amateur. (He had earlier received a PhD in economics.) Schlesinger pursued the existence controversy and grasped the idea that the existence problem was simply not recognizing complementary slackness. It was insisting that supply equals demand when you might have supply greater than demand.

Well, he was no mathematician. So he went to Oskar Morgenstern, who was running a business cycle research institute, financed by Rockefeller. Morgenstern had hired a graduate student in mathematics to do some work— mainly some statistical work—a fellow named Abraham Wald. Wald was Romanian. He was actually born in Hungary, but the boundary had been moved, so he was now a Romanian after World War I. And so there's Wald, who, using Schlesinger's insight about the importance of complementary slackness, came up with a proof of existence. The assumptions were absurdly strong. It clearly left an open problem, and I won't go into the history of that.

The Essential Role of Time

Now, though time is running short, let me turn briefly to the second issue, that is, the big question that comes up, sort of right at the beginning— even in Smith—but is usually skated over: Production takes time. It's not for nothing that the word "capitalism" starts with "capital," which means production taking time. Well, it can take time in an indirect form. You buy durable goods, like your plant and your equipment, which last and are gradually used up in the process. So, one way or another, literally it just simply takes time—or it may use machines that are durable and so are used over time. That means, if I look at a production process, to do it properly, you put in goods at time zero, you put in more goods at time one, and the good comes out at time two, or some such process. So, a production process involves not only different goods but different goods at different times. So, we can say, okay, no problem, we'll just think of the same good at different times as different goods.

The first person, as far as I know, who made this simple observation was Eric Lindahl, a Swedish economist. It was picked up by Hicks. I got it from Hicks. To the young theorists of my generation, Hicks was god. His book, *Value and Capital*, was the most important thing in the world.

Prior to Hicks, the problem was that you read all this discussion about capital theory by Frank Knight and other things like that, and it was all mystical. You didn't know what they were talking about. Pigou was a little bit clearer, but he confined himself to simple questions. Hayek was impenetrable. But when you read Hicks and then went back to Hayek, you could see that's what Hayek was saying. I would never have understood Hayek. I did read Hayek, *Theory of Capital*. It was incomprehensible. But as I say, when you read Hicks, then it's "oh, now I understand Hayek." And I think part of it is that Hicks got something from Hayek. He gives credit in the footnotes but in a very general sort of way.

So, to this question of time. Now, when Gerard (Debreu) and I wrote, for example, our proofs weren't really any different from McKenzie's, or anything like that, but I think we set out—we carried the Walrasian program out—more thoroughly than anybody else did. That was the advantage of what we did. And so, we modernized it. We had utility functions, we had preference orderings, we recognized the ordinalist revolution, things of that kind, and we stated the need for concavity. It was a modernized version of Walras. And we wrote just automatically, but we both thought the same way without even discussing it. We treated goods at different times as though they were just different commodities.

But what does that mean? It means we're talking about a world in which there are markets for everything. In particular, a market for goods tomorrow and goods 10 years from now and 20 years from now. Well, you could wave away a little bit of that, but you need goods markets for everything. Look at the world. What do we see? There are goods for things tomorrow. Agricultural goods, minerals, that's about it. You can't typically buy a car in the future. I mean, obviously, if I'm setting up an automobile plant, it'd be very nice to sell forward the car, a futures market, and credit. Well, the problem is that I don't know what the car is going to be like. I do know it's going to be different. Something's going to happen. Maybe nothing important, maybe just, you know, different styles or something trivial. But maybe it will be significantly better in fuel economy or safety or some other way that is important. So we have this problem. And that's where general equilibrium runs into limits. Somehow you can't carry through the program. And Hicks knew this, and he said, you have expectations of prices. But he's not very good at explaining how you form the expectations.

I'm sorry: I'll wrap up in a minute.

Expectations and the Role of Information

There had been a literature, in the nascent econometric movement, about price expectations. What people were really showing was that price expectations might give rise to trouble. And this is static expectations. Let's say the price tomorrow is going to be the same as the price today. And then they had this famous "corn-hog" cycle. Well, similar versions of this is when you plant your crop, you look at the price prevailing and say that's the price I'm going to sell it for. In fact, the result is, let's say, if the price is high, today you plant a lot, but then the resulting effect is that the price is low tomorrow. So you can wind up with a cyclical movement in people's expectations; of course, they're already being dashed all the time, and people began to develop more and more sophisticated kinds of expectations. But this is the trouble.

The same thing could be extended to uncertainty, but that brings in the question being asked of why information is key. (I don't have time to get to my main theme, but all right). Once you start out on the idea that we're ensuring there's uncertainty, there comes the problem that people know different things. There's asymmetric information. And of course, we've had an enormous development of the theory of asymmetric information, but it tends to be static. You have to laugh at the fact that there's going to be a realization.

So let me conclude by saying that where I find general equilibrium theory most used is as a basis for models. Climate change illustrates it. What have we got there? We have dynamic models, like Nordhaus and others have developed. That is, you have models of the future, and we make it clear that they are price clearing models. In fact, they are optimal, so they clear with full anticipation of what's going to happen in the future. So these models are fully specified. They're used for predictive purposes, and they're used for policy formation purposes. And that's where I think equilibrium theory is having its biggest use now. Thank you.

Comment: Shantayanan Devarajan

It is an honor to be a discussant for Kenneth Arrow's presentation. I learned general equilibrium theory from Gerard Debreu, whom Ken mentioned, and it's nice to hear from the other half of the great Arrow-Debreu pair. I will focus my remarks on the three nouns in the title of the paper, "Equilibrium, Welfare, and Information."

First, equilibrium. The proof of the existence of a general equilibrium, due to Arrow and Debreu, is one of the most powerful contributions in economics. Its power lies not just in its mathematical elegance but in its utility. For we use general equilibrium reasoning every day, including at the World Bank. Without the proof that the interaction among sectors through the price mechanism is a consistent system, we would be spinning tales out of thin air. The idea of the Dutch disease (Corden and Neary 1982), where a booming sector (such as oil) increases prices of nontradables and decreases output of the traditional tradable sector, is not just a random collection of hypotheses. It is a description of the general equilibrium system that, thanks to Arrow, we know the conditions under which it exists. I used a general equilibrium model to estimate the overvaluation of the CFA franc in Africa (Devarajan 1997). That estimate was quite close to the actual devaluation in 1994. Again, we could not have built the model, much less used it, without a coherent theory that this way of describing the economy is analytically founded. This idea of the interdependence of different sectors of the economy, mediated through prices, is central to development. In recent work on cronyism in Tunisia, Rijkers, Freund, and Nucifora (2016) looked at monopoly power in the telecommunications sector, which had been granted because of connections to the then-ruling family. The authors showed that by raising telecoms prices, the monopoly had undermined the competitiveness of Tunisia's garments and electronics manufacturing sectors, which is another example of applied general equilibrium reasoning (and an explanation of why Tunisia's exports are not growing). Perhaps most importantly, the whole notion of inequality, which is currently being hotly debated in rich and poor countries, has to be understood in terms of general equilibrium. This concept is fundamental, because the distribution of income is a function of both the uses and sources of income, which in turn are functions of how prices and quantities adjust in different sectors. For example, in a resource-rich developing country like Zambia, a favorable terms of trade shock can lead to greater inequality, because poor people spend more of their income on nontradable goods (Devarajan and Go 2003)—a general equilibrium result that may deviate from a first-round, partial equilibrium one. In short—and I say this with some trepidation, because many contributors to this volume have made enormous contributions to economics—the proof of the existence of general equilibrium is one of the most powerful contributions, not just to economics but also to the welfare of poor people.

This brings me to the second topic of Arrow's talk, which is welfare. The two fundamental theorems of welfare economics, which state that, under certain assumptions, a competitive equilibrium is Pareto optimal and that any Pareto optimum can be supported by a competitive equilibrium, are, well, fundamental. But as Arrow points out, they are important because of what happens when you relax some of the assumptions. For example, when externalities exist, the competitive equilibrium will not be Pareto optimal. This is the cornerstone of economic policy: The purpose of economic policy is, when the assumptions of the first welfare theorem don't hold, to get us from the competitive equilibrium to the social optimum. Here is where I think we have a problem. Although everyone agrees that our goal should be to maximize social welfare—we've studied the theorems in graduate school and can probably recite them—some of our behavior does not follow suit. Having agreed that our purpose is to increase welfare, we sometimes develop "special initiatives" that include such goals as universal primary enrollment, or universal health care, or universal financial access. To be sure, these are worthy goals, but it is not clear that achieving any one of them is welfare maximizing. You could likely do better by increasing access to something at a very low level than spending the marginal dollar on going from 99 to 100 percent access in one of the other areas. So I think development economists should be vigilant in pursuing the goal of welfare rather than appealing to constituencies or the latest trends.

Finally, despite its appeal, the general equilibrium model, and general equilibrium theory, have come under some criticism. One such criticism, which Arrow alluded to, is that the assumption that you have a complete set of markets for every contingency is unrealistic. It's hard to imagine that everybody knows exactly what they're going to buy under every possible state of the world. This is why a whole body of work has developed on general equilibrium under uncertainty. Joe Stiglitz and other contributors to this volume have made seminal contributions in this area. A second criticism is that people may not follow the optimizing behavior that is assumed in standard general equilibrium models. Consumers may not maximize utility; producers may not maximize profits. People have limited cognitive capacity. This has led to the area of behavioral economics, which my colleague Karla Hoff will discuss next. Despite the great progress that Karla and others have made in this field, we have yet to develop a fully specified theory of general equilibrium where agents are not optimizing, comparable to the traditional theory of general equilibrium. Such a theory would be a fitting tribute to the great work of Kenneth Arrow.

References

Corden, W. Max, and Peter J. Neary. 1982. "Booming Sector and De-Industrialisation in a Small Open Economy." *Economic Journal* 92 (368): 825–848.

Devarajan, Shantayanan. 1997. "Real Exchange Rate Misalignment in the CFA Zone." *Journal of African Economies* 6 (1): 35–53.

Devarajan, Shantayanan, and Delfin S. Go. 2003. "The 123PRSP Model." In *The Impact of Economic Policies on Poverty and Income Distribution: Evaluation Techniques and Tools*, edited by François Bourguignon and Luiz A. Pereira da Silva, 277–300. New York and Washington, DC: Oxford University Press and World Bank.

Rijkers, Bob, Caroline Freund, and Antonio Nucifora. 2017. "All in the Family: State Capture in Tunisia." *Journal of Development Economics* 124: 41–59.

Comment: Karla Hoff

Do Social Factors Determine "Who We Are"?

In a conference that asks where economics is headed, it is natural that the first invited speaker be Kenneth Arrow. As much as anyone else who was alive in 2016, he had advanced the field of economics. He was the first to prove Adam Smith's conjecture that under some conditions, the market economy attains the ideal of Pareto efficiency (Arrow 1951), and his proof was a two-edged sword: It showed that a market equilibrium is Pareto efficient only under conditions so special that they would never be met in reality, even approximately (Greenwald and Stiglitz 1986). What sets Arrow apart from every economist before him is that he understood how unrealistic the conditions must be for market equilibrium to produce a Pareto efficient allocation. He also understood that the impersonal price system supplied a very incomplete description of reality.

Arrow consistently pushed the boundaries of neoclassical economics, in part by going back to earlier traditions that explored how a society as a whole functions. He studied peer influences on preferences (Arrow and Dasgupta 2009). He demonstrated that in a competitive economy, the rate of investment in learning would be too low, since learning benefits future investors who do not pay for it (Arrow 1962). Although he never left the framework of rational choice theory, he pushed the boundaries of the emerging field of behavioral economics, too. Leaders in that field, Richard Thaler and Sendhil Mullainathan (2008), had defined it as one that introduced psychologically more realistic assumptions about decision-making into economics. Arrow (2010, 12) commented: "[T]oday psychology is invading economics—the whole field of behavioral economics. I believe that sociology should play more of a role in economics than it does. The way people behave in economics is partly influenced by how other people behave. It's easy to point out examples, but it's not so easy to construct a broad theory."

Behavioral economics has moved in the direction of sociology in the twenty-first century. The research in behavioral economics has two strands. The first focuses on the *quasi-rational actor*, who is rational when she thinks "slow" but who much of the time thinks "fast" using heuristic principles to reduce to simpler operations the complex task of making decisions (for example, Thaler 2000). The second strand, in which sociology, anthropology, and neuroscience play a role, is concerned with a *quasi-rational, enculturated actor*. The cognitive tools she uses to expand her ability to process information fast are endogenous, not universal. They differ across groups and over time. They are shaped by the socio-cultural environments that she and her ancestors have experienced or been exposed to (Nunn 2012; Hoff and Stiglitz 2016; Demeritt and Hoff 2018).

Each strand is easy to illustrate. Kahneman and Tversky, pioneers of the first strand, showed that the mechanisms of cognition (rather than merely the emotions) produce systematic errors of intuition. For example, when Kahneman (2011) shows us the box on the next page, we think the middle symbol is "B."

But when he shows us the next box, we think the middle symbol is "13." In neither case do we think the middle symbol is ambiguous. The example illustrates that "one does not just see, one *sees as*" (Bacharach 2003, 63).

Kahneman emphasizes that automatic, not deliberate, thinking is the "secret author of many of the choices and judgments you make" (Kahneman 2011, 13). Automatic thinking entails matching a stimulus to known patterns and making associations. It does not entail logic or careful reasoning. If an individual doesn't have useful patterns and concepts that are easily accessible, she won't make good choices and judgments.

Behavioral economics shows that when people are making choices based on automatic thinking, interventions can sometimes nudge them to make choices that leave them better off. "Nudges" have been devised to help people in poor countries save enough for medical expenses and health needs (Dupas and Robinson 2013), buy fertilizer (Duflo, Kremer, and Robinson 2011), treat unclean drinking water regularly with diluted chlorine (Kremer et al. 2011), and complete multiple-stage immunization programs to protect their children from disease (Banerjee et al. 2010).

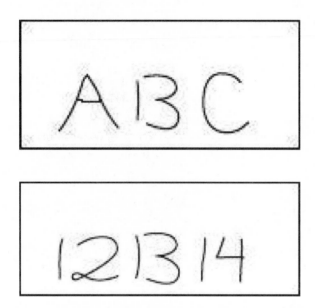

The second strand of behavioral economics goes beyond nudges. It considers how to change the repertoire and the accessibility of cognitive tools—for example, cultural categories and narratives—that individuals use to process information. By expanding the repertoire or making some mental models more accessible, exposure to new social patterns (even in fiction) can induce long-run social change.

At the turn of the twentieth century, about one-fourth of the population in Brazil watched a soap opera at 9:15 each weeknight. Globo was the main producer of soap operas in Brazil. It crafted them with characters who had few or no children in order to reduce the number of characters in the stories. Small family size sharply contrasted with the prevailing patterns in Brazil.

Exposure to the soap operas lowered fertility rates in Brazil! Causal identification of the impact is possible because of the arguably random year that different municipalities obtained access to the Globo transmissions. The fertility rate in a municipality declined after the first year that it had access to transmissions of these soap operas (La Ferrara, Chong, and Duryea 2012). The decline was greatest for women who were within 4 years of the age of a leading female character in the soap operas, which is consistent with a role model effect. The effect was comparable to that of an increase in average education of women by 2 years. Yet the effect was not driven by a change in assets or skills or prices, but only a change in the kinds of lives people imagined for themselves.

Changes in markets can also create new prototypes and thereby induce changes in preferences. A randomized controlled trial by Robert Jensen (2012) indicates that the proportion of young women in an Indian village who have business process outsourcing (BPO) jobs, such as at call centers, influences the average marriage patterns, education, fertility rates, and aspirations in the village. To conduct the experiment, Jensen hired eight call center recruiters and sent them to recruit women in 80 villages randomly chosen from a set of 160 villages about 100 kilometers from Delhi (too remote for profitable visits from recruiters). His experiment created a surge in demand in those 80 villages for women in BPO jobs. Before the experiment, no members of any household in these villages held a BPO job. As a result of the experiment, there were 11 job matches on average per village over 3 years. The proportion of young women with BPO jobs increased from 0 to 5.6 percent in the treatment villages. The surge in demand changed how women in the treatment villages defined their lives and how parents perceived and cared for their daughters, as table 1.1 shows.

The change in choice sets would have rationally changed expectations for women too. But it is plausible that by seeing young women play new roles, the lives that parents and young women imagined were possible for them had changed. The increase in the body mass index (BMI) of girls aged 5–15, shown in table 1.1, is evidence that daughters were better cared for in treatment than in control villages. It is evidence that a cultural shift had occurred. Like the study of the effect on fertility rates of Globo soap operas in Brazil, the randomized controlled trial using call center recruiters in India shows the kind of social influences that Arrow suggested behavioral economics should take into account.

Social influences can, of course, be bad or good. Just as social experience and exposure expanded individuals' sense of "who they were" in the previous two examples, they can also narrow this sense and make a society rigid. In a village in which most girls are uneducated, it is possible to sustain a stereotype of educated women as immoral and a threat to the social order, which sustains the social pattern of low education for girls.

Table 1.1
Social impacts of hiring female villagers in BPO jobs

	Control villages	Treatment villages
Women of age 15–21		
Percentage who married during the 3-year period of the experiment	0.71	0.66
Percentage who gave birth during the 3-year period of the experiment	0.43	0.37
Number of children that the individual desires	3.00	2.65
Girls of age 5–15		
z-score of body mass index for age	−1.25	−1.01

Source: Based on Jensen (2012).

In interviews throughout India, comments of women demonstrate the influence of prevailing education levels on attitudes toward educating girls. When asked why their daughters never went to school, some parents responded, "We don't educate girls in our community." In contrast, when parents in Kerala, a socially progressive state of South India, were asked why they send their children to school, "some of them don't know what to say simply because they take it as self-evident that going to school is what children do" (PROBE Team 1999, 22, 24).

The fact that attitudes and choices about educating girls are widely shared within a village and vary across villages suggests the existence of multiple stable and Pareto-ranked equilibria. Hoff and Stiglitz (2016) formalizes this observation in a simple model. It assumes that in each of the many households in a village, there is a young girl whom the parents have to choose to educate, or not. How they think about the girl's education depends on the village stereotype of an educated woman and on her expected market-determined lifetime earnings, W (call the former their "framed utility," after Kahenman 2011, chapter 34). Consider two stereotypes of an educated woman, denoted A and P. Under stereotype A, a woman's autonomy is held in esteem, and an educated daughter is a source of pride to her parents. Under stereotype P, an educated woman is a threat to the patriarchal social order and to her husband's masculinity, which means that an educated daughter is difficult to marry off. Parents do not have fixed preferences over educating their daughter. Instead, their preferences depend on the stereotype that is cued by the environment. Let $U(s)$ be the weighted sum,

$$U(s) = \omega(s)V^A + [1 - \omega(s)]\ V^P + W,$$

where s is the salience of the mental model A, V^A is the parents' intrinsic valuation of an educated daughter under mental model A, and similarly for V^P. Let s be the fraction of village households that educate their daughters. The weight $\omega(s)$ is increasing in s: If all households educate daughters, $\omega = 1$. If none do, $\omega = 0$. Figure 1.1A illustrates the function $U(s)$.

For simplicity, assume that having an uneducated daughter would give parents utility θ that is independent of the fraction of households in the village that educate their daughters. Across households, θ varies because some parents have greater need than others for a young child to tend to another family member, such as an infant or a sick grandmother. Figure 1.1B assumes a roughly normal distribution of θ above some fixed, low value.

The evolution of the fraction of educated girls closes the model. A long-run interior equilibrium is the fraction of daughters who are educated, s^*, at which the marginal parents are indifferent between educating their daughter or not doing so. In the neighborhood of any value of s^* at a stable equilibrium, parents for whom θ is less than $U(s^*)$ would be strictly better off educating their daughters, and parents for whom θ is more than $U(s^*)$ would be strictly worse off educating their daughters. See figure 1.1C, where the two graphs are superimposed. There are two stable equilibria (marked by circles) and one unstable equilibrium between them. In the bad equilibrium, the village has no educated girls: the patriarchal stereotype P is so salient that no parents want to educate their daughters. In the good equilibrium, stereotype A is so salient that most parents have the opposite preference: most prefer to educate their daughters.

The stereotypes in this model are a linchpin that *reflects* social patterns ("normal" girls do, or don't, get educated) and *affects* individual behavior (the parents' decisions to educate girls) in ways that sustain the stereotypes and the social pattern in a "cycle of mutual constitution" (Markus and Kitayama 2010). The social pattern in the village shapes how people think and the alternatives they can imagine. The social pattern is naturalized, even though other outcomes are possible, perhaps preferable, and prevail in other villages. *Behavioral development economics*, an emerging field in the twenty-first century, sheds light on how dysfunctional social institutions

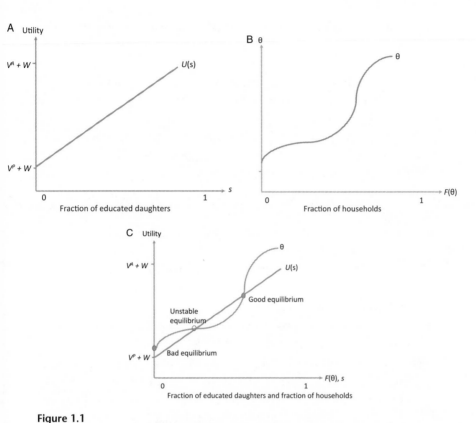

Figure 1.1

Role model effects on parents' decision to educate a daughter

Notes: (A) Parents' "framed utility" U from an educated daughter. The utility depends on the salience of a stereotype A, in which an educated girl is a source of pride to her parents, and a stereotype P, in which an educated girl is perceived to be a threat to the patriarchal social order. The salience of the stereotype A depends on the fraction of educated daughters in the village. W is the market-determined lifetime expected earnings of an educated girl.

(B) Cumulative distribution function of parents' utility from a daughter who is not educated.

(C) Multiple equilibria of the proportion of parents who choose to educate their daughters.

Source: Hoff and Stiglitz (2016).

(such as low education for girls) can persist and affect how people think and what they can imagine. In that sense, social patterns can determine "who we are."

In a famous article on medical care and insurance, Arrow (1963) discusses the problem of asymmetric information. He argued that equilibria in insurance markets are very far from Pareto efficient. Buying insurance for the risk of a car accident will reduce the care that the insured party takes. If she knows she's a bad driver but the insurance company does not, she is likely to fully insure. At the high price at which the insurance company breaks even on bad drivers, good drivers won't be willing to fully insure. Sellers and buyers of insurance do not have the same information and, thus, are not really trading the same things (Rothschild and Stiglitz 1976 show that market equilibrium will thus not be Pareto efficient).

But whatever information decision makers have, neoclassical economics assumes that they process it objectively. Behavioral economics departs from that assumption and recognizes the systematic influence of cultural mental models for *subjectively processing* information. Perception is selective. Depending on the activated mental model, an individual sees different things. Recall the earlier figure that showed that depending on the frame, a person might be sure that a symbol was "B" or "13." That is, "one does not just see, one *sees as*." Culture works through the interaction of shared mental models and the information and context that activate those mental models to varying degrees (DiMaggio 1997, 264, 274).

	Neoclassical Economics	Behavioral Economics	
		Strand 1	Strand 2
Concept of the actor	The rational actor	The quasi-rational actor	The quasi-rational, enculturated actor

The drivers of behavior	Guided by incentives	Also guided by context in the moment of decision, e.g.
		▶ Presentation.
		    ■ Default options
		    ■ Language
		▶ Cues
		    ■ Reminders
		    ■ Mental accounting
			Also guided by experience and exposure, which shape:
			▶ Mental models
			    ■ Categories
			    ■ Concepts
			    ■ Identities
			    ■ Narratives
			▶ What primes certain behaviors

Figure 1.2
Neoclassical economics and the two strands of behavioral economics
Source: Based on Hoff and Stiglitz (2016).

"Nudges" are based on the the idea that a change in a frame changes what is seen and may change what one does. Interventions to change experience or exposure (for example, exposure to new role models) are based on the idea that in the medium-run, they will change the repertoire or accessibility of mental models and thereby change the concepetual frames that one brings to a problem.

Figure 1.2 illustrates the three types of actors assumed in modern work in economics: the rational actor; the quasi-rational actor; and the quasi-rational, enculturated actor. By conceptualizing the last actor, recent work in behavioral economics has taken up Ken Arrow's recommendation that sociology should play more of a role in economics.

References

Arrow, Kenneth J. 1951. "An Extension of the Basic Theorems of Classical Welfare Economics." In *Proceedings of the Second Berkeley Symposium on Mathematical Statistics and Probability*, edited by Jerzy Neyman, 507–532. Berkeley: University of California Press.

Arrow, Kenneth J. 1962. "The Economic Implications of Learning by Doing." *Review of Economic Studies* 29 (3): 155–173.

Arrow, Kenneth J. 1963. "Uncertainty and the Welfare Economics of Medical Care." *American Economic Review* 53 (5): 941–973.

Arrow, Kenneth J. 2010. "The Economy of Trust: An Interview with Kenneth Arrow." *Religion and Liberty* 16 (3): 3, 12–13. https://acton.org/pub/religion-liberty/volume -16-number-3/economy-trust.

Arrow, Kenneth J., and Partha S. Dasgupta. 2009. "Conspicuous Consumption, Inconspicuous Leisure." *Economic Journal* 119 (541): F497–F516.

Bacharach, Michael. 2003. "Framing and Cognition in Economics: The Bad News and the Good." In *Cognitive Processes and Economic Behaviour*, edited by Marcello Basili, Nicola Dimitri, and Itzhak Gilboa, 63–74. New York: Routledge.

Banerjee, Abhijit, Esther Duflo, Rachel Glennerster, and Dhruva Kothari. 2010. "Improving Immunisation Coverage in Rural India: Clustered Randomised Control Evaluation of Immunisation Campaigns with and without Incentives." *British Medical Journal* 340 (1): c2220.

Demeritt, Allison, and Karla Hoff. 2018. "The Making of Behavioral Development Economics." *History of Political Economy* 50 (annual supplement): 303–322. http://bit.ly /2GwyGUK.

DiMaggio, Paul. 1997. "Culture and Cognition." *Annual Review of Sociology* 23: 263–287.

Duflo, Esther, Michael Kremer, and Jonathan Robinson. 2011. "Nudging Farmers to Use Fertilizer: Theory and Experimental Evidence from Kenya." *American Economic Review* 10 (6): 2350–2390.

Dupas, Pascaline, and Jonathan Robinson. 2013. "Why Don't the Poor Save More? Evidence from Health Savings Experiments." *American Economic Review* 103 (4): 1138–1171.

Greenwald, Bruce C., and Joseph E. Stiglitz. 1986. "Externalities in Economics with Imperfect Information and Incomplete Markets." *Quarterly Journal of Economics* 101 (2): 229–264.

Hoff, Karla, and Joseph E. Stiglitz. 2016. "Striving for Balance in Economics: Towards a Theory of the Social Determination of Behavior." *Journal of Economic Behavior and Organization* 126 (Part B, June): 25–57.

Jensen, Robert. 2012. "Do Labor Market Opportunities Affect Young Women's Work and Family Decisions? Experimental Evidence from India." *Quarterly Journal of Economics* 127 (2): 753–792.

Kahneman, Daniel. 2011. *Thinking Fast and Slow.* New York: Farrar, Straus and Giroux.

Kremer, Michael, Edward Miguel, Sendhil Mullainathan, Clair Null, and Alix Peterson Zwane. 2011. "Social Engineering: Evidence from a Suite of Take-Up Experiments in Kenya." Unpublished manuscript, University of California, Berkeley.

La Ferrara, Eliana, Alberto Chong, and Suzanne Duryea. 2012. "Soap Operas and Fertility: Evidence from Brazil." *American Economic Journal: Applied Economics* 4 (4): 1–31.

Markus, Hazel Rose, and Shinobu Kitayama. 2010. "Culture and Selves: A Cycle of Mutual Constitution." *Perspectives on Psychological Science* 5 (4): 420–430.

Nunn, Nathan. 2012. "Culture and the Historical Process." *Economic History of Developing Regions* 12 (27): 108–126.

PROBE Team. 1999. *Public Report on Basic Education in India.* New Delhi: Oxford University Press.

Rothschild, Michael, and Joseph E. Stiglitz. 1976. "Equilibrium in Competitive Insurance Markets: An Essay on the Economics of Imperfect Information," *Quarterly Journal of Economics* 90 (4): 629–649.

Thaler, Richard. 2000. *Misbehaving: The Making of Behavioral Development Economics.* New York: W. W. Norton.

Thaler, Richard H., and Sendhil Mullainathan, 2008. "Behavioral Economics." In *The Concise Encyclopedia of Economics*, edited by David R. Henderson, 34–37. Indianapolis, IN: Liberty Fund.

2   Social Choice and Welfare Economics

Amartya Sen

In the making of acceptable social decisions for a group (such as a nation, a community, a committee, or any other collectivity), the diverse views and interests of members of the group must receive attention and importance. This can be an exacting task, because people's views can differ, and as Horace pointed out a long time ago, there may be as "many preferences as there are people." Choosing actions and policies for a group can be formidably difficult.

And there are, in addition, difficult issues even in describing what exactly is happening to a group as a whole. Is it better off or worse? Are its members happier? Do they have more freedom than before? Is there more poverty or less than in the past? Has social inequality in the group diminished or increased? Can the social decisions that emerge be seen as democratic, or are they, in some important sense, authoritarian? Methods of aggregative assessment are central to the subject of social choice in general and welfare economics in particular.

People have speculated on social aggregation throughout human history. However, social choice theory as a formal discipline first came into its own around the time of the French Revolution. The subject was pioneered by French mathematicians in the late eighteenth century, particularly J.-C. Borda (1781) and Nicolas de Condorcet (1785). They addressed social choice problems in rather mathematical terms and initiated the intellectual discipline of social choice theory in terms of voting and related procedures. The intellectual climate of the period was greatly influenced by the European Enlightenment, with its interest in reasoned construction of a social order.

Indeed, some of the early social choice theorists, most notably Condorcet, were also among the intellectual leaders of the French Revolution. Condorcet noted that Anne Robert Jacques Turgot, the pioneering French economist (and also the governor of the province of Limoges), whom Condorcet greatly admired, was the first statesman who "deigned to treat the people as a society of reasonable beings" (Condorcet 1847, 9, 15, 18). Condorcet admonished Jacques Necker, an opponent of Turgot, for "exaggerating the stupidity of people." Condorcet took great interest, especially in his later works, on interactive decision-making in assemblies, including "assemblées d'administration," charged with making decisions about taxation, public works, militias, the use of public funds, and the management of public goods.

The motivation for the early social choice theorists included the avoidance of authoritarianism as well as arbitrariness in social choice. Their work focused on the development of a framework for rational and democratic decisions for a group, paying adequate attention to the preferences and interests of its members. However, even the theoretical investigations typically yielded rather pessimistic results. Condorcet noted, for example, that majority rule can be caught in an impasse when every alternative is defeated in voting by some other alternative. To illustrate the "voting paradox," first spotted by Condorcet, consider a 3-member community in which person 1 strictly prefers x to y and that to z; person 2 ranks them in the strict order of y, z, and x; and person 3 strictly ranks them as z, x, and y. Then x will defeat y by majority vote, while y defeats z, and z vanquishes x, thereby generating a "cycle." More particularly, every alternative is rejected in a majority vote by some other alternative, and there will be no "Condorcet winner," that is, an alternative that wins against (or at least stays undefeated against) every other alternative.

Even though there is no continuous line of work on social choice theory following the early lead of French mathematicians, the subject received sporadic attention in various writings, often from distinguished intellectuals, such as Lewis Carroll, the author of *Alice in Wonderland* (he wrote some engaging and important papers on group decisions under his real name, C. L. Dodgson (1876, 1884)).

However, in its modern—and fully axiomatized—form, modern social choice theory had to wait until the middle of the twentieth century for its first rigorous foundation in the work of Kenneth J. Arrow. His famous "impossibility theorem," contained in his PhD dissertation, was first reported in a journal article (Arrow 1950). His thesis was published shortly thereafter as a monograph (Arrow 1951), which became an instant classic.

Economists, political theorists, moral and political philosophers, sociologists, and even the general public took rapid notice of what seemed like—and indeed was—a devastating result. And in a comparatively short time, social choice theory in a modernized and systematically axiomatic form was firmly established as a discipline with immediate and extensive implications for economics, philosophy, politics, and the other social sciences. Very rarely in intellectual history has a young graduate student so profoundly influenced the course of social thought in the world.

Like Condorcet with his "voting paradox," Arrow was also concerned with the difficulties of group decisions and the inconsistencies to which they may lead. Arrow's "impossibility theorem" (formally, the "general possibility theorem") is a result of breathtaking elegance and power. The theorem shows that even some very mild conditions of reasonableness could not be simultaneously satisfied by any social choice procedure in the wide family of such procedures that identify a social ordering for any collection of individual preference orderings over social alternatives.

The fundamental challenge that Arrow considered is that of going from individual preferences over the different states of affairs to a social preference over those states, reflecting something like an "aggregation" of the points of views of all members of the society. He wanted the social preference to be an "ordering" (sometimes called a "complete ordering"). A ranking is an ordering if (1) any two alternatives can be ranked—one preferred to the other, or the opposite, or they are indifferent to each other (this is called the "completeness" of the ranking), and (2) the ranking has a requirement of coherence that goes by the name of "transitivity" (a flash of grammatical language in the field of preferences). Transitivity demands that if an alternative x is taken to be at least as good as y, and y to be at least as good as z, then x must be judged to be at least as good as z. Arrow saw these demands on the social choice as requirements of "collective rationality."

A social choice procedure that takes us from a cluster (or "profile") of individual preference orderings (one ordering per person) to a social preference ordering is called a "social welfare function," as defined by Arrow. Interpreting this in the context of welfare economics, if a state of affairs x is socially ranked above another state y, then state x yields more "social welfare" than does y. The impossibility theorem shows that if there are at least three distinct alternatives and at least two different individuals (though only a finite number of them), then a set of very mildly demanding conditions of reasonableness cannot be satisfied together by any possible social welfare function.

Consider the following four axioms characterizing a social welfare function, specifying a social ordering of alternative states of affairs for each profile of individual preference orderings over those states.[1]

Unrestricted domain (U) claims that a social welfare function must work for every profile of individual preferences (that is, it must generate a social ordering for every cluster of individual preferences).

Independence of irrelevant alternatives (I) requires that the social ranking of any pair of alternatives must depend only on the individual rankings over just that pair (the "relevant" pair).

The Pareto principle (P) instructs that if everyone strictly prefers some alternative x to another alternative y, then social ordering too must place x strictly above y.

Non-dictatorship (D) demands that there should be no dictator such that when that person strictly prefers any x to any y, then society must invariably place x strictly above y.

Arrow's impossibility theorem shows that these mild-looking axioms U, I, P, and D cannot be simultaneously fulfilled by any social aggregation procedure (or social welfare function).

This is not only an astonishing analytical result, but also one that generated much despair in the search for rational social choice procedures based on individuals' preferences. It also seemed like an antidemocratic result of profound reach (which, in fact, is not quite the correct interpretation). One common take on this result was that only a dictatorship would avoid social inconsistencies, but a dictatorial rule would, of course, involve (1) an extreme sacrifice of participatory decisions and (2) a gross inability to be sensitive to the heterogeneous interests of a diverse population.

Two centuries after the flowering of the ambitions of social rationality in Enlightenment thinking and in the writings of the theorists of the French Revolution, the subject seemed to be inescapably doomed. Social appraisals, economic evaluations, and normative statistics would have to be, it seemed, inevitably arbitrary or irremediably despotic.

---

1. This is a somewhat simplified version of the set of conditions that Arrow himself used (see Sen 1970a).

The Idea of Social Preference

Arrow's framework makes substantial use of the idea of social preference, and Arrovian conditions of "collective rationality" seen in terms of direct use of maximization based on the binary relation of social preference, or indirect use of the idea through imposing internal consistency conditions of choice that has a binary representation. The binary relation can be seen as an "as-if social preference." James Buchanan (1954) has argued powerfully against the alleged cogency of the idea of social preference, because society is not an individual and so cannot have any self-evident attribute of a "preference." The objection is particularly relevant in dealing with political decisions rather than social welfare evaluation, because the latter demands some notion of a socially acceptable idea of a possibly binary social welfare ranking relation. But the case for relying on institutional outcomes rather than on any implicit idea of social preference can be seen to be strong for political processes.

The possibility of a nonbinary formulation of the social choice has received considerable attention in the literature of social choice theory in recent years, led by contributors like Bergt Hansson, Thomas Schwartz, Peter Fishburn, Donald Campbell, and Charles Plott. In some cases, the impossibility results of the Arrow type seem resolved, and in others, they have been revived in the choice-functional framework. The question that arises, however, is whether the impossibility results, thus derived, have been crucially dependent on imposing conditions of internal consistency of choice, which tend to take us in the direction of a binary representation of the choice function. However, it turns out (see Sen 1993) that Arrow's impossibility theorem can be generalized to hold without any condition of internal consistency of choice and without imposing any demands of collective rationality. Through seeing the fuller implications of the relation between individual preferences and social choice (including seeing independence of irrelevant alternatives in a more demanding light), the Arrow impossibility can be shown to resurface without any use of internal consistency in social choice functions and without any idea—explicit or implicit—of a social preference.

Voting and Majority Decisions

As far as political decisions are concerned (postponing for the moment welfare economic investigations), it seems fair to conclude that there is not going to be any perfect resolution through voting procedures of the social choice dilemmas of the kind identified by Arrow. This leads to two different kinds of questions. First, even though there may not be any fault-less voting procedure, do some of them function much better than others? Second, is voting a good way at all of trying to resolve social choice prob-lems of all kinds?

Majority voting has many rather attractive qualities and is considered by many as a quintessential component of democratic decision making. Can the grip of inconsistent choices—and more particularly, of not having a "Condorcet winner"—be at least partially subdued? One of the ways of coping with this challenge that has been much explored in this context is the use of a "restricted domain" of the social welfare function—through limiting the preference profiles that are allowed—that would avoid prob-lems of inconsistency in voting results and also avoid the nonexistence of a "Condorcet winner." Arrow (1951) himself had initiated, along with Duncan Black (1948, 1958), the search for adequate restrictions that would guarantee consistent majority decisions, and he had identified a class of preference profiles ("single-peaked" preferences) that would work.

In fact, the Arrow-Black identification of sufficiency for consistent majority rule (single-peaked preference profiles) can be vastly expanded through using a process of reasoning not dissimilar to Arrow's own, which results in a much more general condition: "value restriction" (Sen 1966). Value restriction demands that in every triple of alternatives (x, y, z), there is one alternative (say, x) such that everyone agrees that it is either "not best," or "not worst," or "not medium" (the position on which there is such an agreement can vary from one triple to another).

Going from sufficiency conditions to the demands of necessity, the nec-essary and sufficient conditions of domain restriction for consistent major-ity decisions can also be precisely identified (see Sen and Pattanaik 1969). If individual preferences are strict—that is, they have no indifferences—then these rather complex necessary and sufficient conditions boil down simply to value restriction. However, even though these conditions are much less restrictive than the earlier conditions that had been identified, they are still quite demanding; indeed, it can be shown that they can be easily violated in many actual situations.

Even though a voting impasse cannot be generally eliminated, it appears that majority rule is, in fact, far less vulnerable to contradictions than other procedures of voting. It can be shown that if there is a domain restriction for which any voting rule other than the majority rule works well, then so will majority rule (see Maskin 1995, 2014; Dasgupta and Maskin 2008). Furthermore, for any nonmajority voting rule, there is a class of preference profiles for which majority rule works well, but the other voting rules do not. This powerful "dominance result" shows that even though all voting rules are subject to impasse or contradictions, the method of majority rule, which has other attractions too, is the least vulnerable among them. The comparative robustness of majority rule is surely a pointer to its strength that cannot but be important for many social and political decisions. But that comfort may not be available for many other types of social choice. For example, voting rules, including majority rule, may be quite inappropriate as a basis for welfare economic judgments (on which more presently).

Liberty and Rights

Majority rule can also be severe against minority rights and may also work against individual liberty. More than a century and a half ago, John Stuart Mill ([1859] 1959) investigated how a good society should try to guarantee the liberty of each person. Liberty has many different aspects, including two rather distinct features:

1) *The opportunity aspect:* We should be able to achieve what we choose to achieve in our respective personal domains, for example, in our private life.

2) *The process aspect:* We can make our own choices in our personal domains (no matter whether we achieve what we want).

In social choice theory, the formulation of liberty has been primarily concerned with the former, that is, the opportunity aspect.

Seen in the perspective of the opportunity aspect, liberty demands that each person should be decisive in safeguarding certain things in his or her "personal domain," without interference by others (even if a majority is keen to interfere). J. S. Mill considered various examples of such personal domains over which the person involved should be able to prevail, including—for example—in the practice of his or her own religion. Note that the "opportunity aspect" cannot be safeguarded, as it is sometimes wrongly presumed, by leaving to the person the choices to be made in her personal domain, as an alleged "process guarantee." The trouble is that others can interfere in the practice of this person through their own actions (for example, a person may be allowed to choose her religious practices, but others could interfere through making hugely distracting loud noises, or even by organizing disturbing demonstrations outside her home, making life difficult for the person involved). It is the duty of the society, Mill argued, to make sure that the person's own choices over a personal domain prevail (in this case, guaranteeing that the person can perform his or her private religious actions, without being stopped by others, *and also* without being hindered by the actions of others).

It is the conflict of this opportunity aspect of liberty with the Pareto principle (given unrestricted domain) that is the subject matter of an impossibility theorem, which is sometimes referred to as "the liberal paradox," or "the impossibility of the Paretian liberal" (See Sen 1970a, 1970b). Unlike the Arrow theorem, this impossibility theorem does not depend on the independence of irrelevant alternatives (condition I), which is not invoked at all. Instead, it is shown that unrestricted domain (U) and the Pareto principle (P) cannot be combined with "minimal liberty," demanding only that at least two persons are each decisive over the choice over one pair each. There is a huge literature on the subject, including contributions that (1) dispute the result, (2) extend it, (3) attempt to resolve the conflict, and (4) question the interpretation of liberty. The theorem shows the impossibility, given unrestricted domain, of satisfying even a very mild demand for "minimal liberty" when combined with an insistence on Pareto efficiency.

Turning to the process aspect, seeing liberty as a guaranteed process of leaving people free to do certain things in their own personal sphere is a requirement that has been particularly pursued by various writers in this field (led by Robert Nozick (1974), and joined in many distinct ways by others). In this perspective, what liberty demands is that people remain free to choose what to do in their personal domain, but it does not really matter what the actual outcome is (that is, it does not matter as far as liberty is concerned). I cannot pretend that I find this conclusion particularly persuasive, because the opportunity aspect of liberty can also be very important.

In modern societies in particular, it is hard to give people the agency to control what happens in all aspects of their lives. My liberty to fly safely is better guaranteed by leaving many decisions to the pilot, rather than my taking charge of the agencies in the cockpit. Our lives are saved by better policing and effective epidemiology, which involve the agencies of many other people (and not just on what we ourselves do).

However, it is hard to deny that liberty has both opportunity and procedural aspects. If being free to smoke is an important liberty (there can be a debate on this), then surely a procedural system that allows anyone to decide whether to smoke can rightly be seen as a part of liberty. However, if a person who shuns smoking does not want smoke to be blown in her face, her liberty to secure this does not depend primarily on what she does, but mostly on what others do. Leaving her free with her action cannot eliminate this violation of her personal liberty.

In the recent literature, the formulation of process-based liberty has been much refined from the simple statements originally made by Nozick (1974). In particular, the specification of liberty has been given "game-form" formulations (see Gaertner, Pattanaik, and Suzumura 1992), so that agency freedoms are judged by the acceptability of combinations of different persons' actions (e.g., do not smoke if others are present, or—as a stricter demand—do not smoke in places where others can be present if not deterred by the presence and activities of smokers). This refinement is surely an important one, but as Gaertner, Pattanaik, and Suzumura explain, it does not eliminate the impossibility of the Paretian liberal. Its merit lies elsewhere, in particular, in capturing better the common idea of liberty with the assignment of individual agency freedoms. It does not, however, eliminate the relevance of social choice in assessing different game forms (see Sen 1992; Hammond 1996). Game forms do help the specification and analysis of liberty, but the motivation behind social choice theory would continue to apply in the assessment of alternative game forms. And in that context, we must take note of outcomes as well as processes.

Crisis in Welfare Economics

I turn now to welfare economics. Social choice difficulties apply inter alia to what is called "welfare economics"—an old subject aimed at judging social states in terms of the well-being (and other concerns) of the people, on which A. C. Pigou's (1920) distinguished book, *The Economics of Welfare*, had been something of a classic account. The subject, however, had taken quite a hard hit in the 1930s, even before Arrow's impossibility result further darkened—or seemed to darken—the prospects of systematic welfare economics. The initial crises came because of the economists' newfound—but rather hastily argued—conviction that there was something quite unsound in making use of interpersonal comparison of individual utilities, which had been the basis of traditional welfare economics

Welfare economics had been developed by utilitarian economists (such as Francis T. Edgeworth (1881), Alfred Marshall (1890), and Arthur C. Pigou (1920)) and had taken a very different track from the vote-oriented social choice theory. It took inspiration not from Borda (1781) and Condorcet (1785), but from their contemporary, Jeremy Bentham (1789). Bentham had pioneered the use of utilitarian calculus to obtain judgments about social interest by aggregating the personal interests of the different individuals in the form of their respective utilities.

Bentham's concern—and that of utilitarians in general (John Stuart Mill was the exception here)—was with the *total utility* of a community. The focus, which has problems of its own, was on the total sum of utilities, irrespective of the distribution of that total, and in this, we can see a partial blindness of considerable ethical and political import. For example, in the utilitarian best world of maximizing utility, a person who is unlucky enough to have a uniformly lower capability to generate enjoyment and utility out of income (say, because of a physical or mental handicap) would be given even a lower share of a fixed total income, because of her lower ability to generate utility out of income. This is a consequence of utilitarianism's single-minded pursuit of maximizing the sum-total of utilities—no matter how unequally distributed. However, the utilitarian interest in taking comparative note of the gains and losses of different people is not in itself a negligible concern. And this concern makes utilitarian welfare economics deeply interested in using a class of information—in the form of comparison of utility gains and losses of different persons—with which Condorcet and Borda had not been directly involved.

Utilitarianism has been very influential in shaping welfare economics, which was dominated for a long time by an almost unquestioning adherence to utilitarian calculus. But by the 1930s, utilitarian welfare economics came under severe fire. It would have been quite natural to question (as

Rawls (1971) would do masterfully in formulating his theory of justice) the utilitarian neglect of distributional issues and its concentration only on utility sum-totals (in a distribution-blind way). But that was not the direction in which the anti-utilitarian critiques went in the 1930s and in the decades that followed. Rather, economists came to be persuaded by arguments presented by Lionel Robbins and others (who were themselves deeply influenced by the then-fashionable philosophical approach of "logical positivism") that interpersonal comparisons of utility had no scientific basis: "Every mind is inscrutable to every other mind and no common denominator of feelings is possible" (Robbins 1938, 636). Thus, the epistemic foundations of utilitarian welfare economics were seen as incurably defective.

There followed attempts to do welfare economics on the basis of each person's respective ordering of social states, without any interpersonal comparisons of utility gains and losses of different persons. Although utilitarianism and utilitarian welfare economics are quite indifferent to the distribution of utilities among different persons (concentrating, as they do, only on the sum-total of utilities), the new regime, without any interpersonal comparisons in any form, further reduced the informational base on which social choice could draw. The already limited informational base of Benthamite calculus was made to shrink further to the narrow electoral plane of Borda and Condorcet (I should explain that I am referring here to Condorcet as a voting theorist, not as a general social philosopher—in that capacity, his attention was much broader). The use of different persons' utility rankings without any interpersonal comparison is analytically quite similar to the use of voting information—each individual taken separately—in making social choice.

Attempted Repairs and Further Crises

Faced with this informational restriction, utilitarian welfare economics gave way, from the 1940s on, to what came to be called—hugely overambitiously–"new welfare economics," which used only one basic criterion of social improvement: the "Pareto comparison." The Pareto criterion for social improvement only asserts that a situation can be seen as definitely better than another if the change would increase the utility of every one (or at least increase the utility of someone without reducing the utility of anyone else). A good deal of subsequent welfare economics restricted attention to "Pareto efficiency" only (that is, only to making sure that no further Pareto improvements are possible). This criterion takes no interest whatsoever in distributional issues, which would tend to involve conflicts of interests of different persons). So if one person gains while everyone else loses (no matter how many—and by how much), we were not allowed to declare this change to be a deterioration, if we seek only Pareto efficiency.

This remarkable reticence, it seems fair to guess, would have appealed to Emperor Nero, who evidently enjoyed playing his music while Rome burned and all other Romans were plunged into misery. In general, the Pareto efficiency of a state of affairs would not be disturbed even if many people are forced into terribly famished lives, while some others lead lives of extreme luxury, provided the misery of the destitute cannot be reduced without cutting into the lives of the super-rich.

Some further criterion—beyond Pareto efficiency—is clearly needed for making social welfare judgments with a greater reach, and this was insightfully explored by Abram Bergson (1938) and Paul A. Samuelson (1947). This search led directly to Arrow's (1950, 1951) pioneering formulation of social choice theory, relating social preference (or decisions) to the set of individual preferences, that is, to the search for what Arrow called a "social welfare function." It was in the framework of social welfare functions that Arrow (1951, 1963) established his powerful impossibility theorem, showing the incompatibility of some very mild-looking conditions (discussed earlier), including Pareto efficiency, nondictatorship, independence of irrelevant alternatives, and unrestricted domain. This generated further gloom in an already gloomy assessment of the possibility of having a reasoned and satisfactory welfare economics.

To escape the impossibility result, different ways of modifying Arrow's requirements were tried out in the literature that followed, but other difficulties continued to emerge. The force and widespread presence of impossibility results generated a consolidated sense of pessimism, and this became a dominant theme in welfare economics and social choice theory in general. By the middle 1960s, William Baumol, a distinguished contributor to economics in general and welfare economics in particular, judiciously remarked that "statements about the significance of welfare economics" had started having "an ill-concealed resemblance to obituary notices" (Baumol 1965, 2). This was certainly the right reading of the prevailing views.

Welfare Economics and Voting Information

It can be argued that the "obiturial" climate of welfare economics in its postutilitarian phase was related largely to the epistemic penury of welfare economics based on confining informational inflow to voting-like inputs. Voting-based procedures are entirely natural for some kinds of social choice problems, such as elections, referendums, or committee decisions. They are, however, altogether unsuitable for many other problems of social choice. For example, when we want to get some kind of an aggregative assessment of social welfare, we cannot rely on such procedures for at least three distinct reasons.

First, there are some serious problems in the correspondence between actual preferences and the votes cast, which must take note of the possibility of strategic voting, aimed at manipulating the voting outcomes. The impossibility of having strategy-proof voting procedures has been well established.[2] The subject occupies a huge literature.

Second, voting requires active participation, and if some groups tend not to exercise their voting rights (perhaps due to cultural conditioning or because of procedural barriers that making voting difficult and expensive), then the preferences of those groups tend to have quite inadequate representation in social decisions. Because of lower participation, the interests of substantial groups—for example, of African Americans in the United States—can have a quite limited influence on national politics.

Third, even with the active involvement of everyone in voting exercises, we will still be short of important information needed for welfare economic evaluation. It is absurd to think that social welfare judgments can be made without some understanding of issues of inequality and disparities that characterize one society or another. Voting information, taken on its own, turns a blind eye to such comparisons—its takes no direct note of how deprived different voters may be, nor of the extent to which their preference reflects large differences or small ones. These limitations are related to the eschewing of interpersonal comparison of well-being, on the impossibility of which for several decades, professional economists remained prematurely convinced.

---

2. See Gibbard (1973), Satterthwaite (1975), and also Pattanaik (1973, 1978), Maskin (1985) and Maskin and Sjöström (2002).

There was also the exclusion of what economists call "cardinal utility," which takes us beyond relying merely on the ranking of alternatives in terms of being better or worse (or indifferent)—the so-called ordinal utility—to giving us some idea of the relative gaps between the utility values of different alternatives. Utilitarian welfare economics uses cardinality of utilities as well as interpersonal comparison of these utilities, and the new orthodoxy that emerged in the 1930s disputed the scientific status of both cardinality and of interpersonal comparison of utilities of different persons.

Informational Penury as a Cause of Social Choice Problems

It is also worth recollecting that utilitarian philosophy—and influenced by it, traditional welfare economics as well—had huge informational restrictions of their own. It was not allowed to make any basic use of non-utility information, because everything had to be judged ultimately by utility sum-totals in consequent states of affairs. To this informational exclusion was now added the further exclusion of interpersonal comparisons of utilities, along with cardinal utility, which disabled the idea of utility sum-totals without removing the exclusion of non-utility information. This barren informational landscape makes it hard to arrive at any systematic judgment of social welfare, based on informed reasoning. Arrow's theorem can be interpreted, in this context, as a demonstration that even some very weak conditions—in this case, Arrow's axioms—relating individual preferences to social welfare judgments cannot be simultaneously satisfied in a world of such informational privation (see Sen 1977b, 1979).

The problem is not just one of impossibility. Given Arrow axioms U (unrestricted domain), I (independence of irrelevant alternatives), and P (Pareto principle), the relation between the profile of individual preferences and the social ranking emerging from it has to forgo taking any note of the nature of the alternatives (that is, the social states). The relation must simply go by the individual preferences over the alternatives, no matter what they are. If person 1 is decisive in the choice over any pair (a, b)—for whatever reason—then that person would be decisive in the social preference over every other pair of alternatives (x, y) as well, even though the nature of the choice involved may radically differ because of the nature of the social alternatives involved.

This requirement is sometimes called "neutrality" (a usage that had the support—I very much hope only half-hearted—of Arrow (1963) himself). It is, in fact, a peculiarly kind term for what is after all a sanctification of blindness to all information other than utility information. Perhaps the alternative term used for it (namely, "welfarism") is more helpful, in that it focuses on the limitation imposed by forbidding any direct use of any information about the states of affairs other than the individual welfares they respectively generate—and that again only in the form of utilities. Adding to that the further requirement that the utility information used must not involve any cardinality, or any interpersonal comparison of utilities, amounts to insisting that social choices must be made with extremely little information indeed.

The demand of so-called neutrality tends to play havoc with the discipline of reasoned social choice. Consider, for example, a cake division problem, in which everyone prefers to have a larger share of the cake. If, in this cake division problem, an equal division between two persons in the form (50, 50) is socially preferred to person 1 having 99 percent of it, with the other having only 1 percent in the form (99, 1), it is clearly being judged that person 2's preference should prevail over person 1's, in this case. But if so-called neutrality is demanded, then due to the insistence that the nature of the alternatives should not make any difference to whose preference prevails, an opposite type of inequality—with person 2 having nearly all in the form of (1, 99)—should be socially preferred to a (50, 50) division, through the requirement that person 2, decisive over the earlier choice, should be decisive over all other pairwise conflicts as well. It is hard to escape the thought that something has gone badly wrong in the underlying intellectual system—and that problem arises even before any impossibility result emerges.

What is being presumed here is to insist that welfare judgments must be based on something like voting data, taking note of who prefers what but ignoring who is rich and who is poor, and who gains how much from a change compared with what the losers lose. We must go beyond the class of voting rules (explored by Borda and Condorcet as well as Arrow) to be able to address distributional issues, particularly in welfare economics.

Arrow had ruled out the use of interpersonal comparisons, because he had followed the general consensus that had emerged in the 1930s that (as Arrow put it) "interpersonal comparison of utilities has no meaning" (Arrow 1951, 9). The totality of the axiom combination used by Arrow had the effect of confining social choice mechanisms to rules that are, broadly speaking, of the voting type. His impossibility result relates, therefore, to this class of rules with this informational abstinence.

It should be emphasized that, unlike ruling out the use of interpersonal comparison of utilities, which Arrow explicitly invoked, the insistence on restricting social choice procedures only to voting rules is not an assumption that is directly imposed by Arrow. It is, in fact, a combined result—quite startling in its own right—of the different axioms that Arrow uses. It can be seen as an analytical consequence of a set of apparently reasonable axioms postulated for social choice. Interpersonal comparison of utilities is, of course, explicitly excluded, but in the process of proving his impossibility theorem, Arrow also shows that a set of seemingly plausible assumptions, taken together, logically entail other features of voting rules as well, in particular something close to so-called neutrality (discussed earlier). This requires that no effective note be taken of the nature of the social states, and that the social decisions must be based only on the votes that are respectively cast in favor of—and against—them. Although the eschewal of interpersonal comparisons of utilities eliminates the possibility of taking note of the inequality of utilities (and also of differences in gains and losses of utilities), the entailed component of so-called neutrality (or welfarism) prevents attention being indirectly paid to distributional issues through taking explicit note of the nature of the respective social states (for example, of the incomes or wealth levels of different persons, as in the cake-division example discussed earlier).

This also brings out the disanalogy between Condorcet's voting paradox and Arrow's much more general impossibility theorem (in contrast to some common statements in the literature). Condorcet's analysis begins with the world of voting rules, whereas Arrow gets there only after establishing a remarkable analytical theorem showing that the combination of a few very apparently plausible axioms leaves us no option but to confine our vision to voting rules. Some of the hard work in establishing Arrow's theorem ends where the Condorcet exercise begins.

Incorporating More Information in Social Decisions

To lay a broader foundation for a constructive social choice theory (broader than the framework Arrow developed), we have to resist the historical consensus against the use of interpersonal comparisons in social choice that was

dominant when Arrow began his research on social choice. That historical consensus was based on a rather fragile understanding of epistemology,
derived from the short-lived boom of logical positivism. The case for unqualified rejection of interpersonal comparisons of mental states is hard to sustain
(quite aside from the fact that these comparisons need not be of mental states
only—on which more presently).[3] Indeed, as has been forcefully argued by
the philosopher Donald Davidson (1986), it is difficult to see how people can
understand anything much about other people's minds and feelings without
making some comparisons with their own minds and feelings. Such comparisons may not be extremely precise, but then again, we know from analytical investigations that very precise interpersonal comparisons may not be
needed to make systematic use of such comparisons in social choice.

However, aside from doubts about the evidential basis of interpersonal
comparisons, there were also questions about the possibility of a systematic
analytical framework for comparing and using the accounting of different
persons' welfare magnitudes for social decisions, especially because interpersonal comparisons can take many different forms. John Harsanyi (1955)
and Patrick Suppes (1966) made some early departures in that direction.
But they were more concerned with using interpersonal comparisons (of
"units" in the case of Harsanyi and of "levels" in the case of Suppes) rather
than with working out a comprehensive analytical framework for interpersonal comparisons in general, including the possibilities of specific features
of interpersonal welfare calculus.

Inspired by this challenge, I tried my hand at developing a comprehensive analytical framework for interpersonal comparisons in my book *Collective Choice and Social Welfare* (Sen 1970a) and in follow-up contributions
(Sen 1977b, 1982). Happily, the 1970s and 1980s also saw the publication
of major contributions on the subject from a dazzling group of social choice
theorists, including Peter Hammond (1976); Claude d'Aspremont and Louis
Gevers (1977); Eric Maskin (1978, 1979); Louis Gevers (1979); Kevin Roberts
(1980a, 1980b); Kotaro Suzumura (1983, 1997); Charles Blackorby, David
Donaldson, and John Weymark (1984); d'Aspremont (1985); d'Aspremont
and Mongin (1998); and others. Even Kenneth Arrow (1977) joined this

---

3. On this issue and that of making actual interpersonal comparisons with factual
information, see Daniel Kahneman (1999, 2000), Alan Krueger (2009), and Krueger
and Stone (2014).

exploration. It is fair to say that we now have a much clearer understanding of the analytical demands of different kinds and extents of interpersonal comparisons, and the ways and means of making systematic use of that information in social choice.

Without going into the technicalities that have emerged in the literature, it can be said that the extent and reach of different kinds of interpersonal comparisons can be explicitly invoked in a fully axiomatized form (prominent types include full comparability, level comparability, unit compability, ratio-scale comparability, and so on; see Sen 1977b). Each kind of comparability imposes its own demands on combining welfare numbers of different persons. Consider, for example, a case of full comparability, by beginning with well-being numbers 1, 2, 3 for person 1, respectively, for social alternatives x, y, and z, with the corresponding numbers for person 2 being 2, 3, 1. Because there are no naturally fixed units of well-being, we can easily enough alter the well-being numbers of person 1 for x, y, and z to be 2, 4, 6 instead of 1, 2, 3. Full interpersonal comparability would demand that if we rescale person 1's well-being numbers by doubling them, then we must do the same for person 2, and transform her well-being numbers from 2, 3, 1 to a corresponding set 4, 6, 2. With such tying up (they are axiomatized through "invariance conditions") implied by full interpersonal comparability, it would not make any real difference whether we work with the original numbers (1, 2, 3 for person 1, and 2, 3, 1 for person 2), or deal instead with the symmetrically transformed numbers (2, 4, 6 for person 1, and 4, 6, 2 for person 2). As different types of interpersonal comparability (such as "level comparability" or "unit comparability") are considered, we shall have correspondingly different specifications of the invariance conditions (see Sen 1970a, 1977b; Roberts 1980a).

Through the use of "invariance conditions" in a generalized framework that allow the use of interpersonally comparable well-being numbers, going beyond simple rankings (to different extents, depending on the type of interpersonal comparability), we get what are called *social welfare functionals*, which allow the use of much more information than Arrow's social welfare functions permit. Indeed, interpersonal comparisons need not even be confined to all-or-none dichotomies. We may be able to make interpersonal comparisons to some extent, but not in every comparison, nor of every type, nor with tremendous exactness. To illustrate, we may invoke the same example of Nero and the burning of Rome, discussed earlier. It seems reasonable to argue that there should be no great difficulty in accepting that Emperor Nero's welfare gain from the burning of Rome was smaller than the sum-total of the welfare loss of all the other Romans put together—perhaps hundreds of thousands of them—who suffered from the fire. But this does not require us to presume that we can put everyone's welfares in an exact one-to-one correspondence with one another. Thus, there may be room for demanding "partial comparability"— denying both the extremes: full comparability and no comparability at all.

The different extents of partial comparability can be given mathematically exact forms (precisely articulating the extent of the variations that may be permitted). It can also be shown that terribly refined interpersonal comparisons may not be needed for arriving at definite social decisions. Quite often, rather limited levels of partial comparability will be adequate for making social decisions. Thus, the empirical exercise need not be as ambitious as is sometimes feared.

What Difference Does It Make?

How much of a change in the possibility of social choice is brought about by systematic use of interpersonal comparisons? Does Arrow's impossibility theorem (and related results) go away with the use of interpersonal comparisons in social welfare judgments? In brief, the answer is yes. The additional informational availability allows sufficient discrimination to escape impossibilities of this type. For example, with interpersonal comparability we can use the Rawlsian distributive principle of maximin (what he calls "the Difference Principle"), which takes the form of giving priority to the interests of the worst-off person (or persons).[4] And this just demands "level comparability," while the units of different persons' welfares need not be comparable at all.

There is an interesting contrast here. Although interpersonal comparability even without cardinality helps dissolve Arrow's impossibility theorem,

---

4. For compatibility with the Pareto principle (as well as for making reasonable sense), this Rawlsian approach has to be used in what is called a "lexicographic" form, so that in case where the worst-off persons tie with each other in the comparison between two states of affairs, we go by the interests of the second worst-off. And so on. For the wide reach of Rawls's criterion and its widespread relevance in public policy, see Edmund S. Phelps (1973).

cardinality without interpersonal comparability does nothing of the sort. In the absence of interpersonal comparability, Arrow's theorem can, in fact, be generalized to cover the case of fully cardinal utilities or welfares (see Sen 1970a, chapter 8). In contrast, the possibility of only "ordinal" interpersonal comparisons (so that the rankings of well-being between different persons remain invariant) is adequate to end the impossibility, even without any cardinality. We already know of course that with some types of interpersonal comparisons demanded in a full form (including cardinal interpersonal comparability), we can use the classical utilitarian approach. But it turns out that even weaker forms of comparability would still permit making consistent social welfare judgments, satisfying all of Arrow's requirements, in addition to being sensitive to distributional concerns (even though the possible rules may have to be confined to a relatively small class; see Roberts 1980a, 1980b).

Interpersonal Comparison of What?

Even though the analytical issues in incorporating interpersonal comparisons have been fairly well sorted out, there still remains the important practical matter of finding an adequate approach to the empirical discipline of making interpersonal comparisons and then using them in practice. The foremost question to be addressed is: interpersonal comparison of what? Even though the debates about interpersonal comparison of well-being have been, historically, concentrated on the comparison of "utilities" in which utilitarian philosophers were particularly interested, the subject of interpersonal comparison in general is much broader than that.[5]

It must be recognized that the formal structures of social welfare functions are not specific to utility comparisons only, and they can, in fact, incorporate other types of interpersonal comparisons as well. The principal conceptual issue is the accounting of individual advantage. This need

---

5. Along with broadening the coverage of information for a better understanding of poverty, there is also the important question of making sure that the empirical connections used in the informational expansion are appropriately tested and scrutinized. Recently, randomized trials have been skillfully used to make the informational broadening more sure footed, whenever possible (see particularly Banerjee and Duflo 2011).

not take the form of comparisons of mental states of happiness or desires (which have been exclusively championed by utilitarian philosophers). It could instead focus on some other way of looking at individual well-being, or freedom, or substantive opportunities.

Further, if the aggregation considered is that of individual judgments (not of individual interests), then the question can also be raised about how the divergent opinions or valuations of different persons may be combined (this is a social choice exercise of a rather different kind, on which, see Sen 1977a). This exercise, with complexities of its own, has also received some attention (see particularly Christian List and Philip Pettit (2002) and List (2005)). Furthermore, if utility comparisons are taken to be value judgments themselves, rather than purely observational assessments (this was the position strongly advocated by Lionel Robbins), then the assignment of individual utilities for use in social aggregation could itself be seen as involving aggregation of different individuals' assessments of people's utilities (see Roberts 1995).

Capabilities and Primary Goods

The main problem with relying on mental state comparisons may not be their feasibility but their relevance—at least their allegedly exclusive relevance in social choice. There are many difficulties in judging the well-being of a person by his or her mental state. Utilities may sometimes be very malleable in response to persistent deprivation. A hopeless destitute, or a downtrodden laborer living under inescapably exploitative arrangements, or a subjugated housewife in a society with entrenched gender inequality, or a tyrannized citizen under brutal authoritarianism may come to terms with her deprivation. She may take whatever pleasure she can from small achievements and adjust her desires to take note of feasibility (thereby helping the fulfillment of her downwardly adjusted desires). But her success in such adjustments will not make her deprivation go away. The metric of pleasure or desire may sometimes quite inadequately reflect the extent of a person's substantive deprivation.

There may indeed be a case for taking incomes, commodity bundles, or resources more generally to be of direct interest in judging a person's advantage. The interest in incomes or resources can arise for many different reasons—not merely for the mental states that opulence may help generate.

In fact, the Difference principle in Rawls's (1971) theory of "justice as fairness" is based on judging individual advantage in terms of a person's command over what Rawls calls "primary goods," which are general-purpose resources that are useful for anyone to have (no matter what her exact objectives are).

This procedure can be improved on by taking note not only of the holdings of primary goods and resources, but also of interpersonal differences in converting them to the capability to live well. Indeed, I have tried to argue in favor of judging individual advantages in terms of the respective capabilities that the person has reason to value, on which, see Sen (1980, 1985a, 1985b) and Nussbaum (1988, 1992, 2000, 2001, 2011). This approach focuses on the substantive freedoms that people have rather than only on the particular outcomes they obtain. For responsible adults, the concentration on freedom rather than only on achievement has some merit, and it can provide a general framework for analyzing individual advantage and deprivation in a contemporary society.

Normative Measurement

The variety of information on which social welfare analysis can draw can be well illustrated by the study of poverty and the battle against it. The intellectual challenges involved in what Angus Deaton (2013) has called "the great escape" are as important to the subject of social choice as they are central to the basic engagements of the social sciences in general.

In the standard measurement literature, poverty is typically seen in terms of the lowness of incomes, and it has been traditionally measured simply by counting the number of people below the poverty-line income; this is sometimes called the "head-count measure." A scrutiny of this approach, which has been an important part of contemporary social choice literature, yields two different types of questions. First, is it adequate to see poverty as equivalent to lowness of income? Second, even if poverty is seen as low income, is the aggregate poverty of a society best characterized by some index of the head-count measure of the number falling below the chosen cut-off poverty-line income?

I take up these questions in turn. Do we get enough of a diagnosis of individual poverty by comparing the individual's income with a socially given poverty-line income? What about the person with an income well above the poverty line, who suffers from an expensive illness (requiring, say, kidney dialysis)? Is deprivation not ultimately a lack of opportunity to lead a minimally acceptable life, which can be influenced by a number of considerations, including of course personal income but also physical and environmental characteristics, and other variables, related to, say, epidemiological conditions of a person's regional location. It has been argued that poverty can be more sensibly seen as a serious deprivation of certain basic capabilities. This alternative approach leads to a rather different diagnosis of poverty from the ones that a purely income-based analysis can yield.

This is not to deny that lowness of income can be very important in many contexts, because the opportunities a person enjoys in a market economy can be severely constrained by her level of real income.[6] However, various contingencies can lead to variations in the "conversion" of income into the capability to live a minimally acceptable life. And if that is what we are concerned with, there may be good reasons to look beyond income poverty (see Sen 1984, 1992; Foster and Sen 1997) without ignoring the income information. There are at least four different sources of variation: (1) personal heterogeneities (for example, disability or proneness to illness), (2) environmental diversities (for example, living in a storm-prone or flood-prone area), (3) variations in social climate (for example, the prevalence of crime or epidemiological challenges), and (4) differences in relative deprivation connected with customary patterns of consumption in particular societies (for example, being relatively impoverished in terms of income in a rich society can lead to deprivation of the absolute capability to take part in the life of the community—a point that was made with compelling force by Adam Smith (1776)).

I turn now to the second question. The most common and most traditional measure of poverty had tended to concentrate on head counting. But it must also make a difference as to how far below the poverty line the poor individually are, and furthermore, how the deprivation is *shared and distributed* among the poor. The social data on the respective deprivations of the individuals who constitute the poor in a society need to be aggregated

---

6. These issues have been insightfully scrutinized by Philippe Van Parijs (1995).

to arrive at informative and usable measures of aggregate poverty. This is a social choice problem, and axioms can indeed be proposed that attempt to capture our distributional concerns in this constructive exercise.[7]

Among the new developments in the field are multidimensional measures of poverty and inequality, powerfully pursued in different forms by Atkinson and Bourguignon (1982), Alkire and Foster (2011a, 2011b), and others.[8] To understand poverty and inequality, a strong case can be made for looking at real deprivation and not merely at mental reactions to that deprivation. The point has been brought out particularly clearly by recent investigations of gender inequality that focus not just on happiness or unhappiness but also on women's deprivation in terms of undernutrition; clinically diagnosed morbidity; observed illiteracy; even unexpectedly high mortality (compared with physiologically justified expectations); and in an anticipatory context, sex-specific abortion of female fetuses.

Multidimensional interpersonal comparisons can be sensibly—and comfortably—accommodated in a broad framework of welfare economics and social choice theory, enhanced by the removal of informational constraints that are explicitly invoked or implicitly imposed in traditional welfare economics.

A Closing Remark

Broadening of the informational basis has become a major concern in modern social choice theory. This applies, first of all, to addressing Arrow's impossibility result. Second, it is central to being inequality sensitive in welfare economics. Third, it is relevant to being liberty conscious in politics, law, and the pursuit of human rights. Fourth, it is especially important for having better informed normative measurement of the well-being of people.

---

7. I will not survey here the huge axiomatic literature on this subject. The measure of poverty on the income space in Sen (1976) can, in fact, be improved by an important but simple variation illuminatingly proposed by Anthony F. Shorrocks (1995). I have to confess favoring the "Sen-Shorrocks measure" over the original "Sen index." See also Foster and Sen (1997).

8. See also Kolm (1977), Maasoumi (1986), Alkire et al. (2015), and Maasoumi and Racine (2016), among many other contributions to the rich literature on multidimensional aggregation in the context of the measurement of inequality and poverty.

As has been discussed and illustrated in different contexts in this chapter, the reasoned use of appropriate information involves both epistemology and ethics. More engagement in each is crucially important for further progress in social choice and welfare economics.

References

Alkire, Sabina, and James E. Foster. 2011a. "Counting and Multidimensional Poverty Measurement." *Journal of Public Economics* 95 (7–8): 476–487.

Alkire, Sabina, and James E. Foster. 2011b. "Understandings and Misunderstandings of Multidimensional Poverty Measurement." *Journal of Economic Inequality* 9 (2): 289–314.

Alkire, Sabina, James E. Foster, Suman Seth, Maria Emma Santos, Jose Manuel Roche, and Paola Ballon. 2015. *Multidimensional Poverty Measurement and Analysis*. Oxford: Oxford University Press.

Arrow, Kenneth J. 1950. "A Difficulty in the Concept of Social Welfare." *Journal of Political Economy* 58 (4): 328–346.

Arrow, Kenneth J. 1951. *Social Choice and Individual Values*. New York: Wiley.

Arrow, Kenneth J. 1963. *Social Choice and Individual Values*, second edition. New York: Wiley.

Arrow, Kenneth J. 1977. "Extended Sympathy and the Possibility of Social Choice." *American Economic Review* 67 (1): 219–225.

Atkinson, Anthony B., and François Bourguignon. 1982. "The Comparison of Multi-Dimensioned Distributions of Economic Status." *Review of Economic Studies* 49 (2): 183–201.

Banerjee, Abhijit V., and Esther Duflo. 2011. *Poor Economics: A Radical Rethinking of the Way to Fight Global Poverty*. New York: Public Affairs.

Baumol, William J. 1965. *Welfare Economics and the Theory of the State*, second ed. Cambridge, MA: Harvard University Press.

Bentham, Jeremy. 1789. *An Introduction to the Principles of Morals and Legislation*. London.

Bergson, Abram. 1938. "A Reformulation of Certain Aspects of Welfare Economics." *Quarterly Journal of Economics* 52 (2): 310–334.

Black, Duncan. 1948. "The Decisions of a Committee Using a Special Majority." *Econometrica* 16 (3): 245–261.

Black, Duncan. 1958. *The Theory of Committees and Elections*. Cambridge: Cambridge University Press.

Blackorby, Charles, David Donaldson, and John A. Weymark. 1984. "Social Choice with Interpersonal Utility Comparisons: A Diagrammatic Introduction." *International Economic Review* 25 (2): 327–356.

Borda, Jean-Charles de. 1781. *Memoire sur les Elections au Scrutin*. Memoires de l'Academie Royal des Sciences. Translated by A. de Grazia. 1953. *Isis* 44 (1/2): 42–51.

Buchanan, James M. 1954. "Individual Choice in Voting and the Market." *Journal of Political Economy* 62 (4): 334–343.

Condorcet, Nicolas de. 1785. *Essai sur l'Application de l' Analyse à la Probabilité des Decisions Rendues à la Pluralité des Voix*. Paris: L' Impremerie Royale.

Condorcet, Nicolas de. 1847. *Ouvres de Condorce,* edited by A. Condorcet O'Connor and M. F. Arago, vol X1. Paris.

Dasgupta, Partha, and Eric Maskin. 2008. "On the Robustness of Majority Rule." *Journal of the European Economic Association* 6 (5): 949–973.

d'Aspremont, Claude. 1985. "Axioms for Social Welfare Orderings." In *Social Goals and Social Organization: Essays in Memory of Elisha Pazner*, edited by Leonid Hurwicz, David Schmeidler, and Hugo Sonnenschein, 19–76. Cambridge: Cambridge University Press.

d'Aspremont, Claude, and Louis Gevers. 1977. "Equity and the Informational Basis of Collective Choice." *Review of Economic Studies* 44 (2): 199–209.

d'Aspremont, Claude, and Philippe Mongin. 1998. "Utility Theory and Ethics." In *Handbook of Utility Theory*, edited by Salvador Barberá, Peter J. Hammond, and Christian Seidl, Volume 1, 371–481. Dordrecht: Kluwer Academic.

Davidson, Donald. 1986. "Judging Interpersonal Interests." In *Foundations of Social Choice Theory*, edited by Jon Elster and Aanund Hylland, 195–211. Cambridge: Cambridge University Press.

Deaton, Angus S. 2013. *The Great Escape: Health, Wealth, and the Origins of Inequality*. Princeton, NJ: Princeton University Press.

Dodgson, Charles L. 1876. *A Method of Taking Votes on More Than Two Issues*. Oxford: Oxford University Press.

Dodgson, Charles L. 1884. *The Principles of Parliamentary Representation*. London: Harrison and Sons.

Edgeworth, Francis T. 1881. *Mathematical Psychics*. London: Kegan Paul.

Foster, James E., and Amartya K. Sen. 1997. "On Economic Inequality after a Quarter Century." In *Economic Inequality* by Amartya K. Sen, expanded edition, 107–219. Oxford: Oxford University Press.

Gaertner, Wulf, Prasanta K. Pattanaik, and Kotaro Suzumura. 1992. "Individual Rights Revisited." *Economica* 59 (234): 161–177.

Gevers, Louis. 1979. "On Interpersonal Comparability and Social Welfare Orderings." *Econometrica* 47 (1): 75–89.

Gibbard, Allan F. 1973. "Manipulation of Voting Schemes: A General Result." *Econometrica* 41 (4): 587–601.

Hammond, Peter J. 1976. "Equity, Arrow's Conditions, and Rawls' Difference Principle." *Econometrica* 44 (4): 793–804.

Hammond, Peter J. 1996. "Consequentialism, Structural Rationality and Game Theory." In *The Rational Foundations of Economic Behaviour. Proceedings of the IEA Conference held in Turin, Italy,* edited by Kenneth J. Arrow, Enrico Colombatto, Mark Perlman, and Christian Schmidt, 25–42. Basingstoke, UK: Macmillan

Harsanyi, John C. 1955. "Cardinal Welfare, Individual Ethics, and Interpersonal Comparison of Utility." *Journal of Political Economy* 63 (4): 309–321.

Kahneman, Daniel. 1999. "Objective Happiness." In *Well-Being: Foundations of Hedonic Psychology*, edited by Daniel Kahneman, Edward Diener, and Norbert Schwarz, 3–25. New York: Russell Sage Foundation.

Kahneman, Daniel. 2000. "Evaluation by Moments: Past and Future." In *Choices, Values, and Frames*, edited by Daniel Kahneman and Amos Tversky, 673–692. Cambridge: Cambridge University Press.

Kolm, Serge-Christophe. 1977. "Multidimensional Egalitarianism." *Quarterly Journal of Economics* 91(1): 1–3.

Krueger, Alan B., ed. 2009. *Measuring the Subjective Well-Being of Nations: National Accounts of Time Use and Well-Being.* Chicago: University of Chicago Press.

Krueger, Alan B., and Arthur A. Stone. 2014. "Progress in Measuring Subjective Well-Being." *Science* 346 (6205): 42–43.

List, Christian. 2005. "The Probability of Inconsistencies in Complex Collective Decisions." *Social Choice and Welfare* 24 (1): 3–32.

List, Christian, and Philip Pettit. 2002. "Aggregating Sets of Judgments: An Impossibility Result." *Economics and Philosophy* 18 (1): 89–110.

Maasoumi, Esfandiar. 1986. "The Measurement and Decomposition of Multi-Dimensional Inequality." *Econometrica* 54 (4): 991–997.

Maasoumi, Esfandiar, and J. S. Racine. 2016. "A Solution to Aggregation and an Application to Multidimensional 'Well-Being' Frontiers." *Journal of Econometrics* 191 (2): 374–383.

Marshall, Alfred. 1890. *Principles of Economics*. London: Macmillan.

Maskin, Eric. 1978. "A Theorem on Utilitarianism." *Review of Economic Studies* 46 (4): 93–96.

Maskin, Eric. 1979. "Decision-Making under Ignorance with Implications for Social Choice." *Theory and Decision* 11 (3): 319–337.

Maskin, Eric. 1985. "The Theory of Implementation in Nash Equilibrium: A Survey." In *Social Goals and Social Organization: Essays in Memory of Elisha Pazner*, edited by Leonid Hurwicz, David Schmeidler, and Hugo Sonnenschein, 173–204. Cambridge: Cambridge University Press.

Maskin, Eric. 1995. "Majority Rule, Social Welfare Functions, and Games Forms." In *Choice, Welfare, and Development: A Festschrift in Honour of Amartya K. Sen*, edited by Kaushik Basu, Prasanta P. Pattanaik, and Kotaro Suzumura, 100–109. Oxford: Oxford University Press.

Maskin, Eric. 2014. "The Arrow Impossibility Theorem: Where Do We Go from Here?" In *The Arrow Impossibility Theorem*, edited by Eric Maskin and Amartya K. Sen, 43–55. New York: Columbia University Press.

Maskin, Eric, and Tomas Sjöström. 2002. "Implementation Theory." In *Handbook of Social Choice and Welfare*, edited by Kenneth J. Arrow, Amartya K. Sen, and Kotaro Suzumura, 237–288. Amsterdam: Elsevier.

Mill, John Stuart. [1859] 1959. *On Liberty*. New York: Gateway Editions.

Nozick, Robert. 1974. *Anarchy, State, and Utopia*. New York: Basic Books.

Nussbaum, Martha C. 1988. "Nature, Function, and Capability: Aristotle on Political Distribution." *Oxford Studies in Ancient Philosophy* (Supplementary Volume): 145–184.

Nussbaum, Martha C. 1992. "Human Functioning and Social Justice: In Defense of Aristotelian Essentialism." *Political Theory* 20 (2): 202–246.

Nussbaum, Martha C. 2000. *Women and Human Development*. New York: Cambridge University Press.

Nussbaum, Martha C. 2001. "Disabled Lives: Who Cares?" *New York Review of Books*, January 11, 34–37.

Nussbaum, Martha C. 2011. *Creating Capabilities*. Cambridge, MA: Harvard University Press.

Pattanaik, Prasanta K. 1973. "On the Stability of Sincere Voting Situations." *Journal of Economic Theory* 6 (6): 558–574.

Pattanaik, Prasanta K. 1978. *Strategy and Group Choice*. Amsterdam: North-Holland.

Phelps, Edmund S. 1973. *Economic Justice: Selected Readings*. Harmondsworth, UK: Penguin.

Pigou, Arthur C. 1920. *The Economics of Welfare*. London: Macmillan.

Rawls, John 1971. *A Theory of Justice*. Cambridge, MA: Harvard University Press.

Robbins, Lionel. 1938. "Interpersonal Comparisons of Utility: A Comment." *Economic Journal* 48 (192): 635–641.

Roberts, Kevin W. S. 1980a. "Interpersonal Comparability and Social Choice Theory." *Review of Economic Studies* 47 (2): 421–439.

Roberts, Kevin W. S. 1980b. "Possibility Theorems with Interpersonally Comparable Welfare Levels." *Review of Economic Studies* 47 (2): 409–420.

Roberts, Kevin W. S. 1995. "Valued Opinions or Opinionated Values: The Double Aggregation Problem." In *Choice, Welfare, and Development: A Festschrift in Honour of Amartya K. Sen,* edited by Kaushik Basu, Prasanta P. Pattanaik, and Kotaro Suzumura, 100–109. Oxford: Oxford University Press.

Samuelson, Paul A. 1947. *Foundations of Economic Analysis*. Cambridge, MA: Harvard University Press.

Satterthwaite, Mark A. 1975. "Strategy-Proofness and Arrow's Conditions: Existence and Correspondence Theorems for Voting Procedures and Social Welfare Functions." *Journal of Economic Theory* 10 (2): 187–217.

Sen, Amartya K. 1966. "A Possibility Theorem on Majority Decisions." *Econometrica* 34 (2): 491–499.

Sen, Amartya K. 1970a. *Collective Choice and Social Welfare*. San Francisco: Holden Day.

Sen, Amartya K. 1970b. "The Impossibility of a Paretian Liberal." *Journal of Political Economy* 78 (1): 152–157.

Sen, Amartya K. 1976. "Poverty: An Ordinal Approach to Measurement." *Econometrica*, 44 (2): 219–231.

Sen, Amartya K. 1977a. "On Weights and Measures: Informational Constraints in Social Welfare Analysis." *Econometrica* 45 (7): 1539–1572.

Sen, Amartya K. 1977b. "Social Choice Theory: A Re-examination." *Econometrica* 45 (1): 53–89.

Sen, Amartya K. 1979. "Personal Utilities and Public Judgements: Or What's Wrong with Welfare Economics." *Economic Journal* 89 (355): 537–558.

Sen, Amartya K. 1980. "Equality of What?" In *The Tanner Lectures on Human Values*, volume I: 197–220. Cambridge: Cambridge University Press.

Sen, Amartya K. 1982. *Choice, Welfare, and Measurement*. Oxford: Blackwell.

Sen, Amartya K. 1984. *Resources, Values, and Development*. Cambridge, MA: Harvard University Press.

Sen, Amartya K. 1985a. *Commodities and Capabilities*. Amsterdam: North-Holland.

Sen, Amartya K. 1985b. "Well-Being, Agency and Freedom: The Dewey Lectures 1984." *Journal of Philosophy* 82 (4): 169–221.

Sen, Amartya K. 1992. *Inequality Reexamined*. Cambridge, MA: Harvard University Press.

Sen, Amartya K. 1993. "Internal Consistency of Choice." *Econometrica* 61 (3): 495–521.

Sen, Amartya K., and Prasanta K. Pattanaik. 1969. "Necessary and Sufficient Conditions for Rational Choice under Majority Decision." *Journal of Economic Theory* 1 (2): 178–202.

Shorrocks, Anthony F. 1995. "Revisiting the Sen Poverty Index." *Econometrica* 63 (5): 1225–1230.

Smith, Adam. 1776. *An Inquiry into the Nature and Causes of the Wealth of Nations*. London: George Routledge and Sons.

Suppes, Patrick. 1966. "Some Formal Models of Grading Principles." *Synthese* 16 (3–4): 284–306.

Suzumura, Kotara. 1983. *Rational Choice, Collective Decisions, and Social Welfare*. Cambridge: Cambridge University Press.

Suzumura, Kotara. 1997. "Interpersonal Comparisons of the Extended Sympathy Type and the Possibility of Social Choice." In *Social Choice Re-Examined. Proceedings of the International Economic Association Conference held at Schloss Hernstein, Berndorf, Vienna, Austria*, edited by Kenneth J. Arrow, Amartya K. Sen, and Kotaro Suzumura, 202–229. London and New York: Palgrave Macmillan.

Van Parijs, Philippe. 1995. *Real Freedom for All: What (If Anything) Can Justify Capitalism?* Oxford: Oxford University Press.

Comment: Célestin Monga

The Economy of Tastes, Feelings, and Opinions

I still remember vividly the strange mix of excitement and bewilderment that overwhelmed me in my high school years when our professor of accounting taught us the fundamentals of benefit-cost analysis. I immediately went to my dormitory and spent most of the evening trying to apply this powerful technique, not to assess whether the advantages of a hypothetical investment project were likely to outweigh its drawbacks, but to evaluate my own life prospects. Benefit-cost analysis seemed like a rigorous and revealing tool to examine whether my minuscule and uncertain existence was a "profitable" venture, or at least a worthwhile escapade that deserved to be continued. Of course, the few friends to whom I confided this found it a ludicrous idea. They reminded me that a benefit-costs analysis is always controversial, even when circumscribed to real investment decisions or to public policies. They were right: Applying it to one's life opened even more unresolved conceptual questions. But so what?

I kept running the numbers. To ascertain the net effect of an imaginary list of positive and negative changes to come in my well-being, I first had to come up with a way of measuring the gains and the losses. The identified benefits and costs, even though they were expressed in monetary terms, went well beyond changes in my projected individual income: My well-being was to be affected positively or negatively by nonmonetary factors, whether linked to my individual and personal preferences or related to the well-being of people around me (social benefits and costs).

I also had to decide how to imagine and estimate the prospective benefits and costs of my entire life to come. Using my own personal value scale,

I calculated the costs as the amount of compensation required to exactly offset negative consequences of being alive for the 50 years or so of life expectancy ahead. The compensation required was the monetary amount that would leave me just as well off as before engaging in this exercise. Benefits were measured by my willingness to stay alive and enjoy all the things and emotions that I could reasonably expect for the decades ahead. Knowing that, in the end, life always results in death, typically following either an abrupt and tragic event like a car or airplane crash, or a long and painful illness, I could not find many benefits whose present and expected value could match and compensate for the pains and disappointments of the costs. The results of my benefit-cost analysis were not very promising: Taking into consideration all current and expected streams of good and bad news, life did not appear to be a "profitable" investment.

Shocked by the outcomes, I quickly did some sensitivity analyses to check the robustness of the findings: No matter what discount rates I chose, the calculations still yielded disappointing numbers to the question of whether life was a worthwhile venture. This was all the more puzzling, because I actually loved many aspects of my life. Not knowing what to do with the analyses, I concluded that one should either doubt the validity of certain measurement instruments and our ability to use them "objectively," or radically give more weight to whatever we define as "positive" outcomes for our actions or inactions, or accept the very probable hypothesis that happiness may be an illusion but those who choose to live should learn to ignore its downsides. I could only forget the outcomes of my own study by learning to radically change whatever assumptions I used in carrying it out. "Life is impossible without the ability to forget," philosopher Emil Cioran once said. But some memories are just too long lasting to be erased.

Carrying out the same benefit-cost analysis today, even with the same elements and discount rates, would obviously yield different results. This illustrates some of the truly challenging conceptual problems at the heart of the study of well-being, whether it is approached through the lens of welfare, utility, or the standard of living of one individual. The challenges are even more formidable when one tries to assess not just the perspectives and preferences of one person but also the social preferences of people in a group; then one has to aggregate and make sense of the various viewpoints of all members of the society. The complexities are not just "technical" or methodological—after all, these can be addressed with carefully designed quantitative frameworks and clearly formulated assumptions; they also involve ethical and psychological issues that do not fit nicely in any linear models of aggregative social choice theory.

I should not have been surprised to feel lost trying to determine and assess the validity of my own present and future welfare. Cioran also warned about the dangers of loving oneself, which is falling in love with someone about whom we know nothing. If capturing one's own utility, welfare, and standard of living is so challenging, how about doing the same exercise at the level of a group or society? The instability of my preferences and of my own subjectivity, the constantly changing moods and mental states, and the inability to even decide for myself what my objective functions are or should be explain why my schematic benefit-cost analysis was unsatisfactory and inconclusive. These problems are compounded when one gets to the level of social aggregation. How would one confidently compute and aggregate individual tastes and opinions that are moving targets? What is the right approach to ethical decision-making, both at the individual level and at the social/aggregative level? And what are the appropriate ethical stances for comparative analyses of such scope?

Central to the general topic of social aggregation is the issue of interpersonal comparisons of well-being, which has preoccupied economists, social scientists, and philosophers for centuries. At least three types of problems must be addressed to elaborate intellectual and policy frameworks for making socially acceptable decisions. One must obviously start with valid methods for defining, understanding, capturing, and measuring the notion of individual well-being. Second, these methods should be extended to social groups in ways that make them meaningful and credible. Third, one should remember that the very purpose for carrying out such an exercise may affect the answers to the two initial questions posed (Elster and Roemer 1991). All this supposes that individual preferences can be measured at a satisfactory level of confidence that the intrinsic subjectivity in such exercises are more than compensated by objectivity in the methods used.

The various steps that one must go through (from theory to specific concepts and empirical strategies) are therefore both daunting and exciting. Not surprisingly, many of the most creative minds in economics have tried to climb that mountain, a task that requires not only using the traditional quantitative tools of economics but also taking stock of the relevant findings of philosophy, psychology, and even biology. Amartya Sen's chapter,

"Social Choice and Welfare Economics," which builds on several important previous contributions (most notably Sen 1970), is the latest attempt to do so. As always with Sen, the reader is taken on an erudite and insightful journey, intellectually challenging but always rewarding. Before offering a summary exposition of his bold thesis, let me provide an initial overview of some of the elements of the puzzle that he heroically tries to assemble.

My comment offers a brief reassessment of the elements of the debate. Section 1 summarizes the intellectual progress made by economists in the search for a valid social choice theory and outlines a few aspects of Amartya Sen's new contribution on the topic. Section 2 discusses some of the remaining ethical questions and urges economists to be more attuned to the research findings in the other social sciences and the humanities. Section 3 offers a few concluding remarks.

Beyond Utilitarian Calculus: Amartya Sen's Bold Thesis

How to assess and report our own pleasures, utility, state of mind, and opinions? How to make individual and collective choices? How to prioritize and rank them? And how to compare and aggregate our selections with those of other people in a credible and legitimate social welfare function? How should we make collective decisions that reflect optimally the preferences and welfare of everyone in a social group—so that they can all live, if not happily, at least with the feeling that the decisions are made in ways that are acceptable to everyone? Underpinning these questions of social aggregation of utility, tastes, and opinions is the issue of interpersonal comparisons of well-being, which has preoccupied economists, social scientists, and philosophers for centuries. Various waves of research on the topic have basically identified several types of problems that must be addressed to elaborate an intellectual framework for making socially acceptable decisions. Such frameworks obviously start with valid methods for defining, understanding, capturing, and measuring individual preferences and then extend them to social groups, with a satisfactory level of confidence that subjectivity is more than compensated by objectivity.

Capturing one's feelings and converting them into indicators of welfare or utility, measuring them and aggregating opinions from groups of people have long been challenging questions for researchers. In an introduction to one of his books, Jevons ([1871] 1970, 85) warned that:

The reader will find again, that there is never, in any single instance, an attempt to compare the amount of feeling in one mind with that in another. I see no means by which such comparisons can be accomplished. ... Every mind is thus inscrutable to every other mind, and no common denominator of feeling seems to be possible.

Economists followed suit and showed a strong reluctance to carry out interpersonal comparisons of utility that were forcefully promoted by logical positivists. The economists justified their position by arguing that ethical statements were always unverifiable and therefore lacked scientific foundations—see Ayer ([1936] 1971).

Utilitarian economists were particularly adamant in their opposition to interpersonal comparisons of utility, arguing that it is unsound to make use of interpersonal comparisons of individual utilities. Jeremy Bentham, the leading proponent of such utilitarian calculus, was concerned only with maximizing the total utility of a community, irrespective of its distribution. Even the early critics of utilitarianism thought that interpersonal comparisons of utility had no scientific basis: "Every mind is inscrutable to every other mind and no common denominator of feelings is possible" (Robbins 1938, 636). Such views were rooted in *logical positivism*, also called *logical* empiricism, a philosophical movement that emerged in Vienna in the 1920s and considered scientific knowledge to be the only kind of factual knowledge.

The general reluctance of researchers to move to that terrain led to major intellectual impasses in both social choice theory and welfare economics. Although positive economics could be carried out without interpersonal comparisons of utility, social choice theory without interpersonal comparisons of utility could not go very far: The scope of normative economics and welfare economics was basically limited to theoretical developments concerning the identification of Pareto efficient outcomes or Pareto improvements to existing economic situations. "Traditional comparisons of utility have to be made if there is to be any satisfactory escape from Arrow's Impossibility theorem," notes Hammond (1991, 235). But the lingering fundamental question raised by the logical positivists had to be answered: How can one rigorously construct an interpersonally comparable utility function?

Starting in the 1950s, economists, mathematicians, and philosophers took up the task. Alternative methods of making different forms of interpersonal comparisons of utility were offered by several researchers, with various degrees of complexity and success. The really exciting intellectual journey in the quest for a more convincing social welfare function was launched by Arrow ([1951] 1963), who put social choice theory in its modern, fully axiomatized form. He tried to identify the most valid procedures for deriving a collective or "social ordering" of the alternatives (from better to worse) from people's preferences. His search for a "general possibility" theorem, as he called it, led to the conclusion that it was in fact an impossibility—no single procedure could satisfy a few straightforward assumptions concerning the autonomy of the agents and the rationality of their preferences.

Several generations of researchers subsequently attempted to modify Arrow's requirements and come up with a solution to the impossibility theorem (see Maskin and Sen 2014). Generally these solutions led to other difficulties. This research quickly became a journey into the dilemmas and challenges of normative ethics and how economics has struggled with them. It strongly focused on discussions of utilitarianism, understood in its generic definition as the view that the morally right actions are those that generate the most good, with the implication that the social good is the sum of the welfares of individuals in a group—assuming that the latter are interpersonally comparable. Harsanyi (1953, 1955, 1977) provided the most debated axiomatic arguments in support of utilitarianism. His work set the stage for the issues of utility and preferences as seen by economists and mathematicians, and it suggested a framework for modeling moral value judgments.

Harsanyi's main insight has been to imagine an impartial observer who can determine a social ordering of the existing alternatives faced by all members of a given group or society. Although detached from the group, the observer in question is also sympathetic to its concerns, and he imagines how he would determine a social ordering of the available alternatives based on an impartial attitude toward the interests of all members of the group. The neutral observer imagines how he would assess the various alternatives if he were in the shoes of, say, individual i, with i's objective circumstances, tastes, and opinions. Harsanyi makes two additional and important suppositions: The impartial observer has preferences about these hypothetical alternatives that satisfy the expected utility axioms,[1] and these prefer-

---

1. The von Neumann–Morgenstern axioms of the expected utility theory that define a rational decision-maker are as follows: completeness, which assumes that an individual has a set of well-defined preferences and can always decide between any two alternatives; transitivity, which assumes consistency in the decision-making of the

ences are represented by a von Neumann–Morgenstern utility function. It is also assumed that the observer (who plays the role of and seeks the interests of society as a whole) respects the orderings of social alternatives by the individuals. With the adoption of the impartial perspective, the resulting judgments computed from the observer's utility can be considered moral judgments, as they give equal consideration to the interests of each person in the group.[2] Harsanyi used this framework to elaborate aggregation and impartial individual theorems with strong assumptions: the existence of a single profile of *individual* preference orderings and of a single *social* preference ordering of a set of social alternatives (consisting of all lotteries that can be generated from a finite set of alternatives).

Harsanyi's approach is based on the notion of "impersonality," which posits that it is possible for an ethical observer of any situation to free himself from selfish perspectives when weighting moral issues by pretending to be entirely uncertain about which individual the oberver will become after the issue has been decided. In sum, one should be willing and capable of becoming somebody else completely: This is a clever device, comparable to Hare's (1963) principle of "universalizability" and Rawls's (1971) notion of the "veil of ignorance." These ideas paved the way for other influential approaches, which recommended inferring interpersonal comparisons from different aspects of the behavior of individuals. Yet in the end, such behaviorist empirical methods were often found to be unsatisfactory, as they typically required ethical judgments and also led to normative statements that could not be made from empirical observations alone.

Then came Amartya Sen, the most daring theorist among those who have studied the issues surrounding the rationality of economic agents from various angles. In this chapter, he revisits the theme but approaches it obliquely and offers a comprehensive analytical framework for interpersonal comparisons. One obvious and striking feature of the chapter is its

---

individual; independence, which assumes that two lotteries mixed up with an irrelevant third one will maintain the same order of preference as when the two initial lotteries are presented independently of the third one; and continuity, which assumes that when there are three lotteries (1, 2, and 3) and the individual prefers 1 to 2 and 2 to 3, then there should be a possible combination of 1 and 3 in which the individual is indifferent between this particular mix and lottery 2.

2. See Weymark (1991) for an excellent discussion.

style: Sen's prose is always very precise, soft, and elegant. It constantly keeps the reader in focus, even when the issues discussed are technically demanding. Sen is also a master at challenging erroneous ideas without ruffling feathers. It can be said about him what is often said about former US senator Joseph Lieberman: "He is so elegant in his criticism of his opponents that even if he tells you to go to Hell, you would actually enjoy the ride!"

Sen begins with a reexamination of some old questions in the theory of collective decision-making, which he traces back to Jean-Charles de Borda (1781) and de Condorcet (1785). Sen's deconstruction of the problem at hand starts as follows: Suppose a group of people is facing some alternatives to choose among (such as candidates in an election, policy options, projects and programs, and distribution of income). How does one make acceptable social decisions for a group (such as a nation, or a community, or any other collectivity) in a way that the diverse views and interests of members of the group all receive attention and importance? How does one go from individual preferences over different states of affairs to a social preference over those states, reflecting an "aggregation" of the points of views of all members of the society?

In fact, Sen had attempted to answer these questions in many previous works. He gracefully fired multiple salvos to some of the earlier theories of and approaches to social welfare (Sen 1970, 1977, 1986). Building on Arrow's work, Sen did not hesitate to question it, but with elegance and admiration—he always did it in homeopathic doses, relaxing assumptions here, delicately challenging the rigidity of the impossibility theorem there, or taking the tangent whenever he believed that his predecessors' frameworks were erroneous. Sen's analyses have brought new hope to the search for rational social choice procedures based on individuals' own preferences.

Sen begins the chapter with the acknowledgment that there is not going to be any perfect resolution of the social choice dilemmas of the kind identified by Arrow through voting procedures. He rejects the notion that they can be used in all situations: "Voting-based procedures are entirely natural for some kinds of social choice problems, such as elections, referendums, or committee decisions. They are, however, altogether unsuitable for many other problems of social choice."

Sen's reasoning is logical: If it is true that there are no faultless voting procedure out there to be found, the next logical question is whether some of them could yield better results than others. And by the way, is voting itself a good method to resolve social choice problems of all kinds? Didn't Winston Churchill famously say that "The best argument against democracy is a five-minute conversation with the average voter?" (Priest 2017, 3). Sen is an optimistic economist: He is skeptical of the traditional welfare economics developed by the utilitarian researchers. He is very confident that interpersonal utility can be measured satisfactorily. He challenges the historical consensus against the use of interpersonal comparisons in social choice.

Sen's recommendation is bold and hopeful: One must go beyond the class of voting rules (studied by Borda, Condorcet, and Arrow) to address distributional issues, particularly in welfare economics. The decision to reject the philosophical basis of logical positivism and to believe instead, like philosopher Donald Davidson, that people can understand and relate to other people's minds and feelings only by making some comparisons with their own minds and feelings, allows new ways of thinking about social choice. Then Arrow's impossibility theorem and its related results just go away when different kinds of interpersonal comparisons are used in social welfare judgments.

Sen observes that each kind of comparability requires a particular way of combining welfare numbers of different people in a group. Of course, such comparisons need not be very precise before they can be used systematically in social choice. He writes:

> We may be able to make interpersonal comparisons to some extent, but not in every comparison, nor of every type, nor with tremendous exactness.... It can also be shown that terribly refined interpersonal comparisons may not be needed for arriving at definite social decisions. Quite often, rather limited levels of partial comparability will be adequate for making social decisions.

A very clever way of using minimalism to achieve maximum intellectual impact, indeed.

Beyond Aggregation Techniques: Some Ethical Challenges

Developing a legitimate framework for making social decisions—one that accounts "democratically" for the preferences and interests of the members of the group or society under consideration—is likely to remain an elusive quest. It requires much more than an intellectual consensus on the measurement and aggregation techniques that game theory and mathematics have so far offered. It is indeed impossible to carry out any social choice theory without acknowledging the underlying question that is the basic problem of moral philosophy: "What should I do?" Issues of individual and group preferences or interests are likely to collide in ways that cannot be fully captured by the rigid laws of averages, which underpin most aggregative theories. Group decisions are also mired in ethical dilemmas and conceptual inconsistencies that economics is not equipped to handle.

The impossibility theorem, which Sen describes as a result of breathtaking elegance and power, is a very useful tool for assessing which outcome is "right" when thinking about social choices. Each of its axioms is reasonable and compelling, but taken together, they are overwhelming. I agree with Sen that Arrow may have overstated the negative case by insisting that each rule under consideration satisfies all the axioms no matter what people's rankings of their preferences and choices turn out to be.[3] I also agree that to lay a broader foundation for a constructive social choice theory, we have to reject the historical consensus against the use of interpersonal comparisons that was prevalent in the first part of the twentieth century and became conventional wisdom. Sen argues that we should resist such historical consensus, because it "was based on a rather fragile understanding of epistemology." I would suggest that we explore new frameworks for different levels of interpersonal comparisons of utility but remain mindful of the intrinsic limitations of such analytical tools, which clearly rely on rigid and sometimes simplistic assumptions, and that lessons from various disciplines be considered.

Sen believes that the search for a social welfare function may not even need to be very precise. This valid point also leaves open many questions about the "appropriate," acceptable standards of comparability of welfare numbers of different persons. Even in situations of full comparability of self-reported well-being numbers (which Sen would use to justify full interpersonal comparability), one obvious question is how much faith should be given to self-assessments. How much trust should be given to self-reported welfare numbers? The legitimacy of someone judging her own welfare and giving a metric to characterize it doesn't solve the problem of being "wrong" in that self-assessment. As Cioran reminded us, among the many reasons for invalidating narcissism is the fact that it is based on profound

---

3. See Maskin (2009) and Sen and Maskin (2017) for new and interesting ways of approaching voting measures.

uncertainty and randomness, because it is basically an exercise in which we fall in love with someone we know very little about.

Fortunately, Sen also believes that rigorous interpersonal comparisons need not be of mental states only. He is right in his benign neglect of the validity of self-evaluation of mental states in interpersonal utility comparisons. Can we trust ourselves to know what we actually go through in each particular life situation, how we actually feel, what we actually believe in each situation, and how we actually convey it to ourselves and to others? And does what we believe and how we feel matter if our behavior, actions, objective welfare, and standards of living are not really impacted by such perceptions? If the answers to such questions are positive, what are the implications for the analytical frameworks for interpersonal comparisons that rely on self-reported indicators of welfare?

Self-reported welfare and happiness numbers may be too subjective to be relied on. The problem goes beyond narcissism. Recent work on the economics of "motivated" belief distortions, both individual and social, shows how agents often try even unwittingly to maintain positive self-images and identities (Bénabou 2015). It has been shown, for instance, that most people believe they are more likely than others to experience favorable life events and less likely to suffer adverse ones, such as unemployment, accidents, divorce, or major illness (Weinstein 1980).[4] "We also commonly see ourselves as better drivers, better citizens, less biased and more attractive than others. Some widely held beliefs are just plainly implausible or demonstrably false, given publicly available knowledge" (Bénabou 2015, 3). Such departures from objective cognition may have subjective or objective value. Still, the prevalence of overoptimism and the reality of overconfidence has heavy economic and social costs. An illustration of the problem is the fact that large numbers of people in high-income countries who could afford life insurance (given the risks they face) choose not to buy it.

"There are many difficulties in judging the well-being of a person by his or her mental state," Sen rightly points out. "The metric of pleasure or desire may sometimes quite inadequately reflect the extent of a person's substantive deprivation." True. Hence, his recommendations that such variables as incomes, commodities bundles, or resources more generally be

---

4. For a more nuanced analysis, see Harris and Hahn (2011).

"of direct interest in judging a person's advantage." Perhaps. But this pre-scription raises several uncomfortable obvious questions. If mental states (as self-reported) are insufficient or even invalid as metrics of personal util-ity, who has the legitimacy to select the more "relevant" additional or sub-stitute variables to carry out interpersonal comparisons of utilities? Who gives us the right to judge anyone's mental states and to even decide that some "objective" variables of their welfare should be given consideration? Who decides that another person is living "well" or "poorly"?[5]

A sequence in Sergio Leone's epic movie *The Good, the Bad, and the Ugly* shows the main character Tuco (a bandit) is being lectured by his brother Pablo, who is a priest. "Outside of evil, what else have you managed to do?" Pablo asks him. Tuco listens patiently to his sermons and reprimands and then responds vehemently:

> You think you're better than I am. Where we came from, if one did not want to die of poverty…one became a priest or a bandit! You chose your way, I chose mine. Mine was harder. You talk of our mother and father. You remember when you left to become a priest. I stayed behind! I must have been ten, twelve. I don't remember which, but I stayed. I tried, but it was no good. Now I am going to tell you something. You became a priest because you were…too much of a coward to do what I do!

In some ways, Tuco emerges from that scene as more than the cartoonish bandit character that he appears to be in the first half of the movie. He also is revealed to be a humble and thoughtful man who simply faced impos-sible choices in his life and made those that seemed to him to be the most courageous and even "ethical." When Pablo chose to abandon the family to pursue (selfishly) his calling as a priest, Tuco was left to take care of their parents. He tried to the best of his abilities and presumably in the most ethical way but failed. The only other option left for his own survival was to become an outlaw.

This is more than the often derided "situational ethics"—the notion that when assessing human responsibility, one should keep in mind that the "right" or "wrong" thing to do depends on the situation,[6] because there

---

5. See Monga (2015a, 2015b, 2017) for further discussion.
6. Situation ethics (Fletcher 1967) may have its flaws. But one should remember that even John Dewey held views that rejected moral universality: such a stance "would assume the existence of final and unquestionable knowledge upon which we can fall

are no universal moral rules or rights that apply everywhere and always. Tuco's apparently shocking discourse can still be viewed as rational and deeply rooted in moral philosophy—his willingness as a minor child to stay home and take care of his parents when his older brother selfishly left the family home to (egoistically) pursue his personal calling. Tuco may be the worse bandit the West has ever produced, but he would argue that his decision-making is still profoundly moral not just descriptively (in terms of the codes of conduct put forward by his society) but also normatively (the necessary behavior and actions that, given specified conditions, would be put forward by all rational persons). In sum, Tuco is actually a moral agent in the Kantian sense, who simply finds himself expressing what he saw as a "categorical imperative."[7] If Tuco and other comparable characters are indeed justified in their "perverse" moral stance, perhaps one should conclude that rationality cannot be defined at the moral philosophy level in a way that allows for interpersonal comparisons. This would be another real impossibility theorem.

In fact, rationality assumptions (more precisely, *some* conceptions of rationality) are everywhere in the reasoning and modeling of the social choice procedures offered by all social choice theorists. Without such assumptions, no valid ordering of social preferences can take place, because any ranking must be based on preferred alternatives by people who are supposed somehow to be rational agents. Sen's very sophisticated and extremely elegant framework for interpersonal comparison also shows a lot of faith in some generic level of Rationality (with a capital "R"), which

---

back in order to settle automatically every moral problem. It would involve the commitment to a dogmatic theory of morals" (Dewey and Tufts 1908, 488). However, Dewey's skepticism of moral universality mainly reflects his skepticism about one method (the method of abstract moral reasoning) in favor of another (what he calls the "experimental" or the "method of democracy"). His proposed method

> implies that reflective morality demands observation of particular situations, rather than fixed adherence to a priori principles; that free inquiry and freedom of publication and discussion must be encouraged and not merely grudgingly tolerated; that opportunity at different times and places must be given for trying different measures so that their effects may be capable of observation and comparison with one another.

See Dewey and Tufts (1908, chapter XVI (1)) on "Morals and Social Problems."
7. See Kant ([1797] 1993).

presumes that people always have reasons for their actions. Even when people offer reasons for their actions, such reasons may not necessarily need to be validated identically. Infinitely many explanations exist for why people are (or are not) motivated to do the "right" thing.

Economists should be cautious in their faith in rationality, regardless of its scope and use. Some cognitive scientists have conjectured that reason may be an evolutionary attribute to human beings, just like bipedalism—a trait that occurred only over time. Mercier and Sperber (2017) suggest that reason initially emerged in the savannas of Africa when human beings realized that they needed to cooperate among themselves. In their view, reason, which has become the ultimate and unique characteristic of the human race, developed mainly to allow the resolution of problems posed by living in collaborative groups. Reason had a purely utilitarian genesis as "an adaptation to the hypersocial niche humans have evolved for themselves" (Mercier and Sperber 2017, 330). Reason emerged not to help people solve abstract problems but rather to fill their trust deficit, which was the critical criterion for improved living conditions and for survival.

Reason is therefore a constantly changing human trait, a unique faculty that is also moving target. It is therefore an enigma. If one agrees to link human reasoning to evolutionary processes, such as natural selection, then it is understandable that the dynamics of social change always creates distortions between phenomena that human brains can grasp, study, and debate, and real life—even though most phenomena that humans can grasp may be a part of reality—which sometimes occurs at a much more rapid pace. The Neanderthal man didn't have to worry about cyber attacks or the ideal curriculum for training a good economist. His life prescription did not include the need to see a dentist twice a year. He lived in small groups of hunter-gatherers, and his reasoning could be used to focus only on the key elements of such an existence. Today, few people live like Neanderthals and have to confront and solve the problems similar to those from 25,000 years ago. Some wealthy people live in spectacular houses or skyscrapers and mainly worry about finding the time to enjoy all the many comfortable features in their lives, or about what is said about them on Facebook. Other individuals live in poverty and permanently face the burden of social exclusion, stigma, and the destruction of their human dignity. In sum, the differential of pace between social change challenges and the adaptation of human reason to them would explain why many economic agents who seem reasonable often act foolishly—and why reason often fails us.

A good illustration of this differential in pace is the discrepancies often observed in the way societies that strive for morality also seem to tolerate for an inordinate time laws, regulations, and norms of behavior that are subsequently viewed as violating and even damaging their own moral philosophies. Appiah (2010) has examined moral revolutions and campaigns against repugnant practices, and he concludes that appeals to reason, morality, or religion aren't enough to spur fundamental changes in ethical standards. Objectionable practices seem to be eradicated only when they come into conflict with the prevailing conception of honor. Appiah's work convincingly demonstrates how moral codes evolve across space and time, and why we should be skeptical of any form of immanent rationality. Generations of historians have wondered how Thomas Jefferson, the intellectual and visionary humanist who wrote in 1776 the words "all men are created equal," could have been the proud owner of a 5,000 acre working plantation and owned 607 slaves over the course of his life (Thompson 2017). Jefferson, the third president of the United States, was the father of six children of one of his slaves, Sally Hemings. Was he simply another cynical hypocrite? Not necessarily. Simply, perhaps, just another human being going through the tragic contradictions and mysteries of life. One can safely guess that there have always been millions of Thomas Jeffersons and Sally Hemings out there, who would have struggled to define and self-report their well-being, utility, or welfare metrics. If that is the case, then any social choice theory that places too much faith in any conception of rationality runs the risk of being at some level, a non sequitur.

Sen has carefully avoided falling into that trap by making his comparative utility framework broad and flexible enough to accommodate many of the conceptual challenges faced by social choice theorists. His remarkable insights certainly open up interesting new avenues for solving Arrow's impossibility theorem. He also provides valid arguments for ignoring the skepticism of the likes of Lionel Robbins. He emboldens researchers who struggle with the complex issues of social aggregation to rethink utility comparisons at levels that may not require the types of rigid conditions imposed by Arrow. Sen's more relaxed approach makes possible the design of consistent analytical frameworks to assess and measure interpersonal welfare. But one can only take his proposed intellectual route at the (somewhat heavy) cost of accepting the big assumptions that such exercises should be done at several different levels and that the exclusive reliance on mental state comparisons may not be relevant in social choice. These are elegant but big assumptions.

Conclusion

In the end, we should perhaps acknowledge that there are situations in which one simply cannot win. Francis Blanche, the late French comic, often said in one of his sketches: "I was married twice, two catastrophes: The first time my wife left; the second time, she stayed!" He never wondered whether the problem was with his wife-selection skills, or with him more generally. But would it matter? The more serious points are our innate inability to look beyond our intrinsically self-centered natures, our shifting egos and psyches, and our unstable preferences; our inability to consistently define our own tastes, feelings, and opinions; and the structural limitations of any attempt to consistently capture and aggregate the criteria for common well-being.

Such a perspective alters one's view of rationalities. It also allows me to regard rather favorably the various attempts by economists and other social scientists to free their disciplines from the tyrannies of rationality. In this critical endeavor, Sen's contribution in particular, has been salient and spectacular. I still am hopeful that, one day, perhaps using Sen's analytics, I will be able to carry out a rigorous benefit-cost analysis of my life and find out whether it had enough meaning to look like a "profitable" investment. But the constantly shifting values of time, discount rates, and ethical criteria for interpersonal welfare comparisons may render my intellectual journey irrational and foolish.

References

Appiah, Kwame Anthony. 2010. *The Honor Code: How Moral Revolutions Happen.* New York: W. W. Norton & Company.

Arrow, Kenneth J. [1951] 1963. *Social Choice and Individual Values*, second edition. New York: Wiley.

Ayer, A. J. [1936] 1971. *Language, Truth, and Logic.* Harmondsworth, UK: Penguin Books.

Bénabou, Roland. 2015."The Economics of Motivated Beliefs." Jean-Jacques Laffont Lecture, delivered at the Congress of the French Economic Association, June 2014. Forthcoming in *Revue d'Economie Politique* 2015/5 Vol. 125, 665–685.

Borda, Jean-Charles de. 1781. "Mémoire sur les élections au scrutin." *Mémoires de l'Académie Royal des Sciences*, 657–665. Translated by A. de Grazia. 1953. *Isis* 44 (1/2): 42–51.

Condorcet, Jean-Antoine-Nicolas de Caritat. 1785. *Essai sur l'Application de l'Analyse à la Probabilité des Décisions Rendues à la Pluralité des Voix*. Paris: L'Imprimerie Royale.

Dewey, John, and James H. Tufts. 1908. *Ethics*. New York: Henry Holt & Co.

Elster, Jon, and John E. Roemer. 1991. "Introduction." In *Interpersonal Comparisons of Well-Being*, edited by Jon Elster and John E. Roemer, 1–16. New York: Cambridge University Press.

Fletcher, Joseph. 1967. *Moral Responsibility: Situation Ethics at Work*. Philadelphia: Westminster Press.

Hammond, Peter J. 1991. "Interpersonal Comparisons of Utility: Why and How They Are and Should Be Made." In *Interpersonal Comparisons of Well-Being*, edited by John Elster and John E. Roemer, 200–254. New York: Cambridge University Press.

Hare, Richard M. 1963. *Freedom and Reason*. Oxford: Clarendon Press.

Harris, Adam J. L., and Ulrike Hahn. 2011. "Unrealistic Optimism about Future Life Events: A Cautionary Note." *Psychological Review* 118 (1): 135–154.

Harsanyi, John C. 1953. "Cardinal Utility in Welfare Economics and in the Theory of Risk-Taking." *Journal of Political Economy* 61 (5): 434–435.

Harsanyi, John C. 1955. "Cardinal Welfare, Individualistic Ethics, and Interpersonal Comparisons of Utility." *Journal of Political Economy* 63 (4): 309–321.

Harsanyi, John C. 1977. *Rational Behaviour and Bargaining Equilibrium in Games and Social Situations*. Cambridge: Cambridge University Press.

Jevons, William Stanley. [1871] 1970. *The Theory of Political Economy*. London: Macmillan.

Kant, Immanuel. [1797] 1993. *Groundwork of the Metaphysics of Morals: With On a Supposed Right to Lie Because of Philanthropic Concerns*, third edition, translated by J. Ellington. Indianapolis, IN: Hackett.

Maskin, Eric. 2009. "The Arrow Impossibility Theorem: Where Do We Go from Here?" Arrow Lecture presented at Columbia University, New York, December 11.

Maskin, Eric, and Amartya K. Sen. 2014. *The Arrow Impossibility Theorem*. New York: Columbia University Press.

Maskin, Eric, and Amartya K. Sen. 2017. "The Rules of the Game: A New Electoral System." *New York Review of Books*, 64(1): 8–10.

Mercier, Hugo, and Dan Sperber. 2017. *The Enigma of Reason*. Cambridge, MA: Harvard University Press.

Monga, Célestin. 2015a. "Principles of Economics: African Counter-narratives." In *The Oxford Handbook of Africa and Economics. Volume 1: Context and Concepts*, edited by Célestin Monga and Justin Y. Lin, 303–333. New York: Oxford University Press.

Monga, Célestin. 2015b. "Measuring Democracy: An Economic Approach." In *The Oxford Handbook of Africa and Economics. Volume 1: Context and Concepts*, edited by Célestin Monga and Justin Y. Lin, 427–452. New York: Oxford University Press.

Monga, Célestin. 2017. "The Macroeconomics of Marginal Gains: Africa's Lessons to Social Theorists." In *The Political Economy of Everyday Life in Africa: Beyond the Margins*, edited by Wale Adebanwi, 115–132. Woodbridge, Suffolk; Rochester, New York: Boydell and Brewer.

Priest, Kyle. 2017. "Churchill's Argument Against Democracy: The Average Voter. Information Levels and News Sources among Americans." Political Science Senior Thesis. Bemidji State University.

Rawls, John. 1971. *A Theory of Justice*. Cambridge, MA: Harvard University Press.

Robbins, Lionel. 1938. "Interpersonal Comparisons of Utility: A Comment." *Economic Journal* 8 (192): 635–641.

Sen, Amartya K. 1970. *Collective Choice and Social Welfare*. San Francisco: Holden-Day.

Sen, Amartya K. 1977. "On Weights and Measures: Informational Constraints in Social Welfare Analysis." *Econometrica* 45 (7): 1539–1572.

Sen, Amartya K. 1986. "Social Choice Theory." In *Handbook of Mathematical Economics*, volume 3, edited by Kenneth J. Arrow and Michael D. Intriligator, 1073–1181. Amsterdam: North-Holland.

Thompson, Krissah. 2017. "For Decades They Hid Jefferson's Relationship with Her. Now Monticello Is Making Room for Sally Hemings." *Washington Post*, February 19.

Weinstein, Neil D. 1980. "Unrealistic Optimism about Future Life Events." *Journal of Personality and Social Psychology* 39 (5): 806–820.

Weymark, John A. 1991. "A Reconsideration of the Harsanyi–Sen debate on Utilitarianism." In *Interpersonal Comparisons of Well-Being*, edited by John Elster and John E. Roemer, 254–320. New York: Cambridge University Press.

Comment: James E. Foster

Measurement as Social Choice

I am terribly biased when it comes to Professor Sen and hence feel obligated, in the spirit of full disclosure, to let you know why. I first met A. K. Sen in a welfare economics class at New College, Florida, in 1976—not in person, but through his book *Collective Choice and Social Welfare*. The starred chapters captured me and wouldn't let go until I had extended his liberal paradox to a world where groups, rather than persons, were decisive. I sent a draft to Professor Sen, and he responded with guidance on how to revise the paper and where to publish it, which happened soon after. Thus began my journey from mathematics to economics via social choice theory, guided at a distance by Professor Sen.

We met in person a few years later, when I was a graduate student at Cornell. As Andrew D. White Professor-at-Large at Cornell, Professor Sen encouraged me to consider research in poverty measurement, which led to my work with Joel Greer and Erik Thorbecke. He also provided a list of problems on partial orderings to explore along with my thesis advisor (and his coauthor), Mukul Majumdar, which—alas—we never jointly pursued. In 1982, there was a wild ride from London to Oxford in a yellow Alfasud, during which Professor Sen explained how, despite Thatcher's cutbacks, he was able to conduct a research project on gender discrimination in Indian villages by diverting funds from his telephone budget. In 1993 we began a project to expand his classic *On Economic Inequality*, which led to many late nights, as my wife remembers well. Then in 2008, we co-taught Economics 2054, *Social Choice and Welfare Economics*, at Harvard. Now an expanded edition of *Collective Choice and Social Welfare* has been published—the book that began the process some 40 years ago. Professor Sen has been an inspiration to generations of researchers. I have received a full measure of his generosity, for which I am most grateful.

The present chapter is a prime example of why we love to read Sen: remarkably clear summaries of difficult literatures, woven together with entertaining quotes and remarkably apt phrases. On one hand, it is a lucid exposition of the key results from social choice, including Condorcet's voting paradox, Arrow's pathbreaking general possibility theorem, Gibbard's equivalent result on strategic voting, the Arrow-Black theorem on single-peaked preferences and majority voting, and Sen's result on the impossibility of a Paretian liberal. On the other hand, it is a masterful exposition of the downs and ups of welfare economics: including Bentham's utilitarianism, the Robbins "logical positivist" revolution and its progeny, "new welfare economics," which privileged "Pareto efficiency" and its "remarkable reticence" to discuss distributional issues. Then the paper moves on to Bergson-Samuelson social welfare functions and back to Arrovian social welfare and its accompanying informational privations, with no cardinal or interpersonal comparisons allowed and in a world of purely welfarist information. The final section breaks free from the tyranny of impossibility and narrow informational bases, through rigorous definitions of partial comparability and an expansion of the informational basis of comparisons to human capability and freedom. It concludes with a discussion of poverty measurement—both monetary and multidimensional.

All right, you say, this is a fine exercise in the history of economic thought. But what practical lessons does social choice and welfare economics have for the World Bank, or for that matter, policymaking in general? My answer focuses on metrics and measurement, a topic of particular interest to me, and the foundation of policy analysis, wherein data are identified and aggregated in meaningful ways to inform social decisions. Let us examine a few of the messages that are especially pertinent to the process of measurement.

Broadening the informational basis. Sen attributes the impossibility in Arrow's theorem to the paucity of information contained in its preference profiles. His characterization of the Pareto-extension rule also illustrates how restricting consideration to interpersonally noncomparable profiles of individual orderings leaves decision-makers unable to address distributional issues.[1] Broader bases of information are necessary to overcome

---

1. See Sen (2017, Theorem 5*3).

these challenges. The capability approach, which operates in the space of "functionings" and considers achievements as well as "capability sets" of achievements (containing both chosen and unchosen alternatives), is one answer. The approach has become a generally accepted way of conceptualizing well-being, opportunity, and empowerment, and it is the notion of progress underlying Sen's (1999) masterpiece *Development as Freedom*. The approach also leads to measures that are multidimensional and linked across dimensions at the individual level, such as the multidimensional poverty measures of Alkire and Foster (2011). However, it presents challenges to empirical researchers, as traditional datasets and measurement methodologies may not be applicable.

The measurement properties of variables.   Broader information brings with it the need to use that information appropriately. After data have been identified, the next important task is to understand the measurement properties of the data's underlying variables and apply a methodology that is suitable. For example, ordinal variables are commonly used in measurement, whether as part of self-reports (such as self-reported health or life satisfaction) or due to the inherently qualitative characteristics of the indicators (such as the quality of floors or sanitation facilities). In addition, issues of noncomparability or partial comparability can easily arise across persons or dimensions. The variables cannot simply be treated as if they were monetary—fully cardinal and fully comparable across different individuals. An intuitive way of thinking about this issue is to view it as a form of robustness. If many rescalings of the data are possible, or if many ways of relating the data across persons (or across dimensions) could be used, would each of the possibilities yield the same results? The results for a single cardinalization or one way of one of linking data across persons or dimensions are not enough. Meaningful interpretation of the data requires agreement across the full range of possibilities.[2]

Axioms as policy.   A third message pertains to the centrality of axioms and the axiomatic approach in this literature.[3] Although it is not always apparent, axioms are in essence chunks of policy—basic requirements or qualities that an object must exhibit if it is to be seen as functioning appropriately. For an Arrovian social welfare function, axioms can ensure that it is broadly

---

2. See Alkire et al. (2015, section 2.3).
3. See Foster and Sen (1997, 119).

applicable, is appropriately oriented when preferences are in agreement, ignores irrelevant information, or rules out unambiguously problematic methods. For measurement, axioms ensure that a measure is capturing the desired phenomenon. The main axioms come in three varieties: invariance axioms (like anonymity), which identify the sorts of information a measure should ignore; subgroup axioms (like decomposability), which specify how local and national measures are to be linked; and dominance axioms (like the transfer principle), which require the measure to move in a specific direction in the presence of an unambiguous change in the data.[4] Axioms help define what the measure should be measuring.

Desiderata. Some authors also include a list of desiderata or "proto-axioms" to help guide the construction of measurement methodologies.[5] A common desideratum is that the measure should be understandable and easy to describe—a requirement that can trump formal axioms when communication is important. This property might explain: the prevalence of the headcount ratio in poverty measurement despite its axiomatic failings; how the traditional Human Development Index (based on the arithmetic mean) might be preferable to the post-2010 Index (based on the geometric mean); and why the mean of the bottom 40 percent—the measure underlying the World Bank's shared prosperity goal—was selected instead of an Atkinson "equally distributed equivalent" income function or the Sen welfare measure. There is a clear tension between this key desideratum and the more nuanced policy aims embodied in axioms.

The use of partial orderings. Partial orderings are central to Sen's presentation of social choice theory and also are at the core of measurement.[6] To determine whether the income distribution has taken an unambiguous turn for the worse, the Lorenz criterion or the various orders of stochastic dominance can be consulted. Likewise, poverty orderings point out when poverty has fallen for an entire range of poverty lines (or measures). In multidimensional analysis, dashboards of dimensional achievements provide a partial order for assessing well-being when there is little guidance on how to value dimensions.

---

4. See Alkire et al. (2015, section 2.5).
5. See, for example, Székely (2005), who gives the list used in setting the Mexican income poverty methodology.
6. See Sen (2017, xxix–xxxi) and Foster and Sen (1997, 120–121).

Partial orderings identify unambiguous (or unanimous) changes; however, they are also incomplete and unable to decide between certain pairs of options. Axioms and desiderata can help narrow options and reduce the incompleteness. But policy discussion typically demands a headline measure that is real valued as well as complete, facilitates discussion, and encourages policy analysis. Once again, there may be tension between communication and other policy objectives. In some circumstances, however, a partial ordering can actually facilitate the selection of a specific measure. For example, the choice of a specific monetary poverty line seems less problematic when a poverty ordering is available to test robustness for a range of poverty lines.

Measurement as choice. The process of measurement, like that of description, "involves the exercise—possibly difficult—of selection" across the many ways of viewing a phenomenon.[7] Over time, the justification for the choices underlying measurement tends to become "this is how it has always been done." Institutions like the World Bank are the repositories of the art of measurement, and they have the responsibility of being transparent and, from time to time, re-evaluating their methods. With the establishment of its Commission on Global Poverty, the World Bank is working toward fulfilling this goal for the flagship monetary poverty measure and may consider a multidimensional approach to poverty as outlined in the present chapter and other writings. In any event, Professor Sen's many contributions to measurement will undoubtedly prove useful in guiding this and other related efforts.

References

Alkire, Sabina, and James E. Foster. 2011. "Counting and Multidimensional Poverty Measurement." *Journal of Public Economics* 95 (7): 476–487.

Alkire, Sabina, James E. Foster, Suman Seth, Maria E. Santos, Jose M. Roche, and Paola Ballon. 2015. *Multidimensional Poverty Measurement and Analysis.* Oxford: Oxford University Press.

Foster, James E., and Amartya K. Sen. 1997. "On Economic Inequality after a Quarter Century." In *Economic Inequality*, Amartya K. Sen, expanded edition, 107–219. Oxford: Oxford University Press.

---

7. Sen (1980, 353).

Foster, James E., Joel Greer, and Erik Thorbecke. 1984. "A Class of Decomposable Poverty Measures." *Econometrica* 52 (3): 761–766.

Sen, Amartya K. 1980. "Description as Choice." *Oxford Economic Papers* 32 (3): 353–369.

Sen, Amartya K. 1999. *Development as Freedom*. New York: Anchor.

Sen, Amartya K. 2017. *Collective Choice and Social Welfare*, expanded edition. London: Penguin.

Székely, Miguel, ed. 2005. *Números que Mueven al Mundo: La Medición de la Pobreza en México*. City: Miguel Ángel Porrúa.

3   The Revolution of Information Economics: The Past and the Future

Joseph Stiglitz

The economics of information has constituted a revolution in economics, upsetting longstanding presumptions, including the presumption of market efficiency, with profound implications for economic policy. The central models of information economics, developed almost a half century ago but greatly elaborated on in the intervening years, have proven remarkably robust. At the same time, these advances in the economics of information have shown the lack of robustness of the standard competitive paradigm. The models have provided a deeper understanding of other ways in which actual markets differ from the perfect markets paradigm. For instance, the imperfections of competition and risk-sharing are two features that matter a great deal, and the economics of information provided new insights into both of these.

Early work in the economics of information also showed how it would help us understand better the role of institutions and the form that institutions take; work since then has confirmed the promise. So, too, the economics of information has provided new intellectual underpinnings to branches of the subject that seemed devoid of a theoretical framework, such as accounting, finance, and corporate governance, and has helped us understand better why work in these subfields is so important.

Elaborations of the early models and the adaptation of these models to different market contexts have occupied much of the economics profession's attention in the decades since the first models were presented.

Paper presented at the conference "The State of Economics, The State of the World," World Bank, Washington, DC, June 9, 2016. I acknowledge research assistance from Andrew Kosenko and editorial assistance from Debarati Ghosh.

Not surprisingly, the policies derived from the new paradigm are often markedly different from those derived on the basis of the standard model. Most importantly, as I emphasize below, there is no presumption that markets are efficient; quite the contrary, the presumption is that markets are not efficient. And in those sectors where information and its imperfections play a particularly important role, there is an even greater presumption of the need for public policy. The financial sector is, above all else, about gathering and processing information, on the basis of which capital resources can be efficiently allocated. Information is *central*. And that centrality is at least part of the reason that financial sector regulation is so important.

Markets where information is imperfect are also typically far from perfectly competitive (as that concept is understood, say, in the models of Arrow and Debreu).[1] In markets with some—but imperfect—competition, firms strive to increase their market power and to increase the extraction of rents from existing market power, giving rise to widespread distortions. In such circumstances, institutions and the rules of the game matter. Public policy is critical in setting the rules of the game. Distributive effects of alternative rules may outweigh any efficiency gains.

Undoing the adverse distributive effects created by these market imperfections may be very costly, again, largely because of information imperfections.[2]

Many recent changes in the rules may have had both adverse efficiency and distributive effects. The economics of information has explained why distributive effects themselves may have efficiency consequences, especially in the presence of macroeconomic externalities.

Looking forward, changes in the structure of demand (that is, as a country gets richer, the mix of goods purchased changes) and in technology may lead to an increased role for information and increased consequences of

---

1. The market failures referred to in the previous paragraph arise even when firms and households are price takers. I am now describing an important second set of market failures typically arising in markets with imperfect information.
2. In standard economics, the second welfare theorem explains how any Pareto efficient allocation can be achieved simply through the redistribution of initial endowments. When there is imperfect information, the second welfare theorem is in general not true. For an exposition, see Stiglitz (1994).

information imperfections, decreased competition, and increasing inequality. Many key battles will be about information and knowledge (implicitly or explicitly)—and the governance of information. Already, big debates are going on about privacy (the rights of individuals to keep their own information) and transparency (requirements that government and corporations, for instance, reveal critical information about what they are doing). In many sectors, most especially, the financial sector, there are ongoing debates about disclosure—obligations on the part of individuals or firms to reveal certain things about their products. Many of these issues can be framed in terms of property rights—who owns the right to certain pieces of information. But these property rights issues are different from and more complex than those concerning conventional property rights, where it is usually assumed the stronger the better. Here, the ambiguities in the assignment of property rights are apparent, and so-called strong (intellectual) property rights may lead to poorer economic performance.

Globalization has heightened all the associated controversies because now, how the rules are set affects not only distribution among individuals within countries but also the distribution of income between countries. Many in the former colonial world see the attempt by some in the advanced countries to impose their set of rules as not just an attempt to enrich their corporations but also to entrench old inequities.

How we handle these issues will affect inequality, economic performance, and the nature of our polity and society for decades to come.

This paper is divided into seven sections. In the first, we lay out some of the key insights of the New Information Economics, contrasting it with the old paradigm, which assumed perfect information. The central result of the new paradigm is that markets are not, in general, efficient: There is a need for government intervention. Adam Smith's invisible hand failed, simply because it wasn't there. The second section describes several failed but still important attempts to respond—to show that the market was in fact efficient, if not always, at least in relevant cases. The third then describes some of the policy corollaries, and the ongoing policy battles over information. The fourth section sets the Information Revolution in the context of the longstanding battle of how to understand the persistent inequality under capitalism—is it exploitation (as Marx suggested) or just rewards in response to differences in social contribution? We suggest that although Marx had the wrong model of the economy, there is more than a little grain of truth in his exploitation theories. The fifth section describes the role of the information revolution in promoting broader changes in the economic paradigm. The sixth looks forward—to the implications of the new paradigm for the economy that is evolving in the twenty-first century. I end with a few concluding remarks.

The Information Revolution

Economists had, of course, long recognized the importance of imperfect information. Indeed, some economic discussions actually trumpeted the informational efficiency of the market—arguing that efficiency can be achieved in a decentralized price system, so there is no need for a central planner. All the information that a firm or a household needed to know to make its decisions was to be found in the prices. Prices coordinated all economic activity. Yet these statements were made without any formal models of the economy as an information processor. Resource allocations were once-and-for-all decisions. Moreover, the kinds of information imperfections were limited. There was no uncertainty about the quality of a worker or a product.

By and large, formal models made no mention of information—other than to assume that there was perfect information. The hope was that analyses assuming perfect information would still be relevant so long as information was not *too* imperfect.

Some Chicago school economists thought that one could develop an "economics of information"—based on the analysis of the supply and demand for information (much like the "economics of agriculture") and focusing on the particular characteristics of the demand for and production of information (just like agriculture economics focuses on the particular characteristics of the demand for and supply of food). But it should have been clear, even before the formal development of the field described below, that such a development was unlikely. Information (knowledge) is fundamentally different from steel, corn, or the other goods on which ordinary economics focuses. Information is a public good[3]—indeed, more broadly,

---

3. In the sense defined by Samuelson, as a good characterized by nonrivalrous consumption (the enjoyment of a pure public good by one individual does not detract from its enjoyment by others). Pure public goods are also typically characterized by the impossibility (or at least difficulty) of appropriation. As we discuss below,

knowledge is a global public good (Stiglitz 1999), and markets on their own typically are not efficient in the provision of such goods.

Arrow and Debreu provided the key benchmark model describing the behavior of a competitive economy with perfect information through a model of competitive general equilibrium in which all firms were price takers. Most importantly, Arrow and Debreu provided conditions under which Smith's "invisible hand" conjecture was correct, not just the first welfare theorem (showing that market economies were Pareto efficient) but also the second fundamental theorem. The latter showed that every Pareto-efficient outcome could be obtained through a market mechanism, provided that there was an appropriate initial (lump sum) redistribution of wealth. Arrow and Debreu focused on the technical conditions that were required—such as convexity of production sets (making use of the key economic assumption of diminishing returns)—as well on as the economic conditions: perfect competition, a full set of risk markets (subsequently called Arrow-Debreu "AD" securities), and the absence of externalities. They had provided sufficient conditions for the efficiency of the market. The question was: Would results still be true under more general conditions? Were the sufficient conditions necessary, or almost necessary? After several decades of research, it became clear that Arrow and Debreu had essentially discovered the necessary and sufficient conditions.[4]

Most of the limitations on which Arrow and Debreu had focused had in some sense been widely recognized well before their work. They had put these longstanding understandings on sound footings. And there were well-developed public policies in response: environmental regulation or corrective taxes, for instance, to deal with environmental externalities, and anti-trust policies to deal with imperfect competition. The existence

---

intellectual property rights are an attempt to enable the partial appropriation of the returns to the production of knowledge. Inherently, such attempts have a social cost, because the usage of the information or knowledge is restricted, though there is no marginal cost associated with usage.

4. There were a few other sets of uninteresting conditions—conditions that, remarkably, came to play a central role in a particular branch of macroeconomics. The economy would be efficient even in the absence of a complete set of risk markets if all individuals were identical—precisely because when they are identical, there would be no insurance. There would be no one else to whom someone could transfer the risk he faces.

of a natural monopoly required either strong regulation or government ownership.

Absence of a Complete Set of Risk Markets

The one "new" market failure to which Arrow and Debreu called attention was the absence of a complete set of risk markets. It was obvious that individuals and firms could not buy insurance against many of the risks that they faced—workers couldn't buy unemployment insurance, firms couldn't buy insurance against the risk that the demand for their products declined. But economists had not realized the importance of this failure. For Arrow and Debreu to establish the Pareto efficiency of the economy required the existence of a full set of what came to be called "AD securities"—securities delivering a specific amount of some commodity in a particular state at a particular date, in effect, a *complete* set of insurance markets. It was obvious that this was more than a matter of mere technicalities; there were many *important* risks for which households and firms simply couldn't obtain insurance at all. One could think of public provision of social protection as having arisen to partially "correct" this market failure.

Presumption That Markets Are Not Efficient

Arrow and Debreu had, however, shunted aside the key question of information in all of its dimensions. Earlier, I described how market advocates viewed the informational efficiency of the economy as one of its triumphs. These advocates especially celebrated how much one could achieve without anyone knowing anything about any other firm or household: All relevant information was conveyed by prices.

But this model made extraordinarily strong assumptions that were not even stated: Products were homogeneous, and any individual could tell costlessly any deviation of the product from the "specified" characteristics. Cheating on quality was impossible. Everyone knew fully the "true" probability distribution of returns of every asset. There were no asymmetries of information, where a well-informed individual could take advantage of a less informed one.

In the real world, these quality differences are critical. Workers are not homogeneous. A great deal of effort goes into finding workers who are well matched for the job. Insurance firms worry about the risk profile of those they insure. The entire financial industry is focused on identifying "underpriced" assets.

Obviously, these information problems are important to all market participants. The early literature showed that information asymmetries—where one agent had information not available to another—presented a special set of problems. Attempts to extract that information or to exploit the informational advantages gave rise to multiple distortions. A great deal of activity is concerned with addressing these information problems (both the lack of information and asymmetries in information), improving information and reducing asymmetries, if not eliminating them. At the same time, some market participants realize that opportunities for profit can be enhanced by increasing information asymmetries. They devote their efforts to ensuring the existence and persistence of these information asymmetries, as costly as these asymmetries may be to the economy as a whole.[5]

Some two decades after Arrow and Debreu's work, Greenwald and Stiglitz (1986, 1988) showed that information market failures were much more pervasive and consequential. Whenever there was imperfect and asymmetric information or *incomplete risk markets*—that is, essentially always—the economy was not (constrained) Pareto efficient, taking into account the limitations of information. There were always interventions in the market that could make some individuals better off without making anyone else worse off.[6] (For brevity, in the discussion below, I refer to this result as the "GS theorem.") Correcting these market failures is not so easy: They are not isolated,[7] they are diffuse, and they are an integral part of the market economy. In the presence of asymmetries of information and incomplete markets, there are pervasive pecuniary externalities *that matter:* What one firm or individual does has consequences for others, and that is true even when it is only through the price system. Price changes are more than purely redistributive.[8]

---

5. With perfect competition there are no pure profits, and firms realize (as already noted) that markets where information is imperfect are likely to be less than perfectly competitive. This principle holds in other contexts, as we discuss below: Managers may take actions that result in greater information asymmetries to entrench themselves.
6. Geanakoplos and Polemarchakis (1986) provided an alternative proof of the inefficiency of market equilibria when there is an incomplete set of markets.
7. This stands in marked contrast to pollution externalities, where at least in principle, one could ascertain the emissions of pollutants and impose a charge.
8. Greenwald and Stiglitz's proof of market inefficiency focused on these pecuniary externalities, showing that in markets with imperfect information or incomplete risk

Consider a group of seemingly similar people buying health insurance in a world in which smoking is not observable. Should one person smoke, it will increase the risk of disease, driving up the health insurance premiums of everyone. There is a real cost to this externality, which the smoker does not take into account. The market response is to limit the amount of insurance that an individual can obtain, so that she has some incentive to behave well. But a real cost results from this restraint; with risk-averse individuals, restricting the purchase of insurance lowers expected utility.

Information market failures obviously affect resources devoted to collecting, processing, and disseminating information. Information is a public good, with no marginal cost associated with the use of an idea by someone else, so normally one would expect an underinvestment in information. Thus, an idea that had some popularity for a while was that markets were informationally efficient, that is, they transmitted through prices all information from the informed to the uninformed. But in a sense, that idea (popularized by Fama (1970, 1991) but totally discredited by Shiller (1990) as well as Grossman and Shiller (1981)), was intellectually incoherent, as Grossman and Stiglitz (1976, 1980) pointed out: If the market fully transmitted information, no one would devote any resources to its collection.

Moreover, private returns to information often can exceed social returns: If I can prove that I am more able than someone else with whom I would otherwise have been grouped (in the absence of information), my wages will go up, but his wages will go down. My gains are at his expense. Much of the returns to information are thus *distributive*.[9]

In addition, firms will attempt to create barriers to the dissemination of information—politically, they try to create property rights (called "intellectual property rights"). These rights are costly to enforce and seldom enable

---

markets, their effects are markedly different than in the standard model, where such price effects cancel, with the gains of one individual being offset by the losses of others. Arnott, Greenwald, and Stiglitz (1994) explicitly show how changes in prices affect the self-selection constraints with first-order effects. Similar results hold for price effects on incentive compatibility or collateral constraints. The analysis of these effects has been at the center of the macro-externalities literature discussed below.

9. See Hirshleifer (1971) and Stiglitz (1975). While Hirshleifer identified the distributive effects of information, Stiglitz succeeded in analyzing the market equilibria. He showed that there can be multiple equilibria, with a pooling equilibrium (where the two groups are not differentiated) Pareto dominating the "separating" equilibrium (where the two groups are differentiated).

those investing in information to appropriate all the social returns from their information. However, to the extent that they are successful, these rights create a static market inefficiency: Because information, once created, is a public good, any barrier to its free dissemination introduces a distortion in the economy. In practice, the static costs are often increased, because these restrictions create barriers to entry, supporting a less competitive market environment, and yet the incentives provided for the creation of knowledge may be limited. Indeed, because the most important input into the production of knowledge is knowledge, by restricting the use of knowledge, these rights may actually impede innovation itself. More generally, the dynamic benefits are markedly less than the supporters of strong intellectual property rights suggest.[10]

Thus, the key insight of information economics—differing from worlds in which there is perfect information where social and private returns are normally the same—is that *social returns to information expenditures typically differ from private returns*, in some cases they are greater, in other cases less. This insight has many implications, including that privately profitable transactions may not be socially desirable. The subsequent literature has exposed a huge number of distortions in specific contexts. They include marginal inefficiencies, where a Pigouvian corrective tax might induce market participants to do more of the things that they are doing too little of and less of the things that they are doing too much of; and structural inefficiencies, associated with multiple equilibria, with the economy sometimes being in a Pareto dominated equilibrium (Stiglitz 1972, 1975).

Sometimes, limited government actions can ensure that the economy is in the "good" equilibrium.[11]

Information asymmetries can be endogenous Moreover, households and firms have incentives for creating information imperfections (asymmetries)—they may gain from a lack of transparency. So can managers—it can enhance their "market power" by creating an entry barrier to competitive managerial teams (see Edlin and Stiglitz 1995).

Complexity is one way that financial firms in particular introduce opacity. Many financial transactions seem designed more to increase complexity

---

10. See Stiglitz (2008), Stiglitz (2014a) and Baker, Jayadev, and Stiglitz (2017).
11. For instance, discrimination laws can prevent an equilibrium in which some groups are treated worse than others (Stiglitz 1973, 1974b).

and the associated market power than to solve societal problems. Recent research has shown how complexity increases uncertainty even about systemic stability and the effects of regulatory policy. Although society would like a better functioning, more stable financial system, market participants are simply concerned with maximizing profits. The GS theorem emphasizes the disparity between private returns and social returns arising from information asymmetries and incomplete markets. But this recent work has noted other aspects of the market failures in the financial sector: By becoming too big to fail, too interlinked to fail, or to correlated to fail, financial institutions can ensure a bailout, in effect a transfer of resources from the public to themselves. Firms thus have incentives to become too big, too interlinked, too correlated to fail: There is a *systemic* problem.

With a high probability of a bail-out, they can engage in excessive risk taking, in which they realize the upside (the profits), and the public bears the downside (the losses). Moreover, with financial institutions that are too big to fail, too interconnected to fail, or too correlated to fail, success may not be based on relative efficiency but on relative size and linkages. And the huge excessive complexity that they have brought to the financial system makes the consequences of regulations more uncertain. If, as a result, regulators are discouraged from undertaking necessary regulations—for instance, relying on self-regulation—this provides an opportunity for those in the sector to increase further their profits.

These problems would simply not exist if there were perfect information, in which case private contractual arrangements would internalize these information-related externalities. These market failures clearly provide a rationale for government intervention. Much of the intervention has focused on *behavior* (e.g., restricting excessive risk taking and actions that enhance the risk of conflicts of interest). But this analysis has suggested that government needs to go beyond this focus, for example, to regulate the size of banks (to reduce the risk of being too big to fail), linkages among banks (to reduce the risk of being too interconnected to fail), and contractual arrangements (to reduce the risk of excessive complexity).[12] Recent research has also noted that (in part because government cannot monitor the actions of individual banks) what matters is the entire "ecology," that is, the diversity (and interconnectedness) of financial institutions. Regulating this ecology (by, for

---

12. See Battiston et al. (2013, 2016a) and Roukny, Battiston, and Stiglitz (2016).

instance, preventing the creation of universal banks) mitigates the dangers of "too correlated to fail," and provides part of the rationale for *structural regulations* (e.g., the Glass-Steagall Act, which separated commercial and investment banks).

Production and information are interlinked   But the inefficiencies of the market economy go deeper, because production of knowledge and information is intertwined with other activities. Thus, the presumption is that the market is not only inefficient in the production of information/knowledge but also in the production of goods. For instance, knowledge or information is produced as a by-product of the production of goods; if this information leaks out to others, then the value of this information won't be fully internalized in the determination of the levels of production (Stiglitz and Greenwald 2014).

Macro consequences of informational externalities   Keynes provided an explanation of the Great Depression and other deep downturns that had afflicted capitalism from its beginning. But in the 1970s, dissatisfaction grew over the disparity between macroeconomics, as it had developed following Keynes, and standard microeconomics. Information economics provided the necessary underpinnings to reconcile the two. It explained, for instance, why credit and equity rationing occurred,[13] why this led to risk-averse behavior on the part of firms (Greenwald and Stiglitz 1990), and why wages might not adjust even when unemployment is significant. (See Shapiro and Stiglitz 1984 and other variants of efficiency wage theory [Stiglitz 1987c].) These "financial frictions," as they came to be called, gave rise to a financial accelerator, whereby small shocks to the net worth of a firm could give rise to large shifts in both the aggregate demand and supply curves.[14] The effects of a shock could persist—the restoration of balance sheets and thus the recovery of the economy to full employment could take a long time. Moreover, the decentralized adjustment of wages and prices meant that in response to a shock, the economy might not instantaneously move to the new equilibrium set of wages and prices consistent with, say, persistent full employment. Indeed, the economy could persist with wages and prices each adjusting, but real wages and unemployment remaining

---

13. See Greenwald, Stiglitz, and Weiss (1984) and Stiglitz and Greenwald (2003) and the extensive lists of references cited there.
14. See Greenwald and Stiglitz (1993a) and Bernanke and Gertler (1990).

relatively unchanged (Solow and Stiglitz 1968), or even worse, the adjustments might lead to even higher unemployment (Stiglitz 2016).[15]

As already mentioned, Greenwald and Stiglitz (1986) noted that one could describe the market failures associated with adverse selection and moral hazard as giving rise to pecuniary externalities that matter. These microeconomic pecuniary externalities have their macroeconomic manifestation, which have been the center of much recent work in macroeconomics. For instance, the market equilibrium may be characterized by excessive foreign-denominated indebtedness (Jeanne and Korinek 2010). More generally, borrowers may not take fully into account the effects of their decisions on prices in the future, say, if they were forced to liquidate their assets. Each small borrower takes the price distribution as given; but of course, if they all borrow more, then if a crisis occurs, next period prices of certain assets will fall as they all are forced to liquidate more of their assets.

One of the implications of the theory is that it may be (in general will be) optimal to treat differently things that are *observably* different. Thus, contrary to prevailing attitudes, taxes and regulations affecting foreign capital and financial institutions should differ from those affecting domestic capital. The "nondiscrimination" provisions of some trade agreements cannot be justified in the context of a model with imperfect information.

Theory of second best   Long ago, Meade (1955) and Lipsey and Lancaster (1956) warned the profession about the theory of second best. Just because an economy is inefficient doesn't mean that moving the economy closer to a perfect model will improve welfare. In the presence of multiple distortions, removing one may worsen economic welfare. Newbery and Stiglitz (1984) demonstrated this idea in the context of a longstanding presumption by economists in favor of free trade. So long as there are imperfect risk markets, trade integration may lower welfare for everyone. But we will never have full information or a complete set of markets, so we are always in a second best

---

15. This line of work emphasized a quite different aspect of Keynes than that which has been the center of much recent work in macroeconomics, highlighting the consequences of wage and price rigidities. Here, it is price adjustments that give rise to problems (consistent with much of the recent policy concerns over deflation). It can be viewed as reviving Fisher's debt-deflation theories (1933). Information economics also provided an alternative explanation of the slow pace of wage and price adjustments, associated with differential risk (Greenwald and Stiglitz 1989) and of adjustments in employment (Greenwald and Stiglitz 1995). The contrast between the alternative approaches to macroeconomics is discussed in Greenwald and Stiglitz (1987, 1993b).

world. Hence, we need to tread carefully when using the perfect markets paradigm as a guide to policy reform. Often it gives misleading advice.

One example concerns the absence of a complete set of risk markets. The question is: Will creating new financial instruments/markets increase welfare? The advocates of structured finance seem to have suggested that it will. The answer is far from clear. What is clear is that these new financial products give rise to at least three distinct problems.

The first one we have already noted: the increased complexity of the financial system results in financial fragility and reduces the ability of the regulator to effectively regulate the financial system. Financial interlinkages may lead to an increase in *intrinsic uncertainty*—with the possibility of there being multiple equilibria (even with rational expectations.)[16]

The second problem is that differences in beliefs give rise to gambling (risk trading) opportunities. In such cases, both sides of the gamble (which is zero-sum) overestimate the probability of gain and react as if their actual wealth has increased. This gives rise to what Guzman and Stiglitz (2016a, 2016d) call pseudo-wealth, the wealth that only exists in the imagination of the gamblers. Changes in pseudo-wealth can give rise to macroeconomic fluctuations. Guzman and Stiglitz suggest that some of the observed increased volatility may be due to these new structured products, which open up new gambling opportunities.

The third problem is that the interlinkage of finance undermines the decentralizability of the economy, one of the main virtues of the market economy. To know the financial position of any firm requires knowing the financial position of all creditors, which requires knowing the financial positions of all creditors of creditors.[17]

Financial architecture matters   In short, different architectures affect the extent of externalities and the nature of information requirements. There is no evidence that market-driven architectures are efficient: Because of the disparity between private and social incentives, one would not expect efficient outcomes. The design of the architecture can affect the magnitude and

---

16. Indeed, complex derivatives may even result in the nonexistence of equilibria. That is, without coordination, market participants can sign a set of mutually inconsistent contracts.

17. Requiring trading to go through adequately capitalized clearing houses— adamantly opposed by the financial sector—would go a long way toward resolving this problem.

consequences of the disparity of private and social incentives. Many of the new financial products giving rise to greater complexity may result in more "distorted" architectures, which increase the risk of financial fragility.[18]

Structured finance was thus not (as it claimed) really about matching risk.[19] Significant moral hazard can also be associated with increased indebtedness, but there is no presumption that the market-determined contractual bankruptcy provisions are efficient. Indeed, the presumption is to the contrary, as each firm tries to signal that it is better than others. This is one of the reasons bankruptcy laws are necessary. (Advocates of the contractual approach to sovereign debt restructuring seem not to understand this.)[20]

Information and Other Market Failures

Imperfect competition   One of the important insights of the economics of information is that in the absence of good information, typically competition will be imperfect. And with imperfect competition, there is the possibility (likelihood) of firms exploiting market power, and indeed, with imperfect and costly information, of undertaking actions that enhance their market power.

Information is a fixed cost, introducing a natural "nonconvexity" into production. Convexity played a key role in the proofs of Arrow and Debreu. But these mathematical properties have economic implications. The law of diminishing returns long played a central role in economic analysis; but this "law" will not be satisfied when information is endogenous.[21]

With fixed search costs, no matter how small, it pays any firm to raise its price above that of others by a small amount—until the monopoly price is reached, so the only possible equilibrium is the monopoly price (Diamond 1971, Stiglitz 1985). But then it is worthwhile for firms to engage in nonlinear

---

18. Recent research on credit networks (Battiston et al. 2016a) highlights inefficiencies associated with particular architectures, for example, bankruptcy cascades and increased systemic risk with large/correlated shocks (following on earlier work by Allen and Gale (2000) and Stiglitz and Greenwald (2003)). For analogous results for cross-border financial linkages, see Stiglitz (2010c, 2010d).
19. The information that was collected was markedly different from that which would be needed if markets were engaged in "matching." For example, see Stiglitz (1982).
20. See Brooks et al. (2015) and Guzman and Stiglitz (2016b, 2016e).
21. See, for example, Radner and Stiglitz (1984) and Arnott and Stiglitz (1988).

pricing, which extracts some of the remaining consumer surplus—to the point that there exists no market equilibrium (see Stiglitz 2013 and the references cited there).

Indeed, the major distortion of monopoly is in fact associated with its trying to extract information to enable it to extract more surplus from consumers (Stiglitz 1977). With perfect information, monopoly extracts all the consumer surplus, and it can do so (in theory) in a nondistortionary way. Distortions arise because the monopolist cannot easily differentiate those who enjoy different levels of surplus from its products: Marketing strategies, which are distortionary, are designed to maximize its ability to extract this surplus from its customers (Salop and Stiglitz 1977).

More generally, small sunk costs—and expenditures on information are always sunk costs—can give rise to persistent monopoly rents with Bertrand competition (Stiglitz 1987b).

Not only does imperfect information lead to imperfect competition, but also firms' attempts to manage information imperfections reduce competition. Efficient management of adverse selection/moral hazard involves intertemporal linkages—contracts extending over multiple periods, where, say, payments in one period are dependent on events/performance in earlier periods (Stiglitz and Weiss 1983). This limits the scope for the usual competitive mechanisms—where contracts are short term, and the threat of leaving acts as an important discipline device—and enhances scope for monopolistic exploitation. It also gives rise to *institutions* (like banks) responding by internalizing some of the information externalities.

Explanation of some key market failures   The Arrow and Debreu analysis also gave rise to another question: How do we explain key market failures, such as the lack of a complete set of securities markets or limitations in capital markets? Information economics (adverse selection and moral hazard) provides at least part of the answer: Almost surely, the firm knows more about its profits prospects than do possible insurers, and so it would not be expected to buy insurance against a risk of low profit levels unless the terms were favorable—terms that would make it unprofitable for the insurer.[22]

---

22. In the absence of risk aversion, there obviously would be no trade in such securities. This is the implication of the Akerlof (1970) lemons model and the no-trade theorems of Grossman and Stiglitz (1980) and Milgrom and Stokey (1982). See also Stiglitz (1982).

Information economics also provides one of the explanations for why Coasian bargaining would not resolve problems posed by externalities. Coase suggested that through bargaining, an efficient outcome could be achieved only if there were clear property rights. However, bargaining with information asymmetries typically is not efficient, as parties engage in costly actions to convey information about the value of the externality imposed on them.

Responding to Market Failures: The Possibility of Dysfunctional Social Institutions

Information-related externalities are not only pervasive, they are also diffuse, making it difficult to address them with corrective taxation, though corrective taxation should be part of the policy response (see Arnott and Stiglitz 1986).

Sometimes the appropriate response is the public provision of information (or restrictions on withholding information). Thus, when designing systems for leasing oil in different tracts, auctions will suffer greatly if some firm is known to have more information than the others. This provides a rationale for exploratory drilling to be done by the government.

Sometimes the consequences of these market failures are so obvious and severe that society responds through the creation of social institutions. The absence of life insurance led to the creation of burial societies to help families meet the unexpected costs of an untimely death. Such societies, mentioned as early as Ancient Rome, were widespread in Victorian England and still exist today. There was no moral hazard problem here—no one would die just to have his or her family collect burial insurance—and the problem of adverse selection was slight. Perhaps the simplest explanation of this "market failure" is that the transactions costs were high. As a result, it may be more efficient to provide such social protection through the government.

More generally, society responds to market failures by developing institutions and contracts. But there is no presumption that these institutional solutions lead to Pareto efficiency. Indeed, Arnott and Stiglitz (1991) show that institutional interventions may actually be dysfunctional. Imperfect "family" insurance (imperfect because risk is shared only among a few individuals) displaces ("crowds out") more efficient (but limited) market insurance.

Further Key Insights of the Information Paradigm

Robustness of the standard model   As information economics developed, a key question was: How robust is the standard model, which had ignored information imperfections? The answer was: not very, with even slight imperfections of information leading to marked changes in results (e.g., concerning the nature, optimality, and even existence of equilibrium (Rothschild and Stiglitz 1976)). Many of the key characterization results also changed, once information imperfections were recognized. For instance, markets might not clear even in equilibrium, and the Law of Single Price was repealed. Markets could be characterized by a price distribution, even when no source of exogenous noise was present.

Robustness of the new paradigm   It was natural, at this point, to ask: How robust are these new models? The key information problems and modes of analysis that were identified early (adverse selection, moral hazard) have remained the central foci of research for almost a half century. At the same time, the precise characterization of the equilibrium turned out to be dependent on details of markets and, in particular, on assumptions about information. The early literature differentiated between a price equilibrium (in which sellers of, say, insurance had no information about the characteristics of the buyers or their actions, such as how much insurance they purchased),[23] as characterized by Akerlof (1970), and the quantity constrained equilibrium (in which insurance firms had such information, with in effect each buyer buying exclusively from one firm). More recently, Stiglitz, Yun, and Kosenko (2017) have shown that if individuals/firms can decide whether to hide or disclose information, then neither Akerlof/price nor Rothschild-Stiglitz/quantity equilibrium can be sustained. An equilibrium always exists (unlike Rothschild-Stiglitz), and the unique equilibrium is a disclosed pooling contract (the one most favored by low-risk individuals) supplemented by an undisclosed price contract at the high-risk individual's odds purchased only by high-risk individuals.

In the presence of adverse selection and moral hazard, a pooling quantity equilibrium may exist (Stiglitz and Yun 2013), something that could not occur if there were only adverse selection.

---

23. Or, correspondingly, the buyers of cars had no information about the sellers.

One of the significant contributions of information economics was to show the importance of, and to analyze the forms of, contracts (Stiglitz 1974a) and institutions, like banks. Loans are not made through auctions but through institutions like banks, which gather and process information. Information economics also led to a new focus on enforcement and commitment (time consistency). A key issue in contract enforcement, for instance, is verifiability and thus relates to information.

All of this stood in marked contrast to the Arrow-Debreu framework, where not only was the information structure exogenous, with a complete set of markets, but there were also no problems with enforcement and no issues of commitment.

Second fundamental theorem also reversed   As noted earlier, Greenwald and Stiglitz (1986) showed that when there was asymmetric information, markets were not efficient, thus undoing the first fundamental welfare theorem of economics. Rather than the presumption being that markets are efficient, now there is a presumption that they are not.

But what about the second fundamental theorem, which asserts that any feasible Pareto efficient distribution of income could be attained through a market mechanism, with the correct initial redistribution of assets? This theorem was enormously important, because it enabled the separation of issues of efficiency from those of distribution. Economists should focus on efficiency, leaving distribution to politics, or so it was argued.

The new paradigm, however, shows that the distribution of wealth (assets) matters, and distributional effects cannot be undone through (lump sum) redistributions—partly because the information required to achieve those lump sum distributions is not available, and the only feasible redistributive taxes are distortionary.[24]

Key question: What is the critical market failure?   Much of the early literature on imperfect information focused on information asymmetries, with some discussions of imperfect information going so far as to suggest that virtually all distortions associated with imperfect information arise from these information asymmetries. But the real issue is not so much asymmetry of information as the endogeneity of information. For instance, the life insurance firm may know far more about the statistics of life expectancies

---

24. See Mirrlees (1971), Shapiro and Stiglitz (1984), Stiglitz (1987a), and Brito et al. (1990).

than those they are insuring. The individual may not know whether he or she is a high-risk or low-risk individual. The life insurance company may still engage in costly screening activities (including the use of self-selection mechanisms) to identify individuals who have characteristics that are systematically associated with longer life expectancy (see Stiglitz 2002).

Not only is information endogenous but so also are asymmetries of information (in contrast, most of the earlier literature simply assumed that the asymmetries are given exogenously). As already noted, firms and individuals have large incentives to create and enhance market power and to maximize rent extraction through the creation of information asymmetries.

Information and Delegation

Imperfect information implies that the standard analysis of efficient decentralization, based on the AD model with perfect information, is not correct. But it is the costs of collecting and disseminating information that make decentralization necessary and give rise to delegation, with profound implications for economic organization. Delegation means, for instance, that there is a separation of ownership and control: This separation undermines the standard theory of the firm and gives rise to problems of corporate governance.

Among the important market failures are those associated with corporate governance. Managers do not necessarily do what is in the interests of shareholders. Even larger differences arise between social returns and managerial returns, implying that the market solution cannot be presumed to be efficient. There are imperfections in all control mechanisms (e.g., takeovers). That is why the rules of the game—the laws governing corporate governance—matter.[25] These issues are particularly relevant in the financial sector.

Economics of Knowledge

Most of the results I have just described have applicability beyond information economics narrowly defined, to the economics of knowledge.[26] Indeed, knowledge can be thought of as a particular form of information. Knowledge is, of course, at the center of the theory of innovation. With a modern economy often characterized as a knowledge or an innovation economy, it is clear that understanding the economics of knowledge is

---

25. Stiglitz (2015).
26. The ideas in this section are developed more fully in Stiglitz and Greenwald (2014).

key. Knowledge, like information, is different from an ordinary commodity. The tools and insights of standard economics, developed for thinking about the demand and supply of pins, steel, oil, and other conventional products, are of only limited relevance to understanding a knowledge economy.

As I have suggested, knowledge is a form of information with many or most of the latter's key properties. Most importantly, knowledge is a quasi-public good—with, as already noted, no marginal cost associated with the use of an idea by someone else. Hence, there is always an inefficiency associated with restricting usage, such as through intellectual property rights. Like many public goods, the appropriation of returns is also difficult. There are typically large spillovers from an important innovation, such as the laser or the transistor, with the innovators typically capturing a small fraction of the social benefits.

The implication is that the insights that we have gleaned from the study of the economics of information apply to innovation and the production of knowledge. Markets on their own are not likely to be efficient, and competition is likely to be imperfect. This runs contrary to a longstanding view that the real strength of a market economy is the drive for innovation through Schumpeterian competition.

Early Attempts to Broaden Perspective—to Recover Previous Results on Market Efficiency—Failed

Arrow and Debreu had provided sufficient conditions for the efficiency of the economy, but not necessary ones. A search ensued for weaker conditions under which the market was still efficient.

The best-known example was that of Diamond (1967), who established the (constrained) efficiency of an economy with a stock market. Even with the highly restricted notion of optimality and highly restrictive assumptions about risk (each firm fell within a risk class and couldn't change the probability distribution of returns; it could only change the scale of production), the result turned out not to be general. With just two commodities, or with bankruptcy costs, or with decisions that affect the pattern of risk distribution, the result was not true: The market was not (constrained) efficient.

As already noted, this quest for weaker conditions under which markets are efficient ended with the Greenwald-Stiglitz (1986) theorem, which showed that markets were generically inefficient; they would be efficient only in special cases. For instance, the absence of risk markets would make no difference in an economy with a single individual, because there is no one with whom the individual could share or trade risk.[27]

But there was a second issue—how markets dealt (imperfectly) with the consequences of imperfect information, including the absence of state-contingent commodities. Contracts (with payments dependent on observable state outcomes) provided a way of simultaneously sharing risk and providing incentives (Ross 1973; Stiglitz 1974a).

A huge literature ensued, exploring optimal contract design. One interesting result is that the predicted complexity[28] was far greater than what was observed. For instance, because common shocks are among the unobservable variables, optimal contracts should make compensation dependent on others' outcomes: The predicted *forms* of contracts thus are typically different from those which are observed (see Nalebuff and Stiglitz 1983a, 1983b).

New Institutional Economics

Although the contracts that were observed differed markedly from those that were predicted, the information paradigm more generally helped explain many aspects of observed institutions. For instance, sharecropping has long been criticized as attenuating incentives—with half or more of the (marginal) returns going to the landlord. But Stiglitz (1974a) explained sharecropping as balancing out incentives and risk sharing—a "reasonable" contract, given the limitations of information and risk markets.

Although many aspects of contract design are consistent with what theory predicts, the hope that these institutions would lead to Pareto efficiency failed; as already noted, they could even worsen welfare.

---

27. As already noted, the failure of markets to be efficient can be simply explained: with imperfect information, the key constraints—incentive compatibility constraints, self-selection constraints, and collateral constraints—are all affected by what *other* individuals do; each individual fails to take into account how his or her actions affect these constraints. And these effects are of first-order importance. These externalities matter.
28. Except under special and easily rejected specifications of utility functions.

Policy Corollaries

There are many policy corollaries to the ideas that I have just discussed. In particular, Washington Consensus/neoliberal policies were predicated on the Smithian presumption that markets are efficient and the presumption that moving toward a perfect market would be welfare-enhancing, ignoring second best economics. As already noted, it is wrong to presume that moving the economy toward first best economy is welfare-enhancing. But even if this were not the case, there would be winners and losers, the adverse distributive effects could outweigh any gains, and the cost of undoing distributive effects could be large.

Policy Battles over Information: High-Frequency Trading

Today, a new set of battles has emerged, many directly related to information. It is in this arena that social and private returns are most likely to be large, and therefore the insights of this chapter are most likely to be relevant.

Consider, for instance, the development of high-frequency trading. It was often justified by "price discovery"—uncovering prices to enable the efficient allocation of resources.[29] But this was a self-serving justification of the financial sector: No evidence has ever been presented of its importance; no evidence suggests that having slightly more accurate prices a nanosecond earlier than otherwise has led to higher growth or more efficient resource allocations. The reality is that it may be a new form of front-running—those who get information about bids and offers or trades before others can make a profit. Indeed, by extracting some of the rents that would have gone to those who actually do research, high-frequency trading reduces the overall efficiency of the economy à la Grossman-Stiglitz (see Stiglitz 2014b).

Other New Policy Insights: Structured Finance

The new theory changes views about a variety of government policies. For instance, I have already noted how creating additional risk instruments may actually increase risk. So, too, welfare may be increased by requiring

---

29. High-frequency trading is also justified by "liquidity"—enabling individuals to easily move into or out of assets, enhancing willingness to make real investments. But this also seems largely to be a self-serving argument of the financial sector: The evidence is that liquidity dries up when it's needed.

disclosures—market equilibrium disclosures do not suffice. And welfare may be increased by requiring trading to occur in markets (through clearing houses), as long as they are adequately capitalized,[30] because that improves the decentralizability of the economy.

Securitization   The information paradigm helps us understand what went wrong with the securitization market. Before the 2007–2008 financial crisis, there was enormous enthusiasm about securitization because it allowed the dispersion of risk throughout the economy. But securitization entailed the delegation of different aspects of information gathering and analysis to different entities. For securitization to work well required complex contracts (with put backs and warranties). It failed, partly because of massive fraud[31] but also because of extensive problems in contract enforcement: Mortgage originators and even seemingly reputable investment banks simply refused to honor their contracts. This behavior highlights the issues of contracts and enforcement noted earlier and the important role of government in preventing fraud in information markets (Greenwald and Stiglitz 1992).

These failures of securitization (capital markets) should not come as a surprise. What is a surprise is the failure of both markets and government regulators to understand and anticipate the limitations of capital markets and securitization, including the limitations on informational efficiency of markets (Grossman and Stiglitz 1980) associated with the difficulties of appropriating returns.[32]

---

30. Which can be accomplished by requiring joint and several liability among market participants.

31. That is, the information provided to those who bought the mortgages and mortgage products was massively incorrect—with relatively clear evidence that the sellers did so at least partially intentionally.

32. The credit rating agencies not only were massively wrong in their evaluations of the probability of default of different tranches of the structured products (for which they were paid handsomely); again, there is also evidence of fraudulent behavior. I was privy to the evidence on fraud and the failure to comply with contract provisions as an expert witness in several cases against the rating agencies, the investment banks, and other financial institutions. But the federal government and state governments have brought cases in which some of this evidence has been publicly disclosed. The *Final Report of the National Commission on the Causes of the Financial and Economic Crisis in the United States* (2011) identifies the behavior of the credit rating agencies and the structured financial products as two of the main causes of the financial crisis of 2008–2009. See also Stiglitz (2010b, 2010d).

Banks can be viewed as the alternative institutional solution to these informational problems.[33] It is noteworthy that a decade after the collapse of the mortgage securitization market in the United States, it has not been restored. Evidently, the banks—in spite of their belief in free markets—want a structure that entails unacceptable levels of public risk bearing.

Other aspects of financial sector regulation Much of the profits arising from financial activity is associated with market exploitation (much of which would not arise in the presence of perfect information), including creating and exploiting asymmetries of information and market manipulation. In their book *Phishing for Phools*, Akerlof and Shiller (2015) describe the incentives for exploiting "ignorance," irrationalities, and market power.[34] Predatory lending and abusive credit card practices are only the most obvious examples.

I have also noted banks' incentives for increasing complexity—and the disparity between social and private returns in increasing complexity. Increased complexity even gives rise to new opportunities for hard-to-detect fraud. Banks availed themselves of these opportunities. High legal costs, statutes of limitations, and political capture all make it difficult to prosecute.

The financial sector has developed new ways of increasing its rents and new justifications for its exploitive activity that have sometimes prevailed in courts. Changes in technology and knowledge (e.g., about individual irrationalities and how to exploit them) and legal frameworks may have also enhanced the ability of the financial sector to exploit others.

Reconciling Two Long-Competing Theories for Describing Market Equilibrium and Explaining Inequalities

For more than 200 years, there have been two basic strands of economic theory. One emphasizes the role of competition (competitive equilibrium theory); the other, market power (exploitation).

---

33. Advocates of securitization never explained why one could not obtain adequate risk diversification through diversified ownership of banks.

34. Here I am focusing on the consequences of imperfections in information. The financial sector also enjoyed enormous rents from exploiting other sources of market power, for example, from running payment systems (credit and debit cards).

In recent decades, the former theory has dominated in the West. Of course, some constraints are always placed on the exercise of market power, *some* competition exists. But the standard (price-taking) competitive model describes few markets. Many tests of competition are only tests of the presence of some competitive constraints, not tests of how close the economy approximates a perfect competition model.

The imperfect information/imperfect competition model is fundamentally different from either polar case of perfect or no competition. I believe the real world is best described by this mixed model. In an economy that is perfectly competitive, there are, of course, no rents. In an economy where a monopoly exists in each sector, there are no battles over rents: The monopolist simply gets them. In reality, the key battle is over grabbing or limiting rents, over the structuring of markets and the rules of the game, which affect the magnitude and distribution of rents.

The rules of the game matter—markets do not exist in a vacuum. Different rules affect the well-being of different groups; each tries to restrain the feasible set of contracts and actions of others in ways that benefit themselves, and more generally, change the rules to enrich their interests at the expense of others. The public interest, of course, is to create institutional frameworks for corporate and public governance that benefit ordinary citizens and society as a whole. This is why the presumption that markets are basically competitive is a poor starting point for policy analysis, because it shunts aside all issues associated with the grabbing of rents. Governance is crucial—who makes the decisions, and the rules under which the decisions are made. In the AD model, there is no real governance issue—each firm simply maximizes its market value, and all shareholders agree that that is what it should do. With imperfect information and imperfect risk markets, it matters whose judgments are decisive, and how different judgments are "aggregated." Different individuals will have different views about what the firm should do (Grossman and Stiglitz 1977).

Economists have long recognized that governance matters in the public sector and that there is no simple way of aggregating preferences. That was the essential insight of Arrow (1951). For example, monetary policy made by those representing workers, focusing on unemployment, will be markedly different from that made by those representing bond holders, focusing on inflation. Information economics has made it clear that this is true in the private as well as in the public sector.

Indeed, the rules of the game matter in every aspect of the economy—corporate governance, financial sector, monetary policy, bankruptcy, anti-trust, and labor. Workers will do better with rules that facilitate the formation of unions, encourage union membership, and strengthen their collective bargaining rights, recognizing the "public good" they provide (all workers benefit when wages are increased). All consumers benefit with a strong anti-trust policy that recognizes that when there is market power, prices increase, and an increase in prices lowers standards of living of ordinary citizens just as a decrease in wages would. Even bankruptcy law can have important effects: Laws giving derivatives first priority in bankruptcy, even over workers, encourage derivatives and impose greater risks on workers. Laws saying that student loans cannot be discharged, even in bankruptcy, encourage predatory student lending, lead to the immiseration of those at the bottom, discourage investments in education, and increase inequality overall.

Broader Theoretical Impacts of Information Economics

The information revolution played a critical role in some broader changes in economics, beyond those just described, including giving rise to new subfields like contract theory. As noted in the Introduction, it provided for the first time intellectual foundations for fields like accounting. In finance, it created tensions between two branches, one focusing on the benefits of risk diversification, the other on the collection, processing, and dissemination of information. As noted, these branches are often in tension: securitization and structured financial products allegedly led to better risk diversification and matching of risk profiles with individuals' preferences and situations, but they also reduced the incentives for the collection and processing of information. The financial crisis demonstrated that the latter effect dominated the former.

But among the greatest legacies of information economics is its contribution to the growth of behavioral economics. Although models with imperfect and asymmetric information were able to explain many previously unexplained phenomena, models with rational behavior with imperfect information still could not explain some of what was going on (e.g., in financial markets). This provided the impetus for the development of behavioral economics.

The original work (e.g., Kahneman and Tversky 1979; Tversky and Kahneman 1974, 1981) incorporated insights from psychology. Individual decision-making, especially when decisions were made quickly, involved a myriad of biases, such as confirmatory bias, where individuals weight more heavily evidence that is consistent with their priors (Kahneman 2011).

More recent work, focusing on endogenous preferences and beliefs, and emphasizing the role of "mental models" (the lens through which we see the world), has incorporated insights from sociology and social psychology. Both fields have helped provide insights into societal rigidities and social change (Hoff and Stiglitz 2010, 2016). They have provided new instruments for policy, especially in the context of development, as illustrated by the World Development Report, *Mind, Society, and Behavior* (World Bank 2015).

A Look Forward

At one time, it was hoped that advances in technology, including the Internet, would increase competition by lowering search costs. This is true in some areas, which have homogeneous or well-specified commodities and manufactured goods. But new technology has also increased the ability to exploit—increasing asymmetries of information and market power of those who have differential access to information.

More broadly, some of the changes in our economy—in technology, in demand structure, and in our regulatory framework—have exacerbated the disparity between private and social returns to information (knowledge) and enhanced rent seeking and the capacity for rent extraction. These changes in underlying fundamentals will require changes in policy to prevent increasing market power and inequality. There is a risk that the move to the "information economy" may give market power to those who dominate in grabbing information (such as Google and Facebook), distorting both the markets for goods and services (increasing the ability to price discriminate)[35] and innovation. Innovation will be encouraged in areas with high potential for grabbing rents based on information, thereby moving scarce research resources away from areas where social

---

35. Recall our earlier discussion that imperfections in information have fundamental effects on production.

benefits would be higher. The extent to which this occurs will be determined by the rules of the game, for instance, about privacy, transparency, ownership rights of information (data) transmitted over a platform, and constraints on the ability of individuals to give up their rights. This is an area rife with externalities and other market imperfections, so government cannot shy away from taking a role; it cannot just "leave it to the market."

Moreover, partly because of the network externalities, it is hard to displace incumbents or change structures: Decisions today will have long-lasting effects, with the market characterized by having one or at most a few dominant firms whose dominance persists for long periods.

New Technology

The new technologies of the past two decades have played a particularly important role in forcing these issues on us. They are responsible for the creation of the information economy. Network effects and the increasing role of knowledge may naturally lead to more scale economies. When network effects are strong, there is a natural monopoly. The classical literature on natural monopolies states that they either have to be closely regulated or nationalized. Until recently, these new natural monopolies have managed to fend off even the recognition of their market power, and therefore of any serious attempt at regulation. As Europe has taken a closer look at their practices and found them anticompetitive, the United States has complained about the European Union taking an anti-American position. This is wrong. European anti-trust authorities are doing what they should, trying to ensure that market power is not abused. It is partially because of the political influence of these American near-monopolies that the United States has not taken actions.

The abuse of their market power is especially likely and troublesome. I noted earlier that the real distortion associated with monopoly arose from the attempt to differentiate among customers, to extract more of each individual's consumer surplus for the monopoly itself. An understanding of behavioral economics and the theory of discrimination (based on the economics of asymmetric information) plus access to enormous amounts of new data enhance their ability to exploit their market power. Even more troublesome is that their access to and ability to exploit data on individuals raises deep questions about rights to privacy and the nature of our society.

Schumpeter argued that we should not be much worried about monopolies. One monopoly will be succeeded by another, and competition to be that monopolist incentivizes innovation. Those ideas have now been discredited.[36] But the special features of these new technologies, with their access to large amounts of data that cannot be replicated, may have enhanced the ability of incumbents to persist, in spite of some instances of disruptive technology.

The Changing Structure of the Economy

Other changes in the economy may have changed the role of information—again in ways that make the economy less competitive. It is widely noted that we are moving from a manufacturing economy to a service economy. Manufactured goods are produced and sold globally. Thus, it is relatively easy to obtain and transmit information about these products.

By contrast, many of the services that will constitute an increasing fraction of gross domestic product are produced and provided locally. Consumers care about the quality of the services provided, and therefore information about quality is key and reputation effects are critical. But all of this gives rise to local market power.

Interplay between Increased Market Power and Politics

Increased economic inequality arising from the natural market forces I have just described leads to increased political inequality—which in turn leads to restructuring the rules of the game (e.g., rules governing privacy and transparency) to enhance market power and increase inequality. But as the rules of the game are shaped to enhance the incomes of those with market power, not only is inequality increased but also economic performance is likely weakened.

---

36. Dasgupta and Stiglitz (1980) showed that incumbents have the power and incentive to persist, and Fudenberg et al. (1983) showed that they could persist with a low level of expenditures on research, and thus a low level of innovation. For a more general and updated discussion, see Stiglitz and Greenwald (2014), especially chapters 5 and 6 of the 2015 revision.

Concluding Comments

Information economics has had a transformative effect on economics and economic policy, directly giving rise to new sub-branches of economics, such as contract theory, which have developed enormous literatures of their own.

It has provided explanations of phenomena that previously had been unexplained. A century ago, there was a conflict between institutional economics and "theoretical" economics, derived from the work of Smith, Ricardo, Walras, and Cournot. Information economics has, in a sense, united these two schools by highlighting the importance of institutions, at the same time that it has demonstrated the limits of markets. In many cases, it has been able to explain not only the existence of certain institutions but also their structure.

It was also noted that some phenomena could not be explained in a framework of rational individuals making decisions with imperfect information. These "failures" were important in encouraging the development of behavioral economics.

Information economics, together with other work derived from advances in game theory, has strongly suggested that the economy is best viewed through models that highlight market imperfections rather than through the lens of the competitive equilibrium model. These imperfections include imperfect and asymmetric information and the other market failures to which they give rise: incomplete risk markets, market power, and the possibilities for enhanced rent seeking and exploitation.

Most importantly, information economics has questioned—and in many cases reversed—longstanding presumptions of economic policy. The presumption is that market economies are *not* efficient. In the case of pervasive market power, there are interventions that can simultaneously increase efficiency and equity.

These ideas are particularly important for an institution like the World Bank, attempting to promote development in some of the poorest countries of the world. In these countries, markets are often weak or nonexistent, and the institutions that promote the gathering, production, and dissemination of information are particularly weak. For a long time, the Bank predicated its advice on an economic model that ignored the role of imperfect information. Fortunately, for the past two decades, the Bank has been at the forefront in raising questions about that model and enhancing our understanding of the implications of alternative frameworks—like those discussed here—for development policy.[37]

References

Akerlof, George A. 1970. "The Market for 'Lemons': Quality Uncertainty and the Market Mechanism." *Quarterly Journal of Economics* 84 (3): 488–500.

Akerlof, George A., and Robert J. Shiller. 2015. *Phishing for Phools: The Economics of Manipulation and Deception.* Princeton, NJ: Princeton University Press.

Allen, Franklin, and Douglas Gale. 2000. "Financial Contagion." *Journal of Political Economy* 108 (1): 1–33.

Angelides, Phil, et al. 2011. "Final Report of the National Commission on the Causes of the Financial and Economic Crisis in the United States." Financial Crisis Inquiry Commission, U.S. Government Printing Office, Washington, DC, January.

Arnott, Richard, and Joseph E. Stiglitz. 1986. "Moral Hazard and Optimal Commodity Taxation." *Journal of Public Economics* 29 (1): 1–24.

Arnott, Richard, and Joseph E. Stiglitz. 1988. "The Basic Analytics of Moral Hazard." *Scandinavian Journal of Economics* 90 (3): 383–413.

Arnott, Richard, and Joseph E. Stiglitz. 1991. "Moral Hazard and Non-market Institutions: Dysfunctional Crowding Out or Peer Monitoring." *American Economic Review* 81 (1): 179–190.

Arnott, Richard, Bruce Greenwald, and Joseph E. Stiglitz. 1994. "Information and Economic Efficiency." *Information Economics and Policy* 6 (1): 77–88.

Arrow, Kenneth J. 1951a. *Social Choice and Individual Values.* New York: Wiley.

Arrow, Kenneth J. 1951b. "An Extension of the Basic Theorems of Classical Welfare Economics," *Proceedings of the Second Berkeley Symposium on Mathematical Statistics and Probability*, edited by J. Neyman, 507–532. Berkeley: University of California Press.

Arrow, Kenneth J. 1964. "The Role of Securities in the Optimal Allocation of Risk-Bearing." *The Review of Economic Studies* 31(2): 91–96.

Arrow, Kenneth J., and G. Debreu. 1954. "Existence of an Equilibrium for a Competitive Economy." *Econometrica* 22 (3): 265–290.

---

37. See, for example, the 1998 World Development Report, *Knowledge for Development* (World Bank 1998), and the 2015 World Development Report already cited (World Bank 2015).

Baker, Dean, Arjun Jayadev, and Joseph E. Stiglitz. 2017. "Innovation, Intellectual Property, and Development: A Better Set of Approaches for the 21st Century." AccessIBSA, Innovation and Access to Medicines in India, Brazil, and South Africa, Bangalore, India.

Battiston, Stefano, Guido Caldarelli, Co-Pierre Georg, Robert M. May, and Joseph E. Stiglitz. 2013. "Complex Derivatives." *Nature Physics* 9 (1): 123–125.

Battiston, Stefano, Guido Caldarelli, Robert M. May, Tarik Roukny, and Joseph E. Stiglitz. 2016a. "The Price of Complexity in Financial Networks." *Proceedings of the National Academy of Sciences of the United States of America* 113 (36): 10031–10036.

Battiston, Stefano, J. Doyne Farmer, Andreas Flache, Diego Garlaschelli, Andrew G. Haldane, Hans Heesterbeek, Cars Hommes, Carlo Jaeger, Robert M. May, and Marten Scheffer. 2016b. "Complexity Theory and Financial Regulation." *Science* 351 (6275): 818–819.

Bernanke, Ben, and Mark Gertler. 1990. "Financial Fragility and Economic Performance." *Quarterly Journal of Economics* 105 (1): 87–114.

Brito, Dagobert L., Jonathan H. Hamilton, Steven M. Slutsky, and Joseph E. Stiglitz. 1990. "Pareto Efficient Tax Structures." *Oxford Economic Papers* 42: 61–77.

Brooks, Skylar, Martin Guzman, Domenico Lombardi, and Joseph E. Stiglitz. 2015. "Identifying and Resolving Inter-Creditor and Debtor-Creditor Equity Issues in Sovereign Debt Restructuring." CIGI Policy Brief 53, Centre for International Governance Innovation, Waterloo, ON.

Dasgupta, Partha, and Joseph E. Stiglitz. 1980. "Uncertainty, Industrial Structure, and the Speed of R&D." *Bell Journal of Economics* 11 (1): 1–28.

Debreu, G. 1959. *The Theory of Value.* New Haven, CT: Yale University Press.

Diamond, Peter A. 1967. "The Role of a Stock Market in a General Equilibrium Model with Technological Uncertainty." *American Economic Review* 57 (4): 759–776.

Diamond, Peter A. 1971. "A Model of Price Adjustment." *Journal of Economic Theory* 3 (2): 156–158.

Edlin, Aaron S., and Joseph E. Stiglitz. 1995. "Discouraging Rivals: Managerial Rent-Seeking and Economic Inefficiencies." *American Economic Review* 85 (5): 1301–1312.

Fama, Eugene F. 1970. "Efficient Capital Markets: A Review of Theory and Empirical Work." *Journal of Finance* 25 (2): 383–417.

Fama, Eugene F. 1991. "Efficient Capital Markets: II." *Journal of Finance* 46 (5): 1575–1617.

Fisher, Irving. 1933. "The Debt-Deflation Theory of Great Depressions." *Econometrica* 1 (4): 337–357.

Fudenberg, Drew, Richard Gilbert, Joseph E. Stiglitz, and Jean Tirole. 1983. "Preemption, Leapfrogging, and Competition in Patent Races." *European Economic Review* 22 (1): 3–31.

Geanakoplos, John D., and Heraklis M. Polemarchakis. 1986. "Existence, Regularity, and Constrained Suboptimality of Competitive Allocations When the Asset Market Is Incomplete." In *Uncertainty, Information, and Communication: Essays in Honor of Kenneth J. Arrow*, volume III, edited by Walter P. Heller, Ross M. Starr, and David A. Starrett, 65–96. Cambridge: Cambridge University Press.

Greenwald, Bruce, and Joseph E. Stiglitz. 1986. "Externalities in Economics with Imperfect Information and Incomplete Markets." *Quarterly Journal of Economics* 100 (2): 229–264.

Greenwald, Bruce, and Joseph E. Stiglitz. 1987a. "Keynesian, New Keynesian and New Classical Economics." *Oxford Economis Papers* 39 (1): 119–132.

Greenwald, Bruce, and Joseph E. Stiglitz. 1987b. "Examining Alternative Macroeconomic Theories." *Brookings Papers on Economic Activity*, 1, 1988, pp. 207–270.

Greenwald, Bruce, and Joseph E. Stiglitz. 1988. "Pareto Inefficiency of Market Economies: Search and Efficiency Wage Models." *American Economic Review* 78 (2): 351–355.

Greenwald, Bruce, and Joseph E. Stiglitz. 1989. "Toward a Theory of Rigidities." *American Economic Review* 79 (2): 364–369.

Greenwald, Bruce, and Joseph E. Stiglitz. 1990. "Asymmetric Information and the New Theory of the Firm: Financial Constraints and Risk and Behavior." *American Economic Review* 80 (2): 160–165.

Greenwald, Bruce, and Joseph E. Stiglitz. 1992. "Information, Finance, and Markets: The Architecture of Allocative Mechanisms." *Industrial and Corporate Change* 1 (1): 37–68.

Greenwald, Bruce, and Joseph E. Stiglitz. 1993a. "Financial Market Imperfections and Business Cycles." *Quarterly Journal of Economics* 108 (1): 77–114.

Greenwald, Bruce, and Joseph E. Stiglitz. 1993b. "New and Old Keynesians." *Journal of Economic Perspectives* 7 (1): 23–44.

Greenwald, Bruce, and Joseph E. Stiglitz. 1995. "Labor Market Adjustments and the Persistence of Unemployment." *American Economic Review* 85 (2): 219–225.

Greenwald, Bruce, Joseph E. Stiglitz, and Andrew Weiss. 1984. "Informational Imperfections in the Capital Markets and Macroeconomic Fluctuations." *American Economic Review* 74 (2): 194–199.

Grossman, Sanford J., and Robert J. Shiller. 1981. "The Determinants of the Variability of Stock Market Prices." *American Economic Review* 71 (2): 222–227.

Grossman, Sanford J., and Joseph E. Stiglitz. 1976. "Information and Competitive Price Systems." *American Economic Review* 66 (2): 246–253.

Grossman, Sanford J., and Joseph E. Stiglitz. 1977. "On Value Maximization and Alternative Objectives of the Firm." *Journal of Finance* 32 (1): 389–402.

Grossman, Sanford J., and Joseph E. Stiglitz. 1980. "On the Impossibility of Informationally Efficient Markets." *American Economic Review* 70 (3): 393–408.

Guzman, Martin, and Joseph E. Stiglitz. 2016a. "A Theory of Pseudo-Wealth." In *Contemporary Issues in Macroeconomics*, edited by Joseph E. Stiglitz and Martin Guzman, International Economic Association Conference Volume 155-II, 21–33. Basingstoke, UK: Palgrave Macmillan.

Guzman, Martin, and Joseph E. Stiglitz. 2016b. "Creating a Framework for Sovereign Debt Restructuring That Works." In *Too Little, Too Late: The Quest to Resolve Sovereign Debt Crises*, edited by Martin Guzman, José Antonio Ocampo, and Joseph E. Stiglitz, 3–32. New York: Columbia University Press.

Guzman, Martin, and Joseph E. Stiglitz. 2016c. "Pseudo-Wealth and Consumption Fluctuations." NBER Working Paper 22838, National Bureau of Economic Research, Cambridge, MA.

Guzman, Martin, and Joseph E. Stiglitz. 2016d. "A Soft Law Mechanism for Sovereign Debt Restructuring Based on the UN Principles." FES International Policy Analysis Paper, Friedrich Ebert Stiftung, Berlin.

Haldane, Andrew G., and Robert M. May. 2011. "Systemic Risk in Banking Ecosystems." *Nature* 469 (7330): 351–355.

Henry, Claude, and Joseph E. Stiglitz. 2010. "Intellectual Property, Dissemination of Innovation, and Sustainable Development." *Global Policy* 1 (3): 237–251.

Hirshleifer, Jack. 1971. "The Private and Social Value of Information and the Reward to Inventive Activity." *American Economic Review* 61 (4): 561–574.

Hoff, Karla, and Joseph E. Stiglitz. 2010. "Equilibrium Fictions: A Cognitive Approach to Societal Rigidity." *American Economic Review* 100 (2): 141–146.

Hoff, Karla, and Joseph E. Stiglitz. 2016. "Striving for Balance in Economics: Towards a Theory of the Social Determination of Behavior." *Journal of Economic Behavior and Organization* 126 (Part B): 25–57.

Jeanne, Olivier, and Anton Korinek. 2010. "Excessive Volatility in Capital Flows: A Pigouvian Taxation Approach." *American Economic Review* 100 (2): 403–407.

Kahneman, Daniel. 2011. *Thinking, Fast and Slow*. New York: Farrar, Straus and Giroux.

Kahneman, Daniel, and Amos Tversky. 1979. "Prospect Theory: An Analysis of Decisions under Risk." *Econometrica* 47 (2): 263–291.

Lipsey, Richard G., and Kelvin Lancaster. 1956. "The General Theory of Second Best." *Review of Economic Studies* 24 (1): 11–32.

May, Robert M. 2014. "Stability and Complexity in Financial Ecosystems." presentation to British Ecological Society and London School of Economics Joint Annual Symposium: Eco^2: Ecology × Economics=Eco^2 , BMA House, London, September 8–10.

Meade, James E. 1955. *Trade and Welfare*. London: Oxford University Press.

Milgrom, Paul, and Nancy Stokey. 1982. "Information, Trade and Common Knowledge." *Journal of Economic Theory* 26 (1): 17–27.

Mirrlees, James A. 1971. "An Exploration in the Theory of Optimum Income Taxation." *Review of Economic Studies* 38 (2): 175–208.

Nalebuff, Barry J., and Joseph E. Stiglitz. 1983a. "Information, Competition, and Markets." *American Economic Review* 73 (2): 278–283.

Nalebuff, Barry J., and Joseph E. Stiglitz. 1983b. "Prices and Incentives: Towards a General Theory of Compensation and Competition." *Bell Journal of Economics* 14 (1): 21–43.

Newbery, David M. G., and Joseph E. Stiglitz. 1984. "Pareto Inferior Trade." *Review of Economic Studies* 51 (1): 1–12.

Radner, Roy, and Joseph E. Stiglitz. 1984. "A Nonconcavity in the Value of Information." In *Bayesian Models of Economic Theory*, edited by Marcel Boyer and Richard E. Kihlstrom, 33–52. Amsterdam: Elsevier.

Ross, Stephen A. 1973. "The Economic Theory of Agency: The Principal's Problem." *American Economic Review* 63 (2): 134–139.

Rothschild, Michael, and Joseph E. Stiglitz. 1976. "Equilibrium in Competitive Insurance Markets: An Essay on the Economics of Imperfect Information." *Quarterly Journal of Economics* 90 (4): 629–649.

Roukny, Tarik, Stefano Battiston, and Joseph E. Stiglitz. 2016. "Interconnectedness as a Source of Uncertainty in Systemic Risk." *Journal of Financial Stability* 35 (2): 93–106.

Salop, Steven, and Joseph E. Stiglitz. 1977. "Bargains and Ripoffs: A Model of Monopolistically Competitive Price Dispersion." *Review of Economic Studies* 44 (3): 493–510.

Shapiro, Carl, and Joseph E. Stiglitz. 1984. "Equilibrium Unemployment as a Worker Discipline Device." *American Economic Review* 74 (3): 433–444.

Shiller, Robert J. 1990. "Market Volatility and Investor Behavior." *American Economic Review* 80 (2): 58–62.

Solow, Robert M., and Joseph E. Stiglitz. 1968. "Output, Employment and Wages in the Short Run." *Quarterly Journal of Economics* 82 (4): 537–560.

Spence, Michael. 1973. "Job Market Signaling." *Quarterly Journal of Economics* 87 (3): 355–374.

Stiglitz, Joseph E. 1972. "On the Optimality of the Stock Market Allocation of Investment." *Quarterly Journal of Economics* 86 (1): 25–60.

Stiglitz, Joseph E. 1973. "Approaches to the Economics of Discrimination." *American Economic Review* 62 (2): 287–295.

Stiglitz, Joseph E. 1974a. "Incentives and Risk Sharing in Sharecropping." *Review of Economic Studies* 41 (2): 219–255.

Stiglitz, Joseph E. 1974b. "Theories of Discrimination and Economic Policy." In *Patterns of Racial Discrimination*, edited by George M. von Furstenberg, Bennett Harrison, and Ann R. Horowitz, 5–26. Lexington, MA: Lexington Books.

Stiglitz, Joseph E. 1975. "The Theory of Screening, Education and the Distribution of Income." *American Economic Review* 65 (3): 283–300.

Stiglitz, Joseph E. 1977. "Monopoly, Non-linear Pricing and Imperfect Information: The Insurance Market." *Review of Economic Studies* 44 (3): 407–430.

Stiglitz, Joseph E. 1982. "Information and Capital Markets." In *Financial Economics: Essays in Honor of Paul Cootner*, edited by William F. Sharpe and Cathryn M. Cootner, 118–158. Upper Saddle River, NJ: Prentice Hall.

Stiglitz, Joseph E. 1985. "Equilibrium Wage Distributions." *Economic Journal* 95 (379): 595–618.

Stiglitz, Joseph E. 1987a. "Pareto Efficient and Optimal Taxation and the New Welfare Economics." In *Handbook on Public Economics*, edited by Alan J. Auerbach and Martin S. Feldstein, 991–1042. Amsterdam: Elsevier Science.

Stiglitz, Joseph E. 1987b. "Technological Change, Sunk Costs and Competition." *Brookings Papers on Economic Activity* 3 (1): 883–947.

Stiglitz, Joseph E. 1987c. "The Causes and Consequences of the Dependence of Quality on Prices." *Journal of Economic Literature* 25 (1): 1–48.

Stiglitz, Joseph E. 1994. *Whither Socialism?* Cambridge, MA: MIT Press.

Stiglitz, Joseph E. 1999. "Knowledge as a Global Public Good." In *Global Public Goods: International Cooperation in the 21st Century*, edited by Inge Kaul, Isabelle Grunberg, and Marc A. Stern, 308–325. New York: Oxford University Press.

Stiglitz, Joseph E. 2002. "Information and the Change in the Paradigm in Economics." *American Economic Review* 92 (3): 460–501.

Stiglitz, Joseph E. 2008. "Economic Foundations of Intellectual Property Rights." *Duke Law Journal* 57 (6): 1693–1724.

Stiglitz, Joseph E. 2010a. "The Financial Crisis of 2007–2008 and Its Macroeconomic Consequences." In *Time for a Visible Hand: Lessons from the 2008 World Financial Crisis*, edited by Stephany Griffith-Jones, José Antonio Ocampo, and Joseph E. Stiglitz, 19–49. Oxford: Oxford University Press.

Stiglitz, Joseph E. 2010b. "Responding to the Crisis." In *Time for a Visible Hand: Lessons from the 2008 World Financial Crisis*, edited by Stephany Griffith-Jones, José Antonio Ocampo, and Joseph E. Stiglitz, 76–100. Oxford: Oxford University Press.

Stiglitz, Joseph E. 2010c. "Risk and Global Economic Architecture: Why Full Financial Integration May Be Undesirable." *American Economic Review* 100 (2): 388–392.

Stiglitz, Joseph E. 2010d. "Contagion, Liberalization, and the Optimal Structure of Globalization," *Journal of Globalization and Development* 1(2), Article 2, 45 pages.

Stiglitz, Joseph E. 2013. *The Selected Works of Joseph E. Stiglitz, Volume II: Information and Economic Analysis: Applications to Capital, Labor, and Product Markets*. Oxford: Oxford University Press.

Stiglitz, Joseph E. 2014a. "Intellectual Property Rights, the Pool of Knowledge, and Innovation." NBER Working Paper 20014, National Bureau of Economic Research, Cambridge, MA.

Stiglitz, Joseph E. 2014b. "Tapping the Brakes: Are Less Active Markets Safer and Better for the Economy?" Paper presented at the Federal Reserve Bank of Atlanta, Atlanta, GA, April 15.

Stiglitz, Joseph E. 2015. *Rewriting the Rules of the American Economy: An Agenda for Growth and Shared Prosperity*. New York: W. W. Norton.

Stiglitz, Joseph E. 2016. *Towards a General Theory of Deep Downturns*. (Presidential address to the 7th World Congress of the International Economic Association, Dead Sea, Jordan, June 6–10, 2014), IEA Conference volume 155-VI. Houndmills, UK, and New York: Palgrave Macmillan.

Stiglitz, Joseph E., and Bruce Greenwald. 2003. *Towards a New Paradigm for Monetary Policy*. London: Cambridge University Press.

Stiglitz, Joseph E., and Bruce Greenwald. 2014. *Creating a Learning Society: A New Approach to Growth, Development, and Social Progress*. New York: Columbia University Press.

Stiglitz, Joseph E., and Bruce Greenwald. 2015. *Creating a Learning Society: A New Approach to Growth, Development, and Social Progress*. Readers Edition. New York: Columbia University Press.

Stiglitz, Joseph E., and Andrew Weiss. 1983. "Incentive Effects of Terminations: Applications to the Credit and Labor Markets." *American Economic Review* 73 (5): 912–927.

Stiglitz, Joseph E., and Jungyoll Yun. 2013. "Optimality and Equilibrium in a Competitive Insurance Market under Adverse Selection and Moral Hazard." NBER Working Paper 19317, National Bureau of Economic Research, Cambridge, MA.

Stiglitz, Joseph E., Jungyoll Yun, and Andrew Kosenko. 2017. "Equilibrium in a Competitive Insurance Market under Adverse Selection with Endogenous Information." NBER Working Paper 23556, National Bureau of Economic Research, Cambridge, MA.

Tversky, Amos, and Daniel Kahneman. 1974. "Judgment under Uncertainty: Heuristics and Biases." *Science* 185 (4157): 1124–1131.

Tversky, Amos, and Daniel Kahneman. 1981. "The Framing of Decisions and the Psychology of Choice." *Science* 211 (4481): 453–458.

World Bank. 1998. *World Development Report 1998/1999: Knowledge for Development.* New York: Oxford University Press.

World Bank. 2015. *World Development Report 2015: Mind, Society, and Behavior.* Washington, DC: World Bank.

Comment: Ravi Kanbur

Left Field Observations on the Information Revolution in Economics

There is no question that an information revolution has occurred in economics. And there is no question that Joe Stiglitz is a revolutionary leader. The classic papers in this literature bear the names of Stiglitz, Rothschild-Stiglitz, Stiglitz-Weiss, Shapiro-Stiglitz, Grossman-Stiglitz, Greenwald-Stiglitz, Newbery-Stiglitz, and so on.

And there is no question that development economics is closely entwined with the information revolution. The development context provided the spur for the theorizing and conceptualizing of Stiglitz, Akerlof, and others. The information revolution in turn has implications for development economics and development policy, including, for example: (1) share cropping and agrarian relations; (2) credit rationing, moneylenders, and microfinance; (3) asymmetric information and efficiency wages; (4) migration models; (5) commodity price stabilization; and (6) free trade and uncertainty, and many other topics.

So what can you say after Joe Stiglitz has given his account of the information revolution in economics? It is a bit like critiquing Fidel Castro's account of the Cuban Revolution, or taking issue with Dwight Eisenhower's narration of the D-Day landings. Commentary is particularly difficult when you agree with the revolution and the revolutionary on almost everything, and consider yourself to have been a foot soldier, having fought in the "risk taking and inequality" detachment of the revolutionary brigades.[1] So,

---

1. See, for example, Kanbur (1979).

what to do? To make the commentary somewhat interesting, I will come at the revolution from left field and pose some methodological questions for myself, for Joe, and for all of us to ponder.

Expected Utility Analysis

The core analytical tool in the information revolution armory has been expected utility (EU) analysis. As we all know, questions have been raised about the independence axiom that undergirds the EU representation of preference orderings. It is this axiom that allows the representation to be separable in a specific way between the utility of an outcome with certainty and the probability of that outcome. But individuals do not appear to behave according to this axiom, with research on this going back at least as far as the Allais paradox.

At one level, it is remarkable that so many features of the real world, like credit rationing or insurance market failures, can be explained with models in which agents are assumed to behave in a manner that they do not actually behave like in practice. And it may not matter methodologically, so long as the predictions of the models are not falsified by observations. But it does raise the question: How exactly would the iconic results of the classic models in the revolution survive without EU?

In all of the well-known exercises that establish the iconic results of the imperfect information revolution, we use EU. For example, in the classic Rothschild and Stiglitz (1976) paper on insurance, when we show that a pooling equilibrium can be broken by a separating insurance contract, and a separating equilibrium can be broken by a pooling contract, we use EU comparisons. In another classic (Stiglitz and Weiss 1981), when we show that credit rationing is an equilibrium for lenders, we use EU. And so on.

Could we construct these equilibria, or show nonexistence of equilibrium, if agents did not behave according to EU? My instinct is that we could. In the insurance context, for example, non-EU preferences might allow a wider range of contract offers, which could break an existing equilibrium. But the twist is that the candidate equilibrium would first have to be described in a non-EU frame. This is an open and interesting area for research. And note that it is not enough to argue, as Machina (1982) does in a famous paper, that EU works locally as a linearization—many of the results require global comparisons.

Radical Uncertainty and Behavioral Economics

EU analysis, the foundation of Stiglitzian imperfect information analysis, is also confined to risk, where probabilities of outcomes are well defined and known, as opposed to uncertainty, where this is not the case (also known as Knightian uncertainty). Such radical uncertainty was well described by Keynes (1937, 213–214), in an article that introduced the conceptual foundations of the General Theory to American audiences:

> By "uncertain" knowledge, let me explain, I do not mean merely to distinguish what is known for certain from what is only probable. The game of roulette is not subject, in this sense, to uncertainty....The sense in which I am using the term is that in which the prospect of a European war is uncertain, or the price of copper and the rate of interest twenty years hence....About these matters there is no scientific basis on which to form any calculable probability whatever. We simply do not know.

Keynes (1937, 214–215) then goes on to develop the argument further, especially the implications of such radical uncertainty for behavior. Summarizing somewhat:

> How do we manage in such circumstances to behave in a manner which saves our faces as rational, economic men? We have devised for the purpose a variety of techniques, of which much the most important are the three following :(1)......
> (2)..... (3) Knowing that our own individual judgment is worthless, we endeavor to fall back on the judgment of the rest of the world which is perhaps better informed....Now a practical theory of the future based on these three principles has certain marked characteristics. In particular, being based on so flimsy a foundation, it is subject to sudden and violent changes....At all times the vague panic fears and equally vague and unreasoned hopes are not really lulled, and lie but a little way below the surface.

These "behavioral considerations," as they would now be called, are not present in Rothschild-Stiglitz, Stiglitz-Weiss, Grossman-Stiglitz, and so forth. In all of those models, agents are rational choice EU maximizers with risk rather than uncertainty. This leads to a set of questions.

Does it matter that the models that describe so well outcomes in actual markets have models of individual behavior that are so far removed from reality? How different would the outcomes of those models be if agents in them followed the precepts of recent developments in behavioral economics rather than rational choice EU analysis? And would it matter for policy? I believe these are open questions for research and debate.

Keynesian Interventionism or Burkean Conservatism?

Does imperfect information, particularly of the radical uncertainty variety ("We simply do not know"), make one tend towards Keynesian interventionism or Burkean conservatism? Keynes himself was greatly influenced by Edmund Burke. In an as yet unpublished[2] undergraduate essay (Keynes, 1904, 4–15), he lauds Burke's conservatism in considerations of war and other momentous decisions:

> Burke ever held, and held rightly, that it can seldom be right...to sacrifice a present benefit for a doubtful advantage in the future...; we should be very chary of sacrificing large numbers of people for the sake of a contingent end, however advantageous that may appear....We can never know enough to make the chance worth taking.

The direct descendant of this line of thinking is Keynes's famous 1923 statement from his *Tract on Monetary Reform*: "But this *long run* is a misleading guide to current affairs. *In the long run* we are all dead." (Keynes, quoted in Skidelsky, 2013).

Skidelsky (2013) argues that "Keynes would have rejected the claim of today's austerity champions that short-term pain, in the form of budget cuts, is the price we need to pay for long-term economic growth. The pain is real, he would say, while the benefit is conjecture."

So far, so good. Radical uncertainty appears to favor such progressive positions as caution in launching wars and austerity programs. But from Burke's prudence principle also flowed an institutional conservatism, as made clear in a famous passage (quoted in Edlin 2017, 50) from Burke's *Reflections on the Revolution in France*:

> You see, Sir, that in this enlightened age I am bold enough to confess that we [the English]...instead of casting away all our old prejudices, we cherish them ... and, to take more shame on ourselves, we cherish them because they are prejudices; and the longer they have lasted, and the more generally they have prevailed, the more we cherish them.

A modern version of this argument for conservatism is provided by Edlin (2017, 49):

> Decision makers suffer from switcher's curse if they forget the reason that they maintained incumbent policies in the past and if they naively compare rival and

---

2. Brief extracts from it are published in Skidelsky (2016).

incumbent policies with no bias for incumbent policies. I find that conservatism emerges as a heuristic to avoid switcher's curse. The longer a process or policy has been in place, the more conservative one should be. On the other hand, the more conservative were past decision makers, the more progressive one should be today.

Keynes (1904, 15) interpreted the Burkean recoil from revolution in his 1904 undergraduate essay: "We can never know enough to make the chance worth taking, and the fact that cataclysms in the past have sometimes inaugurated lasting benefits is no argument for cataclysms in general. These fellows, says Burke, have 'glorified in making a Revolution, as if revolutions were good things in themselves'."

This is not the place to develop the argument, and others have developed it as well, that an institutional conservatism was also deeply ingrained in Keynes, who wanted to save capitalism, not end it. Actually, what Keynes really wanted was to save the world of late Victorian and Edwardian England, which came to an end in 1914.

Conclusion

So, imperfect information in the form of radical uncertainty, and its consequent undermining of EU analysis, opens up a wide area of research, asking whether the classic Stiglitzian propositions will still hold in this brave new world.

Further, radical uncertainty can be the basis for either Keynesian interventionism or Burkean conservatism or, in Keynes's mind, both! In any event, so far as Joe Stiglitz is concerned, to paraphrase Keynes on Burke, "This fellow has glorified in making a revolution, as if a revolution was a good thing in itself." And there is no question that the information revolution has indeed been a good thing in itself. As a foot soldier in the information revolution, I salute our leader!

References

Edlin, Aaron. 2017. "Conservatism and Switcher's Curse." *American Law and Economics Review* 19 (1): 49–95.

Kanbur, Ravi. 1979. "Of Risk Taking and the Personal Distribution of Income." *Journal of Political Economy* 87 (4): 769–797.

Keynes, John Maynard. 1904. *The Political Doctrines of Edmund Burke*. Keynes papers, *KP: UA/20/315*, Kings College Archives, Cambridge.

Keynes, John Maynard. 1937. "The General Theory of Employment." *Quarterly Journal of Economics* 51 (2): 209–223.

Machina, Mark J. 1982. "'Expected Utility' Analysis without the Independence Axiom." *Econometrica* 50 (2): 277–323.

Rothschild, Michael, and Joseph E. Stiglitz. 1976. "Equilibrium in Competitive Insurance Markets: An Essay on the Economics of Imperfect Information." *Quarterly Journal of Economics* 90 (4): 629–649.

Skidelsky, Robert. 2013. "True, Keynes Cared Little about the Long Run. But That Wasn't Because He Was Gay." Op-Ed, *Washington Post*, May 9.

Skidelsky, Robert. 2016. *The Essential Keynes*. London: Penguin Classics.

Stiglitz, Joseph E., and Andrew Weiss. 1981. "Credit Rationing in Markets with Imperfect Information." *American Economic Review* 71 (3): 393–410.

Comment: Hamid Rashid*

Information Asymmetry, Conflicts of Interest, and the Financial Crisis: Lessons Learned and the Way Forward

Information asymmetry is often the main cause of market failures, as Joe explains earlier in the chapter. Firms, especially financial firms, have incentives to exploit information asymmetries, hiding critical information about their incentives, behavior, and performance. Conflicts of interests—with information asymmetry hiding their existence—can allow financial firms to ignore, misprice, and under-report risks, triggering devastating market failures. This is what we saw in the run up to the financial crisis, the most significant market failure of our lifetime. One lesson from the crisis is that regulators, rating agencies, and investors largely failed to detect widespread conflicts of interest in the mortgage market, when some large banks comingled appraisal, origination, servicing, securitization, underwriting, and even rating functions. A bank originating a mortgage typically relies on an independent third party to appraise the value of the property and thus avoid potential conflicts of interest in the valuation. But this practice changed during the boom years before the financial crisis. If a bank stood to gain more from a higher valuation of the property—earning hefty commissions and fees, as we saw during the mortgage boom—it would use a complicit appraiser willing to inflate the property value. By 2006, 90 percent of the property appraisers felt pressured—often by the originating bank or its agents—to inflate home values.[1] The independent appraiser was supposed

---

*The views expressed here do not reflect the views of the United Nations or its Member States.
1. Financial Crisis Inquiry Commission (2011).

to protect the lender (and by extension, the banks' depositors) against the risk of a mortgage default. But during the mortgage boom, the appraiser and mortgage originator worked together—a clear conflict of interest—to inflate property values and originate as many mortgages as quickly as possible, which exacerbated the risk of a crisis.

Conflicts of interest were also pervasive in transactions between the originator and the mortgage securitizer. Both often worked for the same bank, and the originator knew that the securitizer would buy whatever mortgages she would originate, without raising any question about the quality of the mortgages. In addition, the securitizer knew that he would be able to package any mortgage into AAA-rated securities and sell them to the investor clients of the same bank, then neither the originator nor the securitizer had an incentive to assess underlying risks accurately and price the mortgage-backed securities correctly. With all transactions taking place among related parties and no consequences for ignoring conflicts, due diligence became a waste of time for our banks.

During the mortgage boom, our banks routinely hid conflicts of interest and originated trillions of dollars of subprime mortgages that did not meet minimum underwriting standards. In a "issuer pays" rating model—with manifest conflicts of interest—more than 80 percent of subprime mortgage-backed securities received the highest-possible AAA ratings,[2] making many below-investment-grade securities highly attractive to investors. Had the investors been fully aware of the extent of the conflicts of interests—and how these conflicts contributed to the mispricing of mortgage-backed securities—the mortgage bubble that precipitated a global financial crisis might have been avoided.

It is surprising that the pervasive conflicts of interest that led us to the crisis did not attract the attention of our regulators, given that only 7 years earlier, the Enron scandal exposed widespread and harmful conflicts of interest in corporate America. Drawing on the Enron lessons, the US Congress passed the Sarbanes-Oxley Act in 2002, with the stated objective: "to protect investors by improving the accuracy and reliability of corporate disclosures." Title V of the Act deals with conflicts of interest, requiring a clear separation between the securities analysts and

---

2. Ashcraft, Goldsmith-Pinkham, and Vickery (2010).

underwriting functions of a financial firm. Large banks blatantly disregarded the separation and exploited conflicts of interest in securitization deals. Yet no banker was charged for violating the Sarbanes-Oxley Act, although it contained provisions for holding senior management personally responsible for a breach.

As the issuers of billions of dollars of Alt-A and subprime private-label mortgage-backed securities, our largest banks were fully aware of the quality of underlying assets that backed the securities and yet hid that information from their investors. The banks put their own interests ahead of the interests of their investors to make a quick profit on risky bets. The sheer size and complexity of these banks—financial supermarkets—that combined mortgage, retail, and investment banking activities, allowed them to exploit conflicts of interest with impunity. Their status as "too big to supervise" allowed them to evade regulatory oversight, while being "too big to fail" meant they faced no consequences of a devastating financial crisis.

Aiming to address the root causes of the financial crisis, the US Congress passed the Dodd-Frank Wall Street Reform and Consumer Protection Act in 2010. The Act was intended to mitigate, among other issues, the inherent conflicts of interests in securitization. Section 621 of the Act, for example, prohibits any transaction that could create a conflict of interest with an investor in a securitization transaction. The subsequent rule issued by the Securities and Exchange Commission (SEC) included a negative list of conflicts of interest in securitization that is laden with exceptions and loopholes. For example, the rule provided that a securitization transaction would not represent a conflict of interest if it is for hedging, market-making, or for providing liquidity. This leaves room for subjective interpretation, requiring the regulator to differentiate ex ante between hedging and speculation. There is a growing recognition that it is hard, if not impossible, to detect conflicts of interest in securitization, especially when it involves many parts of a large and complex financial firm.

The Dodd-Frank Act, even if implemented fully, is unlikely to mitigate conflicts of interest in securitization, largely because of its reliance on a narrow set of rules and a long list of exceptions. Instead of prohibiting a limited number of activities, the Dodd-Frank Act needed to effectively address the structural causes of the crisis, such as the "too big to fail" criterion or stock-option based executive compensations, which incentivize banks to hide conflicts of interests and take excessive risks. Conflicts of interest—material, perceived, or potential—are often unobservable until their adverse effects become apparent. But organizational structures, such as bank size and compensation packages of senior executives, are clearly observable. The regulators need to target and regulate the observables instead of trying to regulate unobservable behavior. The Federal Reserve Board, for example, recently imposed a limit on the growth of the assets of a large bank that engaged in inappropriate behavior.[3] This is clearly a bold step in the right direction.

For nearly 70 years, the Glass-Steagall Act managed to keep conflicts of interest under control by enforcing a clear and structural separation between commercial and investment banking activities and making sure— albeit indirectly—that banks were not too big to supervise and regulate. Unlike the Dodd-Frank Act, it incorporated specific measures to address the problems of information asymmetry and conflicts of interest in the financial sector. Although Dodd-Frank recognizes the "too big to fail" problem, it has not prevented the growth of our largest banks. The large banks have since become even larger. In fact, the market share of the top 10 or 15 largest banks has increased relative to the pre-crisis level (figure 3.1). The largest bank in the United States was 57 percent larger in 2014 than it was in 2007.

Dodd-Frank also does not adequately address the problems of incentive structures in large banks. The stock-option based compensation schemes create a conflict of interest, as they encourage managers to act more like investors or speculators and to take excessive risks that boost short-term stock price of the firm, even if doing so undermines the financial stability and interests of the firm. In the run-up to the crisis, large financial firms offered significant amounts of stock options to their senior managers, ostensibly to incentivize best performance. Stock-based compensation also contributes to the "too big to fail" problem, encouraging top managers to aggressively increase size and market share. Although Dodd-Frank introduces certain prohibitions, time-limits, and claw-back provisions, stock-based compensation remains as pervasive as it was before the crisis. If this practice continues unabated, financial firms will continue to find ways to

---

3. See https://www.reuters.com/article/us-usa-wells-fargo-fed/fed-orders-wells-fargo
-to-halt-growth-over-compliance-issues-idUSKBN1FM2V9.

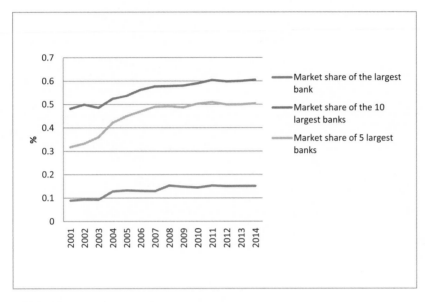

Figure 3.1
Market share of large US banks: 2001–2014
Percentage of total assets of banks with more than $300 million in assets
Source: Author's compilation of data from https://www.federalreserve.gov/releases /lbr/.

make risky bets and boost short-term profits and market valuation. This also perhaps explains the spectacular growth of the market valuation of US financial firms since the crisis, increasing from $2.8 trillion in 2008 to $7.3 trillion in 2015 (figure 3.2).

The financial crisis is a sad testimony to the failure of the revolution in information economics that Joe spearheaded, which should have fostered and enabled effective regulation of our financial sector, where information asymmetry matters the most. The advances in our thinking and understanding of how information shapes market behavior and the scope and intensity of financial regulations have moved in the opposite direction during the past few decades. We now see a starker, and more disconcerting, disconnect between the lessons of information economics and the state of financial regulation. Financial regulation of the past few decades has relied on the imaginary narrative of perfectly competitive financial markets with perfect information. The Dodd-Frank Act is no exception. The revolution

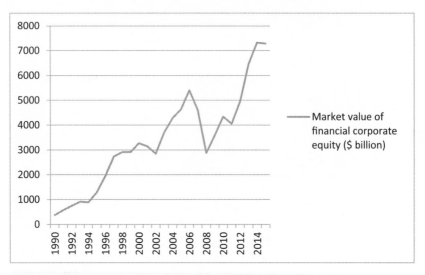

Figure 3.2
Market value of US financial corporate equity ($ billion)
Source: US financial accounts, https://www.federalreserve.gov/releases/Z1/Current
/data.htm.

in information economics will remain incomplete until the economics of
information guides and shapes financial regulation. Unless we bridge the
gap between what we know and how we regulate financial markets, another
financial crisis is just around the corner.

References

Ashcraft, Adam, Paul Goldsmith-Pinkham, and James Vickery. 2010. "MBS Rating
and the Mortgage Credit Boom." Staff Report 449, Federal Reserve Bank of New York.

Financial Crisis Inquiry Commission. 2011. *The Financial Crisis Inquiry Report.* Washington, DC: US Government Publishing Office.

II Macroeconomic Stabilization and Growth

4 From Chronic Inflation to Chronic Deflation: Focusing on Expectation and Liquidity Disarray since World War II

Guillermo Calvo

The organizers of this conference have asked me to distill in a few pages my experience with macroeconomics, focusing on issues that are relevant for policy making. After several false starts, I concluded that I could better serve the objective if I identified a few theoretical topics that helped in the discussion of critical policy issues during the period covered. Rational expectations (RE) stands up, given its role in the flourishing of macroeconomics since the 1970s. Whether or not one endorses its relevance for positive theory, RE has proven to be immensely useful to sort out analytical issues and offer useful insights on applications. Like the Modigliani-Miller theorem or Ricardian equivalence, the RE insights provide benchmarks that shed light even on cases in which RE does not hold.

Macroeconomics is a very rich and varied field. To keep this chapter within reasonable bounds, I confine the discussion to two grand themes, namely, chronic inflation and chronic deflation, and associated issues. Chronic inflation took center stage in developed market economies (DMs) in the 1970s (a period called the "Great Inflation"), and in emerging market economies (EMs) during much of the twentieth century after World War II. The Great Inflation has been subject to a good number of studies (for a recent discussion, see Bordo and Orphanides (2013) and McKinnon (2013)). Therefore I will focus on EM episodes. Simple rules for stopping inflation, inspired by available theory, failed to work and, in several instances, gave

This is an abridged version of a paper, under the same title, prepared for the World Bank conference entitled *The State of Economics, The State of the World*, held in Washington, DC, June 8 and 9, 2016. I am thankful to Edmar Bacha, Sara Calvo, Fabrizio Coricelli, Roque Fernandez, Arvid Lukauscas, and Pablo Ottonello for valuable comments.

rise to serious distortions and costly crises. However, chronic deflation is galvanizing world attention since the dramatic financial crisis episodes in EMs and, more recently, the ongoing Great Recession that started in 2007.

Research on EM chronic inflation focused mostly on local or domestic factors and, as a general rule, assumed that DMs were stable and provided the services of deep capital markets. This view started to be challenged by the rise of EM financial crises in which external factors have a significant, if not necessarily dominant, role (e.g., the debt crisis in the 1980s—partly triggered by Volcker's stabilization program—and Mexico's "Tequila" crisis in 1994/1995, which followed on the heels of a more modest but still important rise in US interest rates). These crises involved a host of financial factors, but the conventional wisdom tended to attribute them to EM weak domestic institutions and domestic policy mistakes. Global capital markets might have played a role, but they were not seen as the main culprit. This view proved harder to defend after the Asia/Russia crises in 1997–1998, because some of epicenter economies had followed the Washington Consensus. At any rate, the succession of these crises gave a strong impetus to research that pointed in a sharply different direction. For example, toward sudden stop (i.e., a severe supply-driven crunch in international capital flows), a phenomenon alien to well-oiled financial markets. Moreover, given that the abovementioned crises involved several economies outside the crisis epicenter, research focused on systemic sudden stop. This set off a search for factors that may turn a regular contraction in international capital flows into systemic sudden stop (e.g., Calvo 1998; Cavallo and Frenkel 2008; Calvo, Izquierdo, and Mejía 2016).

These crises raised the suspicion that the explanation went beyond standard fundamentals and that liquidity phenomena were at work. "Liquidity" is a slippery word. For my purposes here, it will suffice to define liquidity services as the services provided by assets or, more generally, arrangements that may facilitate market transactions. Assets that provide those services will be called "liquid assets." This does not imply that they are mostly employed as means of exchange. Liquid assets can be easily transformed into means of exchange but can be held as store of value or employed as credit collateral, for example. It is important to notice, though, that liquidity services depend on implicit compacts in which the equilibrium value of, say, a liquid asset is a function of the compacts themselves. Therefore, liquidity is inherently illusory. Its value can collapse on the spur of the moment, giving rise to what is usually called a "liquidity crunch." Moreover, the latter can occur in the absence of real shocks. In fact, real and liquidity shocks are seldom independent of each other. The main point is that liquidity shocks can be rationalized without appealing to other kinds of shocks (e.g., total factor productivity shocks). In fact, as argued below, liquidity shocks can give rise to sudden stops, and to issues associated with liquidity traps and price deflation.

In a nutshell, this chapter will be divided into two parts, the motivation of which will become self-evident as we proceed. Expectations, spiced up with chronic inflation issues, will be the theme of the first part of the chapter; while liquidity, spiced up with recent capital market episodes, will be the theme of the second part. Context and more details follow.

Setting the Stage and Overview

Most people would likely agree that Keynes's (1936) General Theory (GT) played a pivotal role in establishing macroeconomics as a field different from, but not incompatible with, microeconomics. The GT was born during the Great Depression and was greatly influenced by issues that have become once again relevant during the Great Recession (e.g., the liquidity trap). The GT downplayed the relevance of monetary policy for the recovery phase and gave rise to the view that "money does not matter." The appeal of this view, however, started to fade in the wake of World War II, when inflation spiked and the world economy recovered from its initial slump and started to grow at relatively high rates, despite the large contraction of public expenditure after the war. As a result, the liquidity trap became a bogeyman of the past, and the view that "money matters" came back with renewed vigor. Friedman and Schwartz (1963), for instance, argue that the Fed caused the Great Depression by ignoring the harmful effects of price collapse and failing to adopt a more aggressive easy-money stance. The relevance of monetary policy got further support from the 1970s Great Inflation episode in DMs (see Bordo and Orphanides 2013; McKinnon 2013), and chronic inflation in EMs (see Calvo and Végh 1995).

First attempts to accommodate inflation in a Keynesian context involved sticking a Phillips curve (an empirical regularity that suggests a trade-off between inflation and unemployment) in Hicks's (1937) IS/LM model, subject to little microeconomic backing (or microfoundations). This approach gave rise to a highly fruitful literature around the question of whether the trade-off could be used to lower unemployment by raising the rate of inflation. This literature is very well known and need not be discussed in great detail here (see Gordon 2011). However, I think it is worth pointing out that the Phillips curve literature brought "expectations" to center stage and helped establish the view that in the long run, inflation is ineffective for lowering unemployment and could even make it worse (see Phelps 1972; Friedman 1977). This view got further support from the RE literature, in which context it can be shown that inflation ineffectiveness could also hold in the short run (Lucas 1972) and, more fundamentally, that empirical regularities like the Phillips curve could be misleading for policy making (Lucas 1976; Sargent and Wallace 1981).

Moreover, the RE literature illustrated the possibility that frank and well-intentioned policy makers could throw the economy into a destructive black hole, given that in the RE context, policy making is subject to a serious birth defect: time inconsistency. Time inconsistency arises when policy makers renege from earlier policy announcements or commitments. It is a birth defect, because policy makers have incentives to engage in time inconsistency, even though cheating is not in their DNA, their foremost objective is to maximize social welfare, and (not a minor detail) RE implies that individuals cannot be easily fooled (see Kydland and Prescott 1977; Calvo 1978). The time inconsistency literature offers support for the adoption of rules rather than discretion, and central bank independence is a natural corollary. All these insights are in the toolkit of modern macroeconomists, and several have already been incorporated in governments' macroeconomic models around the globe.

The RE approach allows analyzing policy credibility issues in isolation from other, perhaps important but disparate, issues like the public's imperfect information about the relevant model. RE does not answer all relevant questions concerning policy credibility but signifies a major step forward compared to the case in which expectations are assumed to be backward looking (e.g., adaptive expectations). I will illustrate this by discussing some key policy roadblocks faced by EMs subject to chronic inflation problems in the next section.

As pointed out in the beginning of this chapter, since the mid-1990s, the world economy has been buffeted by crises in which the role of financial dysfunction has become increasingly evident. Moreover, these crises are severe and bear an eerie resemblance to the Great Depression. Expressions like "liquidity trap" and "price deflation," popular in the 1930s, have become part of the daily lingo. This prompted the economics profession to look back to the 1930s and brush up on the rich menu of new financial instruments that have been created since the 1990s (see Eichengreen 2015; Ohanian 2016). Prior to that, a macroeconomist could get her paper published in a top-ranked journal by assuming, say, that debt contracts took the form of state-contingent bonds, free from default risks. Moreover, she would not have faced major referee's objections if the paper assumed that liquidity was confined to an object called "money," which did not interfere in a major way with the workings of the capital market. Issues in which unplanned over-indebtedness and default are the order of the day could not be accommodated in that type of model—and the long time to recovery that we were experiencing until recently, accompanied by unrelenting deflationary forces (particularly in the Eurozone and Japan) even less so. These issues are very troubling, and policy makers are clamoring for a rapid analytical response.

What to do? Compared to the tame "reality" prior to the Great Recession, the new reality looks extremely complex. Thus it is easy to give in to the temptation of increasing models' complexity. This could be a serious mistake. Taking that route might make macroeconomics look like a feather in the wind—driven by the flow but unable to change the direction of the wind. For macroeconomic policy to have a chance to make a difference, theory has to identify a few key factors that could have a major impact on the direction of the wind. As mentioned at the start of the chapter, I think liquidity is one of them, and I will argue that one can get useful insight tidbits ("intuition pumps," as Krugman (2011) calls them) by setting liquidity at the center of the macro universe. This will be fleshed out in the third section in this chapter.

Much of the literature that I refer to is available in print (especially that in the next section) and, therefore, I thought that it would be more useful if I focus on the flow of ideas and leave out technicalities, unless they are necessary to clarify the argument. I should note, incidentally, that I will confine the discussion to narrow economic models and will have to apologize for not covering attendant and highly relevant political economy issues.

Chronic Inflation: Theory and Practice in EMs

Chronic inflation—that is, high inflation or stop-and-go high inflation epi-sodes that occur over an extended period—has been the nemesis of several large EMs during the twentieth century (see, e.g., Dornbusch and Simon-sen 1983; Bruno et al. 1988, 1991). Many stabilization programs employed the exchange rate as a nominal anchor. This choice was prompted by the existence of shallow domestic capital markets that made interest rates inef-fective monetary policy instruments, and the growing evidence that mon-etary aggregates have a weak and volatile link with inflation—especially when inflation rates are high. In the 1970s, exchange-rate-based stabiliza-tion programs were expected to produce quick results. This view was based on the belief that purchasing power parity will bite and force domestic prices to grow at about the same rate as international prices plus the rate of devaluation. In general, this was not to happen. Domestic prices contin-ued unabated and caused unwanted (and, I must say, unexpected for many well-trained economists) major real currency appreciation. Moreover, many of these programs started with a consumption boom that increased fiscal revenue and gave the impression that fiscal imbalance—a common feature in high-inflation economies—was going away without additional sacrifice. These optimistic expectations were hard to change, because, of course, pol-icy makers (and international financial institutions, especially those that endorsed these stabilization and reform programs) became enthusiastic cheerleaders. Besides, as I argue below, some of the popular monetary models before the 1970s were unsuitable for discussing certain critical issues, like imperfect policy credibility.

Imperfect Credibility and Excessive Inflation

To motivate this section, I start by referring to a provocative paper by Milton Friedman (1971) that, abstracting from credibility issues, concludes that inflation in several seigniorage-dependent economies was excessive, in the sense that a lower rate of inflation would collect higher seigniorage. This looks puzzling. However, the puzzle is a result of focusing on a restricted set of policy options. Friedman (1971) focuses on permanent or steady state inflation paths and thus rules out inflation spikes. If the public is taken by surprise, for example, it can easily be shown that inflation spikes could be effective in further increasing revenue from inflation.

To illustrate, consider a standard model in which the demand for money is a decreasing function of the expected rate of inflation. Suppose inflation is set to maximize seigniorage à la Friedman (1971), and consider an unexpected once-and-for-all spike in the rate of inflation, coupled with a credible policy announcement that future inflation will remain unchanged. The inflation spike lowers the stock of real money, but it does not affect the demand for money, because expected inflation would stay the same. Thus, the public will be willing to spend extra resources to restore the steady-state demand for money, which results in seigniorage higher than what would be attained if authorities stuck to Friedman's seigniorage-maximizing inflation rate.

Repeated use of surprise inflation is unlikely to be successful in increasing seigniorage, because the public will start to expect a rate of inflation larger than the one that optimizes steady-state revenue from inflation. Thus, eventually the economy may land on the excessive-inflation territory highlighted in Friedman (1971). However, this is not due to an elementary economics error on the part of the central bank, as Friedman's results might lead us to conclude. An inflation spike is, in the short run, one of the cheapest and most expeditious methods for securing additional fiscal revenue. Moreover, this "carrot" is always there. As noted, though, a problem arises if the government repeatedly reaches out for the carrot. But even in this case, the evidence presented in Friedman (1971) does not prove that authorities were making an error. To assess that, one needs information about how quickly the public catches up with the inflation-spike strategy.

The central lesson from the above example is that there are harmful incentives that lead policy makers to implement inflation levels that they may eventually come to regret. These incentives are no rarity; they are very common in economies that do not have the instruments to reach a first best equilibrium. Moreover, these incentives cannot be ruled out even under RE. This is shown in the time inconsistency literature (see, e.g., Kydland and Prescott 1977; Calvo 1978). However, there is room for policy. In the above example, one could try to neutralize these harmful incentives if the central bank is banned from extending loans to the fiscal authority.[1]

Inflation surprise is effective for liquidating the real value of financial assets other than high-powered money. Important examples are public debt obligations denominated in nominal terms (e.g., principal or coupon not indexed to the price level). Thus, in designing public debt instruments, policy makers should take these seigniorage incentives into account, especially if the fiscal authority is constrained to have small fiscal latitude. Calvo and Guidotti (1990) address these issues and discuss public debt configurations in terms of maturity and indexation. Price indexation, for example, would remove incentives for surprise inflation; however, it may make public debt service too rigid in the face of real shocks (more on this in the next subsection). Moreover, short-maturity nominal debt may also remove incentives for surprise inflation if fiscal cost grows exponentially with the rate of inflation (e.g., making the cost of a price-change surprise much higher if it takes place, say, in a day rather than in a month). However, the government gives up the resilience provided by long-term debt.[2]

Remark 1. An embarrassing error and a warning. These insights were not common knowledge at the time of Friedman (1971), partly because the profession did not have the instruments for modeling forward-looking expectations. At the time, adaptive expectations, a backward-looking scheme, was in vogue. It was employed to model inflation expectations. Thus, inflation expectations at time t were assumed to be a function of the path of inflation prior to t, weighted by a factor that declined geometrically with the distance between time t and the time of the inflation realization. The rate of decline was determined by a parameter that I denote by $\gamma > 0$, such that the larger is γ, the steeper the decline of the weighting factor will be. Cagan (1956) showed, in the context of a simple monetary model, that there is a critical $\gamma = \bar{\gamma}$, such that if $\gamma > \bar{\gamma}$, the system becomes unstable. This implies,

---

1. However, this is not a foolproof solution to the excessive inflation problem. See Calvo (1986a) for a discussion of an episode in which the central bank of Argentina was banned from lending to the treasury and, hence, private banks took that role. When the treasury went bankrupt, though, the central bank bailed out private banks, which was equivalent to taking a long and tortuous route to lending to the treasury.
2. These ideas were developed at the International Monetary Fund (IMF) and helped make debt indexation and maturity part of the IMF's program design. See Guidotti and Kumar (1991) and Calvo (1991).

for example, that if the economy starts off in steady state, it is possible for the model to generate hyperinflation even though money supply is constant over time! This counterfactual implication led to the conclusion that the RE approach was incompatible with realistic monetary models, because RE was identified with the case in which $\gamma \to \infty$. This is, of course, wrong, because no matter how large the weight given to very recent observations, it does not make adaptive expectations rational: They are doomed to be backward looking! It is interesting to note, though, that it took around 15 years and the RE revolution to get rid of this error (see Sargent and Wallace 1973).[3] This episode should send a warning to the profession, because it shows emphatically that formal models can be dangerously misleading if they are not disciplined by a good dosage of common sense.

Inflation Stabilization and Incredible Reforms

In the 1980s, several EM exchange-rate-based stabilization programs failed to achieve their objectives (see Little et al. 1993; Kiguel and Liviatan 1994). An unwanted side effect was a large real currency appreciation accompanied by a consumption boom and large current account deficits. This took policy makers—and the profession at large—by surprise, because according to the (then) prevalent conventional wisdom—much of it based on DM experience—inflation stabilization is associated with a slump in economic activity. The opposite happened. The disconnect between conventional wisdom and practice was dramatic and, as happens on these occasions, brought to the surface a myriad of lightweight and even opportunistic comments. Neoclassical theory and "monetarism" were easy targets, but an answer from the beleaguered camp did not take long to come. It relied on the assumption that these stabilization programs were likely imperfectly credible. The analysis is very simple, thanks to the RE revolution. Calvo (1986b) shows, for example, that if the public expects that the stabilization program will eventually be abandoned and high inflation stages a comeback, it might be rational for the public to anticipate consumption. This anticipation obviously enlarges the current account deficit and, under normal circumstances, lowers the real exchange rate (i.e., the relative price of tradable goods with respect to nontradable goods). The model assumes that

---

3. This does not invalidate the relevance of adaptive expectations. In fact, it can be a useful complement to RE.

the total cost of consumption includes the purchase price plus the cost of holding money in advance to carry out the transaction (i.e., Clower 1967). The latter is an increasing function of the nominal interest rate, which rises with expected inflation, and causes the expectation that the total cost of consumption will be higher after the program is abandoned. Intertemporal substitution trivially follows and gives a rationale for the consumption boom. For a recent version of the model, which can accommodate the usually sizable consumption booms, see Buffie and Atolia (2012).[4] The argument would also go through if inflation increased the cost of credit as a result of high price volatility, for example.[5]

This model can also be employed to study the impact of temporary trade liberalization (see Papageorgiou, Michaely, and Choksi 1991). Consider the case in which the government announces that trade tariffs will be permanently eliminated, but the public believes that they will eventually be reestablished. As in the monetary example, this amounts, in the opinion of the private sector, to making tradable goods cheaper today relative to tomorrow. Calvo (1986b), for example, shows that this brings about a current account deficit that would not take place if the government's announcement was fully credible. Moreover, the implied intertemporal substitution is Pareto inefficient, because it is based on an intertemporal distortion. Even if the government does not intend to abandon trade liberalization, lack of credibility brings about the same deleterious effects. The government could disappoint expectations by never reestablishing trade barriers, but that will not undo the damage! This is, thus, a glaring example of the power of credibility for the success or failure of economic reform, a phenomenon that I coined in the (tongue-in-cheek) phrase "Incredible Reforms" (see Calvo 1989).

An implication of these models that policy makers should take into account is that lack of credibility could give rise to short-run effects that might give the impression that policies are highly successful. For example,

---

4. Calvo and Drazen (1998) extend the basic model to account for uncertainty about the duration of announced policies.
5. Sargent (1982) is closely linked to this literature and makes a strong case for credible stabilization programs. However, the paper focuses on short-lived astronomic inflation episodes that could hardly be called "chronic." Moreover, it seems unlikely that individuals believe in the sustainability of hyperinflation, which would tend to enhance the credibility of any reasonable stabilization program and, thus, its effectiveness.

the consumption boom that follows the announcement of an exchange-rate-based stabilization program brings about an increase in the demand for money, which gives rise to larger international reserves. If the program is prompted by high inflation, these developments are likely to be interpreted as stemming from greater trust that those in charge are serious and able to carry out the necessary reforms.

It is worth noting that the deleterious effects of lack of credibility highlighted here depend on the existence of intertemporal trade (e.g., credit). Without this channel, the economy would not benefit from intertemporal trade geared to the fundamentals stressed by conventional trade theory; however, the economy would be free from credibility distortions. Thus, these types of models are especially relevant for EMs that have access to financial markets but have not succeeded in developing resilient market-friendly institutions. Depending on the circumstances, the model may justify imposing controls on capital mobility, for instance. But a major contribution of this literature is to highlight the relevance of expectation management and, above all, ensuring policy credibility.[6]

Expectations Dominance

Chronic inflation is typically associated with fiscal dominance (i.e., a situation in which the central bank loses control of money supply because it is forced to finance the fiscal deficit by issuing domestic money, as in the previous subsection). The phenomenon is especially relevant when the central bank faces a recalcitrant fiscal authority that, say, for political reasons, is not willing to lower the fiscal deficit. But (what appears to be) fiscal dominance can also arise in an analytically much more interesting situation in which the fiscal authority is fully committed to support the inflation stabilization program, as announced.

This is illustrated in Calvo (1998), which was motivated by trying to understand why Brazil struggled to stop high inflation when public debt and the primary deficit were not grossly out of line. Let b, π, and π^e denote real public debt, one-period forward-looking inflation, and expected

---

6. The consumption boom phenomenon associated with stabilization programs has received a lot of attention. Some outstanding alternative explanations do not rely on imperfect credibility but on a combination of lower nominal interest rates, as a result of lower inflation expectations and sticky prices. For example, see Rodriguez (1982).

inflation, respectively. For simplicity, I assume that, at RE equilibrium, the real one-period interest rate is equal to zero. Thus, under risk neutrality, the equilibrium interest rate will equal expected one-period inflation, π^e, in which case, the next-period debt service bill (including amortization) in real terms equals

$$b\frac{1+\pi^e}{1+\pi}. \tag{1}$$

Therefore, given the rate of inflation, the larger expected inflation is, the larger will be the real debt service burden. For simplicity, let us assume that the government is bound to service debt in its totality at the end of next period and that the central bank is obliged to rebate seigniorage to the private sector in the form of a lump sum subsidy (so that seigniorage net of rebate equals zero). The government is assumed to manage the rate of inflation, π, by manipulating the rate of devaluation. Thus, for instance, if output is homogeneous, there are no barriers to trade, and international prices are constant in foreign exchange, it follows that inflation equals the rate of devaluation: $\pi = \varepsilon$, where ε stands for the rate of devaluation.

Under the above assumptions, expression (1) denotes the real tax revenue necessary for debt service. I assume that the fiscal authority can comfortably generate tax revenue to service its debt if $\pi = \pi^e$, but not a cent more.[7] It follows that the government will have to default if it sets $\pi < \pi^e$ and, if default is too costly, it will be forced to make $\pi \geq \pi^e$ and become hostage to inflation expectations. For the casual observer, this would be a case of fiscal dominance but, in essence, the situation is better characterized as a case of expectations dominance, which becomes effective through the credit channel. Notice that across RE equilibriums in which $\pi = \pi^e$, investors get the same revenue. Hence, if the economy generates inflation higher than the government's target, the solution is Pareto inefficient. This problem holds even in a world of RE, in which individuals are fully aware that the government's inflation target is feasible if expectations are equal to the target. In this case, however, RE depends on beliefs about market expectations. A single individual has no command over the latter, and rationally aligns her expectations to the expectations of others, a phenomenon that the GT calls "expectations of expectations."

---

7. In Calvo (1988), government is allowed to collect higher tax revenue.

An interesting implication of the above example is that RE equilibrium may be validated, not because individuals are rational but because policy makers are forced to corroborate individuals' expectations.

Calvo (1988) also shows that the problem would go away if the interest rate on government bonds were indexed to the rate of inflation. In terms of the above example, it is clear that if the rate of interest ex post was set equal to the realized rate of inflation, the government would be able to implement the target inflation rate independently of market inflation expectations![8] This rule has been adopted in Chile through the Unidad de Fomento (a unit of account) and may have helped to support inflation targeting. Moreover, there seems to be wide consensus that eliminating inflation uncertainty in financial contracts has helped financial deepening and the development of the mortgage market (Fontaine 1996; Shiller 1998). In other instances (e.g., the 1989 Bonex plan in Argentina), expectations dominance led to denominating financial contracts in terms of US dollars. In the simple model developed here, US dollar indexation gives similar results, but this would not be the case if one allows for the existence of nontradable goods, for example.

Expectations dominance can also have a deleterious effect on the private sector. For example, if the economy comes from high inflation and people have structured their contracts on the expectation that inflation will continue unabated, a cold turkey stabilization program, which stops inflation in its tracks, will cause the same kinds of problems highlighted above. At one point in the 1980s, for example, Brazil inflation was about 30 percent per month. Imagine the impact of lowering inflation to single digits, annually! Several stabilization programs had to be abandoned, because keeping the course meant sky-high ex post real interest rates that would wreak chaos in the financial sector and the payments system. This phenomenon has been recently discussed in Lara Resende (2016). It bears some resemblance to Irving Fisher's (1933) debt deflation theory. The latter, inspired by the Great Depression, is a case in which the real value of debt skyrockets as a result of a sharp and unexpected fall in the price level (during the Great Depression, wholesale prices fell by more than 30 percent). In contrast, the

---

8. In practice, inflation indexation is applied with a lag. This may make indexation less effective for shielding investors from inflation risk, especially during periods of high and accelerating inflation. Moreover, financial indexation may lower policy makers' incentives for price stability.

harmful effects of cold turkey stabilization highlighted here would arise even though prices do not fall and may continue rising, albeit at a sharply lower rate than expected.

These problems are akin to what is called the "peso problem," an expression popularized in the 1970s and 1980s as Mexico's interest rates exceeded the rate of devaluation by a wide margin (Lewis 2016). An explanation that, in a way, foreshadowed RE was that the phenomenon was triggered by the expectation that Mexico's peso would exhibit a maxi-devaluation. This type of devaluation involves isolated jumps in the exchange rate. Thus, interest rates will look "too large" during stretches in which the exchange rate is constant. The peso problem is indeed closely related to the example discussed above. However, in Calvo (1988), the authorities are forced to validate devaluation expectations, despite the existence of another, more benign, RE equilibrium. The latter has important policy implications, because, for instance, it highlights the relevance of indexation for stopping high inflation, even though policy makers are fully credible. Notice that these implications would be missed in models displaying equilibrium uniqueness, a feature that policy-oriented macro models tend to favor.[9]

So far, the discussion has abstracted from debt default. A government that is adamant on stabilizing inflation but is facing high inflation expectations may entertain the idea of default. This case is analyzed in Calvo (1988) and further developed by Corsetti and Dedola (2016). A sketch follows.

Debt default can be analyzed in the context of a nonmonetary economy employing the framework developed above. I will reinterpret inflation, π, and inflation expectations, π^e, as rate of default and expected rate of default, respectively. In this instance, the expectation that the government will default would force the government to default. In contrast to the inflation example, solving this problem is likely to be more difficult. In the inflation example, the problem would go away by adopting new types of contracts (i.e., indexation). This approach is less likely to work if default is in the cards, because the private sector may be less predisposed to believe the government will honor its contracts. Therefore, to improve the situation,

---

9. The literature also abounds with backward-looking "wage indexation" as a factor preventing speedy price stabilization. Although this could be reinterpreted as a case of backward-looking expectations, I will refrain for discussing this issue here, given this chapter's emphasis on RE.

it may be necessary to bring in independent parties that are willing and capable to credibly insure investors against sovereign default. This is not easy, given the legal privileges enjoyed by sovereign states. But it seems to have worked in the Eurozone. Worried about the high interest rate premium in satellite Eurozone economies, reflecting investors' concerns about the solvency of those economies, Mario Draghi, president of the European Central Bank (ECB), gave a speech on July 26, 2012, pledging to "do whatever it takes" to lower those interest rates. This was read by the market as an ECB commitment to purchase as much of those sovereign debt instruments as necessary to squash their risk premium to default-free levels. It resulted in an astonishing fall in those rates of interest, as predicted by the model. Why the ECB can muster such impressive muscle is an important issue. A common conjecture is that Germany is the actual credible lender of last resort, in view of Germany's strong fundamentals. But another conjecture that cannot be dismissed is that the ECB can print credible liquidity. I will revisit that issue in the next section.

Once again, intertemporal trade and nonstate-contingent financial contracts are at the heart of these problems. Fortunately, there is room for policy, as illustrated by the Chile and ECB experiences mentioned above.

Remark 2. Staggered prices. Calvo and Végh (1993) extend the credibility discussion to the case in which prices are set in advance in a staggered and uncoordinated manner à la Calvo (1983). Results are in line with the above analysis, but the richer environment helps show that, for instance, a noncredible inflation stabilization program faces an additional powerful challenge. If agents fail to be persuaded that authorities have the determination and public support to carry out the program, prices may continue rising at a high rate despite tight monetary policy.

The results in Calvo and Végh (1993), taken at face value, imply that controlling inflation might become easier if prices/wages were flexible. However, this conclusion, which enjoys widespread appeal among policy makers, would be hasty. In the next section, I argue that staggered prices could play a fundamental role in a monetary economy. They could provide a stable output anchor to fiat monies and units of account, without which a monetary economy may become unstable, unless the currency is credibly anchored (but not necessarily pegged) to a resilient foreign currency, for example, the US dollar. This is common practice in EMs (see, e.g., Calvo and Reinhart 2002), but credibility usually calls for large and costly holdings of international reserves (see Calvo, Izquierdo, and Loo-Kung 2013).

Sudden Stop, Chronic Deflation, and Sluggish Recovery: Liquidity Explanations

The discussion in the previous section was framed in terms of conventional macro theory under the assumption of RE. Until recently, the corresponding models were taken with a high degree of confidence by policy makers. However, amid that placid scenario, the Great Recession rose with shattering force, putting into question everything, from RE to the feasibility of capitalism. Minsky's (2008) nightmares could no longer be discounted!

In this section, I start to explore the new issues by giving "liquidity" a more central role than it had in mainstream macro theory prior to the Great Recession. Otherwise, however, the models stick to the assumption of RE and other assumptions of traditional economic theory. This smoothes out the transition from the previous section, but the reader must be prepared for a sharp turn, because the new vistas that the liquidity approach conveys are anything but ordinary.

Liquidity is an issue that only recently has been given serious attention in the literature (see, e.g., Holmström and Tirole 2011; Calvo 2016). This situation may be partly because mainstream models appeared to be adequate for monetary policy before the Great Recession, at least for DMs. But I would not discard the possibility that model builders were reluctant to focus on liquidity issues because they cannot be easily accommodated in canonical general equilibrium models. In other words: intellectual inertia was at work.

This section argues that liquidity offers promising insights, but we have to make sure that we are treading on firm ground. Although liquidity has become a ubiquitous word, "fashion over substance" seems to dominate. For example, several observers claim that the Lehman 2008 crisis involved a phenomenal liquidity crunch on financial assets backed up by real assets (e.g., asset-backed securities (ABS)). And they seem undisturbed to say, in the same breath, this shock was accompanied by a flight to quality involving the US dollar, a fiat money. Something is amiss here and forces us to delve into the reasons for fiat money to hold positive value in terms of output, a characteristic of fiat money that conventional macroeconomics tends to take for granted.

The next subsection considers Frank Hahn's (1965) fundamental observation that, as a general rule, conventional general equilibrium monetary models cannot rule out the existence of barter equilibria. This result makes the flight-to-US-dollars phenomenon even more puzzling and enhances the relevance of finding plausible explanations for the resilience of money. The flight-to-money phenomenon was a central issue in Keynes's GT (and it is associated with what was elsewhere called the "liquidity trap").[10] In an isolated and wholly ignored paragraph, the GT puts forward a simple, but in my opinion insightful, conjecture that I labeled the price theory of money (PTM).[11] The PTM claims that money derives its liquidity and positive purchasing power from the existence of staggered prices. Staggered prices provide an output backing to money that, as a general rule, governments fail to give. Notice that this output backstop does not extend to other liquid assets with flexible nominal prices.

Although staggered prices give a real platform for liquidity of money that helps explain its resilience during episodes of financial crisis, this does not rule out liquidity fragility or liquidity shortage—because money's output backstop is anything but ironclad. This leads naturally (in the second subsection below) to considering a world with multiple monies and a variety of nominal liabilities (e.g., asset-backed securities, EM US dollar-denominated bonds). Under these conditions, resilient and fragile liquid assets live next to each other. Since, by definition, liquid assets are transactions facilitators, a liquidity crunch of a subset of liquid assets generates a sudden deceleration of transaction flows that rely on those assets. In practice, this takes the form of a credit sudden stop—a large and largely unexpected fall in credit flows—that could become systemic, given that liquidity is in the eye of the beholder.[12] These insights can also be employed as a guide for monetary policy. It can be shown, for instance, that standard open-market operations could be ineffective for restoring potential output—and that the latter may

---

10. I conducted a search in a Kindle edition of Keynes's *General Theory* and could not find the expression "liquidity trap."

11. See Calvo (2012, 2016).

12. As noted at the start of the chapter, "sudden stop" is an expression introduced to refer to severe contraction in international capital flows. The phenomenon has also been observed in Europe during the Great Recession (see Merler and Pisani-Ferry 2012). Nowadays it has been extended to credit flows. To avoid confusion, I choose to dub the latter "credit sudden stops."

be better served by unconventional monetary policy instruments, which do not call for lowering the central bank's policy interest rate.

The third subsection below focuses on the case in which the official sector is unable to increase the stock of real liquidity. This could be the result of having increased liquid public debt far beyond its output backing. I show that this situation may generate chronic deflation. Finally, the fourth subsection below argues that liquidity shortage can also help rationalize "sluggish recovery" (also known as "secular stagnation").

Hahn's Problem, the Price Theory of Money, and Fear of Floating

The typical mainstream macro model assumes that there exists an object called "money"—usually denoted M—that provides liquidity services. A popular assumption in the literature is "cash-in-advance," according to which, to conduct market transactions, agents have to bring to market a quantity of M proportional to the monetary (or nominal) market value of planned purchases (e.g., the Clower (1967) constraint). In simple models, the proportionality coefficient is assumed to be constant. Despite its simplicity, the cash-in-advance assumption dramatizes an important fact that is easily ignored in nonmonetary economics, namely, that liquidity services are essential for trade. In this setup, if $M=0$, no trade is possible!

Let planned purchases be denoted by c (in terms of homogeneous real output), and the real (or output) price of money (i.e., the inverse of the price level) by Γ. Then, setting the factor of proportionality $= 1$, the cash-in-advance condition can be expressed as:

$$M\Gamma = c. \tag{2}$$

Thus, as pointed out above, in equilibrium, if $M=0$, then $c=0$, and there cannot be trade. But, what if $\Gamma=0$? Clearly, the result is the same: Agents will be doomed to operate under full autarky. Is $\Gamma=0$ a possible equilibrium outcome? Hahn (1965) shows that it is. The proof is trivial if M has no intrinsic market value, because in that case, money cannot buy output and the situation is equivalent to bringing no money to the market.[13] This is a deep observation that does not apply to regular goods: If the price of bread is zero in terms of other goods, say, there is likely to be excess demand for bread.

---

13. Notice that if holding M were a minor nuisance, its demand would be nil, causing excess supply in the money market. However, by Walras's Law, that does not generate excess demand in the rest of the economy, because the real price of money $\Gamma=0$.

There have been attempts to show conditions under which zero-output value of money can be ruled out; for example, assuming that real monetary balances (i.e., $M\Gamma$) enter utility functions that satisfy Inada-type conditions.[14] These conditions sound somewhat artificial in this case; moreover, I do not think they are enough to rule out $\Gamma=0$ If the latter holds, then $M\Gamma=0$, independently of how large M is. No matter how valuable monetary balances would be for individual agents, there is nothing single individuals can do to make $M\Gamma>0$. In fact, as noted in a note in the previous paragraph, if holding worthless M involves just a minor nuisance, agents would dump M even though they are starving for $M\Gamma>0$!

The GT offers a conjecture for why $\Gamma>0$. In short, the conjecture is that $\Gamma>0$ because agents employ nominal prices to communicate to the market the quantity of units of account (money, in this case) at which they are ready to sell their staples. Moreover, they are prepared to keep those prices "live" for some interval of time. Hence, nominal prices come first: We are in the world of "prices-in-advance." For an individual agent to have incentives to set her price in advance, it helps that a substantial number of other agents have already posted their prices in similar fashion, and that most of those prices can be taken for granted by present price setters. So this is also a world of "staggered prices." In this world, individual price setters have a clear reference when setting their prices in terms of money, because at time t, say, Γ_t is (essentially) predetermined and positive.[15] Moreover, keeping their price quotations live for a period of time does not involve great risks of price misalignment if the expected rate of inflation is low.[16]

The PTM can be criticized for being no more than a tautology: $\Gamma>0$ because $\Gamma>0$. But the case is subtler than this. The PTM states: $\Gamma_t>0$ because $\Gamma_{t-1}>0$, and just a few agents can or will change their prices at t. This mechanism is incentive compatible: Price setters at t will have no incentives to set their money prices $=\infty$ (which is equivalent to refusing to quote their prices

---

14. See Obstfeld and Rogoff (1983, 1986).

15. However, this does not necessarily imply inflation in advance. Thus, the output backup of money will also be a function of inflation expectations, and the issues raised in the second section of this chapter still apply.

16. However, the risks of setting prices in advance could be large in periods in which, say, the economy is buffeted by large swings in its terms of trade, which involve prices set outside the domestic economy.

in terms of money). Compare this with canonical models like the cash-in-advance model, or models in which real monetary balances are an argument in utility or production functions—and prices are perfectly flexible. Even if $\Gamma_{t-1} > 0$, in these canonical models, individuals have no incentives that would rule out $\Gamma_t = 0$! Notice that the PTM does not rely on the existence of physical money. It is a theory that applies equally well to a cashless economy with a unit of account in terms of which prices are set in a staggered manner (see Woodford 2003). To be sure, it would be interesting to explore the process by which units of account are established, but that does not make canonical models superior to the PTM, because models that are anchored on M instead of Γ also need a rationale for the choice of a particular unit of account.

The PTM helps rule out $\Gamma = 0$ but does not guarantee that Γ will be stable in realistic situations, because not all prices are set in terms of the same unit of account.[17] To wit, the world displays many units of account subject to variable bilateral exchange rates. Interestingly, though, there is more stability in bilateral exchange rates than the existence of multiple currencies would lead one to expect. For example, Calvo and Reinhart (2002) show that EMs tend to peg their currencies to so-called reserve currencies, a phenomenon called "fear of floating." Reserve currencies are units of accounts that are employed as invoice currencies in a wide variety of international trade and financial transactions (see Gopinath 2016). Consequently, pegging to a reserve currency strengthens EM currencies output backing, making them more reliable as stores of value, which, in turn, enhances the liquidity of reserve currencies. The US dollar is the king among reserve currencies and has shown its muscle during the Lehman crisis, as the dollar appreciated relative to other currencies, even though the US economy was at the epicenter of the crisis. The US dollar privilege is rooted in considerations that fall outside the scope of the present chapter, and I will not discuss them here. However, it is worth pointing out that, especially in small EMs, the realm of their national units of account is very limited. Thus, unless their currencies are pegged to a reserve currency, their currencies' output backing would be very narrow, which could make them easy targets of currency

---

17. The PTM does not ensure uniqueness of the Γ path even if there exists a unique unit of account. Uniqueness may require rules like the Taylor rule, a central topic in New Keynesian literature. See Woodford (2003) and also Calvo (2016) for a skeptical assessment of the relevance of New Keynesian models in that respect.

runs' episodes, and large currency devaluations or appreciations (recall the sharp and surprising appreciation of the Swiss franc in January 2015).

To make the previous statements more intuitive, it is useful to think of currencies in terms of a T-account with the stock of money on the liability side and a pot of goods (output) on the asset side. The pot of goods stands for the currency's output backing. This is similar to a bank's balance sheet with deposits on the right-hand side and illiquid loans on the left-hand side. In the present case, the pot of goods stands for the goods and services that money holders can grab in exchange for money if they wish. The pot of goods is likely to be smaller than the output value of money, ΓM. Hence, as in banking models, there may exist multiple equilibriums (see, e.g., Diamond and Dybvig 1983). In a "good" equilibrium, ΓM could far exceed the pot of goods; in a "bad" one, ΓM would just be equal to the pot of goods.[18] Accumulating international reserves in terms of reserve currencies increases the pot of goods. It is intuitive that pegging, especially if accompanied by reserve accumulation, is likely to diminish the probability of currency runs and thus lowers the need for trade to rely on derivative markets, which are costly and not easily available to small and medium-sized enterprises. This helps give a rationale to "fear of floating" and international reserve accumulation.

It should be noted that fear of floating is not unique to EMs. During the Lehman crisis, for example, the Fed signed a large currency swap agreement with the ECB to prevent a wave of massive bankruptcies in the Eurozone (with possible spillover effects on the United States), given that the Eurozone was undergoing a severe shortage of US dollars. Thus, despite the large menu of national currencies, the world economy appears to be groping toward a Bretton Woods–like scheme with the US dollar as the nominal (and hence, real) anchor.

A Larger Set of Liquid Assets: Sudden Stop

In practice, national currencies' own rates of interest are nil. Thus, unless price deflation is rampant, there are incentives to create quasi-monies. This process goes back to at least medieval banking (see Cipolla 1989) and ran at full steam prior to the Great Recession. The phenomenon has already

---

18. Equilibria could be Pareto ranked by ΓM in models in which ΓM is an argument in utility or production functions (or both) and exhibits positive partial derivatives.

been covered in multiple sources (e.g., Brunnermeier 2009), so here I just highlight some salient features that relate to the discussion in the previous subsection. A common characteristic is that quasi-monies take the form of fixed-income obligations denominated in terms of a unit of account. The age-old example is bank deposits backed up by a credible lender of last resort (typically, a central bank able to print currency or public liabilities denominated in the bank deposits' unit of account). A more recent example is mortgage-backed securities (MBS), which are large pools of mortgage contracts denominated in terms of a unit of account. Barring systemic shocks, pooling allows MBS to take advantage of the law of large numbers, reducing the need for information about individual contracts and exhibiting low return volatility in terms of the corresponding unit of account. As a result, securitized assets like MBS can come to resemble interest-bearing money.

The similarity between money and quasi-monies does not stop there. Hahn's problem also applies to quasi-monies, because they are subject to runs that are akin to those discussed in the banking literature (see Diamond and Dybvig (1983) and the notes about national monies in previous section). In those models, bank deposits provide liquidity services, but unless there is a credible lender of last resort, other equilibriums exist in which a sizable share of depositors tries to get their money out of the bank at the same time, the bank goes bankrupt, and the liquidity services of the associated deposits evaporate. Runs on quasi-monies can occur even though their fundamentals show no fissure prior to the run, similar to the phenomenon referred to under Hahn's problem. Except for bank deposits fully ensured by a lender of last resort, most other liquid assets have flexible prices in terms of the unit of account. Hence, if the market refuses to take them as a means of exchange, their price may plunge. Prices may not go to zero because, say, MBS involve obligations that will eventually be at least partially honored, but the price fall of these securities may still be significant.

Quasi-monies play an important role as credit collateral (e.g., repurchase agreements or repos). They do not circulate as fiat money or bank deposits, but they are important transaction facilitators for intertemporal trade transactions. Therefore, quasi-monies fall under the category of liquid assets as defined here. Positive welfare effects generated by stable liquid assets are bound to be very large, given that credit is essential for trade in modern capitalist economies. Without liquid assets, it would be hard to realize gains from trade. A major problem, though, is that these assets are subject to liquidity crunch without warning and can cause major interruption of credit flows. There is still no good understanding of how liquidity crunch takes place, which leaves the credit market at the mercy of large shocks that are hard or impossible to insure against. This problem is exacerbated by the fact that, given that liquidity is only partially linked to standard fundamentals, a credit crunch triggered by a liquidity crunch in one corner of the market can easily spread to the rest of the economy. Thus, a local liquidity crunch episode could become systemic, a situation for which insurance markets are ineffective. This phenomenon was clear in the 1998 Russian and 2007–2008 subprime crises (see Calvo 2016). As noted above, a large interruption of credit flows under these circumstances is called "sudden stop" and typically causes (1) large capital loss in the financial sector and, more importantly, (2) casts serious doubts on the reliability of liquid assets. The latter, in particular, contributes to making these crises highly persistent (see Reinhart and Reinhart 2010; Calvo 2016, chapter 6). The Great Recession is a telling example.

The above observations were not central to the DM policy discussion prior to the Great Recession. Instead, the opposite view prevailed. There was wide consensus that DM financial systems ran like clockwork driven by the hand of sophisticated operators (see Andrews 2008). And, moreover, if crisis erupted, the view was that reserve-currency central banks could rapidly stabilize the situation by lowering their interest rates by a few basis points. This view was partly based on the highly influential conjecture by Friedman and Schwartz (1963) that the Great Depression would have been a regular US recession if the Fed had kept the price level from plunging (e.g., in the Great Depression, the Wholesale Price Index fell by more than 30 percent, peak to trough). Unfortunately, the Great Recession put a question mark on the Friedman-Schwartz conjecture. The Fed and other reserve-currency central banks followed the advice, and price-level deflation was avoided. But these actions did not prevent a deep and long-lasting recession. In the Eurozone, for example, GDP recovered its level prior to the Lehman crisis only in 2016. To be sure, the evidence suggests that monetary expansion was helpful, perhaps because it partially prevented a replay of I. Fisher (1933) debt deflation,[19] but the results are much worse than expected. What is missing? The above discussion offers a clue: Central banks' liquidity does

---

19. However, the Fed did not prevent debt deflation in the housing market, where dollar prices fell by about 30 percent.

not necessarily solve liquidity problems triggered by the liquidity crunch, unless such liquidity is directed to restore the market for liquid assets hit by crisis (see Calvo 2012). Without that directed restoration policy, credit flows stop and can cause major damage. Liquid assets are not born equal, indeed!

DM central banks became aware that something was seriously amiss when they hit the zero lower bound, and they adopted policies aimed at unclogging the credit channel in a more direct fashion. It took the form of quantitative easing (QE), such as central bank purchases of MBS and measures that directly stimulate credit to the private sector. The ECB, for example, announced a modus operandi on March 7, 2016, that among other things, expands the scope of a liquidity window for some corporate bonds, and de facto subsidizes loans to the private sector. All of these actions are consistent with the view that the liquidity crunch calls for heterodox central bank policy (which, incidentally, is dangerously close to being catalogued as a surreptitious form of fiscal policy).

Remark 3. Some microfoundations.   To clarify the discussion, let us consider a simple case in which there is an asset-backed security, which underlying asset I identify as "land." Land, denoted by k, is in fixed supply and is subject to no maintenance costs. Output is a function of land as a standard factor of production, but in addition, land is a transactions facilitator for firms; land's liquidity (measured in terms of output) also has a positive effect on output. Hence, I assume that output is given by $f(\theta q k)$, where q and θ are the output price of land and a liquidity coefficient, respectively; θ is between 0 and 1. Let the real interest rate (i.e., the own-interest rate on output) be denoted by r. Then, at a steady state in which q is expected to be constant over time, profit maximization at $k > 0$ implies the following first-order condition with respect to k: $f'(\theta q k)\theta = r$. One can show that if function f is Cobb-Douglas, the price of land q rises with the liquidity coefficient θ. Hence, a liquidity crunch on land could bring about a collapse in the relative price of land with respect to output. In this simple setup, money supply has no role to play. Therefore, if the price of land causes side effects like unplanned over-indebtedness, standard monetary policy cannot help. One needs instruments that can have an impact on q. The unconventional purchase of toxic assets, as in the Fed's initial quantitative easing program, is a possible, albeit not foolproof, example.[20]

---

20. These issues are discussed in greater detail in Calvo (2012) and Calvo (2016, chapters 3 and 5).

As noted above, liquidity crunch is no DM monopoly. The systemic EM crises in the 1990s can also be characterized in the same way. But there are important differences. Consider the 1997/1998 Asian/Russian crises, which involved a run against EM bonds floated in the international capital market. First and foremost, unlike in DMs, those bonds were denominated in US dollars or other reserve currencies, not EM domestic monies. The meltdown could have been prevented by a massive purchase by EM bonds using international reserves, or drawing on credit lines from an international lender of last resort (e.g., the IMF). But the latter was not available, and EMs had neither the resources (i.e., international reserves) nor the ability to launch a coordinated counteroffensive. Therefore, this gave rise to a sudden stop episode that, employing the metaphor in an earlier subsection, lowered the pot of goods backing up domestic EM money and triggered currency devaluation, not appreciation—in sharp contrast with the United States during the Lehman crisis. Furthermore, currency devaluation weakened EM balance sheets, because foreign-currency-denominated debt is partly employed to fund projects denominated in domestic currency. Thus, large devaluation—a hallmark of EM sudden stops—brought about harmful effects that are akin to I. Fisher debt deflation, as the value of debt obligations skyrocketed relative to the flow of domestic currency revenue, exacerbating the depth of the financial crisis. Clearly, high initial debt and low levels of international reserves enhance the severity of the crisis. These conditions prevailed prior to the Russian crisis, because, in my opinion, few investors and policy makers foresaw the massive systemic meltdown that occured in the Russian crisis.

Interestingly, after the Asian/Russian crises, favorable circumstances that gave rise to improving current account balances and large accumulations of international reserves in several Asian and Latin American economies placed those economies on a stronger footing to face the 2008 Lehman crisis (see International Monetary Fund 2010, chapter 2). The shock was felt, but recovery was fast and was followed by a string of relatively high growth rates, which suggests that the size of the "pot of goods" makes a difference. This idea is also borne out by empirical research (see Calvo, Izquierdo, and Loo-Kung 2013; Calvo 2016; Calvo, Izquierdo, and Mejía 2016).

As argued in an earlier subsection, fear of floating could be traced back to an attempt by EMs to anchor their currencies on reserve currencies. This works for regular shocks but it is probably too costly to prevent currency runs in a sudden stop episode. Still, sizable international reserves could help contain runaway inflation. The reason is simple: Employing the metaphor in an earlier subsection, devaluation increases the nominal value of the asset side of the balance sheet (the "pot of goods") without, in principle, changing the supply of money. Therefore, money's output backup becomes stronger and gives the central bank more ammunition to stop inflation from spiraling out of control. However, it is easy to show that if the central bank intervenes and stops devaluation in its tracks, money's output backup would weaken, in the normal situation in which monetary domestic liabilities exceed international reserves. This helps explain why, during the recent sizable contraction of capital flows to EMs, many countries in Latin America decided to meet the shock with large devaluations and only modest sacrifices of international reserves. Spiraling inflation, the nemesis of these economies in the 1980s, has not been a major problem (see International Monetary Fund 2016, chapter 2).

Remark 4. Endogenous liquidity: Currency substitution. Liquid assets have a long history in which tyrants and wars play a major role. But liquid assets also owe their existence to much more friendly technical change and run-of-the-mill incentives. EMs are a rich laboratory that illustrates that high inflation, for instance, can give rise to the creation of local liquid assets in the form of foreign currencies, a phenomenon labeled "currency substitution" (see the Calvo-Végh discussion in Calvo 1996). The foreign currencies in question are typically reserve currencies, but they need some help from domestic agents to become liquid at the local level. Incentives for the creation of liquid assets or arrangements can also take very different forms. Gorton and Metrick (2012), for instance, claim that shadow banks were partly prompted by attempting to offer more reliable deposit insurance arrangements for large depositors, such as pension funds.

The topic of endogenous liquidity is still in its infancy. The currency substitution literature calls attention to some constraints that the phenomenon imparts to monetary policy, but I feel that the literature has scarcely scratched the surface. Taking an approach similar to that of the micro banking literature (e.g., Diamond and Dybvig 1983), for instance, suggests the existence of sharp discontinuities or nonlinearities that I do not think have been fully exploited in the currency substitution literature. Moreover, a better understanding of endogenous liquidity could help establish a more solid grasp on the implications of low reserve-currency interest rates, a highly topical issue. For instance, this type of theory may help rationalize the commonly heard statement that low international interest rates are spawning EM fragile liquid assets that are subject to costly runs.

The Deflation Cycle: Chronic Deflation

Price deflation has pushed chronic inflation from center stage, and issues from the distant past, like liquidity traps, have come back with a vengeance. Thus, momentarily at least, the voluminous inflation literature will be swapped for old-fashioned deflation papers and a few essays by economic historians of the Great Depression. It is worrisome, though, that past deflation episodes occurred under very different circumstances and data are scant. Moreover, although chronic deflation could be partly explained by over-indebtedness and balance sheet problems (e.g., Koo 2009), these problems could well have arisen in a hyperinflationary context, as highlighted in Sargent (1982). This motivated me to try alternative explanations.

In this subsection, I explore a tentative road inspired by the PTM. The basic idea is straightforward. Consider an economy in which (fiat) money is the only liquid asset. Money enjoys some output backup thanks to the existence of sticky prices. In that context, doubling the stock of money supply doubles real monetary balances—but it does not necessarily double money's output backup. If money's output backup stays constant, for instance, the expected purchasing power of money may less than double. In Calvo (2016), I call this effect "liquidity deflation." It is tantamount to a pecuniary externality for atomistic agents. The initial doubling of the money supply may make people feel that their monetary wealth has doubled in real terms, but they will soon be disabused of this notion as they realize that they would have to share money's output backup with the rest of the agents, even if prices are sticky.

It is interesting to compare the above situation to the conventional one in monetary theory, in which individuals assess money's liquidity services by their individual holdings of real monetary balances. Suppose, for simplicity, that prices are flexible and the demand for the liquidity of real monetary balances is constant. Hence, in the conventional model, doubling money supply, will double the equilibrium price level. In contrast, if liquidity deflation is at work, prices may less than double. Therefore, liquidity deflation gives a rationale for the difficulties central banks may find in stopping deflationary forces by expanding their balance sheets. This reasoning applies with special force to reserve currencies, for which it is difficult to find more reliable alternative liquid assets. Formal details follow.

To stay on familiar ground, I will start focusing on the Pigou effect, a pivotal concept for the classical (as defined in the GT) argument against the relevance of the liquidity trap, according to which wage and price flexibility could help restore full employment. Formally, the argument is that the liquidity of real monetary balances, $M\Gamma$, rises without bound as the price level falls (i.e., as Γ rises). Under normal circumstances, the associated wealth effect will lift aggregate demand (this is the Pigou effect), a process that will not stop until full employment is restored. This argument ignores I. Fisher's (1933) debt deflation, but I will not let this distract us, because the main point is to show that the argument could be fallacious nonetheless.

The Pigou effect relies on the assumption that economic agents will take $M\Gamma$ as a highly reliable yardstick of how much output can be fetched in the market by exchanging $M\Gamma$ for output, even in cases where aggregate $M\Gamma$ exceeds total nonmonetary wealth by a large margin. This assumption is consistent with individual rationality under the assumption that there is no run against money. The latter may not sound like a strong assumption for the US dollar, but runs cannot be discounted if M contains quasi-monies, even if the latter are indexed to the US dollar (as illustrated by ABS's meltdown in the Lehman crisis; see Gorton and Metrick 2012). Thus, if runs are in the cards, it is plausible to argue that, beyond a certain point, an increase in $M\Gamma$ may be equivalent to less output in case of a run, as individuals rush to exchange money for output and take advantage of price stickiness while it lasts (recall the metaphor in an earlier subsection). Therefore, agents that take runs into consideration will attach a liquidity coefficient to $M\Gamma$ that is less than unity. This corresponds to the liquidity deflation effect mentioned above. Following these lines, I assume that the liquidity of money for a single individual is given by the expression:

$$M\Gamma + Z((M\Gamma)^e), \ Z' < 0, \tag{3}$$

where $(M\Gamma)^e$ stands for equilibrium aggregate real monetary balances, and the function Z captures liquidity deflation. This is equivalent to assuming that it is rational for a single individual in an atomistic environment to take her own $M\Gamma$ as real wealth but adjusts liquidity services of money downward as a function of aggregate $M\Gamma$. Liquidity deflation opens the possibility that the expansionary effect of a larger stock of real monetary balances fizzles out as monetary balances become large.

To couch the discussion in more familiar terms, consider the cash-in-advance equation (2), and stick on the left-hand side the new definition of liquidity services from equation (3). Because $(M\Gamma)^e = M\Gamma$ in an RE equilibrium with a representative individual, we get

$$M\Gamma + Z(M\Gamma) = c. \tag{4}$$

Clearly, it is now conceivable that the Pigou effect is nil, because the wealth effect is offset by the negative liquidity effect. Hence, a fall in the price level, or an increase in money supply, given the price level, could have no effect on aggregate demand. Suppose, for example, that real liquidity hits the upper bound and the associated aggregate demand is below full capacity output. This would tend to depress the price level, which exacerbates liquidity deflation—lowering money's output backup and eventually triggering a run against M that destroys money's liquidity. Notice that the failure of the Pigou effect—and the resulting liquidity trap—highlighted here is due to supply-side considerations. I will call it the "supply-side liquidity trap." This is radically different from the GT rationale, which relies on the assumption that the demand for money is infinitely elastic with respect to "the" interest rate. It is worth noting, though, that GT liquidity traps and liquidity deflations are complementary rationales for situations in which increasing money supply has a hard time stimulating output.

Remark 5. ECB puzzle. At the end of a previous subsection, I referred to the highly successful ECB strategy for lowering risk premiums on some Eurozone sovereign bonds, which consisted of announcing that the bank "would do whatever it takes" to achieve this objective. Given the small ECB capital relative to the stock of sovereign bonds from vulnerable economies (e.g., those of Italy and Spain), a popular and plausible conjecture is that success of the strategy stems from the expectation that Germany would bail out the ECB if necessary. This conjecture is in accord with the above discussion, because Germany would be providing the "pot of goods" behind the ECB liabilities. It is interesting, though, that in 2007/2008, when the Great Recession reached a boiling point, the actual lender of last resort happened to be the Fed! The Fed's comparative advantage over Germany under those circumstances was its capacity to print US dollars, an asset toward which the whole world was running for safety. This suggests that even though the ECB was very successful in lowering risk premiums in the Eurozone, it may again need the support of the Fed if, for instance, the federal funds rate rises faster than expected. Thus, it would be a mistake to think that the euro is run-free, simply because the ECB was able to lower risk premiums. This observation implies that the assumption behind liquidity deflation above is not vacuous, even in the case of a reserve currency like the euro.

Remark 6. More on the supply-side liquidity trap.   The above results may look confusing to those familiar with the standard approach in monetary theory (see, for instance, Patinkin 1965, where individuals internalize the pecuniary externalities introduced in expression (3)). Thus, if one follows the standard approach, the cash-in-advance constraint would take the form of equation (4) above. Let $\overline{M\Gamma}$ denote the value of real monetary balances that maximize $M\Gamma + Z(M\Gamma)$. If $\overline{M\Gamma}$ is not large enough to generate full capacity utilization, then the situation would be one of real money shortage. But it would not correspond to a liquidity trap, because an increase in money supply will paradoxically generate excess supply of money and, if nominal prices are upwardly flexible, it would result in a fall in Γ (i.e., an increase in the price level) that pushes real monetary balances back to $\overline{M\Gamma}$. This would validate the view, popular among well-trained economists, that an increase in the supply of money raises nominal prices, unless the GT liquidity trap holds and the demand for money is infinitely interest elastic.

In contrast, if the pecuniary externality is not internalized, as assumed in expression (4), increasing M when $M\Gamma = \overline{M\Gamma}$, given Γ, implies of course that $M\Gamma > \overline{M\Gamma}$. The larger stock of real monetary balances $M\Gamma$ yields lower, not higher, liquidity services, because $M\Gamma + Z(M\Gamma)$ is maximized at $\overline{M\Gamma}$, and individuals will vie for more real monetary balances—not less, as implied in the standard approach. This situation, if anything, will put downward pressure on the price level, raising $M\Gamma$ even further and driving the system into a vicious chronic deflation cycle.

An interesting extension of the model that can also help to make the new results more intuitive is to assume that $(M\Gamma)^e$ runs behind $M\Gamma$. Consider the following example:

$$(M\Gamma)^e_{t+1} = M\Gamma_t, \tag{5}$$

which, taking equations (3) and (5) into account, implies

$$M\Gamma_t + Z(M\Gamma_{t-1}) = c_t. \tag{6}$$

Hence, an increase in money supply will succeed in stimulating aggregate demand at time t, but money stock will have to continue rising to prevent liquidity deflation from catching up.

In this example, even if initially $M\Gamma = \overline{M\Gamma}$ (recall remark 6), the central bank would be able to generate full capacity utilization by helicopter money, say, but it will have to continue doing so to prevent renewed recessionary pressures and possibly price deflation. This scenario is interesting, because it is an example in which deflation is a persistent threat requiring an endless expansion of money supply: Pigou meets Sisyphus!

An interesting twist is to replace equation (4) by

$$M\Gamma + Z(M\Gamma) = L(i - i^m, y), L_{i-i^m} < 0, L_y > 0, \tag{7}$$

where L is the standard textbook liquidity preference function, and i^m stands for the interest rate on money. The latter is a shortcut of the Calvo and Végh (1995) model in which money is a mix of cash and treasury bills, and i^m can be interpreted as the interest rate controlled by the central bank (e.g., the federal funds rate in the United States).[21] To put equation (7) through its paces, note that in the IS/LM apparatus, equation (7) corresponds to the LM curve. Thus, a rise in i^m will increase the demand for money (i.e., will shift up the LM curve) and generate output contraction. Note that contraction holds even in the case in which QE is ineffective. This helps rationalize the opinion, popular in current debate, that QE is no longer effective, but a rise in the Fed's rate can deepen the extent of recession.

However, the impact of increasing i^m could have the opposite effect. For the sake of the exposition, I will assume equation (5). Suppose that money (including other safe assets) has a role as a medium of exchange for firms' transactions. This can be captured by assuming that real monetary balances, $M\Gamma$, enter the production function. Let the latter be denoted by $F(M\Gamma_t + Z(M\Gamma_{t-1}))$, where the function F is strictly concave and satisfies

---

21. Technical note. The absence of the Liquidity Deflation term Z from the demand side in equation (7) holds if derived from a standard representative-individual model in which $M\Gamma + Z((M\Gamma)^e)$ is an argument in the utility function. However, this would not hold true if the Z function *multiplies* $M\Gamma$.

Inada conditions around 0. The representative firm's profit (in real terms) is given by:

$$F(M_t\Gamma_t + Z(M_{t-1}\Gamma_{t-1})) - (i - i^m)M_t\Gamma_t. \tag{8}$$

Thus, the first-order condition with respect to M_t is

$$F'(M_t\Gamma_t + Z(M_{t-1}\Gamma_{t-1})) = i - i^m. \tag{9}$$

Hence, lowering the central bank interest rate, i^m, leads to a fall in output (and the zero lower bound is a nonissue), because it increases the opportunity cost of money holdings. The negative output effect from lower i^m would also hold if money had a role as credit collateral. I find it curious that the literature and policy debate systematically assumes that "easy money" is expansionary, despite the popularity of the literature that highlights collateral assets (e.g., Kiyotaki and Moore 1997) and the central role of collateral meltdown in the Lehman crisis (see Gorton and Metrick 2012).[22] Notice that under these assumptions, maximum steady-state output is achieved at $M\Gamma = \overline{M\Gamma}$. If this output level is thought to be too low, interest rate policy alone could not help take the economy out of that rut. As in the previous case, the central bank will be doomed to rely on unconventional monetary policy in aeternum.

In sum, liquidity deflation could generate chronic deflation. Standard and unconventional monetary policy may fail to generate the liquidity necessary to restore full employment. Moreover, as deflation proves to be much more resilient than expected and output is dragged down by lack of aggregate demand, the private sector may start considering money as an attractive investment vehicle, exacerbating price deflation. These effects will be less acute if the economy operates below $\overline{M\Gamma}$, but they may start to be felt, leading policy makers to turn their attention to alternatives like fiscal policy. This may be the right way to go. However, given credit market difficulties, it would be misleading to analyze the effects of fiscal policy while ignoring financial constraints. Liquidity shortage could have a major impact on the size of the Keynesian multiplier. Ilzetzki, Mendoza, and Végh (2013), for instance, found that the multiplier is negative in highly indebted economies.

---

22. For further discussion on this topic, see Calvo (2016).

Remark 7. Spillover effects. Liquidity shortage and deflation in DMs could spill over to EMs, generating new liquid assets centered on EM liabilities (Gorton 2017; Calvo 2016). For EMs that display large international reserves, this situation may enhance the liquidity of public sector obligations, for example, leading to lower pass-through coefficients and making inflation targets easier to achieve. This is, in principle, good news for EMs but as usual, there is also a dark side: Liquidity of EM liabilities is likely to be sensitive to DM interest rates.

In closing, it is worth pointing out that the supply-side liquidity trap phenomenon discussed here is a close relative to the burgeoning safe-asset shortage literature (see Caballero, Farhi, and Gourinchas 2016). Both emphasize difficulties in stimulating aggregate demand or output supply due to supply-related factors. The value-added of the approach in this chapter is that these factors are linked to liquidity, traced to the large loss of liquidity (in e.g., the inception of the Great Recession) and the difficulty of increasing liquidity by pumping in reserve currency public sector liabilities, or a fall in the international (e.g., US dollar-denominated) price level. Moreover, the discussion suggests that the supply-side liquidity trap for reserve currencies is linked to collateral trouble in the credit channel that lowers the output backstop of liquid assets, a topic addressed next.

Sluggish Recovery

Empirical evidence shows that economies may take long to recover from severe financial crises (e.g., Reinhart and Reinhart 2010). The Great Recession is a striking example. In 2016 the European Union was still struggling to recover its output peak in 2008. The United States has been more successful, but output is still now below trend. This phenomenon has been attributed to the credit boom prior to the crisis and resulting over-indebtedness (e.g., Koo 2009; Reinhart and Reinhart 2010; Taylor 2015). Naturally, theory has put financial frictions and imperfections at center stage—although, it should be noted, more as amplifiers than as main triggering factors (see, e.g., Queraltó 2013). Less attention has been paid to liquidity fragility, a birth defect of the financial sector. I am afraid that this bias may result in losing sight of some valuable "low-hanging fruits" that help explain not only sluggish recovery but also other central features of systemic financial crises (e.g., nominal price deflation). A model displaying those features is discussed in Calvo (2016, chapter 5). I will sketch it out in what follows.

Consider a closed-economy, representative-agent model under perfect price flexibility. Output can be allocated on a one-to-one basis to consumption or raw materials, and households are subject to a cash-in-advance constraint, similar to equation (2) above, where now M stands for fiat money. The representative firm is also subject to a liquidity-in-advance constraint for its raw material purchases. Moreover and realistically, I assume that the firm can hold both fiat money and highly liquid securities, say, ABS. The return on ABS, including liquidity services, is also a function of its liquidity coefficient, indicated by θ in the formal model ($0 \leq \theta \leq 1$). Clearly, if $\theta = 0$, ABS cannot be employed to satisfy the firm's liquidity constraint, and the firm will hold liquidity entirely in the form of fiat money. In contrast, if $\theta = 1$, ABS would be perfect substitutes for fiat money and, under normal circumstances, will return-dominate the latter. Thus, I assume that if $\theta = 1$, firms would prefer to hold their entire liquidity portfolio in ABS. The formal model considers intermediate cases, but the two limit cases are enough for illustration.

Liquidity crunch is defined as a sudden exogenous fall in the parameter θ. For motivation, this can be thought of as a run on ABS along Diamond-Dybvig (1983) lines. Consider the case in which, initially, $\theta = 1$, and as a result of the liquidity crunch, θ goes all the way down to 0. Because the return on ABS prior to the crisis is higher than the return on fiat money, the return on the liquid portfolio that the firm is constrained to hold in advance will be lower after the liquidity crunch. This increases the cost of raw materials and, if the production function satisfies Inada's conditions, induces a fall in output. If consumers were the only holders of fiat money and money supply was given, the slump would cause a rise in the price level, because output contraction would bring about a fall in the demand for fiat money. But in this model, an additional effect points in the opposite direction, because as noted, the liquidity crunch provokes a massive switch in firms' liquid portfolio from ABS to fiat money. This switch can offset the fall in the demand for money from households and cause price deflation. Thus, the model can rationalize price deflation, even though the cards were stacked against it by the assumption that households are subject to a cash-in-advance constraint.

The model can be extended to a growth context in which the liquidity-in-advance constraint applies to investment. In a model in which output is proportional to the stock of capital, one can show that the rate of capital accumulation is a negative function of the opportunity cost of liquidity. Thus, for instance, a liquidity crunch would bring about a fall in growth (i.e., sluggish recovery). Moreover, if liquidity-in-advance also applies to the purchase of raw materials, the liquidity crunch will bring about output contraction on impact, possibly accompanied by price deflation (as discussed in the previous paragraph).

Some policy experiments in terms of this model are conducted in Calvo (2016, chapter 5). Here I just note that, despite its simplicity, the model captures several realistic features associated with liquidity crunch. This suggests that policies that aim at restoring the economy's vitality after a liquidity crunch should pay special attention to factors that caused the crunch and moderate its effects. Actually, some popular policies that do not address those issues may fail to work. For instance, an increase in money supply or government expenditure would be totally ineffective, unless they help to restore the liquidity of ABS without simultaneously provoking a large drop in their pure rates of return (i.e., rates of return that do not include liquidity services).

References

Andrews, Edmund L. 2008. "Greenspan Concedes Error on Regulation." *New York Times*, October 23.

Bordo, Michael D., and Athanasios Orphanides, eds. 2013. *The Great Inflation: The Rebirth of Modern Central Banking.* Chicago: University of Chicago Press.

Brunnermeier, Markus K. 2009. "Deciphering the Liquidity and Credit Crunch 2007–2008." *Journal of Economic Perspectives* 23 (1): 77–100.

Bruno, Michael, Guido Di Tella, Rudiger Dornbusch, and Stanley Fischer. 1988. *Inflation Stabilization: The Experience of Israel, Argentina, Brazil, Bolivia and Mexico.* Cambridge, MA: MIT Press.

Bruno, Michael, Stanley Fischer, Elhanan Helpman, and Nissan Liviatan, with Leora (Rubin) Meridor. 1991. *Lessons of Economic Stabilization and Its Aftermath.* Cambridge, MA: MIT Press.

Buffie, Edward F., and Manoj Atolia. 2012. "Resurrecting the Weak Credibility Hypothesis in Models of Exchange-Rate-Based Stabilization." *European Economic Review* 56 (3): 361–372.

Caballero, Ricardo J., Emmanuel Farhi, and Pierre-Olivier Gourinchas. 2016. "Safe Asset Scarcity and Aggregated Demand." *American Economic Review* 106 (5): 513–518.

Cagan, Phillip. 1956. "The Monetary Dynamics of Hyperinflation." In *Studies in the Quantity Theory of Money*, edited by Milton Friedman, 25–117. Chicago: University of Chicago Press.

Calvo, Guillermo A. 1978. "On the Time Consistency of Optimal Policy in a Monetary Economy." *Econometrica* 46 (6): 1411–1428.

Calvo, Guillermo A. 1983. "Staggered Prices in a Utility Maximizing Framework." *Journal of Monetary Economics* 12 (3): 383–398.

Calvo, Guillermo A. 1986a. "Fractured Liberalism: Argentina under Martínez de Hoz." *Economic Development and Cultural Change* 34 (3): 511–533.

Calvo, Guillermo A. 1986b. "Temporary Stabilization: Predetermined Exchange Rates." *Journal of Political Economy* 94 (6): 1319–1329.

Calvo, Guillermo A. 1988. "Servicing the Public Debt: The Role of Expectations." *American Economic Review* 78 (4): 647–671.

Calvo, Guillermo A. 1989. "Incredible Reforms." In *Debt, Stabilization and Development*, edited by Guillermo A. Calvo, Robert Findlay, Pentti Kouri, and Jorge Braga de Macedo, 217–234. New York: Basil Blackwell.

Calvo, Guillermo A. 1991. "The Perils of Sterilization." *IMF Staff Papers* 38 (4): 921–926.

Calvo, Guillermo A. 1996. *Money, Exchange Rates, and Output*. Cambridge, MA: MIT Press.

Calvo, Guillermo A. 1998. "Capital Flows and Capital-Market Crises: The Simple Economics of Sudden Stops." *Journal of Applied Economics* 1 (1): 35–54.

Calvo, Guillermo A. 2012. "Financial Crises and Liquidity Shocks: A Bank-Run Perspective." *European Economic Review* 56 (3): 317–326.

Calvo, Guillermo A. 2016. *Macroeconomics in Times of Liquidity Crises: Searching for Economic Essentials*. Cambridge, MA: MIT Press.

Calvo, Guillermo A., and Allan Drazen. 1998. "Uncertain Duration of Reform: Dynamic Implications." *Macroeconomic Dynamics* 2 (4): 443–455.

Calvo, Guillermo A., and Pablo Guidotti. 1990. "Indexation and Maturity of Government Bonds: An Exploratory Model." In *Capital Markets and Debt Management*, edited by Rudiger Dornbusch and Mario Draghi, 52–82. New York: Cambridge University Press.

Calvo, Guillermo A., and Carmen M. Reinhart. 2002. "Fear of Floating." *Quarterly Journal of Economics* 117 (2): 379–408.

Calvo, Guillermo A., and Carlos A. Végh. 1993. "Exchange-Rate-Based Stabilisation under Imperfect Credibility." In *Proceedings of the IEA Conference on Open-Economy Macroeconomics*, edited by H. Frisch and A. Worgötter, 3–28. Hampshire, UK: Macmillan. Reprinted in Calvo (1996, chapter 18).

Calvo, Guillermo A., and Carlos A. Végh. 1995. "Fighting Inflation with High Interest Rates: The Small-Open-Economy under Flexible Prices." *Journal of Money, Credit, and Banking* 27 (1): 49–66.

Calvo, Guillermo A., Alejandro Izquierdo, and Rudy Loo-Kung. 2013. "Optimal Holdings of International Reserves: Self-Insurance against Sudden Stop." *Monetaria* 35 (1): 1–35.

Calvo, Guillermo A., Alejandro Izquierdo, and Luis-Fernando Mejía. 2016. "Systemic Sudden Stop: The Relevance of Balance-Sheet Effects and Financial Integration." In *Macroeconomics in Times of Liquidity Crises: Searching for Economic Essentials*, edited by Guillermo A. Calvo, 143–200. Cambridge, MA: MIT Press.

Cavallo, Eduardo A., and Jeffrey A. Frenkel. 2008. "Does Openness to Trade Make Countries More Vulnerable to Sudden Stops, or Less? Using Gravity to Establish Causality." *Journal of International Money and Finance* 27 (8): 1430–1452.

Cipolla, Carlo M. 1989. *Money in Sixteenth-Century Florence*. Berkeley: University of California Press.

Clower, Robert. 1967. "A Reconsideration of the Microfoundations of Monetary Theory." *Western Economic Journal* 6 (1): 1–9.

Corsetti, Giancarlo, and Luca Dedola. 2016. "The 'Mystery of the Printing Press': Monetary Policy and Self-Fulfilling Debt Crises." CEPR DP11089, Centre for Economic Policy Research, London.

Diamond, Douglas W., and Philip H. Dybvig. 1983. "Bank Runs, Deposit Insurance and Liquidity." *Journal of Political Economy* 91 (3): 401–419.

Dornbusch, Rudiger, and Mario Henrique Simonsen. 1983. *Inflation, Debt, and Indexation*. Cambridge, MA: MIT Press.

Eichengreen, Barry. 2015. *Hall of Mirrors: The Great Depression, the Great Recession, and the Uses—and Misuses—of History*. Oxford: Oxford University Press.

Fisher, Irving. 1933. "The Debt-Deflation Theory of Great Depressions." *Econometrica* 1 (4): 337–357.

Fontaine, Juan Andres. 1996. "La Construcción de un Mercado de Capitales. El caso de Chile." EDI Learning Resources Series. Washington, DC: World Bank.

Friedman, Milton. 1971. "Government Revenue from Inflation." *Journal of Political Economy* 79 (4): 846–856.

Friedman, Milton. 1977. "Nobel Lecture: Inflation and Unemployment." *Journal of Political Economy* 85 (3): 451–472.

Friedman, Milton, and Anna J. Schwartz. 1963. *A Monetary History of the United States, 1867–1960*. Princeton, NJ: Princeton University Press.

Gopinath, Gita. 2016. "The International Price System." In *Inflation, Dynamics and Monetary Policy, Proceedings of the Federal Reserve Bank of Kansas City, August 27–29, 2015, Jackson Hole, WY*, 71–150.

Gordon, Robert J. 2011. "The History of the Phillips Curve: Consensus and Bifurcation." *Economica* 78 (309): 10–50.

Gorton, Gary. 2017. "The History and Economics of Safe Assets." *Annual Review of Economics* 9 (1): 547–586.

Gorton, Gary, and Andrew Metrick. 2012. "Securitized Banking and the Run on Repo." *Journal of Financial Economics* 104 (3): 425–451.

Guidotti, Pablo E., and Manmohan S. Kumar. 1991. "Domestic Public Debt of Externally Indebted Countries." IMF Occasional Paper 80, International Monetary Fund, Washington, DC.

Hahn, F. H. 1965. "On Some Problems of Proving the Existence of an Equilibrium in a Monetary Economy." In *The Theory of Interest Rates*, edited by F. H. Hahn and F. P. R. Brechling, 125–135. London: Macmillan.

Hicks, John R. 1937. "Mr. Keynes and the 'Classics'; A Suggested Interpretation." *Econometrica* 5 (2): 147–159.

Holmström, Bengt, and Jean Tirole. 2011. *Inside and Outside Liquidity*. Cambridge, MA: MIT Press.

Ilzetzki, Ethan, Enrique G. Mendoza, and Carlos A. Végh. 2013. "How Big (Small?) Are Fiscal Multipliers?" *Journal of Monetary Economics* 60 (2): 239–254.

International Monetary Fund. 2010. *World Economic Outlook (WEO): Recovery, Risk and Rebalancing*. Washington, DC.

International Monetary Fund. 2016. *World Economic Outlook (WEO): Too Slow for Too Long*. Washington, DC.

Keynes, John M. [1936] 1961. *The General Theory of Employment, Interest and Money*. London: Macmillan & Co.

Kiguel, Miguel A., and Nissan Liviatan. 1994. "Exchange-Rate Based Stabilizations in Argentina and Chile: A Fresh Look." In *Frameworks for Monetary Stability*, edited by Tomás J. T. Baliño and Carlo Cottarelli, 162–185. Washington, DC: International Monetary Fund.

Kiyotaki, Nobuhiro, and John Moore. 1997. "Credit Cycles." *Journal of Political Economy* 105 (2): 211–248.

Koo, Richard C. 2009. *The Holy Grail of Macroeconomics: Lessons from Japan's Great Recession.* Hoboken, NJ: John Wiley and Sons.

Krugman, Paul. 2011. "Mr. Keynes and the Moderns." Voxeu.org, June 21.

Kydland, Finn, and Edward C. Prescott. 1977. "Rules Rather Than Discretion: The Inconsistency of Optimal Plans." *Journal of Political Economy* 85 (3): 473–493.

Lara Resende, André. 2016. "A Teoria da Política Monetária: Reflexões sobre um caminho sinuoso e inconclusivo." In *A Crise Fiscal e Monetária Brasileira: Ensaios em homenagem a Fábio O. Barbosa*, edited by E. Bacha, 483–506. Rio de Janeiro: Editora Civilização Brasileira. English version online: http://iepecdg.com.br/wp-content/uploads/2016/03/The-Theory-of-Monetary-Policy5.pdf.

Lewis, Karen K. 2008. "Peso Problem." In *The New Palgrave Dictionary of Economics*, second edition, edited by Steven N. Durlauf and Lawrence E. Blume. New York: Palgrave-Macmillan.

Little, I. M. D., Richard N. Cooper, W. Max Corden, and Sarath Rajapatirana. 1993. *Boom, Crisis, and Adjustment: The Macroeconomic Experience of Developing Countries.* New York: Oxford University Press.

Lucas, Robert E., Jr. 1972. "Expectations and the Neutrality of Money." *Journal of Economic Theory* 4 (2): 103–124.

Lucas, Robert E., Jr. 1976. "Econometric Policy Evaluation: A Critique." *Carnegie-Rochester Conference Series on Public Policy* 1: 19–46.

McKinnon, Ronald I. 2013. *The Unloved Dollar Standard: From Bretton Woods to the Rise of China.* Oxford: Oxford University Press.

Merler, Silvia, and Jean Pisani-Ferry. 2012. "Sudden Stops in the Euro Area." Bruegel Policy Contribution 2012/6, Bruegel, Brussels; http://bruegel.org.

Minsky, Hyman P. 2008. *Stabilizing an Unstable Economy.* ebook, McGraw Hill.

Obstfeld, Maurice, and Kenneth Rogoff. 1983. "Speculative Hyperinflations in Maximizing Models: Can We Rule Them Out?" *Journal of Political Economy* 91 (4): 675–687.

Obstfeld, Maurice, and Kenneth Rogoff. 1986. "Ruling Out Divergent Speculative Bubbles." *Journal of Monetary Economics* 17 (3): 349–362.

Ohanian, Lee E. 2016, "The Great Recession in the Shadow of the Great Depression: A Review Essay on 'Hall of Mirrors: The Great Depression, The Great Recession and the Uses and Misuses of History'." NBER Working Paper 22239, National Bureau of Economic Research, Cambridge, MA.

Papageorgiou, Demetris, Michael Michaely, and Armeane M. Choksi. 1991. *Liberalizing Foreign Trade*. Oxford: Basil Blackwell.

Patinkin, Don. 1965. *Money, Interest, and Prices*. New York: Harper and Row.

Phelps, Edmund S. 1972. *Inflation Policy and Unemployment Theory*. New York: W. W. Norton.

Queraltó, Albert. 2013. "A Model of Slow Recoveries from Financial Crises." FRB International Finance Discussion Paper 1097, Federal Reserve Board, Washington, DC.

Reinhart, Carmen M., and Vincent R. Reinhart. 2010. "After the Fall." NBER Working Paper 16334, National Bureau of Economic Research, Cambridge, MA.

Rodríguez, Carlos Alfredo. 1982. "The Argentine Stabilization Plan of December 20th." *World Development* 10 (9): 801–811.

Sargent, Thomas J. 1982. "The Ends of Four Big Inflations." In *Inflation: Causes and Effects*, edited by Robert E. Hall, 41–98. Chicago: University of Chicago Press.

Sargent, Thomas J. 1983. "Stopping Moderate Inflations: The Methods of Poincaré and Thatcher." In *Inflation, Debt, and Indexation*, edited by Rudiger Dornbusch and Mario Henrique Simonsen, 54–98. Cambridge, MA: MIT Press.

Sargent, Thomas J., and Neil Wallace. 1973. "The Stability of Models of Money and Perfect Foresight." *Econometrica* 41 (6): 1043–1048.

Sargent, Thomas J., and Neil Wallace. 1981. "Some Unpleasant Monetarist Arithmetic." *Quarterly Review* 5 (3): 1–17, Federal Reserve Bank of Minneapolis.

Shiller, Robert J. 1998. "Indexed Units of Account: Theory and Assessment of Historical Experience." NBER Working Paper 6356, National Bureau of Economic Research, Cambridge, MA.

Taylor, Alan M. 2015. "Credit, Financial Stability, and the Macroeconomy." *Annual Review of Economics* 7: 309–339.

Woodford, Michael. 2003. *Interest and Prices: Foundations of a Theory of Monetary Policy*. Princeton, NJ: Princeton University Press.

Comment: Gita Gopinath

Without a doubt, the 2008–2009 global financial crisis and its lingering effects have changed the lens through which macroeconomists view the world. Previously, developed markets had been characterized as having frictionless and benign financial markets, but the 2008–2009 financial crisis that originated in the developed world dispelled all notions of this. As a consequence, it is now nearly impossible to discuss macroeconomics without explicitly describing the interactions of economic agents and the imperfect world of finance.

However, it is important to note that for international macroeconomists, of which Guillermo Calvo is most prominent, the failures of financial markets has been at the center of understanding the economies of emerging markets, economies that have routinely been buffeted by financial and debt crises. This gives Guillermo, who is one of the leading experts on emerging market crisis, an edge over other macroeconomists in analyzing this crisis and pointing out to us lessons for the future of macroeconomics. This is why his contribution to this volume is so valuable, and I thoroughly enjoyed reading his chapter.

Guillermo makes several important points, of which I will highlight a few, but I encourage the reader to delve into the many other contributions in the chapter. Guillermo flags two major blind spots that policy makers have ignored at the peril of their economies. The first is the power of expectations to drive self-fulfilling crises when policy makers suffer the original sin of not being able to commit so-called expectations dominance. The second is that liquidity scarcity can arise rapidly and have long-lasting effects on the economy, and conventional monetary policy can fail to rescue the economy. As Guillermo goes on to describe, two important policy recommendations that follow from these observations. The first is the need to ensure sufficient supply of safe and liquid assets. The second is that the world benefits from a global coordination of policies, so that expectations are coordinated on the good equilibria. I will reinforce both these points.

As Guillermo highlights, the inability of even social welfare maximizing central bankers to commit to policy was a major factor in the hyperinflations of the past. This is tied to the time inconsistency problem, where monetary authorities would like to commit to not inflating ex ante but then ex post have every incentive to general surprise inflation so as to stimulate the economy, increase seignorage, and lower the real value of nominal debt. Forward-looking private agents of course expect this behavior and raise prices in anticipation, thereby raising equilibrium inflation.

Similarly, expectations can generate temporary booms that eventually go bad, and governments can misinterpret the cause of the boom. As an example, Guillermo points to the consumption booms that followed exchange-rate-based stabilizations in emerging markets. He argues that it is expectations of the failure of the stabilization reform measures that generate a temporary consumption boom as agents front-load purchases of goods in anticipation of a return to high inflation in the future.

The importance of expectations dominance and self-fulfilling crises was evident in the 2012 debt crisis in the Eurozone. As yields on government debt rose rapidly in Greece and spilled over to Ireland, Portugal, Spain, and Italy, the European Central Bank's (ECB) president Mario Draghi promised to do whatever it takes to save the euro, including possibly buying stressed government debt. The mere promise of this brought yields down rapidly, even in the absence of any purchases by the ECB (figure 4.1). This event not only highlights the role of expectations dominance in generating crisis, it also importantly points out the errors of the framers of the common currency area who restricted the ECB from being the lender of last resort. Aguiar et al. (2015) describe self-fulfilling crisis in monetary unions and the important role of central banks to intervene in a state-contingent manner to alleviate such crises.

Aguiar et al. (2013) also describe how the ability to inflate does not necessarily reduce the potential for self-fulfilling crises. In the midst of the Greek crisis, it was argued by several leading economists that the problem arose because Greek debt was real, as the Greek's did not control the supply of the currency in which the debt was denominated, and required fiscal surpluses to pay it down. In contrast, if the debt had been denominated

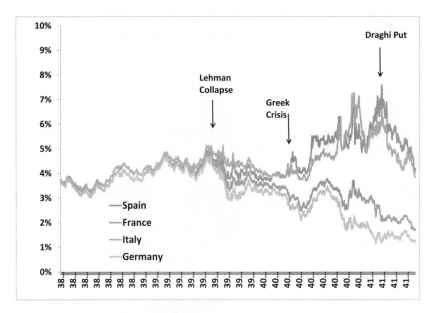

Figure 4.1
Sovereign 10-year yields

in a currency over which the country has direct control, as in the case of U.S. and Japanese debt, then governments also have the option of inflating some of the debt so as to make it easier to repay. This argument is flawed to the extent that it ignores the role of expectations. When debt is in nominal terms and lenders expect the use of inflation to reduce the real value of debt, then this expectation gets priced into nominal interest rates. Consequently, there is no additional gain from being able to control the currency in which the debt is denominated.

A second theme in Guillermo's chapter is about liquidity and its fragility. Clearly it can be tricky to describe what a liquid asset is, something Guillermo gets into at some length. But the point that sudden collapse can occur in liquidity relative to the demand for it, which in turn can have important negative and lasting consequences for the economy, is a point that has been emphasized recently by many economists. In the "safe assets" literature, Caballero and Farhi (2014) point to the collapse in safe assets following the 2008–2009 financial crisis as important for understanding the decline in real interest rates, the drop in output, and the increase in risk premia in equity markets. The excess demand for safe assets also calls for unconventional monetary interventions, such as the purchase by the central bank of toxic assets as opposed to the more conventional purchase of safe treasuries.

Whether there continues to be a liquidity crisis is up for debate. However, there is little doubt that the world needs to be prepared for future financial crises that may arise from China. With China's debt exceeding 240 percent of its GDP and the ongoing credit boom there is sufficient cause for concern.

A theme in the chapter that I have spent little time discussing is the price theory of money. Guillermo argues that the reason people hold certain currencies is because prices denominated in that currency tend to be preset and staggered and therefore deliver predictable output. This is an appealing argument, but of course one could ask what comes first. The reason prices are sticky in a currency is plausibly because of the faith in the monetary authorities that manage the currency to keep inflation low.

I look forward to reading future work by Guillermo on this and related issues so as to gain important insights into the functioning of the world economy, something Guillermo has delivered in spades over many years.

References

Aguiar, Mark, Manual Amador, Emmanuel Farhi, and Gita Gopinath. 2013. "Crisis and Commitment: Inflation Credibility and the Vulnerability to Sovereign Debt Crises." NBER Working Paper 19516, National Bureau of Economic Research, Cambridge, MA.

Aguiar, Mark, Manuel Amador, Emmanuel Farhi, and Gita Gopinath. 2015. "Coordination and Crisis in Monetary Unions." *Quarterly Journal of Economics* 130 (4): 1727–1779.

Caballero, Ricardo, and Emmanuel Farhi. 2014. "The Safety Trap." NBER Working Paper 19927, National Bureau of Economic Research, Cambridge, MA.

Comment: Luis Servén

The 2008–2009 global financial crisis and the ensuing Great Recession have prompted a critical reassessment of mainstream macroeconomic models. Among their key weaknesses, many observers have singled out the virtual neglect of the financial system. Indeed, the description of the financial side in the pre-crisis mainstream macro model was pretty much limited to a demand function, presumed stable, for a well-defined concept of "money." Financial frictions and amplification mechanisms, two ingredients widely seen at core of the financial crisis and its propagation, were altogether absent.

These themes at the nexus of macroeconomics and finance have long attracted Guillermo Calvo's attention. His chapter brings together a broad array of big macrofinancial issues that reflects the wide range of his contributions to macroeconomic thinking, and it showcases his mastery at drawing insights from highly stylized analytical settings. The common threads that tie the chapter together are expectations and, especially, liquidity and its role in past and recent crises. This is the focus of my comments below. Needless to say, it has been a longstanding concern for Guillermo Calvo, as proven, for example, by his seminal work on sudden stops.

The chapter argues that liquidity should take center stage in macroeconomics and places it at the root of the global crisis and the post-crisis slump. The central role of liquidity reflects two key facts. The first is that liquid assets are essential to the operation of modern economies. They facilitate market transactions, can (almost) always be transformed into means of exchange at full face value, and exchanged for goods and services or other assets. In particular, their widespread use as collateral in financial transactions makes them essential to a well-functioning credit market. But the second key fact is that liquidity is also fragile: Liquid assets—especially those privately produced, with bank deposits as the classic example—are vulnerable to self-fulfilling runs. This puts the spotlight on the role of expectations and coordination mechanisms in triggering sudden shifts in the valuation of liquid assets.

These two issues—liquid assets as the key to the credit mechanism in the context of financial frictions and the vulnerability of those assets to shifts in expectations—have been explored by an ample literature, which could have featured more prominently in the chapter. Recent examples that come to mind are those of Martin and Ventura (2012), who show how bubbles can unlock credit and growth, and Gorton and Ordoñez (2013), who analyze the endogenous nature of financial fragility.

The Backing of Money

As the chapter reminds us, fragility is a fundamental feature of fiat money, the ultimate liquid asset. Fiat money is an intrinsically worthless asset, valuable only to the extent that it is (or is expected to be) valued by others. Thus, it fits the standard definition of a bubble. This in turn opens the door to the existence of multiple self-fulfilling equilibria in monetary economies— including barter equilibria, in which the price of money is zero.

The question of why money is valuable attracted considerable attention from monetary theory during the 1960s and 1970s. Yet flight away from money has been a rare occurrence in modern times. It has not been a feature of recent crises; indeed, if anything, the opposite has been the case. The chapter sets out a "price theory of money" (or PTM for short) to explain this resilience of money: What anchors the value of money is nominal price stickiness. In a world of staggered price setting, the positive value of money is just a result of hysteresis: Money is valuable today, because it was valuable yesterday. Because only a limited number of individual prices may have changed in the interim, the general price level (the inverse of the value of money) cannot have moved much. By the same reasoning, if money is valuable today, it can be anticipated to remain valuable tomorrow. Thus, staggered price setting provides an output backing for money.

This approach casts nominal rigidities in an unusual light. In the macroeconomic literature they routinely get the blame for hampering adjustment to shocks, but the PTM holds instead that they also deserve credit for preserving monetary stability. Put differently, much-hyped price flexibility is not an unmixed blessing after all, as it may come with increased monetary fragility.

But there is some circularity underlying the PTM. Pricing arrangements are themselves not invariant to perceptions about monetary and aggregate price stability. For example, if (for whatever reason) the price level is expected to rise quickly, more agents are likely to revise upward their individual prices, and by larger amounts, than if they expect the overall price level to rise slowly (Burstein 2006). Thus, as a result of the combined actions of individual agents, the degree of price level stickiness, and hence its contribution to the backing of money, in effect depends on expectations. Ultimately, this suggests that the power of the PTM to explain the backing of money—that is, the degree of monetary and price stability—may itself depend on the perceived degree of monetary and price stability. In other words, the PTM may not take us too far in resolving the indeterminacy surrounding the value of money.

Liquidity and Fragility

In modern economies, other assets beyond fiat money provide liquidity services. Much of the recent literature (e.g., Gorton and Ordoñez 2013; Caballero and Fahri 2018) refers to them as "safe assets." They include public debt backed by the government's taxation capacity, as well as privately produced debt backed by either a lender-of-last-resort guarantee (as in the case of insured bank deposits) or by credible collateral (as in the case of asset-backed securities).

What distinguishes safe assets from the rest is the fact that they can (almost) always be exchanged at full face value. They retain (much of) their value in large systemic events. Also, their value is information insensitive—there is no benefit to producing private information about it. In other words, they are free from adverse selection, that is, concerns that the counterparty may have superior private information about their value.

Private-label assets help meet the overall demand for liquidity, but their use also raises financial fragility. They can be close, but not perfect, substitutes for safe public debt. Their value is impaired in systemic events. In particular, unless fully backed by a lender of last resort, short-term private-label safe assets are vulnerable to runs, as shown in the global financial crisis (Brunnermeier 2009; Gorton 2010).

All these issues are touched on, to varying extents, in Guillermo Calvo's chapter. But they have important implications for public debt, a missing theme. The fragility of private-label liquidity implies that safe public debt has a key role to play in protecting the credit mechanism. More specifically, public debt is net wealth, to the extent that it allows sustaining credit at times of crisis—when privately produced assets cease to be accepted as collateral (Gorton and Ordoñez 2013). Even if the choice between taxes and debt to finance government expenditure may be inconsequential in normal times, Ricardian equivalence still breaks down when financial crises can occur. Failure to recognize this may result in an undersupply of safe public debt.

Another important policy question is the ability of financial regulation to mitigate the fragility of privately produced liquid assets. This subject has focused the attention of financial regulators worldwide after the crisis, although it receives limited attention in the chapter. Yet, as Guillermo Calvo notes, the tightening of regulatory requirements post-crisis has gone in the direction of raising the mandated liquidity holdings of financial institutions, which will likely have the unintended consequence of increasing the aggregate shortage of safe assets.

Expectations and Fragility

Investor runs are often attributed to "shifts in sentiment." But the causes of those shifts remain poorly understood. This echoes the fact that theoretical work on models with multiple equilibria typically has little to say on what prompts jumps across them—for example, what causes transition from a bubbly to a bubbleless equilibrium in a model of asset bubbles. In practice, the factors responsible are often difficult to determine even in ex post forensic analysis of financial crashes. The Minsky moment that marks their onset does not usually follow large shocks to fundamentals or major news about their future path. Instead, it tends to occur after the arrival of relatively minor, sometimes almost irrelevant, news.

The subprime crash is a case in point. The sharp increase in the default rate of subprime mortgages in the United States is commonly viewed as the trigger of the global crisis. But it is hard to see how the souring of a fairly minor segment of the US mortgage market could have reversed expectations about the future prices of broad categories of assets so dramatically as to trigger runs on a wide variety of leveraged investors across the financial system.

What makes for this disproportionate effect of seemingly innocuous news? The literature on amplification mechanisms in financial crises (e.g., Brunnermeier and Oehmke 2013) offers some hints. One example can be found in Guillermo's own work on the interplay between informed and uninformed investors (Calvo and Mendoza 2000). The latter investors infer the state of fundamentals from the actions of the former. In appropriate conditions, the uninformed investors may stage a run just because informed investors are redeeming assets to meet their liquidity needs, which uniformed investors misinterpret as a sudden worsening of fundamentals.

A related mechanism arises when rational investors hold heterogeneous expectations due to the presence of private information about the fundamentals. Asset prices then reflect average market expectations, and rational investors have to face Keynes's "beauty contest" (i.e., they need to form expectations about the expectations of others). In such settings, noisy public signals about the fundamentals drive a wedge between asset prices and fundamental values (Bacchetta and van Wincoop 2008). In particular, asset prices may overreact to public signals (Allen, Morris, and Shin 2006) and experience abrupt shifts in response to nearly irrelevant news.

From this it would seem tempting to conclude that steps aimed at improving the reliability and accuracy of public information—such as enhanced disclosure rules for leveraged investors—might help reduce asset price volatility and stem investor panics. It is doubtful, however, that such measures would make much of a material contribution to anchor investor expectations and deter runs. Calvo's chapter points in a different direction. For example, he suggests more use of pegs to limit the indeterminacies surrounding flexible exchange rates or of backward indexation to anchor inflationary expectations. How, if at all, this could translate to the case of asset prices—which are fundamentally forward looking—is not discussed, but it seems like a natural follow-up question. For example, should policy make more systematic use of floors (or ceilings) to the levels, or the changes, of asset prices?

The Post-Crisis

Almost 10 years after the global crisis, world economic growth remains sluggish, and advanced economies continue to exhibit deflationary pressures. This disappointing performance has attracted a wide variety of explanations (see Teulings and Baldwin 2014). They range from those that portray the post-crisis as a new normal, driven by slow-moving supply or demand factors (i.e., the "secular stagnation" view) to others that take more of a short-term perspective and attach a central role to Keynesian aggregate demand deficiencies. Yet others find the post-crisis sluggishness well in accordance with the past history of major financial crashes, which are typically followed by protracted recessions.

The chapter takes a liquidity-centered view: The crisis was driven by the collapse of liquid assets, which brought the financial system to the verge of collapse. As credit supply dried up, output and employment fell across the globe. Low growth in the post-crisis world reflects the continuing liquidity shortage and malfunction of the credit market.

Few dispute the key role of the liquidity crunch in the onset of the crisis, but there is much less agreement on whether the shortage of credit remains the main cause of the subsequent sluggish growth. Casual observation suggests that many firms in the United States and Japan are awash with liquidity, yet investment has been slow to recover. Empirical tests by Mian and Sufi (2014) indicate that the credit crunch cannot explain the US employment collapse. On the whole, the seeming implication is that aggregate demand shortages, actual or anticipated, might also be a major factor behind the weak growth recovery.

Most observers believe that the powers of monetary policy to reignite growth have been weakened in the post-crisis as the economy fell into a liquidity trap posed by the zero lower bound on interest rates. Although the chapter shares this perspective, its distinguishing feature is the view that what is at work is a supply-side liquidity trap—as distinct from the Keynesian demand-side liquidity trap. The latter arises from an insatiable demand for liquidity; the former, according to Calvo, from the inability of monetary policy to raise the supply of liquidity services.

In this narrative, expansionary monetary policy may be able to raise real money balances but fail to raise liquidity or even reduce it; such policy may prompt deflation rather than inflation, as individuals vie for yet more liquidity. The mechanism responsible for this intriguing result is not fleshed out, but it appears to rely on agents' competition for liquidity services in a setting with pecuniary externalities and anticipated runs on liquid assets. In a variation on the same idea, the central bank might be able to raise liquidity, and thereby output, only as long as it keeps expanding the money supply indefinitely.

Strictly speaking, it is not clear if this really qualifies as a supply-side liquidity trap, because the underlying mechanism seems to rely on the behavior of liquidity users on the demand side. And, on the whole, it seems doubtful that central banks' attempts to implement expansionary policies really belong among the chief factors behind the deflationary pressures in advanced countries.

Leaving aside these issues, however, Calvo's perspective on the post-crisis has a lot in common with the recently proposed "safety trap" view (e.g., Caballero and Fahri 2018). In that narrative, the market for safe assets witnessed a long-term increase in demand, largely driven by the growing liquidity needs of financial intermediaries, as well as the self-insurance needs of emerging-country governments around the world in the face of global external disturbances (Gourinchas and Jeanne 2012). The growth of demand far outstripped the available supply of safe public debt and led to a boom in the supply of private-label (quasi-)safe assets, through securitization and similar mechanisms. Indeed, the US evidence confirms that the net supply of private-label liquid assets is negatively correlated with the supply of government debt (Krishnamurty and Vissing-Jorgensen 2012).

These assets unraveled in the crisis and brought down with them large volumes of formerly safe sovereign debt, notably that of European periphery countries struggling to rescue their financial systems. By some estimates, the supply of safe assets relative to global GDP fell by half, opening up a massive gap vis-à-vis their demand and pushing down into negative territory their "natural" rate of return (i.e., that consistent with full employment; Caballero and Fahri 2018). With the actual rate constrained by the zero lower bound, the economy fell into a safety trap, and equilibrium in the safe asset market was restored through an output fall.

This story seems to have a lot in common with that outlined in the chapter. The safety trap is akin to a liquidity trap, with the added feature of an endogenous risk premium that shapes the output effects of macro-economic policy. And some policy implications seem broadly similar—in particular, the scope for conventional monetary policy is limited in both narratives. In truth, however, the "supply-side liquidity trap" perspective in the chapter is not developed in sufficient detail to allow the reader to see how, or why, appropriate policy actions to revive liquidity would differ from those needed under a demand-side liquidity trap or a safety trap.

In a safety trap, for example, issuance of (safe) public debt, quantitative easing through central bank purchases of risky assets, or inflation target increases are all effective for raising output (see Caballero and Fahri 2018 for details). In turn, Calvo's chapter seems skeptical regarding risky asset purchases. Because such purchases essentially amount to changing the relative supply of safe and risky assets, one may conclude that (safe) public debt issuance, which is not explicitly discussed, may be ineffective, too—in sharp contrast with the "safety trap" optic. This seems puzzling, although strictly speaking, both risky asset purchases and public debt issuance should be expected to be similarly unhelpful in conventional liquidity traps. In turn, inflation target increases are not contemplated either, although one would conjecture that they should be of help, as in standard liquidity traps.

What about the international perspective? Many central banks, especially from emerging markets, hold massive amounts of safe assets at present, in most (but not all) cases for self-insurance purposes. This tends to worsen the global asset shortage. Improved reserve-pooling arrangements, through the IMF or in other ways, might help reduce self-insurance needs, as Calvo notes. But these steps may also require higher levels of mutual trust than currently exist. A more intriguing option, recently proposed by Rogoff (2016), would partly reallocate emerging-market reserve holdings to gold, which is a highly liquid asset whose rate of return is not subject to a zero lower bound—thus potentially helping release the safety trap. In addition, reforms to enhance emerging markets' ability to supply safe assets, rather than just demand them, would seem worth considering too, but they are not discussed in the chapter.

Final Thoughts

Over the past decades, the overall demand for liquid assets has grown steadily, largely driven by the growing liquidity demand of the global financial system. Demand has far outpaced the supply of outside liquid assets (i.e., fiat money and safe public debt), resulting in an increasing resort to inside assets (i.e., private-label assets) that is seen by many observers as one of the key ingredients behind the global crisis and its disappointing aftermath. Much of the policy debate has centered on how to engineer a commensurate increase in asset supply to bridge the gap with demand.

This view prompts two concluding questions. First, because much of the growth in demand stems from the increasing collateral needs of an expanding financial system, we may wonder whether such expansion really is welfare-increasing. In other words, is it possible for financial intermediation, and thus its derived collateral needs, to grow "too large" from a social welfare viewpoint?

In practice, externalities are at work that may easily lead to excessive financial intermediation in a general equilibrium setting. Eden (2016) offers an example, based on the fact that, although both fiat money and quasi-monies can be used to facilitate socially efficient transactions, it is cheaper to use fiat money, because it is costless to produce. The private incentives for spending resources on the production of quasi-monies are always greater than the social incentives, as they do not internalize the equilibrium adjustment of the price level. A similar reasoning applies to credit: Although it facilitates efficient transactions, its production requires real resources in the form of monitoring services. Thus, the private incentives to produce credit are likely to be excessive, because they do not internalize equilibrium price adjustments.

It is easy to think of situations in which financial intermediation grows too large because of other externalities. A prominent example is that of intermediation facilitating socially excessive risk taking, driven by the fact that individual intermediaries do not take into account their contributions to systemic risk and hence to the likelihood of adverse scenarios—a theme explored by the macro-prudential literature.

Leaving aside the scale of the financial system, the second question concerns the roots of its collateral needs. These ultimately arise from the presence of frictions, such as asymmetric information, monitoring costs, and imperfect contract enforcement. The natural question is whether the primary focus of policy should be just to meet the collateral needs imposed by these frictions, possibly at the cost of increasing financial fragility. Granted, it is not likely that frictions can be eliminated altogether. But there probably is ample room for regulatory and other policies to substantially limit their scope, and thereby contain the ever-expanding collateral needs of financial intermediation.

References

Allen, Franklin, Stephen Morris, and Hyun Song Shin. 2006. "Beauty Contests and Iterated Expectations in Asset Markets." *Review of Financial Studies* 19 (3): 719–752.

Bacchetta, Philippe, and Eric van Wincoop. 2008. "Higher Order Expectations in Asset Pricing." *Journal of Money, Credit and Banking* 40 (5): 837–866.

Brunnermeier, Markus K. 2009. "Deciphering the 2007–2008 Liquidity and Credit Crunch." *Journal of Economic Perspectives* 23 (1): 77–100.

Brunnermeier, Markus K., and M. Oehmke. 2013. "Bubbles, Financial Crises, and Systemic Risk." In *Handbook of the Economics of Finance*, volume 2B, edited by George M. Constantinides, Milton Harris, and Rene M. Stulz, 1221–1288. Boston: Elsevier.

Burstein, Ariel T. 2006. "Inflation and Output Dynamics with State-Dependent Pricing Decisions." *Journal of Monetary Economics* 53 (7): 1235–1257.

Caballero, R., and E. Fahri. 2018. "The Safety Trap." *Review of Economic Studies* 85 (1): 223–274.

Calvo, Guillermo A., and Enrique Mendoza. 2000. "Rational Contagion and the Globalization of Securities Markets." *Journal of International Economics* 51 (1): 79–113.

Eden, Maya. 2016. "Excessive Financing Costs in a Representative Agent Framework." *American Economic Journal: Macroeconomics* 8 (2): 215–237.

Gorton, Gary. 2010. *Slapped by the Invisible Hand: The Panic of 2007*. New York: Oxford University Press.

Gorton, Gary, and Guillermo Ordoñez. 2013. "The Supply and Demand for Safe Assets." NBER Working Paper 18732, National Bureau of Economic Research, Cambridge, MA.

Gourinchas, Pierre-Olivier, and Olivier Jeanne. 2012. "Global Safe Assets." BIS Working Papers 399, Bank of International Settlements, Basel.

Krishnamurty, Arvind, and Annette Vissing-Jorgensen. 2012. "The Aggregate Demand for Treasury Debt." *Journal of Political Economy* 120 (2): 233–267.

Martin, Alberto, and Jaume Ventura. 2012. "Economic Growth with Bubbles." *American Economic Review* 102 (6): 3033–3058.

Mian, Atif, and Amir Sufi. 2014. "What Explains the 2007–2009 Drop in Employment?" *Econometrica* 82 (6): 2197–2223.

Rogoff, Kenneth. 2016. "Emerging Markets Should Go for the Gold." Project Syndicate, May 3. https://www.project-syndicate.org/commentary/gold-as-emerging-market-reserve-asset-by-kenneth-rogoff-2016-05.

Teulings, Coen, and Richard Baldwin. 2014. *Secular Stagnation: Facts, Causes and Cures*. London: CEPR Press.

5 Global Liquidity and Procyclicality

Hyun Song Shin

It is an honor to join this distinguished group and to take part in this event. I feel especially privileged to have Maurice Obstfeld and Aslı Demirgüç-Kunt as my discussants. I have learned a lot from Aslı and Maury over the years and no doubt will learn much from their comments today.

Exchange rates are back in the news. It is a cliché that the world has become more connected, but the external dimension of monetary policy has figured more and more prominently in central bankers' speeches lately. Financial markets, for their part, appear to be tethered more closely than ever to global events, and the real economy appears to dance to the tune of global financial developments rather than the other way round. If you will excuse a rather extravagant metaphor, the financial tail appears to be wagging the real economy dog. This is not how things are supposed to work. According to the traditional approach to international finance, financial flows are no more than the accounting counterparts to savings and investment decisions. The current account is the borrowing need of the country as a whole, and exchange rates steer net exports to restore external balance. When a country experiences an *appreciation* of its currency, this is presumed to be *contractionary*, as net exports fall.

I am grateful to Raphael Auer, Fernando Avalos, Stefan Avdjiev, Morten Bech, Claudio Borio, Michael Chui, Ben Cohen, Dietrich Domanski, Peter Hoerdahl, Krista Hughes, Jonathan Kearns, Catherine Koch, Bob McCauley, Pat McGuire, Andreas Schrimpf, Ilhyock Shim, Vlad Sushko, and Philip Turner for comments on earlier drafts and to Bat-el Berger, Anamaria Illes, Emese Kuruc, Denis Petre, Jeff Slee, and Agne Subelyte for excellent research assistance. The views expressed here are my own and not necessarily those of the Bank for International Settlements.

However, events have not always played out this way, especially in emerging economies. Rather than dampening economic activity, episodes of sustained currency appreciation often go hand in hand with buoyant economic activity on the back of strong capital inflows. The boom may be accompanied by the buildup of financial vulnerabilities. Think back to the years before the latest bout of financial turbulence in emerging markets. My discussant Maurice Obstfeld has a well-known empirical paper with Pierre-Olivier Gourinchas (Gourinchas and Obstfeld 2012) that sheds much light on this phenomenon. The combination of a rapid increase in leverage and a sharp appreciation of the currency emerges as a strong indicator of financial vulnerability and of subsequent crises.

There is also a flip side to the argument based on the current account. If a country is running current account surpluses, the argument goes, then its currency will tend to appreciate unless the authorities are keeping the currency artificially low. This is the familiar argument heard around the G20 table, directed at economies running current account surpluses. By the same token, the currency of a deficit country should *depreciate*. However, again, events do not always play out this way. In the mid-2000s, the US current account deficit widened to historical highs, and many commentators expected an imminent depreciation of the dollar. In the event, the dollar went in the opposite direction. It appreciated strongly with the onset of the crisis, wrong footing many commentators. The appreciation of the dollar was accompanied by a tightening of global financial conditions.

The wheel has turned full circle, and financial markets are once again keeping a wary eye on a stronger dollar. Observers are keenly attuned to every twist and turn in the monetary policy debate in the United States. Markets rally and the dollar weakens on any temporary reprieve from the normalization of US interest rates, only to reverse course when monetary tightening is back on the agenda.

Why are global financial conditions so attuned to the strength of the dollar? And why is the real economy so sensitive to global financial conditions? These are the two questions addressed in this chapter.

The chapter starts by describing a market anomaly in the currency market that is symptomatic of the strains currently being placed on global capital markets. In spite of the outward tranquillity, tensions lurk beneath the surface. Market anomalies offer a window on these strains.

A Telling Market Anomaly

There is an intriguing market anomaly in the foreign exchange market right now: the widespread failure of *covered interest parity*. Covered interest parity (CIP) is the proposition that interest rates implicit in foreign exchange markets should be consistent with market interest rates.[1]

Before 2008, CIP held as an empirical regularity with very few exceptions worth mentioning. As an academic, I used to tell my students that CIP is about the only relationship that can be relied on in international finance. I know better than to say this now. Textbooks still say that CIP holds, but it is no longer true.

Figure 5.1 shows the evidence. A foreign exchange swap (FX swap) is an arrangement where one party borrows US dollars by pledging another currency as collateral—that is, lending the other currency in exchange for dollars. The *forward rate* is the agreed exchange rate at which repayment takes place. From the forward rate and the current spot rate, we can calculate the implied interest rate on the US dollar. The top panels of figure 5.1 plot the implied 3-month interest rate on the dollar from forward rates embedded in FX swaps. Each series shows the particular currency pledged as collateral. Figure 5.1 plots the comparison of the 3-month US dollar LIBOR, the market interest rate for dollars. When the implied dollar interest rate from FX swaps is above LIBOR, then the borrower of dollars in the FX swap is paying more than the rate available in the open market. This has been the case for the yen, Swiss franc, and euro.

CIP held with barely a blip until the crisis (Akram, Rime, and Sarno 2008). Large deviations from CIP did take place during the 2008–2009 global financial crisis and the euro area crisis of 2011–2012. However, these were periods when financial intermediaries came under severe stress (Baba and Packer 2009; Baba and Shim 2010; Avalos and Moreno 2013). What is remarkable now is that deviations from CIP have appeared during periods of relative calm. Recent deviations have been especially large for the yen,

---

1. Formally, CIP is the statement that $1 + r_A = \dfrac{F}{S}(1 + r_B)$, where r_A and r_B are the market interest rates on two currencies A and B, and S and F are the spot and forward exchange rates, respectively, of A in terms of B.

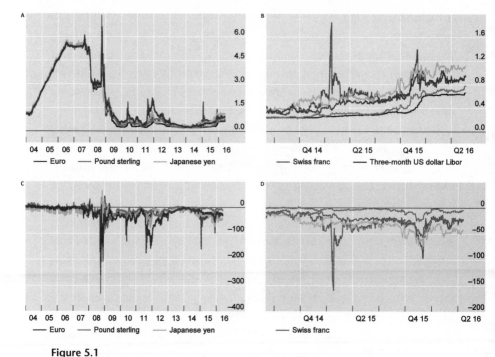

Figure 5.1
US dollar interest rate implied by FX swaps
A., B. Three-month US dollar interest rate implied by FX swaps[1]
C., D. FX swap spread, 3-month[2]

1. Implied US dollar interest rate in an FX swap involving the indicated currency. The 3-month US dollar LIBOR is plotted for comparison.

2. Spread between the 3-month US dollar LIBOR and 3-month dollar rate implied by FX swaps.
Source: Bloomberg; Datastream; BIS calculations.

although the Swiss franc also had a large deviation following the surprise revaluation of the Swiss franc in January 2015.

The bottom two panels of figure 5.1 show the magnitude of the deviation from CIP, where the deviation is measured as US dollar LIBOR minus the FX swap-implied dollar interest rate. The difference is called the "cross-currency basis," and for the currencies listed in figure 5.1, the cross-currency basis is negative, meaning that dollar borrowers in FX swaps pay more than LIBOR.

Traditionalists will be surprised—shocked even—to discover that CIP fails. But there it is, in the full glare of daylight. Not only does CIP fail systematically, the observed deviations from CIP have become more pronounced in the past 18 months or so.[2] In textbook settings where someone could borrow and lend without limit at prevailing market interest rates, the cross-currency basis could not deviate from zero, at least not by much and not for too long. This is because someone could borrow at the cheaper dollar interest rate and lend out at the higher dollar interest rate. However, executing such a trade entails a sequence of transactions, often through intermediaries. Thus, it makes demands on the risk-taking capacity of dealer banks as well as on counterparties.[3]

What is the link between CIP violations and the dollar? One can draw a parallel with recent strains in emerging markets. At first sight, advanced economy currency markets seem a million miles away from stresses in emerging markets, but the common element is that a stronger dollar and tighter credit conditions go together.

Figure 5.2 plots the value of the US dollar (in light gray), calculated as the simple average of the exchange rates against six advanced economy currencies as indicated. When the light gray line goes up, the dollar strengthens. On the same chart, plotted in dark gray, the average cross-currency basis. Notice how the cross-currency basis is the mirror image of the strength of the dollar. When the dollar strengthens, the cross-currency basis widens. This is especially so in the past 18 months or so, reflecting the stronger dollar.

The relationship is even clearer if we plot changes in exchange rates and changes in the cross-currency basis. Figure 5.3 shows this for the bilateral exchange rate of the euro against the dollar. See the reflected symmetry in the left panel, just like mountains reflected in a lake, where a strengthening of the dollar is associated with a widening of the deviation from CIP. The

---

2. The recent evidence is examined by Du, Tepper, and Verdelhan (2016), who find that the cross-currency basis is not confined to LIBOR and appears across many market interest rates. Borio et al. (2016) show that that the sign of the cross-currency basis depends on the net swap position of the banking sector.

3. Gabaix and Maggiori (2015) propose a theory of exchange rate determination based on intermediary balance sheet constraints. More generally, a bank's risk-taking capacity is limited by its capital, as described in two of my recent speeches (Shin 2016a, 2016b).

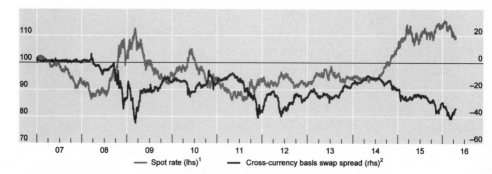

Figure 5.2
US dollar exchange rate and the cross-currency basis
[1]Simple average of bilateral exchange rate of the dollar against CAD, EUR, GBP, SEK, CHF, and JPY. Higher values indicate a stronger US dollar.
[2]Simple average of the five-year cross-currency basis swaps against CAD, EUR, GBP, SEK, CHF and JPY vis-à-vis the US dollar.
Source: Avdjiev et al. (2016); Bloomberg; BIS calculations.

right panel shows the same information as a scatter chart. The negative slope is clear to see; a strengthening of the dollar goes hand in hand with a widening of the deviation from CIP.

The key takeaway is that a stronger dollar is associated with more severe market anomalies. The amazing thing is that this is true not only for emerging markets but also for "safe haven" currencies, such as the yen and the Swiss franc. To understand the nature of this relationship, we need to cast the net wider and take in the larger picture concerning the role of the dollar in the global banking system.

The Global Banking System and the US Dollar

The global role of the US dollar is reflected in its preeminent role in the global banking system. The dollar is the unit of account in debt contracts in that borrowers borrow in dollars and lenders lend in dollars, irrespective of whether the borrower or lender is located in the United States.

Figure 5.4 gives a sense of the size of cross-border bank claims denominated in US dollars, arranged by region. The size of the arrows represents the size of the claims. In 2002, the arrow from the United States to Europe was $462 billion, meaning that banks resident in the United States had

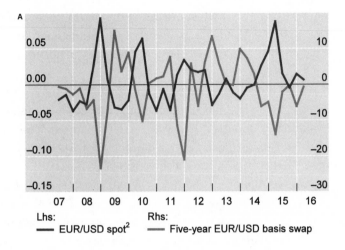

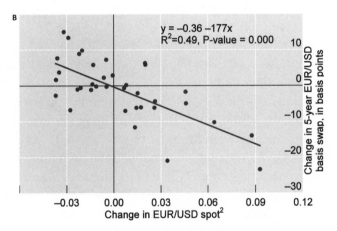

Figure 5.3
Change in euro/US dollar exchange rate and change in cross-currency basis[1]
[1]Changes in quarterly averages.
[2]An increase represents an appreciation of the US dollar against the euro.
Source: Avdjiev, Du, Koch, and Shin (2016); Bloomberg; BIS calculations.

claims of $462 billion to borrowers in Europe. This grew to $1.54 trillion by 2007. The return leg from Europe to the United States went from $856 billion in 2002 to more than $2 trillion in 2007.[4]

4. McGuire and Tarashev (2007) and McCauley, McGuire, and von Peter (2010) map the geography of cross-border lending.

I will return to figure 5.4 when discussing the macro implications. For now, notice that the US dollar is used widely throughout the global banking system, even when neither the lender nor the borrower is a US resident.

Why is the US dollar so important in the global banking system? One answer invokes the dollar's broad international role in cross-border transactions, including its dominant role as an invoicing currency for international trade.[5] Trade financing or associated hedging activity can account for some of the US dollar-denominated bank credit.

A second answer builds on the first. The dollar's role as an invoicing currency spills over to the currency denomination of lending that finances real assets. For export firms, if the invoice is in dollars, it may make sense to borrow in dollars. Figure 5.4 shows only the bank claims, but an important funding source for emerging market firms has been dollar-denominated bonds. This is especially so for the oil and gas sector. Caruana (2016) and Chui, Kuruc, and Turner (2016) provide further evidence.

The story does not end there, however. This reasoning has a third level. The role of the dollar as the funding currency of choice means that the universe of dollar-denominated assets extends beyond the United States. For large institutional investors with a global portfolio of assets, there may be a currency mismatch between the assets they hold and the commitments they have to their domestic stakeholders. For instance, pension funds and life insurance companies have obligations to their beneficiaries and policy holders. These obligations are denominated in domestic currency—in euros, yen, or Swiss francs. However, a large investor will not be limited to domestic assets and will look abroad to form a diversified portfolio of global assets, including securities issued in US dollars.

To the extent that investors face currency risk, they will hedge that risk. We know that investors from emerging economies with large funded pension systems hedge actively.[6] However, institutional investors from rich economies will face the problem most acutely, as they have the largest portfolios of global assets. The hedging counterparty is typically a bank, and the bank lays off its own currency risk by borrowing dollars. That way, dollar claims are counterbalanced by dollar debts.

---

5. Goldberg and Tille (2009) and Gopinath (2015).
6. See Avalos and Moreno (2013) for evidence from Chile.

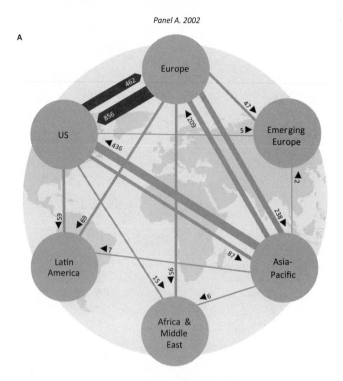

Panel A. 2002

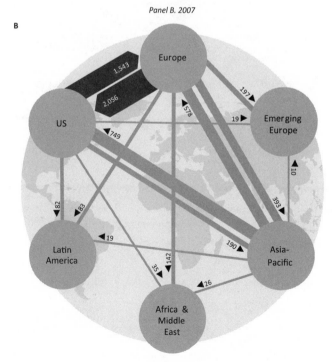

Panel B. 2007

Figure 5.4
US dollar-denominated cross-border claims (billions of US dollars)
Source: BIS locational banking statistics.

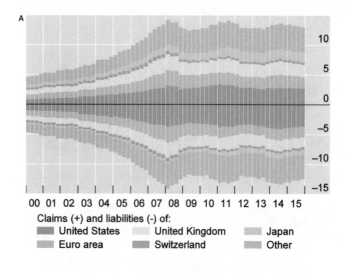

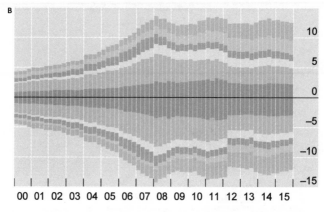

Figure 5.5
Cross-border US dollar denominated credit, all sectors (trillion US dollars)
[1]The break in the series between Q1 2012 and Q2 2012 is due to the Q2 2012 introduction of a more comprehensive reporting of cross-border positions (for more details, see http://www.bis.org/publ/qtrpdf/r_qt1212v.htm).
Source: BIS locational banking statistics, tables A5 (by residence) and A7 (by nationality).

The upshot is that banks take on liabilities denominated in dollars in the process of providing hedging services. This is the third level of the argument. The consequence of the dollar's international role in transactions is that the global banking system runs on US dollars.

Figure 5.5 provides a window on the total dollar-denominated cross-border bank credit arranged by region. The two panels are plotted using

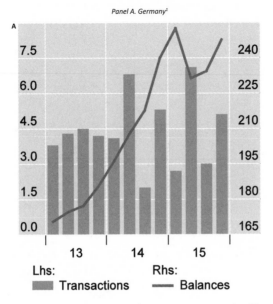

Panel A. Germany[1]

Lhs: Transactions   Rhs: Balances

[1]For Germany, long-term debt securities of insurance companies. Transactions indicate acquisitions minus external financing.

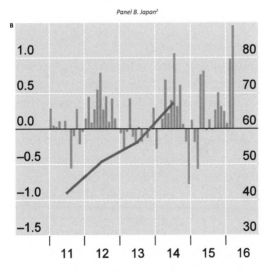

Panel B. Japan[2]

[2]For Japan, life insurance companies. Positive (negative) transactions indicate a net purchase (sale) of medium- and long-term bonds.

Figure 5.6
Outward bond investment of insurance companies
Source: Deutsche Bundesbank; Japanese Ministry of Finance; Statistics Sweden; Life Insurance Association of Japan; BIS calculations.

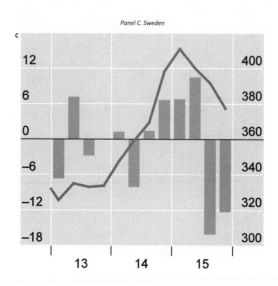

Figure 5.6
(continued)

data that we have started posting on the BIS website as part of our effort to make more detailed data available.[7]

In both panels, upward-pointing bars indicate assets, and downward-pointing bars indicate liabilities. The left panel breaks out the total by residence, and the right panel breaks out the total by nationality, meaning the location of the headquarters. So, for instance, the cross-border claims of a German bank office in London would be classified as "UK" in the left panel, but as "euro area" in the right panel. By comparing the two panels of figure 5.5, we see that Swiss and euro area banks have been active in other jurisdictions, especially in the United Kingdom and the United States.

Notice how the undulations in cross-border dollar liabilities track global financial conditions. The totals in figure 5.5 grew strongly up to 2008 but contracted with the onset of the global financial crisis, and then also with the euro area crisis of 2011–2012. Interestingly, the most recent period of dollar strength from mid-2014 has been associated with a decline in the

7. See BIS locational banking statistics, tables A5 and A7, www.bis.org/statistics /bankstats.htm.

aggregate cross-border liabilities. The inference is that banks have been less willing to roll over hedges put in place by institutional investors during the earlier period of more ample dollar liquidity.

Direct evidence of institutional investor holdings is not very comprehensive. However, some evidence from national data from a few countries indicates that institutional investors have increased their holding of external bonds. Figure 5.6 gathers some evidence on the outward portfolio flows of insurance companies from Germany (panel A), Japan (panel B), and Sweden (panel C). The bars indicate flows, and the line plots outstanding amounts, where available. The outstanding amounts of foreign bond holdings have fluctuated in recent years, but the general trend has been upward.

Another source of information on foreign exchange hedging comes from the twice-yearly BIS surveys of over-the-counter foreign exchange derivatives. Panel A of figure 5.7 shows the outstanding notional amounts by instrument, and panel B shows the breakdown by counterparty. There was a sharp pull-back during the 2008 crisis, but strong growth in its aftermath. We see, however, that there has been a decline since end–2014, coinciding with the period when the cross-currency basis has widened.

The category consisting of nonreporting financial institutions has seen the largest decline in notional amounts since the end of 2014. This decline has come after a period of strong growth and is consistent with the market having entered a phase where foreign exchange derivative stocks have declined amid a strengthening dollar and subdued risk-taking in the banking sector more generally.

Thus far, the activities of advanced economy banks and investors have been described. But a consistent theme also runs through to events in emerging economies. For this reason, we will broaden the perspective by considering recent events in emerging economies, especially the activities of emerging market economy (EME) corporate borrowing in dollars. Swiss and Japanese life insurance companies could not be more different from emerging market corporates, but they all have in common their strong links to the banking system and their exposure to the procyclical tendencies driven by the "risk-taking channel" of exchange rate changes. Let us consider this now. It is the core of this chapter.

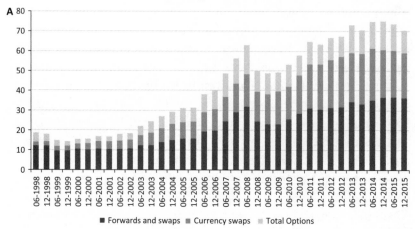

Panel A. By instrument

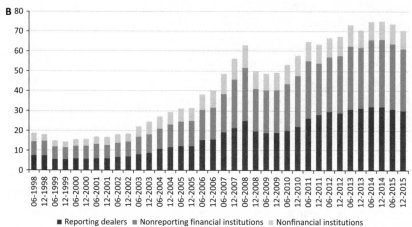

Panel B. By sector of counterparty

Figure 5.7

Over-the-counter foreign exchange derivatives—Notional principal[1]

[1] At half-year end (end June and end December). Amounts denominated in currencies other than the US dollar are converted to US dollars at the exchange rate prevailing on the reference date.

Source: BIS over-the-counter derivatives statistics.

The Risk-Taking Channel and the Exchange Rate

In a nutshell, the proposition is this: *When an international currency depreciates, there is a tendency for foreigners to borrow more in that currency.* Figure 5.8, which is taken from Avdjiev, Koch, and Shin (2016), illustrates the risk-taking channel for the US dollar. The precise mechanism will depend on the context, but the key feature of the risk-taking channel is that when the dollar depreciates, banks lend more in US dollars to borrowers outside the United States. Similarly, when the dollar appreciates, banks lend less or even shrink outright the lending of dollars. In this sense, the value of the dollar is a barometer of risk-taking and global credit conditions.

A weaker dollar is associated with greater lending in dollars, lower volatility, and more risk taking, but a stronger dollar is associated with higher volatility and a recoiling from risk taking. For instance, a standard carry trade motive would be consistent with the risk-taking channel (Menkhoff et al. 2012).

Panel B of figure 5.8 shows the coefficients of rolling regressions with a 20-quarter sample window. What is notable is that the coefficient has become more negative in the recent post-crisis period. Before the 2008–2009 crisis, the coefficient hovered around –0.2 to –0.3, but after the crisis, the coefficient has been around –0.5. In other words, a 1 percent appreciation of the dollar in terms of the nominal effective exchange rate is associated with a 0.5 percent decline in the quarterly growth rate of dollar cross-border credit. In this sense, the value of the dollar is a key barometer of global dollar credit conditions.

We saw earlier in figures 5.2 and 5.3 how the deviation from CIP tracked closely the value of the US dollar. We now have a way of making sense of this relation. The breakdown of CIP is a symptom of tighter dollar credit conditions putting a squeeze on accumulated dollar liabilities built up during the previous period of easy dollar credit. During the period of dollar weakness, global banks were able to supply hedging services to institutional investors at a reasonable cost, as cross-border dollar credit was growing strongly and was easily obtained. However, as the dollar strengthens, the banking sector finds it more challenging to roll over the dollar credit previously supplied.

One way to summarize the finding is that a "triangle" links a stronger dollar, more subdued dollar cross-border flows, and a widening of the

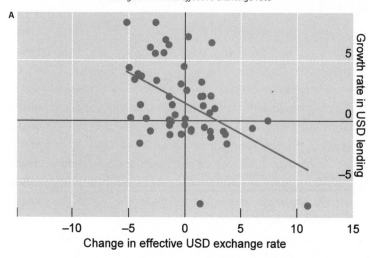

Panel A. Cross-border bank lending to nonresidents versus change in nominal effective exchange rate[1]

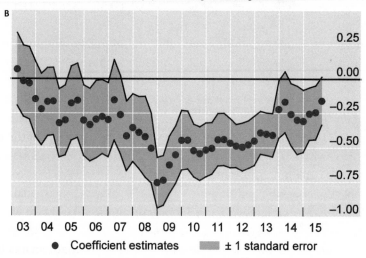

Panel B. Twenty-quarter rolling window regressions[2]

● Coefficient estimates   ▢ ± 1 standard error

Figure 5.8
US dollar cross-border bank lending and the dollar exchange rate
[1] Plot of quarterly growth rate of cross-border bank lending in US dollars on quarterly changes in the US dollar nominal effective exchange rate for Q1 2003–Q3 2015. Lending refers to loans by BIS reporting banks to all (bank and nonbank) borrowers outside the United States. The line is a fitted regression line. Positive changes indicate an appreciation of the dollar.
[2] Rolling regression coefficient for 20-quarters window.
Sources: BIS locational banking statistics; BIS effective exchange rate indices; BIS calculations.

cross-currency basis against the dollar. This is the main theme explored in Avdjiev et al. (2016). The preeminent role of the US dollar as the global funding currency means that US monetary policy has an especially important place in the determination of global financial conditions.

The euro, after a slow start, is showing signs of joining the dollar as an international funding currency. Borrowers outside the euro area are borrowing more in euros, taking advantage of very low long-term interest rates, just as borrowers outside the United States have been borrowing in US dollars for some time. To be sure, the sums are still small for the euro. The stock of euro-denominated debt of nonbanks outside the euro area is only about a quarter of the equivalent US dollar amount. But the trajectory is steep. US companies have been particularly active in borrowing in euros. This type of borrowing is common enough to have its own name: "reverse Yankee" borrowing.

Figure 5.9 shows that the risk-taking channel for the euro is starting to show the telltale negative relationship between a weaker currency value and expanding cross-border lending in that currency; it was not there before but has emerged since the crisis. The coefficient of the rolling regression is now negative. At about –0.7, the coefficient is even larger in absolute terms than for the dollar. For the Japanese yen, Avdjiev, Koch, and Shin (2016) find that its role as an international funding currency has waxed and waned over the decades, but the telltale signs of the risk-taking channel have reappeared in recent years with monetary easing in Japan.

As the euro and yen join the dollar in the ranks of international funding currencies, we are left with a dilemma. With each successive wave of monetary easing since the financial crisis, greater demands are being made on international capital markets. One important task that remains is to investigate how much of the observed market anomalies can be attributed to exchange rate pressures and changing market dynamics wrought by monetary spillovers. Spillovers and "spillbacks" have been an important theme in international finance,[8] and it looks to stay that way for the time being.

---

8. This theme has been tackled by Caruana (2012), Rajan (2014), Rey (2015), and Borio (2016).

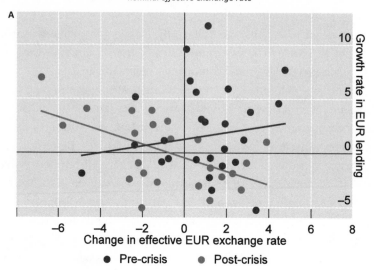

Panel A. Cross-border bank lending to nonresidents versus nominal effective exchange rate[1]

A

Growth rate in EUR lending

Change in effective EUR exchange rate

● Pre-crisis ● Post-crisis

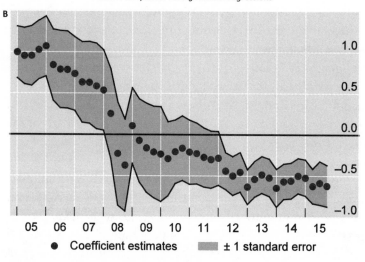

Panel B. 20-quarter rolling window regressions[2]

B

● Coefficient estimates ▨ ± 1 standard error

Figure 5.9

Euro-denominated cross-border bank lending

[1] Plot of quarterly growth rate of cross-border bank lending in euros on quarterly changes in the euro nominal effective exchange rate for Q1 2003–Q3 2015. Lending refers to loans by BIS reporting banks to all (bank and nonbank) borrowers outside the euro area. Positive changes indicate an appreciation of the euro.

[2] Rolling regression coefficient for 20-quarter window.

Sources: BIS locational banking statistics; BIS effective exchange rate indices; BIS calculations.

Macro Implications of the Risk-Taking Channel

The risk-taking channel has macro implications, too, and may explain why currency appreciation in emerging markets may sometimes be expansionary rather than contractionary. Exchange rate fluctuations influence the economy through both real and financial channels. The real effects through the net exports channel are well known and are standard in open economy macro models, such as the textbook Mundell-Fleming model. However, exchange rate fluctuations influence the economy through a financial amplification channel as well as through net exports.

The financial channel of exchange rates operates when currency appreciation elicits valuation changes on borrower balance sheets. For instance, if the borrower has local currency assets but has borrowed in dollars, there is a naked currency mismatch. Even if the assets generate dollar cash flows, an empirical association may exist between a stronger dollar and weaker cash flows, as in the case of oil firms. For whatever reason, when the potential for valuation mismatching arises from exchange rate effects, a weaker dollar flatters the balance sheets of dollar borrowers, whose liabilities fall relative to assets. From the standpoint of creditors, the stronger credit position of the borrowers creates spare capacity for credit extension even with a fixed exposure limit, for instance, through a value-at-risk constraint. The spare lending capacity is filled through an expansion in the supply of dollar credit (see Bruno and Shin 2015a, 2015b).

There are knock-on effects of the risk-taking channel on the government's fiscal position, too. When credit supply expands, so does the set of investment projects, raising economic activity and improving the fiscal position (Turner 2014; Chui, Kuruc, and Turner 2016). If corporate dollar borrowing is done through state-owned enterprises (as is the case for the oil and gas sector in many EMEs), then the fiscal impact may be even more direct through the dividends that are paid into government coffers.

Figure 5.10 shows how sovereign credit default swap (CDS) spreads for a group of EMEs have moved with shifts in the bilateral exchange rate against the US dollar. The horizontal axis in each panel is the percentage change in the bilateral exchange rate against the US dollar from the end of 2012. The vertical axis gives the change in the local currency 5-year sovereign CDS spread. The size of the bubbles indicates the total dollar-denominated debt owed by nonbanks in the country.

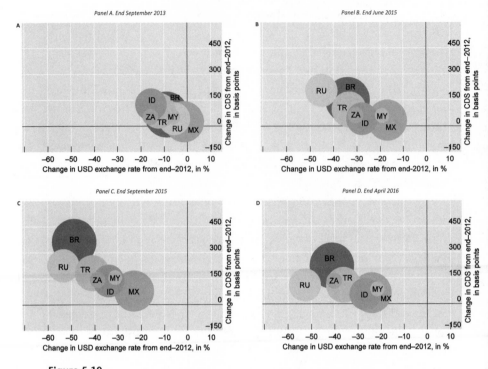

Figure 5.10
The risk-taking channel for EMEs: Bilateral US dollar exchange rate and 5-year sovereign CDS, change from end–2012
BR = Brazil; ID = Indonesia; MX = Mexico; MY = Malaysia; RU = Russia; TR = Turkey; ZA = South Africa. The size of the bubbles indicates the size of US dollar-denominated credit to nonbanks in the respective economies in Q4 2015.
Source: Avdjiev, McCauley, and Shin (2016); Datastream; Markit; national data; BIS; BIS calculations.

We see from figure 5.10 that both time series and cross-section relationships exist between the CDS spread and the bilateral dollar exchange rate. In the cross-section, the bubbles line up along a downward-sloping line, indicating that those countries that have depreciated more against the US dollar tend to have CDS spreads that are higher. Over time, as the US dollar appreciates, the bubbles migrate toward the upper left-hand corner of the graph; in other words, as the domestic currency weakens against the US dollar, EME sovereign CDS spreads have tended to rise.

Interestingly, these results go away when we consider instead the trade-weighted effective exchange rate that is unrelated to the US dollar (Hofmann, Shim, and Shin 2016). When we consider the component of the effective exchange rate that is unrelated to the US dollar, there is no evidence that a currency appreciation is associated with loosening of financial conditions. Indeed, we actually find the opposite result for some measures of financial conditions. Again, the takeaway is that dollar strength is key for financial conditions in emerging markets.

Beyond the Current Account

Capital flows are traditionally viewed as the financial counterpart to savings and investment decisions, and exchange rates are the automatic stabilizers. In textbook models, a current account deficit can be remedied when the exchange rate depreciates, raising net exports and closing the current account gap.

Going back to 2002, figure 5.4 shows a snapshot of the cross-border banking claims denominated in US dollars around the world. Even then, the two-way flow was quite active between Europe and the United States. The two-way flow resulted from the "round-tripping" of dollars intermediated by the large European banks. These banks raised wholesale funds by using their US branches to borrow from US money market funds, shipping the funds back to headquarters, and then recycling the proceeds back to the United States by purchasing securities based on mortgages of US households. A large chunk of US subprime mortgages were financed this way. In 2002, the arrow from the United States to Europe was $462 billion (see figure 5.4). This grew to $1.54 trillion by 2007. The return leg of the round trip went from $856 billion in 2002 to more than $2 trillion in 2007.

The outflows to Europe were matched by the inflows from Europe, and so the net flows were small compared to the gross flows. The current account between Europe and the United States remained broadly in balance, even though the gross capital flows from Europe into the United States grew enormously. Lending standards, though, are based on the size of the balance sheet. So, gross flows are what count for lending standards. Gross flows surged, easing lending standards and fueling the rapid increase in credit to subprime borrowers. Borio and Disyatat (2011, 2015) give a detailed account of why current account reasoning led some commentators astray. My discussant Maury Obstfeld was one of the first to highlight the importance of gross flows (Obstfeld 2010, 2012).

Why did policy makers miss the surge in subprime funding coming from Europe? For once, we cannot blame the lack of data. Figure 5.4 was constructed from the BIS locational banking statistics, but the BIS simply aggregates the data supplied by central banks. In fact, the cross-border position data between Europe and the United States actually comes from the central banks in those regions.

If it's not the lack of data, then why did we miss this? The blind spot is most likely due to our accounting conventions in international finance. When we do international finance, we often buy into the "triple coincidence," where the GDP area, decision-making unit, and the currency area are one and the same (Avdjiev, McCauley, and Shin 2016). Textbooks therefore start with the assumptions that each GDP area has its own currency and the use of that currency is largely confined to that economic area. The Mundell-Fleming model is a classic example of the triple coincidence, but even in sophisticated macroeconomic models, the triple coincidence is rarely questioned. Currency appreciation or depreciation then acts on the economy through changes in net exports.

One reason that triple coincidence reasoning has led researchers astray comes from another common error that economists were making before the crisis. As the US current account deficit grew to historically high levels, triple coincidence reasoning would point to a depreciation of the dollar. Many commentators wondered aloud whether there would be "sudden stop" in the capital flows to the United States, just as in emerging market crises (Summers 2004; Edwards 2005; Obstfeld and Rogoff 2005; Roubini and Setser 2005; Krugman 2007).

In the event, the US dollar appreciated sharply with the onset of the 2008–2009 global financial crisis. The dollar's surge was associated with a deleveraging of financial market participants outside the United States that had used short-term dollar funding to invest in risky long-term dollar assets, with the European banks mentioned above being the most prominent example. As the crisis erupted, these financial institutions found themselves short the dollar and overleveraged, and they sought to reduce their dollar liabilities, bidding up the value of the dollar in the process.

Looking Back and Looking Ahead

The strengthening of the dollar since mid-2014 brings us back full circle to the mechanisms at play today. But meanwhile the protagonists have changed. The dollar borrowers are not European banks, but emerging market corporates. And the borrowing is done through corporate bonds rather than wholesale bank funding.

The stock of US dollar-denominated debt of nonbanks outside the United States currently stands at $9.7 trillion. Of this, the US dollar-denominated debt of nonbanks in EMEs stands at $3.3 trillion. This overhang of US dollar-denominated debt has been weighing on macroeconomic conditions in emerging market economies since the dollar started to strengthen in 2014.

To be sure, there are some mitigating factors. For one thing, much of the recent increase in dollar debt in EMEs has been in the form of debt securities issued by emerging market corporates. These debt securities have long maturities. In addition, many emerging economies hold substantial foreign exchange reserves, in contrast to their situation in past crises. Demirgüç-Kunt and Detragiache (1998) is a classic reference on the determinants of banking crises, and many of the factors identified there do not show up currently.

Nevertheless, we have no room for complacency. Even if the bonds have long maturities, there are other repercussions on the economy if US dollar-denominated borrowing begins to unwind. Nonfinancial firms are deeply embedded in the economy, and their financial activities spill over into the rest of the economy. Bruno and Shin (2015c) find that dollar borrowing by emerging market corporates has had the attributes of a "carry trade," where for every dollar raised through a bond issue, around a quarter ends up as cash on the firm's balance sheet. Here, cash could mean a domestic currency bank deposit or a claim on the shadow banking system, or indeed a financial instrument issued by another firm. So, dollar borrowing will spill over into the rest of the economy in the form of easier credit conditions. When the dollar borrowing is reversed, these easier domestic financial conditions will be reversed, too.

Furthermore, even if a country has large foreign exchange reserves, the corporate sector itself may find itself short of financial resources and may cut investment and curtail operations, resulting in a slowdown of growth. So, even a central bank that holds a large stock of foreign exchange reserves may find it difficult to head off a slowing real economy when global financial conditions tighten. Arguably, such a slowdown is part of what we are seeing right now in emerging market economies.

All this goes to show that international financial developments have to be placed in the broader context of past and anticipated central bank actions. We will undoubtedly have more opportunities to discuss these issues in policy circles in the months ahead.

References

Akram, Farooq, Dagfinn Rime, and Lucio Sarno. 2008. "Arbitrage in the Foreign Exchange Market: Turning on the Microscope." *Journal of International Economics* 76 (2): 237–253.

Avalos, Fernando, and Ramon Moreno. 2013. "Hedging in Derivatives Markets: The Experience of Chile." *BIS Quarterly Review* (March): 53–64. www.bis.org/publ/qtrpdf /r_qt1303g.htm.

Avdjiev, Stefan, Catherine Koch, and Hyun Song Shin. 2016. "Exchange Rates and the Transmission of Global Liquidity." Paper presented at the Central Bank of the Republic of Turkey Conference on Global Liquidity, March, Istanbul.

Avdjiev, Stefan, Robert N. McCauley, and Hyun Song Shin. 2016. "Breaking Free of the Triple Coincidence in International Finance." *Economic Policy* 31 (87): 409–451.

Avdjiev, Stefan, Wenxin Du, Catherine Koch, and Hyun Song Shin. 2016. "The Dollar, Bank Leverage, and the Deviation from Covered Interest Parity." BIS Working Paper 592, Bank for International Settlements, Basel. https://www.bis.org/publ /work592.htm.

Baba, Naohiko, and Frank Packer. 2009. "Interpreting Deviations from Covered Interest Parity during the Financial Market Turmoil of 2007–08." *Journal of Banking and Finance* 33 (11): 1953–1962.

Baba, Naohiko, and Ilhyock Shim. 2010. "Policy Responses to Dislocations in the FX Swap Market: The Experience of Korea." *BIS Quarterly Review* (June): 29–39. www.bis .org/publ/qtrpdf/r_qt1006e.htm.

Borio, Claudio. 2016. "More Pluralism, More Stability?" Speech at the Seventh High-Level SNB-IMF Conference on the International Monetary System, May 10, Zurich. www.bis.org/speeches/sp160510.htm.

Borio, Claudio, and Piti Disyatat. 2011. "Global Imbalances and the Financial Crisis: Link or No Link?" BIS Working Paper 346, Bank for International Settlements, Basel. www.bis.org/publ/work346.htm.

Borio, Claudio, and Piti Disyatat. 2015. "Capital Flows and the Current Account: Taking Financing (More) Seriously." BIS Working Paper 525, Bank for International Settlements, Basel. www.bis.org/publ/work525.htm.

Borio, Claudio, Robert N. McCauley, Patrick McGuire, and Vladyslav Sushko. 2016. "Covered Interest Parity Lost: Understanding Cross-Currency Basis." *BIS Quarterly Review* (September): 45–64. https://www.bis.org/publ/qtrpdf/r_qt1609e.htm.

Bruno, Valentina, and Hyun Song Shin. 2015a. "Cross-Border Banking and Global Liquidity." *Review of Economic Studies* 82 (2): 535–564.

Bruno, Valentina, and Hyun Song Shin. 2015b. "Capital Flows and the Risk-Taking Channel of Monetary Policy." *Journal of Monetary Economics* 71: 119–132.

Bruno, Valentina, and Hyun Song Shin. 2015c. "Global Dollar Credit and Carry Trades: A Firm-Level Analysis." BIS Working Paper 510, Bank for International Settlements, Basel. www.bis.org/publ/work510.htm.

Caruana, Jaime. 2012. "Policymaking in an Interconnected World." Speech at Federal Reserve Bank of Kansas City Economic Policy Symposium, August 31, Jackson Hole, WY. www.bis.org/speeches/sp120903.htm.

Caruana, Jaime. 2016. "Credit, Commodities and Currencies." Lecture at the London School of Economics, February 5. www.bis.org/speeches/sp160205.htm.

Chui, Michael, Emese Kuruc, and Philip Turner. 2016. "A New Dimension to Currency Mismatches in the Emerging Markets–Non-financial Companies." BIS Working Paper 550, Bank for International Settlements, Basel. www.bis.org/publ/work550 .htm.

Demirgüç-Kunt, Aslı, and Enrica Detragiache. 1998. "The Determinants of Banking Crises: Evidence from Industrial and Developing Countries." *IMF Staff Papers* 45 (1): 1–109.

Du, Wenxin, Alexande Tepper, and Adrien Verdelhan. 2016. "Deviations from Covered Interest Rate Parity." papers.ssrn.com/sol3/papers.cfm?abstract_id=2768207.

Edwards, Sebastian. 2005. "Is the US Current Account Deficit Sustainable? If Not, How Costly Is Adjustment Likely to Be?" *Brookings Papers on Economic Activity* 1: 211–288.

Gabaix, Xavier, and Matteo Maggiori. 2015. "International Liquidity and Exchange Rate Dynamics." *Quarterly Journal of Economics* 130 (3): 1369–1420.

Goldberg, Linda, and Cedric Tille. 2009. "Macroeconomic Interdependence and the International Role of the Dollar." *Journal of Monetary Economics* 56 (7): 990–1003.

Gopinath, Gita. 2016. "The International Price System." In *Inflation, Dynamics and Monetary Policy, Proceedings of the Federal Reserve Bank of Kansas City, August 27–29, 2015, Jackson Hole, WY*, 71–150.

Gourinchas, Pierre-Olivier, and Maurice Obstfeld. 2012. "Stories of the Twentieth Century for the Twenty-First." *American Economic Journal: Macroeconomics* 4 (1): 226–265.

Hofmann, Boris, Ilhyock Shim, and Hyun Song Shin. 2016. "Sovereign Yields and the Risk-Taking Channel of Currency Appreciation." BIS Working Paper 538, Bank for International Settlements, Basel. http://www.bis.org/publ/work538.htm.

Krugman, Paul. 2007. "Will There Be a Dollar Crisis?" *Economic Policy* 22 (51): 436–467.

McCauley, Robert, Patrick McGuire, and Goetz von Peter. 2010. "The Architecture of Global Banking: From International to Multinational?" *BIS Quarterly Review* (March): 25–37. www.bis.org/publ/qtrpdf/r_qt1003e.htm.

McGuire, Patrick, and Nikola Tarashev. 2007. "International Banking with the Euro." *BIS Quarterly Review* (December): 47–61. www.bis.org/publ/qtrpdf/r_qt0712f.htm.

Menkhoff, Lukas, Luciano Sarno, Maik Schmeling, and Andreas Schrimpf. 2012. "Carry Trades and Global Foreign Exchange Volatility." *Journal of Finance* 67 (2): 681–718.

Obstfeld, Maurice. 2010. "Expanding Gross Asset Positions and the International Monetary System." Panel Remarks at Federal Reserve Bank of Kansas City Economic Policy Symposium at Jackson Hole, August 27.

Obstfeld, Maurice. 2012. "Does the Current Account Still Matter?" *American Economic Review* 102 (3): 1–23.

Obstfeld, Maurice, and Kenneth S. Rogoff. 2005. "Global Current Account Imbalances and Exchange Rate Adjustments." *Brookings Papers on Economic Activity* 1: 67–146.

Rajan, Raghuram. 2014. "Competitive Monetary Easing: Is It Yesterday Once More?" Remarks at the Brookings Institution, April 10, Washington, DC.

Rey, Hélène. 2015. "International Channels of Transmission of Monetary Policy and the Mundellian Trilemma." Mundell-Fleming Lecture presented at the International Monetary Fund Fifteenth Jacques Polak Annual Research Conference: Cross-Border Spillovers, November 13–14, Washington, DC. *IMF Economic Review* 64 (1): 6–35.

Roubini, Nouriel, and Brad Setser. 2005. "Our Money, Our Debt, Our Problem." *Foreign Affairs* 84 (4): 194–200.

Shin, Hyun Song. 2016a. "Bank Capital and Monetary Policy Transmission." Panel remarks at the ECB and Its Watchers XVII Conference, April 7, Frankfurt. www.bis.org/speeches/sp160407.htm.

Shin, Hyun Song. 2016b. "Market Liquidity and Bank Capital." Remarks at the Perspectives 2016: Liquidity Policy and Practice Conference, April 27, London Business School. www.bis.org/speeches/sp160506.htm.

Summers, Lawrence H. 2004. "The US Current Account Deficit and the Global Economy." Per Jacobsson Lecture at the International Monetary Fund, October 3, Washington, DC.

Turner, Philip. 2014. "The Global Long-Term Interest Rate, Financial Risks and Policy Choices in EMEs." BIS Working Paper 441, Bank for International Settlements, Basel. www.bis.org/publ/work441.htm.

Comment: Aslı Demirgüç-Kunt

It was a pleasure to read Hyun Shin's chapter on global liquidity and procyclicality. Indeed, any paper that starts with emphasizing the importance of finance for the real economy is music to my ears, as I have spent a large part of my professional life arguing that "finance matters for economic development," rather than merely the other way around. In the beginning of the chapter, Hyun says "the financial tail is wagging the real economy dog." For many of us in the finance and development field, finance is the brain anyway, not the tail, so this is not very surprising from that perspective.[1] Hence I like the emphasis on the role of the financial system in the international economy and how problems in the financial system and the intermediation process might spill over to the rest of the economy. Therefore I am predisposed to agree with the arguments and the main conclusion of the chapter.

However, the job of the discussant is to think of ways to sharpen the arguments and strengthen the chapter, so that is what I will try to do in my comments. My first observation is that although there is a lot to like in this chapter, there are also a lot of moving parts. It pulls together a lot of data and analysis from different pieces of work. Indeed, I would characterize it as a collection of interesting, provocative hypotheses rather than a fully developed argument. So, although the data and evidence presented are compelling, it is not always clear how the links are made, and sometimes possible alternative explanations are not adequately covered to present a

I am grateful to Sergio Schmukler and Ha Nguyen for helpful comments.
1. See, for example, Levine (2005); Demirgüç-Kunt and Levine (2008, 2009); Cull, Demirgüç-Kunt, and Morduch (2011); Ayyagari, Demirgüç-Kunt, and Maksimovic (2013); and Cihak and Demirgüç-Kunt (2014); among others.

coherent storyline. This approach leaves the reader with more questions than answers. Nevertheless, the ideas presented here are very thought provoking, which no doubt will lead to much more research in these areas.

Identification Issues

The chapter starts by asking two main questions. Why are global financial conditions so attuned to the strength of the US dollar? And why is the economy so sensitive to global financial conditions? These are important yet complicated questions, and drawing from my own area of expertise, they are immediately subject to the identification problem. In other words, when we try to answer these types of questions looking at equilibrium outcomes, it is very difficult to figure out the direction of causality. It could simply be that the global financial conditions are sensitive to the economy, or what we observe could simply be reflecting other factors at play.

It is not that different here. Take, for example, the centrality of the dollar in the global banking system. Although the dollar certainly plays a large part in the world economy, transactions in other currencies are also growing, as the chapter also mentions. Hence the dollar may not be the only driving factor.

Shin observes that when an international currency depreciates, there is a tendency for foreigners to borrow more in that currency. Hence, banks lend more internationally when the dollar is weak. But again, how much of this trend is a mere reflection of other currencies strengthening? For example, as emerging markets boom, capital flows in, their currencies appreciate, and the dollar depreciates vis-à-vis these currencies. This process is not necessarily driven by the dollar; instead, the dollar exchange rate is just a reflection of this process.

Another observation made in the chapter is that during the 2008–2009 global financial crisis, the dollar appreciated strongly with the onset of the crisis, despite the large US current account deficit. But again, we need to remember that these developments coincided with a run toward safe assets (notably, US treasuries), so it is not possible to disentangle how much of this appreciation was due to dollar per se, which was surely attractive for other reasons.

Overall, it is not clear that causality goes from the dollar to other markets; the dollar may not be as central as Shin argues, but may be just a reflection of an entirely different set of factors at play. Indeed, Shin also mentions that similar patterns are observed with other currencies, like the yen and Swiss franc.

Limits to Arbitrage, Portfolio and Foreign Direct Investment Flows, Gross versus Net Flows

Other points would also benefit from a more detailed explanation in the chapter. First, an interesting market anomaly that is highlighted is the failure of covered interest parity (CIP). We generally expect market interest rates and the implied interest rates from forward rates embedded in foreign exchange swaps to be more or less consistent. But as Shin reports, this has not been the case in recent years, particularly for periods of a strong dollar. Unfortunately, there is little explanation of why we observe this phenomenon. The chapter mentions in passing issues of risk-taking capacity (or limits to arbitrage) and counterparty risk, which could play important roles in explaining this anomaly. But given that a big part of the story depends on the inability of financial markets to hedge risk, it seems that this should deserve more attention than it gets in the chapter. For example, why does a dollar appreciation lead to a more negative cross-currency basis swap spread?

Second, why is the central focus of the chapter on bank flows as opposed to other flows? Shin focuses mostly on the importance of bank flows, which are, of course, highly relevant. However, a significant part of the increasing flows are portfolio and foreign direct investments. And for many countries around the world, these other two components have grown more quickly and might now surpass bank flows. The chapter should at least acknowledge this and discuss the implications.

Third, Shin makes a distinction between net versus gross flows, which is welcome.[2] But a significant part of the story is related to net financing. As home bias diminishes and residents have more wealth to invest, gross flows will expand as individuals diversify their portfolios internationally and hold one another's portfolios. Figure 5.11 illustrates that as countries

---

2. Shin relies on BIS data for this analysis, but gross flows are also available from balance of payments data by type of flow. Gross investment, issuance, and portfolio positions are available, too. See for example, World Bank (2015).

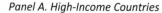

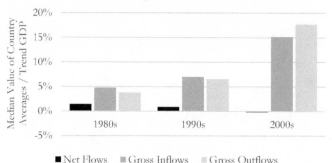

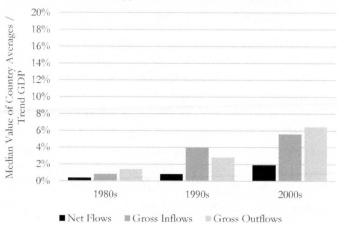

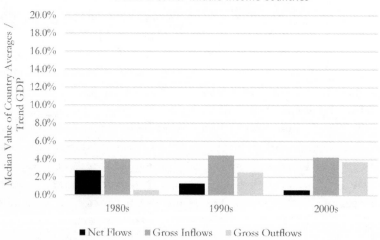

Figure 5.11

Net and gross capital flows

A. High-income countries

B. Upper-middle-income countries

C. Lower-middle-income countries

become richer, we expect gross flows to grow, although the trends in net flows are much less clear (Broner et al. 2013).

The effects of a shock may play out very differently depending on the reallocation between foreign and domestic investors as they retrench from the expansion period. To the extent that gross flows expand, what is important is how the asset and liability positions expand. As many emerging market economies have accumulated reserves, reduced sovereign borrowing, and received foreign direct investment and equity inflows, dollar appreciations and market collapses have been accompanied by a strengthening of their net foreign positions.

Overborrowing by Emerging Market Corporates?

Looking ahead, the chapter also tries to identify sources of fragility. One interesting conjecture is whether emerging market corporates will cause the next crisis. Shin asks whether we are going to see another East Asian crisis, where corporates were at the heart of the problem. Though the chapter does not devote much space to this discussion, it is nevertheless worth commenting on. Excessive borrowing to finance risky investments can be exacerbated by global liquidity conditions and may be a valid source of concern. However, there are mitigating factors, and some questions need to be answered to ascertain whether this concern is serious.

First, measuring risk taking in financial markets is difficult, because positions can be hedged. So an important question is: What proportion of these positions are open or unhedged? It is also difficult to decide what should be the benchmark level of indebtedness when discussing whether corporations are overborrowing.[3]

Second, as discussed at length in *Global Financial Development Report 2015/2016 on Long-Term Finance* (World Bank 2015), the emerging market corporates that borrow abroad do so through bond issuance in foreign currency, but this means they also extend their maturity at the same time, as foreign corporate bond markets are longer than domestic ones. Indeed, as figure 5.12 shows, in developing countries, maturity of international bond issues tends to be longer than that of domestic issues, although the reverse

---

3. See, for example, Alfaro et al. (2016) for a discussion of different benchmarks and the sensitivity of conclusions to the choice of these benchmarks.

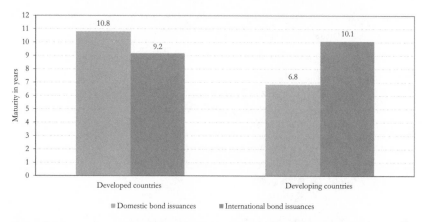

Figure 5.12
Maturity of domestic and international issuances, corporate-bond market
Notes: This figure reports the weighted average maturity of domestic and interna-
tional corporate bonds issued by firms from developed and developing countries.
The sample period is 1991–2014.
Source: Cortina, Didier, and Schmukler (2016).

is true for developed countries (Cortina, Didier, and Schmukler 2016). This
is only briefly mentioned in the chapter.

Third, the important role of reserve accumulation by emerging markets
is also mentioned in passing in the chapter, but it deserves more elaboration. To the extent that governments hold foreign reserves, they benefit
from an appreciation of the US dollar, compensating for the potential losses
that the corporates might suffer. The dollar appreciation may have fiscal
costs (due to a potential bailout), but the government will have additional
resources. Whether this is enough will depend on the size of government
assets versus unhedged corporate liabilities. Otherwise on net, it is not clear
whether the result would be gains or losses from an appreciation of the US
dollar due to funding abroad. At any rate, only a very few of the largest
corporates in emerging markets are able to access international markets.

Fourth, the main concern expressed in the chapter is that firms engage
in carry trade (i.e., they issue bonds at low rates to accumulate cash and
undertake risky financial intermediation activities in their home countries). But according to Bruno and Shin (2015), at most firms accumulate
23 percent of each dollar raised through bond issues (the estimates vary
substantially and can be as low as 4 percent). This does not seem to be a

large enough figure to be concerned about this effect. Clearly, the majority of the finance raised is used to finance growth opportunities through capital investment, growth in employment, mergers and acquisitions, and the like, as expected.

Fifth, large firms could indeed be using some of the cash to finance other firms, such as their suppliers. This intermediation process might channel funds from large companies to small and medium enterprises that cannot access capital markets directly because of information asymmetries; as a result, it could relax their financing constraints. If large companies have better information and are able to overcome information asymmetries that these smaller firms often face, this activity may be beneficial.

Finally, the fact that the Bruno and Shin (2015) results are driven by emerging markets makes the reader wonder what is special about these countries. Another important question is what the role of financial firms is. One would think they would be in a better position to engage in carry trade.

Trade-Offs and Parallels

One implication of the chapter is that although it is potentially an important source of economic benefits, financial globalization also has potential downsides. It worsens the trade-offs that monetary policy faces in navigating among multiple domestic objectives. There is the basic one between inflation and unemployment. But financial stability considerations are also important. So, for example, optimal monetary policy may have to be pulled away from the traditional macroeconomic goals of price stability and full employment to restrain debt buildups, particularly in the absence of effective macro-prudential tools.

These problems only become worse in an open economy, because openness to global financial markets will inevitably reduce the effectiveness of the macro-prudential tools that are available. So the trade-off between macro stabilization and financial stability becomes even more difficult. If a bigger interest rate change is required to bring about a given demand response in an open economy, this may worsen the macro-prudential problem by increasing the fragility of banks and encouraging gross financial flows.

This discussion has important parallels to banking globalization, which is the topic of the *Global Financial Development Report 2017/18* (World Bank 2018). It, too, describes an inherent tension between risk diversification and sharing as capital flows from low- to high-return countries and the implied necessity for exposing oneself to shocks and trends from abroad.

The benefits are many: In addition to resource mobilization and risk sharing, importantly, the entry of international banks can increase competition in the domestic banking industry, improving the efficiency of resource allocation, which is key to promoting economic development. When entry happens through brick and mortar, foreign banks often bring new technical knowledge, improve human capital in the industry, generate demand for improving regulation and supervision, and are generally less subject to political manipulation. These findings are quite well established in the literature.

But there are also potential costs. As in the global financial crisis, host countries might be exposed to external shocks transmitted by international banks, endangering their stability. It is also true that international banks might fuel excessive credit booms in host countries that end up in busts, because domestic financial systems are not capable of handling such flows. Such behavior—amplified by global liquidity conditions—might be harmful for the financial stability of home and host countries, ending up in costly boom and bust cycles and cross-border contagion risks.

For example, in a recent paper, we use bank-level data from more than 100 countries during 1999–2010 to study bank lending behavior over the business cycle (Bertay, Demirgüç-Kunt, and Huizinga 2015). Of all the banks in the sample, lending by foreign banks is the most procyclical, increasing their lending much more during upswings compared to domestic banks (figure 5.13). This is potentially because they can access funding from their international parent firms to take advantage of local lending opportunities during economic growth periods.

A Research Agenda for Developing Countries

It is useful to frame this discussion in the context of recent trends in bank internationalization (namely, the dramatic growth of foreign banking in the 1990s), followed by the retrenchment as a result of the crisis and the increase in south-south flows to at least partially compensate this retrenchment. Thus viewed, this discussion raises important policy questions for developing countries and lays out a research agenda. Several questions are in the minds of policy makers.

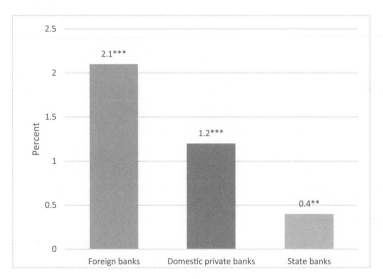

Figure 5.13
Change in bank lending associated with 1 percent growth in GDP per capita, 1999–2010
Note: The figure shows marginal effects from a regression of bank lending on GDP
per capita growth and number of control variables, estimated using a sample of
1,633 banks from 111 countries. Significance level: ** 5 percent, *** 1 percent.
Source: Bertay, Demirgüç-Kunt, and Huizinga (2015).

First: Are international banks too fickle to be heavily relied on by developing countries? Especially if they enter through acquisition, is there a risk that they will hollow out existing banks by substituting for local provision key functions from foreign headquarters? If so, information technology, certain aspects of payments capability, and even risk management skills could be lost or substantially eroded locally if the bank decides to exit the country. Although this question is age old, it has been receiving increased policy attention since the global financial crisis, as capital regulations on many European and US international banks induce them to retrench from international business (for example, the recent retreat of Barclays from Africa). So with the retrenchment after the crisis, has our policy advice to developing countries on foreign banking changed?

Second: Given the rise of south-south entry, should developing country authorities be especially cautious in their approach to admitting south-south international banking activities? For example, Chinese banks may be beginning to expand into Africa, Southeast Asia, and Latin America.

Should one worry about the lack of experience and perhaps insufficient home country prudential and AML-CFT supervision in some south-south cases? Or does the cost base and region-specific knowledge give these banks a better potential to provide banking services on a solid basis in the host countries?

Third: What is the development impact of international banking, particularly when it comes to access and inclusion? Does allowing foreign banks a larger share risk reducing the access and increasing the price of banking services to small and medium enterprises (SMEs) and lower income households? This is an old question, but not as much work has been devoted to it as has been to analyzing efficiency and stability concerns. Yet it is still one of the big policy questions.

And finally: What is the future going to look like? How do we expect technological advances and fin-tech to modify global banking? How would potential blurring of cross-border and brick and mortar banking change our answers to the questions above? What should financial regulation and supervision look like in a world in which international banking is much larger?

Overall financial globalization, including banking globalization, can lead to important trade-offs. The challenge of policy will be to maximize the benefits of bank internationalization while minimizing the costs. It is an exciting agenda, which we will be working on over the coming years.

References

Alfaro, Laura, Gonzalo Asis, Anusha Chari, and Ugo Panizza. 2016. "Lessons Learned? Corporate Debt in Emerging Markets." NBER Working Paper 3407, National Bureau of Economic Research, Cambridge, MA.

Ayyagari, Meghana, Aslı Demirgüç-Kunt, and Vojislav Maksimovic. 2013. "Financing in Developing Countries." In *Handbook of the Economics of Finance*, volume 2B, edited by George Constantinides, Milton Harris, and Rene Stulz, 683–757. Boston: Elsevier.

Bertay, Ata, Aslı Demirgüç-Kunt, and Harry Huizinga. 2015. "Bank Ownership and Credit over the Business Cycle: Is Lending by State Banks Less Procyclical?" *Journal of Banking and Finance* 50 (C): 326–339.

Broner, Fernando, Tatiana Didier, Aitor Erce, and Sergio L. Schmukler. 2013. "Gross Capital Flows: Dynamics and Crises." *Journal of Monetary Economics* 60 (1): 113–133.

Bruno, Valentina, and Hyun Song Shin. 2015. "Global Dollar Credit and Carry Trades: A Firm-Level Analysis." BIS Working Paper 510, Bank for International Settlements, Basel.

Cihak, Martin, and Aslı Demirgüç-Kunt. 2014. "Revisiting the State's Role in Finance and Development." In *Handbook of Banking*, second edition, edited by Allen N. Berger, Philip Molyneux, and John O. S. Wilson, 777–806. New York: Oxford University Press.

Cortina, Juan Jose, Tatiana Didier, and Sergio L. Schmukler. 2016. "How Long Is the Maturity of Corporate Borrowing? Evidence from Bond and Loan Issuances across Markets." Policy Research Working Paper 7815, World Bank, Washington, DC.

Cull, Robert, Aslı Demirgüç-Kunt, and Jonathan Morduch. 2011. "Microfinance Tradeoffs: Regulation, Competition, and Financing." In *Handbook of Microfinance*, edited by Beatriz Armendariz and Marc Labie, 141–157. Hackensack, NJ: World Scientific.

Demirgüç-Kunt, Aslı, and Ross Levine. 2008. "Finance, Financial Sector Policies, and Long Run Growth." M. Spence Growth Commission Background Paper 11, Washington, DC.

Demirgüç-Kunt, Aslı, and Ross Levine. 2009. "Finance and Inequality: Theory and Evidence." *Annual Review of Financial Economics* 1: 287–318.

Levine, Ross. 2005. "Finance and Growth: Theory and Evidence." In *Handbook of Economic Growth*, volume 1A, edited by Philippe Aghion and Steven Durlauf, 865–934. Amsterdam, Boston: Elsevier, North-Holland.

World Bank. 2015. *Global Financial Development Report 2015/16: Long-Term Finance*. Washington, DC: World Bank.

World Bank. 2018. *Global Financial Development Report 2017/18: Banker without Borders*. Washington, DC: World Bank.

Comment: Maurice Obstfeld

Thank you, Kaushik, for inviting me to comment on this chapter by Hyun Song Shin. It's always a pleasure to come across 19th Street to the World Bank. This is a very nice chapter that summarizes and brings together material about global liquidity and credit that Hyun Song Shin and the Bank for International Settlements (BIS), more generally, have been calling to our attention for a while. There are two main themes. One is that US financial conditions drive global conditions. The second is that the US dollar's value is a key barometer of global liquidity conditions and hence of risk taking.[4] In establishing propositions one and two above, the chapter looks at a number of pieces of evidence, such as CIP deviations, US dollar denominated bank lending data, and sovereign CDS spreads. The underlying driver put forth to explain the facts is that the US dollar has a unique role as an international currency: as an invoice currency, as a funding currency, as a vehicle currency, and as a reserve currency.

My comments will be based on four observations, some of which are macro comments and some are finance comments. Before covering these, let me flag the chapters's important observation with respect to CIP deviations. My interest in this should not be a surprise, given that my textbook (Krugman, Obstfeld, and Melitz 2017) is one that commits the sin of claiming that CIP holds (more precisely, held quite closely for about three decades up until the 2008–2009 global financial crisis). We will have to be

I gratefully acknowledge helpful assistance from and discussions with Eugenio Cerutti. All opinions and errors are mine alone.
4. One subtheme in the chapter that was not emphasized is that the euro and yen may be growing in international importance. I won't have time to go into this issue, but I'm a bit skeptical, given the challenges that those economies currently face.

sure in the next edition of the book to acknowledge more fully the seeming arbitrage opportunities that have persisted long after the end of the crisis; more on these below.

My *first* observation concerns the relation between the exchange rate and the current account. Even in theory, a current account deficit does not necessarily signal future depreciation over any specific time frame. Even in the simplest model with perfect substitution among assets, and where portfolio effects therefore are not important, the relationship is not straightforward. A current account deficit could arise because of a fall in foreign demand or a rise in domestic demand, and these two events will have completely opposite effects on the exchange rate and output in the short run. The point is that the exchange rate movements are going to be endogenous, so we cannot really speak of an exchange rate change leading to a contractionary effect. This really depends on what is driving it. Now, if we go to the kind of world that Hyun is talking about, where there are also two-way gross capital flows and a rich array of different assets and liabilities traded, then indeed, life is going to become much more complicated. We can think about portfolio shifts between asset classes, possibly due to changes in preferences, policy liquidity conditions, and the like. But here again, currency appreciation need not be contractionary, as a more traditional approach to international economics might indicate through its exclusive focus on the net export effect. For example, one very important channel that Hyun and others have stressed arises from the presence of dollar liabilities, such that domestic net worth can increase when the currency appreciates. Any resulting easing of binding credit constraints will be expansionary. More recently, Olivier Blanchard and coauthors (Blanchard et al. 2016) have suggested a different channel. They look at nonbond inflows and show that these can be expansionary. So, more generally, I see here a very interesting research agenda that looks more deeply to understand the complex links among the current account, the exchange rate, and the macroeconomic conjuncture.

Let me turn to my *second* comment, which is about CIP violations. This is a fascinating anomaly. In perspective, there are many other asset market anomalies that have arisen since 2008, some of which do not obviously have much to do with the international economy specifically, but likely have to do with liquidity and asset markets in general. Part of the rethinking we've been doing since the global financial crisis centers on figuring

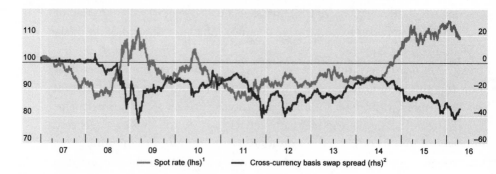

Figure 5.14
US dollar exchange rate and the cross-currency basis
[1]Simple average of bilateral exchange rate of the dollar against CAD, EUR, GBP, SEK, CHF and JPY. Higher values indicate stronger US dollar.
[2]Simple average of the five-year cross-currency basis swaps against CAD, EUR, GBP, SEK, CHF, and JPY vis-à-vis the US dollar.
Sources: Bloomberg; BIS calculations. This chart is from S. Avdjiev, W. Du, C. Koch, and H. S. Shin, 2016. Exchange rates, currency hedging and the cross-currency basis.

out how things that we thought were true and obvious seem not so true or obvious anymore. But CIP is a particularly fascinating case, because, since Keynes (1923) first explained covered interest parity in 1923, it has been an article of faith (despite deviations over long stretches, when currency markets and international arbitrage were restricted). But what you see in figure 5.14, which is a repeat of figure 5.2 from the Shin chapter, is that since the global financial crisis, CIP no longer works very well. The upper line graphs an average exchange rate against the dollar, and when it rises, the US dollar appreciates. The lower line is the swap basis, which as Hyun explains, is the difference between the gross LIBOR interest rate, which is denoted $1 + i_{US}$, and the covered foreign gross interest rate. This gap has generally been negative and substantial in absolute magnitude since the financial crisis. Why? Hyun argues that the gap shrinks when the dollar is weaker—and presumably when Fed policy is relatively easy—owing to the easier global liquidity conditions that result. My guess, however, is that different factors are of greater or lesser importance over different periods.[5]

---

5. For an exploration of the changing factors driving CIP deviations over time, see Cerutti, Obstfeld, and Zhou (2019).

For example, we see a big widening of the swap basis in the period of the euro crisis. During that period, the dollar is actually somewhat weak, compared to its period average, because this is also the period before the temper tantrum unwinds. So it is likely that the story is more complex than in Hyun's account—other things may be going on. One very interesting theory, one that focuses on the euro crisis, is told by Ivashina, Scharfstein, and Stein (2015). Interestingly, it is based on a structural factor that is very central to Hyun's story: the large extent of dollar financial intermediation in the world economy. Ivashina and coauthors point out that European banks have a structural deficit of US dollar funding in the sense that they want to lend a lot of dollars, but their natural (explicitly and implicitly insured) deposit base, which therefore is somewhat cheaper to tap, is in euros. Please look at figure 5.15, based on a paper out of the IMF Research Department by Eugenio Cerutti and coauthors. As you can see, there is a lot of bank lending to emerging markets, euro area banks play a key role, and they lend predominantly in US dollars. This snapshot is very consistent with the story that Hyun is telling.

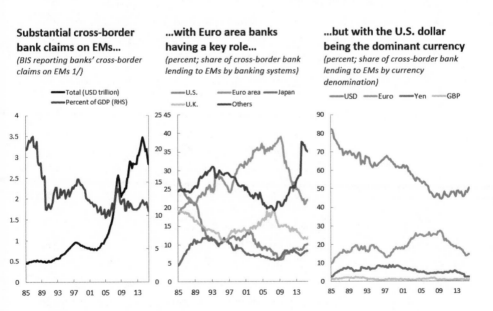

Figure 5.15

Cross-border bank lending to emerging markets

Sources: BIS Banking Statistics; and Cerutti, Claessens, and Ratnovski (2017). The sample of emerging markets includes 49 large emerging markets.

So, what do these banks do when they have a deposit base in euros, but they want to lend US dollars? They borrow euros and swap them into dollars, and then they can keep rolling over those swaps. This imbalance, however, gives rise to a structural excess supply of forward dollars, and thus, the pattern of CIP deviations that Hyun has shown us. Why does classical arbitrage not eliminate these gaps? Given even small repayment frictions, but in a much different environment since the global financial crisis, limits to arbitrage (which can be due to liquidity, limited capital, market structure, etc.) allow CIP gaps to persist. In the Ivashina, Scharfstein, and Stein (2015) work, when euro area banks become more stressed, as they certainly seem to be now, they may find that the comparative advantage of euro over US dollar funding rises, which will induce them to do more synthetic US dollar borrowing through the swap market. The result of what is basically a demand effect will push up the cost of such funding.

Hyun's chapter does not go into a lot of detail here, but my reading is that he puts more emphasis on the suppliers of these swaps, which are likely to be other banks. These banks also face limited capital and other impediments to arbitrage, impediments that recede when US monetary policy is easier. So, both forces—demand and supply—are going to be in play. The big central banks have recently changed the architecture of some of these markets quite substantially through the introduction of standing swap lines among themselves, but it is unclear in the very short run whether disruptions could occur nonetheless. I would join Hyun in the plea for more research on this general topic, and more work on developing a general-equilibrium picture.

I would also observe, putting a macro hat back on, that there could be a real channel that works against Hyun's hypothesized mechanism. When the US dollar strengthens due to tighter Fed policy, the euro weakens, which has positive effects on the real euro area economy and thereby helps its banks. So a range of complex macro and financial effects are in play. One interesting question that Hyun does not address is evident from the figures in the chapter: some currencies (like sterling) have pretty small basis deviations, but for others they are quite large. For the Swiss franc, we see some huge spikes, because it is now a safe haven and the Swiss National Bank's interventions in currency markets have been associated with considerable turbulence. What is going on across currencies? We have no good sense of that, but the fact that euro area banks appear especially challenged should not surprise us.

My comment *number three* is also a macro comment: Is the US Federal Reserve really all-powerful? There are powerful global forces at work, but they also lie behind the global level of the natural real interest rate, and one can argue that the latter is driving monetary policies worldwide. Sure, the US dollar's role is important; but is it really the central fact here? I think back to the mid-2000s, when Alan Greenspan was lamenting the conundrum of raising short-term dollar interest rates, with little apparent impact on long-term dollar interest rates. At the same time, there was widespread discussion of global saving gluts and global imbalances, and the limits of US monetary policy in the face of those global flows, which were held to have depressed real interest rates worldwide. In light of current debates over the role of the Fed in the global economy, it is useful to recall those debates of the past decade.

In a related vein, Hyun mentions some work by his colleague Claudio Borio, and Hyun himself has also done some work along the same lines. A strand of macro-financial analysis, of which I think Hyun's chapter is representative, downplays the role of the Wicksellian natural or neutral real interest rate in favor of the primacy of financing conditions. That approach does help make sense of issues like US dollar funding and liquidity, is critical for short-term market dynamics, and certainly illuminates problems that macroeconomists missed before the global financial crisis. But the old conventional macroeconomic issues still remain important. For example, beyond other measures of financial conditions, we have seen that global real interest rates—mostly driven by nominal interest rates—have shown a powerful downward trend since at least the 1990s, as shown in figure 5.16, and macroeconomic flow factors seem likely to be key drivers.

When I think about the interaction of complex financing and macro issues, I find it helpful to remember Tobin's work, which was very influential at the time but at some level never became totally mainstream. Tobin's research program aimed to reconcile stock and flow equilibrium phenomena in models with a rich menu of assets. (See, for example, Tobin 1981.) Taking Tobin seriously, one would acknowledge the mutual consistency of stock equilibrium and flow equilibrium, as well as their tendency to interact over time and thereby determine the economy's dynamic path. The conditions of stock equilibrium matter, because changes there (for example, a rise in the portfolio demand for safe assets) change asset prices and affect flows of saving and investment, with effects that alter the entire future path of

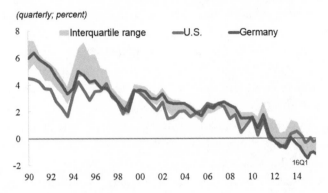

Figure 5.16

Global 10-year real interest rates

Notes: Calculated as nominal 10-year bond yields minus 10-year-ahead CPI inflation forecast (consensus forecast). Sample includes Australia, Canada, France, Germany, Italy, Japan, Netherlands, New Zealand, Norway, Spain, Sweden, Switzerland, United Kingdom, and United States.

Sources: IMF, *Global Data Source*; Bloomberg L.P.; and Consensus forecasts.

the economy. In contrast, the fundamental Wicksellian natural rate, which is established in the flow equilibrium of global saving and investment, is the foundation for the whole array of risky rates of return that the economy's available assets offer. If Tobin were here, he would certainly endorse adding realistic financial constraints and financing frictions to the models we use, as those also feed into the flow equilibrium. When I call for developing general-equilibrium models, I am calling for a reconciliation of the stock and flow points of view, because I do not think they are contradictory. However, it is important to recognize that in some situations, shocks to the flow equilibrium will dominate. For example, China's entry into the world economy is a stock story, but it also represents a big flow shock. It was a flow shock in the first instance, because China started out not being integrated into world markets. Now that China is rebalancing and is somewhat more integrated financially, we are seeing stock shocks galore emanating from China—some through direct Chinese financial relationships; most through expectation effects in foreign asset markets.

My *fourth* and final comment is on the implications of Hyun's findings for emerging market monetary independence. I will keep an open mind about the real-world pertinence of the following argument, but it is one implication of thinking hard about the questions on CIP that Hyun is raising. Assume the pattern that Hyun describes—of costs being lower when borrowing in the US currency market versus borrowing dollars by borrowing foreign currency, buying dollars with it, and using forward transactions to offset currency risk. Then $1 + i_{US} < \dfrac{F}{S}(1 + i^{\star})$, where F is the forward dollar price of the foreign currency, S is the spot dollar price of foreign currency, and $1 + i^{\star}$ is the gross foreign-currency interest rate. But in that case also, you get another inequality: $\left(\dfrac{F^{-1}}{S^{-1}}\right)(1 + i_{US}) < 1 + i^{\star}$. This expression states that if you reside in an emerging market and Hyun's pattern of forward rates, spot rates, and interest rates holds for emerging market currencies, then it is going to be cheaper to borrow US dollars and swap into local currency than to borrow local currency. Importantly, however, this will be true not because the dollar borrowing rate is low, but because domestic financial frictions make the effective domestic-currency borrowing rate high. This idea is also consistent with other research on the prevalence of swap-covered foreign borrowing in some emerging markets (for example, Munro and Wooldridge 2009). Clearly further research is needed, but one implication concerns the transmission to emerging markets of changes in US monetary policy. Imagine that the US raises interest rates: i_{US} goes up, and the emerging market central bank raises its short term interest rate to match that. If Hyun's empirical regularity holds—the swap basis rises when US monetary policy tightens—then the basis gap will widen, making it relatively more attractive to borrow US dollars and swap into domestic currency. In turn, this widening has the effect of cushioning the impact of the domestic interest rate rise on domestic financial conditions. Is this correct? If so, is it likely to be important? In truth, I have no idea. But the possibility illustrates that in this world where CIP does not hold, the process through which US dollar liquidity conditions are transmitted across borders—particularly to emerging markets—is likely to be complex and subtle and involve transmission mechanisms that we do not yet fully understand.

In sum, Shin's chapter is very useful and thought provoking, one that will surely help to encourage much future research.

References

Blanchard, Olivier, Jonathan D. Ostry, Atish R. Ghosh, and Marcos Chamon. 2016. "Capital Flows: Expansionary or Contractionary?" *American Economic Review, Papers and Proceedings* 106 (5): 565–569.

Cerutti, Eugenio, Stijn Claessens, and Lev Ratnovski. 2017. "Global Liquidity and Cross-Border Banking Flows." *Economic Policy* 89 (32): 81–125.

Cerutti, Eugenio, Maurice Obstfeld, and Haonan Zhou. 2019. "Covered Interest Parity Deviations: Macrofinancial Determinants." IMF Working Paper 19–14, January.

Ivashina, Victoria, David S. Scharfstein, and Jeremy C. Stein. 2015. "Dollar Funding and the Lending Behavior of Global Banks." *Quarterly Journal of Economics* 130 (3): 1241–1281.

Keynes, John Maynard. 1923. *A Tract on Monetary Reform.* London: Macmillan.

Krugman, Paul, Maurice Obstfeld, and Marc Melitz. 2017. *International Economics: Theory and Policy*, eleventh edition. New York: Pearson.

Munro, Anella, and Philip Wooldridge. 2009. "Motivations for Swap-Covered Foreign Borrowing." BIS Symposium on Internationalisation of Asia-Pacific Bond Markets, Paper One.

Tobin, James. 1981. "Money and Finance in the Macroeconomic Process." Nobel Memorial Lecture, December, Stockholm. http://www.nobelprize.org/nobel_prizes /economic-sciences/laureates/1981/tobin-lecture.pdf.

6 Growth and Development from a Schumpeterian Perspective

Philippe Aghion

Thirty years ago, Peter Howitt and I elaborated a new theory, now known as the "Schumpeterian theory," of economic growth. Why did we need a new theory of economic growth? What did we find unsatisfactory with the dominant theory at the time, both theoretically and empirically?

In this chapter, we shall revisit some current debates about the growth and development process and about growth policy design, using the lenses of the Schumpeterian growth paradigm.

Thus, in the first part of this chapter, I touch on four open questions on which the Schumpeterian approach sheds new light: the relationship between competition and innovation-led growth, the debate on secular stagnation, the recent rise in top income inequality, and firm dynamics.

In the second part of the chapter, I argue that the Schumpeterian growth paradigm can be used to further bridge the existing gap between growth and development economics.

And finally, in a third part, I will show how the paradigm can be used to think about (or rethink) growth policy design.

Why Elaborate a New Theory of Economic Growth?

During my student years, the dominant paradigm in growth economics was the neoclassical growth model, which would be taught first under the assumption of a constant savings rate (the Solow model) and then in the context of an economy where a representative consumer decides about consumption, savings, and investment by maximizing her intertemporal utility (the Ramsey-Cass-Koopmans model).

The Solow model is the true template in growth economics, just as Modigliani-Miller is the benchmark in corporate finance. This is first due to it being a model of elegance and parsimony: The whole dynamics of the economy is described in two equations. The second reason is that the model shows very clearly why there can be no long-run growth without technical progress. The model was published in 1956 (I was born that same year) and was rewarded by a Nobel Prize to its author in 1987.

No need to go into the details of this model, which economists all know too well. But in a nutshell, the model describes an economy where final output is produced using capital as input, and where therefore it is the accumulation of capital that generates output growth. This corresponds to the first equation of the model. Then the question is: Where does capital accumulation come from? This in turn is answered with the second equation of the model: from savings (aggregate savings equal aggregate investment in equilibrium), and savings in the Solow model are a constant fraction of final output (i.e., of aggregate GDP).

You might think that everything should go well in such an economy: More capital stock financed by savings will produce more final output, which will translate into more savings (as savings are proportional to final output) and therefore in still more capital stock, and so on.

The problem is that we run into decreasing returns when trying to increase output by increasing the capital stock: The higher the existing stock of capital (number of machines) is, the lower will be the marginal increase in output from increasing the stock of capital by one unit (i.e., from adding one more machine). Thus, the lower the increase in savings and therefore the lower the induced increase in capital stock will be.

At some moment, the process of capital accumulation runs out of steam (it stops when capital depreciation catches up with marginal savings), at which point the economy stops growing. To generate sustained long-term economic growth, there must be continuous technical progress to increase the quality (productivity) of machines. But Solow does not tell us where technical progress is coming from.

In addition, if the model predicts conditional convergence, it does not give us the tools to understand why the distribution of per capita income has kept spreading out over time, why some countries converge to the standards of living (per capita GDP) of developed countries whereas other countries do not converge, or why some countries start converging and then stop at midway. It does not explain why some countries with lower capital stocks grow less rapidly than other countries with higher capital stocks, or why capital does not necessarily flow from rich to poor countries (the so-called Lucas Paradox).

Moreover, the model does not look at growth from the point of view of firms and entrepreneurs: How does growth relate to the size distribution of firms, to the creation and destruction of firms and jobs, to firm dynamics more generally? It does not provide keys to understand how institutions or policies affect growth by affecting innovation and entrepreneurship.

These shortcomings motivated Peter Howitt and I to elaborate a new paradigm.

The Schumpeterian Paradigm

The paradigm Howitt and I formalized in the fall of 1987 revolved around three important ideas laid out by the Austrian economist Joseph Schumpeter.[1]

First idea: Long-run growth is primarily generated by innovations (this is the natural counterpart of Solow's conclusion that no long-run growth can be expected without sustained technological progress).

Second idea: Innovations result from entrepreneurial investments (R&D, training, computer purchase, and so forth), and entrepreneurs respond to the economic incentives (positive or negative) that result from economic policies and economic institutions. Thus, innovation-based growth typically will be discouraged in environments with poor property right protection or with hyperinflation, as these conditions will damage the profitability from innovation. In other words, innovation-based growth is a social process, and we can talk about policies of growth and institutions of growth.

Third idea: creative destruction. New innovations replace old technologies, and Schumpeterian growth is a conflictual process between the old and the new: It tells the story of all these incumbent firms and interests that permanently try to prevent or delay the entry of new competitors in their sector. Hence there is something called "the political economy of growth."

Thus, a first distinctive prediction of the Schumpeterian growth model is that firm or job turnover should be positively correlated with productivity growth. Another distinctive implication of the model is that innovation-led growth may be excessive under laissez-faire. Growth is excessive (resp.

---

1. See Aghion and Howitt (1992).

insufficient) under laissez-faire when the business-stealing effect associated with creative destruction dominates (resp. is dominated by) the intertemporal knowledge spillovers from current to future innovators.

Four Growth Enigmas

In this section, I show how the Schumpeterian paradigm can be used to shed light on four important enigmas associated with the growth process: (1) the relationship between competition and innovation-led growth, (2) the debate on secular stagnation, (3) the dynamics of income inequality, and (4) firm dynamics.

Competition and Innovation-Led Growth

Our original model predicted that more competition should be detrimental to growth by reducing monopoly rents from innovation and thus entrepreneurs' incentives to invest in innovation in the first place (incidentally, this latter argument has been used by Bill Gates when facing antitrust action). However, Blundell, Griffith, and Van Reenen (1995, 1999) used UK firm-level data to regress firm-level innovation intensity and/or productivity growth on the degree of product market competition in the firm's sector. And they found a positive correlation between competition and innovation/growth.

How could we reconcile theory and evidence? Should we just dismiss the Schumpeterian paradigm and start again from scratch? Should we simply ignore the empirical evidence? I went for a third way: to look more closely at the model and try to identify the assumption or assumptions that generate this counterfactual prediction of a negative relationship between competition and growth.[2]

Having tried several alternative stories,[3] we finally identified the main culprit: In our initial model, only currently inactive firms innovate, not the currently active firms (i.e., not the current technological leaders). Thus, an innovating firm in our model would move from zero profit (pre-innovation) to a positive profit (post-innovation). Then, not surprisingly, competition

---

2. See Aghion, Harris, and Vickers (1997) and Aghion et al. (2001).
3. For example, see Aghion, Dewatripont, and Rey (1999).

would discourage innovation: Competition reduces the post-innovation profit, which here is equal to the net profit from innovation.

However, in practice we find at least two types of firms in most sectors of the economy, and these two types of firms do not react in the same way to increased competition. You first have what we call "frontier firms," that is, firms that are close to the current technological frontier in their sector. These firms are currently active, and they make substantial profits even before innovating this period. Second, you have what we call the "laggard firms," which are firms far below the current technological frontier. These firms make low profits and try to catch up with the current technology frontier.

To try to understand why these two types of firms react differently to competition, imagine for a moment that what you are looking at are not firms but students in a classroom. And among them, you have the top students and the bottom of the class. And suppose that you are opening the class to an additional student, who turns out to be a very good student. This is how I represent an increase in competition in this context. How will the students react to this new student joining the classroom? The answer (here I refer to important work by Caroline Hoxby, who studied precisely this scenario) is that letting the new student in will encourage the other top students to work harder to remain the best, whereas it will further discourage students at the bottom of the class, as they will find it even harder to catch up.

Quite strikingly, firms react like classroom students: Faced with a higher degree of competition in their sector, firms that are close to the technology frontier will innovate more to escape competition, whereas firms that are far from the technological frontier and try to catch up will be discouraged by the higher degree of competition, and as a result innovate less: the latter firms behave like those in the basic Schumpeterian model.

Overall, the effect of competition on innovation and productivity growth is an inverted U, which synthetizes the positive escape competition effect and the negative discouragement effect. The prediction of opposite reactions of frontier versus nonfrontier firms to competition, and of an inverted U overall, were tested and confirmed in joint work with Richard Blundell, Nick Bloom, and Rachel Griffith (see Aghion et al. 2005) using the same kind of firm-level data as in the empirical studies I mentioned above.

To reconcile theory with evidence, we extended our basic Schumpeterian model by allowing for step-by-step innovation in the Schumpeterian growth model.[4] Namely, a firm that is currently behind the technological leader in the same sector or industry must catch up with the leader before becoming a leader itself. This step-by-step assumption implies that firms in some sectors will be neck-and-neck. In turn, in such sectors, increased product market competition, by making life more difficult for neck-and-neck firms, will encourage them to innovate to acquire a lead over their rival in the sector. This we refer to as the "escape competition effect." In contrast, in unleveled sectors where firms are not neck-and-neck, increased product market competition will tend to discourage innovation by laggard firms, as it decreases the short-run extra profit from catching up with the leader. This we call the "Schumpeterian effect." Finally, the steady-state fraction of neck-and-neck sectors will itself depend on the innovation intensities in neck-and-neck versus unleveled sectors. This we refer to as the "composition effect."

This extended model predicts that in the aggregate, the relationship between competition and innovation should follow an inverted-U pattern. Intuitively, when competition is low, innovation intensity is low in neck-and-neck sectors; therefore most sectors in the economy are neck-and-neck (the composition effect). But it is in precisely those sectors that the escape competition effect dominates. Thus overall aggregate innovation increases with competition at low levels of competition. When competition is high, innovation intensity is high in neck-and-neck sectors. Therefore most sectors in the economy are unleveled sectors, so that the Schumpeterian effect dominates overall. This inverted-U prediction is confirmed by Aghion et al. (2005), using panel data on UK firms.

The prediction that more intense competition enhances innovation in frontier firms but may discourage it in nonfrontier firms was tested by Aghion et al. (2009a), again using panel data on UK firms.

Another prediction from our extended model is that there is complementarity between patent protection and product market competition in fostering innovation. Intuitively, competition reduces the profit flow of non-innovating neck-and-neck firms, whereas patent protection is likely to enhance the profit flow of an innovating neck-and-neck firm. Both contribute to raising the net profit gain of an innovating neck-and-neck firm;

---

4. See Aghion, Harris, and Vickers (1997) and Aghion et al. (2001).

in other words, both types of policies tend to enhance the escape competition effect.

That competition and patent protection should be complementary in enhancing growth rather than mutually exclusive is at odds both with our first model and with Romer (1990), where competition is always detrimental to innovation and growth (as we discussed above) for exactly the same reason that intellectual property rights in the form of patent protection are good for innovation: Namely, competition reduces post-innovation rents, whereas patent protection increases these rents. But it is also at odds with Boldrin and Levine (2008), who hold that patent protection is always detrimental to innovation and growth in their model where competition is good for growth.

Our prediction of a complementarity between competition and patent protection was tested by Aghion, Howitt, and Prantl (2013) using OECD country-industry panel data.

The Debate on Secular Stagnation
In 1938, economist Alvin Hansen explained in his presidential address before the American Economic Association[5] that in his opinion, the United States faced inexorable weak growth in the long term. The nation was just emerging from the Great Depression, and Hansen did not anticipate another world war that would stimulate a rebound in public spending and thereby of aggregate demand.

Since then, we have experienced another major financial crisis, the 2007–2008 crisis, which led Larry Summers (2013) and others to revive the expression "secular stagnation" to characterize a situation that they assimilated to the one described by Hansen in 1938. Summers's argument is that investment demand was so weak that negative interest rates were necessary for a return to full employment.

Robert Gordon (2012), however, believes that the risk of secular stagnation reflects a supply problem. Gordon proposes that the age of great innovations is past. He uses the metaphor of a fruit tree: The low-hanging fruit is the best; after that, the fruit is harder to pick and less juicy.

Schumpeterian economists are more optimistic about the future than Summers and Gordon are. A first argument (Jorgenson) is that the

---

5. See Hansen (1939).

revolution in information and communications technologies (ICT) has radically and durably improved IT-producing technology; meanwhile, globalization (which was concomitant with the ICT revolution) has substantially increased the potential returns on innovation—the scale effect—as well as the potential downside of not innovating—the competition effect. A second argument against the secular stagnation view is that we have witnessed an acceleration in innovation over the past several decades, which has not been fully reflected by measured productivity growth.

In particular, Aghion et al. (2017) argue that innovation involving creative destruction is not properly taken into account by current measures of total-factor productivity (TFP) growth. Whenever old products in the producer price index are replaced by new entrants, statistical offices typically resort to imputation. For each product category in the economy, imputation uses the rate of quality-adjusted price growth for a set of surviving products in that category (i.e., products that were not subject to creative destruction) to compute the inflation rate for the whole product category.

Using the Schumpeterian growth paradigm, together with the assumption that the statistical office cannot observe the innovation coming from creative destruction and instead computes the aggregate quality-adjusted price growth for the entire economy as being equal to the average price growth over existing products that are not subject to creative destruction, Aghion et al. (2017) provide an explicit expression for economywide missing growth from creative destruction. Then they use this expression to quantify missing growth based on two different approaches. In the first exercise, they use micro data from the US Census on the employment shares of incumbents, entrants, and exiters in all nonfarm business sectors. In the second exercise, they use data on the flow and quality of patents (exploiting information from patent citations) to directly estimate the arrival rates and step sizes of the various kinds of innovations and from there calculate the missing productivity growth from imputation. These two exercises yield missing growth of comparable magnitudes, of about 0.5 percentage points on average per year over the past 30 years.

My third and last argument for optimism regarding future growth prospects is also based on the observation that many countries have taken only belated and incomplete advantage of technological advances (e.g., because of structural rigidities or inappropriate economic policies).

We do not question the existence of long-run technological waves, with their acceleration and slowdown phases. These waves are typically associated with the diffusion of new general purpose technologies, defined as generic technologies that affect most sectors of the economy.[6] Obvious examples include steam energy in the early and mid-nineteenth century, electricity and chemistry in the early twentieth century, and the information and communication technology revolution in the 1980s.

And indeed, using annual and quarterly data for 1890–2012 on labor productivity and TFP for 13 advanced countries (the G7 plus Spain, the Netherlands, Finland, Australia, Sweden, and Norway) plus the reconstituted euro area, Bergeaud, Cette, and Lecat (2014) show the existence of two big productivity growth waves during this period. The first wave culminates in 1941, the second culminates in 2001. The first wave corresponds to the second industrial revolution: that of electricity, internal combustion, and chemistry. The second wave is the ICT wave.

However, Cette and Lopez (2012) show that the euro area and Japan experienced the waves with a lag compared to the United States. Thus the first wave fully diffused to the current euro area, Japan, and the United Kingdom only post–World War II. As for the second productivity wave, so far it has not shown up in the Euro area or in Japan. Moreover, through an econometric analysis, Cette and Lopez show that this lag of ICT diffusion in Europe and Japan, compared to the United States, is explained by institutional aspects: a lower educational level, on average, of the working-age population and more regulations on labor and product markets. This in turn suggests that by implementing structural reforms, these countries could benefit from a productivity acceleration linked to a catch-up to the US ICT diffusion level. The lower quality of research and higher education in the euro area and Japan compared to the United States also appears to matter for explaining the diffusion lag.

One can contrast the evolution of TFP in Sweden versus Japan over the past decades. In particular, there has been a positive break in TFP growth in Sweden after 1990, in contrast with the case of Japan, where we see no such break but instead decelerating TFP growth since 1980. Our explanation is that Sweden implemented sweeping structural reforms in the early 1990s:

---

6. See Bresnahan and Trajtenberg (1995).

in particular, a reform of the public spending system to reduce public deficits and a tax reform to encourage labor supply and entrepreneurship. No significant reform has taken place in Japan over the past 30 years.

To conclude this discussion on secular stagnation, although we do not question the existence of long-run technological waves, what leads us to be somewhat more optimistic than Gordon is that (1) the ICT revolution has improved the technology to produce ideas, and globalization has increased the potential rents to successful innovators; (2) measured TFP growth does not properly take into account innovation involving creative destruction; and (3) some developed countries, particularly in Europe, have not yet implemented the structural reforms that would allow them to fully take advantage of the most recent wave of innovation.

Innovation, Inequality, and Social Mobility

Over recent decades, developed nations have experienced an accelerated increase in income inequality, especially at the top tier, with the top 1 percent capturing a rapidly growing share of total income.[7] What explains this evolution?

Figure 6.1 compares the evolution of innovation in the United States since 1960 (as measured by the number of patents registered annually with the United States Patent and Trademark Office), with extreme inequality (as measured by the share of income attributed to the top 1 percent of earners). The similarity in the two curves (innovation and the top 1 percent's share of income) is striking.

A new study by Antonin Bergeaud, Richard Blundell, Ufuk Akcigit, David Hemous, and myself[8] shows that this strong correlation reflects a causal link between innovation and extreme inequality: Income from innovation contributes significantly to the increase in the share of income going to the top 1 percent.

The observation that the observed increase in the top 1 percent results in part from innovation, and not solely from returns from real estate and speculation, provides an important insight, because innovation has virtues that the other sources of high income do not necessarily share.

---

7. See Atkinson, Piketty, and Saez (2011) and Piketty (2013).
8. See Aghion et al. (2015a).

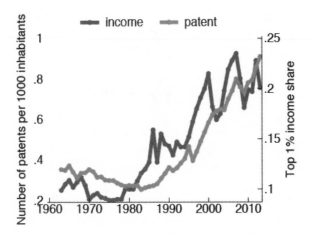

Figure 6.1
Evolution of top income share and patents per capita in the United States
Source: Aghion et al. (2015b).

First, as previously mentioned, innovation is the main motor of growth in developed economies. Second, although in the short term innovation benefits those who generated or enabled the innovation, in the long term its returns are dissipated due to imitation and creative destruction. In other words, the inequality induced by innovation is temporary. Third, because of the link between innovation and creative destruction, innovation generates social mobility: It enables new talent to enter the market and to displace (partially or totally) the firms in place. Thus in the United States, California (currently the most innovative state in the union) far outpaces Alabama (which is among the least innovating states) both in terms of the inequality of income going to the top 1 percent and in terms of social mobility.

The two figures below are especially eloquent. Figure 6.2 describes the relationship between innovation and social mobility by comparing American municipalities. Social mobility is defined as the probability that an individual from a modest background (i.e., one whose parents were in the lowest quintile in the earnings scale between 1996 and 2000) will reach the highest quintile in 2010 on reaching adulthood (based on the work of Chetty et al. (2014)). Innovation is measured by the number of patents filed with the United States Patent and Trademark Office per resident in the municipality. The resulting graph shows a strong positive correlation between innovation and social mobility.

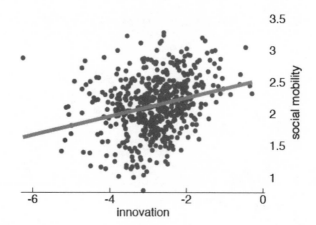

Figure 6.2
Relationship between innovation and social mobility across municipalities in the
United States
Source: Aghion et al. (2015b).

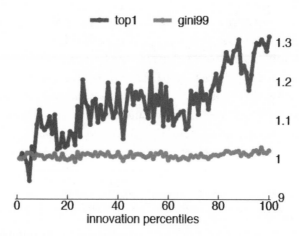

Figure 6.3
No correlation between innovation and the Gini measure of inequality
Source: Aghion et al. (2015b).

Figure 6.3 shows that there is no correlation between innovation and the
broader measures of inequality, such as the Gini coefficient, which measures the deviation between the actual distribution of income in an economy and a perfectly equal distribution.

By taking into account all pieces of the puzzle, we can respond to the
question of whether we should object to innovation on the grounds that it

contributes to income inequality. The response is no, because innovation generates growth. It does not increase inequality in broader terms; instead, it stimulates social mobility. As a corollary to this discussion, tax policy must differentiate between innovation and other sources of top income. Put differently, we must distinguish between a Steve Jobs and a Carlos Slim. Tax policy that discourages innovation would not only inhibit growth but also reduce social mobility, whereas innovation does not increase inequality measured broadly.

Firm Dynamics and Economic Development

The empirical literature has documented various stylized facts about firm size distribution and firm dynamics using micro firm-level data. In particular: (1) the firm size distribution is highly skewed; (2) firm size and firm age are highly correlated; and (3) small firms exit more frequently, but the ones that survive tend to grow faster than the average growth rate.

These are all facts that non-Schumpeterian growth models cannot account for. In particular, the first four facts listed require a new firm to enter, expand, then shrink over time, and eventually be replaced by new entrants: These and the last fact on the importance of reallocation are all embodied in the Schumpeterian idea of creative destruction.

The Schumpeterian model by Klette and Kortum (2004) can account for these facts. This model adds two elements to the baseline model: First, innovations come from both entrants and incumbents; and second, firms are defined as a collection of production units where successful innovations by incumbents will allow them to expand in product space (see figure 6.4).

This model allows us to explain the above stylized facts:

Prediction 1:   The size distribution of firms is highly skewed.

Recall that in this model, firm size is summarized by the number of product lines of a firm. Hence, to become large, a firm needs to have succeeded in many of its attempts to innovate in new lines and at the same to have survived many attempts by potential entrants and other incumbents at taking over its existing lines. This is turn explains why there are so few very large firms in steady-state equilibrium (i.e., why firm size distribution is highly skewed), as shown in a vast empirical literature.

Prediction 2:   Firm size and firm age are positively correlated.

In the model, firms are born with a size of 1. Subsequent successes are required for firms to grow in size, which naturally produces a positive correlation between size and age. This regularity has been documented extensively in the literature.

Prediction 3:   Small firms exit more frequently. The ones that survive tend to grow faster than average.

In the above model, it takes only one successful entry to make a one-product firm exit, whereas it takes two successful innovations by potential entrants to make a two-product firm exit. The facts that small firms exit more frequently and grow faster conditional on survival have been widely documented in the literature.

Various versions of this framework have been estimated using micro-level data by Lentz and Mortensen (2008), Acemoglu et al. (2013), and Akcigit and Kerr (2010).[9]

In more recent work, Acemoglu et al. (2013) analyze the effects of various industrial policies on equilibrium productivity growth, including entry subsidy and incumbent R&D subsidy, in an enriched version of the above framework. Their extended framework also sheds new light on whether or how one should conduct industrial policy. In particular, allowing for high- and low-ability innovators, they argue that subsidizing incumbent firms has a detrimental effect on aggregate innovation and productivity growth by inducing a bias in favor of (low-ability) incumbents at the expense of high-ability entrants.

Growth Meets Development

Michael Kremer, Abhijit Banerjee, and Esther Duflo have revolutionized development economics by introducing experimental random methods of analysis drawn from pharmaceutical science to evaluate the effectiveness of new medicines and vaccines.[10] In particular, their work has enabled us to understand better the behavior of individuals and households in extreme poverty and to see how they react to different policies of aid and assistance.

However, this line of research suffers from two main limitations. First, firms and firm dynamics play little role in these analyses of the development process. Second, the link between micro and macro development is

---

9. See Aghion, Akcigit, and Howitt (2014) and Akcigit and Kerr (2010) for more references.
10. See Banerjee and Duflo (2012).

not fully spelled out. However, my own view is that one cannot disregard macroeconomic and systemic factors, or the effects of firm dynamics and resource reallocation, when the goal is to eradicate poverty at a national or regional level.

To see why macroeconomics matters, consider the following example. The rate of poverty in urban zones of India (the fraction of the population living on less than $1 per day) fell from 39 percent in 1987–1988 to 12 percent in 1999–2000. Over the same period, growth took off: From less than 0.8 percent in the mid-1980s, it climbed to 3.2 percent in the 1990s. This upswing in growth in India resulted less from local actions than from systemic reforms, such as the liberalization of trade and of the market for goods and services, with the suppression of the "raj license."[11]

But looking at the systemic and macroeconomic aspects of a problem by no means implies that we should ignore the microeconomic aspects, in particular, at the level of the firm or sector. Specifically, our discussion of growth enigmas in the previous section has implications for how Schumpeterian growth theory can help bridge the gap between growth and development economics: first, by capturing the idea that growth-enhancing policies or institutions vary with a country's level of technological development; and second, by analyzing how institutional development (or the lack of it) affects firm size distribution and firm dynamics.

Appropriate Institutions and the Transition Trap

In 1890, Argentina enjoyed a GDP per capita approximately 40 percent that of the United States, which made it a middle-income country. This level was three times the GDP per capita of Brazil and Colombia and equivalent to that of Japan at the time. Argentina sustained this level of 40 percent of the GDP per capita of the United States through the 1930s. To be precise, Chow's test (a statistical test) shows a break around 1938, after which Argentina's productivity declines relative to American productivity by approximately 21 percent per year. What explains this drop-off?

Schumpeterian growth theory offers the following explanation. Countries like Argentina either had institutions or had implemented policies (in particular, import substitution) that fostered growth by accumulation of capital and economic catch-up. They did not, however, adapt their

---

11. See Aghion et al. (2008).

institutions to enable them to become innovating economies. As demonstrated in joint work with Daron Acemoglu and Fabrizio Zilibotti,[12] the greater the level of development is in a country (i.e., the closer it gets to the technology frontier), the greater the role of cutting edge innovation becomes as the motor of growth, replacing accumulation and technological catch-up.

This phenomenon also exists in Asia. Japan, where the state has always tightly controlled competition, is another example: Japan's Ministry of Economy, Trade and Industry caps the number of import permits, and the state subsidizes investment by the big industrial-financial consortia known as keiretsu. It is thus not surprising that from an extremely high level between 1945 and 1985—the envy of other developed countries—Japan's growth has fallen to a very low level since 1985.

In the previous subsection, I discussed the prediction that competition and free entry should be more growth enhancing in more frontier firms, which implies that they should be more growth enhancing in more advanced countries, because such countries have a larger proportion of frontier firms. Similarly, using a cross-country panel of more than 100 countries over the 1960–2000 period, Acemoglu, Aghion, and Zilibotti (2006) test the following predictions from the Schumpeterian prediction between imitation and innovation-driven growth:

Prediction 1: Average growth should decrease more rapidly as a country approaches the world frontier when openness is low.

Acemoglu, Aghion, and Zilibotti (2006) repeat the same exercise using entry costs faced by new firms instead of openness. They show:

Prediction 2: High entry barriers become increasingly detrimental to growth as the country approaches the frontier.

These two empirical exercises point to the importance of interacting institutions or policies with technological variables in growth regressions: Openness is particularly growth enhancing in countries that are closer to the technological frontier; entry is more growth enhancing in countries or sectors that are closer to the technological frontier.

Next, to the extent that frontier innovation makes greater use of research education than imitation, the prediction is:

---

12. See Acemoglu, Aghion, and Zilibotti (2006).

Prediction 3: The more frontier an economy is, the more growth in this economy will rely on research education.

And indeed, Aghion et al. (2009b) show that research-type education is always more growth enhancing in US states that are more frontier, whereas a bigger emphasis on 2-year colleges is more growth-enhancing in US states that are farther below the productivity frontier. Similarly, using cross-country panel data, Vandenbussche, Aghion, and Meghir (2006) show that tertiary education is more positively correlated with productivity growth in countries that are closer to the world technology frontier.

In the same spirit, one can look at the relationship between technological development, democracy, and growth. An important channel is Schumpeterian, namely, democracy reduces the scope for expropriating successful innovators or for incumbents to prevent new entry by using political pressure or bribes. In other words, democracy facilitates creative destruction and thereby encourages innovation.[13]

To the extent that innovation matters more for growth in more frontier economies, the prediction is:

Prediction 4: The correlation between democracy and innovation/growth is more positive and significant in economies that are closer to the frontier.

This prediction is confirmed by Aghion, Alesina, and Trebbi (2007) using employment and productivity data at industry level across countries and over time.

Innovation, Institutions, and Firm Dynamics in Developing Countries

The two figures below, from the work of Chang-Tai Hsieh and Peter Klenow (2009), illustrate the importance of firm dynamics and firm size distribution in the process of economic development. Figure 6.4 compares the distribution of Indian firms by productivity with that of American firms. Note that many more firms have low productivity in India than in the United States. Figure 6.5 represents the evolution of the average size of a company as a function of its age in India, Mexico, and the United States. It shows that US firms continue to grow, whereas the growth of Indian firms drops

---

13. Acemoglu and Robinson (2006) formalize another reason, also Schumpeterian, as to why democracy matters for innovation, namely, new innovations do not only destroy the economic rents of incumbent producers, they also threaten the power of incumbent political leaders.

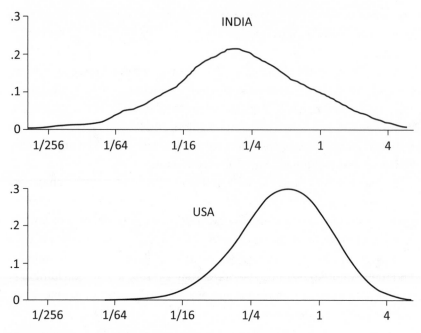

Figure 6.4
Distribution of firm productivity, India and the United States
Source: Hsieh and Klenow (2009).

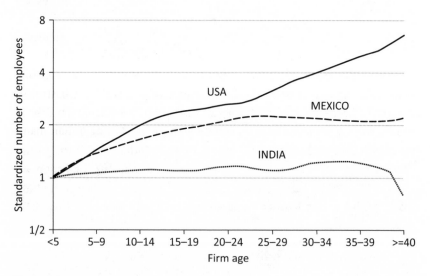

Figure 6.5
Link between the age and size of firms
Source: Hsieh and Klenow (2009).

off. In fact, Hsieh and Klenow show that although US establishments grow five times relative to their entry size by the age of 30, Indian counterparts barely show any growth.

Both these figures look at microeconomic characteristics. Yet when placed side by side, they tell a story that has consequences for the Indian economy as a whole: The inability of Indian firms, even the most innovative and productive ones, to grow beyond a certain size enables firms with low productivity to survive. But in the aggregate, innovation, and thereby the growth of the Indian economy overall, suffers.

To explain these two figures, we must consider the systemic characteristics of the Indian economy. Why do establishments not grow in India? Bloom et al. (2013) show that lack of trust and the weak rule of law are major obstacles to firm growth.

More recently, Akcigit, Alp, and Peters (2014) extend the Klette-Kortum model of firm dynamics discussed in the previous section by adding two major ingredients: (1) production requires managers, as owners' time is limited, and therefore owners face an overload constraint; (2) firm owners can be of high or low ability, where high-ability owners are more creative and therefore have the potential to expand much faster than can low-ability owners (but this potential for expansion materializes more when the scope for delegation is higher).

Their model generates the following predictions:

Prediction 1:   The expected number of outside managers is (1) increasing in firm size and (2) increasing in the rule of law.

Larger firms involve a higher degree of overload for firm owners, which in turn increases the returns from hiring outside managers. Finally, stronger rule of law implies higher net return to delegation. Akcigit, Alp, and Peters (2014) provide empirical support for these predictions using Indian manufacturing establishments.

Prediction 2:   The average firm size increases with the rule of law.

Firm value is increasing in owner time, and therefore the firms are willing to innovate and expand more when firm value is higher. The empirical support for this prediction is provided by Bloom et al. (2013). The positive link between firm size and the rule of law has been extensively documented in the literature (see, for instance, Bloom, Sadun, and Van Reenen (2012) for a detailed discussion). Finally, Akcigit, Alp, and Peters (2014) show that the link between firm size and family size is weaker in high-trust regions in India.

Prediction 3: Firm growth decreases with firm size, and the more so the weaker the rule of law.

Indeed in larger firms, the span of control is larger, and therefore the owner has less time to allocate to each product line. This in turn implies that any constraint limiting the scope for delegation will have more dramatic effects on large firms. In particular, the weaker the rule of law is, the lower the larger firms' incentive to grow will be, which in turn implies that the difference in growth incentives between large and small firms will be higher in countries with weaker rule of law. Akcigit, Alp, and Peters (2014) show that growth decreases faster in firm size in low-trust regions in India.

Prediction 4: Everything else being equal, creative destruction and reallocation among firms will be higher in economies where the rule of law is stronger.

Clearly this last prediction is in line with the main findings of Hsieh and Klenow's work, which showed the missing growth and reallocation in developing countries. Understanding the reasons behind the lack of reallocation and creative destruction is essential when designing the right development policies. The Schumpeterian growth framework provides a useful framework to conduct counterfactual policy exercises, which can shed light on this important debate.

I see this approach as potentially quite fruitful. For example, one could look at the extent to which characteristics (such as the quality of education, infrastructure, or labor market regulations) also affect firm dynamics and the ability of better performing firms to grow faster. More generally, a better understanding of the process of growth of firms and the reallocation of resources among firms or sectors would undoubtedly provide new keys to understand the relationship between growth and development and to find lasting remedies for underdevelopment and poverty in the world.

Rethinking Growth Policy

Economists have responded in different ways to the question of whether to get involved in economic policy debates or to stay out of the debates and concentrate on basic research. My work lies between these two attitudes.

Although I am first and foremost a researcher and a teacher, I find economic policy debates compelling for two reasons. First, as a strictly scientific matter, analyzing public policy and action enables us to better understand the mechanisms of growth. Second, theoretical and empirical economic analysis combats "false good ideas" by clarifying the terms of the policy debate, and it helps suggest guidelines for growth policy design.

The Growth Diagnostics Approach
In an influential paper titled "Growth Diagnostics," Hausmann, Rodrik, and Velasco (2005), henceforth HRV, have proposed an attractively simple methodology to design growth-enhancing policy. In this section, I first summarize the methodology, point out some of its potential limitations, and then propose an alternative approach based on growth regressions that are themselves suggested by the theory, particularly the Schumpeterian paradigm outlined above.

HRV start from the relevant observation that growth-enhancing policies should vary from one country or region to another. For example, growth in the United States and other industrialized countries over the past 10 years appears to have benefited from market deregulations and privatizations. However, in Asian countries (including China) high growth rates have been promoted under limited competition or limited privatizations. The next question then is: Can one use existing new growth theory to provide a flexible guide to growth policy making, one that fully takes cross-country variability into account? HRV provide a positive and attractively simple answer to this question: namely, to use price comparisons to infer the importance of each potential constraint to growth. To illustrate their methodology, HRV consider a few Latin American examples, including Brazil and El Salvador.

In Brazil, returns to capital are high (with a net interest margin equal to 11.5 in 2001). This leads HRV to point to the low level of local savings (with very negative public savings) and the high tax rates as the main constraints on growth (the importance of the former is further supported by the positive and significant correlation between the interest rate and the current account deficit over time). The rate of return on education is also high in Brazil, which suggests that the rate of return on capital, and thereby growth, could be further increased by investing more on education. However, the argument goes, the already high rate of return on capital suggests that investing in education may not be a priority in Brazil.

In El Salvador, interest rates are low (a net interest margin equal to 3.7 in 2001), but so is the tax rate on capital. Is the lack of education responsible for the rate of return on capital? The HRV answer is no, given that the rate of return on education in El Salvador is low. Nor is there a lack of contractual enforcement that would reduce profitability. Lack of savings cannot be the binding constraint either, otherwise the interest margin would be high. Having failed to identify true obstacles to growth in El Salvador, HRV mention the "absence of profitable investment opportunities" as yet another potential suspect to consider.

Now suppose we used the same growth diagnostic approach to deal with the slow EU growth problem. The return to education is lower in the European Union than it is in the United States, which HRV would interpret as an indication that education is the most binding constraint to growth. Instead, they would presumably point to the high European tax rates as the main suspect, and thereby advocate lower tax rates as the primary cure to the growth problem in the European Union.

The simple and ingenious approach proposed by HRV raises at least two concerns. First, equilibrium prices do not necessarily reflect a constraint on growth. Consider interest rates. A low interest rate does not mean that the local credit market is not constrained. In fact, low interest rates may reflect a high degree of credit rationing, as shown by Aghion and Bolton (1997). Indeed, the more restricted the access to credit is (that is, the more individuals are barred from undertaking their own projects), the more supply of loanable funds there will be in the economy, as all credit-rationed individuals will end up lending to a few entrepreneurs. But this in turn should result in a lower domestic equilibrium interest rate. Next, consider the rates of return on labor, which are measured by the so-called Mincerian wages, that is, by the forgone wage income of 1 more year in education at different levels of education. Mincerian wages of course provide some useful indication on the marginal value of private investments in education in different fields and at different levels of education. However, a big shortcoming of the Mincerian approach is that the Mincerian wage does not account for externalities. In particular, it does not account for the intertemporal knowledge externalities that lie behind the positive relationship between education and growth. That intertemporal externalities matter is evidenced by the large effects of education on growth.

More generally, current prices reflect a current state of the economy. They do not inform directly about the growth dynamics that would result for various types of policies.

A second concern with the HRV approach is that it cannot lead to growth prescriptions that would affect simultaneously the demand side and the supply side of markets. Thus, for example, HRV would never recommend that a country invest in education (thereby increasing the supply of research labor) and at the same time invest in structural reforms that increase the profitability of innovations (thereby fostering the demand for R&D labor by firms).[14]

An alternative to the above methodology is to use theory to construct growth regressions that are meant to inform us directly about the impact of different institutions or policies on growth.

Pillars of Innovation-Led Growth

To enhance innovation-led growth and thereby avoid the middle-income trap, the Schumpeterian paradigm and our discussion in the previous two sections suggest policy priorities such as:

1. Liberalize entry and increase competition among existing firms. This policy favors creative destruction and also encourages incumbent firms to innovate to escape competition from their rivals.

2. Liberalize labor markets to make it easier for labor to reallocate from old to new activities. This policy in turn requires active labor policies that combine unemployment support with retraining programs. This approach is quite intuitive: The more advanced a country is, the more productivity growth will rely on frontier innovation. But frontier innovation in turn entails more creative destruction, and thus more job turnover, than does technological catch-up.

3. Invest in well-funded and autonomous universities to promote frontier research and innovation-led growth. Indeed, frontier innovation requires frontier researchers and therefore good universities and research centers, whereas good undergraduate education is sufficient for imitation.

---

14. Incidentally, HRV would never recommend more active competition policies whose effect in the simple growth paradigm they consider is simply to reduce the rate of return on capital.

4. If a bank-based financial system enhances productivity growth more for less advanced countries, a more market-based financial system enhances productivity growth more in more frontier countries where growth is driven by frontier innovation. Intuitively, frontier innovation, which breaks new ground, entails a higher level of risk than imitation activities, which are already well defined. But this in turn implies that outside financiers involved in frontier innovation will ask for a higher share of upside revenues and also for higher control rights: hence the role of equity in financing frontier innovation.

To enhance productivity growth based on imitation or adaptation in less developed (catching up) countries, the examples of China, India, or the Asian Tigers suggest that reallocation and technology transfers are key. These properties in turn appear to benefit from good basic education systems and from institutional features—access to infrastructure, access to (bank) finance, and labor market flexibility—that favor factor mobility and the creation and growth of new business activities. Thus Aghion et al. (2008) showed that the delicensing reforms in India spurred productivity growth particularly in provinces with higher degrees of labor market flexibility.

Conclusion

In this chapter, we have seen how Schumpeterian growth theory can shed light on key growth enigmas: in particular, the relationship between competition and innovation-led growth; the existence of transition traps; secular stagnation; the relationship between growth and inequality; and the relationship between growth and firm dynamics. We also discussed how growth theory can guide growth policy design. Finally, I argued that the theory can further contribute to reconciling growth with development economics: first, by bringing out the notion of appropriate growth institutions and policies; and second, by looking at how institutional development shapes the relationship among firm size distribution, reallocation, and growth.

Numerous paths have yet to be explored to better understand the enigmas of growth, the relationship between growth and innovation, and the role of institutions and economic policy in the process of development. Understanding this process will benefit not only science but also society as a whole, because we are less fearful of what we understand.

References

Acemoglu, Daron, and James A. Robinson. 2006. "Economic Backwardness in Political Perspective." *American Political Science Review* 100 (1): 115–131.

Acemoglu, Daron, Philippe Aghion, and Fabrizio Zilibotti. 2006. "Distance to Frontier, Selection, and Economic Growth." *Journal of the European Economic Association* 4 (1): 37–74.

Acemoglu, Daron, Ufuk Akcigit, Nicholas Bloom, and William R. Kerr. 2013. "Innovation, Reallocation and Growth." NBER Working Paper 18993, National Bureau of Economic Research, Cambridge, MA.

Aghion, Philippe, and Patrick Bolton. 1997. "A Theory of Trickle-Down Growth and Development." *Review of Economic Studies* 64 (2): 151–172.

Aghion, Philippe, and Peter Howitt. 1992. "A Model of Growth Through Creative Destruction." *Econometrica* 60 (2): 323–351.

Aghion, Philippe, Ufuk Akcigit, and Peter Howitt. 2014. "What Do We Learn from Schumpeterian Growth Theory?" In *Handbook of Economic Growth*, volume 2, edited by Philippe Aghion and Steven N. Durlauf, 515–563. Amsterdam: Elsevier.

Aghion, Philippe, Alberto Alesina, and Francesco Trebbi. 2007. "Democracy, Technology, and Growth." NBER Working Paper 13180, National Bureau of Economic Research, Cambridge, MA.

Aghion, Phillipe, Mathias Dewatripont, and Patrick Rey. 1999. "Competition, Financial Discipline, and Growth." *Review of Economics and Statistics* 66(4): 825–852.

Aghion, Philippe, Christopher Harris, and John Vickers. 1997. "Competition and Growth with Step-by-Step Innovation: An Example." *European Economic Review* 41 (3–5): 771–782.

Aghion, Philippe, Peter Howitt, and Susanne Prantl. 2013. "Patent Rights, Product Market Reforms, and Innovation." NBER Working Paper 18854, National Bureau of Economic Research, Cambridge, MA.

Aghion, Philippe, Robin Burgess, Stephen J. Redding, and Fabrizio Zilibotti. 2008. "The Unequal Effects of Liberalization: Evidence from Dismantling the Raj License in India." *American Economic Review* 98 (4): 1397–1412.

Aghion, Philippe, Christopher Harris, Peter Howitt, and John Vickers. 2001. "Competition, Imitation and Growth with Step-by-Step Innovation." *Review of Economic Studies* 68 (3): 467–492.

Aghion, Philippe, Nick Bloom, Richard Blundell, Rachel Griffith, and Peter Howitt. 2005. "Competition and Innovation: An Inverted-U Relationship." *Quarterly Journal of Economics* 120 (2): 701–728.

Aghion, Philippe, Richard Blundell, Rachel Griffith, Peter Howitt, and Susanne Prantl. 2009a. "The Effects of Entry on Incumbent Innovation and Productivity." *Review of Economics and Statistics* 91 (1): 20–32.

Aghion, Philippe, Leah Boustan, Caroline Hoxby, and Jerome Vandenbussche. 2009b. "The Causal Impact of Education on Economic Growth: Evidence from the U.S." Unpublished manuscript, Harvard University, Cambridge, MA.

Aghion, Philippe, Ufuk Akcigit, Antonin Bergeaud, Richard Blundell, and David Hemous. 2015a. "Innovation and Top Income Inequality." NBER Working Paper 21247, National Bureau of Economic Research, Cambridge, MA.

Aghion, Philippe, Ufuk Akcigit, Antonin Bergeaud, Richard Blundell, and David Hemous. 2015b. "Innovation, Income Inequality, and Social Mobility." https://voxeu.org/article/innovation-income-inequality-and-social-mobility.

Aghion, Philippe, Antonin Bergeaud, Timo Boppart, Peter J. Klenow, and Huiyu Li. 2017. "Missing Growth from Creative Destruction." NBER Working Paper 24023, National Bureau of Economic Research, Cambridge, MA.

Akcigit, Ufuk, and William R. Kerr. 2010. "Growth Through Heterogeneous Innovations." NBER Working Paper 16443, National Bureau of Economic Research, Cambridge, MA.

Akcigit, Ufuk, Harun Alp, and Michael Peters. 2014. "Lack of Selection and Limits to Delegation: Firm Dynamics in Developing Countries." Unpublished manuscript, University of Pennsylvania, Philadelphia.

Atkinson, Anthony B., Thomas Piketty, and Emmanuel Saez. 2011. "Top Incomes in the Long-Run History." *Journal of Economic Literature* 49 (1): 3–71.

Banerjee, Abhijit V., and Esther Duflo. 2012. *Repenser la Pauvreté*. Paris: Seuil.

Bergeaud, Antonin, Gilbert Cette, and Remy Lecat. 2014. "Productivity Trends from 1890 to 2012 in Advanced Countries." Working Paper 475, Banque de France, Paris.

Bloom, Nicholas, Raffaella Sadun, and John Van Reenen. 2012. "The Organization of Firms across Countries." *Quarterly Journal of Economics* 127 (4): 1663–1705.

Bloom, Nicholas, Benn Eifert, Aprajit Mahajan, David McKenzie, and John Roberts. 2013. "Does Management Matter? Evidence from India." *Quarterly Journal of Economics* 128 (1): 1–51.

Blundell, Richard, Rachel Griffith, and John Van Reenen. 1995. "Dynamic Count Data Models of Technological Innovation." *Economic Journal* 105 (429): 333–344.

Blundell, Richard, Rachel Griffith, and John Van Reenen. 1999. "Market Share, Market Value and Innovation in a Panel of British Manufacturing Firms." *Review of Economic Studies* 66 (3): 529–554.

Boldrin, Michele, and David K. Levine. 2008. *Against Intellectual Monopoly*. Cambridge: Cambridge University Press.

Bresnahan, Timothy F., and M. Trajtenberg. 2005. "General Purpose Technologies: 'Engines of Growth'?" *Journal of Econometrics* 65 (1): 83–108.

Cette, Gilbert, and Jimmy Lopez. 2012. "ICT Demand Behavior: An International Comparison." *Economics of Innovation and New Technology* 21 (4): 397–410.

Chetty, Raj, Nathaniel Hendren, Patrick Kline, and Emmanuel Saez. 2014. "Where Is the Land of Opportunity? The Geography of Intergenerational Mobility in the United States." *Quarterly Journal of Economics* 129 (4): 1553–1623.

Gordon, Robert J. 2012. "Is U.S. Economic Growth Over? Faltering Innovation Confronts the Six Headwinds." NBER Working Paper 18315, National Bureau of Economic Research, Cambridge, MA.

Hansen, Alvin H. 1939. "Economic Progress and Declining Population Growth." *American Economic Review* 29 (1): 1–15.

Hausmann, Ricardo, Dani Rodrik, and Andrés Velasco. 2005. "Growth Diagnostics." Working Paper, John F. Kennedy School of Government, Harvard University, Cambridge, MA.

Hsieh, Chang-Tai, and Peter J. Klenow. 2009. "Misallocation and Manufacturing TFP in China and India." *Quarterly Journal of Economics* 124 (4): 1403–1448.

Klette, Tor Jakob, and Samuel Kortum. 2004. "Innovating Firms and Aggregate Innovation. *Journal of Political Economy* 112 (5): 986–1018.

Lentz, Rasmus, and Dale T. Mortensen. 2008. "An Empirical Model of Growth Through Product Innovation." *Econometrica* 76 (6): 1317–1373.

Piketty, Thomas. 2013. *Le Capital au XXIᵉ Siècle*. Paris: Seuil.

Romer, Paul M. 1990. "Endogenous Technical Change." *Journal of Political Economy* 98 (5): S71–S102.

Summers, Lawrence H. 2013. "Why Stagnation Might Prove to Be the New Normal." *Financial Times*, December 15.

Vandenbussche, Jérôme, Philippe Aghion, and Costas Meghir. 2006. "Growth, Distance to Frontier, and Composition of Human Capital." *Journal of Economic Growth* 11 (2): 97–127.

Comment: Francesco Caselli

Philippe Aghion's paper is a wonderful introduction to some of his contributions in the area of growth theory and empirics over the past 30 years. Everybody knows, of course, that Philippe is a major figure in this field. But even those who have followed his work fairly closely cannot fail to be inspired anew by the ambition, cohesiveness, and ultimate success of his efforts as they emerge from the account he gives in the preceding pages. Indeed, the feeling of awe is only magnified by the knowledge that there are many other important contributions that Philippe has chosen not to discuss here.

The chapter lays out an understanding of the growth process that encompasses a broad set of phenomena, including the role of competition in fostering (or, in some cases, discouraging) innovation; the need for institutions to evolve to keep the growth process going; the implications of innovation and growth for income inequality and for the evolution of the size distribution of firms, and so forth. It is one of the hallmarks of Philippe's work to raise the bar for the set of regularities that a theory of growth should be required to address. In that spirit, while Phillippe's paper rightly and convincingly celebrates the successes of the modern growth agenda, and of his many contributions to it, my brief remarks will try to look at the work ahead. Which challenges, or "enigmas" in Phillipe's parlance, still await growth theory? Think of it as my wish list for Phillipe's next 30 years of work.

With some huge oversimplification, it is possible to create a taxonomy of growth experiences. All parts of the world, as far as we know, experienced many centuries of Malthusian, or near-Malthusian growth. In the Malthusian era, most increases in aggregate output translated into larger populations, resulting in relatively modest (if any) increases in living standards over very long horizons. A plot of GDP per capita against time looks nearly flat. The taxonomy of growth experiences I alluded to before is based on when and whether countries exited the Malthusian regime, and what happened after they left it. It features four groups.

The first category is composed of a small number of economies that experienced an industrial revolution at the beginning of the nineteenth century. After the industrial revolution, the rate of growth in per capita income picked up very markedly and has remained roughly steady, when averaged over decades or twenty-year periods, ever since. In a plot of (log) income per capita against time, we see something of a "kink" at the time of the industrial revolution, and a remarkably straight upward-sloping line ever since. We might call these countries the "pioneers."

A second group is made up of countries that underwent a similar industrial revolution at later dates, and subsequently (broadly) converged to the pioneers. The date at which these later industrializations took place varied enormously, from the mid-nineteenth century for some European countries to the mid-twentieth century for some East Asian ones. However, the common feature is that subsequent to their industrial revolution, these countries experienced a sustained period in which they grew faster than the pioneers, so that eventually living standards became quite similar for the first and second groups. In a plot against time, (the log of) per capita income shows a kink, followed by an upward-sloping, concave trajectory, asymptoting to a straight line that runs close to the straight line of the pioneers. I'll call these countries the "convergents."

In the third bin are countries that, similar to the convergents, experienced industrialization followed by a period of growth exceeding the growth of the leaders, but whose convergence process, unlike the convergents, aborted prematurely. That is, these countries were able to make up some of the income gap with the pioneers, but then their growth rate stabilized at a rate similar to those of the pioneers well before living standards became similar. The plot of their (log) income per capita against time is similar to that of the convergents, except that the linear section is well below the linear path followed by the pioneers. We may refer to this group as the "middle-income trapped."[1]

---

1. I am implicitly defining the "middle-income trap" in terms of income relative to the pioneers, not in terms of absolute income. The hypothesis of a middle-absolute-income trap does not withstand even a modest amount of scrutiny: Most of the countries cited as poster boys for the middle-income trap (e.g., Brazil, South Africa)

The fourth and final group includes those countries that never underwent a proper industrialization stage. As a result, these countries did not even exhibit the temporary phase of convergence that the middle-income trapped experienced. I do not mean to suggest that most of these countries are still stuck in the Malthusian regime. Some structural transformation from agriculture to services is happening, as is a fair amount of urbanization. Nevertheless, these changes do not seem able to ignite a sustained catching-up process, and as a result, countries in this group tend, at best, to maintain their relative position and, at worst, to diverge from the leaders. Figuratively if not technically, the plots for these countries' GDP per capita never shows the kink. We can call the countries in this group the "poverty trapped."

How well does modern growth theory explain these four types of experiences, individually and collectively? My view is that it gets full marks in some areas, passing marks in some others, and bad fails in a few.

The biggest achievement of modern growth theory is its ability to rationalize the pattern of sustained, steady growth in the pioneers (and in the convergents after the completion of the catch-up phase)—the linear growth in the plots. Steady per capita income growth over the span (in some cases) of two centuries is an astonishing fact, and the success of growth theory in illustrating the mechanisms that make this possible is one of the greatest achievements in macroeconomics. The theory centers on innovation and clarifies the roles of R&D, property rights protection, competition, and many other elements. Needless to say, Philippe has been a key force in developing this body of work.

Another part of the growth landscape that growth theory does pretty well with is the tendency of later industrializers to convergence to the pioneers. The modern understanding still largely builds on the old tradition centered on the "advantage of backwardness," which has been successfully incorporated in contemporary growth models (much as theories of growth at the frontier incorporate older arguments based on creative destruction). In this view, which seems hard to refute, later industrializers can grow faster, because they can imitate and adopt technologies already invented by the leaders.

---

have reasonably steady growth rates when averaged over long periods. What they are failing to do is to close the gap with the high-income countries.

Overall, the postindustrialization experiences of the pioneers and the convergents are the areas where modern growth theory deserves full marks. This may be because these are the success stories, and economics often seems to do better at explaining successes than failures.

With the question of why some initially promising catching-up experiences petered out, ending in a middle-income trap, we have some ideas but no consensus and little evidence. Philippe does offer a hypothesis, and others have advanced their own. The good news is that this is an active area of research, and I am optimistic that a greater understanding will emerge in the not-too-distant future.

I would offer a similar assessment on the question of why the industrial revolution happened in the first place (the first "kink"). This is of course a classic question both in macro and in economic history, and countless books and articles have been written about it. Although a consensus account still eludes us, I do sense considerable progress in recent years. The emerging vision features some combination of intellectual developments (scientific discoveries combined with the enlightenment mindset), political developments (particularly in terms of the power relations between landed aristocracy and emerging urban bourgeoisie), and possibly evolutionary forces.

In sum, both on the question of the middle-income trap and on the reasons for the transition from the Malthusian to the modern growth regime, I'd give growth theory a passing mark—for effort if not for success.

And now for the bad fail: the later "kinks" and, in particular, the lack thereof. Why did some countries manage to properly industrialize and others never do so? What is the difference between the convergents and the (eventually) middle-income trapped, on one hand, and the poverty-trapped on the other? I hope I am not too harsh in saying that not only do we not know, but we are not even trying to know. Perhaps, as I mentioned, modern macroeconomics is so bad at explaining failures that we are not even willing to try. But the question of the failure to industrialize is too important to give up on. Our friends on the microeconomic development side know this and are working hard on finding out how individuals in poverty-trapped countries can do a little bit better. We macroeconomists should join them and try to figure out ways in which the whole country can get that "kink."

Comment: Aart Kraay

Philippe Aghion's paper for this conference provides a concise and insightful summary of his fundamental contributions to the theory and empirics of economic growth over the past 25 years. It is challenging for Philippe to do justice to such an impressive body of work in the short space of a conference presentation, but he succeeds remarkably in doing so. It is even more challenging to follow Philippe as a discussant, so my expectations for this discussion are appropriately modest.

We have known since the fundamental work of Solow and Swan in the 1950s that, in the presence of diminishing returns, sustained growth in output in the long run requires sustained growth in technology. But it took another 30 years for the profession to begin to articulate theories that spelled out mechanisms through which improvements in technology came about. Philippe Aghion, in work with Peter Howitt, was at the forefront of this movement in the 1980s, formalizing earlier insights from Joseph Schumpeter about the process of creative destruction into well-articulated and elegant models of innovation and growth.

By spelling out the incentives for innovation, these models not only provided a theoretical basis for technology growth, but they also generated a rich set of insights for policy makers contemplating changes to laws and regulations affecting property rights, competition, and firm entry and exit. As discussed in Philippe's paper, the insights of Schumpeterian growth theory also have implications for current debates about secular stagnation, trends in inequality, and much more.

I focus my discussion on the fundamental underlying theme in Philippe's paper—the importance for growth of technology growth and the importance of Schumpeterian creative destruction in generating the innovations that lead to growth in technology. Given my professional background as a World Bank economist, I want to reflect particularly on the relevance of these themes for policy makers in developing countries. I organize my discussion around three questions: (1) How important are cross-country and over-time differences in technology? (2) What is "inside" the differences in technology that we can isolate at the aggregate level?, and (3) What do the answers to these questions imply for development policy?

How Important Are Differences in "A"?

A basic premise in Philippe's work is the importance of understanding the forces that drive differences across countries and changes over time in the level of technology, conventionally referred to as A in a neoclassical production function $Y = AF(K, H)$, where K and H represent physical and human capital, respectively. Various recent accounting exercises have contributed to the view that cross-country differences in A are large (for example, see Caselli (2005), whose notation I follow here). These typically are based on a decomposition of income differences between rich and poor countries along the following lines:

$$\frac{Y_{RICH}}{Y_{POOR}} = \frac{A_{RICH}}{A_{POOR}} \times \frac{F(K_{RICH}, H_{RICH})}{F(K_{POOR}, H_{POOR})}.$$

Depending on how "rich" and "poor" are defined, one can easily confront the task in such a decomposition of explaining up to 40-fold differences in incomes between rich and poor countries, i.e. $\frac{Y_{RICH}}{Y_{POOR}} \approx 40$. Baseline assumptions that (a) the production function is Cobb-Douglas, (b) physical capital stocks are related to the accumulation of observable past investments, and (c) human capital stocks are some straightforward linear aggregate of workers with productivity differences adjusted for some observed measure of schooling,can be used to evaluate the contribution of cross-country differences in factors of production to these differences.Under these baseline assumptions, it is typically possible to generate something in the range of 5- to 8-fold cross-country differences in the contribution of factors of production to cross-country income differences,i.e. $\frac{F(K_{RICH}, H_{RICH})}{F(K_{POOR}, H_{POOR})} \approx 5-8$ *This in turn implies that cross-country differences in the level of technology A must* also be in the five- to eightfold range to account for observed cross-country differences in output.

Thus taking the data at face value suggests a very large role for cross-country differences in technology, and therefore a comparably great importance for imposing structure on these differences through theories of innovation that lead to differences in technology levels across countries. Although I do not spell it out in detail here, one can of course perform similar decompositions in countries across time, leading to measures of the growth rate of A in countries over time. Such growth (as opposed to development) accounting exercises often reveal very large cross-country differences in measured growth rates of technology.

However, as with many things, the devil is in the details, and one does not have to go very far into the literature to find careful consideration of measurement issues that, when properly addressed, suggest that we should take a more nuanced view of the importance of cross-country and over-time differences in A. One early and very well-known example comes from Alwyn Young's meticulous growth accounting exercises for rapidly growing East Asian economies, which suggested that once increases in factors of production were more comprehensively measured, the productivity growth underlying the extraordinary output growth in these countries was actually quite ordinary (Young 1995). Perhaps the starkest case is that of Singapore over the 25-year period 1966–1990 studied by Young: Although output grew at nearly 9 percent per year, productivity growth was indistinguishable from zero, once such factors as increasing labor force participation, increased human capital, and a more efficient allocation of resources across sectors were taken into account.

Turning to more recent examples, Jones (2014) and Manuelli and Seshadri (2014) tackle in different ways the question of the contribution of human capital to differences in output per capita across countries. Jones (2014) emphasizes the consequences of considering alternatives to the standard linear human capital aggregator. The standard aggregator plausibly assumes that skilled workers are X times more productive than unskilled woirkers, but it implausibly assumes that skilled and unskilled workers are perfectly substitutable after this rescaling by productivity levels is taken into account—a skilled task can be accomplished by one skilled worker or by X unskilled workers. It does not take much introspection to realize the implausibility of this benchmark assumption, and Jones (2014) spells out a variety of more realistic human capital aggregators that recognize the complementarity between different skill types. These in turn lead to much greater differences in aggregate human capital across countries, which in turn imply a greater role for cross-country differences in factors of production and a commensurately smaller role for cross-country differences in productivity.

In a related paper, Manuelli and Seshadri (2014) take seriously incentives to invest in human capital. Although their paper is much richer than this, the basic insight is simple—if individuals rationally take into account the quality of human capital formed through investments in education, then low observed investments in education signal not just that the level of human capital is low but also that the quality of human capital is low. Calibrating their model seriously to cross-country data suggests a much larger role for human capital differences to per capita output differences across countries, and therefore again a smaller role for productivity differences.

All of this is not to say that cross-country or over-time differences in productivity are unimportant. Rather, it emphasizes that (1) careful, theory-consistent measurement of factors of production is important, and (2) understanding the forces that create incentives for investments in physical and human capital is at least as important from a policy perspective as is understanding better the incentives for innovation that lead to increases in A.

What Is "Inside" A?

As noted above, careful measurement suggests that cross-country differences in A may not be quite as large as a naïve first look at the data might suggest. However, even after careful measurement, they likely are nontrivial and therefore worth understanding more deeply. The literature on Schumpeterian innovation that Philippe has made seminal contributions to has offered an innovation-based view of these differences. But cross-country differences in the abilities of society to allow innovation to take place and bear fruit are not the only reason why A may be different. These alternative explanations are worth taking seriously, because they may suggest alternative policy levers to promote sustained growth.

A first set of explanations that has attracted considerable empirical attention over the past decade hinge on misallocation of resources across firms or sectors of the economy, particularly in response to policies that favor some firms or sectors over others. To the extent that such policies prevent marginal products of factors from being equalized across alternative uses, they can contribute to cross-country differences in A even when measured aggregate factors of production, such as K and H , are the same. In one of the seminal contributions to this literature, Hsieh and Klenow (2009) document differences in marginal products of capital across manufacturing firms in narrowly defined industries. Their results suggest that a country such as China could effectively double its level of aggregate productivity in manufacturing simply by reducing its level of resource misallocation to that observed in the United States.

Another set of explanations for what might contribute to low values of A revolves around managerial incompetence rather than lack of access to the best technology or dulled incentives to innovate at the technological frontier. Bloom et al. (2013) document extremes of mismanagement in a set of Indian firms, such as basic failures to manage inventories and materials, or failures to maintain minimal standards of cleanliness and safety in and around factories. Bloom et al. (2013) go on to show that an experimental intervention that provided management training to firms resulted in a significant improvement in productivity in these firms.

In fairness, misallocation and mismanagement are probably not fully separate causal factors in driving the low levels of A, and indeed, one might argue that they are in part a manifestation of the same lack of competitive pressures that also contribute to low innovation. In an environment with weak competition, the incentives to ensure that resources are efficiently deployed in and between firms may also be weak. However, this is a somewhat different mechanism than the effect of competition on incentives to innovate that is stressed in the Schumpeterian approach.

Finally, although it is perhaps not so surprising that a lack of Schumpeterian innovation may not be the main reason behind low productivity in a developing country, it seems more plausible that it is an important factor in advanced economies. Yet in a recent paper, Garcia-Macia, Hsieh, and Klenow (2016) study the dynamics of innovation at the firm level in the United States and document some patterns that seem at odds with Schumpeterian dynamics. For example, contrary to the Schumpeterian view of "creative destruction," where innovative new firms replace existing firms that fail to innovate, they document that most of growth in the United States seems to come from growth in incumbent firms rather than from new firms replacing old ones. They also document that much of innovation seems to take the form of improvements in existing products rather than creation of new products. Both of these observations suggest that a more nuanced interpretation of the Schumpeterian emphasis on innovation and creative destruction is in order.

Implications for Development Policy?

Philippe's paper concludes with a set of policy prescriptions designed to unleash Schumpeterian growth. The list is short, sound, and sensible: (1) liberalize entry and encourage competition, (2) liberalize labor markets, (3) promote institutions such as autonomous universities that foster research, and (4) develop a policy framework to encourage equity finance of risky investments in R&D in richer countries near the technology frontier. One does not have to squint very hard at this list to see key elements of traditional policy advice included in the "Washington Consensus," nor is it very hard to provide a Schumpeterian interpretation of key ingredients in the Washington Consensus. For example, classic elements on John Williamson's list—but not on Philippe's list—such as competitive exchange rates, trade liberalization, and deregulation, can all be thought of as fostering competitive pressures that drive Schumpeterian innovation and growth.

In fact, this raises the question of whether the four policy prescriptions in Philippe's paper are uniquely Schumpeterian, or whether they are just plain sensible. For example, liberalization of entry and deregulation of labor markets arguably have direct effects on resource misallocation, which through this channel may raise productivity, even if they do not directly promote competition. Conversely, the emphasis on property rights protection in the Washington Consensus can be interpreted as a key factor in promoting Schumpeterian innovation (because innovators require assurance of their property rights over the new ideas they develop). But at the same time, it is hardly a uniquely Schumpeterian policy prescription—there are many other channels through which the protection of property rights promotes economic growth that do not operate through the channel of innovation.

Another issue raised by Philippe's list is the question of prioritization, particularly when one considers developing countries, and especially those very far below the frontier, who face much more primordial challenges than the lack of innovation. Prescriptions to foster autonomous universities are probably sensible advice for advanced economies and a handful of emerging economies near the frontier, but they are unlikely to be priorities in the many developing countries that struggle to provide even minimal education and health care to kids.

A final difficult question that merits serious consideration when turning Schumpeterian insights into development policy advice concerns the political feasibility of this advice. Recall that the fundamental Schumpeterian insight is that when firms face competitive pressures, they are forced to innovate to escape these competitive pressures, unleashing a virtuous circle of innovation, competition, and further innovation that raises growth. But the reality, particularly in many developing countries facing governance challenges, is that well-connected firms have at their disposal tools other than innovation to escape competitive pressures, and these tools lead to less virtuous outcomes. There are many such possibilities, but a particularly vivid example comes from recent work by Rijkers, Freund, and Nucifora (2014). They meticulously document the incidence of policy-induced barriers to entry across different sectors in Tunisia and then go on to show that the presence of these barriers is strongly associated with the presence of firms connected to the family of then-President Ben Ali. More generally, how to implement procompetitive Schumpeterian growth policies in environments in which politically powerful incumbents are precisely the ones benefiting from the absence of competition remains a deeply challenging question for development policy makers.

References

Bloom, Nicholas, Benn Eifert, Aprajit Mahajan, David McKenzie, and John Roberts. 2013. "Does Management Matter? Evidence from India." *Quarterly Journal of Economics* 128 (1): 1–51.

Caselli, Francesco. 2005. "Accounting for Cross-Country Income Differences." In *Handbook of Economic Growth*, volume 1A, edited by Phillipe Aghion and Steven Durlauf, 679–741. Amsterdam: Elsevier.

Garcia-Macia, Daniel, Chang-Tai Hsieh, and Peter J. Klenow. 2016. "How Destructive Is Innovation?" Unpublished manuscript, University of Chicago.

Hsieh, Chang-Tai, and Peter J. Klenow. 2009. "Misallocation and Manufacturing TFP in China and India." *Quarterly Journal of Economics* 124 (4): 1403–1448.

Jones, Benjamin F. 2014. "The Human Capital Stock: A Generalized Approach." *American Economic Review* 104 (11): 3752–3777.

Manuelli, Rodolfo, and Ananth Seshadri. 2014. "Human Capital and the Wealth of Nations." *American Economic Review* 104 (8): 2736–2762.

Rijkers, Bob, Caroline Freund, and Antonio Nucifora. 2014. "All in the Family: State Capture in Tunisia." World Bank Working Paper 6810, World Bank, Washington, DC.

Young, Alwyn. 1995. "The Tyranny of Numbers: Confronting the Statistical Realities of the East Asian Growth Experience." *Quarterly Journal of Economics* 110 (3): 641–680.

III New Areas of Research and Inquiry

7   Climate Change, Development, Poverty, and Economics

Sam Fankhauser and Nicholas Stern

The past three decades have seen an unprecedented increase in world living standards and a fall in poverty across many fundamental dimensions. Increased confidence in what was possible together with greater acceptance of moral responsibilities led to the adoption of the Millennium Development Goals at the turn of the century. They provided a real basis for international cooperation and development. In the Sustainable Development Goals (SDGs), agreed on in September 2015, there is now a common platform for the next phase of the fight against poverty.

The SDGs make it clear that environmental protection will be a key feature of this next phase, since it is increasingly intertwined with poverty reduction. Thirteen of the seventeen SDGs are directly concerned with the natural environment, climate, or sustainability. Environment, climate, and sustainability were not prominent in the Millennium Development Goals. With hindsight, we can now see that this omission was a mistake.

A key factor in all this is climate change. Climate change is not the only environmental problem we face, nor is it the only threat to global prosperity. But climate change is unique in its magnitude and the vast risks it poses. It is a potent threat-multiplier for other urgent concerns, such as habitat loss, disease, and global security (IPCC 2014). And it puts at risk

We thank Gael Girard, Mike Toman, Bob Ward, and the participants of the World Bank conference on The State of Economics, the State of the World (Washington, DC, June 2016) for their thoughtful comments. Patrick Curran and Isabella Neuweg have provided outstanding research support. We also acknowledge financial support from the Grantham Foundation for the Protection of the Environment and the UK Economic and Social Research Council (ESRC), through its support of the Centre for Climate Change Economics and Policy (CCCEP).

the development achievements of the past decades (Hallegatte et al. 2016). If unchecked, climate change could fundamentally redraw the map of the planet, and where and how humans and other species can live.

Climate change is also unique in the scale of the response that is needed. Reducing climate risks requires cooperation from all countries, developed and developing, to reorient their economic systems away from fossil fuels and harmful land-use practices. This reorientation is urgent. Our activities in the next two decades will determine whether our successes in development will be sustained or advanced, or whether they will be undermined or reversed in a hostile environment.

The nature of the climate problem has implications for economic analysis. Economics has much to offer, and indeed continues to provide important insights, but there has been a dangerous tendency to force climate change into narrow conventional ways of thinking. This must change. We need to construct theories and models that reflect the structure and scale of the problem and the contexts in which it occurs.

Climate change also has implications for development policy. In the Paris Agreement—negotiated at the end of 2015—there is now an international platform through which global climate action can be advanced and coordinated. The Paris Agreement has been ratified by 185 countries (as of April 2019). It sets out a process through which the rise in global mean temperatures may be curtailed to "well below" 2° C above pre-industrial levels and perhaps as low as 1.5° C. In 2018 the Intergovernmental Panel on Climate Change advised that 1.5° C would have substantial benefits for people and the natural environment, compared with 2° C (IPCC 2018).

Meeting the Paris objectives requires sustained action over many decades. It also requires the reorientation of investment. At least US$100 trillion will be invested over the next two or three decades in buildings and urban infrastructure, roads, railways, ports, and new energy systems. It is imperative that these investment decisions are taken with climate change in mind.

If they are, there will be substantial benefits for development and poverty reduction—living spaces where we can move, breathe, and be productive and better protection for fragile ecosystems, as well as the fundamental reduction of the risks of climate change.

Putting the SDGs and Paris together, the agreements of 2015 have given us, for the first time, a global agenda for sustainable development applying to all countries. This chapter sets out the implications of this agenda, and climate change in particular, for development economics and development policy. It emphasizes the nature of the required changes and their implications. We start with an examination of what economics has had to say about the link between economic prosperity and the environment. We then explain why climate change is a different kind of problem, and why it requires a new approach to both analysis and policy. The final two sections explore how this new approach might look.

Prosperity and the Environment

Environmental concerns entered development policy relatively late. The World Bank created the Office of the Environmental Advisor in 1970, but in the early years, this was very much an advisory function. Over time, the role evolved and the environment grew in importance, culminating in the creation of the Environmentally Sustainable Development vice presidency in 1993.[1] In parallel, environmental economics began to emerge as a new field of academic study (Pearce 2002).

Understanding the interactions between economic growth and environmental protection is crucial to development in all countries, but especially in poor ones. Careful environmental management is a critical ingredient of any viable path to poverty reduction. Bad environmental management results in environmental degradation, poor public health, and lost economic output. Poor people are the primary victims of these trends, though we should recognize that poverty also contributes to them (Pearce and Warford 1993).

Environment and Growth
Knowledge about the link between economic development and the environment of course goes back much further than the 1970s. The economics pioneers of the eighteenth and nineteenth centuries were well aware of environmental resources as an essential source of wealth, and indeed as a potential constraint to economic growth. For David Ricardo, differences in land quality were the main source of rent for landowners. Thomas Malthus, more pessimistically, predicted widespread poverty as a consequence of

---

1. See https://archivesholdings.worldbank.org/.

population growth and decreasing returns to agriculture. Montesquieu speculated at length about the influence of the climate on society and the "temper of the mind" (Montesquieu [1748, Book XIV] 2011), but the link to economic performance was cursory. The early economists were more interested in resource endowments than climate factors.

Unlike Montesquieu's theories on climate, Malthus's concern about natural resource constraints has remained a constant feature of the growth debate. In the 1860s, William Stanley Jevons worried about the future of industrial England when its coal reserves would run out. In the 1970s, the Club of Rome made headlines with *The Limits to Growth* (Meadows et al. 1972). Inspired by Kenneth Boulding's (1966) notion of "spaceship Earth," the interdisciplinary field of ecological economics has continued to probe the natural boundaries that the laws of science impose on economic processes (e.g., Rockström et al. 2009).

So far, Malthus and the resource pessimists have generally appeared to be wrong. Human ingenuity has mostly managed to outpace natural resource constraints. This does not mean that environmental resources are not overexploited. They are, including not least in developing countries. However, in most cases this overexploitation appears, in large measure, to be the result of policy mismanagement and market failure rather than resource scarcity per se.

The Management of Natural Resources

From the outset, economists have devoted considerable attention to the effective management of natural resources. In the nineteenth century, Knut Wicksell and Martin Faustmann were among the first to study the optimal harvesting cycle for slow-maturing resources like forests (Hedlund-Nyström et al. 2006). However, it was Harold Hotelling (1931) who produced the defining treatise on natural resource management. According to his Hotelling rule, the value of natural resources, if optimally used, must rise at the rate of interest. This insight has formed the basis of natural resource economics to this day. It also informs the analysis of stock pollution problems like climate change.

The Hotelling rule was revisited in the 1970s, when it became apparent that it may not be consistent with an emerging development concept, that of sustainable development. The notion of sustainable development was popularized by the Brundtland Commission on Environment and

Development, which defined it as "development which meets the needs of current generations without compromising the ability of future generations to meet their own needs" (World Commission on Environment and Development 1987).

For economists, this meant consumption (or utility) could not be allowed to decrease over time. Robert Solow and John Hartwick worked out what nondecreasing utility meant for resource depletion. The rents from natural resource extraction had to be reinvested in other forms of capital, so that the total stock of environmental, physical, and human capital remained constant (Solow 1974; Hartwick 1977). The World Bank has been at the forefront of translating the Hartwick-Solow rule into practical policy advice (World Bank 2011).

Environmental Management and Public Policy

If Harold Hotelling is the forefather of natural resource economics, Arthur Cecil Pigou deserves the credit for incorporating environmental concerns into welfare economics. Drawing on his teacher Alfred Marshall, Pigou systematically introduced into economics the notion of externalities, that is, costs or benefits that are not captured in the market price of goods. Later writers added nuance and extensions—such as open access problems, common property resources, and public goods—that refine our understanding of environment-related market failures, but the core concept of externalities remains central to modern environmental economics.

Pigou's observations on the environment were prescient. He discussed at length the negative effects of pollution, which "inflicts a heavy uncharged loss on the community" (Pigou (1920), as cited in Sandmo (2015, 53)). The concern remains valid to this day. Urban air pollution, linked to particulate matter and other pollutants, remains a major issue in most countries (New Climate Economy 2014). In another perceptive comment, Pigou praised the external value of forests, whose "beneficial effect on climate often extends beyond the borders of the estates owned by the person responsible for the forest," though he probably had the local climate in mind (cited in Sandmo (2015, 55)).

Pigou also identified the requisite remedy to address these market failures: a corrective tax levied in proportion to the externality. This was later complemented by the work of Ronald Coase, who showed that problems of externalities could also be managed via clearer (and perhaps tradable) property rights (Coase 1960). Both writers were drawing on John Stuart Mill, who already in 1848 had called for government intervention to ensure the "common enjoyment" of the world's natural riches (Sandmo 2015). Today, variants of Pigouvian taxes and Coasean trading schemes are in use throughout the world (for an overview, see Sterner (2003); Freeman and Kolstad (2007)).

Following in Pigou's footsteps, John Hicks and Nicholas Kaldor developed the theory for a systematic comparison of the costs and benefits of policy intervention. James Meade (1955) provided the defining general equilibrium approach and analysis in his seminal book *Trade and Welfare* (see also Drèze and Stern (1987, 1990)). Cost-benefit analysis soon became the standard tool for project appraisal, including in development organizations like the World Bank (e.g., Little and Mirrlees 1974).

In environmental economics, the extensive body of work on welfare economics gave rise to the field of environmental valuation—the use of techniques that monetize the external value of the environment, so it can be appropriately reflected in cost-benefit analysis (for an overview, see Hanley and Barbier (2009)).

It soon became clear that nature's contribution to human welfare goes well beyond the provision of food and materials, which had exercised Malthus and the Club of Rome. The modern theory of ecosystem services (e.g., TEEB 2010) distinguishes between provisioning services (food, water, materials), cultural services (spiritual value, recreation, mental and physical health), regulating services (air quality, water treatment, carbon sequestration) and support services (genetic diversity, habitats). The full extent of this rich range of services is not yet fully understood—or indeed, always appreciated—by policy makers. It remains an active and important area of interdisciplinary research.

A central test for any economic prescription on environmental management is the health of the natural environment. Against this yardstick, the economics of Hotelling, Pigou, Meade, and their successors has serious limitations. There have been notable successes, but on the whole, environmental protection in practice has been much harder than the solutions embodied in simple theory. The political economy of poverty and the environment is particularly complex and has to include factors like power, exclusion, land rights, market access, and gender relations.

Unfortunately, the environment–development nexus has become more complex still. The environmental problems of the twenty-first century could be of a different order of magnitude and generality than those of the past, and none more so than climate change.

Why Climate Change Is Different

Climate change is different from past environmental problems in terms of its scale, the magnitude of risks, and the urgency of action. We are all involved both in the generation of the problems and in our vulnerability to its impacts. Climate change is also different in terms of its complexity and the difficulty of identifying a "solution." To appreciate the nature and scale of the challenge, it is necessary to set out some basic science about climate change.

Science

The science of climate change is based on almost two centuries of theory and evidence. The basic physics of the greenhouse effect—that there are heat-trapping gases in the atmosphere, which leads to the earth retaining heat—were established by Jean-Baptiste Fourier and John Tyndall in the second half of the nineteenth century. Studying the earth's heat balance, the former showed that something was preventing the escape of energy, and the latter identified the key gases at work. At the start of the twentieth century, Svante Arrhenius made the link to fossil fuel-based emissions by showing that they intensified the magnitude of the natural greenhouse effect. In the first half of the twentieth century, with the rise of quantum theory, it was established that the mechanism at work was the frequency of oscillation of greenhouse gas molecules, which interfered with that of infrared energy. The systematic monitoring of atmospheric CO_2 concentrations began in 1958.

This part of the physics and chemistry of the atmosphere is basic and clear. Important uncertainties remain, but we increasingly understand the main driving forces in the inherently complex and chaotic system that is the earth's climate. From this evidence, which continues to be gathered, published, and presented, we understand that the current, unprecedented climate change starts and ends with people.

Human activity, through the extraction and combustion of fossil fuels, removal of forests, or agricultural activities contributes to the emission (or "flow") of greenhouse gases. The increased flows lead to increased quantities (or "stocks") of greenhouse gases in the atmosphere, and with them, an increase in the amount of heat energy trapped by the atmosphere. As the heat energy increases, so too do the average global land and sea temperatures. With higher temperatures and more energy, there is increased intensity and variability in the global climate system, leading to fluctuations or changes in local and regional weather patterns.

Risks

The implications of this complex causal chain are difficult to comprehend in their entirety, and the specifics cannot be predicted with certainty. However, it is clear that the effects in terms of human lives and livelihoods are potentially severe.

Since the beginning of the Industrial Revolution in the mid-1800s, global mean surface temperatures have risen by about 0.9°C (IPCC 2018). The atmospheric concentration of the main greenhouse gases has increased from about 285 parts per million (ppm) of carbon dioxide equivalent (CO_2e) to more than 450 ppm of CO_2e today, of which over 400 ppm is CO_2. About 70 years ago, we were adding approximately 0.5 ppm of CO_2e per year, and now we are adding about 2.5 ppm of CO_2e per year. If this trend continues, the median temperature increase over the next one or two centuries would be in the region of 4° C, with a substantial probability of well over 4° C (IPCC 2013).

To put these numbers into context, our civilization has developed during the climatically benign Holocene period, following the last ice age, which came to an end about 9,000 or 10,000 years ago. The Holocene has had relatively stable temperatures that fluctuated in a range of ±1–1.5° C relative to the late nineteenth century benchmark. We are now near the edge of that range. If the temperature increase reaches 3 or 4° C, we would be outside the range of experience of our species, *Homo sapiens*, which is about 250,000 years old. The planet has not seen a 3° C increase in temperature for about 3 million years (when the sea level was about 20 meters higher than it is today; IPCC (2013)), and 4° C for tens of millions of years.

Along with the physical science, the natural and social sciences are rapidly developing models to investigate the risks of rising temperatures for economies, ecosystems, cultures, and social structures. The specifics cannot be known with certainty, but risks to people and the environment will rise rapidly above 1.5°C of warming (IPCC 2018). There is an increased risk of tipping points (Drijfhout et al. 2015) and of exacerbating and compounding other threats, like habitat loss, political instability, and disease (IPCC 2014).

Poor countries and poor people would be hit particularly hard. They rely more heavily on climate-sensitive economic activities like agriculture and have reduced capacity to adapt effectively. Poor people are also more likely to live in hazard zones, such as floodplains, and their assets are more likely to be damaged in extreme weather events. They are also more susceptible to the pests and diseases that follow heat waves, floods, and drought (Hallegatte et al. 2016).

The Urgency

Limiting temperature rises to any specific level requires the restriction of the accumulation of long-lived greenhouse gases in the atmosphere. The concentration of greenhouse gases in the atmosphere cannot exceed a certain threshold and must stabilize at a lower level. The lower the temperature target is, the lower the threshold and stabilization level will be and the sooner emissions will have to peak.

Eventually, global annual emissions will have to reach "net-zero," that is, a balance must be established between the release of greenhouse gases into the atmosphere from human activities and their removal (for example, through reforestation).

The 2° C upper temperature bound in the rise in global mean surface temperature is associated with a remaining "budget" for carbon dioxide, the most important greenhouse gas, of maybe 600–1100 gigatons of CO_2 over the period to 2100, depending on the probability we seek of keeping to the 2° C target; the higher the probability the lower the budget. A 1.5° C target would involve lower budgets in the order of 400–750 gigatons of Co_2 and require reaching net zero by around 2050 (IPCC 2018).

To remain within an emissions budget of 600–1100 gigatons CO_2, global emissions would have to peak before 2020 and decline rapidly from then on. Negative emissions technology (not just expanded forest cover but also, e.g., bioenergy combined with carbon capture and storage) will likely be required later in the century to avoid warming of more than 2° C.

The global emissions budget creates a zero-sum game. The higher one country's emissions are, the lower those of other countries will have to be. It is here that disagreements occur. Developed countries are responsible for the majority of historical greenhouse gas emissions. But the balance of annual emissions has shifted in recent years. Developing countries (led by China) now account for about 60 percent of total annual emissions and will be responsible for most future emissions growth (New Climate Economy 2014). Six of the top 10 emitters are developing countries (World Resources Insititute 2014).

Cooperation

Tackling climate change thus requires efforts from all countries and strong international cooperation. Experience tells us that such cooperation can be hard to secure. International cooperation on climate change has historically been difficult,.

The benefits that accrue from reduced climate risks are a global public good. Countries cannot be excluded from profiting and have incentives to free ride if they perceive reducing emissions to be costly to themselves and disregard the benefits to others. Moreover, the group that would benefit is large and diverse, and the impacts of accelerated climate change affect countries unevenly. These are strong reasons for why reaching an agreement is difficult, but they are also the reasons that international cooperation is needed (Barrett 2003).

Against this backdrop, the Paris Agreement is a remarkable breakthrough in international climate cooperation. To illustrate this, compare Paris to another agreement that seemed almost impossible at the time. The Bretton Woods Agreement brought together 44 countries in an attempt to rebuild the international economic and financial system after World War II in a more cooperative form.

In 1944, Keynes (cited in Braithwaite and Drahos (2001, 98)) described it as "forty-four nations…actually able to work together at a constructive task in amity and unbroken concord. Few believed it possible. If we can continue in a larger task as we have begun in this limited task, there is hope for the world."

Although the Bretton Woods agreement should be regarded as a crucial achievement, it is important to recognize that the urge for collaboration in the post–World War II era and the call for international coordination were almost omnipresent. The grave experience of two world wars and a great depression in 30 years taught some clear and strong lessons. The consequences of the failure to work together were demonstrated to be catastrophic; the evidence was hard and real. Furthermore, the United States was in a dominant position. In contrast, the Paris Agreement brings together more than 180 countries in *anticipation* of future harm, which makes it all the more remarkable. And no one country was dominant.

That an agreement was formed lies not only in the increased understanding of the gravity of the risks but also, and crucially, in an understanding of the attractiveness of alternative pathways to sustainable development. This has changed the calculus of self-interested action. But the agreement also includes features that enhance the willingness to cooperate by increasing the benefits of cooperation and realizing them more quickly, such as international collaboration on low-carbon research and development (Keohane and Victor 2016). Moreover, transfers between country coalitions (in the form of funds, commitments, etc.) helped make the agreement more profitable to participants. However, we should also not underestimate a shared sense of responsibility. Much of the motivation appeared to be beyond narrow self-interest and was about responsibility to future generations.

Yet, however remarkable, the deal struck in Paris must be seen as only the beginning of a long process of international cooperation. The effectiveness of the agreement is yet to be tested. The building blocks that have led to the agreement will need to be expanded and deepened. The pledges submitted ahead of Paris, if fully implemented, still put the world on an emissions path that is closer to 3° C warming than the Paris objective of "well below" 2° C, let alone 1.5° C (Rogelj et al. 2016). Without even closer cooperation by and action from all countries over the next 10–15 years, the chance of remaining well below 2° C is slim.

The Analytical Challenge: Beyond the Marginalist Approach

Economists were slow to recognize the enormity of climate change and its relevance to economic development. Climate change has yet to reach the mainstream in many economics departments. Yet a small number of pioneers have engaged with the topic from an early stage (Nordhaus 1982, 1991a, 1991b; Edmonds and Reilly 1983; Cline 1992; Manne and Richels 1992; Schelling 1992).

The authors of those early works applied the tools of their trade. The groundbreaking work of William Nordhaus was inspired by the growth theory of Ramsey and Solow.[2] The accumulation of greenhouse gases in the atmosphere was understood as an exhaustible resource problem in the spirit of Hotelling. The likely impacts of climate change were enumerated, monetized, and aggregated in the tradition of Pigou and Meade. To correct the externality, economists advocated Pigouvian carbon taxes or Coasean emissions trading schemes (see Fankhauser 1995 for an overview of early climate economics).

Their contributions were essential to building the argument for action. However, by placing a strong focus on the marginalist tools of welfare economics, economists have tended to underestimate both the potential impacts of climate change and the wider benefits of a transition to low-carbon growth, to the point where their models were increasingly at odds with the science. They have focused on fairly marginal perturbations to long-term growth when the question at hand is the management of immense risk and the longer term. Growth itself could be severely disrupted and reversed—not simply perturbed on the margin.

The Precautionary Economics of Climate Change Risks

Initial estimates of the economic costs of climate change began to emerge in the 1990s. They were both derived from and provided input into integrated assessment models. These models attempt to combine the key elements of biophysical and economic systems and represent the full cycle from socioeconomic activity to emissions, temperature change, and impacts that then feed back into the socioeconomics. It was a valiant endeavor, but the early models suffered from a poor evidence base. Many important impacts either had to be omitted or were extrapolated from single data points (Tol and Fankhauser 1998). This had the effect of marginalizing or ignoring some of the most worrying risks identified by scientists.

Today, our evidence base is much better (IPCC 2014). More solid empirical evidence is beginning to emerge on the impacts of moderate climate change, for example, in regard to agricultural impacts (e.g., Schlenker, Hanemann, and Fisher 2005; Schlenker and Lobell 2010) and labor productivity

---

2. Nordhaus's work on climate change economics was recognized with the 2018 Nobel Prize in economics.

(e.g., Heal and Park 2013; Burke, Hsiang, and Miguel 2015). Case study evidence also links climate and conflict (Hsiang and Burke 2014; Kelley et al. 2015).

However, there are inherent limits to the empirical investigation of severe climate impacts on people. The nature of the problem is precisely that it will take us outside the range of the empirically observed in the history of *Homo sapiens* (see above). To understand the consequences of the large temperature changes, we might have to go back further in time and study the evidence from paleoclimatology, for example, on sea levels.

The Intergovernmental Panel on Climate Change therefore concluded that the results of integrated assessment models depend on a number of "disputable" assumptions (IPCC 2014). This is hard to disagree with, when, in one common specification, a temperature increase of 5°C is associated with damages equivalent to just 5–10% of GDP. Temperatures at that level have not been seen for tens of millions of years. The transformation would likely be traumatic.

Integrated assessment models still have a role to play. However, their value does not lie in producing specific estimates of economic damage, which can be profoundly misleading. Instead it lies in documenting the high levels of risk we face. Multiple model runs and some understanding of the omitted impacts show that the balance of uncertainty is heavily tilted toward the downside. Negative surprises relative to the effects that are incorporated are much more likely than positive ones. Economic tools can be used to translate these uncertainties into prescriptions for risk management.

An important strand of research, pioneered by Martin Weitzman, is demonstrating the importance of looking not just at the most likely outcomes but also at the tail of the distribution (Weitzman 2012). However, although the focus on the tails is welcome, the central estimates of potential change over the long term—beyond past human experience—are themselves deeply worrying and offer sufficient grounds for strong action (Stern 2016).

The Dynamic Economics of a Low-Carbon Transition

The economic models available to study low-carbon development paths often, in structure and approach, predate the debate on climate change and have their origin in energy sector planning. At the core of many models are estimates of marginal abatement costs, that is, the incremental costs of reducing emissions by an additional ton. Models based on marginal abatement costs have been useful in informing the low-carbon strategies of many countries. However, by focusing on emission reduction efforts at the margin, they often ignore the inherently systemic nature and dynamic force of transformative change.

Some systemwide effects will make carbon abatement more expensive than would be the case in their absence. We should not underestimate the difficulty of deep structural change. One key concern is rigidities in the labor market, both in terms of labor mobility and wages (Bowen and Kuralbayeva 2015). There are also rigidities in the capital stock. Carbon-intensive capital is often long lived, and assets might get stranded unless investment decisions are sufficiently forward looking (Pfeiffer et al. 2016). And finally, inertia is associated with innovation, which appears to be heavily path dependent (Aghion et al. 2016). Few of these effects are properly modeled as yet, but they point to the dangers of locking in high-carbon capital and infrastructure.

However, there are potentially very large gains from future innovations on cheaper and sustainable paths. We have the potential to harness the large dynamic benefits of low-carbon innovation—unlocking the process of "creative destruction," which Joseph Schumpeter described back in the 1940s. This includes not just technological innovation but also changes in business practices and social behavior (Stern 2016). As engineers learn how to install, connect, and repair technology cheaply, unit costs fall faster for many new technologies than for existing ones. Also influential will be the emergence of new networks, such as the integration of electric-vehicle energy storage into smart grids. Dechezleprêtre, Martin, and Mohnen (2014) find that clean technology innovation creates much higher spillovers than conventional innovation does, on a par with those in transformative sectors like information technology and nanotechnology. New technologies plus wise management and investment can both produce very large gains in energy efficiency. Indeed, nearly half of the required action on climate change could come from energy efficiency.

The low-carbon transition also has other environmental benefits, from reduced fossil-fuel pollution (air and water) to the preservation of the world's forests. In China and India, probably close to 2 million people die each year as a result of poor air quality (New Climate Economy 2014). These are environmental priorities of immense significance that could and should be pursued in their own right, but the low-carbon transition offers opportunities for synergies and coordination.

The Ethics of Intervention

The magnitude of climate risks and the lasting impact of policy choices on lives and livelihoods, both today and in the future, raise issues of equity and justice that are more consequential and difficult than we usually encounter in policy analysis.

Different ethical approaches guide the actions of individuals and communities, but they all provide consistent normative support for strong action (Stern 2007, 2015). Moral guidance is also offered in the teachings of major religions. Concern about future generations, deep respect for the environment, and the duties of the current generation as stewards of the earth are consistent themes.[3]

The ethics discourse in economics has, for the most part, made little accommodation or room for these wider philosophical, ethical, and religious perspectives. It has focused heavily on technical issues, unusually narrowly defined, in particular on the intergenerational question of discounting and the intragenerational issue of burden sharing or dividing up the remaining carbon space.

Discounting is of course a central issue and requires rigorous, analytical scrutiny from economic, philosophical, and political perspectives. It is discussed in great detail elsewhere, and readers are referred to Stern (2007, 2015). Those works argue strongly against pure time-discounting, because it is essentially "discrimination by date of birth" that would be unacceptable, for example, in criminal courts, voting procedures, and human rights. If it were to be introduced as an ethical criteria, it would require direct and convincing argument: Such argument is usually conspicuous by its absence.

These writings also point out that speaking of "the discount rate" as if it were something introduced entirely from outside the debate is a serious conceptual mistake. The discount factor is a relative price between goods

---

3. This can be seen from the Papal encyclical *Laudato Si: On Care for Our Common Home*, the Islamic Declaration on Global Climate Change, the *Bhumi Devi Ki Jai!* (A Hindu Declaration on Climate Change), and the Buddhist Climate Change Statement to World Leaders.

now and in the future. It depends on which goods and which dates. It is a relative price logically prior to the concept of the discount rate, which is the rate of fall of the discount factor. Discount factors, and thus, discount rates, like other prices and values, depend on where we turn out to be, and that depends on our decisions. They are endogenous to our decision-making.

The ethics of "burden sharing" are also often misconstrued. There is a powerful argument that developed countries have a moral obligation, from their history, their wealth, and their technology, to take a strong lead in cutting emissions. However, the current arguments tend to see rights and allocations only in terms of a single dimension: greenhouse gas emissions. The focus on this one dimension ignores a multitude of other relevant influencing factors and the dynamics and co-benefits of the alternative low-carbon transition.

There is no evidence that greenhouse gas emissions are needed for development. Although energy is an essential requirement for development (Fankhauser and Jotzo 2017), it does not necessarily, at least in a technical sense, have to be associated with greenhouse gas emissions, because it is possible to source energy with low or zero emissions. It can be argued that each country or individual has a right to development, a right to energy, and a right to basic human needs, but these rights neither separately nor together imply a right to emit or degrade the environment.

The Policy Challenge: Beyond Incremental Action

The development community is increasingly aware of the risks of climate change (e.g., World Bank 2010, 2012; Hallegatte et al. 2016). However, it has yet to respond to the threat with sufficient purpose and scale. Climate policy is not about incremental initiatives that can be attached to existing development plans. It requires deep structural and systemic change, implemented over many decades, both to reduce emissions and to adapt to remaining climate risks.

Climate-Resilient Development

It is well recognized that even a moderate degree of climate change can pose risks to development. What is less appreciated is the extent to which the rapid development that many developing countries are undergoing—for example, along urban coastlines (Hanson et al. 2011)—is shaping their future vulnerability to climate change.

The pace of development means that the greatest opportunities for achieving climate resilience lie in influencing these trends. Policy makers should incorporate climate risks into long-term development, infrastructure, and spatial planning decisions. This macro-level approach is an important departure from traditional analysis, which has tended to treat adaptation to climate change as a set of independent, threat-specific responses, such as coastal protection schemes.

How does climate-resilient development differ from conventional development? Thomas Schelling, one of the first economists to engage with climate change, famously claimed that economic development was the best form of adaptation, implying that conventional and climate-resilient development are one and the same (Schelling 1992, 1997).

Climate resilience and economic progress are indeed heavily intertwined. However, not all forms of development have the same effect on climate resilience. As countries develop, the structure of their economy evolves, typically away from agriculture. Sectors become more productive, and the location of economic activity may shift to urban centers. Income per capita rises, and with higher incomes the demand for climate protection goes up.

Of these changes, only the increased demand for adaptation unequivocally reduces climate change risks. The net effect of the other trends is unclear. Although agriculture is highly sensitive to climate change, a structural shift into industry and urban living improves resilience only if those sectors and locations encounter fewer climate risks than agriculture, which they may not do (Fankhauser and McDermott 2014, 2016). For example, much urban development has involved building on flood plains.

Pursuing climate-resilient development at the macro scale has institutional consequences. The responsibility for adaptation shifts from environment departments and hydro-meteorological offices to planning and economic ministries. These tend to be more powerful and better able to instigate the necessary reforms. This shift is an important and sometimes overlooked side effect of moving from project-level adaptation to climate-resilient development.

When integrating development and climate action, we should recognize that development (conventionally understood), mitigation, and adaptation are closely intertwined. For example, low-till agriculture and approaches like Sustainable Rice Intensification save energy and water, reduce emissions and are more resilient. There are many further examples in energy, urban planning, and building design.

The Low-Carbon Transition

Fossil fuel-based energy has been such a powerful force of growth and poverty reduction that it seems reasonable to ask, in the words of Dercon (2012), whether "green growth is good for the poor." It is a longstanding concern. The original text of the UN Framework Convention on Climate Change deals extensively with the question of who bears the incremental costs, implying that there is a "horse race" between growth and environmental responsibility.

We now know that the notion of a "horse race" represents a false dichotomy. We have highlighted above the dynamic benefits of an innovation-driven growth model, where learning processes and economies of scale create investment and employment opportunities. We have also outlined the environmental benefits of such a course of action, for example, in terms of air quality, and the great scope for improving resource efficiency. We have emphasized the intertwining of development, mitigation, and adaptation.

The challenge for development policy is to guide economic decisions in this new direction. Even if it is beneficial, structural transformation is never easy. Policy makers will have to tackle fundamental market failures not just in relation to greenhouse gases, but also in networks, capital markets, clean innovation, and the provision of information, and with respect to the local, regional, and global environment. There are harmful policy distortions, not least the subsidization of fossil fuels and the underpricing of energy, which amount to hundreds of billions of dollars each year (Coady et al. 2015; OECD 2015). The vested interests can be very powerful. Political skills and systems will be tested severely.

The choice of policies is important. Carbon pricing has proven to be an effective tool to incentivize emission reductions with very limited effects, so far, on competitiveness (Dechezleprêtre and Sato 2014). The breakthrough of low-carbon technology requires additional support for clean research and early deployment (Dechezleprêtre, Martin, and Bassi 2016). Thoughtful regulation (and its enforcement) also has a role to play, for example, in the form of efficiency standards, planning rules, and building codes. Another essential part of the policy mix is strategies to reduce structural adjustment costs by supporting labor mobility, providing social safety nets, and protecting low-income households.

Spurring low-carbon growth requires the redirection of financial flows and investment. Private investors will only do this if the balance of risks and returns is attractive, and the direction of travel is clear. The consistency, clarity, and credibility of climate policies therefore matter hugely. This is not something current political processes always deliver. Government-induced policy risk is an immense disincentive around the world. However, it is possible to reduce policy uncertainty, for example, through statutory carbon targets enshrined in legislation and monitored by an independent nonpolitical body (Fankhauser 2013).

A key concern is infrastructure. Over the next 20 years, the required investment in infrastructure will be in the region of US$100 trillion or more (Bhattacharya, Oppenheim, and Stern 2015). This new capital will be long lasting, and the choices made now will have enduring consequences for growth, development, and the climate. Currently about 60 percent of global annual greenhouse gas emissions can be attributed to the investment in and use of infrastructure. Very rapid urbanization (likely to rise from about 3.5 billion people now to about 6.5 billion people by mid-century) demonstrates the immense dangers of lock-in of wasteful and polluting structures. These numbers show that investment over the next 20 years will shape the future profoundly: It will determine whether we have cities where we can move and breathe, and whether we can hold the global temperature rise to well below 2° C.

Conclusions

Human ingenuity has succeeded in overcoming natural resource constraints that were once thought binding. That extraordinary progress has not been sufficient to eradicate global poverty, and the natural environment has suffered, but human welfare has improved markedly. However, the environment and development challenges of the twenty-first century are likely to be more difficult than those of the past.

Nowhere is this more evident than for climate change. Climate change is a threat of a completely different magnitude and character from those of the past. To continue our progress in the face of climate risks, we need both strong policy action and a radical deepening of economic analysis. We need to construct theories and models that reflect the unique challenges we now face and the contexts in which they arise.

The response to the threat is not the cessation of economic growth (Jackson 2011; Klein 2015). It is possible to advance economic prosperity and combat climate change at the same time. We argue that an approach to growth driven by clean innovation and investment can create new growth and employment opportunities. The economic, structural, and technological challenges of sustainable growth are massive, but the opportunities are real and very attractive.

However, time is short. Over the next two decades, the emerging markets of Asia, Africa, and Latin America will build their cities, infrastructure, and energy systems. Developed nations will need a major renewal of theirs. The way we make decisions on these issues will determine whether we have a chance of keeping climate change well below 2° C.

There is some reason for optimism. In the Paris Agreement (December 2015) and the Sustainable Development Goals (September 2015), the international community now has a platform through which climate change, environment, and development can be integrated into planning, financing, and investment decisions. We have a global agenda for the first time in which virtually all countries are involved.

To guide these decisions, we call for a *radical deepening of economic analysis*. Climate change is the biggest and most important example of systemic global risk, but it is not the only one, and we, in economics, have to learn to think about and investigate these issues much more carefully. Standard growth theory, general equilibrium, and marginal methods will, as ever, have much to contribute. But they will not be sufficient. We should seek a dynamic economics where we tackle directly issues involving pace and scale of change in the context of major and systemic risks.

We also call for a *departure from development business as usual*. Poor countries have a large pent-up demand for modern forms of energy, transport, and essential consumption goods that must now be met in a low-carbon way. They will suffer most from the adverse effects of climate change and need a form of economic development that manages their climate exposure and increases their capacity to adapt. A key focus must be investment in sustainable infrastructure. The world needs strong and clear policies to foster those investments and a major expansion in finance to undertake them. With their range of instruments, the confidence inspired by their presence, and the ability to take a long-term view, the development banks have a vital role to play.

Managing climate change and reducing poverty are the defining challenges of the twenty-first century. Both can be tackled, and the alternative paths to sustainable growth are very attractive. We know what needs to be done, we know how to begin, and we will learn along the way.

References

Aghion, Philippe, Antoine Dechezleprêtre, David Hémous, Ralf Martin, and John Van Reenen. 2016. "Carbon Taxes, Path Dependency, and Directed Technical Change: Evidence from the Auto Industry." *Journal of Political Economy* 124 (1): 1–51.

Barrett, Scott. 2003. *Environment and Statecraft: The Strategy of Environmental Treaty-Making*. Oxford: Oxford University Press.

Bhattacharya, Amar, Jeremy Oppenheim, and Nicholas H. Stern. 2015. "Driving Sustainable Development through Better Infrastructure: Key Elements of a Transformation Program." Global Working Paper 91, Brookings Institution, Washington, DC.

Boulding, Kenneth E. 1966. "The Economics of the Coming Spaceship Earth." In *Environmental Quality in a Growing Economy: Essays from the Sixth RFF Forum*, edited by Henry Jarrett, 3–14. Baltimore: Resources for the Future, Johns Hopkins University Press.

Bowen, Alex, and Karlygash Kuralbayeva. 2015. "Looking for Green Jobs: The Impact of Green Growth on Employment." Policy brief, Grantham Research Institute on Climate Change and the Environment, London School of Economics and Political Science, London.

Braithwaite, John, and Peter Drahos. 2001. *Global Business Regulation*. Cambridge: Cambridge University Press.

Burke, Marshall, Solomon M. Hsiang, and Edward Miguel. 2015. "Global Non-Linear Effect of Temperature on Economic Production." *Nature* 527 (7577): 235.

Cline, William. 1992. *The Economics of Global Warming*. Washington, DC: Peterson Institute for International Economics.

Coady, David, Ian Parry, Louis Sears, and Baoping Shang. 2015. "How Large Are Global Energy Subsidies?" IMF Working Paper 15/105, International Monetary Fund, Washington, DC.

Coase, Ronald H. 1960. "The Problem of Social Cost." *Journal of Law & Economics* 3 (October): 1–44.

Dechezleprêtre, Antoine, and Misato Sato. 2014. "The Impacts of Environmental Regulations on Competitiveness." Policy brief, Grantham Research Institute on Climate Change and the Environment, London School of Economics and Political Science, London.

Dechezleprêtre, Antoine, Ralf Martin, and Samuela Bassi. 2016. "Climate Change Policy, Innovation and Growth." Policy brief, Grantham Research Institute on Climate Change and the Environment, London School of Economics and Political Science, London.

Dechezleprêtre, Antoine, Ralf Martin, and Myra Mohnen. 2014. "Knowledge Spillovers from Clean and Dirty Technologies: A Patent Citation Analysis." Working Paper 135, Grantham Research Institute on Climate Change and the Environment, London School of Economics and Political Science, London.

Dercon, Stefan. 2012. "Is Green Growth Good for the Poor?" Policy Research Working Paper 6231, World Bank, Washington, DC.

Drèze, Jean, and Nicholas H. Stern. 1987. "The Theory of Cost-Benefit Analysis." In *Handbook of Public Economics*, volume 2, edited by Alan J. Auerbach and Martin Feldstein, 909–989. Amsterdam: North-Holland.

Drèze, Jean, and Nicholas H. Stern. 1990. "Policy Reform, Shadow Prices, and Market Prices." *Journal of Public Economics* 42 (1): 1–45.

Drijfhout, Sybren, Sebastian Bathiany, Claudie Beaulieu, Victor Brovkin, Martin Claussen, Chris Huntingford, Marten Scheffer, Giovanni Sgubin, and Didier Swingedouw. 2015. "Catalogue of Abrupt Shifts in Intergovernmental Panel on Climate Change Climate Models." *Proceedings of the National Academy of Sciences* 112 (43): E5777–E5786.

Edmonds, Jae, and John Reilly. 1983. "A Long-Term Global Energy-Economic Model of Carbon Dioxide Release from Fossil Fuel Use." *Energy Economics* 5 (2): 74–88.

Fankhauser, Sam. 1995. *Valuing Climate Change: The Economics of the Greenhouse.* London: Earthscan.

Fankhauser, Sam. 2013. "A Practitioner's Guide to a Low-Carbon Economy: Lessons from the UK." *Climate Policy* 13 (3): 345–362.

Fankhauser, Sam, and Frank Jotzo. 2017. "Economic Growth and Development with Low-Carbon Energy." *Wiley Interdisciplinary Review Climate Change*: e495.

Fankhauser, Sam, and Thomas K. J. McDermott. 2014. "Understanding the Adaptation Deficit: Why Are Poor Countries More Vulnerable to Climate Events Than Rich Countries?" *Global Environmental Change* 27 (Supplement C): 9–18.

Fankhauser, Sam, and Thomas K. J. McDermott, eds. 2016. *The Economics of Climate-Resilient Development.* Cheltenham, UK: Edward Elgar.

Freeman, Jody, and Charles D. Kolstad. 2007. *Moving to Markets in Environmental Regulation: Lessons from Twenty Years of Experience.* Oxford: Oxford University Press.

Hallegatte, Stephane, Mook Bangalore, Laura Bonzanigo, Marianne Fay, Tamaro Kane, Ulf Narloch, Julie Rozenberg, David Treguer, and Adrien Vogt-Schilb. 2016. *Shock Waves: Managing the Impacts of Climate Change on Poverty.* Washington, DC: World Bank.

Hanley, Nick, and Edward B. Barbier. 2009. *Pricing Nature: Cost-Benefit Analysis and Environmental Policy.* Cheltenham, UK: Edward Elgar.

Hanson, Susan, Robert Nicholls, N. Ranger, S. Hallegatte, J. Corfee-Morlot, C. Herweijer, and J. Chateau. 2011. "A Global Ranking of Port Cities with High Exposure to Climate Extremes." *Climatic Change* 104 (1): 89–111.

Hartwick, John M. 1977. "Intergenerational Equity and the Investing of Rents from Exhaustible Resources." *American Economic Review* 67 (5): 972–974.

Heal, Geoffrey, and Jisung Park. 2013. "Feeling the Heat: Temperature, Physiology & the Wealth of Nations." NBER Working Paper 19725, National Bureau of Economic Research, Cambridge, MA.

Hedlund-Nyström, Torun, Lars Jonung, Karl-Gustaf Löfgren, and Bo Sandelin. 2006. "Knut Wicksell on Forestry: A Note." In *Swedish Economic Thought: Explorations and Advances,* edited by Lars Jonung, 46–65. London and New York: Routledge.

Hotelling, Harold. 1931. "The Economics of Exhaustible Resources." *Journal of Political Economy* 39 (2): 137–175.

Hsiang, Solomon M., and Marshall Burke. 2014. "Climate, Conflict, and Social Stability: What Does the Evidence Say?" *Climatic Change* 123 (1): 39–55.

IPCC (Intergovernmental Panel on Climate Change). 2007. *Climate Change 2007: Synthesis Report. Contribution of Working Groups I, II and III to the Fourth Assessment Report of the Intergovernmental Panel on Climate Change.* Geneva: Intergovernmental Panel on Climate Change.

IPCC (Intergovernmental Panel on Climate Change). 2013. *Climate Change 2013: The Physical Science Basis: Working Group I Contribution to the Fifth Assessment Report of the Intergovernmental Panel on Climate Change.* Cambridge: Cambridge University Press.

IPCC (Intergovernmental Panel on Climate Change). 2014. *Climate Change 2014: Impacts, Adaptation and Vulnerability. Part A: Global and Sectoral Aspects. Contribution of Working Group II to the Fifth Assessment Report of the Intergovernmental Panel on Climate Change.* Cambridge: Cambridge University Press.

IPCC (Intergovernmental Panel on Climate Change). 2018. *Global Warming of 1.5°.* An IPCC Special Report, Intergovernmental Panel on Climate Change, Geneva.

Jackson, Tim. 2011. *Prosperity without Growth: Economics for a Finite Planet*. London: Routledge.

Kelley, Colin P., Shahrzad Mohtadi, Mark A. Cane, Richard Seager, and Yochanan Kushnir. 2015. "Climate Change in the Fertile Crescent and Implications of the Recent Syrian Drought." *Proceedings of the National Academy of Sciences* 112 (11): 3241–3246.

Keohane, Robert O., and David G. Victor. 2016. "Cooperation and Discord in Global Climate Policy." *Nature Climate Change* 6 (6): 570–575.

Klein, Naomi. 2015. *This Changes Everything: Capitalism vs. The Climate*. New York: Simon & Schuster.

Little, Ian, Malcolm David, and James A. Mirrlees. 1974. *Project Appraisal and Planning for Developing Countries*. New York: Basic Books.

Manne, Alan Sussmann, and Richard G. Richels. 1992. *Buying Greenhouse Insurance: The Economic Costs of Carbon Dioxide Emission Limits*. Cambridge, MA: MIT Press.

Meade, James Edward. 1955. *Trade and Welfare*. London, New York: Oxford University Press.

Meadows, Donella H., Dennis L. Meadows, Jørgen Randers, and William W. Behrens. 1972. *The Limits to Growth*. New York: Universe Books.

Montesquieu, Charles Baron de. [1748] 2011. *The Spirit of Laws*. Translated by Thomas Nugent. New York: Cosimo Classics.

New Climate Economy. 2014. *Better Growth, Better Climate: The New Climate Economy Report*. London: Global Commission on the Economy and Climate.

Nordhaus, William D. 1982. "How Fast Should We Graze the Global Commons?" *American Economic Review* 72 (2): 242–246.

Nordhaus, William D. 1991a. "A Sketch of the Economics of the Greenhouse Effect." *American Economic Review* 81 (2): 146–150.

Nordhaus, William D. 1991b. "To Slow or Not to Slow: The Economics of the Greenhouse Effect." *Economic Journal* 101 (407): 920–937.

OECD (Organisation for Economic Co-operation and Development). 2015. *OECD Companion to the Inventory of Support Measures for Fossil Fuels 2015*. Paris: OECD Publishing.

Pearce, David W. 2002. "An Intellectual History of Environmental Economics." *Annual Review of Energy and the Environment* 27: 57–81.

Pearce, David W., and Jeremy J. Warford. 1993. *World without End: Economics, Environment, and Sustainable Development*. Oxford: Oxford University Press.

Pfeiffer, Alexander, Richard Millar, Cameron Hepburn, and Eric Beinhocker. 2016. "The '2°C Capital Stock' for Electricity Generation: Committed Cumulative Carbon

Emissions from the Electricity Generation Sector and the Transition to a Green Economy." *Applied Energy* 179 (Supplement C): 1395–1408.

Pigou, Arthur C. 1920. *The Economics of Welfare*. London: Macmillan.

Rhode, Robert A., and Richard A. Muller. 2015. "Air Pollution in China: Mapping of Concentrations and Sources." *PLoS ONE* 10 (8): e0135749.

Rockström, Johan, Will Steffen, Kevin Noone, Åsa Persson, F. Stuart Chapin III, Eric F. Lambin, Timothy M. Lenton, et al. 2009. "A Safe Operating Space for Humanity." *Nature* 461 (7263): 472–475.

Rogelj, J., M. Den Elzen, N. Höhne, T. Fransen, H. Fekete, H. Winkler, R. Schaeffer, F. Sha, K. Riahi and M. Meinshausen. 2016. "Paris Agreement Climate Proposals Need a Boost to Keep Warming Well Below 2 C." *Nature* 534 (7609): 631–639.

Sandmo, Agnar. 2015. "The Early History of Environmental Economics." *Review of Environmental Economics and Policy* 9 (1): 43–63.

Schelling, Thomas C. 1992. "Some Economics of Global Warming." *American Economic Review* 82 (1): 1–14.

Schelling, Thomas C. 1997. "The Cost of Combating Global Warming." *Foreign Affairs* 76 (6): 8–14.

Schlenker, Wolfram, and David B. Lobell. 2010. "Robust Negative Impacts of Climate Change on African Agriculture." *Environmental Research Letters* 5 (1): 014010.

Schlenker, Wolfram, W. Michael Hanemann, and Anthony C. Fisher. 2005. "Will U.S. Agriculture Really Benefit from Global Warming? Accounting for Irrigation in the Hedonic Approach." *American Economic Review* 95 (1): 395–406.

Solow, Robert M. 1974. "Intergenerational Equity and Exhaustible Resources." *Review of Economic Studies* 41 (5): 29–45.

Stern, Nicholas H. 2007. *The Economics of Climate Change: The Stern Review*. Cambridge: Cambridge University Press

Stern, Nicholas H. 2015. *Why Are We Waiting?: The Logic, Urgency, and Promise of Tackling Climate Change*. Cambridge, MA: MIT Press.

Stern, Nicholas H. 2016. "Economics: Current Climate Models Are Grossly Misleading." *Nature News* 530 (7591): 407–409.

Sterner, Thomas. 2003. *Policy Instruments for Environmental and Natural Resource Management*. Washington, DC: Resources for the Future.

TEEB (The Economics of Ecosystems and Biodiversity). 2010. *The Economics of Ecosystems and Biodiversity*. London: Earthscan.

Tol, Richard S. J., and Sam Fankhauser. 1998. "On the Representation of Impact in Integrated Assessment Models of Climate Change." *Environmental Modeling & Assessment* 3 (1–2): 63–74.

Weitzman, Martin L. 2012. "GHG Targets as Insurance Against Catastrophic Climate Damages." *Journal of Public Economic Theory* 14 (2): 221–244.

World Bank. 2010. *World Development Report 2010: Development and Climate Change.* Washington, DC: World Bank.

World Bank. 2011. *The Changing Wealth of Nations: Measuring Sustainable Development in the New Millennium.* Washington, DC: World Bank.

World Bank. 2012. *Turn Down the Heat: Why a 4°C Warmer World Must Be Avoided.* Washington, DC: World Bank.

World Commission on Environment and Development (Brundtland Commission). 1987. *Our Common Future.* Oxford: Oxford University Press.

World Resources Institute. 2014. "CAIT Climate Database." http://cait.wri.org/.

Comment: Michael Toman

In their paper, Fankhauser and Stern (hereafter FS) do a fine job of demonstrating the urgent need to address the threat of global climate change, a view that I very much share. Climate change will be a particular threat for World Bank client countries with greater vulnerabilities due to their location (e.g., in low-lying coastal areas); the prevalence of at-risk sectors in their economic activity (e.g., low-productivity subsistence agriculture); a lower level of access to more resilient technologies; and less developed institutional capacities for adapting to climate change (e.g., in delivering public health programs). Similar arguments have also been made in a flagship report by the Bank on climate change and poverty risks (Hallegatte et al. 2016). Although many of the major risks will materialize in the future, inertia in the earth's climate system and in the adjustment of capital stocks in the economy mean that actions need to start in earnest now to stem the risks, even though their magnitudes are uncertain.

FS also argue that now is the time for a major push to stem climate change risks through deep and rapid cuts in global greenhouse gas emissions. For reasons described below, I am less sanguine about this possibility—though I would be glad to be wrong. FS base their conclusion on several premises:

1. The ethical argument for the responsibility of this generation to protect future generations from the serious adverse effects of climate change is unambiguous.

2. The political aspects of obtaining international agreement on concerted action to mitigate greenhouse gas emissions have become more favorable (New Climate Economy 2015), particularly in light of the Paris Agreement established at the United Nations conference on climate change in late 2015 (UNFCCC 2015, Addendum).

3. Rapid decarbonization can be undertaken in ways that actually create economic opportunity over the medium and longer terms, for developing and developed countries alike, through new opportunities for technical advance and creation of markets for new goods and services (New Climate Economy 2014).

4. There are near-term benefits of mitigating greenhouse gas emissions as well—most notably, "co-benefits" obtained when switching to renewable energy and improving energy efficiency reduce local pollutants from fossil fuel burning that damage human health and the environment.

With respect to the first point, I do not think there is yet a widely shared view of what it means in practice to assume an intergenerational responsibility. Is the obligation of the current generation to do as much as possible to mitigate cumulative emissions in an attempt to forestall catastrophic impacts of climate change, an option discussed in (Barrett 2013)? What is the responsibility to reduce noncatastrophic risks as well? Are there different ethical obligations between mitigating greenhouse gas emissions and strengthening resilience to climate change?

Greater complexity comes in addressing unavoidable questions about how nearer-term costs of emissions mitigation and improved resilience to climate change are to be shared among members of the current generation. Almost 25 years of analytical work and policy wrangling have not led to practical resolution of the burden-sharing issue, other than the general recognition that better-off countries should carry more of the burden. Funding for cost-sharing remains inadequate, and there continues to be advocacy for expensive low-carbon energy projects in low-income developing countries whose contributions to global emissions are minimal.

With respect to the second point, the degree of engagement among developing and developed countries in the 2015 Paris Agreement is indeed a significant achievement. Going forward, it remains to be seen how well countries do in implementing their "Nationally Determined Contributions" (NDCs) to reducing global greenhouse gas emissions. Moreover, mitigating the serious risks from climate change will require substantially deeper cuts than will follow even under full implementation of NDCs. The basic paradox of international agreements holds: Finding ways to agree on and deliver significant mitigation commitments across many countries is quite difficult.

With respect to the third point, analysis reported in the most recent IPCC assessment indicates relatively modest cumulative effects on consumption over time from greenhouse gas mitigation, *if* everything goes right (IPCC 2014, table SPM2). That means the ready availability *and* public acceptance of cost-effective decarbonization technologies that remain controversial (notably geological carbon sequestration, as well as greatly expanded nuclear power). It also means extremely cost-effective coordinated implementation of national policies to curb greenhouse gas emissions. Costs are considerably higher if these strong assumptions do not hold.

Beyond these challenges, it is important to be circumspect about the economics of rapidly and massively scaling up decarbonization. A great deal can be accomplished with improvements in energy efficiency. On the other hand, although solar power in particular seems to be increasingly inexpensive these days, the cost of overcoming intermittency—through combinations of back-up fossil fuel generation, smart grids (which help only for uncorrelated intermittency), and evolving but still-costly storage—also must be taken into account.

The 2014 New Climate Economy report makes much of the broader possibilities for "creative destruction" from more stringent limits on greenhouse gas emissions, leading to economic gains from increased innovation and new markets. I think the breadth of applicability of this argument needs further validation. Although retiring a significant amount of fossil-fuel-based power generation capacity would lead to expanded markets for replacement technologies and competitive gains for some suppliers, such a policy is not likely to be a near-term win across the board. How much innovation would take place also depends critically on the extent to which greenhouse gases are appropriately priced, and what complementary policies for supporting basic and applied R&D are deployed.

The fourth point is a popular argument in climate policy debates, but I think we need to consider more carefully the economic and ethical aspects of counting environmental co-benefits as an argument for greenhouse gas mitigation. Developing countries currently face numerous environmental challenges, including major public health threats from air pollution. However, air pollution can be reduced cost-effectively with established technologies, without the delay or uncertain cost associated with scaling-up low-polluting renewable alternatives to fossil energy. Why not make the strong economic case for cutting these emissions anyway, regardless of what is done with respect to low-carbon energy? From an ethical perspective, there are intense debates about who has a greater responsibility to pay for steps to cut current greenhouse gases in order to protect the welfare of future generations. What can we say about the morality of not pushing for readily available and relatively affordable life-saving pollution control measures today?

FS make the valid and important point that macro and micro scales of analysis need to be better integrated for assessing greenhouse gas mitigation possibilities and for enhancing resilience to climate change. What is needed is more of an "environmental macroeconomics" than is currently within the scope of environmental and natural resource economics. They also argue that at this juncture, it is important to "get the big decisions right"—like how to implement carbon pricing and increase assistance for adaptation measures.

To have a realistic chance to make the deep cuts in future global greenhouse gas emissions that FS rightly advocate, the development of a favorable technological environment is crucial. There is a vital need especially to provide more cost-competitive low-carbon energy technology options. Low-carbon energy sources—renewables, nuclear, and fossil energy use with carbon capture and storage—must increase from less than 20 percent of total energy use to more than 70 percent or even 90 percent by 2100, depending on the stringency of the limit on temperature increase sought (IPCC 2014, figure 7.16). Such a transformation will not be possible without fundamental changes in the cost and performance of low-carbon energy technologies.

The call by some prominent observers (including Stern) for a "Global Apollo Programme to Tackle Climate Change" (King et al. 2015) draws welcome attention to the need for greatly expanding international R&D for greenhouse gas mitigation. The proposal is to do this through voluntary participation in a kind of "Low-Carbon Technology Innovation Club." Keohane and Victor (2016) describe in more detail such an approach for international cooperation to develop technologies needed for deep cuts in greenhouse gas emissions, as part of a larger framework for different types of climate change policy coordination. However, the initial target proposed by King et al. (2015) of $15 billion per year, or about 0.02 percent of global GDP, is roughly an order of magnitude smaller than the required investment levels per year that the International Energy Agency has calculated to be necessary for a low-carbon transition (IEA 2014). How to mobilize such large sums of money in order to make rapid and deep cuts in global greenhouse gas emissions is an urgent but still-unanswered question.

References

Barrett, Scott. 2013. "Climate Treaties and Approaching Catastrophes." *Journal of Environmental Economics and Management* 66 (2): 235–250.

Hallegatte, Stephane, Mook Bangalore, Laura Bonzanigo, Marianne Fay, Tamaro Kane, Ulf Narloch, Julie Rozenberg, David Treguer, and Adrien Vogt-Schilb. 2016. *Shock Waves: Managing the Impacts of Climate Change on Poverty.* Washington, DC: World Bank.

IEA (International Energy Agency). 2014. *World Energy Investment Outlook.* Paris: International Energy Agency. https://www.iea.org/publications/freepublications/public ation/WEIO2014.pdf.

IPCC (Intergovernmental Panel on Climate Change). 2014. *Climate Change 2014: Mitigation of Climate Change. Contribution of Working Group III to the Fifth Assessment Report of the Intergovernmental Panel on Climate Change.* Cambridge: Cambridge University Press.

Keohane, Robert, and David Victor. 2016. "Cooperation and Discord in Global Climate Policy." *Nature Climate Change* 6 (6): 570–575.

King, David, John Browne, Richard Layard, Gus O'Donnell, Martin Rees, Nicholas Stern, and Adair Turner. 2015. "A Global Apollo Programme to Combat Climate Change." London: London School of Economics, Centre for Economic Performance. http://cep.lse.ac.uk/pubs/download/special/Global_Apollo_Programme_Report.pdf).

New Climate Economy. 2014. *Better Growth, Better Climate: Charting a New Path for Low-Carbon Growth and a Safer Climate.* London: Global Commission on the Economy and Climate. http://newclimateeconomy.report/2014/.

New Climate Economy. 2015. *Seizing the Global Opportunity: Partnerships for Better Growth and a Better Climate.* London: Global Commission on the Economy and Climate. http://newclimateeconomy.report/2015/.

UNFCCC (United Nations Framework Convention on Climate Change). 2015. "Report of the Conference of the Parties on Its Twenty-First Session," Paris, November 30–December 15, Addendum. Document FCCC/CP/2015/10/Add.1. http://unfccc.int/resource/docs/2015/cop21/eng/10a01.pdf.

Comment: Gaël Giraud

The Trouble with Climate Economics

Here I briefly comment on the main points raised by the nice and thought-provoking paper by Sam Fankhauser and Nicholas Stern (FS hereafter). The next section deals with the ongoing debate on the seriousness of economic damages induced by climate change. I argue in section 2 that the gravity of the physical risk creates a funding problem that can hardly be expected to be solved solely by conventional means, such as national budgets. Section 3 provides some brief thoughts on the ethical questions raised by FS. Section 4 echoes the strong call made by the authors for a "radical deepening" of integrated economic models aimed at assessing the impact of global warming (and how we can avoid its disastrous effects). For that purpose, the last section offers a tentative suggestion of a dynamic model that could be used as a complement—or an alternative—to more conventional ones.

Climate: It's Serious!

The first and main lesson to be taken away from the FS paper is pretty clear: Economic damages caused by global warming are probably going to be considerably greater than our current economic models predict. This makes it more important than ever to take urgent and drastic action to curb temperature change by reducing carbon emissions. What is more, the authors emphasize the "double inequity" that plagues the challenge

This work benefited from the support of the Energy and Prosperity Chair, under the aegis of the Fondation du Risque (Institut Louis Bachelier, 28 place de la Bourse, 75002 Paris, France). All errors are, of course, mine.

of coping with climate change: Rich countries are responsible for most of the current stock of greenhouse gases in the atmosphere, but poor people in southern countries (and to a lesser extent, in northern ones) will be hit earliest and hardest. On this issue, the index for physical vulnerability to climate change provides an interesting, albeit perfectible, tool for measuring the exposure of poor countries to the consequences of global warming (Guillaumont 2013). Figure 7.1 illustrates the geographical distribution of physical climate risk, as estimated according to this index.

Even a country like France is acutely concerned, through its overseas geographies (Goujon, Hoarau, and Rivière 2015) of course, but also with respect to its metropolitan territory (Le Treut 2013). Hallegatte et al. (2016) estimate that about 100 million people in the world may be relegated to below the poverty line by 2030 because of climate change. Obviously, as stressed by FS, "mitigation, adaptation, and development are intertwined," such that the "horse-race" between climate policy and development represents a "false dichotomy." Some concrete experiences confirm that development and climate policy can—and actually ought to—be achieved at the same time. Many of the projects in which Agence Française de Développement (AFD) is involved reflect this conjugacy, from urban planning (in Porto Novo, Benin, or the Philippines) and addressing rising sea levels, to building the solar power plant near Ouarzazate (Morocco). Additional examples include agroecological micro-projects in Zimbabwe or sanitation programs in the slums of Santo Domingo's Barquita district, aimed at children suffering from leptospirosis, a disease spread by alternating periods of drought and devastating typhoons. As a consequence, adaptation to global warming and resilience are of utmost importance for southern countries, whereas mitigation should be a priority for emerging and advanced economies. Unfortunately, this does not mean that developing countries could be exempted from any efforts regarding mitigation. Greenhouse gas emissions stemming from Sub-Saharan Africa today represent less than 3.4 percent of the world's emissions. But Liousse et al. (2014) suggest that by 2030, this continent's contribution could account for up to 20 percent of global emissions, or even more—at least in a business-as-usual scenario. Thus, even for some countries that have not yet emerged, a path toward emergence that would simply mimic Western "dirty" production modes and life style should not be considered a valid option. This is particularly true in Asia, where the already planned coal-fired power plants—if they do indeed

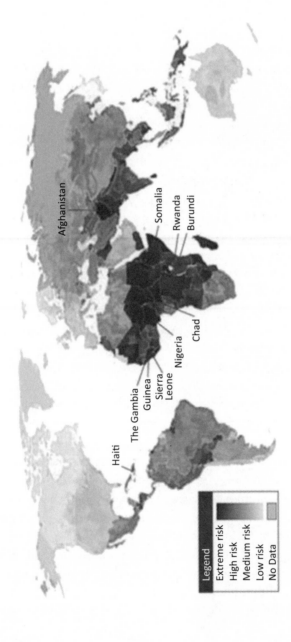

Figure 7.1
Physical vulnerability to climate change
Source: Guillaumont (2013).

start operating in the near future—would absorb the entire carbon budget left available at world level, if we want the average planetary temperature increase to have reasonable chances of remaining below 2° C.

On this count, my feeling is that we urgently need more data on the regional and local impacts of climate change: Global integrated assessment models, however powerful they might be, will remain of middling help for the political agenda as long as we are not able to increase the granularity of our understanding of the consequences of global warming. Climatologists are devoting valuable efforts to this central issue: Vautard et al. (2014) and Le Treut (2013), among many others, show that, at least for some territories, it is possible to get a relatively clear picture of the consequences of climate change in the foreseeable future, provided a truly interdisciplinary methodology is adopted.

Reducing greenhouse gases is far from easy, but efficient adaptation is actually an even more challenging task, because resilience to climate change means shaping infrastructure and institutions so that they evolve according to a phenomenon that is itself dynamic and highly nonlinear. A single example can illustrate this point: The coast of Danang and Hoïan, in Vietnam, is heavily eroded by the rise of the sea level. One immediate answer that comes to mind—inspired, say, by the secular experience of Dutch polders—would involve building dikes so as to protect the coast. This, however, might prove to be a short-sighted and even counterproductive answer. Indeed, as the sea level rises, the direction of flows and waves might change in the coming decades. Being the result of complex turbulence phenomena related to the nonlinear Navier-Stokes partial differential equation, these changes are hard to predict. Dikes that would be efficient in the short-term might promote a disaster in the medium run. A smart answer therefore calls for some kind of adaptive process. It seems to me that we are just beginning to realize how demanding this challenge is.

Let me close this section on the physical risks arising from the coming increased frequency and severity of climate- and weather-related events by stressing one particularly important point that might well be overlooked in a hasty reading of the FS paper. Mentioning the celebrated debate about Malthusian pessimism, the authors rightly argue: "So far, Malthus and the resource pessimists have generally appeared to be wrong. Human ingenuity has mostly managed to outpace natural resource constraints."

That the carefulness of this statement is not a mere rhetorical precaution is confirmed by the conclusions of the thirty-third report to the Club of Rome (Bardi 2014): Today, the world's mining industry is already starting to show worrying signs of difficulty. The mineral resources that are the least expensive to extract and process have mostly been exploited and depleted.[1] Whilst there are plenty of minerals left to extract, they will come at higher financial and energy cost and be increasingly difficult to extract. Thus, the depletion of minerals (in the economic rather than geological sense, meaning the unsustainable cost of today's plundering of the planet) has to be weighed up when planning the path towards societies based on renewable energies (Vidal, Goffé, and Arndt 2013; Giraud 2014).[2]

Mobilizing Climate Finance

Insurers are on the frontline of physical risks. This engagement is illustrated by the Insurance Development Forum—a partnership formed in 2015 between the UN Development Programme, the World Bank, and the insurance sector with the intention of using the industry's expertise to insure people in developing countries who are unprotected but vulnerable to climate change risk. According to Bank of England's Governor Mark Carney, "this protection gap currently represents 90 percent of the economic costs of natural disasters that are uninsured."[3]

But beyond the physical risk, and because of its very gravity, the financial stake should not be neglected. As argued by Carney, too rapid a movement toward a low-carbon economy could materially damage financial stability: "A wholesale re-assessment of prospects, as climate-related risks are re-evaluated, could destabilise markets, spark a pro-cyclical crystallisation of losses and lead to a persistent tightening of financial conditions: a climate Minsky moment" (Carney 2016). Conversely, insufficient adoption

---

1. To take the example of copper (a widely used mineral still difficult to substitute in many industrial applications), the density of copper resources exploited so far had been greater than 5 percent on average. That of today's remaining resources is at most 1 percent (Vidal, Goffé, and Arndt 2013).
2. Depletion is not the only problem: pollution induced by mining takes many forms and produces many consequences, including the aggravation of climate change.
3. Carney (2016).

of adequate financial tools may prevent the world economy from investing at the required scale.

The strong warnings expressed by FS are in line with those of the Bank of England's governor, as well as with the message put forward by the New Climate Economy (2014) report. According to the latter, US$90 trillion are needed at the world level over the next 15 years to fund clean infrastructures; US$2 trillion per year in high-income countries, and between US$3 and 4 trillion in low- and middle-income countries. These numbers prompt a daunting question: How will the world economy finance such monetary flows? The first difficulty lies probably in the huge Knightian uncertainty that plagues any cost-benefit analysis of the opportunity to devote costly efforts today to addressing climate change challenges.

FS rightly claim that the international community needs now to "get the big decisions right." One could object, however, that given the pervasive deep uncertainty we are facing, big decisions might also lead to big mistakes. At the analytical level at least, this issue has been successfully tackled in the field of financial measures of risk. Value at risk, as is well known, provides a poor measure of the tail of a risk distribution. However, Artzner et al. (1999) laid the axiomatic foundation of a family of alternative coherent risk measures, whose essence is the following. In a situation where we do not even know with sufficient accuracy the probability distribution of risk, a rational approach consists of envisaging the worst distribution of risk and optimizing our expected outcome according to it. Thus it would not be fair, I believe, to claim that deep uncertainty prevents us from taking action along the lines advocated by FS.

That being said, the question as to how the international community is going to fund the required financial efforts remains open. The Green Climate Fund established at the Conference of the Parties (known as COP 16) in Cancun in 2011 is quite a promising tool but, in its current design, its size may not suffice to reach an adequate order of magnitude, even when due account is taken of the leverage effect of additional private capital markets. Thus, complementary solutions are called for. Two reports published before and after the Paris agreement (Canfin et al. 2015; Canfin, Grandjean, and Mestrallet 2016) consider some alternative proposals. Let me just mention two of them.

Canfin, Grandjean, and Mestralle (2016) make a strong case in favor of orienting international negotiations toward a corridor of carbon prices.

Indeed, the quest for a unique, universally relevant price is probably a dead end: Why should the (real) marginal costs of producing 1 ton of carbon be equal across countries? Beyond obvious cross-sectional differences between national industry and agricultural sectors, the lack of methodological robustness surrounding the purchasing power parity calculus and the long-standing noncoincidence of these rates with market exchange rates are well known. There is probably very little hope of ever being able to identify "the" market carbon price that would provide the right incentives for efficient decarbonization in Maputo, Buenos Aires, or Osaka, for example. Moreover, the financial transfers from northern to southern countries that would be required to compensate for the losses incurred by the latter seem to exceed the limits of any politically reasonable transaction. In contrast, the corridor approach requires the international community to agree on three variables: a cap, a floor, and the slope of the tubular neighborhood (i.e., the speed at which the median price would increase, keeping the cap-and-floor diameter constant). At the time these lines were written, a US$20–50 interval, together with a 5 percent yearly growth rate seem to be reasonable figures on which an international consensus would not be out of reach.

Next, Canfin et al. (2015) suggest setting up a financing tool that uses the ability of the International Monetary Fund to create new international reserve money in the form of Special Drawing Rights (SDRs). In contrast to some proposals dealing with SDRs (e.g., Bredenkamp and Pattillo 2010), the plan of Canfin et al. (2015) is not to create new and additional SDRs but rather to use already existing ones. In fact, in 2009, the International Monetary Fund "printed" about US$300 billion to sustain countries shackled by the financial turmoil of the 2008–2009 global financial crisis. A large fraction of this "money" is stored today as currency reserves and could be turned into full-blown money provided the countries that received this manna in 2009 would agree to convert it and thus pay the (low) interest due to the International Monetary Fund as soon as the SDR-option is exercised.[4] This is admittedly quite an unconventional proposal, and more analysis is needed to understand its macroeconomic implications.[5] It should never-

---

4. An SDR can indeed be viewed as a call on one of the four currencies into which SDRs are convertible—the US dollar, the euro, the pound sterling, and the yen—with an unspecified maturity.
5. See, however, the section on "The Trouble with Macroeconomics" in these comments.

theless be clear from FS's paper that overcoming the climate challenge will not be cheap. As most countries currently confronted with huge public deficits are reluctant to spend money on medium-term climate-related issues, a genuinely effective climate policy to reduce global warming as much as still possible probably has to rely on unconventional tools.

Can Ethical Traditions Cooperate?

As pointed out by FS, when assessing financial risks associated with the transition to a low-carbon economy, ethical issues inevitably come to the fore. Indeed, due to the intergenerational gap between polluters and victims,[6] standard incentives (e.g., carbon taxes) are key tools, as ever, but are probably insufficient to provide the right impetus. Some spiritual or moral resources are needed—at the cost, however, of having to face today's proliferation of spiritual experimentations in our globalized postsecular societies (Giraud 2015). Could the rich diversity of ethical traditions prevent these efforts from unifying on the front of the climate change "tragedy" (Carney 2016), and therefore from providing a clear call to action?

On this aspect of the climate change problem, social choice theory can be helpful. In fact, at least to a first analytical approximation, modern consequentialist theories of distributive justice can be encapsulated in two extremal points. On the one hand is the utilitarian viewpoint, which claims that justice consists of maximizing the average welfare of people's normalized utility functions (see, e.g., Dhillon and Mertens 1999);[7] on the other is the Rawlsian (maximin) approach, which asserts that fairness is best captured by optimizing the fate of the less advantaged citizens (Fleurbaey and Maniquet 2008). A continuum of intermediate theories of justice can be conceived, lying somewhere between these two extreme standpoints

---

6. One could also add the geographic gap that prevailed until recently between polluters (mostly in the north) and their contemporaneous victims (mostly in the south). But the magnitude of this second gap is currently shrinking, as emerging economies are now contributing more to greenhouse gas emissions than countries from the Old World, as FS remind us.

7. Citizens' utility functions need to be normalized in some way or other, because otherwise, the arbitrariness of the cardinal representation of ordinal preferences potentially leads to distortions in the respective weight of each individual utility. In a broad sense, Dhillon and Mertens (1999) essentially offer a quite general axiomatic that leads to a unique, well-defined normalization procedure.

(Giraud and Gupta 2016). With each of these theories, a specific social welfare function can be associated, whose optimization (under standard constraints) potentially leads to diverging guidelines for action.

For the sake of concreteness, let us examine this point with respect to the specific (but decisive) issue of choosing the "right" discount rate with which future expected profits and losses can be valued. As argued by Sterner and Persson (2008), there actually is no reason to assume a priori that the discount rate must be constant across time. Let us nevertheless assume that it is, for the sake of simplicity (and because this is still the current practice in the financial industry today). Then, if one is utilitarian (in the sense of Jean-François Mertens's relative utilitarianism), the discount rate, r, that should be adopted ought to be equal to the real growth rate, g, of the economy.[8] In the context of our current debates, this choice means that the discussion about the "correct" discount measure boils down to the plausibility of secular stagnation. If there are good reasons to believe that g will remain low (and even close to zero) in the future, then there are equally good reasons—at least in a utilitarian Weltanschauung—to choose a low (or even zero) discount rate. For those who, on the contrary, adhere to the Rawlsian perspective, things might seem to be completely different. But in fact they are not. Indeed, Roemer (2011) has shown that the "correct" discount rate that should be deduced from a normative maximin approach is zero. As a result, the practical difference between two apparently antagonistic ethical postures, such as utilitarianism versus the Rawlsian viewpoint, might not be as large as initially suspected.

The Trouble with Macroeconomics

Beyond warning that emissions are presumably going to be very high and, on top of that, that the economic damage from temperature change will presumably be much worse than most of the literature would so far admit, Fankhauser and Stern (2016, 23) argue that the economic models that have

---

8. In other words, the normalization of citizens' utility functions boils down to the unitary normalization of the risk aversion premium (or, geometrically, the curvature of utility functions), γ, in the "golden rule" formula, $r = \theta + \gamma g$, with θ being the normative exchange rate between the welfare of today's generations and that of future generations (or, equivalently, the psychological rate of time preference). I assume here that $\theta = 0$.

been used to calculate the fiscal fallout from climate change are woefully inadequate and severely underestimate the scale of the threat: "This is why we call for a radical deepening of economic analysis, including a development economics that begins to understand and incorporate climate change. Standard growth theory, general equilibrium and marginal methods will, as ever, have much to contribute but they will be nowhere near sufficient. This is about immense risks and radical change where time is of the essence. We should seek a dynamic economics where we tackle directly issues involving pace and scale of change in the context of major and systemic risks."

Indeed, several of the standard economic models used so far to assess the impact of global warming rest on assumptions that simply do not reflect current knowledge about climate change. The difficulty encountered today by the community of physicists in their dialog with the scientific tribe of economists (e.g., in the UN Intergovernmental Panel on Climate Change circles) is not new, however. It was already acknowledged by Wassily Leontief in the early 1980s "How long will researchers working in ajoining fields…abstain from expressing serious concern about the splendid isolation in which academic economics now finds itself?" (Leontief 1982, 104).

FS's call for a "radical deepening" is also in line with the even harsher considerations recently expressed by Narayana Kocherlakota (2016) on macroeconomics as such:

> The premise of "serious" modelling is that macroeconomic research can and should be grounded in an established body of theory. My own view is that, after the highly surprising nature of the data flow over the past ten years, this basic premise of "serious" modelling is wrong: we simply do not have a settled successful theory of the macroeconomy. The choices made 25–40 years ago—made then for a number of excellent reasons—should not be treated as written in stone or even in pen. By doing so, we are choking off paths for understanding the macroeconomy.

The former president of the Federal Reserve of Minneapolis concludes that we should prefer toy models to "serious modeling." The difference between the two lies in their relationships to data and their normative usage: "Users of toy models can often gauge the magnitude of key forces using simple calculations. (Mehra and Prescott 1985 is a nice example of what I have in mind.) But toy models are not designed to allow users to reach definitive quantitative answers to policy questions of interest" (Kocherlakota 2016).

The criticism expressed by Romer (2016) about what he calls "post-real macroeconomics" rather nicely complements Kocherlakota's viewpoint. At the core of Romer's critique lies the idea that "macroeconomists got comfortable with the idea that fluctuations in macroeconomic aggregates are caused by imaginary shocks, instead of actions that people take, after Kydland and Prescott (1982) launched the real business cycle (RBC) model." Regarding dynamic stochastic general equilibrium (DSGE) models, the harsh judgment recently formulated by Blanchard (2016) suggests that, despite being widely used in advising policy makers, this specific class of quantitative tools is not immune to the in-depth questioning of contemporaneous macroeconomics raised by the past decade of evidence. Even though, to the best of my knowledge, DSGE models are rarely used for assessing the economic impact of global warming, some of the critiques that Blanchard (2016) levels at them also hold for alternative (computable) equilibrium models—in particular, the difficulty of providing a convincing story for price inertia, the lack of robustness of certain Bayesian estimations, and the relative neglect of issues related to the distribution of wealth. These critiques suggest that FS's call for a "radical deepening" is actually part of a larger revision of current macroeconomics. In this context, however, it raises specific challenges linked to climate and development economics. Which features should realistic macro models share if they are to be used for climate-related assessments?

First, they probably ought to be based on some nonlinear dynamics.[9] Why dynamics? Because, as underlined by FS, the timing of mitigation is key: We need to find the correct speed at which our economies must transit toward low-carbon institutions. This issue can hardly be dealt with in a static framework. One might add a second reason: because economic resilience requires an adaptive process, as I suggested above. And a third reason: because fluctuation of most macroeconomic variables is a trivial matter of

---

9. By this, I mean an out-of-equilibrium dynamics in the sense given to this word in the mathematics of dynamical systems after Poincaré, or in recent developments of thermodynamics. Indeed, although the Boltzman-Gibbs law of classical thermodynamics is an equilibrium theory, out-of-equilibrium thermodynamical systems had only been understood, until recently, in the vicinity of an equilibrium, thanks to Onsager's linear formalism. To the best of my knowledge, the first consistent theory of far-from-any-equilibrium (and therefore nonlinear) thermodynamics goes back to Mallick (2009) (see also the references therein).

fact and, as advocated by Romer (2016), should not be explained by imaginary shocks—which are assumed to temporarily perturb some otherwise stable fixed point—but rather by the interplay of endogenous forces.

Why nonlinear? Because, as also stressed by FS, we unfortunately need much more than marginal adjustments to address climate issues. The size of the shift required from our economies is potentially large. Although linearity is often a good proxy for small changes, we need to take due account of the full nonlinearity of the phenomena at stake when studying the possibility of large disruptions.

Second, we certainly need these models to make explicit the dynamics of debt—be it public or private. As already stated, the cost of the energy transition toward a post-carbon economy might reach US$90 trillion. Undoubtedly, this immense amount of wealth will require more debt in significant segments of the world economy. The potentially depressing consequences of this additional leverage need to be addressed if we want to have a realistic narrative of the energy shift. Moreover, given the nontrivial role played by money and debt, our models should be able to capture Fisherian debt-deflation (see Eggertsson and Krugman 2010; Giraud and Pottier 2016) and the Minskian instability hypothesis (Minsky 1992). This is important for at least two reasons. In the first place, because Japan, southern Europe, and possibly a larger number of advanced economies are stuck in a liquidity trap (mostly resulting from the financial crisis) or are on the verge of becoming so. This specific situation might impede the funding of the needed green investments alluded to in the third section above. Any analysis of the way in which the world economy might address the climate issue but which neglects the essence of today's "new normal" (negative interest rates, saving glut, etc.) would indeed be of little help.

Third, despite its enormous influence on the literature over about four decades, we may have to give up the mathematical elegance of the rational expectations hypothesis. Why? Because of the huge (Knightian) uncertainty surrounding climate change issues. I have already touched on this topic in section 3 above, but because relaxing rational expectations is so controversial, let me illustrate it with a (well-known) example. As recalled by FS, there is still no consensus in the scientific community regarding the climate sensitivity that links the increase in CO_2 concentration in the atmosphere and the change in average temperature at the surface of the planet. The parameter capturing this sensitivity (economists would speak in terms of elasticity) varies between 1 and 6, depending on the climate model we are referring to.[10]

Today, there is no clear-cut indication as to which value is the most probable one. Nor do we have a meta-model that would provide the probability distribution telling us how likely it is that this parameter takes any given value. We just do not know.[11] So how can prices publicly convey information that is held by nobody? As public transmission of privately held information is what rational expectations are all about (Dubey, Geanakoplos, Shubik 1987), this suggests that rational expectations cannot be the relevant concept for analyzing climate change issues.

Fourth, markets should not be assumed prima facie to clear automatically. As Joseph Stiglitz made evident in chapter 3 of this book, asymmetric information, hence price stickiness, may prevent markets from clearing instantaneously, the labor market in particular. Again, a simple example might help explain why this is crucial for the global warming issue. Some emerging countries ran large computable models to assess their intentional Nationally Determined Contribution (NDC) for the Paris summit by December 2015. By now, most of these contributions are no longer just intentional, but have become genuine NDCs. Almost all of the macro models that have been used for this exercise fail to specify private debts (often simply because they rely on the "representative consumer" assumption, despite ubiquitous emergence phenomena in economics; more on this below) and, moreover, assume full employment throughout. Now, what will happen if the path that one of these countries wants to follow to keep its promises requires its private debt to skyrocket up to, say, 400 percent of its GDP, together with a 70 percent rate of unemployment (which is hard to believe will be entirely voluntary)? This country will simply never put its NDC into practice, because the path that would lead to its fulfilment is simply politically infeasible. Thus, it is of utmost importance to check whether our narratives of the transition to low-carbon economies is compatible with actual political feasibility. This might require abandoning the elegance of

---

10. Snyder (2016) even recently argued that climate sensitivity could reach the catastrophic value of 9.

11. This contrasts even with quantum mechanics, where Heisenberg's uncertainty principle goes hand in hand with a probabilistic theory of where and how fast particles move.

topological fixed-point theory (e.g., Giraud 2001), but it might be the price to pay for making economic science relevant to today's climate challenges.

That said, we should certainly not throw the baby of general equilibrium theory out with the bathwater of unsatisfactory macroeconomics. Indeed—and this is my fifth point—we should probably not forget the wisdom of the old-fashioned Arrow-Debreu theory, namely, that economics does admit emergence phenomena—exactly in the same way as statistical physics does. "Emergence" should be understood here more or less as a synonym for complexity, that is, in the following, rather weak, sense: aggregate micro-behavior may lead to macro-behavior that cannot be reduced a priori to that of any "representative" creature. This was precisely the content of the celebrated results of Sonnenschein, Mantel, and Debreu, published in the 1970s (e.g., Sonnenschein 1972): Any inward-pointing continuous vector field on the positive part of the unit sphere (of normalized prices) can be viewed as the aggregate excess demand of some well-chosen economy. My viewpoint is that there are at least two escape routes from this quandary: the numerical simulations of agent-based models (see, e.g., Axelrod 1997) or a more phenomenological standpoint based on the empirical estimation of aggregate behavioral functions. I shall end these comments by briefly introducing this second perspective.

The Nonlinear Dynamics of Debt with Global Warming Economics

Giraud et al. (2016) introduce a toy model (in the sense of Kocherlakota; see above) based on some stock-flow consistent, nonlinear dynamics. Its basic building blocks are provided by a short-run Phillips curve relating the growth rate of nominal wages to underemployment (Mankiw 2001, 2014) and an aggregate investment function. The mere reduction of the aggregate investment function to a finite sum of individual outputs induced by some intertemporal profit-maximizing program would be problematic, because we know from Mas-Colell (1989) that the analog of a Sonnenschein-Mantel-Debreu theorem holds on the production side as well. Thus, one lets the data speak, and aggregate investment is empirically estimated. Of course, investment may happen to exceed current profits, and we know that this will presumably be the rule in the coming years for the required green investments. Private debt therefore finances investment in excess of profits. In the monetary sphere, sticky prices in the sense of Guillermo

Calvo (see chapter 4 in this book) dynamically relax along the (endogenously determined) unitary production cost augmented by some markup, which reflects the imperfect competitiveness of the commodity market. Finally, the model is completed by adopting the UN median scenario for world population growth.

The model boils down to a three-dimensional nonlinear dynamics of the Kolmogorov type, where the wage share and underemployment rate play a key role. Thus, welfare issues—beyond the mere evolution of GDP—lie at the heart of the dynamics, as recommended by Blanchard (2016). Somewhat more precisely, the dynamical system can be paraphrased by the three following and hardly disputable statements:

1. Employment will rise (resp. decline) if output growth exceeds (resp. remains lower than) the sum of population plus labor productivity growth.

2. Wage share of output will rise (resp. decline) if wage rise exceeds (resp. remains lower than) growth in labor productivity.

3. Private debt ratio will rise (resp. decline) if the rate of growth of debt exceeds (resp. remains lower than) that of GDP.

The simplicity of this presentation of the core dynamics differs sharply from that of DSGE models, for example, which, in the words of Blanchard (2016), "are bad communication devices." More importantly, its long-run analysis shows that, in general circumstances, it admits several locally stable equilibria whose basin of attraction can be geometrically described.

Depending on the initial conditions, and absent any exogenous shocks, the state of the economy will be trapped in one of these basins and ultimately converge toward its associated attractor (Grasselli and Costa Lima 2012; Bastidas, Fabre, and Mclsaac 2016). This methodological simplicity stands in sharp contrast to the equilibrium literature of monetary economies, for which, as Guillermo Calvo reminds us in chapter 4 in this volume, multiple equilibria are also the rule, but where one is often at pains to explain how a static economy can switch from one equilibrium to the other. Next, the interaction between the monetary and the real spheres of the economy in Giraud et al. (2016) leads to endogenous monetary business cycles without relying on exogenous shocks. Furthermore, the good piece of news provided by the empirical estimation of the model at the world scale is that, absent climate change, the world economy would presumably converge to some relatively safe long-run equilibrium. Simulations suggest, however, that the climate back-loop induced by global warming could drive the world economy out of the basin of attraction of this safe steady state, which is a scenario with disastrous consequences.

To grasp the circumstances under which this might happen, let us first assume that labor productivity grows exponentially at a rate of 1.5 percent per year, the climate damage function is quadratic, and climate sensitivity is 2.9 (its average estimation according to IPCC), as in Nordhaus and Sztorc (2013). We then get a reassuring view on the future of the planet as shown in figure 7.2: World real GDP grows exponentially and reaches 4.62 times its 2010 level by the end of this century. Inflation stabilizes at about 2 percent, the employment rate oscillates in the vicinity of 70–75 percent (close to its current value), and the private debt-to-GDP ratio converges slowly toward a stationary level slightly below 200 percent. By 2050, the average yearly CO_2e emission per capita is 5.6 tons. The temperature change in 2100 is $+4.95$ °C, and the CO_2 concentration is 732.8 ppm. Despite these last frightening numbers, the world economy seems to be doing rather well: Damages induced by global warming are reducing the final world real GDP

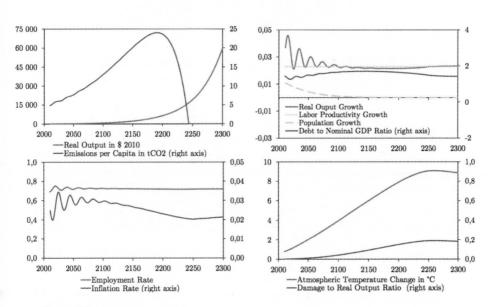

Figure 7.2
Scenario 1: exponential growth
Source: Giraud et al. (2016).

by only one quarter—a fraction higher than the 5 percent losses first envisaged by Stern (2007), but a much smaller relative loss than the one experienced, say, by Russia in the 1990s. As a consequence of this hardly credible
scenario of exponential growth, CO_2e emissions peak only in about the
middle of the twenty-second century, and the zero-emission level reached
one century later!

The picture changes dramatically as soon as growth is made endogenous. Suppose, indeed, that the growth rate of labor productivity is
affected by the rise in temperature, as empirically estimated by Burke et
al. (2015): The hotter the planet becomes, the slower average productivity growth will be. Keeping all other parameters of the model unchanged,
this endogenization of technological progress suffices to provoke a forced
de-growth (figure 7.3): Around 2100, world real GDP peaks at 225 percent of its 2010 value and then inexorably declines. By the end of the
twenty-second century, it becomes even lower than its 2010 value. As a
counterpart, debt-to-GDP ratio explodes: It is already greater than 300 percent by 2100 and grows exponentially after that. Due to a lower pace of
growth, the temperature increase in 2100 is lower than in the exponential
growth scenario (+4.92°C). De-growth, however, has no disruptive effect
on the labor market, because the employment rate only decreases slightly
below 70 percent at the end of the twenty-second century. As for inflation,
it remains wisely close to 2 percent.[12] If such a scenario is considered a
plausible outcome, it logically implies that, above a certain maturity, the
long-term discount rate should be negative (cf. the discussion in section 4
above). Do the negative rates exhibited by financial markets today reflect
the fact that investors are correctly forecasting the potentially disastrous
consequences of the business-as-usual path most of the world economy is
still following?

---

12. Of course, de-growth is an implausible scenario given the astonishingly innovative character of advanced economies and especially the ICT (Information and
Communications Technology) revolution of the past two decades or so. The ongoing
debate on secular stagnation initiated, among others, by Robert Gordon and Larry
Summers does not, however, take climate change into account. That the coupling of
a lack of substantial technological innovation in the coming decades and damages
provoked by climate change might lead to de-growth (by disaster, not by design)
should, at the least, sound like a warning.

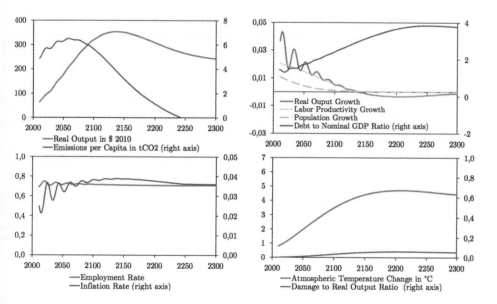

Figure 7.3
Scenario 2: Forced de-growth
Source: Giraud et al. (2016).

So what happens if one takes due account of the probable strong convexity of the damage function, as advocated by Dietz and Stern (2015), together with a climate sensitivity equal to 6? This time, numerical simulations lead to a debt-deflationary collapse of the world economy starting not later than in the 2050s (figure 7.4). As for the employment rate, this fluctuates around 70 percent up to the middle of this century, and then plunges below 50 percent around 2100. Twenty years earlier, the world has entered a strongly deflationary phase, as the inflation rate stabilizes around −5 percent at the turn of the century. At this time, the debt-to-output ratio is above 800 percent. This disaster, however, is not even good news for the climate, as the peak of emissions around 2045 does not prevent the temperature from rising up to +4.62°C in 2100—essentially because of the strong inertia of the response of the world's ecosystem to carbon emissions.

Again, such a breakdown might seem inconceivable, given the current prosperity of so many people, both in advanced and emerging economies.

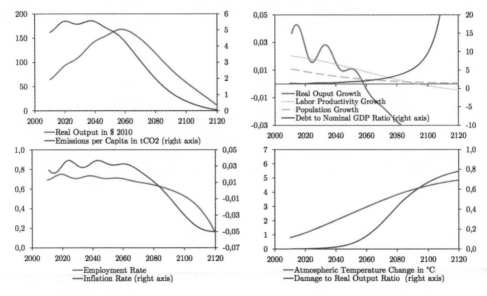

Figure 7.4
Scenario 3: Debt-deflationary collapse
Source: Giraud et al. (2016).

And it is not the intention of Giraud et al. (2016) to claim that such a simulated scenario is even probable. But it could be used as a tool to better understand how the world economy is going to avoid such a collapse. In particular, the public sphere is absent from the model envisaged in Giraud et al. (2016). At the very least, this quite pessimistic perspective means that the funding of the US$90 trillion investment identified in New Climate Economy (2014) can presumably not rely solely on the private sector. The public sphere will have to be involved at some stage. Numerical simulations in Giraud et al. (2016) also suggest that a strongly increasing carbon price would be sufficient to allow an escape from a collapse—at least within the clearly narrow limits of this model. Converted into 2005 US dollars, a value of $74 per ton of CO_2e in 2015 and $306 in 2055 would suffice to drive the world economy onto a safe trajectory in the third scenario sketched above. Note that this implies a price of about $900 for a ton of carbon before the middle of this century.

Of course, Giraud et al. (2016) is definitely a toy model: It aims to gauge "the magnitude of key forces using simple calculations" and "is not designed to allow users to reach definitive quantitative answers to policy questions of interest" (Kocherlakota 2016). It should not be perceived as a tool to forecast the path of the world economy in the twenty-first century. Not only because of its evident modeling limitations, but also because institutional changes, technological shocks, and political complications will most probably play a major role in the future, just as they have always done in the past. In this modest perspective, however, Giraud et al. (2016) undoubtedly confirm some of the points forcefully made by FS:

The business-as-usual scenario might look uglier than many of us believe.

A "radical deepening" of macroeconomics may shed light on issues that, so far, have remained largely ignored by standard approaches, such as the role of private debt along the path toward resilient economies.

The "correct price of carbon"—or for that matter, the correct barycenter of the corridor of prices (see section 3 above)—is probably much higher than more standard simulations would suggest.

References

Artzner, Philippe, Freddy Delbaen, Jean-Marc Eber, and David Heath. 1999. "Coherent Measures of Risk." *Mathematical Finance* 9 (3): 203–228.

Axelrod, Robert. 1997. *The Complexity of Cooperation: Agent-Based Models of Competition and Collaboration*. Princeton, NJ: Princeton University Press.

Bardi, Ugo. 2014. *Extracted: How the Quest for Mineral Wealth Is Plundering the Planet*. White River Junction, VT: Chelsea Green Publishing.

Bastidas, Daniel, Adrien Fabre, and Florent McIsaac. 2016. "Minskyan Classical Growth Cycles: Stability Analysis of a Stock-Flow Consistent Macrodynamic Model." Mathematics and Financial Economics website, https://doi.org/10.1007/s11579-018 -0231-6

Blanchard, Olivier. 2016. "Do DSGE Models Have a Future?" Policy Brief 16-11, Peterson Institute for International Economics, Washington, DC.

Bredenkamp, Hugh, and Catherine A. Pattillo. 2010. "Financing the Response to Climate Change." IMF Staff Position Note 10/06, International Monetary Fund, Washington, DC.

Burke, Marshall, Solomon M. Hsiang, and Edward Miguel. 2015. "Global Non-Linear Effect of Temperature on Economic Production." *Nature* 527 (7577): 235.

Canfin, Pascal, Alain Grandjean, and Gérard Mestrallet. 2016. "Proposals for Aligning Carbon Prices with the Paris Agreement." Ministère de l'environnement, de l'énergie et de la mer, July. https://www.ladocumentationfrancaise.fr/rapports-publics/164000418/index.shtml.

Canfin, Pascal, Alain Grandjean, Ian Cochran, and Mireille Martini. 2015. "Mobilizing Climate Finance—A Road Map to Finance a Low-Carbon Economy." Report of the Canfin-Grandjean Commission, June (INIS-FR--15-0680), France.

Carney, Mark. 2016. "Resolving the Climate Paradox." Arthur Burns Memorial Lecture, September 22, Berlin. http://www.bankofengland.co.uk/publications/Documents/speeches/2016/speech923.pdf.

Dhillon, Amrita, and Jean-François Mertens. 1999. "Relative Utilitarianism." *Econometrica* 67 (3): 471–498.

Dietz, Simon, and Nicholas H. Stern. 2015. "Endogenous Growth, Convexity of Damage and Climate Risk: How Nordhaus' Framework Supports Deep Cuts in Carbon Emissions." *Economic Journal* 125 (583): 574–620.

Dubey, Pradeep, John Geanakoplos, and Martin Shubik. 1987. "The Revelation of Information in Strategic Market Games: A Critique of Rational Expectations Equilibrium." *Journal of Mathematical Economics* 16 (2): 105–137.

Eggertsson, Gauti B., and Paul Krugman. 2010. "Debt, Deleveraging, and the Liquidity Trap: A Fisher-Minsky-Koo Approach." Mimeo, Princeton University, Princeton, NJ.

Fankhauser, Sam, and Nicholas Stern. 2016. "Climate Change, Development, Poverty and Economics." Grantham Research Institute on Climate Change and Environment.

Fleurbaey, Marc, and Francois Maniquet. 2008. "Fair Social Orderings." *Economic Theory* 34 (1): 25–45.

Giraud, Gaël. 2001. "An Algebraic Index Theorem for Non-smooth Economies." *Journal of Mathematical Economics* 36 (4): 255–269.

Giraud, Gaël. 2014. "Le Découplage Énergie-PIB, Ou Le Rôle (Sous-Estimé) de l'Energie dans la Croissance du PIB." In *Produire Plus, Polluer Moins: L'Impossible Découplage?* by Thierry Caminel, Philippe Frémeaux, Gaël Giraud, Aurore Lalucq, and Philippe Roman, 27–43. Paris: Les Petits Matins.

Giraud, Gaël. 2015. "Préface." In *L'Économie En Question. Regards et Apports des Spiritualités et des Religions*, edited by Jan-Luc Castel and Vincent Pilley, 1–35. Paris: L'Harmattan.

Giraud, Gaël, and Rakesh Gupta. 2016. "Coherent Multidimensional Poverty." Chair Energy and Prosperity Working Papers. http://www.chair-energy-prosperity.org/publications/coherent-multidimensional-poverty-measurement/.

Giraud, Gaël, and Antonin Pottier. 2016. "Debt-Deflation versus the Liquidity Trap: The Dilemma of Nonconventional Monetary Policy." *Economic Theory* 62 (1): 383–408.

Giraud, Gaël, Florent McIsaac, Emmanuel Bovari, and Ekaterina Zatsepina. 2016. "Coping with the Collapse: A Stock-Flow Consistent Monetary Macrodynamics of Global Warming." AFD Research Paper 2016/29, Agence Française de Développement, Paris.

Goujon, Michaël, Jean-François Hoarau, and Françoise Rivière. 2015. "Vulnérabilités Comparées Des Économies Ultramarines." AFD Working Paper 45, Agence Française de Développement, Paris.

Grasselli, Matheus R., and B. Costa Lima. 2012. "An Analysis of the Keen Model for Credit Expansion, Asset Price Bubbles and Financial Fragility." *Mathematics and Financial Economics* 6 (3): 191–210.

Guillaumont, Patrick. 2013. "Measuring Structural Vulnerability to Allocate Development Assistance and Adaptation Resources." FERDI Working Paper 68, Fondation por les Etudes et Recherches sur le Développement International, Paris.

Hallegatte, Stephane, Mook Bangalore, Laura Bonzanigo, Marianne Fay, Tamaro Kane, Ulf Narloch, Julie Rozenberg, David Treguer, and Adrien Vogt-Schilb. 2016. "Shock Waves: Managing the Impacts of Climate Change on Poverty." Washington, DC: World Bank.

Kocherlakota, Narayana. 2016. "Toy Models." July 17. https://t.co/8dS85Nlpg9.

Kydland, Finn E., and Edward C. Prescott. 1982. "Time to Build and Aggregate Fluctuations." *Econometrica* 50 (6): 1345–1370.

Leontief, Wassily. 1982. "Academic Economics." *Science* 217 (4555): 104–107.

Le Treut, Hervé. 2013. *Les Impacts du Changement Climatique en Aquitaine: Un Etat des Lieux Scientifique.* Pessac, France: Presses Universitaires de Bordeaux.

Liousse, Catherine, Eric Assamoi, Patrick Criqui, Claire Granier, and Robert Rosset. 2014. "Explosive Growth in African Combustion Emissions from 2005 to 2030." *Environmental Research Letters* 9 (3): 035003, doi:10.1088/1748–9326/9/3/035003.

Mallick, K. Pramana. 2009. *J Phys* 73: 417. https://doi.org/10.1007/s12043-009-0098 -4 ----- source: https://link.springer.com/article/10.1007/s12043-009-0098-4#citeas.

Mankiw, N. Gregory. 2001. "The Inexorable and Mysterious Tradeoff between Inflation and Unemployment." *Economic Journal* 111 (471): 45–61.

Mankiw, N. Gregory. 2014. *Principles of Macroeconomics.* Boston: Cengage Learning.

Mas-Colell, Andreu. 1989. "Capital Theory Paradoxes: Anything Goes." In *Joan Robinson and Modern Economic Theory*, edited by George R. Feiwel, 505–520. London: Palgrave Macmillan.

Mehra, Rajnish, and Edward C. Prescott. 1985. "The Equity Premium: A Puzzle." *Journal of Monetary Economics* 15 (2): 145–161.

Minsky, Hyman P. 1992. "The Financial Instability Hypothesis." Levy Economics Institute Working Paper 74, Levy Economics Institute, Annandale-on-Hudson, NY.

New Climate Economy. 2014. "Better Growth, Better Climate: The New Climate Economy Report." London: Global Commission on the Economy and Climate.

Nordhaus, William D., and Paul Sztorc. 2013. DICE 2013R: Introduction and User's Manual. https://www.google.com/url?sa=t&rct=j&q=&esrc=s&source=web&cd=1&ved =2ahUKEwjkzZ2poPLgAhXn2eAKHX58CVkQFjAAegQICRAC&url=http%3A% 2F%2Fwww.econ.yale.edu%2F~nordhaus%2Fhomepage%2Fhomepage%2Fdocument s%2FDICE_Manual_100413r1.pdf&usg=AOvVaw2D1La96WGlSgoIm2Ka-Q1a.

Roemer, John E. 2011. "The Ethics of Intertemporal Distribution in a Warming Planet." *Environmental and Resource Economics* 48 (3): 363–390.

Romer, Paul M. 2016. "The Trouble with Macroeconomics." *American Economist* 20: 1–20.

Snyder, Carolyn W. 2016. "Evolution of Global Temperature over the Past Two Million Years." *Nature* 538 (7624): 226–228.

Sonnenschein, Hugo. 1972. "Market Excess Demand Functions." *Econometrica* 40 (3): 549–563.

Stern, N. H. 2007. *The Economics of Climate Change: The Stern Review*. Cambridge: Cambridge University Press.

Sterner, Thomas, and Martin U. Persson. 2008. "An Even Sterner Review: Introducing Relative Prices into the Discounting Debate." *Review of Environmental Economics and Policy* 2 (1): 61–76.

Vautard, Robert, Françoise Thais, Isabelle Tobin, François-Marie Bréon, Jean-Guy Devezeaux de Lavergne, Augustin Colette, Pascal Yiou, and Paolo Michele Ruti. 2014. "Regional Climate Model Simulations Indicate Limited Climatic Impacts by Operational and Planned European Wind Farms." *Nature Communications* 5, doi:10.1038/ncomms4196.

Vidal, Olivier, Bruno Goffé, and Nicholas Arndt. 2013. "Metals for a Low-Carbon Society." *Nature Geoscience* 6 (10): 894–896.

8 Behaviorally Informed

Cass R. Sunstein

In recent decades, behavioral economists have been incorporating empirical findings about human behavior into economic models (Kahneman 2011; Thaler 2015). Those findings have transformed our understandings of economic theory. They have also greatly affected our understandings of the role of economic incentives (Chetty et al. 2012) and the content of policy instruments. At the same time, they are providing instructive lessons about the appropriate design of "nudges"—low-cost, choice-preserving, behaviorally informed approaches to regulatory problems, including disclosure requirements, default rules, and simplification (Thaler and Sunstein 2008; Halpern 2015).

Economists have long emphasized the importance of incentives. Behavioral economists do not disagree that incentives matter, but they emphasize the need to see that choice architecture, understood as the background against which decisions are made, can have major consequences for both decisions and outcomes (Thaler 2015). Small, inexpensive policy initiatives, making modest design changes, can have large and highly beneficial effects in areas that include health, energy, the environment, savings, and much more. My main purposes here are to explore relevant evidence, to explore its implications for standard economic theory, to catalog behaviorally informed practices and reforms, and to discuss some lessons for policy. In the United States, numerous policies have been directly informed by behavioral findings, and behavioral economics has played an unmistakable role in countless domains (Sunstein 2013).

The relevant initiatives enlist such tools as disclosure, warnings, norms, and default rules, and they can be found in multiple areas, including fuel economy, energy efficiency, consumer protection, financial regulation, environmental protection, health care, and obesity prevention (Sunstein

2013). As a result, behavioral findings have become an important reference point for regulatory and other policy making in the United States (Sunstein 2016).

In the United Kingdom, then–Prime Minister Cameron created a Behavioural Insights Team with the specific goal of incorporating an understanding of human behavior into policy initiatives (Halpern 2015). The team has used these insights to promote initiatives in numerous areas, including smoking cessation, energy efficiency, organ donation, consumer protection, and compliance strategies in general (Halpern 2015). A great deal of money is being saved. Other nations have expressed keen interest in the work of the team, and its operations are expanding (Halpern 2015).

Behavioral economics has drawn attention in Europe more broadly. The Organisation for Economic Development and Co-operation has published a consumer policy toolkit that recommends initiatives rooted in behavioral findings (OECD 2010). In the European Union, the Directorate-General for Health and Consumers has also shown the influence of behavioral economics (DG SANCO 2010). A report from the European Commission, called "Green Behavior," enlists behavioral economics to outline policy initiatives to protect the environment (European Commission 2012; iNudgeYou.com n.d.). Private organizations are making creative use of behavioral insights to promote a variety of environmental, health-related, and other goals (see iNudgeYou.com n.d.).

It is clear that behavioral findings have greatly affected economic theory (Thaler 2015) and are having a large impact on regulation, law, and public policy all over the world (Sunstein 2016). With increasing global interest in low-cost tools, that impact will inevitably grow over the next decades. In these circumstances, it is particularly important to have a sense of what we know, what we do not know, and how emerging understandings can inform sensible policies and reforms.

What We Know

Findings
Consider a simple view: Human beings try to maximize utility. To understand their behavior, two questions are important. (1) What do they care about? (2) What incentives do they face? On one view, if you can answer those questions, that is all ye need to know on earth (more or less).

Behavioral economics has cast serious doubt on that view. Even if analysts have full information about (1) and (2), they may have little or no idea about what people will choose. At a minimum, there are two more questions. (3) How do people deviate from full rationality? (4) What is the relevant choice architecture? Without answers to (3) and (4), we might be at sea, or make predictions that go badly wrong.

For purposes of policy, the central findings of behavioral economics fall into four categories. What follows is not meant to be a comprehensive account; the focus is on those findings that have particular importance to what governments do.

Inertia and procrastination

a) Default rules often have a large effect on social outcomes. Both private and public institutions often establish "default rules"—rules that determine the result if people make no affirmative choice at all (Sunstein 2015). According to a well-known view in economics and the economic analysis of law, default rules have no effect, at least when transactions costs are zero: People will bargain their way to the efficient result, and that result will be the same, whatever the content of the default.

That view is not correct. In part because of the power of inertia, default rules can be extremely important, because they tend to stick. If the goal is to affect behavior, the right advice is often simple: Create a default rule that puts people in the situation that you favor. Where they start will often be where they end up.

In the domain of retirement savings, for example, the default rule has significant consequences. When people are asked whether they want to opt in to a retirement plan, the level of participation is far lower than if they are asked whether they want to opt out. Automatic enrollment significantly increases participation (Thaler 2015). Something similar is true in the environmental context. If people are automatically enrolled in green energy, there can be major effects on pollution levels (Sunstein 2016).

More generally, people may decline to change from the status quo even if the costs of change are low (or essentially zero) and the benefits substantial. In the context of energy and the environment, for example, we might predict that people might neglect to switch to fuel-efficient alternatives even when it is in their interest to do so (Sunstein 2015). It follows that complexity can have serious adverse effects by increasing the power of inertia, and that ease and simplification (including reduction of paperwork burdens) can produce significant benefits. These benefits include increased compliance with law and greater participation in public programs. Often people do not act in advisable ways, not because they do not want to do so, but because the best path is obscure or difficult to navigate. Behavioral economists suggest that people will often use a GPS device, even when rational people might be expected not to need one.

b) Procrastination can have significant adverse effects, even when it is in people's interest not to procrastinate. According to standard economic theory, people will consider both the short term and the long term. They will take account of relevant uncertainties; the future may be unpredictable, and significant changes may occur over time. They will appropriately discount the future; it may be better to have money, or a good event, a week from now than a decade from now. In practice, however, some people procrastinate or neglect to take steps that impose small short-term costs but that would produce large long-term gains (Thaler 2015). They may, for example, delay enrolling in a retirement plan, starting to exercise, ceasing to smoke, or using some valuable, cost-saving technology.

When procrastination is creating significant problems, automatic enrollment in relevant programs might be helpful. Moreover, complex requirements, inconvenience, and lengthy forms are likely to make the situation worse and perhaps unexpectedly so.

c) When people are informed of the benefits or risks of engaging in certain actions, they are far more likely to act in accordance with that information if they are simultaneously provided with clear, explicit information about how to do so (Leventhal, Singer, and Jones 1965; Nickerson and Rogers 2010). On one view, such information should not matter, at least if it is easy to find. People will consider the costs of search, of course, but if those costs are low and the potential benefits are high, they will search.

But not always. For example, those who are informed of the benefits of a vaccine are more likely to become vaccinated if they are also given specific plans and maps describing where to go (Leventhal, Singer, and Jones 1965). Similarly, behavior has been shown to be significantly affected if people are informed, not abstractly of the value of "healthy eating," but specifically of the advantages of buying 1 percent milk as opposed to whole milk (Heath and Heath 2010). In many domains, the identification of a specific, clear, unambiguous path or plan has an important effect on social outcomes; complexity or vagueness can ensure inaction, even when people are informed about risks and potential improvements. What appears to be skepticism or recalcitrance may actually be a product of ambiguity.

Framing and presentation

a) People are influenced by how information is presented or "framed" (Levin, Schneider, and Gaeth 1998). According to standard theory, "frames" should not matter. What matters is expected value. But psychologists and behavioral economists have found otherwise (Kahneman 2011).

If, for example, people are informed that they will gain a certain amount of money by using energy efficient products, they may be less likely to change their behavior than if they are told that they will lose the same amount of money by not using such products. When patients are told that 90 percent of those who have a certain operation are alive after 5 years, they are more likely to elect to have the operation than when they are told that after 5 years, 10 percent of patients are dead (Redelmeier, Rozin, and Kahneman 1993). It follows that a product that is labeled "90 percent fat-free" may well be more appealing than one that is labeled "10 percent fat." It also follows that choices are often not made based solely on their consequences; assessments may be affected by the relevant frame.

b) Information that is vivid and salient usually has a larger impact on behavior than information that is statistical and abstract. With respect to public health, vivid displays can be more effective than abstract presentations of statistical risks. This point bears on the design of effective warnings. Attention is a scarce resource, and vivid, salient, and novel presentations may trigger attention in ways that abstract or familiar ones cannot.

In particular, salience greatly matters—far more so than standard economic theory has predicted. Why, for example, do people pay bank overdraft fees? One of the many possible answers is that such fees are not sufficiently salient to people, and the fees are incurred as a result of inattention or inadvertent mistakes. One study suggests that limited attention is indeed a source of the problem, and that once overdraft fees become salient, they are significantly reduced (Stango and Zinman 2011). When people take surveys about such fees, they are less likely to incur a fee in the following month, and when they take multiple surveys, the issue becomes sufficiently salient that overdraft fees are reduced for as much as 2 years. In many areas, the mere act of being surveyed can affect behavior by, for example, increasing the use of water treatment products (thus promoting health) and the take up of health insurance; one reason is that being surveyed increases the salience of the action in question (Zwane et al. 2011).

A more general point is that many costs (or benefits) are less salient than purchase prices; they are "shrouded attributes," to which some consumers do not pay much attention. Such add-on costs may matter a great deal but receive little consideration, because they are not salient.

c) People display loss aversion; they may well dislike losses more than they like corresponding gains   (Thaler, Kahneman, and Knetsch 1991; McGraw et al. 2010; Card and Dahl 2011). Standard economic theory emphasizes the importance of expected value. A 90 percent chance of gaining $500 is not any more good than a 90 percent chance of losing $500 is bad. But human beings turn out to be loss averse; they much dislike losses, and they will do a great deal to avoid them (Kahneman 2011).

Whether a change counts as a loss or a gain depends on the reference point, which can be affected by mere description or by policy decisions, and which is often the status quo. A small tax—for example, on grocery bags—can have a large effect on behavior, even if a promised bonus has no effect at all; one reason is loss aversion. It follows that very small charges or fees can be a surprisingly effective policy tool. Partly as a result of loss aversion, the initial allocation of a legal entitlement can affect people's valuations. Those who have the initial allocation may value a good more than they would if the allocation were originally elsewhere, thus showing an endowment effect (Thaler 2015).

Social influences

a) In multiple domains, individual behavior is greatly influenced by the perceived behavior of other people   (Hirshleifer 1995). With respect to obesity, proper exercise, alcohol consumption, smoking, becoming vaccinated, and much more, the perceived decisions of others have a significant influence on individual behavior and choice. The behavior of peers has been found to have a significant effect on risky behavior among adolescents, including tobacco smoking, marijuana use, and truancy (Bisin, Moro, and Topa 2011; Card and Giuliano 2011).

In particular, food consumption is greatly affected by the food consumption of others, and indeed, the body type of others in the relevant group can affect people's responses to their food choices, with a greater effect from those who are thin than from those who are heavy (McFerran et al. 2011).

Perception of the norm in the pertinent community can affect risk taking, safety, and health (Sunstein 2015; Thaler 2015). The norm conveys significant information about what ought to be done; for that reason, those who lack private information may follow the apparent beliefs and behavior of relevant others, sometimes creating informational cascades.

In addition, people care about their reputations. Thus they may be influenced by others so as not to incur their disapproval. In some contexts, social norms can help create a phenomenon of compliance without enforcement—as, for example, when people comply with laws forbidding indoor smoking or requiring buckling of seat belts, in part because of social norms or the expressive function of those laws. These points bear on the value and importance, in many domains, of private–public partnerships.

b) In part because of social influences, people are more likely to cooperate with one another, and to contribute to the solution of collective action problems, than standard economic theory predicts (Camerer 2003). People's willingness to cooperate is partly a product of an independent commitment to fairness, but it is partly a product of a belief that others will see and punish a failure to cooperate or to act fairly. Norms of reciprocity can be exceedingly important. In many contexts, the result is a situation in which people cooperate on the assumption that others are cooperating as well—and might punish those who fail to do so.

Difficulties in assessing probability

a) In many domains, people show unrealistic optimism (Jolls 1998; Sharot 2011). Standard economic theory does not see human beings as having systematically skewed probability judgments. But there is a systematic tendency toward optimism (Sharot 2011). The "above average" effect is common (Weinstein 1987); many people believe that they are less likely than others to suffer from various misfortunes, including automobile accidents and adverse health outcomes. One study found that although smokers do not underestimate statistical risks faced by the population of smokers, they nonetheless believe that their personal risk is less than that of the average smoker (Slovic 1998). Unrealistic optimism has neurological foundations, with people incorporating good news far more readily than bad news (see Sharot (2011) for an overview). A predictable result of unrealistic optimism is a failure to take appropriate precautions.

b) People often use heuristics, or mental shortcuts, when assessing risks (Kahneman and Frederick 2002; Kahneman 2011). For example, judgments about probability are often affected by whether a recent event comes readily to mind (Tversky and Kahneman 1973). If an event is cognitively "available," people may well overestimate the risk. If an event is not cognitively available, people might underestimate the risk. In short, "availability bias" can lead to inaccurate judgments about the probability of undesirable outcomes.

c) People sometimes do not make judgments on the basis of expected value, and they may neglect or disregard the issue of probability, especially when strong emotions are triggered (Loewenstein et al. 2001). When emotions are strongly felt, people may focus on the outcome and not on the probability that it will occur (Loewenstein et al. 2001). (This point obviously bears on reactions to extreme events of various sorts.) Prospect theory, which does not depend on emotions at all, suggests that for low and moderate changes, people may be risk averse with respect to gains but risk seeking with respect to losses; for very large changes, people may be risk seeking with respect to gains but risk averse for losses (Kahneman and Tversky 1979; Kahneman 2011).

Incentives and Choice Architecture

These various findings are hardly inconsistent with the conventional economic emphasis on the importance of material incentives; actual and perceived costs and benefits certainly matter. When the price of a product rises, or when it becomes clear that use of a product imposes serious health risks, the demand for the product is likely to fall (at least, and this is a significant qualification, if these effects are salient). But apart from strictly material incentives of this kind, evidence suggests the independent importance of (1) the social environment and (2) prevailing social norms. If, for example, healthy foods are prominent and easily accessible, people are more likely to choose them; one study finds an 8 to 16 percent decrease in intake simply by making food more difficult to reach (as, for example, by varying its proximity by 10 inches or altering the serving utensil; Rozin et al. 2011). The problem of childhood obesity is, at least in part, a result of the easy availability of unhealthy foods. The same point bears on smoking and alcohol abuse.

In fact, small nudges can have surprisingly large effects (Halpern 2015; Thaler 2015). For example, automatic enrollment in savings programs can have far larger effects than significant economic incentives do—a clear testimonial to the potential power of choice architecture and its occasionally larger effect than standard economic tools (Chetty et al. 2012). Some evidence suggests that if people are asked to sign forms first rather than last—an especially minor change—the incidence of honesty increases significantly (Shu et al. 2012).

Markets, Government, and the Vexing Problem of Paternalism

It is natural to wonder whether an understanding of the findings outlined above justify paternalism or operate as a defense of more regulation (Conly 2013). With respect to paternalism in particular, it is true that some of the relevant findings supplement the standard accounts of market failures, suggesting that in some settings, markets may fail, in the sense that they may not promote social welfare even in the presence of perfect competition and full information. We are now in a position to identify a series of behavioral market failures, and these do appear to justify regulatory controls (Sunstein 2016). Responses to behavioral market failures might be counted as paternalistic.

If, for example, people focus on short-term costs and neglect long-term benefits, it is possible that disclosure policies that specifically emphasize the long term, or even regulatory requirements (involving, for example, energy efficiency), may be justified. It is also possible to identify "internalities"— problems of self-control and errors in judgment that produce within-person harms, as, for example, when smoking behavior leads to serious risks because of the victory of short-term considerations over the longer view. These too count as behavioral market failures, and responses may be paternalistic in character.

Richard Thaler and I have argued in defense of "libertarian paternalism" (Thaler and Sunstein (2008); see also Sunstein (2013)), understood as approaches that preserve freedom of choice while also steering people in directions that will make their lives go better (by their own lights). And it would be possible to think that at least some behavioral market failures justify more coercive forms of paternalism.

It should not be necessary to emphasize that public officials are subject to error as well. Indeed, errors may result from one or more of the findings traced above; officials are human and capable of error, too. Behavioral public choice explores this problem. The dynamics of the political process may or may not lead in the right direction. It would be absurd to say that behaviorally informed regulation is more aggressive than regulation that is not so informed, or that an understanding of recent empirical findings calls for more regulation rather than less. The argument is instead that such an understanding can help inform the design of regulatory programs.

Behaviorally Informed Disclosure

Actually Informing Choice

Examples Many statutory programs recognize that information disclosure can be a useful regulatory tool, replacing or complementing other approaches. Recent initiatives have drawn directly from behavioral economics, emphasizing the importance of plain language, clarity, and simplicity.

a) Credit cards. The Credit Card Accountability, Responsibility, and Disclosure Act of 2009 (Credit CARD Act 2009) is designed in large part to ensure that credit card users are adequately informed. Among other things, the Act prohibits an increase in annual percentage rates without 45 days' notice, prohibits the retroactive application of rate increases to existing balances, and also requires clear notice of the consumer's right to cancel the credit card when the annual percentage rate is raised.

The Act also requires several electronic disclosures of credit card agreements. Specifically, it requires that (1) "each creditor shall establish and maintain an Internet site on which the creditor shall post the written agreement between the creditor and the consumer for each credit card account under an open-end consumer credit plan"; (2) "each creditor shall provide to the Board, in electronic format, the consumer credit card agreements that it publishes on its Internet site"; and (3) the "Board shall establish and maintain on its publicly available Internet site a central repository of the consumer credit card agreements received from creditors pursuant to this subsection, and such agreements shall be easily accessible and retrievable by the public" (Credit CARD Act 2009). The overall effect of the CARD Act has been extremely impressive, with more than $20 billion in annual savings for consumers (Agarwal et al. 2013).

b) Nutrition. In the domain of nutrition, various disclosure requirements are in place. To take just one example, a final rule has been issued by the US Department of Agriculture (USDA), requiring provision of nutritional information to consumers with respect to meat and poultry products. Nutrition facts panels must be provided on the labels of such products. Under the rule, the panels must contain information with respect to calories and both total and saturated fats (9 CFR § 317.309).

The rule clearly recognizes the potential importance of framing. If a product lists a percentage statement such as "80% lean," it must also list its fat percentage. This requirement should avoid the confusion that can result from selective framing; a statement that a product is 80 percent lean, standing by itself, makes leanness salient, and may therefore be misleading.

c) Health care. The Patient Protection and Affordable Care Act of 2010 (Affordable Care Act) contains many disclosure requirements designed to promote accountability and informed choice with respect to health care. Indeed, the Affordable Care Act is, in significant part, a series of disclosure requirements, many of which are meant to inform consumers and to do so in a way that is alert to behavioral findings. Under the Act, a restaurant that is part of a chain with twenty or more locations doing business under the same name is required to disclose calories on the menu board. Such restaurants are also required to provide in a written form (available to customers on request) additional nutrition information pertaining to total calories and calories from fat, as well as amounts of fat, saturated fat, cholesterol, sodium, total carbohydrates, complex carbohydrates, sugars, dietary fiber, and protein (Affordable Care Act 2010). Early results suggest significant effects from calorie labels, concentrated among people who are overweight (Deb and Vargas 2016).

How, not only whether As social scientists have emphasized, disclosure as such may not be enough; regulators should devote care and attention to how, not only whether, disclosure occurs. Clarity and simplicity are often critical. In some cases, accurate disclosure of information may be ineffective if the information is too abstract, vague, detailed, complex, poorly framed, or overwhelming to be useful. If disclosure requirements are to be helpful, they must be designed to be sensitive to how people actually process information.

A good rule of thumb is that disclosure should be concrete, straightforward, simple, meaningful, timely, and salient. If the goal is to inform people about how to avoid risks or to obtain benefits, disclosure should avoid abstract statements (such as, about "healthy eating" or "good diet") and instead clearly identify the steps that might be taken to obtain the relevant goal (by specifying, for example, what specific actions parents might take to reduce the risk of childhood obesity).

In 2010, the Department of Health and Human Services emphasized the importance of clarity and salience in connection with its interim final rule titled "Health Care Reform Insurance Web Portal Requirements," which "adopts the categories of information that will be collected and displayed as Web portal content, and the data we will require from issuers and request from States, associations, and high risk pools in order to create this content." (Department of Health and Human Services 2010). That web portal can be found at http://www.healthcare.gov/.

Behavioral economics, cognitive illusions, and avoiding confusion

If not carefully designed, disclosure requirements can produce ineffective, confusing, and potentially misleading messages. Behaviorally informed approaches are alert to this risk and suggest possible improvements. For instance, automobile manufacturers are currently required to disclose the fuel economy of new vehicles as measured by miles per gallon (MPG). This disclosure is useful for consumers and helps promote informed choice. As the Environmental Protection Agency (EPA) has emphasized, however, MPG is a nonlinear measure of fuel consumption (Environmental Protection Agency 2009). For a fixed travel distance, a change from 20 to 25 MPG produces a larger reduction in fuel costs than does a change from 30 to 35 MPG, or even from 30 to 38 MPG. To see the point more dramatically, consider the fact that an increase from 10 to 20 MPG produces more savings than an increase from 20 to 40 MPG, and an increase from 10 to 11 MPG produces savings almost as high as an increase from 34 to 50 MPG.

Evidence suggests that many consumers do not understand this point and tend to interpret MPG as linear with fuel costs. When it occurs, this error is likely to produce inadequately informed purchasing decisions when people are making comparative judgments about fuel costs. For example, people may well underestimate the benefits of trading a low-MPG car for one that is even slightly more fuel efficient. By contrast, an alternative fuel economy metric, such as gallons per mile, could be far less confusing. Such a measure is linear with fuel costs and hence suggests a possible way to help consumers make better choices.

Recognizing the imperfections and potentially misleading nature of the MPG measure, the Department of Transportation and EPA proposed in 2010 two alternative labels that are meant to provide consumers with clearer and more accurate information about the effects of fuel economy on fuel expenses and on the environment (Environmental Protection Agency 2009). After a period of public comment, the Department of Transportation and EPA ultimately chose a label that borrows from both proposals (Environmental Protection Agency 2009). This approach calls for disclosure of the factual material included in the first option but adds a clear statement about anticipated fuel savings (or costs) over a 5-year period.

In a related vein, the USDA has abandoned the "Food Pyramid," used for decades as the central icon to promote healthy eating. The Pyramid has long been criticized as insufficiently informative; it does not offer people any kind of clear "path" with respect to healthy diet. According to one critical account (Heath and Heath 2010, 61),

> its meaning is almost completely opaque.... To learn what the Food Pyramid has to say about food, you must be willing to decipher the Pyramid's markings.... The language and concepts here are so hopelessly abstracted from people's actual experience with food... that the message confuses and demoralizes.

In response to these objections, and after an extended period of deliberation, the USDA replaced the Pyramid with a new, simpler icon, consisting of a plate with clear markings for fruit, vegetable, grains, and protein (Sunstein 2013).

The plate is accompanied by straightforward guidance, including "make half your plate fruits and vegetables," "drink water instead of sugary drinks," and "switch to fat-free or low-fat (1%) milk." This approach has the key advantage of informing people what to do, if they seek to have a healthier diet.

In some circumstances, the tendency toward unrealistic optimism may lead some consumers to downplay or neglect information about statistical risks associated with a product or an activity. Possible examples include smoking and distracted driving. In such circumstances, disclosure might be designed to make the risks associated with the product less abstract, more vivid, and salient. For example, the Family Smoking Prevention and Tobacco Control Act of 2009 requires graphic warnings with respect to the risks of smoking tobacco, and the Food and Drug Administration has finalized such warnings for public comment, with vivid and even disturbing pictures of some of the adverse outcomes associated with smoking.

Behaviorally Informed Tools: Summary Disclosure and Full Disclosure

Disclosure requirements of this kind are designed to inform consumers at the point of purchase, often with brief summaries of relevant information. Such summary disclosures are often complemented with more robust information, typically found on public or private websites. For example, the EPA offers a great deal of material on fuel economy online, going well beyond the information that is available on stickers, and the nutrition facts label is supplemented by a great deal of nutritional information on government websites. Approaches of this kind provide information that private individuals and institutions can adapt; reassemble; and present in new, helpful, imaginative, and often unanticipated ways. Some of the most valuable and creative uses of full disclosure are made by the private sector.

Other disclosure requirements are not specifically directed at consumers or end users at all. They promote public understanding of existing problems and help produce possible solutions by informing people about current practices. One example is the Emergency Planning and Community Right-to-Know Act (1986). At first, this law seemed to be largely a bookkeeping measure, requiring a "Toxic Release Inventory," in which firms reported what pollutants they were using. But available evidence indicates that it has had beneficial effects, helping spur reductions in toxic releases throughout the United States (Hamilton 2005). One reason involves public accountability: Public attention can help promote behavior that fits with statutory purposes.

To be sure, mandatory disclosure can impose costs and burdens on both private and public institutions, and to the extent permitted by law, those costs and burdens should be considered when deciding whether and how to proceed. Empirical evidence on the actual effects of disclosure policies is indispensable (Greenstone 2009; Sunstein 2010; Schwartz et al. 2011).

Default Rules and Simplification

Social science research provides strong evidence that starting points, or "default rules," greatly affect social outcomes. Default rules are one way of easing people's choices, and they are used in countless domains by both public and private institutions.

Automatic Enrollment and Default Rules: Examples

Savings In the United States, employers have long asked workers whether they want to enroll in 401(k) plans; under a common approach, the default rule is nonenrollment. Even when enrollment is easy, the number of employees who enroll, or opt in, has sometimes been relatively low (Madrian and Shea 2001; Gale, Iwry, and Walters 2009). In the United States, some employers have responded by changing the default to automatic enrollment, by which employees are enrolled unless they opt out. The results are clear: Significantly more employees end up enrolled with an opt-out design than with opt-in (Gale, Iwry, and Walters 2009). This is so even when opting out is easy. Importantly, automatic enrollment has significant benefits for all groups, with increased anticipated savings for Hispanics, African Americans, and women in particular (Chiteji and Walker 2009; Orszag and Rodriguez 2009; Papke, Walker, and Dworsky 2009).

The Pension Protection Act of 2006 (Pension Protection Act 2006) draws directly on these findings by encouraging employers to adopt automatic enrollment plans. The Pension Protection Act does this by providing nondiscrimination safe harbors for elective deferrals and for matching contributions under plans that include an automatic enrollment feature, as well as by providing protections from state payroll-withholding laws to allow for automatic enrollment. Building on these efforts, then-President Obama asked the Internal Revenue Service and the Treasury Department to undertake initiatives to make it easier for employers to adopt such plans (Internal Revenue Service 2009; Obama 2009).

School meals The National School Lunch Act (Healthy, Hunger-Free Kids Act 2012) takes steps to allow "direct certification" of eligibility, thus reducing complexity and introducing what is a form of automatic enrollment. Under the program, children who are eligible for benefits under certain programs will be "directly eligible" for free lunches and free breakfasts and hence will not have to fill out additional applications (Healthy, Hunger-Free Kids Act 2012). To promote direct certification, the USDA has issued an interim final rule that is expected to provide up to 270,000 children with school meals (Department of Agriculture 2011). In total, the program is enrolling more than 12 million children in the relevant program.

Payroll statements The Department of Homeland Security has changed the default setting for payroll statements to electronic from paper, thus reducing costs (Orszag 2010). In general, changes of this kind may save significant sums of money for both the private and public sectors.

Automatic Enrollment and Default Rules: Mechanisms and Complexities

A great deal of research has attempted to explore exactly why default rules have such a large effect on outcomes (Carroll et al. 2009; Dinner et al. 2009; Gale, Iwry, and Walters 2009). There appear to be three contributing factors. The first involves inertia and procrastination. To alter the effect of the default rule, people must make an active choice to reject the default. In view of the power of inertia and the tendency to procrastinate, people may simply continue with the status quo.

The second factor involves what might be taken to be an implicit endorsement of the default rule. Many people appear to conclude that the default was chosen for a reason; they believe that they should not depart from it unless they have particular information to justify a change.

Third, the default rule might establish the reference point for people's decisions; the established reference point has significant effects, because people dislike losses from that reference point. If, for example, the default rule favors energy-efficient light bulbs, then the loss (in terms of reduced efficiency) may loom large, and the tendency will be to continue with energy-efficient light bulbs. But if the default rule favors less efficient (and initially less expensive) light bulbs, then the loss in terms of upfront costs may loom large, and the tendency will be to favor less efficient light bulbs. In a significant number of domains, it might be possible to achieve regulatory goals, and to do so while maintaining freedom of choice and at low cost, by selecting good default rules and avoiding harmful ones (Sunstein 2015).

Some default rules apply to all of the relevant population, subject to the ability to opt out. Other default rules are personalized, in the sense that they draw on available information about which approach best suits individuals in the relevant population. A personalized default might be based on geographical or demographic variables; for example, income and age might be used in determining appropriate default rules for retirement plans. Alternatively, a personalized default might be based on people's own past choices to the extent that they are available.

An advantage of personalized default rules is that they may well be more accurate than "mass" default rules. As technology evolves, it should be increasingly possible to produce personalized defaults, based on people's own choices and situations; such rules are likely to be far more accurate than more general ones. There will be excellent opportunities to use default rules to promote people's welfare (Sunstein 2016). To be sure, any such rules must respect the applicable laws, policies, and regulations involving personal privacy and should avoid unduly crude proxies.

Simplification

Where it is not possible or best to change the default, a similar effect might be obtained merely by simplifying and facilitating people's choices. Complexity can have serious unintended effects (including indifference, delay, and confusion), potentially undermining regulatory goals by reducing compliance or by decreasing the likelihood that people will benefit from various policies and programs (Sunstein 2013).

For example, a series of steps have been taken recently toward simplifying the Free Application for Federal Student Aid (FAFSA), reducing the number of questions through skip logic (a survey method that uses previous responses to determine subsequent questions) and allowing electronic retrieval of information (Office of Management and Budget 2010). Use of a simpler and shorter form is accompanied by a pilot initiative to permit online users to transfer data previously supplied electronically in their tax forms directly into their FAFSA applications.

These steps are intended to simplify the application process for financial aid and thus to increase access to college; there is good reason to believe that such steps will enable many students to receive aid for attending college when they previously could not do so. Similar steps might be taken in many other domains. And indeed, there is reason to believe that imperfect take-up of existing benefit programs, including those that provide income support, is partly a product of behavioral factors, such as procrastination and inertia. It follows that efforts to increase simplicity, including automatic enrollment, may have substantial benefits.

Well Beyond Incentives

My goals here have been to outline some of the key findings in behavioral economics, to show how they depart from standard economic theory, and to sketch some lessons for policy. A general conclusion is that although material incentives (including price and anticipated health effects) greatly matter, outcomes are independently influenced by choice architecture, including (1) the social environment and (2) prevailing social norms.

Because complexity can often have undesirable or unintended side effects—including high costs, noncompliance with law, and reduced participation in useful programs—simplification helps promote regulatory goals. Indeed, simplification can often have surprisingly large effects.

Reduced paperwork and form-filling burdens (as, for example, through fewer questions, use of skip patterns, electronic filing, and prepopulation) can produce significant benefits, not merely by reducing burdens but also by making programs more readily available. It is thus desirable to take steps to ease participation in such programs by increasing convenience and by giving people clearer signals about what, exactly, they are required to do.

References

Affordable Care Act. 2010. The Patient Protection and Affordable Care Act of 2010. Pub L No 111–148, 124 Stat 119, codified in various sections of Title 42.

Agarwal, Sumit, Souphala Chomsisenghphet, Neale Mahoney, and Johannes Stroebel. 2013. "Regulating Consumer Financial Products: Evidence from Credit Cards." NBER Working Paper 19484, National Bureau of Economic Research, Cambridge, MA.

Bisin, Alberto, Andrea Moro, and Giorgio Topa. 2011. "The Empirical Content of Models with Multiple Equilibria in Economies with Social Interactions." NBER Working Paper 17196, National Bureau of Economic Research, Cambridge, MA.

Camerer, Colin F. 2003. *Behavioral Game Theory: Experiments in Strategic Interaction.* Princeton, NJ: Princeton University Press.

Card, David, and Gordon B. Dahl. 2011. "Family Violence and Football: The Effect of Unexpected Emotional Cues on Violent Behavior." *Quarterly Journal of Economics* 126 (4): 1879–1907.

Card, David, and Laura Giuliano. 2011. "Peer Effects and Multiple Equilibria in the Risky Behavior of Friends." NBER Working Paper 17088, National Bureau of Economic Research, Cambridge, MA.

Carroll, Gabriel D., James J. Choi, David Laibson, Brigitte C. Madrian, and Andrew Metrick. 2009. "Optimal Defaults and Active Decisions." *Quarterly Journal of Economics* 124 (4): 1639–1674.

Chetty, Raj, John N. Friedman, Soren Leth-Petersen, Torben Heien Nielsen, and Tore Olsen. 2012. "Active vs. Passive Decisions and Crowdout in Retirement Savings Accounts: Evidence from Denmark." NBER Working Paper 18565, National Bureau of Economic Research, Cambridge, MA.

Chiteji, Ngina, and Lina Walker. 2009. "Strategies to Increase the Retirement Savings of African American Households." In *Automatic: Changing the Way America Saves*, edited by William G. Gale, J. Mark Iwry, David C. John, and Lina Walker, 231–260. Washington, DC: Brookings Institution Press.

Conly, S. 2013. *Against Autonomy*. Cambridge: Cambridge University Press.

Credit CARD Act. 2009. Pub L No 111–24, 123 Stat 1734, codified in various sections of Titles 15 and 16.

Deb, Partha, and Carmen Vargas. 2016. "Who Benefits from Calorie Labeling? An Analysis of its Effects on Body Mass." NBER Working Paper 21992, National Bureau of Economic Research, Cambridge, MA.

Department of Agriculture. 2011. "Direct Certification and Certification of Homeless, Migrant and Runaway Children for Free School Meals." 76 Federal Register 22785–02, 22793.

Department of Health and Human Services. 2010. Centers for Disease Control and Prevention, Community Health Status Indicators (CHSI) to Combat Obesity, Heart Disease and Cancer, May 1. Retrieved from http://www.data.gov/raw/2159.

DG SANCO (European Commission's Directorate General for Health and Consumers). 2010. *Consumer Behaviour: The Road to Effective Policy-Making*. Retrieved from http://ec.europa.eu/consumers/docs/1dg-sanco-brochure-consumer-behaviour -final.pdf.

Dinner, Isaac, Daniel G. Goldstein, Eric J. Johnson, and Kaiya Liu. 2009. "Partitioning Default Effects: Why People Choose Not to Choose." Unpublished manuscript.

Emergency Planning and Community Right to Know Act. 1986. Pub L No 99–499, 100 Stat 1728, codified at 42 USC § 11001 et seq.

Environmental Protection Agency. 2009. "Fuel Economy Labeling of Motor Vehicles: Revisions to Improve Calculation of Fuel Economy Estimates." 74 Federal Register 61537–01, 61542, 61550–53 (amending 40 CFR Parts 86, 600).

European Commission. 2012. "Green Behavior." Future Brief 4, Science for Environment Policy, October. http://ec.europa.eu/environment/integration/research/news alert/pdf/FB4.pdf.

Gale, William G., J. Mark Iwry, and Spencer Walters. 2009. "Retirement Savings for Middle- and Lower-Income Households: The Pension Protection Act of 2006 and the Unfinished Agenda." In *Automatic: Changing the Way America Saves*, edited by William G. Gale, J. Mark Iwry, David C. John, and Lina Walker, 11–27. Washington, DC: Brookings Institution Press.

Greenstone, Michael. 2009. "Toward a Culture of Persistent Regulatory Experimentation and Evaluation." In *New Perspectives on Regulation*, edited by David Moss and John Cisternino, 111–125. Cambridge: The Tobin Project.

Halpern, David. 2015. *Inside the Nudge Unit.* London: Ebury.

Hamilton, James T. 2005. *Regulation through Revelation: The Origin, Politics, and Impacts of the Toxics Release Inventory Program.* Cambridge: Cambridge University Press.

Healthy, Hunger-Free Kids Act. 2012. Pub L No 111–296, 124 Stat 3183.

Heath, Chip, and Dan Heath. 2010. *Switch: How to Change Things When Change Is Hard.* New York: Broadway.

Hirshleifer, David. 1995. "The Blind Leading the Blind: Social Influence, Fads, and Informational Cascades." In *The New Economics of Human Behavior*, edited by Mariano Tommasi and Kathryn Ierulli, 188–215. Cambridge: Cambridge University Press.

Internal Revenue Service. 2009. "Retirement and Savings Initiatives: Helping Americans Save for the Future." http://www.irs.gov/pub/irs-tege/rne_se0909.pdf.

iNudgeYou.com. n.d. "Resources." http://www.inudgeyou.com/resources.

Jolls, Christine. 1998. "Behavioral Economics Analysis of Redistributive Legal Rules." *Vanderbilt Law Review* 51 (6): 1653–1677.

Kahneman, Daniel. 2011. *Thinking, Fast and Slow.* New York: Farrar, Straus, and Giroux.

Kahneman, Daniel, and Shane Frederick. 2002. "Representativeness Revisited: Attribute Substitution in Intuitive Judgment." In *Heuristics and Biases*, edited by Tom Gilovich, Dale Griffin, and Daniel Kahneman, 49–81. Cambridge: Cambridge University Press.

Kahneman, Daniel, and Amos Tversky. 1979. "Prospect Theory: An Analysis of Decision under Risk." *Econometrica* 47 (2): 263–292.

Leventhal, Howard, Robert Singer, and Susan Jones. 1965. "Effects of Fear and Specificity of Recommendation upon Attitudes and Behavior." *Journal of Personality and Social Psychology* 2 (1): 20–29.

Levin, Irwin P., Sandra L. Schneider, and Gary J. Gaeth. 1998. "All Frames Are Not Created Equal: A Typology and Critical Analysis of Framing Effects." *Organizational Behavior and Human Decision Processes* 76 (2): 149–188.

Loewenstein, George F., Elke U. Weber, Christopher K. Hsee, and Ned Welch. 2001. "Risk As Feelings." *Psychological Bulletin* 127 (2): 267–286.

Madrian, Brigitte C., and Dennis F. Shea. 2001. "The Power of Suggestion: Inertia in 401(k) Participation and Savings Behavior." *Quarterly Journal of Economics* 116 (4): 1149–1187.

McFerran, Brent, Darren W. Dahl, Gavan J. Fitzsimons, and Andrea C. Morales. 2011. "How the Body Type of Others Impacts Our Food Consumption." In *Leveraging Consumer Psychology for Effective Health Communications*, edited by Rajeev Batra, Punam Anand Keller, and Victor J. Strecher, 151–170. Armonk, NY: M. E. Sharpe.

McGraw, A. Peter, Jeff T. Larsen, Daniel Kahneman, and David Schkade. 2010. "Comparing Gains and Losses." *Psychological Science* 21 (10): 1438–1445.

Nickerson, David W., and Todd Rogers. 2010. "Do You Have a Voting Plan? Implementation Intentions, Voter Turnout, and Organic Plan Making." *Psychological Science* 21 (2): 194–199.

Obama, Barack H. 2009. Weekly address, September 5.

Office of Management and Budget, Office of Information and Regulatory Affairs. 2010. Information collection budget of the United States government. http://www.whitehouse.gov/sites/default/files/omb/inforeg/icb/icb_2010.pdf.

OECD (Organisation for Economic Co-operation and Development). 2010. *Consumer Policy Toolkit*. Paris: OECD Publishing.

Orszag, Peter. 2010. OMB, Director, SAVEings, March 29. http://www.whitehouse.gov/omb/blog/10/03/29/SAVEings/.

Orszag, Peter, and Eric Rodriguez. 2009. "Retirement Security for Latinos: Bolstering Coverage, Savings, and Adequacy." In *Automatic: Changing the Way America Saves*, edited by William G. Gale, Mark J. Iwry, David C. John, and Lina Walker, 173–198. Washington, DC: Brookings Institution Press.

Papke, Leslie E., Lina Walker, and Michael Dworsky. 2009. "Retirement Security for Women: Progress to Date and Policies for Tomorrow." In *Automatic: Changing the Way America Saves*, edited by William G. Gale, J. Mark Iwry, David C. John, and Lina Walker, 199–230. Washington, DC: Brookings Institution Press.

Pension Protection Act. 2006. Pub L No 109–280, 120 Stat 780, codified in various sections of Titles 26 and 29.

Redelmeier, Donald A., Paul Rozin, and Daniel Kahneman. 1993. "Understanding Patients' Decisions: Cognitive and Emotional Perspectives." *Journal of the American Medical Association* 270 (1): 72–76.

Rozin, Paul, Sydney Scott, Megan Dingley, Joanna K. Urbanek, Hong Jiang, and Mark Kaltenbach. 2011. "Nudge to Nobesity I: Minor Changes in Accessibility Decrease Food Intake." *Judgment and Decision Making* 6 (4): 323–332.

Schwartz, Janet, Jason Riis, Brian Elbel, and Dan Ariely. 2011. "Would You Like to Downsize That Meal? Activating Self-Control Is More Effective Than Calorie Labeling in Reducing Calorie Consumption in Fast Food Meals." Unpublished manuscript.

Sharot, Tali. 2011. *The Optimism Bias: A Tour of the Irrationally Positive Brain*. New York: Knopf.

Shu, Lisa L., Nina Mazar, Francesca Gino, Dan Ariely, and Max H. Bazerman. 2012. "Signing at the Beginning Makes Ethics Salient and Decreases Dishonest Self-Reports in Comparison to Signing at the End." *Proceedings of the National Academy of Sciences* 109 (38): 15197–15200.

Slovic, Paul. 1998. "Do Adolescent Smokers Know the Risks?" *Duke Law Journal* 47 (6): 1133–1141.

Stango, Victor, and Jonathan Zinman. 2011. "Limited and Varying Consumer Attention: Evidence from Shocks to the Salience of Bank Overdraft Fees." Working Paper 11–17, Federal Reserve Bank of Philadelphia.

Sunstein, Cass R. 2010. "Administrator, OIRA, Memorandum for the Heads of Executive Departments and Agencies, Disclosure and Simplification as Regulatory Tools." http://www.whitehouse.gov/sites/default/files/omb/assets/inforeg/disclosure_prin ciples.pdf.

Sunstein, Cass R. 2013. *Simpler*. New York: Simon and Schuster.

Sunstein, Cass R. 2015. *Choosing Not to Choose*. Oxford: Oxford University Press.

Sunstein, Cass R. 2016. *The Ethics of Influence*. New York: Cambridge University Press.

Thaler, Richard H. 2015. *Misbehaving*. New York: Norton.

Thaler, Richard H., and Cass R. Sunstein. 2008. *Nudge*. New Haven, CT: Yale University Press.

Thaler, Richard H., Daniel Kahneman, and Jack L. Knetsch. 1991. "Experimental Tests of the Endowment Effect and the Coase Theorem." In *Quasi Rational Economics*, edited by Richard H. Thaler, 167–188. New York: Russell Sage.

Tversky, Amos, and Daniel Kahneman. 1973. "Availability: A Heuristic for Judging Frequency and Probability." *Cognitive Psychology* 5 (2): 207–232.

Weinstein, Neil D. 1987. "Unrealistic Optimism about Susceptibility to Health Problems: Conclusions from a Community-Wide Sample." *Journal of Behavioral Medicine* 10 (5): 481–500.

Zwane, Alix Peterson, Jonathan Zinman, Eric Van Dusen, William Pariente, Clair Null, Edward Miguel, Michael Kremer, et al. 2011. "Being Surveyed Can Change Later Behavior and Related Parameter Estimates." *Proceedings of the National Academy of Sciences* 108 (5): 1821–1826.

9 CFR § 317.309.

Comment: Robert Hockett

Choice Architectures: An Appreciation and a Provisional Suggestion

I.

I have long been intrigued, and occasionally maddened, by certain idiomatic crazes or fads that seem constantly to break out and spread through American society. Advertisers now hawk "solutions," for example, rather than goods and services. And of course, it has been decades by this point that we have been bringing past conversations up into the present by saying "I'm like…," not "I said.…"

A recent development along these lines that I find especially amusing is the now oft-heard expression, "a thing." Each of "Benghazi" and "the 47 percent," for example, for a time was said to have become "a thing." Likewise Hillary Clinton's emails and Donald Trump's "Tweets." Pretty much every new entrant to the Grand Guignol theater of public consciousness and conversation these days is a "thing" in the requisite sense. By this criterion, I suppose that "a thing" is itself now a thing—perhaps a sort of recursive, reflexive, or self-referential thing.

II.

In the academy, behavioralism seems to have become "a thing" by the late 1970s or early 1980s at latest, notwithstanding the fact that discoveries such as the Allais and Ellsberg "paradoxes," then Herbert Simonian "bounded

Broad thanks to participants at the "State of the Economy, State of the World" conference held at the World Bank in Washington, DC, in June 2016. Special thanks to Kaushik Basu and Cass Sunstein.

rationality,"[1] evidenced certain systematic departures from orthodox models of choice behavior much earlier.

In my own case, I think behavioralism became something of "a thing" with the reading of two authors during the late 1990s: first, a man who later became one of my dissertation advisors, Bob Shiller at Yale; and second, the man on whose vast and still growing body of work I am to comment today—the phenomenal Cass Sunstein.

Bob first got me to thinking about the work of Dick Thaler in particular—especially what I call "endowment psychology" (not to mention Cornell coffee mugs),[2] which I thought a helpful way of explaining my own longstanding intuition that what is now coming to be called "predistribution" might prove more politically stable than redistribution as a means of redressing distributive injustice.[3] This in turn harmonized well with what had drawn me to Bob as a mentor in the first place, for my aim was to develop means of financially engineering justice-improving predistributive schemes, the ultimate upshot of which is a book now forthcoming from Yale University Press.[4]

Cass came into the picture for me with what I suppose was then merely his eight-hundredth book—*Free Markets and Social Justice*, published in 1998. I virtually devoured this rich, rich collection of previously published essays and articles, and learned much from it. But what I think stuck with me most was Cass's emphasis on the endogeneity of preferences, as well as his patient tracing of normatively interesting consequences therefrom.

Now of course, I'd been aware of preference-endogeneity as an objection to certain attempts at theorizing justice, thanks to Amartya's celebrated "tame housewife" objection, and Jerry Cohen's cognate "Tiny Tim" objection, to certain assumptions that figured centrally in liberal accounts of justice.[5] (John Roemer and Jerry were, like Bob Shiller, very patient mentors.) And I'd been aware of Gary Becker's work on tastes in micro theory. But it

---

1. See Allais (1953), Ellsberg (1961), and Simon (1991). It should be noted that Ellsberg's paradox effectively appears earlier in Keynes (1921, 75–76, n. 2).
2. See, for example, Hockett (2005, 2006, 2007, 2008a).
3. See sources cited in Hockett (2005, 2006, 2007, 2008a).
4. See Hockett (2017, forthcoming).
5. See Cohen (1989) and Sen (1995).

was Cass and his reflections that most aided me in thinking comprehensively, in both a broadly transdisciplinary and a more systematically programmatic manner, about preference-endogeneity and its implications. So my remarks here will be one part encomium, one part elaboration, and one part halfway provocative suggestion for further work—perhaps in the direction of what I'll call a sort of "behavioral macro" or "liberal collectivism."[6]

III.

Let me begin, then, by noting a certain family resemblance between classical liberalism in political theory and the classical choice model in welfare-economic theory. If we take Rawlsian justice theory as emblematic of liberalism in the modern era, then in liberalism we find a political ideal that is essentially indifferent to the origins or nature of preferences and is concerned instead with what Rawlsians call "the basic structure" in which preference-satisfactions or "lifeplans" are pursued or executed.[7] This concern finds partial—though, as I shall claim, misleading—programmatic expression in the Rawlsian doctrine's commitment to what Rawls called "the priority of the right over the good."[8]

Analogously, in classical welfare theory, we find preferences to be likewise bracketed—placed outside of—the field of disciplinary inquiry. They are, that is to say, treated as exogenous—no more subject to rational critique than Rawlsian life plans are subject to normative political critique. Discussion and disputation accordingly center on the formal properties of the social welfare function or functional that aggregates preferences. The social welfare function aggregation rule, pursuant to the dominant research program, accordingly plays a role here analogous to "basic structure" in normative liberal political theory à la Rawls.[9]

Now, as is well known, Rawlsian liberalism came under sustained scrutiny and critique during the 1970s and after. One grounds for criticism was the account's implausibly denuded conception of the choosing liberal self behind the Rawlsian (or should we say Harsanyian)[10] veil of ignorance. The

---

6. See, for example, Hockett (2013a).
7. See generally Rawls (1971).
8. Rawls (1971).
9. For more on this link, see Hockett (2008b, 2009).
10. See Harsanyi (1953, 1955).

"unsituated self," as Michael Sandel later canonically dubbed it,[11] became something of an albatross for liberal justice theory, both for reasons of normative attractiveness (cf. Cohen 1897; Sen 1995) and for reasons of theoretic intelligibility (cf. Sandel (1982) and others).[12] So-called communitarians and, more broadly, communicative action theorists, actuated by critiques of this general form, in consequence steadily wrought a manner of "contextualizing" revolution in justice theory—a revolution whose best-known exponents at present are probably Jürgen Habermas, Axel Honneth, and Rainer Forst.[13]

Against this backdrop, I think, one helpful way of viewing the behavioralist revolution in normative economics and economic analysis of law—particularly as systematized, interpreted, and further developed by Cass—is as a thoroughly and programmatically-minded choice-theoretic analog to the "communitarian" revolt against liberal justice theory. Situating the Rawlsian unsituated self is, perhaps, best and most thoroughly done by first comprehensively endogenizing the classical choice-theoretic chooser.

This is, in part, precisely what Cass's thoroughly cataloging, systematizing, and further advancing of behavioralist learning does. For what are careful attention to choice-inertia, framing, salience-attending, loss-aversion, social influences, heuristics, implicit probability assumptions, and so forth if not ways of thoroughly endogenizing preferences and, therefore, more fully situating actual choosing selves? And if, with Cass and his co-authors, we can do this both comprehensively and with an eye to normative significance, then we stand to develop both better positive and better normative microeconomic, welfare economic, and justice theory. Pretty exciting stuff!

IV.

But now here is what I think might be most exhilarating of all in Cass's recent work: His achievements, although they began as theoretic advances, have rapidly opened the door to more practical, "applied" advances as well.

---

11. See Sandel (1982).
12. My colleague Steve Shiffrin often says that "children are the Achilles Heal of liberalism." This seems to me nicely to capture both preference-endogeneity and intelligibility objections in a single slogan.
13. See, for example, Habermas (1996), Forst (2002), and Honneth (2014).

By attending to the whole of the "choice architecture," as Cass dubs it, which the many forms of preference-shaping he studies jointly constitute, we soon spot a novel way to skirt a particularly vexed clash of values in modern Western and, especially, US intellectual and political history.

I allude to the clash between what Rawls would call "liberalism and perfectionism," and what Cass and Thaler call "libertarianism and paternalism."[14] In effect, Cass and Thaler note, we can, by carefully studying and incrementally improving choice architecture, both improve aggregate welfare—something like what Rawls would call "the good"[15]—and avoid any serious, non de minimus affront to individual freedom—what Rawls would call respect for "the priority of liberty."[16]

We can, in other words, act on a sort of commonsense, nonperfectionist and nondogmatic view of the collective good while still allowing for individual opt-outs by those who, upon consideration, still prefer to choose as they would have done under an earlier architecture. In this way, we get to have a bit of our cake while eating it, too, sidestepping irresoluble conflicts over totalizing visions of "the Good," rather as Cass recommended long ago, in a different context, under the rubric of what he called "incompletely theorized agreements."

We encourage or facilitate the making of choices that most would think wise, in other words, without outright coercing them. This is an achievement on par, in my view, with Lock's classic work on toleration and Mill's on liberty many decades ago. And it is apt to be rather more effective, in my humble opinion, than Rawls's late 1990s offering of a "political, not metaphysical" account of liberal justice.[17]

All right, so there's the encomium. Now for a brief closing suggestion that might be a little—but I think only a little—provocative. I want to suggest that we might also encourage some socially beneficial choices without outright coercing them through means additional to Cass's style of

---

14. See Thaler and Sunstein (2008).
15. Though Rawls himself of course tends not to aggregate, since he *brackets* "the good." (A possible exception comes in the form of "the good of the worst-off," whose lot Rawls's "difference principle" aims to optimize. If the "worst-off" embraces a class rather than a person—Rawls doesn't tell us which—then of course there is aggregation at least with respect to the good of this class.)
16. Rawls (1971).
17. See Rawls (1996).

choice-architecture reconstruction. Here I allude to work I've been doing in recent years, some with my colleague Saule Omarova, on what I call "private means to public ends." In particular, I have in mind making more thoughtful, deliberate use of certain market-acting roles that government instrumentalities often play in our macroeconomy.

Here's what I mean. I've worked on and off at the Federal Reserve Bank of New York (or "New York Fed") in the past, and I am struck by how few people seem to know anything about what is, by any measure, the most critical function discharged by this remarkable institution each day. I mean the actual implementation of monetary policy, on a literal day-by-day basis, by the New York Fed trading desk in lower Manhattan. By transacting in massive quantities of (mainly) US Treasury securities with private dealer banks each morning, this desk injects money into, or retracts money out of, our banking and broader financial markets each day, thereby determining borrowing costs and, we hope, the pace of activity throughout the broader economy.[18]

Now, one way to conceive and then generalize from this literally quotidian quasi-governmental activity is to think of it as something that I call "market-moving." A particularly important variable—what in other work I call a "systemically important price or index," or "SIPI"—is deliberately "moved" by a government instrumentality that acts pursuant to the same modalities as do other, nongovernmental actors in the very same markets. All that differs is the object of the activities in question.

Once we recognize that prevailing interest rates are but one of many publicly cognizable SIPIs out there in our markets, it is easy to imagine why and how we might wish to generalize from the New York Fed's open market operations to something that I call "open market operation plus" in connection with other SIPIs.[19] We might wish to move particularly important commodity prices (e.g., foodstuffs or fuel) during a period of dangerous volatility,[20] for example, or prevailing wage rates during a deflationary slump.[21] Or we might have acted to put downward pressure on secondary credit or mortgage markets during the junk bond and mortgage-backed

---

18. See, for example, Hockett and Omarova (2014).
19. See Hockett and Omarova (2015).
20. See Hockett (2011).
21. Hockett and Omarova (2014, 2015).

security (MBS) hyperinflations of the late 1980s and early 2000s, respectively, or on health insurance prices right now through a "public option" add-on to "Obamacare."[22]

Once you start thinking about it, broadly welfare-enhancing market-moving strategies of this kind come quite rapidly to mind. But my taxonomy includes other modalities additional to what I call "market-moving." One such I call "market-making," in the sense meant by financial market participants. This is partly what Fannie Mae was established to do in 1938—to make a secondary market in mortgage loans so as to lower credit costs in the primary markets and thereby stabilize Depression-era real estate markets and the home construction industry while raising home ownership rates.[23] That was a system that worked wonderfully for nearly 60 years until underregulated private investment banks got into the act and blew everything up.[24] The New York Fed's Maiden Lane funds, specially created for the purpose, acted similarly in connection with MBSs to stem an individually rational but collectively irrational run on MBSs from 2008 into 2012, in what I call a "market-preserving" role that was effectively taken over by the Fed Board itself via the third round of quantitive easing in October 2012.

V.

These are but a few of the many examples that I elaborate elsewhere. I won't bore you with more of them here; those who are interested can take a look at the works I cite in the footnotes. My object for present purposes is simply to suggest that in some cases, there might be other avenues, additional to Cass's style of choice architecture, through which to influence preferences in what nearly all would agree to be socially desirable ways, without outright coercing them.

It is true that my "big market actor" strategy might, if used for some conceivable purposes, edge closer to coercion than do Cass's strategies, inasmuch as it imposes higher costs on contrarians than do Cass's default-switches from opt-ins to opt-outs. But these seem to me differences of

---

22. Hockett (2010) and Hockett and Omarova (2014, 2015).
23. See Hockett (2006).
24. Hockett (2006) and also Hockett (2013b).

degree rather than of kind. And because most (if not all) entries on my proposed menu of market actor roles aim to solve what I call "recursive collective action problems" that everyone can plausibly be presumed to wish to solve, rather than systematically to coerce choice,[25] it might even be the case that my proposals "impose" no more on individual choosers than do Cass's.

We have barely begun to explore these proposals' potentials. I suspect now that once we do, we shall see quickly that they can both complement and supplement the impressive array of entries on Cass's proposed menu.

VI.

And with that I shall close. To the vanishingly few of you here who might not be familiar with Cass's vast oeuvre—astonishing, proceeding as it does from one still so young—I'll say no more at present than please take a look! And to Cass himself, I say one more time: Thank you, and please keep it coming!

References

Allais, Maurice. 1953. "Le Comportement de L'homme Rationnel Devant le Risque: Critique des Postulats et Axiomes de L'Ecole Américaine." *Econometrica* 21 (4): 503–546.

Cohen, G. A. 1989. "On the Currency of Egalitarian Justice." *Ethics* 99 (4): 906–944.

Ellsberg, Daniel. 1961. "Risk, Ambiguity, and the Savage Axioms." *Quarterly Journal of Economics* 75 (4): 643–669.

Forst, Rainer. 2002. *Contexts of Justice.* Berkeley, Los Angeles: University of California Press.

Habermas, Jürgen. 1996. *Between Facts and Norms.* Cambridge, MA: MIT Press.

Harsanyi, John. 1953. "Cardinal Utility in Welfare Economics and in the Theory of Risk-Taking." *Journal of Political Economy* 61 (5): 434–435.

Harsanyi, John. 1955. "Cardinal Welfare, Individualistic Ethics, and Interpersonal Comparisons of Utility." *Journal of Political Economy* 63 (4): 309–321.

Hockett, Robert C. 2005. "Whose Ownership? Which Society?" *Cardozo Law Review* 27 (1): 1–103.

---

25. See Hockett (2015).

Hockett, Robert C. 2006. "A Jeffersonian Republic by Hamiltonian Means." *Southern California Law Review* 79 (1): 45–164.

Hockett, Robert C. 2007. "What Kinds of Stock Ownership Plans Should There Be?" *Cornell Law Review* 92 (5): 865–952.

Hockett, Robert C. 2008a. "Insource the Shareholding of Outsourced Employees: A Global Stock Ownership Plan." *Virginia Law & Business Review* 3 (2): 357–426.

Hockett, Robert C. 2008b. "Pareto Versus Welfare." Cornell Legal Studies Research Paper 08–031, Cornell University, Ithaca, NY.

Hockett, Robert C. 2009. "Why Paretians Can't Prescribe: Preferences, Principles and Imperatives in Law and Policy." *Cornell Journal of Law and Public Policy* 18 (2): 391–476.

Hockett, Robert C. 2011. "How to Make QE More Helpful: By Fed Shorting of Commodities." *Benzinga*, October 11. https://www.benzinga.com/news/11/10/1988109/how-to-make-qe-more-helpful-by-fed-shorting-of-commodities.

Hockett, Robert C. 2013a. "The Libertarian Welfare State." *Challenge* 56 (2): 100–114.

Hockett, Robert C. 2013b. "Paying Paul and Robbing No One: An Eminent Domain Solution for Underwater Mortgage Debt." *Current Issues in Economics and Finance* 19 (5): 1–12.

Hockett, Robert C. 2015. "Recursive Collective Action Problems." *Journal of Financial Perspectives* 3 (2): 113–128.

Hockett, Robert C. 2017. *A Republic of Producers*. Forthcoming.

Hockett, Robert C., and Saule Omarova. 2014. "'Private' Means to 'Public' Ends." *Theoretical Inquiries in Law* 15 (1): 530–576.

Hockett, Robert C., and Saule Omarova. 2015. "'Public' Actors in 'Private' Markets." *Washington University Law Review* 93 (1): 103–176.

Honneth, Axel. 2014. *Freedom's Right*. New York: Columbia University Press.

Keynes, John Maynard. 1921. *A Treatise on Probability*. London: Macmillan & Co.

Rawls, John. 1971. *A Theory of Justice*. Cambridge, MA: Belknap Press of Harvard University Press.

Rawls, John, 1996. *Political Liberalism*. New York: Columbia University Press.

Sandel, Michael J. 1982. *Liberalism and the Limits of Justice*. Cambridge: Cambridge University Press.

Sen, Amartya K. 1995. "Equality of What?" In *Equal Freedom: Selected Tanner Lectures on Human Values*, edited by Stephen Darwall. Ann Arbor: University of Michigan Press.

Simon, Herbert. 1991. "Bounded Rationality and Organizational Learning." *Organization Science* 2(1): 125–134.

Thaler, Richard H., and Cass Sunstein. 2008. *Nudge.* New Haven, CT: Yale University Press.

Comment: Varun Gauri

Nudging Goes Global

All over the world, policy making is being nudged. A partial list of governments that have begun, systematically, to use behavioral economics in their policies and programs comprises the United Kingdom, the United States, Chicago, New York, Washington, DC, Rio de Janeiro, New South Wales, New Zealand, the Western Cape, Guatemala, the Netherlands, France, Peru, Canada, Denmark, Indonesia, Lebanon, the UAE, Poland, Latvia, Moldova, Japan, Germany, Singapore, and India. World Bank teams, including the Mind, Behavior, and Development Unit (eMBeD), are involved in dozens of ongoing projects that incorporate social and behavioral insights. Cass Sunstein's work, crystallized in his book *Nudge* with Richard Thaler, has been seminal; it has genuinely changed policy making the world over.

As the use of behavioral economics has moved from the periphery to the mainstream, it is worth reflecting on some of the outstanding questions and criticisms that confront the practice. Sunstein's essay in this volume is, like his work more broadly, not only thorough (in the sense that it successfully organizes a wide range of theory and evidence), but also thoughtful (in the sense that it rewards close reading). In what follows, I use excerpts from Sunstein's essay as a point of departure to raise, in a preliminary way, four issues related to the behavioral economics and policy making agenda. It is also the case, as I will make clear, that Sunstein's own work has anticipated the pathways through which one can make advances on some of these questions.

For Which People Are Nudges Liberty Preserving?

> Suppose, for example, that a particular default rule would place a strong majority of the relevant population in the situation that they would favor if they made an informed choice. If so, there is a legitimate decision reason to adopt that default rule (with the understanding that for those who differ from the majority, it remains possible to opt out).
>
> —Cass Sunstein, (forthcoming)

Because most people are myopic and/or otherwise inattentive, because they view default savings plans as authorized or as important reference points, automatic enrollment in a retirement savings plan increases mean retirement savings. Subsequently allowing people to opt out preserves their liberty to make significant choices regarding their own lives. Because there must be a default rule of some sort—either individuals are not enrolled and can opt in, or they are enrolled and can opt out—why not choose the default rule that increases savings? This is the logic of libertarian paternalism.

Notice, however, that the formulation trades on two different understandings of liberty: positive and negative (Berlin 1969). Automatic enrollment appeals to positive liberty: Myopia and inattention are external sources of "control or interference," to use Berlin's language, that affect what people do. Automatic enrollment helps them achieve their true objectives. But the power to opt out, once one is automatically enrolled, is a negative liberty: Factors external to the will, such as myopia or inattention, still limit the capacity of an automatically enrolled saver to opt out. These enrolled savers are free in the negative sense that they can choose to disenroll without any obstruction by other persons.

Although space is insufficient to spell out the argument in detail, it seems to be the case, then, that automatic retirement savings is not "liberty preserving" in a simple way. Elsewhere, Sunstein (2012) comes to a similar conclusion by referencing a continuum between soft and hard paternalism, which is scaled by the sum of material and psychic costs imposed. He describes most "nudges" as a kind of soft (if not entirely liberty-preserving) paternalism and argues that most people in fact opt out of defaults that are welfare-decreasing (Beshears et al. 2010).

But the paternalism challenge to the long-term "nudge" agenda, particularly in developing countries, will require further elaboration on the part of those of us engaged in it. To take up just two points. First, it will not be enough to say that most people opt out of bad defaults. We also need to know who opts out, and much more about how the capacity to identify welfare-improving choices and take advantage of information disclosure is related to poverty (Mani et al. 2013), as well as to gender and other normatively important social categories.

Second, as nudging goes global and begins to work in cultural environments very different from the United States and the United Kingdom, where it began, it may be that in many contexts, what is ethically salient is not the extent to which a behavioral intervention constrains liberty, understood as the sum of material and psychic costs imposed by a policy, but the intrinsic ethical value of the program itself. Indeed, informal conversations suggest that policy makers in many countries are not particularly troubled by the paternalism question, because liberalism is not the assumed background of ethical evaluation. Other goals—such as "development" or "harmony" or "social justice"—are often more prominent. Indeed, it might be helpful if policy makers were more troubled than they are by nudging policies. Those working in the field might make a contribution to democratic policy making around the world by insisting that nudgers disclose and debate their nudge policies.

How Social Norms Change

> Consider as well the problem of distracted driving. On October 1, 2009, the president issued an executive order that bans federal employees from texting while driving. Such steps can help promote a social norm against texting while driving, thus reducing risks.
>
> —Cass Sunstein, (forthcoming)

We know that social norms are crucial drivers of behavior, but how can policy makers shift them? One approach has been to activate existing social norms, particularly empirical knowledge or expectations regarding modal behavior in a group. Interventions in that vein have reduced road accidents (Habyarimana and Jack 2011), increased tax compliance (Hallsworth et al. 2014), and successfully promoted energy conservation (Allcott and Rogers 2014).

Sunstein's interpretation of the White House order on texting while driving, however, is more ambitious. It is about creating a new social norm, not merely activating an existing one. One analogy in developing countries is a law requiring candidates for village council elections in Haryana, India, to have a functioning toilet in their homes.[1] The idea, as in the texting law, is that public officials can serve as role models or otherwise inspire a shift in the behavior in the general population. But social norms operate in reference groups, and if public officials are not in the reference group of the target population, their behavior might not motivate people to behave differently, or may even even backfire. For instance, villagers in Haryana might come to think that toilets are just for government workers and other important people, not for ordinary folk.

Another analogy is early legislation in American states that made it illegal for anyone who had engaged in a duel from holding public office (Lessig 1995). Those laws, though not successfully enforced, were intended to allow a gentleman to decline a challenge to a duel by appealing to, rather than shrinking from, the honor code—he could say that because honor required him to serve the public, and dueling would make public service impossible, he had no choice but to decline.

The target of the antidueling rules was elite behavior, but duels were highly visible events, so it was possible that their disappearance would promote democratic sensibilities and the ethos of nonviolence more generally. In contrast, texting is not easily observed; even if public officials stop texting, the general public may not realize it.

The general point is that scholars have taught us some things about social norms (Sunstein 1996), and policy makers are coming to recognize the value of activating them. But we know much more about the comparative statics of social norms, and about norm unraveling through bandwagon effects and pluralistic ignorance, than about norm emergence and creation.

---

1. The law also requires minimum educational qualifications, not having defaulted in cooperative loans or having outstanding dues on rural domestic electricity connections, and not having been charged by a court for a grave criminal offense. The Supreme Court of India upheld the law in December 2015. See http://www.livemint .com/Politics/KTRLWs6xYd6OlfSKC3SRHL/Supreme-Court-upholds-Haryana-law -on-Panchayat-polls.html.

Outcomes

> If people learn that they are using more energy than similarly situated others, their energy use may decline—saving money while also reducing pollution.
>
> —Cass Sunstein, (forthcoming)

A full assessment of the effects of home energy reports includes, in addition to lower pollution and savings, the expenditures associated with efficiency-improving capital investments (as when a homeowner purchases new appliances or windows) and, to the extent it can be accurately measured, the hedonic cost of tolerating a hotter or colder living environment in the home (Allcott and Kessler 2015). Although everyone might agree that in theory, those factors should also be included when evaluating the overall effects of a behavioral intervention, they are not usually included in practice. Too often, evaluations of behavioral policies focus almost exclusively on the intended behavioral change. When possible, assessments of behavioral policies should focus on the effects on overall well-being, and not just on behavior itself. Similarly, although there are good reasons to think that some behavioral interventions can have long-term impact (Madrian and Shea 2001; Yeager and Walton 2011), practitioners would like to know more about the kinds of interventions and circumstances under which long-term as opposed to ephemeral effects are achieved.

Nudging the Nudgers

> It should not be necessary to emphasize that public officials are subject to error as well.
>
> —Cass Sunstein, this volume

Although the potential value of behavioral insights in developing countries is substantial (World Bank 2014), one concern is that the successful formulation and implementation of all policies, behaviorally informed or not, requires the capacity to recruit, motivate, and supervise an effective bureaucracy. Opt-out retirement savings plans, for example, are built on financial, regulatory, and informational infrastructure that cannot be taken for granted in many countries. More generally, few now question the negative impact of government failure—and not just market failure—on economic development (Bardhan 2015). Bureaucrats are subject to many of the cognitive biases that everyone else is, including sunk cost bias, cultural cognition, and inaccurate assessment of risks (Banuri, Dercon, and Gauri 2016). Can social and behavioral insights improve governance? Some preliminary evidence suggests that they can. For instance, unexpected payments can motivate workers, even if the money is not tied to performance (Hossain and List 2012); peer effects seem to improve productivity (Mas and Moretti, 2009); and social recognition can improve performance (Ashraf, Bandiera, and Lee 2014).

There remains to be developed an extremely interesting and potentially very useful agenda related to the use of social and behavioral insights to promote professional norms, bureaucratic identities, impartial and sound decision making, and productivity in the public sector. As elsewhere, Sunstein's writings have anticipated this line of research (Sunstein and Hastie 2015). With luck, this commentary will nudge him to expand it.

References

Allcott, Hunt, and Judd B. Kessler. 2015. "The Welfare Effects of Nudges: A Case Study of Energy Use Social Comparisons." NBER Working Paper 21671, National Bureau of Economic Research, Cambridge, MA.

Allcott, Hunt, and Todd Rogers. 2014. "The Short-Run and Long-Run Effects of Behavioral Interventions: Experimental Evidence from Energy Conservation." *American Economic Review* 104 (10): 3003–3037.

Ashraf, Nava, Oriana Bandiera, and Scott S. Lee. 2014. "Awards Unbundled: Evidence from a Natural Field Experiment." *Journal of Economic Behavior and Organization* 100 (April): 44–63.

Banuri, Sheheryar, Stefan Dercon, and Varun Gauri. 2017. "Biased Policy Professionals." World Bank Policy Research Working Paper WPS 8113.

Bardhan, Pranab. 2015. "State and Development: The Need for a Reappraisal of the Current Literature." *Journal of Economic Literature* 54 (3): 862–892.

Berlin, Isaiah. 1969. "Two Concepts of Liberty." In *Four Essays on Liberty*, edited by Isaiah Berlin, 118–172. Clarendon Press.

Beshears, John, James Choi, David Laibson, and Brigitte Madrian. 2010. "The Limitations of Defaults." NBER Retirement Research Center Paper NB 10-02, National Bureau of Economic Research, Cambridge, MA.

Habyarimana, James, and William Jack. 2011. "Heckle and Chide: Results of a Randomized Road Safety Intervention in Kenya." *Journal of Public Economics* 95 (11): 1438–1446.

Hallsworth, Michael, John A. List, Robert D. Metcalfe, and Ivo Vlaev. 2014. "The Behavioralist as Tax Collector: Using Natural Field Experiments to Enhance Tax Compliance." NBER Working Paper 20007, National Bureau of Economic Research, Cambridge, MA.

Hossain, Tanjin, and John A. List. 2012. "The Behavioralist Visits the Factory: Increasing Productivity Using Simple Framing Manipulations." *Management Science* 58 (12): 2151–2167.

Lessig, Lawrence. 1995. "The Regulation of Social Meaning." *The University of Chicago Law Review* 62: 943.

Madrian, Brigitte C., and Dennis F. Shea. 2001. "The Power of Suggestion: Inertia in 401(k) Participation and Savings Behavior." *Quarterly Journal of Economics* 116 (4): 1149–1187.

Mani, Anandi, Sendhil Mullainathan, Eldar Shafir, and Jiaying Zhao. 2013. "Poverty Impedes Cognitive Function." *Science* 341 (6149): 976–980.

Mas, Alexandre, and Enrico Moretti. 2009. "Peers at Work." *American Economic Review* 99 (1): 112–145.

Sunstein, Cass R. 1996. "Social Norms and Social Roles." *Columbia Law Review* 96: 903.

Sunstein, Cass R. 2012. "Storrs Lectures: Behavioral Economics and Paternalism." *Yale Law Journal* 122 (7): 1826–1899.

Sunstein, Cass R. Forthcoming. Nudges.gov: Behavioral Economics and Regulation (February 16, 2013). In *Oxford Handbook of Behavioral Economics and the Law*, edited by Eyal Zamir and Doron Teichman. Available at SSRN: https://ssrn.com/abstract=2220022 or http://dx.doi.org/10.2139/ssrn.2220022.

Sunstein, Cass R., and Reid Hastie. 2015. *Wiser: Getting beyond Groupthink to Make Groups Smarter*. Boston: Harvard Business Review Press.

World Bank. 2014. *World Development Report 2015: Mind, Society, and Behavior*. Washington, DC: World Bank.

Yeager, David S., and Gregory M. Walton. 2011. "Social-Psychological Interventions in Education: They're Not Magic." *Review of Educational Research* 81 (2): 267–301.

9 Morality: Evolutionary Foundations and Policy Implications

Ingela Alger and Jörgen W. Weibull

Act only according to that maxim whereby you can, at the same time, will that it should become a universal law.

—Immanuel Kant, *Groundwork of the Metaphysics of Morals*, 1785

One general law, leading to the advancement of all organic beings, namely, multiply, vary, let the strongest live and the weakest die.

—Charles Darwin, *On the Origin of Species*, 1859

The academic discipline of economics has over many years provided policy makers all over the world with a powerful toolbox. Conceptual, philosophical, and methodological disagreements are relatively rare, and the discipline is not torn by fights between disparate schools of thought. Whether this monolithic character of the field is a sign of strength or weakness is not easy to say, but this methodological unity and power has, arguably, given the discipline great influence on policy. The strong methodological core of economics—in the 1950s–1960s epitomized by general equilibrium theory and later incorporating game theory—has enabled positive and normative analysis of a wide range of economic and social issues.

So what, more exactly, does this core consist of? In a nutshell, it has two main components. The first is that it views economic agents—who may be individuals, households, firms, or organizations—as goal-oriented,

This manuscript was prepared for the conference "The State of Economics, The State of the World," held at the World Bank in Washington, DC, on June 8–9, 2016. The authors thank Daniel Chen, Jean-François Laslier, Assar Lindbeck, Erik Mohlin, Paul Seabright, Jean Tirole, Nicolas Treich, Yu Wen, and Peter Wikman for valuable comments and suggestions.

as if they each had some goal function that they strive to maximize under the constraints they face, given the information they have, and given their beliefs about relevant aspects of the world they live in. The second component is that interactions between these economic agents are taken to meet certain consistency requirements, formalized as equilibria, that is, collections of action plans, one for each agent, such that no agent can unilaterally improve the expected value of her goal function (usually profit or utility).

Both components can and have been contested. Individuals may not be so systematic and consistent, and interactions may be chaotic and volatile. Having a theoretically well-founded and empirically accurate understanding of human motivation is, arguably, in any case of utmost relevance for analysis and policy recommendations.

Among the more noticeable new methodological developments in economics is the emergence of behavioral and experimental economics, where the first strand endows economic agents with richer motivations than in traditional economics, usually in the form of prosocial or other-regarding preferences. The second strand tests such models, old and new, in controlled laboratory experiments and in randomized field experiments. The external validity of laboratory experiments can be questioned, and field experiments may depend on local and historical factors with little generality, but this development of the discipline of economics toward becoming an empirically founded science appears to be essentially very healthy. It was not long ago that economics was thought of as similar to meteorology and astronomy: All it could do was to observe what is happening, without the possibility of experimenting. Moving away from mere observation of data that happen to come about to carefully designed controlled experiments is reminiscent of how Galileo Galilei once lead the way from Aristotelean scholastic discourse to modern science.

Behavioral and experimental economics no doubt will improve the predictive power and the usefulness of economics, but further improvements could certainly be made if the underlying factors that shape human motivation were better understood. The literature on the evolutionary foundations of human motivation aims at providing such understanding by asking: What preferences should humans be expected to have if these are transmitted in society from generation to generation? If certain prosocial or antisocial preferences, or moral values, give their carriers on average better material outcomes than other preferences or values (all else being equal), then one would expect the former to spread in the population (be it by biological or cultural mechanisms). Our aim in this chapter is to discuss a recent theoretical result concerning such evolutionary preference selection and to examine its implications for a range of social and economic issues.

Milton Friedman (1953, 22) claimed that "unless the behavior of businessmen in some way or other approximated behavior consistent with the maximization of returns, it seems unlikely that they would remain in business for long." In a similar vein, one may claim that unless the behavior of an individual is consistent with the maximization of own material payoffs, other, materially more successful behaviors will take over in the interacting population. Economists have shown that this claim is theoretically valid when (1) the population at hand is very large, (2) interacting individuals do not know each other's goal functions, and (3) interactions are perfectly random in the sense that each encounter is just as likely (Ok and Vega-Redondo 2001; Dekel, Ely, and Yilankaya 2007).

In reality, however, populations are not always large, and interacting individuals sometimes know or learn about each other's preferences (for instance, think of the great number of interactions that take place in families or small communities). It has been shown that in such settings, preferences or goal functions can usually serve as effective commitment devices, and evolution will almost always favor goal functions that differ from own material payoffs.[1] Furthermore—and this is what we will focus on here—encounters are only rarely perfectly random; geographic location, language, culture, and religion often have an impact on the likelihood of specific encounters. For example, business partners may know each other from college, and neighbors may have chosen to live in the same place because they share socioeconomic or cultural backgrounds or have similar location preferences and so forth. In such structured populations, some encounters are more likely than others, even if the overall population is large. In two recent theoretical studies (Alger and Weibull 2013, 2016), we show that such *assortative matching* makes evolution favor individuals who are not purely self-interested but who attach some value to "doing the right thing," even though the population is large, and interacting individuals

---

1. Seminal articles on preference evolution, or indirect evolution, are Frank (1987) and Güth and Yaari (1992). See also Banerjee and Weibull (1995); Heifetz, Shannon, and Spiegel (2007), and Alger and Weibull (2010).

do not know one another's preferences. This (for us, initially surprising) finding suggests an evolutionary foundation for a psychologically plausible form of morality, in line with Immanuel Kant's categorical imperative.

In the next section, we describe this novel class of preferences and their evolutionary foundations. In the second section, we discuss the implications of such preferences for some much-studied social and economic behavior and policy issues, including public goods provision and behaviors that affect the environment. The third section discusses other social preferences and contrasts morality with altruism. The final section concludes.

Evolution and Kantian Morality

Imagine a population that has evolved for many generations in a stationary environment and that in each generation, individuals engage in some social or economic interaction. For instance, in a population of self-subsistence farmers, the interaction could be teamwork in the fields, the extraction of resources from a commonly owned lake or piece of land, lending activities, or the maintenance of institutions. In Alger and Weibull (2013, 2016), we propose a theoretical model of precisely such populations. We formalize the interaction by assuming that individuals are now and then randomly matched into groups of arbitrary (but fixed and given) size n to interact with each other in the group. (There are no interactions between groups and hence no group selection takes place.) The interaction may involve elements of cooperation and/or conflict, asymmetric information, repetition or interaction of arbitrary duration, possibility of helping, rewarding and/or punishing others, and so forth. Essentially only two restrictions are imposed on the interaction. First, the material payoff consequences for a participant depend only on the participant's own actions and on some aggregate of other group members' actions (not on who of them does what). In game theory, such interactions are called *aggregative* games. Examples are market competition where only competitors' aggregate output or lowest price matters, contributions to public goods where only the sum of others' contributions matters, some environmental externalities, and the like. Second, the material payoff function is the same for all individuals.

We follow standard economic theory by assuming that each individual acts so as to maximize some goal function. Different goal functions may be present in the population where each goal function represents some preference. Depending on the preference distribution and the process by which interaction groups are formed, individuals may end up in more or less homogeneous groups. For a given material interaction, a given preference distribution, and a given group formation process, the average material payoff consequences for individuals with a particular goal function are well determined in each equilibrium. In our evolutionary stability analysis, we ask: What kind of goal function, if any, would be favored by natural selection? Specifically, we determine which such functions are evolutionarily stable in the sense that, if almost all individuals in the population have such preferences, these individuals would materially outperform individuals with other preferences. Thus, the material payoffs are taken to be the drivers of evolution.

This approach is a generalization of the work of Maynard Smith and Price (1973), from the notion of an evolutionarily stable strategy (ESS), to that of an *evolutionarily stable goal function*.[2] A major challenge arises with this generalization. In any *population state*—the preference distribution in the population—there may be multiple equilibrium behaviors, and hence several possible material payoff allocations. We define a goal function to be *evolutionarily stable against another goal function* if in every population state where the latter goal function is rare, individuals equipped with the former goal function outperform those with the latter in terms of the resulting material payoffs in all equilibria.[3] Conversely, a goal function is *evolutionarily unstable* if there exists another goal function such that, no matter how small its population share, there is some equilibrium in which the latter goal function materially outperforms the former. In both definitions, the test scenario is to let in a small population share of "mutants," who may be migrants or carriers of spontaneously and randomly arising alternative goal functions, into the population of incumbents or residents. We impose minimal constraints on the nature of potential goal functions. They are not required to take any particular parametric form or even to depend on the material payoffs. Hence, individuals may be selfish, altruistic, spiteful,

---

2. In our approach, it is thus as if "mother nature" delegates to individuals to choose their actions, and instead equips them with goal functions that will guide their choice of action.
3. By "equilibrium" we mean Bayesian Nash equilibrium under incomplete information.

fairness-minded, inequity averse, environmentalists, moralists, and the like. Our only assumption is that each individual's goal function is continuous in all group members' courses of action.

A second key feature of our approach is that it allows the random matching to be *assortative*. Geographic, cultural, linguistic, and socioeconomic distances impose (literal or metaphoric) transportation costs, which imply that (1) individuals tend to interact more with individuals in their (geographic, cultural, linguistic, or socioeconomic) vicinity,[4] and (2) cultural or genetic transmission of types (say, behavior patterns, preferences, or moral values) from one generation to the next also has a tendency to take place in the vicinity of where the type originated.[5] Taken together, these two tendencies imply that individuals who interact with each other are likely to be of the same type. We formalize such potential assortativity in the random matching process in terms of a vector we call the *assortativity profile*. This vector consists of probabilities for the events that none, some, or all individuals in a vanishingly rare mutant's group also are mutants.[6]

Our analysis delivers two main results. First, although we impose virtually no restrictions on permissible utility functions, evolution favors a particular class of utility functions, which we call *Homo moralis*. Individuals with preferences in this class attach some weight to their own material payoff but also to what can be interpreted as a probabilistically generalized version of Kantian morality. In his *Grundlegung zur Metaphysik der Sitten*, Immanuel Kant ([1785] 2002, 37) wrote: "Act only according to that

---

4. Homophily has been documented by sociologists (e.g., McPherson, Smith-Lovin, and Cook 2001; Ruef, Aldrich, and, Carter 2003) and economists (e.g., Currarini, Jackson, and Pin 2009, 2010).

5. In biology, the concept of assortativity is known as *relatedness*, and the propensity to interact with individuals locally is nicely captured in the infinite island model, originally due to Wright (1931). Hamilton (1964) provided a first formalization of what is now known as Hamilton's rule: Evolution will select for behaviors whereby the external effects on others are internalized at a rate provided by the relatedness (see also Dawkins (1976), for a popular account of this idea, as well as Rousset (2004), for a comprehensive treatment). In an article on the evolution of behaviors in interactions among siblings, Bergstrom (1995) was probably the first to bring Hamilton's rule into the economics literature.

6. This concept generalizes Bergstrom's (2003) definition of the *index of assortativity* for pairwise encounters. See also Bergstrom (2012) and Alger and Weibull (2013) for further discussions of assortativity under pairwise matchings.

maxim whereby you can, at the same time, will that it should become a universal law." Similarly, paraphrasing Kant, *Homo moralis* attaches some weight to the goal of acting according to that maxim whereby you can, at the same time, will that it should become a universal law, even if followed only probabilistically by others. More precisely, a *Homo moralis* individual in a group of arbitrary size n maximizes a weighted average of equally many terms, indexed $j = 0, \ldots, n-1$, where each term is the material payoff that she would obtain if, hypothetically, she could replace the strategies of j other individuals in the group by her strategy. We call the vector of these probability weights the individual's *morality profile*.

The class of *Homo moralis* preferences has two extremes: *Homo oeconomicus*, who considers only her own material payoff,[7] and *Homo kantiensis*, who considers only the material payoff that she would obtain if all others were to act like she does. In between these two extremes is a whole range of *Homo moralis* preferences with different morality profiles, whereby an individual examines what would happen if some but not all the others were to act like him- or herself. *Homo moralis* partly evaluates her own actions in this probabilistic Kantian sense. In other words, she is to some extent concerned with the morality of her own acting, irrespective of what others do. She asks herself, before taking her action, what action she would prefer if, hypothetically, others would also probabilistically choose the same action in her situation.

Our first main result is that *Homo moralis* with a morality profile identical to the assortativity profile is evolutionarily stable. The intuition behind this result is *not* based on group selection, an old argument (appearing already in Charles Darwin's writings; see also Alexander (1987)) that essentially says that evolution will lead to behaviors that enhance the survival of the group. Quite on the contrary; the intuition is that natural selection will lead to utility functions that *preempt entry* into the population in the sense that the best a potential rare mutant can do, if striving for material payoff, is to mimic the residents.

---

7. Note that we define *Homo oeconomicus* as individuals who always seek to maximize their own material payoff. Some writers define *Homo oeconomicus*, or "economic man," more generally as an individual who always acts in accordance with some goal function, whether this be pure self-interest or not. All agents in the present study are varieties of *Homo oeconomicus* in this broad sense.

Our second main result is that any preferences that are behaviorally distinct from those of *Homo moralis* with the stable morality profile are evolutionarily unstable. Hence, although we made no parametric or structural assumption about utility functions, it appears that natural selection—as represented by evolutionary stability in our abstract and simplified framework—favors the utility function of *Homo moralis*. In particular, our results imply that *Homo oeconomicus*—pure material self-interest—is evolutionarily unstable under any random matching process with positive assortativity. Rare mutants may indeed garner a higher material payoff than *Homo oeconomicus*, on average, by behaving somewhat prosocially, because when there is positive assortativity, the benefits of this prosocial behavior are sometimes bestowed on other mutants, whereas the residents almost never benefit from it.

Homo moralis is easily defined for pairwise interactions, $n=2$. Let $\pi(x, y)$ denote the material payoff to an individual who plays strategy x when the opponent plays strategy y. Then the utility function of *Homo moralis* is

$$U_\kappa(x, y) = (1 - \kappa) \cdot \pi(x, y) + \kappa \cdot \pi(x, x), \tag{1}$$

where $0 \le \kappa \le 1$ is the individual's *degree of morality*. The two extreme degrees of morality represent *Homo oeconomicus* ($\kappa=0$) and *Homo kantiensis* ($\kappa=1$), respectively, and intermediate degrees of morality correspond to individuals who attach some weight to their own material payoff, $\pi(x, y)$, and some weight to "the right thing to do if everyone were to choose the same behavior," $\pi(x, x)$.

For $n > 2$, the precise definition of *Homo moralis* is fairly involved,[8] but it is analytically straightforward in the special case where the random matching is such that the types of any other two group members are statistically independent, given the member's own type. The morality profile is then a binomial distribution, and the utility function of a *Homo moralis* individual i is the expected value of i's material payoff if, hypothetically, other members of the group would randomly and statistically independently switch to use i's strategy with probability κ, which is then i's degree of morality. At one end of the interval of such *Homo moralis*, $\kappa=0$, we find *Homo oeconomicus*; at the other end, $\kappa=1$, we find *Homo kantiensis*.

---

8. The general definition of *Homo moralis* is given in Alger and Weibull (2016).

Moreover, in large groups, the share of mutants in a mutant's group is, by the de Moivre–Laplace theorem, approximately normally distributed with mean value κ and variance $\kappa(1-\kappa)/(n-1)$. Hence, the share of other mutants is then almost deterministic and is equal to κ. A *Homo moralis* with degree of morality κ then acts (approximately) as if she hypothetically assumed that her behavior were to become, if not a "universal law,", then a "random law" applying to a randomly sampled share of size κ out of her group's other members.[9]

It is worth noting that the utility function of *Homo moralis* differs sharply from any utility function that only depends on the payoffs to all participants, such as altruism, inequity aversion, or a concern for social efficiency. We illustrate this by way of a simple example at the end of the third section.

Morality and ethics in connection with economics have been discussed at great length by many economists and philosophers, including Smith ([1759] 1976), Edgeworth (1881), Rawls (1971), Arrow (1973), Sen (1977), and Harsanyi (1980), to mention a few. But to the best of our knowledge, *Homo moralis* preferences have not been previously studied, or even known, with one exception. Bergstrom (1995) shows that evolutionary stability of strategies in interactions between siblings induces behavior that he calls "semi-Kantian," which corresponds to $\kappa = 1/2$ in our equation (1).[10]

Kantian Morality and Economics

Economists' policy advice traditionally relies on models in which individuals have *Homo oeconomicus* preferences. What if economists' models instead were populated by the more general *Homo moralis*? In this chapter, we will merely scratch the surface by studying only a few examples.

---

9. This claim is not fully general and deserves further analysis, because even small perturbations of continuous (utility) functions may lead to "jumps" in behavior.
10. Bergstrom thus differs from us in studying stability of strategies rather than of utility functions. However, in Alger and Weibull (2013, corollary 5), we establish a link between these approaches by showing that *Homo moralis* equilibrium strategies are stable under strategy evolution. For a discussion of several ethical principles in relation to strategy evolution, see Bergstrom (2009).

Trust

There is variation across countries in the extent to which people are trusting, and trust is correlated with economic growth (Algan and Cahuc 2010).[11] In economics, the so-called *trust game* has been used extensively in controlled laboratory experiments as a way to measure trust and trustworthiness in different countries and cultures. This literature was pioneered by Berg, Dickhaut, and McCabe (1995) and has received a lot of attention among behavioral economists and experimentalists. The trust game is succinctly described by Cesarini et al. (2008, 3721):

> Many mutually beneficial transactions involve an element of interpersonal trust and may fail to materialize in the absence of an expectation that trust will be reciprocated. The prevalence of trust in a society has therefore been assigned primacy in a number of domains, for instance empirical and theoretical studies of economic growth. In recent years, the trust game has emerged as a favorite instrument to elicit an individual's interpersonal trust and willingness to reciprocate trust. More generally, the game has been widely used to study cooperative behavior. In a trust game, an individual (the investor) decides how much money out of an initial endowment to send to another subject (the trustee). The sent amount is then multiplied by some factor, usually three, and the trustee decides how much of the money received to send back to the investor. The standard game-theoretic prediction for a single anonymous interaction between two purely self-interested individuals is for the investor to send nothing, rationally anticipating that the trustee will not reciprocate. Yet, experiments consistently show that cooperation flourishes in the trust game; the average investor sends a significant share of her endowment, and most trustees reciprocate.

What will *Homo moralis* do in such an interaction? Consider a situation in which two ex ante identical individuals are randomly paired. With equal chance, one of them is offered an endowment and an investment opportunity as described above. The other individual then has to act in the role of

---

11. A situation where trust is key is that of informal personal lending. In many developing countries, large fractions of the populations are still shut out from formal credit markets; see, for example, Kendall, Mylenko, and Ponce (2010). Then informal lending, in the form of not legally binding loans between individuals, can sometimes be enforced by the threat of future nonrenewal of lending (Ghosh and Ray 2016), social disapproval, or both. Evidence from laboratory experiments suggests that such informal lending may in fact even take place in one-shot interactions (Charness and Dufwenberg 2006). The trust game we analyze here can be interpreted as informal lending.

the trustee. A *strategy* for an individual in such a symmetric interaction then has two components. First, if given the endowment, what share $s \in [0, 1]$ of it is to be invested? Second, if not given the investment opportunity, what "payback rule" $p \in [0, 1]$ is to be used? Here, such a payback rule prescribes for any invested share $t \in [0, 1]$ chosen by the other party what share p of the gross return to pay back. Let $u(c)$ be an individual's hedonic utility from own consumption c, and take this to represent the material payoff in our evolutionary framework. In the standard version of the trust game, the material payoff from using a strategy $x = (s, p)$ when the other individual uses strategy $y = (t, q)$ is then

$$\pi(x, y) = \frac{1}{2}u(1 - s + 3sq) + \frac{1}{2}u(3t - 3tp). \tag{2}$$

In an interaction between two *Homo oeconomicus*, no party is trustworthy; they will choose $p = q = 0$ for all s, $t > 0$. Thus, if each party knows the other's type, no investment is made in equilibrium ($t = s = 0$). The resulting expected material payoff to each party is $u(1)/2$, the probability of being given the initial endowment times the utility from keeping it. If instead both parties were *Homo kantiensis*, then they would each invest all the money if given the opportunity ($t = s = 1$) and return half of the gross return (i.e., use payback rules p and q such that $p = q = 0.5$). The resulting expected material payoff to each party is then $u(1.5)$, much higher than what *Homo oeconomicus* obtains.

Full morality is not necessary to induce full investment, however. For a pair of equally moral *Homo moralis*, full investment ($t = s = 1$) obtains in equilibrium for any sufficiently high degree of morality, although as soon as morality is less than full ($\kappa < 1$), the trustee pays back less than half the gross returns from investment, in which case the trustee ends up being better off than the investor. As the degree of morality κ falls, the amount paid back decreases, and it eventually falls short of the amount originally invested, in which case the investor makes a material loss; nonetheless, morality makes the investor accept this loss and invest anyway, up to some point.[12] Indeed, for sufficiently low degrees of morality, the investor invests

---

12. To see this, note that the derivative of $U_\kappa(x, y)$ with respect to s, where $x = (s, p)$ and $y = (t, q)$, and evalutated when $t = s = 1$, is positive even for $p < 1/3$ for $\kappa < 1$ large enough.

less than his full endowment, and eventually, when morality drops below a certain level, he invests nothing.

Public Goods

Many situations that are important for economic growth may be represented as situations in which people can make voluntary contributions to a public good, including the generation and dissemination of knowledge, and institution building. We examine the behavior of individuals in a community of n members, each of whom is in a position to make a voluntary contribution to a public good (the contribution may be monetary or in kind). A standard concern in economics is that free riding is enhanced as groups become larger, so our aim here is to analyze how group size affects the behavior of *Homo moralis*.

Suppose, then, that i obtains material payoff

$$\pi(x_i, y) = B\left(x_i + \sum_{j \neq i} y_j\right) - C(x_i) \tag{3}$$

if she makes the contribution x_i and the sum of the contributions from the other community members is $\sum y_j$. Here B is a production function for the public good; and C a cost function for a contributing individual, representing forgone private consumption, income, or leisure. We take the marginal cost of making a contribution to be increasing, and the marginal benefit of the aggregate contribution to be decreasing.

Consider first the socially optimal individual contribution, x^*. With a conventional production function of the power form $B(X) = X^a$, where $0 < a < 1$, the necessary first-order condition for the sum of all members' material payoffs to be maximized,

$$nB'(nx^*) = C'(x^*), \tag{5}$$

implies that the socially optimal individual contribution x^* is increasing in n. By contrast, in a community of *Homo oeconomicus*, the first-order condition for the unique Nash equilibrium contribution, $\hat{x}_0$, is

$$B'(n\hat{x}_0) = C'(\hat{x}_0), \tag{5}$$

which implies that in communities with more members, each individual contributes less. As a consequence, free riding—the tendency for people to under-provide public goods—is exacerbated when group size increases. The intuition is that if all contributions were to remain unchanged, then the marginal benefit from each contribution would fall. Thus, each individual will have a weaker incentive to contribute.

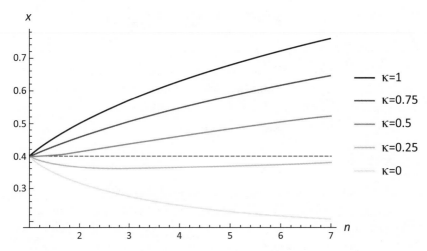

Figure 9.1
The unique Nash equilibrium contribution in the public-goods game for different degrees of morality

Suppose now instead that everyone in the community is a *Homo moralis* with the same degree of morality $\kappa \in [0, 1]$. Then their unique individual equilibrium contribution, $\hat{x}_\kappa$, can be shown to satisfy

$$[1+(n-1)\kappa]\cdot B'(n\hat{x}_\kappa)=C'(\hat{x}_\kappa), \tag{6}$$

For any positive degree of morality, group size has two counteracting effects on the individual contribution. The negative effect is, as before, due to the decreasing marginal productivity. The positive effect is that in larger groups, each individual's contribution benefits a larger number of individuals. The "right thing to do," as the group increases, is thus to increase one's contribution. The positive effect may outweigh the negative.

To see this, consider again the conventional production function used above, and note that for purely Kantian individuals ($\kappa=1$), the individual contribution always increases with n. For intermediate values of κ, the individual contribution decreases with n when small but increases with n when large. See figure 9.1, which shows the equilibrium contribution of *Homo moralis* with degree of morality κ as a function of community size n, with higher curves for higher degrees of morality (when $B(X) = \sqrt{X}$ and $C(x) = x^2$).

These predictions may potentially help explain observations made in laboratory experiments, in which group size sometimes has a positive effect and sometimes a negative effect on individual contributions (see Nosenzo, Quercia, and Sefton (2015) for a review).

Does the extent of free riding increase or decrease as group size increases? In the parametric specification used in figure 9.1, the individual contribution relative to the first-best contribution is

$$\frac{\hat{x}_\kappa}{x^*} = \left(\kappa + \frac{1-\kappa}{n}\right)^{2/3}, \tag{7}$$

a ratio that decreases as group size n increases (for any given degree of morality $\kappa < 1$).[13] A smaller ratio indicates more free riding, so this equation shows that as morality κ increases, the effect of group size n on the extent of free riding declines.[14] Moreover, the extent of free riding is bounded from below; as seen in (7), the ratio $\hat{x}_\kappa/x^*$ exceeds $\kappa^{2/3}$ for all group sizes n. Hence, compared to the outcome under *Homo oeconomicus*, an important policy implication is that, when κ is positive, the contributions from *Homo moralis* decline less with group size and remain positive even in infinitely large groups.

Environmental Economics

According to World Bank president Jim Yong Kim, "If we don't confront climate change, we won't end poverty."[15] Some instruments have been proposed to help mitigate climate change, such as a carbon tax, regulation of production technologies, subsidies to public transportation, and support for R&D concerning environmentally friendly technologies for different forms of green energy. Determining the "right" carbon tax requires knowing how it will affect behavior and welfare. Here we briefly analyze the behavior of *Homo oeconomicus* and more generally, *Homo moralis*, in a standard model of consumption that has an external effect on the environment (Musgrave 1959, Arrow 1970). In this model, the group is taken to be so large that each individual's impact on the group's environment is negligible.

More specifically, there is a continuum of consumers, indexed $i \in I = [0, 1]$, and there are two consumption goods, goods 1 and 2, where good 1

---

13. Formally, $d(\hat{x}_\kappa/x^*)/dn < 0$ when $0 < \kappa \le 1$.
14. Formally, $d^2(\hat{x}_\kappa/x^*)/(dndk) > 0$.
15. See http://www.worldbank.org/en/news/feature/2014/03/03/climate-change -affects-poorest-developing-countries.

is environmentally neutral (that is, its consumption has no effect on the environment) and good 2 is environmentally harmful. Aggregate consumption of these goods are

$$X_1 = \int_I x_1(i)\,d\mu \quad \text{and} \quad X_2 = \int_I x_2(i)\,d\mu$$

where $x(i) = (x_1(i), x_2(i))$ is the consumption bundle of individual i, and μ is a density on I. Because all consumers are infinitesimally small, aggregate consumption is unaffected by any individual's personal consumption.

We take the material payoff to each individual i to be that individual's hedonic utility from own consumption, $x(i)$, and from the quality of the environment, which in turn depends on aggregate consumption, X_2, of the environmentally harmful good. We write $u(x_1(i), x_2(i), X_2)$ for this hedonic utility and assume that it is increasing in consumption of each good and decreasing in aggregate consumption of the environmentally harmful good. Using good 1 as the numeraire, writing p for the price of good 2, and assuming that all individuals have the same income, a socially efficient consumption bundle, x^*, the same for all individuals i, satisfies

$$\frac{u_2(x_1^*, x_2^*, X_2^*)}{u_1(x_1^*, x_2^*, X_2^*)} = p - \frac{u_3(x_1^*, x_2^*, X_2^*)}{u_1(x_1^*, x_2^*, X_2^*)}, \tag{8}$$

where subscripts on the personal utility function denote partial derivatives. The marginal rate of substitution between the environmentally harmful and environmentally neutral goods should thus equal the relative price of the harmful good net of the marginal rate of substitution between the utility from the quality of the environment and the neutral good. In other words, social efficiency requires that, at given prices, consumers consume less of a good the more harmful it is to the environment.

By contrast, in a population consisting entirely of *Homo oeconomicus*, an (interior) equilibrium allocation in which everybody consumes the same bundle x^0 necessarily satisfies the first-order condition

$$\frac{u_2(x_1^0, x_2^0, X_2^0)}{u_1(x_1^0, x_2^0, X_2^0)} = p. \tag{9}$$

Under decreasing marginal utility of consumption, this means that *Homo oeconomicus*, not surprisingly, consumes more of the environmentally harmful good than required by socially efficiency.

As observed above, for interactions in infinitely large groups, the utility function of an individual *Homo moralis* with degree of morality $\kappa \in [0,$

1] is the material payoff that would obtain if a share κ of the group would behave in the same way as the individual himself. In the present context, if an individual consumes the bundle $x = (x_1, x_2)$ and all the others consume some bundle $y = (y_1, y_2)$, then the utility to a *Homo moralis* with degree of morality κ would be

$$U_\kappa(x, y) = u(x_1, x_2, (1 - \kappa) y_2 + \kappa x_2),\qquad(10)$$

where, in this expression, we have normalized the total mass of individuals in the group (which could be a village, region, country, continent, or the whole world) to unity. In a group consisting entirely of *Homo moralis* with the same degree of morality κ, an (interior) equilibrium allocation, everybody consumes the same bundle x^κ, and this satisfies the first-order condition

$$\frac{u_2(x_1^\kappa, x_2^\kappa, x_2^\kappa)}{u_1(x_1^\kappa, x_2^\kappa, x_2^\kappa)} = p - k \cdot \frac{u_3(x_1^\kappa, x_2^\kappa, x_2^\kappa)}{u_1(x_1^\kappa, x_2^\kappa, x_2^\kappa)}.\qquad(11)$$

Compared to *Homo oeconomicus*, for any positive degree of morality κ, each individual refrains somewhat from consuming the environmentally harmful good, although each individual—knowing that she is negligible—is fully aware that her own consumption has no effect on the overall quality of the environment! Hence, if people are in fact somewhat moral, then policy advice based on models inhabited by *Homo oeconomicus* may exaggerate the need for pecuniary incentives, such as carbon taxes. If people are more like *Homo moralis* with some positive degree of morality, then, in addition to some carbon taxes, it may be effective to provide individuals with information about how aggregate consumption (and production) creates carbon dioxide and what we know about how this affects the climate.[16] By contrast, such information in this stylized example would have no effect at all on the behavior of *Homo oeconomicus*.[17]

---

16. Note that equations (8) and (9) are the special cases of (10) when $\kappa = 0$ (*Homo oeconomicus*) and $\kappa = 1$ (*Homo kantiensis*). Laffont (1975) considers these two extreme cases of self-interested individuals (our *Homo oeconomicus*) and "Kantian individuals" (our *Homo kantiensis*).

17. Note further that if good 2 does not cause any externality ($u_3 = 0$), then *Homo moralis* would behave precisely as the classical *Homo oeconomicus*; equation (10) would boil down to equation (9). For such goods, there is no "right thing to do," and hence, morality has no bite.

Voting

Another class of situations in which *Homo moralis* may make a difference is collective decision-making by voting. By and large, countries with more developed economies tend to have more democratic political systems (see, e.g., Persson and Tabellini (2006) and Acemoglu et al. (2014)). For democracy to work, it is important that citizens participate in elections, committee work, and related activities; it is still much debated in economics and political science why and how people vote. As has been pointed out by economists, high participation rates in large elections appear incompatible with rational *Homo oeconomicus* behavior. The reason being that the act of voting usually has some personal cost, say, lost income or leisure, and this cost easily outweighs the expected benefit to the individual of participating in the election, because the probability of being pivotal is virtually nil. This is the well-known *voters' paradox*. Despite this, the turnout in general and local elections in many countries is often impressive. So what then motivates people to participate in elections? Can *Homo moralis* provide an explanation?

A closely related and arguably equally important issue is participation and voting in committees, such as parliamentary bodies, company boards, court juries, and central bank boards. As shown by Austen-Smith and Banks (1996), when committee members have private information and are *Homo oeconomicus*, then voting may fail to aggregate information efficiently, even when the members have the same preferences. This observation challenges the so-called Condorcet jury theorem (Condorcet 1785), which states that democracy in the form of majority rule in such situations is a great institution, because it implies that the right decision is almost always taken if the electorate is large enough. How would *Homo moralis* vote in such committees?

Other Social Preferences

Theoretical work on the evolutionary foundations of human motivation provides insights about potential *ultimate* causes of human behavior—the forces in the environment that have shaped our preferences, not only for the foods that contain the nutrition that we need to survive but also for behaviors in social interactions. This line of research is complementary to behavioral economics, the branch of economics that investigates the explanatory power of richer motivations than mere self-interest. In the language of evolutionary biology, the focus in behavioral economics is on the *proximate* causes of observed human behaviors—the neurological, hormonal, and psychological mechanisms and triggers that induce us to behave in certain ways. Here we briefly discuss how *Homo moralis* preferences compare with those considered in this literature, which is inspired by research in psychology and sociology.

In the 1970s and 1980s, altruistic preferences were proposed to explain intra-family transfers, transfers to the poor, and contributions to public goods (Becker 1974, 1976; Andreoni 1988; Lindbeck and Weibull 1988). However, altruism turned out to be insufficient to explain the data, and "warm glow" was then proposed to enhance the understanding of voluntary contributions to public goods (Andreoni 1990). In the 1990s, inequity aversion, or a preference for fairness, was introduced by Fehr and Schmidt (1999) as an explanation for why people have a tendency to turn down low offers in the ultimatum bargaining game (Güth, Schmittberger, and Schwarze 1982). Still other forms of human motivation that have been proposed, and sometimes tested, include conformity (Bernheim 1994), conditional altruism (Levine 1998), identity (Akerlof and Kranton 2000), and honesty and truth telling (Alger and Ma 2003; Alger and Renault 2006; Demichelis and Weibull 2008).

Although conceptually very different from *Homo moralis*, these preferences would be compatible with evolutionary stability if they gave rise to the same equilibrium behaviors as those of *Homo moralis*.[18] For what class of material payoff functions such behavioral equivalence obtains remains to be analyzed. Here we limit ourselves to pointing out that *Homo moralis* preferences sometimes give rise to radically different behaviors compared to preferences that may appear to be similar. For example, consider altruistic preferences. An altruistic individual's preferences are usually represented as a utility function that attaches unit weight to the individual's own material payoff and a positive weight, less than 1, to other individuals' material payoffs. An altruist hence internalizes some of the external effects of her behavior on others. Let the latter weight be denoted α, the individual's *degree of altruism* toward the other party.[19] For some material payoff func-

---

18. However, the preferences of *Homo moralis* are the only ones that are evolutionarily stable in the whole class of interactions analyzed in Alger and Weibull (2013, 2016).
19. For $n=2$, an altruist's utility is $u_\alpha(x, y) = \pi(x, y) + \alpha\pi(x, y)$. Note that this function can also be interpreted as the individual having a concern for efficiency, because it is a monotone transformation of $v_\alpha(x,y) = \pi(x,y) + \dfrac{\alpha}{1-\alpha}[\pi(x,y) + \pi(y,x)]$.

tions, an altruist with degree of altruism α behaves exactly like *Homo moralis* with a degree of morality $\kappa = \alpha$ (see Alger and Weibull 2013). Hence, in some interactions, one cannot discriminate between moralism and altruism as explanations for observed behavior. However, the two classes of preferences are conceptually quite distinct and induce radically different behaviors in some interactions. This difference is particularly striking in interactions with many participants and in coordination problems among few or many participants.

To illustrate the first case, consider again the environmental economics and the public goods examples. In the environmental example, morality induced consumers to reduce their consumption of the harmful good, even though the effect of each individual's consumption was negligible. In the public goods example, as the number of participants tends to infinity, the individual contribution to the public good tends to a positive amount for any positive degree of morality. By contrast, Andreoni (1988) has shown that in a population of altruists, the proportion of individuals who make positive donations shrinks to zero as the number of individuals grows infinitely large, because each individual donation then has a negligible effect on the total value of the public good. There is thus a sharp distinction between morality and altruism when groups are large. Even if an individual is highly altruistic and cares about the consequences of her behavior for others, she will behave very much like *Homo oeconomicus* if her impact is marginal. By contrast, *Homo moralis* cares directly about his own behavior, beyond the effects that this behavior has on his own material payoff, and this consideration for "the right thing to do" makes him behave differently from both selfish and altruistic individuals in these situations.

This observation may have important implications for other policy issues as well, such as tax compliance. It has been noted by some economists (see Sandmo 2005), that less tax evasion appears to occur in certain countries than would be compatible with *Homo oeconomicus*'s behavior. The risk of being caught is often small and the penalties mild, so maximization of expected personal utility would suggest rampant tax evasion. So why do people in those countries, and perhaps many in other countries, not evade taxes more? Because the marginal effect of any change in an individual's tax payment is, with few exceptions, negligible, prosocial preferences such as altruism or inequity aversion may fail to explain why individuals evade taxes. However, as suggested by the analysis above,

Homo moralis may supply an explanation, because a *Homo moralis* may, to a certain extent, prefer to pay taxes, since she cares about the moral quality of her actions.

Let us now turn to the second situation in which *Homo moralis* preferences give rise to radically different behaviors compared to altruism, namely, coordination problems. Consider an example from Alger and Weibull (2013), a simple 2×2 coordination game in terms of material payoffs:

	A	B
A	2,2	0,0
B	0,0	1,1

. (12)

When individuals pair up to play this game, two alternative potential societal "conventions" are available: Either both parties take action A, or both parties take action B. Clearly, the first convention is Pareto superior to the second. However, under each convention, *Homo oeconomicus* has no incentive to unilaterally deviate. Granted that a sufficiently large population share act according to the going convention, an individual deviator would lose material payoff and, in addition, inflict a payoff loss on the unfortunate opponent.[20] Therefore, an altruist would also stick to the going convention, even if this happened to be the socially inferior convention to always take action B. But not so a *Homo moralis* of high enough degree of morality. For suppose a *Homo kantiensis* were to visit a country where (by and large) every citizen takes action B in every encounter, and suppose that the visitor is indistinguishable from a citizen. Then *Homo kantiensis* would take action A in each encounter, because this would be "the right thing to do" if upheld as a universal law of conduct.[21] This moralistic visitor will earn material payoff zero in each encounter, and so will the unfortunate citizens who meet him. The citizens would very much wish that the visitor instead had been a *Homo oeconomicus* or an altruist.

---

20. These are strict Nash equilibria in terms of material payoffs. The game also has a mixed equilibrium, in which each individual plays A with probability 1/3. However, this equilibrium is unstable in all plausible population dynamics. See Young (1993) and Myerson and Weibull (2015) for formal models of stable conventions in large populations.

21. Indeed, to take action A is optimal for all *Homo moralis* individuals with degree of morality $\kappa \geq 1/3$.

A final point before concluding. Some researchers have developed models in which individuals care about norms, have a concern for their image (in the eyes of others and perhaps also in their own eyes), or a desire to avoid social stigma (Lindbeck, Nyberg, and Weibull 1999; Brekke, Kverndokk, and Nyborg 2003; Bénabou and Tirole 2006; Ellingsen and Johannesson 2008; Huck, Kübler, and Weibull 2012). In these models, individuals are assumed to have a baseline intrinsic wish to "behave well" and in addition a wish to be viewed favorably by others, image concerns that may strengthen the wish to behave well (Bénabou, Falk, and Tirole 2018). Evidently, we humans are very complex creatures, and our behavior is most likely driven by many motives (what biologists would call "proximate causes" for our actions). Biologists distinguish such proximate causes from ultimate causes, by which is meant the reasons we exist in the evolutionary race. Our derivation of *Homo moralis* was based entirely on such ultimate causes. A closer examination of relations between proximate and ultimate causes in human motivation is an avenue for future research. Eventually, evolutionary theory may help close the open-endedness of behavioral economics by providing testable predictions regarding which preferences are more likely to be sustained.

Conclusion

In this chapter, we have discussed the evolutionary foundations for human motivation, how evolution favors the class of *Homo moralis* preferences, and the implications for economics and policy of such preferences compared to other preferences. We have presented the following main points:

1. Economics possesses powerful analytical tools that enable positive and normative analyses of a wide range of social and economic phenomena. These tools should not be abandoned but instead brought to more general use.

2. The conventional assumption among economists, since the days of Adam Smith's ([1776] 1976) *Wealth of Nations*, is that economic agents are purely self-interested and focused on their own consumption. Yet behavioral and experimental economics, insights from the other social and behavioral sciences, everyday observation, and introspection suggest that human motivation is much more complex, sometimes systematically deviating from narrow self-interest.

3. First principles in evolutionary biology, formalized in terms of evolutionary stability along the lines of Maynard Smith and Price (1973) suggest
that, in our simple model framework, evolution favors human motivation
in the form of *Homo moralis*, a generalization of *Homo oeconomicus* that
allows for varying degrees of morality along with self-interest.

4. Applying the powerful analytical tools of economics to *Homo moralis*
results in new predictions and policy recommendations. In particular,
because *Homo moralis* is not only motivated by her material gains and
losses, policy based on *Homo oeconomicus* may lead to exaggerated use
of pecuniary incentives, such as distortionary taxes. If people do have a
natural inclination for moral concerns, it may be more effective to provide the public with information about the consequences of our actions,
for ourselves and others.

Our results being purely theoretical, empirical and experimental work will
be necessary to determine the empirical validity of *Homo moralis*. To this
end, further theoretical analysis is also needed: Even though we have here
examined the behavior of *Homo moralis* in some common situations, we
have only scratched the surface. Moreover, many fundamental questions
have not been addressed at all. In particular, one fundamental issue that
we have not (yet) addressed is welfare. For economic and social policy, this
is a most important and philosophically nontrivial issue, especially when
individuals have social preferences. If individuals have *Homo moralis* preferences, perhaps idiosyncratic degrees of morality, should welfare then be
defined in terms of the material payoffs or in terms of individuals' utility
functions?

This philosophically and methodologically difficult issue may be related
to that addressed by John Harsanyi in two wonderful essays that deal with
game theory, utilitarianism and ethics (Harsanyi (1980, 1992). In these
essays, he advocates what he calls "rule utilitarianism," an approach we
find also appealing for *Homo moralis*. Harsanyi distinguishes between an
individual's "personal preferences" and his or her "moral preferences." He
advocates that, when defining welfare in a society, one should only consider
personal preferences. When individuals' preferences can be represented by
an additive utility function, where one term can be taken to represent "personal utility," Harsanyi argues that welfare should be defined as the sum of
all individuals' expected personal utilities, behind the veil of ignorance as to

what societal position each individual will end up in. This appears to be in line with *Homo moralis*. If we take the material payoff function to represent personal utility, then welfare in a society consisting of *Homo moralis* individuals (each with his or her degree of morality) should be defined simply as the sum of their expected material payoffs, just as in ordinary utilitarian welfare theory.

To wit, suppose a parent has one selfish and one altruistic child, and has a cake to divide between them. Suppose also that both children have the same hedonic utility from consumption, and that this is increasing in the amount consumed, with decreasing marginal utility.[22] Should the parent give a bigger slice to the selfish child, thus maximizing the sum of their altruistic and selfish utilities, or should the parent give them equally large slices, thus maximizing the sum of only their hedonic utilities? The second alternative undoubtedly seems more appealing. The same could be said with one selfish and one spiteful child; taking into account both children's total utility, a bigger slice should be given to the spiteful child, but equal division is, arguably, more reasonable. By contrast, if one child is selfish, and the other instead is inequity averse or a *Homo moralis* (with any degree of morality), it makes no difference if the parent considers the children's total or hedonic (personal) utilities; in every case, their joint welfare is maximized by equal division. Further study of the welfare economics of *Homo moralis* and other social preferences is a topic for future research.

A final point we make concerns the status of economics as a discipline, in the eyes of the general public and among the other behavioral and social sciences. Conventional economics textbooks may give the false impression that selfishness is part of economic rationality (see the discussion in Rubinstein (2006) and the references therein). This misreading of conventional economics probably hurts the reputation of economists. If economists would instead use partly morally motivated agents, such as *Homo moralis*, then such misunderstandings could be avoided, and the critique would fall flat to the ground. The economist's analysis would then not be prejudiced in favor of either selfishness or morality. Instead it would allow for the whole spectrum of intermediate degrees of morality, spanning from pure self-interest to pure Kantian morality.

---

22. This example is due to Peter Diamond, discussed in a conversation many years ago with one of the authors.

References

Acemoglu, Daron, Suresh Naidu, Pascual Restrepo, and James A. Robinson. 2014. "Democracy Does Cause Growth." NBER Working Paper 20004, National Bureau of Economic Research, Cambridge, MA.

Akerlof, George, and Rachel E. Kranton. 2000. "Economics and Identity." *Quarterly Journal of Economics* 115 (3): 715–753.

Alexander, Richard D. 1987. *The Biology of Moral Systems*. New York: Aldine De Gruyter.

Algan, Yann, and Pierre Cahuc. 2010. "Inherited Trust and Growth." *American Economic Review* 100 (5): 2060–2092.

Alger, Ingela, and Albert Ma. 2003. "Moral Hazard, Insurance, and Some Collusion." *Journal of Economic Behavior and Organization* 50 (2): 225–247.

Alger, Ingela, and Régis Renault. 2006. "Screening Ethics When Honest Agents Care about Fairness." *International Economic Review* 47 (1): 59–85.

Alger, Ingela, and Jörgen W. Weibull. 2010. "Kinship, Incentives, and Evolution." *American Economic Review* 100 (4): 1725–1758.

Alger, Ingela, and Jörgen W. Weibull. 2013. "*Homo Moralis*—Preference Evolution under Incomplete Information and Assortativity." *Econometrica* 81 (6): 2269–2302.

Alger, Ingela, and Jörgen W. Weibull. 2016. "Evolution and Kantian Morality." *Games and Economic Behavior* 98: 55–67.

Andreoni, James. 1988. "Privately Provided Public Goods in a Large Economy: The Limits of Altruism." *Journal of Public Economics* 35 (1): 57–73.

Andreoni, James. 1990. "Impure Altruism and Donations to Public Goods: A Theory of Warm-Glow Giving." *Economic Journal* 100 (401): 464–477.

Arrow, Kenneth. 1970. "Political and Economic Evaluation of Social Effects and Externalities." In *The Analysis of Public Output*, edited by Julius Margolis, 1–23. New York: Columbia University Press.

Arrow, Kenneth. 1973. "Social Responsibility and Economic Efficiency." *Public Policy* 21: 303–317.

Austen-Smith, David, and Jeffrey S. Banks. 1996. "Information Aggregation, Rationality, and the Condorcet Jury Theorem." *American Political Science Review* 90 (1): 34–45.

Banerjee, Abhijit, and Jörgen W. Weibull. 1995. "Evolutionary Selection and Rational Behavior." In *Learning and Rationality in Economics*, edited by Alan Kirman and Mark Salmon, 343–363. Oxford: Basil Blackwell.

Becker, Gary S. 1974. "A Theory of Social Interaction." *Journal of Political Economy* 82 (6): 1063–1093.

Becker, Gary S. 1976. "Altruism, Egoism, and Genetic Fitness: Economics and Sociobiology." *Journal of Economic Literature* 14 (3): 817–826.

Bénabou, Ronald, and Jean Tirole. 2006. "Incentives and Prosocial Behavior." *American Economic Review* 96 (5): 1652–1678.

Bénabou, Ronald, Armin Falk, and Jean Tirole. 2018. "Narratives, Imperatives and Moral Reasoning." Mimeo, Toulouse School of Economics, France.

Berg, Joyce, John Dickhaut, and Kevin McCabe. 1995. "Trust, Reciprocity, and Social History." *Games and Economic Behavior* 10 (1): 122–142.

Bergstrom, Theodore C. 1995. "On the Evolution of Altruistic Ethical Rules for Siblings." *American Economic Review* 85 (1): 58–81.

Bergstrom, Theodore C. 2003. "The Algebra of Assortative Encounters and the Evolution of Cooperation." *International Game Theory Review* 5 (3): 211–228.

Bergstrom, Theodore C. 2009. "Ethics, Evolution, and Games among Neighbors." Working Paper, University of California, Santa Barbara.

Bergstrom, Theodore C. 2012. "Models of Assortative Matching." Working Paper, University of California, Santa Barbara.

Bernheim, B. Douglas. 1994. "A Theory of Conformity." *Journal of Political Economy* 102 (5): 841–877.

Brekke, Kjell A., Snorre Kverndokk, and Karine Nyborg. 2003. "An Economic Model of Moral Motivation." *Journal of Public Economics* 87 (9): 1967–1983.

Cesarini, David, Christopher T. Dawes, James H. Fowler, Magnus Johannesson, Paul Lichtenstein, and Björn Wallace. 2008. "Heritability of Cooperative Behavior in the Trust Game." *Proceedings of the National Academy of Sciences* 105 (10): 3721–3726.

Charness, Gary, and Martin Dufwenberg. 2006. "Promises and Partnership." *Econometrica* 74 (6): 1579–1601.

Condorcet, Nicolas de. 1785. *Essai sur l'Application de l'Analyse à la Probabilité des Décisions Rendues à la Pluralité des Voix.* Paris: L'Imprimerie Royale.

Currarini, Sergio, Matthew O. Jackson, and Paolo Pin. 2009. "An Economic Model of Friendship: Homophily, Minorities and Segregation." *Econometrica* 77 (4): 1003–1045.

Currarini, Sergio, Matthew O. Jackson, and Paolo Pin. 2010. "Identifying the Roles of Race-Based Choice and Chance in High School Friendship Network Formation." *Proceedings of the National Academy of Sciences* 107 (11): 4857–4861.

Darwin, Charles. 1859. *On the Origin of Species by Means of Natural Selection.* London: John Murray.

Dawkins, Richard. 1976. *The Selfish Gene*. Oxford: Oxford University Press.

Dekel, Eddie, Jeffrey C. Ely, and Okan Yilankaya. 2007. "Evolution of Preferences." *Review of Economic Studies* 74 (3): 685–704.

Demichelis, Stefano, and Jörgen W. Weibull. 2008. "Language, Meaning, and Games: A Model of Communication, Coordination, and Equilibrium." *American Economic Review* 98 (4): 1292–1311.

Edgeworth, Francis Y. 1881. *Mathematical Psychics: An Essay on the Application of Mathematics to the Moral Sciences*. London: Kegan Paul.

Ellingsen, Tore, and Magnus Johannesson. 2008. "Pride and Prejudice: The Human Side of Incentive Theory." *American Economic Review* 98 (3): 990–1008.

Fehr, Ernst, and Klaus Schmidt. 1999. "A Theory of Fairness, Competition, and Cooperation." *Quarterly Journal of Economics* 114 (3): 817–868.

Frank, Robert H. 1987. "If *Homo Economicus* Could Choose His Own Utility Function, Would He Want One with a Conscience?" *American Economic Review* 77 (4): 593–604.

Friedman, Milton. 1953. *Essays in Positive Economics*. Chicago: University of Chicago Press.

Ghosh, Parikshit, and Debraj Ray. 2016. "Information and Enforcement in Informal Credit Markets." *Economica* 83 (329): 59–90.

Güth, Werner, Rolf Schmittberger, and Bernd Schwarze. 1982. "An Experimental Analysis of Ultimatum Bargaining." *Journal of Economic Behavior and Organization* 3 (4): 367–388.

Güth, Werner, and Menahem E. Yaari. 1992. "Explaining Reciprocal Behavior in Simple Strategic Games: An Evolutionary Approach." In *Explaining Process and Change: Approaches to Evolutionary Economics*, edited by Ulrich Witt, 23–24. Ann Arbor: University of Michigan Press.

Hamilton, William D. 1964. "The Genetical Evolution of Social Behaviour." *Journal of Theoretical Biology* 7 (1): 1–16.

Harsanyi, John C. 1980. "Rule Utilitarianism, Rights, Obligations and the Theory of Rational Behavior." *Theory and Decision* 12 (2): 115–133.

Harsanyi, John C. 1992. "Game and Decision Theoretic Models in Economics." In *Handbook of Game Theory with Economic Application*, volume 1, edited by Robert J. Aumann and Sergiu Hart, 669–707. Amsterdam: North-Holland.

Heifetz, Aviad, Chris Shannon, and Yossi Spiegel. 2007. "What to Maximize If You Must." *Journal of Economic Theory* 133 (1): 31–57.

Huck, Steffen, Dorothea Kübler, and Jörgen W. Weibull. 2012. "Social Norms and Economic Incentives in Firms." *Journal of Economic Behavior and Organization* 83 (2): 173–185.

Kant, Immanuel. [1785] 2002. *Groundwork for the Metaphysics of Morals*. Edited and translated by Allen W. Wood. New Haven, CT: Yale University Press.

Kendall, Jake, Nataliya Mylenko, and Alejandro Ponce. 2010. "Measuring Financial Access around the World." World Bank Policy Research Working Paper 5253, World Bank, Washington, DC.

Laffont, Jean-Jacques. 1975. "Macroeconomic Constraints, Economic Efficiency and Ethics: An Introduction to Kantian Economics." *Economica* 42 (168): 430–437.

Levine, David K. 1998. "Modelling Altruism and Spitefulness in Experiments." *Review of Economic Dynamics* 1 (3): 593–622.

Lindbeck, Assar, and Jörgen W. Weibull. 1988. "Altruism and Time Consistency: The Economics of Fait Accompli." *Journal of Political Economy* 96 (6): 1165–1182.

Lindbeck, Assar, Sten Nyberg, and Jörgen W. Weibull. 1999. "Social Norms and Economic Incentives in the Welfare State." *Quarterly Journal of Economics* 114 (1): 1–35.

Maynard Smith, John, and George R. Price. 1973. "The Logic of Animal Conflict." *Nature* 246 (November): 15–18.

McPherson, Miller, Lynn Smith-Lovin, and James M. Cook. 2001. "Birds of a Feather: Homophily in Social Networks." *Annual Review of Sociology* 27: 415–444.

Musgrave, Richard A. 1959. *The Theory of Public Finance: A Study in Public Economy*. New York: McGraw-Hill.

Myerson, Roger, and Jörgen W. Weibull. 2015. "Tenable Strategy Blocks and Settled Equilibria." *Econometrica* 83 (3): 943–976.

Nosenzo, Daniele, Simone Quercia, and Martin Sefton. 2015. "Cooperation in Small Groups: The Effect of Group Size." *Experimental Economics* 18 (1): 4–14.

Ok, Efe A., and Fernando Vega-Redondo. 2001. "On the Evolution of Individualistic Preferences: An Incomplete Information Scenario." *Journal of Economic Theory* 97 (2): 231–254.

Persson, Torsten, and Guido Tabellini. 2006. "Democracy and Development: The Devil in the Details." *American Economic Review* 96 (2): 319–324.

Rawls, John. 1971. *A Theory of Justice*. Cambridge, MA: Harvard University Press.

Rousset, François. 2004. *Genetic Structure and Selection in Subdivided Populations*. Princeton, NJ: Princeton University Press.

Rubinstein, Ariel. 2006. "A Sceptic's Comment on the Study of Economics." *Economic Journal* 116: C1–C9.

Ruef, Martin, Howard E. Aldrich, and Nancy M. Carter. 2003. "The Structure of Founding Teams: Homophily, Strong Ties, and Isolation among U.S. Entrepreneurs." *American Sociological Review* 68 (2): 195–222.

Sandmo, Agnar. 2005. "The Theory of Tax Evasion: A Retrospective View." *National Tax Journal* 58 (4): 643–663.

Sen, Amartya K. 1977. "Rational Fools: A Critique of the Behavioral Foundations of Economic Theory." *Philosophy & Public Affairs* 6 (4): 317–344.

Smith, Adam. [1759] 1976. *The Theory of Moral Sentiments*. Edited by David D. Raphael and Alec L. Macfie. Oxford: Oxford University Press.

Smith, Adam. [1776] 1976. *An Inquiry into the Nature and Causes of the Wealth of Nations*. Edited by William B. Todd. Oxford: Oxford University Press.

Wright, Sewall. 1931. "Evolution in Mendelian Populations." *Genetics* 16 (2): 97–159.

Young, H. Peyton. 1993. "The Evolution of Conventions." *Econometrica* 61 (1): 57–84.

Comment: Lawrence E. Blume

The topic of this chapter has been central to the research agendas of Ingela Alger and Jörgen Weibull. Both separately (Lindbeck, Nyberg, and Weibull 1999; Alger 2010) and together (Alger and Weibull 2012), they have made important contributions to the study of prosocial preferences and behavior. The Alger-Weibull research program on the social construction of other-regarding preferences (Alger and Weibull 2013, 2016, this chapter) is exciting both for its formal development of the foundations of evolutionary game theory and for its findings concerning a cultural evolution model of the development of other-regarding preferences. It is conventional to assume that individuals' preferences over social states are concerned only with their own material outcomes. This assumption makes possible the powerful duality between social optimality and market outcomes expressed in the "welfare theorems" and is the baseline environment in which social policy is examined. It is nonetheless naïve in its assumption that preferences are primitives, exogenous in a model of social behavior. The recognition that preferences are to some degree socially constructed challenges many fundamental findings of economic theory; in particular, anything having to do with welfare conclusions. Alger and Weibull have significantly enriched the literature on the social construction of preferences by examining the evolutionary foundations of preference relations.

Evolutionary Game Theory

The Alger and Weibull research program develops new evolutionary game theory tools to say something about the kinds of preferences that would persist in a social system. In the conventional noncooperative theory of

N-person symmetric games, a symmetric Nash equilibrium is a strategy that is a best response for any one individual if it is being used by all the other participants. The fundamental equilibrium concept of evolutionary game theory is that of an evolutionarily stable strategy (ESS).[1] Intuitively, an ESS is a strategy that cannot be "invaded" by another strategy. What does "invasion" mean? Suppose that a large population of individuals are matched at random to participate in the game. An ESS has the property that if a sufficiently large fraction of the population uses it while the remainder of the population uses any other strategy, the expected payoffs to the ESS players are greater than those of the residual population. Evolutionary game theory arose first in biology, and so the strategy alternative to the ESS is said to be invading, and the motivation for the concept is that payoffs measure fitness. Higher payoffs mean higher fitness, and the part of the population using the ESS will have higher average fitness and therefore will outreproduce the group using the invading strategy. To see how the two concepts of Nash equilibrium and ESS fit together, one can check that in any finite and symmetric game, every ESS is a Nash equilibrium of the game. The converse, however, is false.

Alger and Weibull's program is in the tradition of Güth and Yaari's (1992) indirect evolutionary approach.[2] Whereas in traditional evolutionary game theory, preferences are fixed and the evolution of the distribution of actions is governed by the distribution of utility payoffs, in indirect evolutionary models, selection pressure on actions causes the distribution of utilities to evolve. This is analogous to biological models in which selection on phenotypes regulates the distribution of genotypes. In the Güth and Yaari program, behaviors correspond to phenotypes and preferences to genotypes. Payoffs in the game correspond to reproductive fitness.

In the Alger-Weibull program, a strategic interaction is described by a material payoff function π that assigns to each strategy profile a material payoff, (e.g., profit in a model of firm competition).[3] Players' choices are

---

1. Maynard Smith and Price (1973).
2. See also Güth and Kliemt (1998).
3. Material payoffs, like von Neumann-Morgenstern payoff functions, are linear in the distribution of pure strategy profiles. The present chapter mostly discusses symmetric two-person interactions, but Alger and Weibull (2016) considers multiplayer interactions under an aggregative assumption that in the material payoff of an agent's choices, the choices of others are exchangeable.

governed not by material payoff π, however, but by a payoff function u that represents subjective expected utility preferences over outcomes.

Alger and Weibull repurpose the ESS solution concept from evolutionary game theory as an equilibrium concept for the distribution of von Neumann–Morgenstern payoff functions in the population rather than for the distribution of strategies. In the Alger-Weibull research program, a payoff function u is an ESS if when a sufficiently large fraction of the population uses it while the remainder of the population uses any other payoff function, the expected material payoffs to those with the u payoff function are greater than those of the residual population. A second feature of the Alger and Weibull program—and this is key for their results—is that matching is not random but assortative: Like tends to match with like.[4]

The indirect evolution of preferences with assortative matching produces novel results. The authors label a payoff function a *Homo moralis* payoff function if $u(x, y)$ is an average of $\pi(x, y)$, the material benefit of playing x when others play y, and $\pi(x, x)$, the material benefit when everyone plays according to x. One end of this class is *Homo oeconomicus*, where the averaging weights puts all weight on $\pi(x, y)$, and the other end they label *Homo kantiensis*, where all weight is put on the material benefits assuming everyone plays the same.

Other work on the evolution of preferences is close in spirit to the Alger and Weibull program, but different assumptions lead to different outcomes. For instance, Ely and Yilankaya (2001) consider the evolution of preferences in a population using a static stability concept motivated much as is ESS. Because they consider only random matching, they find that outcomes are stable if and only if they are equilibria of the game described by material payoffs; that is, the stable preferences are those of *Homo oeconomicus*. The evolution of social behavior, as opposed to other-regarding preferences, is by now an old topic in evolutionary biology. Hamilton (1964) sees inclusive fitness as an explanation for prosocial behavior, and Grafen (1979) attempts to provide formal support for this idea by considering ESS with nonrandom matching. Bergstrom (1995) considers nonrandom matching for the evolution of altruistic play in a

---

4. This is not simple to describe in depth, so following the Alger and Weibull essay in this chapter, I shall not attempt to describe it. It is clearly defined in Alger and Weibull (2016, 61).

explicitly biological context and derives *Homo moralis* preferences with
$\kappa = 1/2$. He called these preferences "semi-Kantian." There is also some
support favoring antisocial preferences. Koçkesen, Ok, and Sethi (2000)
introduce a class of payoff functions that depend increasingly on material
returns and on relative material returns. Thus if everyone else's material
returns decline while mine do not, then my utility increases. They find
that in every equilibrium in a class of games much like those considered
by Alger and Weibull but with complete rather than incomplete information, those players with antisocial preferences do materially better than do
players who maximize material returns. This is not an evolutionary analysis, but it suggests one. Finally, the Alger and Weibull results work because
those with the "right" payoff function receive more material benefits than
do others, and sometimes the "right" payoff function is not that of *Homo
oeconomicus*. Bester and Güth (1998) and Eshel, Samuelson, and Shaked
(1998) develop models where other-regarding preferences do materially
worse than does *Homo oeconomicus*, and yet they survive because of group
selection effects. The conclusion to draw from this is that details matter for
the results of evolutionary models, and we are far from having a complete
understanding of how different configurations of environmental characteristics collectively determine evolutionary outcomes. Thus conclusion
3 in the final section of the Alger and Weibull essay in this chapter[5] is an
overstatement. Natural selection does not "favor human motivation in the
form of *Homo oeconomicus*." Different models of natural selection favor different preference relations. *Homo moralis* and *Homo oeconomicus* are two.
Nonetheless, Alger and Weibull are to be commended for filling in a new
and important part of this landscape.

The promise of the indirect evolutionary approach goes far beyond
selection over payoff functions. In evolutionary game theory as received
from the biologists, selection forces act on payoffs, and the distribution
of strategies evolve. A second level of selection is the indirect evolutionary paradigm. In this case, preferences (which is to say the game itself)
evolve in some fashion. Mechanisms for preference evolution include such
phenomena as social learning, imitation and other adaptive processes, and

---

5. p. 410.

the sorting of individuals across roles. These processes operate on a system level rather than at the level of the individual. For instance, Blume and Easley (1992, 2006) show how the redistribution of wealth through repeated trading can drive some kinds of traders from the market. Thus although there are nearly as many behavioral models of choice as there are behavioral economists, only some of them can pass the market survival test. Yet a third level has both strategy choices and the strategic environment coevolve through time. For instance, some papers look at evolution where the community structure, represented by a social network, coevolves with strategic choice and not payoff functions (e.g., Ely 2002; Goyal and Vega-Redondo 2005; Staudigl and Weidenholzer 2014). A novel paper by Sandholm (2002) applies the idea of coevolution of strategies and the game to mechanism design. Moving beyond the Alger and Weibull program, the coevolution of preferences and game forms could contribute much to central questions in political economy in particular and, more generally, the analysis of institutions.

Symmetry

One limitation of their current essay and indeed, the research program, is that Alger and Weibull have so far studied only symmetric environments; that is, for two-player games, those in which the roles of player 1 and player 2 are identical. This limitation is disappointing, because ESS can certainly be generalized to asymmetric games.[6] Knowing that *Homo moralis* arises in symmetric models—a "one-population" model, one wonders what would emerge from a multiple-population model.

Alger and Weibull consider an asymmetric problem in the third section of their essay in this chapter. I am dissatisfied with their treatment for reasons that foreshadow issues I raise in the sections below having to do with the distinction between positive and normative claims. The strategic situation of their third section imagines a borrower and a lender; the lender has to decide whether to make the loan, and the borrower has to decide whether to pay it back. This is a great example (despite my qualms),

---

6. See, for instance, Fishman (2008) and citations therein.

because one can see the surprising power of the ESS in preferences. A more conventional analysis would consider repeated interactions between borrowers and lenders. Loans would be made and paid back, because in ongoing relations, reciprocity has value. The borrower understands that if he pays back today, he may be able to get a loan tomorrow. In equilibrium, the lender understands that the borrower understands this, and so she is willing to make the loan. Furthermore, it is her willingness to make future loans that validates the borrower's belief. Alger and Weibull consider only one-shot interactions—there is no possibility of history-dependent behavior. Nonetheless, lending and borrowing can be sustained.

So what is wrong with this? To apply their tools, Alger and Weibull must symmetrize the situation. They state that a canonical way to do this is to initially cover the interaction under a "veil of ignorance" as to who will be in what role. They assume that these roles are contingent. At any moment, a given individual from a single population can either be a borrower or a lender; essentially determined by the flip of a coin. The justification for this move is hinted at by the phrase "veil of ignorance." They call on the usual suspects—Harsanyi (1953), Rawls (1958), and Vickrey (1945)—who introduced this move in the analysis of social systems. However, the suspects introduced the veil of ignorance, the original position, ex ante randomness, for purposes of normative analyses. The original position, behind the veil of ignorance, is a counterfactual hypothetical that provides a frame outside the social system for evaluating the moral consequences of its outcomes. We do not pretend that individuals are actually randomized in such a way. The evolutionary model, however, is concerned with real environments rather than counterfactuals. Of course, there could be situations where roles really are random; a given individual could play one role today and another role tomorrow. But I do not believe that this is a useful way to think about the evolution of preferences where each individual's role is known and certain, set in stone. The use of normative analyses to justify positive claims is one example of the conflation of positive and normative that, I believe, obscure the significance of Alger and Weibull's findings.[7]

---

7. Their Kantian claims would be much more compelling if a given individual considered the situation of the other party even though she will never ever be in that role. This seems to be required by several of Kant's expressions of his fundamental law.

Welfare Economics

Alger and Weibull have uncovered some powerful results in the positive theory of socially constructed preferences. Their treatment of normative questions, however, and the distinctly normative cast of their entire essay, raises some issues. For instance, how should we view *Homo moralis* preferences from the consequentialist perspective that is traditional in economics? The examples of their third section suggest that a *Homo moralis* world may be materially better than an *Homo oeconomicus* world. To see that this is not the case, consider a variant of the public goods game they discuss. In this variant, N individuals can give, an outcome that is either 0 or 1. The material benefit of the public good is ϱ to each person, the material cost of giving is $0 < c < 1$, and the public good will be provided if and only if the sum of the contributions is at least 1.

Thus, letting $y_{-i} = \sum_{j \neq i} x_j$,

Suppose that $N\varrho > c$, so that the aggregate material benefit exceeds the cost of provision. It is socially optimal for one individual to provide the good, and the net benefit will be $N\varrho - c$.

The analysis breaks down into three cases (ignoring boundaries). If $\varrho > c$, one person on his or her own should be willing to give. At one extreme, *Homo kantiensis* chooses to maximize $\pi(x, x)$. The optimum is, $x = 1$, everyone gives, and the public good will be massively oversubscribed. If utilities are interpersonally comparable, the optimum achievable welfare is $N\varrho - c$, and *Homo kantiensis* society achieves $N(\varrho - c)$, for a material payoff loss of $(N-1)c$. At the other extreme, *Homo oeconomicus* can achieve efficiency in N distinct asymmetric Nash equilibria. In each equilibrium, one and only one individual gives.

If $\varrho < c$, then *Homo kantiensis* gives zero. The asymmetric pure Nash equilibria of *Homo oeconomicus* also disappear, and *Homo oeconomicus* also gives zero. Both, then, are inefficient.

When $\varrho > c$, there is also a symmetric mixed Nash equilibrium in which the probability of choosing zero is $c^{1/(n-1)}$. In this case, the expected value of the equilibrium to an individual *Homo oeconomicus* is $p - c - (p-1)c^{n/(n-1)}$. Comparing this payoff to that of *Homo kantiensis*, we see that it is materially worse when $\varrho > 1$ but materially better when $c/N < \varrho < 1$.

In summary, for $\varrho < c$, both preference types achieve the efficient outcome. For $c < \varrho < 1$, a *Homo kantiensis* society does materially worse than every Nash equilibrium outcome of a *Homo oeconomicus* society. And for $\varrho > 1$, some *H. oeconomicus* equilibria are efficient, with higher material payoff than that of the *H. kantiensis* society, but the symmetric mixed *oeconomicus* equilibrium is worse.[8]

The general point is that there are problems that, despite being posed symmetrically, have optimal solutions that are asymmetric. Minority games and the related El Farol game provide further examples. This example serves as a caveat to conclusion 4 of the Alger and Weibull essay in this chapter that designing policies for *Homo oeconomicus* when individuals are in fact *Homo moralis* may overincentivize them. Yes, it can, but it may not.

Alger and Weibull's examples in their third section raise the interesting question of how welfare economics should be conducted when preferences are other-regarding. They follow Harsanyi (1980, 1992) and argue that welfare should be measured as the sum of individual material utilities. I followed them in my preceding public good example for purposes of comparison, but this is controversial. To see why, ask: Why exactly is one's desire for a drink of water for herself more necessary to the social welfare calculation then her desire to offer her companion a drink? I can think of two arguments in favor of this claim: one, that water is a necessity for life, and if anything is fundamental, survival needs should be; the other, that to count the companion's welfare in her utility is to double count it. The first argument is nothing more than a statement about marginal rates of substitution at the boundary of the consumption set. At the survival boundary, water for one's self is critical. The second argument says that the utility a decision maker gets from a drink is different from the utility she gets from giving someone else utility. If you take a drink of water, you get some utility. If I offer you that drink, the utility that I get does not count in the social calculation. But if I expend my own resources to do it, the opportunity cost

---

8. One can derive similar results for the middle-ground cases. The treatment of mixing with *Homo moralis* preferences is unusual, except in the extreme *oeconomicus* case. In Alger and Weibull (2016), we are told that the set X on which $\pi(x, x)$ is defined is the set of mixed strategies in the material game. I understand this to mean that if I were, say, *kantiensis* (just for clarity), and if I chose 1 with probability p, then I assume everyone else is too, and when I consider what happens if I were to choose 1 with probability p' instead, I assume everyone else chooses p' too. This leads to a symmetric randomized equilibrium with an expected social net material benefit that converges upward to $n(\rho - c)$ as n increases.

of providing the gift does again count. Apparently, only certain actions are allowed to generate utility for welfare purposes. In my view, neither of these arguments holds water.

Alger and Weibull adopt Harsanyi's distinction between personal and social preferences, and they note that one might understand *Homo moralis* as an individual whose personal preferences are the material preferences π and whose social preferences are given by the *Homo moralis* utility function with its degree κ of morality. Ken Arrow famously wrote,[9] "I am old-fashioned enough to retain David Hume's view that one can never derive 'ought' propositions from 'is' propositions." The findings of evolutionary game theory are "is" propositions. Alger and Weibull are eager to derive from them "oughts." The conflation of "is" and "ought" perhaps undercuts the "is" exercise of their research program.

Alger and Weibull write:

> If we take the material payoff function to represent personal utility, then welfare in a society consisting of *Homo moralis* individuals (each with his or her degree of morality) should be defined simply as the sum of their expected material payoffs, just as in ordinary utilitarian welfare theory.

Harsanyi takes personal preferences to be those preferences that guide individuals' choices, their "everyday behavior."[10] If this is what Alger and Weibull mean by personal preferences, then the *moralis* payoff function should represent personal preferences and not material payoffs, and Alger and Weibull's and my welfare calculations are incorrectly done. Harsanyi's description of personal preferences can certainly allow for externalities. If Alger and Weibull believe, following Harsanyi's paradigm, that *moralis* preferences represent what he calls "moral preferences," then I do not understand why they would appear in an evolutionary analysis; decisions are not made based on moral preferences, and so they cannot be selected on.[11]

If *Homo moralis* preferences are the right preferences to undertake calculations with, then one cannot make welfare comparisons across populations with different degrees κ of morality. By analogy, we might consider two different production economies that differ only in consumers' preferences.

---

9. In his Ely Lecture, Arrow (1994, 1).
10. Harsanyi (1992, 675).
11. Harsanyi (1992, 671) says that "rational behavior is not a descriptive concept but rather is a normative concept." So he is an odd partner for evolutionary game theory.

We might observe that one economy has a higher GDP than the other, but this gives no guide for comparing the welfare of the two economies, even if utility is interpersonally comparable.

Homo moralis as a Moral Theory

Alger and Weibull write that their work "suggests an evolutionary foundation for a psychologically plausible form of morality, in line with Immanuel Kant's categorical imperative" (page 392, this chapter). Strictly speaking, they provide "an evolutionary foundation for" preferences that describe behavior consistent with "a psychologically plausible form of morality." What kind of moral theory? They suggest it is "in line with Immanuel Kant's categorical imperative." Bergstrom (1995) uses the phrase "semi-Kantian" to describe *Homo moralis* preferences with $\kappa = 1/2$. I believe this Kantian affiliation comes from a misreading of Kant. The idea of Kantian preferences exists outside evolutionary game theory. Roemer (2010) calls a strategy profile in a certain class of games "Kantian" if it is immune to simultaneous proportional deviations from all the players.

Broadly speaking, moral theories fall into one of three classes: consequentialist theories, deontological theories, and virtue theories. Consequentialism emphasizes the consequences of actions. Welfare economics is consequentialist. Deontological theories emphasize duties, rules, and obligations. Most philosophers, including Kant, consider(ed) Kantian theories to be deontological.[12] Virtue ethics emphasizes virtues or moral character. To illustrate, suppose someone's life is in danger and can be saved by my telling a lie. A consequentialist would lie, because he believes that saving a life is a good outcome. A deontologist would lie if he believed that saving a life when one can without doing injury to others is a universal law. However, if he believed "never lie" is a universal maxim, then he would not lie even to save a life. A virtue ethicist would lie because saving a life is benevolent; a virtue. I claim that *Homo moralis* has much more to do with virtue ethics than with any deontological moral theory.

---

12. Kagan (2002, 112).

The fundamental moral principle, according to Kant, is a categorical imperative: imperative because it is a command, and categorical because it is required of us unconditionally. That moral principle is, "act only in accordance with that maxim through which you can at the same time will that it become a universal law," or, in another formulation by Kant, to "act as if the maxim of your action were to become through your will a universal law of nature." Where does this come from? Kant wrote:[13]

> Everyone must admit that a law, if it is to be valid morally, i.e., as the ground of an obligation, has to carry absolute necessity with it; that the command "You ought not to lie" is valid not merely for human beings, as though other rational beings did not have to heed it; and likewise all the other genuinely moral laws; hence that the ground of obligation here is to be sought not in the nature of the human being or the circumstances of the world in which he is placed, but a priori solely in concepts of pure reason, and that every other precept grounded on principles of mere experience, and even a precept that is universal in a certain aspect, insofar as it is supported in the smallest part on empirical grounds, perhaps only as to its motive, can be called a practical rule, but never a moral law.

In other words, it is to be rationally derivable, assuming that every human were to heed it. The law is based entirely on reason and is not a consequence of any facts on the ground. In particular, moral propositions are to be independent of whom they are applied to; their preferences make no difference. These propositions are independent of our desires and uncoupled from the consequences that ensue. Clearly, however, the rules that one would derive from *Homo moralis* preferences depend on what the material payoffs are: Consequences matter. To put this somewhat differently, Kant's categorical imperative has a game-theoretic nature: An assumption about the behavior of others enters into your calculation about how you should behave. But *Homo kantiensis* is not Kantian, because his evaluation of the act is independent of his preferences. If a given maxim survives the categorical imperative test, one is obliged to act according to it, even if it is preference minimal. Thus the moral theory for which Alger and Weibull "provide an evolutionary foundation" is not Kantian. Quite the opposite. Harsanyi (1980) calls individuals who maximize a class of utility functions

---

13. Kant ([1785] 2002, 5).

containing *Homo moralis* payoff functions rule "utilitarians." It appears to be consequentialist.[14]

To the extent that we use the language of choice theory to talk about moral choices of individuals, any such theory will appear to be consequentialist. One can read virtue ethics this way. Our preferences are shaped by our character. Thus in some situations, preferences of individuals who have internalized particular virtues will look different than those of individuals who have not. And so the choices of those of virtuous character— sympathetic, charitable, etc.—will reflect these virtues. These are moral choices. One school of modern virtue ethics, so-called agent-based ethics,[15] "understands rightness in terms of good motivations and wrongness in terms of the having of bad (or insufficiently good) motives." Alger and Weibull's evolutionary account of preference evolution supports this view. They tell us that, as a consequence of the social condition, as a result of social interaction, preferences must in the long run take on a certain form, and that form is other-regarding.

Adam Smith ([1759] 2004, 1) begins *The Theory of Moral Sentiments* by claiming the universality of certain virtues:

> How selfish soever man may be supposed, there are evidently some principles in his nature, which interest him in the fortune of others, and render their happiness necessary to him, though he derives nothing from it except the pleasure of seeing it. Of this kind is pity or compassion, the emotion which we feel for the misery of others, when we either see it, or are made to conceive it in a very lively manner. That we often derive sorrow from the sorrow of others, is a matter of fact too obvious to require any instances to prove it; for this sentiment, like all the other original passions of human nature, is by no means confined to the virtuous and humane, though they perhaps may feel it with the most exquisite sensibility. The greatest ruffian, the most hardened violator of the laws of society, is not altogether without it.

He goes on to argue[16]

> that this is the source of our fellow-feeling for the misery of others, that it is by changing places in fancy with the sufferer, that we come either to conceive or to

---

14. In fairness, I should say that the contrast between deontology and consequentialism is not as sharp as it is often made out to be and is somewhat contested. See Kagan (2002) and Cummiskey (1990).

15. Slote (2001, 14).

16. Smith ([1759] 2004, 4).

be affected by what he feels, may be demonstrated by many obvious observations, if it should not be thought sufficiently evident of itself.

This expression of sympathy is, for Smith, the source of our moral decision-making. In a passage that is reminiscent of *Homo moralis*, he states:[17]

> The principle by which we naturally either approve or disapprove of our own conduct, seems to be altogether the same with that by which we exercise the like judgments concerning the conduct of other people. We either approve or disapprove of the conduct of another man according as we feel that, when we bring his case home to ourselves, we either can or cannot entirely sympathize with the sentiments and motives which directed it.

Assuming others behave as x, how do we feel about x?

Finally, it is interesting to note that perhaps Smith in the *Theory of Moral Sentiments* would be sympathetic to the Alger and Weibull program. He writes: [18]

> It is thus that the general rules of morality are formed. They are ultimately founded upon experience of what, in particular instances, our moral faculties, our natural sense of merit and propriety, approve, or disapprove of. We do not originally approve or condemn particular actions; because, upon examination, they appear to be agreeable or inconsistent with a certain general rule. The general rule, on the contrary, is formed, by finding from experience, that all actions of a certain kind, or circumstanced in a certain manner, are approved or disapproved of.

Our moral views emerge from experience, a social process. It would be asking too much of the mid-seventeenth-century Smith to distinguish between social learning and social evolution, and even today, it is not clear that, as classes, these are observationally distinct. But Alger and Weibull need not commit to a mechanism for their ESS analysis beyond the fact that it is monotone in payoffs, and so they are not inconsistent with Smith.

Conclusion

Although I have reservations about Alger and Weibull's (and many other economists) assertions about moral theory, the Alger and Weibull research program is among the most ambitious and promising to date on the exploration of the evolution of other-regarding preferences. The results are

---

17. Smith ([1759] 2004, 151–152).
18. Smith ([1759] 2004, 206).

exciting both for what they find and for the extent of the environments in which they hold.[19] Received game and market theory is of the take-all-comer's variety; equilibrium exists no matter what preferences agents hold. But if preferences are socially constructed, the forces described by Alger and Weibull should limit the kinds of preferences that are prevalent. Game and market theory should take advantage of this fact to make sharper predictions about the behavior of social systems. Finally, Jörgen Weibull has contributed significantly to the literature on evolutionary dynamics, and so I look forward to seeing this program progress from the static analysis of ESS to the much harder (but potentially richer) dynamic analyses that have emerged in recent years.

References

Alger, Ingela. 2010. "Public Goods Games, Altruism, and Evolution." *Journal of Public Economic Theory* 12 (4): 789–813.

Alger, Ingela, and Jörgen W. Weibull. 2012. "A Generalization of Hamilton's Rule—Love Others How Much?" *Journal of Theoretical Biology, Evolution of Cooperation* 299: 42–54.

Alger, Ingela, and Jörgen W. Weibull. 2013. "*Homo moralis*—Preference Evolution under Incomplete Information and Assortative Matching." *Econometrica* 81 (6): 2269–2302.

Alger, Ingela, and Jörgen W. Weibull. 2016. "Evolution and Kantian Morality." *Games and Economic Behavior* 98: 56–67.

Arrow, Kenneth. 1994. "Methodological Individualism and Social Knowledge." *American Economic Review* 84 (2): 1–9.

Bergstrom, Theodore C. 1995. "On the Evolution of Altruistic Ethical Rules for Siblings." *American Economic Review* 85 (1): 58–81.

Bester, Helmut, and Werner Güth. 1998. "Is Altruism Evolutionarily Stable?" *Journal of Economic Behavior and Organization* 34 (2): 193–209.

Blume, Lawrence, and David Easley. 1992. "Evolution and Market Behavior." *Journal of Economic Theory* 58 (1): 9–40.

---

19. This is not apparent in the present chapter, but can be seen in Alger and Weibull (2016).

Blume, Lawrence, and David Easley. 2006. "If You're So Smart, Why Aren't You Rich? Belief Selection in Complete and Incomplete Markets." *Econometrica* 74 (4): 929–966.

Cummiskey, David. 1990. "Kantian Consequentialism." *Ethics* 100 (3): 586–615.

Ely, Jeffrey C. 2002. "Local Conventions." *Advances in Theoretical Economics* 2 (1): 1–32.

Ely, Jeffrey C., and Okan Yilankaya. 2001. "Nash Equilibrium and the Evolution of Preferences." *Journal of Economic Theory* 97 (2): 255–272.

Eshel, Ilan, Larry Samuelson, and Avner Shaked. 1998. "Altruists, Egoists, and Hooligans in a Local Interaction Model." *American Economic Review* 88 (1): 157–179.

Fishman, Michael A. 2008. "Asymmetric Evolutionary Games with Non-linear Pure Strategy Payoffs." *Games and Economic Behavior* 63 (1): 77–90.

Goyal, Sanjeev, and Fernando Vega-Redondo. 2005. "Network Formation and Social Coordination." *Games and Economic Behavior* 50 (2): 178–207.

Grafen, Alan. 1979. "The Hawk-Dove Game Played between Relatives." *Animal Behaviour* 27 (3): 905–907.

Güth, Werner, and Hartmut Kliemt. 1998. "The Indirect Evolutionary Approach: Bridging the Gap between Rationality and Adaptation." *Rationality and Society* 10 (3): 377–399.

Güth, Werner, and Menahem E. Yaari. 1992. "Explaining Reciprocal Behavior in Simple Strategic Games: An Evolutionary Approach." In *Explaining Process and Change: Approaches to Evolutionary Economics*, edited by Ulrich Witt, 23–34. Ann Arbor: University of Michigan Press.

Hamilton, William D. 1964. "The Genetical Evolution of Social Behavior, I and II." *Journal of Theoretical Biology* 7 (1): 1–52.

Harsanyi, John C. 1953. "Cardinal Utility in Welfare Economics and in the Theory of Risk-Taking." *Journal of Political Economy* 61 (5): 434–435.

Harsanyi, John C. 1980. "Rule Utilitarianism, Rights, Obligations and the Theory of Rational Behavior." *Theory and Decision* 12 (2): 115–133.

Harsanyi, John C. 1992. "Game and Decision Theoretic Models in Ethics." In *Handbook of Game Theory with Economic Applications*, volume 1, edited by Robert J. Aumann and Sergiu Hart, 669–707. Amsterdam: North-Holland.

Kagan, Shelly. 2002. "Kantianism for Consequentialists." In *Groundwork for the Metaphysics of Morals*, edited by Allen W. Wood, 111–156. New Haven, CT: Yale University Press.

Kant, Immanuel. [1785] 2002. *Groundwork for the Metaphysics of Morals*. Edited and translated by Allen W. Wood. New Haven, CT: Yale University Press.

Koçkesen, Levent, Efe A. Ok, and Rajiv Sethi. 2000. "Evolution of Interdependent Preferences in Aggregative Games." *Games and Economic Behavior* 31 (2): 303–310.

Lindbeck, Assar, Sten Nyberg, and Jörgen W. Weibull. 1999. "Social Norms and Economic Incentives in the Welfare State." *Quarterly Journal of Economics* 114 (1): 1–35.

Maynard Smith, John, and George R. Price. 1973. "The Logic of Animal Conflict." *Nature* 246 (November): 15–18.

Rawls, John. 1958. "Justice as Fairness." *Philosophical Review* 67 (2): 164–194.

Roemer, John E. 2010. "Kantian Equilibrium." *Scandinavian Journal of Economics* 112 (1): 1–24.

Sandholm, William H. 2002. "Evolutionary Implementation and Congestion Pricing." *Review of Economic Studies* 69 (3): 667–689.

Slote, Michael. 2001. *Morals from Motives*. Oxford: Oxford University Press.

Smith, Adam. [1759] 2004. *The Theory of Moral Sentiments*. New York: Barnes and Noble.

Staudigl, Mathias, and Simon Weidenholzer. 2014. "Constrained Interactions and Social Coordination." *Journal of Economic Theory* 152: 41–63.

Vickrey, William. 1945. "Measuring Marginal Utility by Reactions to Risk." *Econometrica* 13 (4): 319–333.

Comment: Xavier Giné

Morality: Evolutionary Foundations and Policy Implications

Positive economic theories typically model agents interacting in markets as self-interested individuals. This chapter summarizes the work of the authors in Alger and Weibull (2013, 2016), which questions this assumption by investigating the preferences that humans would exhibit if these preferences were transmitted from generation to generation.

In the case of interactions between two agents, the utility function of humans would be a linear combination of the material payoff of a *Homo oeconomicus* (or self-interested individual) and that of a *Homo kantiensis* (an individual who "does the right thing" by assuming the other agent will behave as he or she does). Facing a set of choices similar to that of the other agent, in practice, *Homo kantiensis* does not solve the Nash equilibrium but rather chooses the payoff with highest value from the diagonal of the matrix of the game. Remarkably, these preferences called *Homo moralis* preferences are the only ones that are evolutionarily stable when the matching protocol among agents is exogenous.

But where does the weight that defines the linear combination between the two payoff functions come from? Alger and Weibull (2013) argue that the weight, or the "degree of morality," is related to the probability that individuals are matched with others of same type relative to the probability that they are matched with others of a different type. The model thus predicts that individuals will not behave as self-interested agents as long as this probability is positive and that everyone in a society will share same preferences (with the same degree of morality).

Taking Predictions to Data

The first prediction is consistent with experimental evidence showing robust deviations in behavior from the assumption of *Homo oeconomicus* agents. It is unclear, however, whether these deviations reflect universal social preferences or whether instead social preferences are shaped by the economic, social, and cultural environment. Henrich et al. (2004) set out to distinguish between these two hypotheses by conducting a large cross-cultural study of behavior using several standard experimental games in fifteen small-scale societies, ranging from foraging to sedentary agricultural societies.

The results confirm that there are violations of *Homo oeconomicus*, as individuals seem to care about fairness and reciprocity. In addition, there is dispersion across and within societies (of roughly equal magnitude) in the degree to which the assumption of *Homo oeconomicus* is violated. The dispersion across societies can be explained by the *Homo moralis* preferences if we assume that different societies exhibit different degrees of morality. But the dispersion within societies cannot be explained, because all individuals of a society share the same preferences.

Henrich et al. (2004) also suggest that prosocial behavior is correlated with market integration. *Homo moralis* preferences, however, are correlated with the degree of morality. It is unclear whether market integration is positively or negatively correlated with the degree of morality. One argument suggests they are negatively correlated: market integration may increase the probability of matching with individuals of another type, thus decreasing the degree of morality.

The findings from Henrich et al. (2004) should perhaps be taken with caution, as the relationship between market integration and values in the cross-section may suffer from endogeneity, because institutions and values may coevolve. For example, Alesina and Fuchs-Schündeln (2007) compare the attitudes toward redistribution of East and West Germans after the reunification. They find that communism instilled in people the view that the state was essential for their well-being. This suggests that institutions and political regimes can shape preferences, and therefore the degree of morality may change even if the matching protocol did not.

Falk and Szech (2013) run an experiment in which individuals choose between keeping money or saving a mouse. Decisions are made individually (involving the simple choice of getting money or saving the mouse) or through a market mechanism involving many buyers and sellers. Sellers are endowed with the mice and buyers with money. The mouse was killed if a trade occurred, the seller kept the sale price, and the buyer the endowment minus the sale price. If no trade occurred, the mouse survived, and earnings for both players were zero. The authors find that the willingness to keep the money (and thus to kill the mouse) is higher when decisions are made through a market with many buyers and sellers compared to when the market only has one buyer and seller. Put differently, Falk and Szech (2013) suggest that market interaction may be negatively correlated with the degree of morality.

Role of Institutions and Incentives

Contracts, subsidies, taxes, and other public policy issues are designed to induce self-interested individuals to act in the common interest. David Hume, the Scottish philosopher and economist (and friend of Adam Smith), said it best when arguing that public policy should be designed for "knaves" motivated by the private interest.[1] As Bowles (2008) puts it, the invisible hand needs a helping hand.

In this chapter, *Homo moralis* individuals are not knaves. But could institutions designed for knaves end up turning individuals into knaves? In other words, when individuals are not knaves, can incentives backfire? There is certainly a literature suggesting that this is the case. One example is the well-known study of six day-care centers in Haifa by Gneezy and Rustichini (2000). The day-care centers decided to impose a fine on parents who were late picking up their kids at the end of the day. Parents reacted to the fine by doubling the fraction of time they arrived late. More importantly, once the fine was removed, parents continued to be late when picking up the kids. In another example, Giné, Mansuri, and Sreshtra (2018) study the impacts of a monetary incentive given to the staff of a microfinance institution if

---

1. The quote is "in contriving any system of government [...] every man ought to be supposed a knave, and to have no other end, in all his actions, than private interest. By this interest we must govern him, and, by means of it, make him, notwithstanding his insatiable avarice and ambition, co-operate to public good." (David Hume 1777), http://oll.libertyfund.org/titles/hume-essays-moral-political-literary-lf-ed.

they achieved certain "social" goals related to the empowerment and well-being of their clients. For staff who worked in teams, such incentives led to a worsening of social outcomes.

The critical assumption when designing incentive schemes is that although other-regarding motives may be present, they are not affected by the schemes individuals face. This "separability" assumption fails in both examples above, as they underscore the fact that monetary incentives may diminish the intrinsic motivation of individuals to comply with social norms (Bowles 2008; Bowles and Hwang 2008).

The preferences of *Homo moralis* individuals discussed in this chapter maintain the separability assumption and therefore predict that policies designed for self-interested individuals will not backfire when applied to *Homo moralis*. But one cannot help but wonder whether the degree of regulation should be different across societies with different degrees of morality. Indeed, although regulation may be essential in a society of *Homo oeconomicus*, it may not be needed in a society of *Homo kantiensis*. This observation points to another hypothesis that could be tested in future empirical research.

References

Alesina, Alberto, and Nicola Fuchs-Schündeln. 2007. "Good-Bye Lenin (or Not?): The Effect of Communism on People's Preferences." *American Economic Review* 97 (4): 1507–1528.

Alger, Ingela, and Jörgen W. Weibull. 2013. "*Homo moralis*—Preference Evolution Under Incomplete Information and Assortative Matching." *Econometrica* 81 (6): 2269–2302.

Alger, Ingela, and Jörgen W. Weibull. 2016. "Evolution and Kantian Morality." *Games and Economic Behavior* 98: 56–67.

Bowles, Samuel. 2008. "Policies Designed for Self-Interested Citizens May Undermine 'the Moral Sentiments': Evidence from Economic Experiments." *Science* 320 (5883): 1605–1609.

Bowles, Samuel, and Sung-Ha Hwang. 2008. "Social Preferences and Public Economics: Mechanism Design When Social Preferences Depend on Incentives." *Journal of Public Economics* 92 (8): 1811–1820.

Falk, Armin, and Nora Szech. 2013. "Morals and Markets." *Science* 340 (6133): 707–711.

Giné, Xavier, Ghazala Mansuri, and Slesh Sreshtra. 2018. "Mission and the Bottom Line: Performance Incentives in a Multi-goal Development Organization." Working Paper, World Bank, Washington, DC.

Gneezy, Uri, and Aldo Rustichini. 2000. "A Fine Is a Price." *Journal of Legal Studies* 29 (1): 1–17.

Henrich, Joseph, Robert Boyd, Samuel Bowles, Colin F. Camerer, Ernst Fehr, Herbert Gintis, and Richard McElreath. 2004. "Overview and Synthesis." In *Foundations of Human Sociality: Economic Experiments and Ethnographic Evidence from Fifteen Small-Scale Societies*, edited by Joseph Henrich, Robert Boyd, Samuel Bowles, Colin F. Camerer, Ernst Fehr, and Herbert Gintis. New York: Oxford University Press.

Hume, David. 1777. "Essay VI: Of the Independency of Parliament." In *Essays and Treatises on Several Subjects*. http://oll.libertyfund.org/titles/hume-essays-moral-political-literary-lf-ed.

10   The Influence of Randomized Controlled Trials on Development Economics Research and on Development Policy

Abhijit Vinayak Banerjee, Esther Duflo, and Michael Kremer

Many (though by no means all) of the questions that development economists and policy makers ask themselves are causal in nature: What would
be the impact of adding computers in classrooms? What is the price elasticity of demand for preventive health products? Would increasing interest rates lead to an increase in default rates? Decades ago, the statistician
Fisher proposed a method to answer such causal questions: randomized
controlled trials (RCTs; Fisher 1925). In an RCT, the assignment of different
units to different treatment groups is chosen randomly. This ensures that
no unobservable characteristic of the units is reflected in the assignment,
and hence that any difference between treatment and control units reflects
the impact of the treatment. Although the idea is simple, the implementation in the field can be more involved, and it took some time before randomization was considered to be a practical tool for answering questions
in social science research in general and in development economics more
specifically.

About 20 years ago, the idea of randomized controlled trials was just
starting to make its way into development economics. Starting in 1994,
Glewwe, Kremer, and Moulin (2009) kick-started the use of randomized
evaluations among development economists and practitioners (Kremer

The views expressed in this document express the personal opinions of the author
and are entirely the authors' own. They do not necessarily reflect the opinions of the
U.S. Agency for International Development (USAID) or the United States Government. USAID is not responsible for the accuracy of any information supplied herein.
We thank Alison Fahey, Noor Iqbal, Sasha Gallant, Joaquin Carbonell, Adam Trow-
bridge, and Anne Healy for their support. We thank Rachel Glennerster for useful
comments, and Francine Loza and Laura Stilwell for excellent research assistance.

2003). In 1997, the PROGRESA randomized controlled trial began, marking the first evaluation of a large-scale policy effort in a developing country. With the launch of these randomized evaluations, we, perhaps naively, expressed the hope that RCTs would revolutionize social policy in the twenty-first century, much as they had revolutionized medicine in the twentieth century (Duflo and Kremer 2005; Duflo 2004; Banerjee et al. 2007). With the century less than 20 years old, it seems a little premature to evaluate this claim. Randomized evaluations clearly take a larger place in the policy conversation now than they did at the turn of the century, and they receive substantially more funding from donor organizations and local governments. Policy innovations that have been tested with RCTs have reached millions of people. However, the amount of money involved is still small. Development policy, moreover, is known for its twists and turns; many have predicted that RCTs are just the current fad and, soon enough, will have their comeuppance.

Something that we did not anticipate, however, has undoubtedly happened: Randomized controlled trials have, if not revolutionized, at least profoundly altered, the practice of development economics as an academic discipline. Some scholars applaud this change (we are obviously in that camp), while others rue it (Deaton 2010; Ravallion 2012), but the fact is not really in dispute. In this essay, we start by quantitatively documenting this remarkable evolution. Here we discuss the ways in which the field has been affected by the practice of RCTs and what we see as their main contributions to the practice of development economics.

The popularity of RCTs as a research tool has sometimes been seen as conflicting with their potential (or ambition) for changing the world. The view is that the "academic" desire to come up with the cleverest research design may not line up with the practitioners need to identify scalable innovations (the next cell phone), or change "systems" (health care) or reform institutions (democracy). Using the USAID Development Innovation Ventures (DIV) portfolio as a case study, we identify the policy innovations tested with DIV funding that have eventually led to large-scale reach (more than 100,000 people). The analysis suggests that the proposed opposition between interesting and important is not particularly pertinent. In practice, many of the interventions supported by DIV that have reached this scale started as small research projects driven by academics. These projects also had the greatest

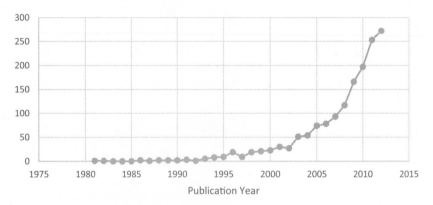

Figure 10.1
Number of published RCTs
Source: Cameron, Drew B., Anjini Mishra, and Annette N. Brown. 2016. "The Growth of Impact Evaluation for International Development: How Much Have We Learned?" *Journal of Development Effectiveness* 8 (1): 1–21.

"bang for the buck" evaluated in terms of lives eventually reached per USAID initial funding dollars.[1] We conclude this essay by discussing what this tells us about the policy process and the role RCTs can have in it.

Rapid Growth

Over the past 15 years, the use of experiments has expanded in academia and in international organizations: The DIME group at the World Bank lists more than 200 studies, nearly all of them randomized, and Arianna Legovini, the head of DIME, estimates that if we take the World Bank as a whole, there are at least 475 RCTs going on (Legovini, personal communication). Tables 10.1 and 10.2 and the figures in the chapter summarize some trends in the use of experiments over time.

We start with a review of impact evaluations conducted by Cameron, Mishra, and Brown (2016; figures 10.1 and 10.2). They compiled a repository of 2,259 impact evaluation studies in development economics that were published between 1981 and 2012 by searching all major academic databases in health, economics, public policy, and the social sciences. They

---

1. This does not necessarily imply they have the highest social return.

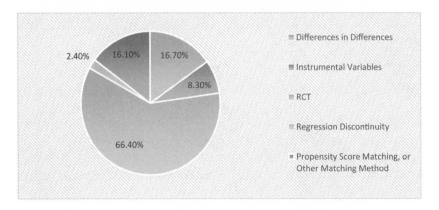

Figure 10.2
Evaluations by type
Source: Cameron, Drew B., Anjini Mishra, and Annette N. Brown. 2016. "The Growth of Impact Evaluation for International Development: How Much Have We Learned?" *Journal of Development Effectiveness* 8 (1): 1–21.

supplemented this with an online crowdsourcing effort, which offered a $10 gift certificate per qualifying paper that was not already in the database. They then classified the papers by sector and by type. Overall, 66 percent (1,491) of those evaluations are RCTs. Figure 10.1 shows that the number of RCTs has grown rapidly over time.

Next, we look at the data compiled by Aidgrade (Vivalt 2015). Aidgrade compiles the results of impact evaluations of development interventions. According to Vivalt:

> The evaluations included in the AidGrade database were carefully selected from a number of different databases and online sources, the detailed process for which is outlined in Vivalt (2015). AidGrade.org employees first chose 30 topics they felt were important development issues. Those lists were combined and made into one large list of topics. The list was then narrowed down based on whether or not there were likely to be enough evaluations for a meta-analysis. The search universe includes search aggregators, such as Google Scholar and EBSCO, but also includes the J-PAL, IPA, CEGA, and 3ie online databases.

Figure 10.3a shows the number of evaluations per year, and figure 10.3b shows how the evaluations are distributed over time among RCTs in economics, RCTs in other fields (e.g., medical trials), and non-RCTs. Both figures show a clear trend in both the number and the fraction of RCTs among the impact evaluations that are surveyed.

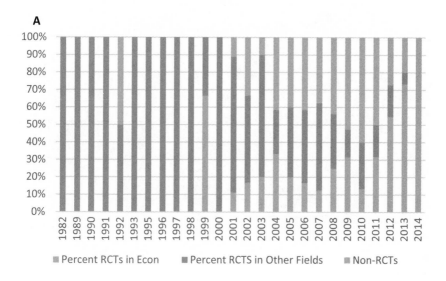

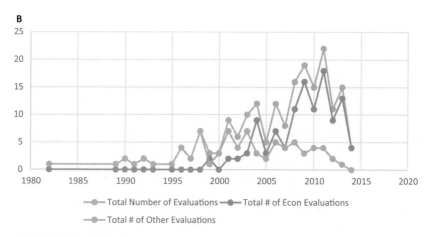

Figure 10.3
Aidgrade.org evaluations
Source: Aidgrade.org.

RCTs are particularly popular among younger researchers. Figures 10.4 and 10.5 show the number and the fraction of researchers who carry out RCTs among the fellows and associates of the Bureau for Research and Economic Analysis of Development (BREAD), the association of development economists, by the year in which they obtained their PhDs. The number clearly increases among the recent PhDs, and although this is in part driven

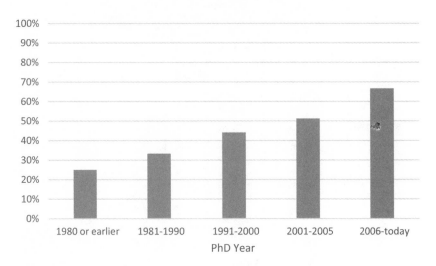

Figure 10.4
Fraction of BREAD affiliates and fellows with one or more RCTs
Source: Aidgrade.org.

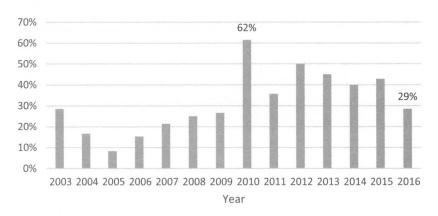

Figure 10.5
Percentage of BREAD conference papers using an RCT
Source: Aidgrade.org.

by a larger number of recent fellows and associates, the fraction of them who conduct RCTs increases as well.

The number of RCTs presented at development economics conferences grew rapidly until 2010 and then stabilized (or decreased) after that. At the annual conference of BREAD (the flagship conference in development economics), the fraction of papers featuring RCTs increased from 8 percent in

Table 10.1
North East Universities Development Consortium conference papers

Year	Total number of RCTs	Share of RCTs (percent)
2015	40	18.20
2014	36	17.90
2013	49	24.30
2012	27	16.00

Source: Data from neudc.org.

2005 to 63 percent in 2010, and hovered around 40–50 percent after that (except for the last conference, at Georgetown, where it was 28 percent). At the North East Universities Development Consortium Conference, a larger conference attended by many junior researchers, the fraction of RCTs has been fairly stable, ranging between 16 and 24 percent for the years 2012 to 2015 (the years for which we could get the papers) and showing no particular trend (table 10.1).

RCTs have made a clear entry in top academic journals. Looking at the *American Economic Review (AER)*, the *Quarterly Journal of Economics (QJE)*, *Econometrica, Review of Economic Studies*, and the *Journal of Political Economy (JPE)*, the number of RCT studies was 0 in 1990, 0 in 2000, and 10 in 2015 (table 10.2). At the same time, the number of development papers published in these journals almost doubled (from 17 in 1990 to 32 in 2015). Table 10.2 also provides the details by journal. This is not driven by any particular journal (except that *Econometrica* does not seem to contribute much). Note that this does not mean that RCT studies have supplanted other types of work: Nearly all published work on development is still non-RCT (if we look at lower-ranked journals), and even in top journals, the experiments have been in addition to the (limited number of) papers that were published on development.

Beyond the growth in the number of experiments and in the number of researchers who carry them out, what also stands out is the range and the ambition of the projects that are attempted: Few topics seem off limits, and scale does not seem to be a barrier.

Researchers work directly with governments to randomize aspects of their work. Finan, Olken, and Pande (2015) describe several of these ambitious experiments. For example, Dal Bó, Finan, and Rossi (2013) randomize the wages at which new government employees are hired; Khan, Khwaja, and Olken (2016) randomize incentives for tax collectors in Pakistan; and

Table 10.2

Papers in top journals

Journal	Year	Total number of papers	Number of development papers	Number of which are RCTs
American Economic Review	2015	101	15	4
	2000	48	6	0
	1990	57	2	0
Quarterly Journal of Economics	2015	40	1	1
	2000	43	5	0
	1990	52	3	0
Journal of Political Economy	2015	36	4	3
	2000	51	7	0
	1990	65	9	0
Restud	2015	48	7	2
	2000	36	3	0
	1990	40	1	0
Econometrica	2015	46	5	0
	2000	37	0	0
	1990	64	2	0
Total	2015	271	32	10
	2000	215	21	0
	1990	278	17	0

Source: Data from neudc.org.

Ashraf, Bandiera, and Lee (2015) work on how government health workers are recruited for their jobs. In experiments covering several districts and millions of workers, Muralidharan, Niehaus, and Sukhtankar (2016) and Banerjee et al. (2016) evaluate two separate process changes in the payment of wages of India's major workfare program the Mahatma Gandhi National Rural Employment Guarantee Act (MGNREGS), while Banerjee et al. (2014) randomize reforms in the police department in India, and Duflo et al. (2013a, 2013b) randomize the enforcement of pollution regulation on industrial firms in India.

Researchers work at a scale that is sufficient to capture market equilibrium effects: Muralidharan and Sundararaman (2015) randomize a private school voucher at the school market level, while Muralidharan, Niehaus, and Sukhtankar (2016), in their aforementioned experiment, are able to look at the impact of MGNREGS on wages and productivity.

The range of topics keeps expanding. Development economists study alcohol addiction (Schilbach 2015), electoral fraud in Afghanistan (Callen and Long 2015), Cognitive Behavioral Therapy for ex-combatants (Blattman, Jamison, and Sheridan 2015), and early childhood stimulation and development (Attanasio et al. 2014).

In summary, randomized experiments have become not so much the "gold standard" as just a standard tool in the toolbox. Running an experiment is now sufficiently commonplace that by itself, it does not guarantee that the paper will get into a top journal or even the BREAD conference. However, researchers from all sorts of perspectives have come to consider RCTs as a feasible option for answering the questions they are interested in. This level of comfort is in part due to the growth of several entities that help researchers with their fieldwork, including by codifying and standardizing experimental practices, and training enumerators. The leader for this is Innovation for Poverty Action, with its vast network of country offices and experienced staff workers, but also J-PAL, CEGA, and the World Bank. There is also more funding available, from USAID (DIV in particular), the World Bank (SIEF and DIME), DFID, The Bill and Melinda Gates Foundation, The William and Flora Hewlett Foundation, The International Initiative for Impact Evaluation, in particular and, more recently, the Global Innovation Fund. But part of it also has to do with the appeal of the technique. In the next section, we reflect on the influence that RCTs have had on development economics research and why.

The Influence of RCTs on Development Economics Research

The remarkable growth in the number of RCTs, and more generally in the importance of empirical development economics as a field, are in themselves dramatic changes. The type of development research that is carried out today is significantly different from research conducted even 15 years ago. A reflection of this fact is that many researchers who were openly skeptical of RCTs, or simply belonged to an entirely different tradition in development economics (e.g., Daron Acemoglu, Derek Neal, Martin Ravallion, and Mark Rosenzweig) have become involved in one or more RCTs in a developing country.

Early discussions of the merits (or lack thereof) of randomization put a lot of emphasis on its role in the reliable identification of internally valid causal effects and the external validity of such estimates. We, and others, have had these discussions in other places (Heckman 1992; Banerjee 2008; Duflo, Glennester, and Kremer 2007; Banerjee and Duflo 2009; Deaton 2010), and we will not reproduce them here. As we began to argue in Banerjee and Duflo (2009), we actually think that these discussions somewhat miss the point about why RCTs are really valuable and why they have become so popular with researchers.

A Greater Focus on Identification across the Board

The original motivation of randomized experiments, starting with Neyman ([1923] 1990; as a theoretical device) and Fisher (1925; who was the first to propose physically randomizing units), was a focus on the credible identification of causal effects. As Athey and Imbens (2017, 78) write in their chapter for *The Handbook on Field Experiments*:

> There is a long tradition viewing randomized experiments as the most credible of designs to obtain causal inferences. Freedman (2006) writes succinctly "experiments offer more reliable evidence on causation than observational studies." On the other hand, some researchers continue to be skeptical about the relative merits of randomized experiments. For example, Deaton (2010) argues that "evidence from randomized controlled trials can have no special priority.... Randomized controlled trials cannot automatically trump other evidence, they do not occupy any special place in some hierarchy of evidence..." Our views align with that of Freedman and others, who view randomized experiments as playing a special role in causal inference. Whenever possible, a randomized experiment is unique in the control that the researcher has over the assignment mechanism, and by virtue of this control, selection bias in comparisons between treated and control units can be eliminated. That does not mean that randomized experiments can answer all causal questions. There are a number of reasons randomized experiments may not be suitable to answer particular questions.

For a long time, observational studies and randomized studies progressed on largely parallel paths: In agricultural science and then biomedical studies, randomized experiments were quickly accepted, and a vocabulary and statistical apparatus to think about them were developed. Despite the adoption of randomized studies in other fields, in the social sciences, most researchers continued to reason exclusively in terms of observational data. The main approach was to estimate associations and then to try to assess the extent to which these associations reflect causality (or to explicitly give up on causality). Starting with Rubin's (1974) fundamental contribution, researchers started to use the experimental analog to reason about observational data, which set the stage for thinking about how to analyze observational data through the lens of the "ideal experiment."

Through the 1980s and 1990s, motivated by this clear thinking about causal effects, labor economics and public finance were transformed by the introduction of new empirical methods for estimating causal effects (matching, instrumental variables, difference-in-differences, and regression discontinuity designs). Development economics also embraced those methods starting in the 1990s, but unlike in labor economics and public finance, some researchers also decided that it may be possible to go directly to the "ideal" experiment or to go back and forth between experimental and nonexperimental studies. As a result, the two literatures developed in close relationship, constantly cross-fertilizing each other.

The nonexperimental literature was completely transformed by the existence of this large RCT movement. When the gold standard is not just a twinkle in someone's eyes but the clear alternative to a particular empirical strategy and a benchmark for it, researchers feel compelled to think harder about identification strategies, and to be more inventive and rigorous about them. As a result, researchers have become increasingly clever at identifying and using natural experiments, and at the same time, much more cautious in interpreting the results from them. Not surprisingly, the standards of the nonexperimental literature have improved tremendously over the past few decades without necessarily sacrificing their ability to ask broad and important questions. For example, Alesina, Giuliano, and Nunn (2013) use suitability to the plow to study the long-run determinants of the social attitudes toward the role of women; Padró i Miquel, Qian, and Yao (2014) use a difference-in-difference strategy to study village democracy; and Banerjee and Iyer (2005) and Dell (2010) use a spatial discontinuity to look at the long-run impact of extractive institutions. In each of these cases, the questions are approached with the same eye for careful identification as other more standard program evaluation questions.

Meanwhile, the RCT literature was also influenced by work done in the nonexperimental literature. The understanding of the power (and limits) of instrumental variables allowed researchers to move away from the basic experimental paradigm of the completely randomized experiment with perfect follow-up and use more complicated strategies, including encouragement designs. Techniques developed in the nonexperimental literature offered ways to handle situations in the field that are removed from the ideal setting of experiments (e.g., imperfect randomization, noncompliance, attrition, spillovers, and contamination). Structural methods were combined with experiments to estimate counterfactual policies (Todd and Wolpin 2006; Attanasio, Meghir and Santiago 2012).

More recently, machine learning techniques have also been combined with experiments to model treatment effect heterogeneity (see Athey and Imbens 2017 for a recent review of the econometrics of experiments).

Of course, the broadening offered by these new techniques comes at the cost of making additional assumptions on top of the original experimental assignment, and those assumptions may or may not be valid. Thus the difference in the quality of identification between a very well-identified, nonexperimental study and a randomized evaluation that ends up facing lots of constraints in the field or tries to estimate parameters beyond pure treatment effects is a matter of degree. In this sense, there has been a convergence across the empirical spectrum in terms of the quality of identification, mostly because experiments have pulled the remaining study designs up with them.

Assessing External Validity

In the words of Athey and Imbens (2017, 79): "External validity is concerned with generalizing causal inferences, drawn for a particular population and setting, to others, where these alternative settings could involve different populations, different outcomes, or different contexts."

The question of the external validity of RCTs is even more hotly debated than that of their internal validity. This is perhaps because, unlike internal validity, there is no clear endpoint to the debate: Heterogeneity in treatment effects across different types of individuals could always occur, or heterogeneity in the effect may result from ever-so-slightly different treatments. As Banerjee, Chassang, and Snowberg (2016, 25) acknowledge: "External policy advice is unavoidably subjective. This does not mean that it needs to be uninformed by experimental evidence, rather, judgment will unavoidably color it."

It is worth noting that very little here is specific to RCTs (Banerjee 2008). The same problem afflicts all empirical analysis with the one exception of what Heckman (1992) calls the "randomization bias." "Randomization bias" refers to the fact that experiments require the consent of both the subjects and the organization that is carrying out the program, and these people may be quite different. Glennerster (2017), in her chapter in the *Handbook of Field Experiments*, provides the list of the characteristics of the ideal partner, and they are clearly not representative of the typical nongovernmental organization (NGO). But it is worth pointing out that any naturally occurring policy that gets evaluated (i.e., not an RCT) is also selected: The evaluation requires that the policy did take place, and that was presumably because someone thought it was a good idea to try it out.

In general, any study takes place at a particular time and place, and that affects results. This does not imply that subjective recommendations by experts, based both on their priors and the results of their experiments, should not be of some use to policy makers. Most policy makers know how to combine the data that is presented to them with their own prior knowledge of their settings. From our experience, we have often observed that when presented with evidence from an RCT on a program of interest, the immediate reaction of a policy maker is to ask whether an RCT could be done in their own context.

There is one clear advantage that RCTs do offer for external validity, although it is not often discussed and has not been systematically exploited as yet. To assess any external validity issues, it is helpful to have well-identified causal studies in multiple settings. These settings should vary in terms of the distribution of characteristics of the units—and possibly in terms of the specific nature of the treatments or the treatment rate—in order to assess the credibility of generalizing to other settings. With RCTs, because we can, in principle, control where and over what sample experiments take place (and not just how to allocate the treatment in a sample), we can get a handle on how treatment effects might vary by context. By itself, this is not sufficient to say anything much, if we account for the infinite unstructured variation in the world. But there are several ways to make progress.

A first approach is to combine existing evaluations and make assumptions about the possible distribution of treatment effects. Rubin (1981) proposes modeling treatment effect heterogeneity as stemming from a normal distribution: At each site, the causal effect of the treatment is a site-specific effect drawn from a normal distribution. The goal is to estimate the mean and variance of the treatment effect, and the implied specific site effect, taking into account the fact that we have other effects, too. An interesting case study is the effect of microfinance programs. Meager (2016) analyzes data from seven randomized experiments, including six published in a special issue of the *American Economic Journal: Applied Economics* in 2015. She finds remarkable consistency in the mean effects across these studies, but much more heterogeneity in their variance. Of course, to carry out this exercise properly, we need access to an unselected sample of studies, and because there is publication bias in economics, the sample of published studies may not be representative of all studies that exist. This is where another advantage of RCT kicks in: Because they have a defined beginning and end, they can in principle be registered. To this end, the American Economic Association recently created a registry of randomized trials (www .socialscienceregistry.org), which, as of June 1, listed 699 studies. The hope is that all projects will be registered, preferably before they are launched, and that results will be clearly linked to the study, so that in the future, meta-analysts can work from the full universe of studies.

A second approach is to conceive projects as multisite projects from the start. One recent example of such an enterprise is the "graduation" approach—an integrated, multifaceted program with livelihood promotion at its core that aims to "graduate" individuals out of extreme poverty and onto a long-term, sustainable higher consumption path. BRAC, the world's largest nongovernmental organization, has scaled up this program in Bangladesh (Bandiera et al. 2013), and NGOs around the world have engaged in similar livelihood-based efforts. Six randomized trials were undertaken over the same period around the world (in Ethiopia, Ghana, Honduras, India, Pakistan, and Peru). The teams regularly communicated with one another and with BRAC to ensure that their local adaptations remained true to the original program. The results suggest that the integrated multifaceted program was "sufficient" to increase long-term income, where "long-term" is defined as 3 years after the productive asset transfer (Banerjee et al. 2015a). Using an index approach to account for multiple hypotheses testing, positive impacts were found for consumption, income and revenue, asset wealth, food security, financial inclusion, physical health, mental health, labor supply, political involvement, and women's decision-making after 2 years. After a third year, the results remained the same in eight of ten outcome categories. There is country-by-country variation (e.g., the program was ineffective in Honduras), and the team is currently working on a meta-analysis to quantify the level of heterogeneity.

One issue is that there is little that the researcher can do ex post to reliably identify the source of differences in findings across countries. A third possible approach would be to take guidance from the first few sites to make a prediction on what the next sites would find. To discipline this process, researchers would be encouraged to use the results from existing trials to make some explicit predictions about what they expect to observe in other samples (or with slightly different treatments). These can serve as a guide for subsequent trials. This idea is discussed in Banerjee, Chassang, and Snowberg (2016), who call it "structured speculation." They propose the following broad guidelines for structured speculation:

1. Experimenters should systematically speculate about the external validity of their findings.
2. Such speculation should be clearly and cleanly separated from the rest of the paper, maybe in a section called "speculation."
3. Speculation should be precise and falsifiable.

Structured speculation has three advantages, according to Banerjee, Chassang, and Snowberg (2016, 27). First, it ensures that the researcher's specific knowledge is captured. Second, it creates a clear sense of where else experiments should be run. Third, it creates incentives to design research that has greater externality. They write:

> To address scalability, experimenters may structure local pilot studies for easy comparison with their main experiments. To identify the right sub-populations for generalizing to other environments, experimenters can identify ahead of time the characteristics of groups that can be generalized, and stratify on those. To extend the results to populations with a different distribution of unobserved characteristics, experimenters may elicit the former using the selective trial techniques discussed in Chassang, Padró-i-Miquel, and Snowberg (2012), and run the experiments separately for each of the groups so identified.

As this approach was just proposed recently, there are few examples as yet. A notable example is Dupas (2014). Dupas (2014) studies the effect of short-term subsidies on long-run adoption of new health products and reports that short-term subsidies had a significant impact on the adoption of a more effective and comfortable class of bed nets. The paper then provides a clear discussion of external validity. It first spells out a simple and transparent argument relating the effectiveness of short-run subsidies to: (1) the speed at which various forms of uncertainty are resolved and

(2) the timing of user's costs and benefits. If the uncertainty over benefits is resolved quickly, short-run subsidies can have a long-term effect. If uncertainty over benefits is resolved slowly, and adoption costs are incurred early on, short-run subsidies are unlikely to have a long-term effect.

Dupas (2014) then answers the question: For what types of health products and contexts would we expect the same results? The paper does so by classifying potential technologies into three categories based on how short-run (or one-time) subsidies would change adoption patterns. Clearly, there could be such discussions at the ends of all papers, not just ones featuring RCTs. But because RCTs can be purposefully designed and placed, there is a higher chance of follow-up in this case.

Observing the Unobservable

If the main benefit of randomization is not the identification of causal effect, what is it? And what explains its remarkable success among researchers?

We agree with Athey and Imbens (2017, 78) that "a randomized experiment is unique in the control that the researcher has over the assignment mechanism," and we would take the argument one step further: Randomization is also unique in the control that the researcher (often) has over the treatment itself. In observational studies, however beautifully designed, the researcher is limited to evaluating what has been implemented in the world. In a randomized experiment, she can manipulate the treatment in ways that we do not observe in reality. This has a number of advantages. First, she can innovate (i.e., design new policies or interventions that she thinks will be effective based on prior knowledge or theory) and test these innovations, even if no policy maker is thinking about putting them in practice yet. Development economists have many ideas, often inspired by what they have read or researched, and many of the randomized experiment projects come out of those ideas: They test in the field an intervention that simply did not exist before (for example, a kilogram of lentil for parents who vaccinate their kids; stickers to encourage riders to speak up against a bad driver; free chlorine dispensers).

Second, the researcher can introduce variations that will help her establish facts that could not otherwise be established. The well-known Negative Income Tax (NIT) experiment was designed with precisely that idea in mind: In general, a raise in wages creates both income and substitution effects that cannot easily be separated (Heckman 1992), but randomized manipulation of the slope and the intercept of a wage schedule makes it possible to estimate both together. Interestingly, after the initial NIT and the Rand Health Insurance experiment, the tradition of social experiments in the United States, as Judy Gueron (2017) describes in her chapter in the *Handbook of Field Experiments*, has mainly been to obtain causal effects of social policies that were often fairly comprehensive packages. In contrast, development economists have worked both on evaluations of real policies (e.g., the PROGRESA evaluation, or, more recently, the evaluation of the graduation program) but also on what Congdon et al. (2017, 394) describe as "mechanism experiments":

> Broadly, a mechanism experiment is an experiment that tests a mechanism—that is, it tests not the effects of variation in policy parameters themselves, directly, but the effects of variation in an intermediate link in the causal chain that connects (or is hypothesized to connect) a policy to an outcome. That is, where there is a specified policy that has candidate mechanisms that affect an outcome of policy concern, the mechanism experiment tests one or more of those mechanisms. There can be one or more mechanisms that link the policy to the outcome, which could operate in parallel (for example when there are multiple potential mediating channels through which a policy could change outcomes) or sequentially (if for example some mechanisms affect take-up or implementation fidelity). The central idea is that the mechanism experiment is intended to be informative about some policy but does not involve a test of that policy directly.

In other words, mechanism experiments do not confine themselves to testing feasible (or desirable) policies. For example, cars with broken windows could be put in the street to test the broken window theory. Once we realize that we are not limited to a set of realistic policy options (though we are constrained by what is ethically acceptable), this opens up a wide range of possibilities.

Banerjee and Duflo (2009) discuss some examples of mechanism experiments. One prominent example in development is a project conducted by Karlan and Zinman (2008) in collaboration with a South African lender that makes small loans to high-risk borrowers at high interest rates. The experiment was designed to test the relative weights of ex post repayment burden (including moral hazard) and ex ante adverse selection in loan default. Potential borrowers with the same observable risk are randomly offered a high or a low interest rate in an initial letter. Individuals then decide whether to borrow at the solicitation's offer rate. Of those who apply at the higher rate, half are randomly offered a new, lower contract interest rate when they are actually given the loan, whereas the remaining half continue at the offer rate. Individuals did not know ex ante that the contract rate could differ from the offer rate. The researchers then compared repayment performance of the loans in all three groups. The comparison of those who responded to the high-offer interest rate with those who responded to the low-offer interest rate in the population that received the same low contract rate allows the identification of the adverse selection effect; comparing those who faced the same offer rate but differing contract rates identifies the repayment burden effect. The basic idea of varying prices ex post and ex ante to identify different parameters has since been replicated in several different studies (e.g., Ashraf, Berry, and Shapiro 2010; Cohen and Dupas 2010). The experimental variation was key here, and not only to avoid bias: In the world, we are unlikely to observe a large number of people who face different offer prices but receive the same actual price.

Experiments can also be devised to understand how institutions function. An example is Bertrand et al. (2007), who set up an experiment to understand the structure of corruption in the process of obtaining a driving license in Delhi. They recruited people who were aiming to get a driving license and set up three groups, one that receives a bonus for obtaining a driving license quickly, one that gets free driving lessons, and a control group. They found that those in the "bonus" group got their licenses faster, but those who received the free driving lessons did not. They also found that those in the bonus group were more likely to pay an agent to get the license (who, they conjecture, bribed someone). They also found that the applicants who hired an agent were less likely to have taken a driving test before getting a license. Although they did not appear to find that those in the bonus group who get licenses are systematically less likely to know how to drive than those in the control group (which would be the litmus test that corruption does result in an inefficient allocation of driving licenses), this experiment provides suggestive evidence that corruption in this case does more than "grease the wheels" of the system.

Such designs do not always directly lead to actionable policy, but they have allowed us to describe or understand how the world works. For example, in the seminal Bertrand and Mullainathan (2004) study, researchers sent resumes to prospective employers. The resumes are paired, such that there are identical resumes, except for the name of the job applicants, who can either be white sounding or African American sounding. They find that "applicants" with black sounding names are half as likely to be called back as those with white sounding names. Furthermore, being highly educated does not help, which suggests that something other than statistical discrimination is at play. This design has been replicated hundreds of times in different settings, providing extensive evidence of discrimination against different people and in different markets. This large body of evidence does not necessarily point to a specific solution to this problem, or even help determine the root of this behavior, but, unlike the previous literature, it provides clear evidence that the phenomenon exists.

Data Collection

Experiments have also spurred creativity in measurement. In principle, there is no automatic link between careful and innovative collection of microeconomic data and the experimental method. And, indeed, it is a long tradition in development economics to collect data that is specifically designed to test theories: Both the breadth and the quantity of microeconomic data collected in development economics has exploded in recent decades, and not only in the context of experiments (see Udry 1995 for a prominent early example).

However, one specific feature of experiments that serves to encourage the development of new measurement methods is high take-up rates and a specific measurement problem. In many experimental studies, a large fraction of those who are intended to be affected by the program are actually affected. Thus, the number of units on which data needs to be collected to assess the impact of the program does not have to be very large, and the data are typically collected especially for the purpose of the experiment. Elaborate and expensive measurement of outcomes is therefore easier to obtain than in the context of a large multipurpose household or firm survey. By contrast, observational studies must often rely on variation for identification (e.g., policy changes, market-induced variation, natural variation, and supply shocks) that cover large populations, requiring the use of a large data set often not collected for a specific purpose. This makes it more difficult to fine tune the measurement to the specific question at hand. Moreover, even if it is possible ex post to do a sophisticated data collection exercise specifically targeted to the question, it is generally impossible to do it for the preprogram situation. This precludes the use of a difference-in-differences strategy for these types of outcomes, which again limits the incentives to collect them ex post.

Some of the most exciting recent developments in empirical development economics have to do with measurement. Researchers have turned to other subfields of economics, as well as entirely different fields, to borrow tools for measuring outcomes. Examples include soil testing and remote sensing in agriculture (see de Janvry, Sadoulet, and Suri 2017 for a review of agriculture); techniques developed by social psychologists for difficult-to-measure outcomes, such as audit and correspondence studies, implicit association tests, Goldberg experiments, and List experiments (see Bertrand and Duflo 2016 for a review of their use to measure discrimination); tools developed by cognitive psychologists for child development (Attanasio et al. 2014); tools inspired by economic theory, such as Becker-DeGroot-Marshak games to infer willingness to pay (see a discussion in Dupas and Miguel (2017)); biomarkers in health, beyond the traditional height, weight, and hemoglobin (cortisol to measure stress, for example); and wearable devices to measure mobility or effort (Kreindler 2018; Rao, Schilbach, and Schofield n.d.).

Specific methods and devices that exactly suit the purpose at hand have also been developed for experiments. Olken (2007) is one example of the kind of data that can be collected in an experimental setting. The objective was to determine whether audits or community monitoring were effective ways to curb corruption in decentralized construction projects. Getting a reliable measure of actual levels of corruption was thus necessary. Olken focused on roads and had engineers dig holes in the road to measure the material used. He then compared that with the level of material reported to be used. The difference is a measure of how much of the material was stolen or never purchased but invoiced, and thus is an objective measure of corruption. Olken then demonstrated that this measure of "missing inputs" is affected by the threat of audits, but not, except in some circumstances, by encouraging greater attendance at community meetings. Rigol, Hussam, and Regianni (n.d.) provide another example of clever data collection methods. For their experiment, they designed soap dispensers that could track when the pump was being pushed in order to accurately measure whether and when people wash their hands and hired a Chinese company to manufacture the dispensers. Similar "audit" methodologies are used to measure the impact of interventions in health, such as patients posing with specific diseases to measure the impact of training (Banerjee et al. 2016) or ineligible people attempting to buy free bed nets (Dizon-Ross et al. 2017). Even a partial list of such examples would be very long.

In parallel, greater use is being made of administrative data, which are often combined with large-scale experiments. For example, Banerjee et al. (2016) make use of both publicly available administrative data on a workfare program in India and restricted expenditure data made available to them as part of the experiment; Khan, Khwaja, and Olken (2016) use administrative tax data; and Attanasio et al. (2017) use unemployment insurance data to measure the long-term effect of job training in Colombia.

The bottom line is that great progress has been made in our understanding of how to creatively and accurately collect or use existing data that go beyond the traditional survey, and these insights have led both to better projects and to innovations in data collection that have been adopted in nonrandomized work as well.

Iterate and Build on Previous Research in the Same Settings

The next methodological advantage of RCTs also relates to the control that researchers have over the assignment and, often enough, over the treatments themselves. Well-identified policy evaluations often leave us with many questions about why things turned out the way they did. For example, some papers using regression discontinuity designs find that the impact of "elite" schools on the marginal child who is admitted tends to be very low. These results seem to hold both in rich and in poor countries (Clark 2009; Abdulkadiroglu, Angrist, and Pathak 2014; Dobbie and Fryer 2014; Lucas and Mbiti 2014; Dustan, de Janvry, and Sadoulet 2015). But these results leave some questions pending: Does this mean that the impact is zero for all students or just the marginal student? Is it because peers don't matter and curriculum doesn't matter, or because they both matter but cancel out?

Although some progress can be made (e.g., Abdulkadiroglu, Angrist, and Pathak (2014) exploit the fact that students take two different tests to get a handle on the impact of the program for different types of students), one is necessarily limited by the type of policy variation that is actually available. The result from a single RCT often likewise raises more questions than it can actually answer. For example, when Duflo, Kremer, and Robinson (2008) found that the return to fertilizer appears to be very large, even when used by the farmers themselves on their own fields (and not just on experimental plots), one possible policy response might have been to follow Jeff Sachs's idea of distributing fertilizer for free. But this was not their next step. Instead, they started wondering why farmers are not using more fertilizer. This set them down a path that led them to set up experiments in the same setting: Some focused on learning and social networks, and some on the difficulty to save even over short periods of time. This latter inquiry led them down the path of designing and implementing a specific product, for which the household was offered the option of buying fertilizer in advance (Duflo, Kremer, and Robinson 2008). The social network interventions found surprisingly little diffusion of agricultural innovation to immediate friends, and this observation set the experimenters down another path: How could it be the case, given all we know about how much people talk about agriculture? To unpack this further, they introduced a simple device designed to address a problem that they noticed in their first set of experiments: Households tend to overuse fertilizer (conditional on using it), relative to what appears to be the profit-maximizing application rate. They then set up experiments to study in what conditions this device does spread, and what this tells us about how farmers decide whether to talk to and trust one another (Duflo et al. 2017).

Analyzing these results will no doubt spur new questions and experiments. All empirical science is of course iterative, with studies building on each other. But the ability to work in the same setting, with the same outcome and measurement, is extremely precious and is not available outside a controlled setting.

Unpacking the Interventions

Finally, RCTs, allow the possibility to "unpack" a program to its constituent elements. Here again, the work may be iterative. For example, all the initial evaluations of the BRAC ultra poor program were done using their "full package," as were a large number of evaluations of the Mexican conditional cash transfer (CCT) program PROGRESA. But both for research and for policy, once we know that the full program works, it is clearly of interest to know why it works. In recent years, some papers have looked "inside" CCT, relaxing the conditionality, for example. Some work has been conducted on the role and the type of conditionality (see Baird, McIntosh, and

Özler 2011; Bursztyn and Coffman 2012; and Benhassine et al. 2015 for examples), followed by many papers experimentally varying other features (we return to the impact of this work below).

Similarly, the early results of the evaluation of the ultra poor program have set the stage both for a more theoretically grounded understanding of exactly which market failures led to a poverty trap, as well as for a more practically grounded understanding of whether all the interventions were truly necessary or if certain components could be removed. In the event that some components are unnecessary, costs could be lowered considerably, allowing the program to reach more people using the same budget. Hanna and Karlan (2017, 539–540) discuss how one could go from the initial "full package" evaluation to this greater understanding:

> The ideal method, if unconstrained by budget and organizational constraints, is a complex experimental design that randomizes all permutations of each component.
>
> The productive asset transfer, if the only issue were a credit market failure, may have been sufficient to generate these results, and if no other component enabled an individual to accumulate sufficient capital to acquire the asset, the transfer alone may have been a necessary component. The savings component on the other hand may have been a substitute for the productive asset transfer, by lowering transaction costs to save and serving as a behavioral intervention which facilitated staying on task to accumulate savings. Clearly it is not realistic in one setting to test the necessity or sufficiency of each component, and interaction across components: Even if treated simplistically with each component either present or not, this would imply 2x2x2x2 = 16 experimental groups.

Several studies have tackled pieces of the puzzle, and more are underway (see the review in Hanna and Karlan 2017). The way forward is clearly going to be the development of a mosaic, rather than any one definitive study that both tests each component and also includes sufficient contextual and market variations that it can help set policy for myriad countries and populations. More work is needed to tease apart the different components: asset transfer (addresses capital market failures), savings account (lowers savings transaction fee), information (addresses information failures), life-coaching (addresses behavioral constraints, and perhaps changes expectations and beliefs about possible return on investment), health services and information (addresses health market failures), consumption support (addresses nutrition-based poverty traps), among other possibilities. Furthermore, for several of these questions, there are key, open issues about *how* to address them; for example, life-coaching can take on an infinite number of manifestations. Some organizations conduct life-coaching through religion, others through interactive problem solving, and others through psychotherapy approaches (Bolton et al. 2003, 2007; Patel et al. 2010). Much remains to be learned not just about the promise of such life-coaching components but also about how to make them work (if they work at all).

In some settings, particularly when working on a large scale with a government, it is actually possible to experiment from the beginning with various versions of a program. This serves two purposes: It gives us a handle on the theory behind the program; and it has operational value for the government, which can pick the most cost-effective combination. Banerjee et al. (2015b) is an example of this approach. The government of Indonesia was interested in reducing corruption in their rice distribution program (Raskin), which is infamous for reaching few of its intended beneficiaries and for not always being sold at the right price. They thought that delivering a card to the beneficiaries with the eligibility information might ameliorate this problem and lead to greater benefits. Working with the Government of Indonesia, the authors designed a set of field experiments to provide information directly to eligible households. In 378 villages (randomly selected from among 572 villages spread over three provinces), the central government mailed "Raskin identification cards" to eligible households to inform them of their eligibility and the quantity of rice that they were entitled to. To unbundle the mechanisms through which different forms of information may affect program outcomes, the government also experimentally varied how the card program was run along three key dimensions—whether an additional rule (the copay price) was also listed on the card, whether information about the beneficiaries was also made very public, and whether cards were sent to all eligible households or only to a subset of them. The researchers then collected data on eligible and ineligible rice purchases and prices paid for all villages. On net, they found that the card did lead to large increases in the amount of subsidies received by the households. Further, they found that the information on the card mattered: the price paid was lower when the price was indicated on the card. They also found that the card was more effective when the information was made public. Finally, public information was not sufficient on its own: The physical card also mattered.

Knowing all of this is important for understanding the mechanisms at play. It was also immediately actionable for the government, which proceeded to scale up the program and to provide cards with price information to all eligible households accompanied by posters. Cards were distributed to more than 65 million individuals. This is one occasion where the researchers' and the government's interests were exactly aligned. Is it more generally true?

Have RCTs Become Too Academic to Lead to Any Real World Changes?

RCTs have changed development economics, but have they also had significant influence in the world? If RCTs are pushing forward the frontiers of academic research by seeking to understand mechanisms and testing ideas generated by academics themselves, does this make them too academic and less useful for policy?

In this section, we argue that RCTs can contribute to policy not only by providing evidence on specific programs that can be scaled but also by changing the general climate of thinking about an issue. We then examine a case study of a funder, Development Innovations Ventures at USAID. Some of the innovations that it has funded were driven by social entrepreneurs without researcher involvement and some were tested using RCTs or had close involvement with development economics researchers. A review of this portfolio suggests that several programs involving development economics researchers and RCTs had substantial real-world influence.

Are RCTs That Are More "Academic" Less Useful for Policy?

Many studies seek not just to test a particular program but also to contribute to a body of literature that seeks to test different theories of human behavior. If citizens vote for candidates based on their ethnicity or caste, is that because of very strong preferences, clientelistic networks, or a combinations of weak preferences and no alternative information on candidate quality? Do people only value what they pay for? How important are liquidity constraints, as opposed to lack of information or low human capital, in explaining poor child health and low business profitability in low-income families?

The studies that seek to answer these questions do not always test standard development programs, although some may become development ideas. De Mel, McKenzie, and Woodruff (2012) gave cash to businesses in Sri Lanka without conditions, repayment requirements, or mentoring, something unheard of in finance programs at the time (of course, eventually, the idea of unconditional cash transfers caught on as a realistic policy option, as indicated by the success of GiveDirectly). As we have discussed above, a series of studies that focused on pricing of health goods first asked households whether they were willing to purchase a good at one price and then gave them the good at a lower price or for free, not something a regular program would do. Researchers pushed to test unconditional cash transfers (Baird, McIntosh, and Özler 2011; Haushofer and Shapiro 2013; Benhassine et al. 2015; Blattman, Fiala, and Martinez 2014), even though at the time, the political consensus favored conditional transfers.

The reason this is potentially important for policy, and not just for academic curiosity, is that even where certain program specifics do not generalize, underlying patterns in human behavior may. The finding that small incentives are effective in encouraging people to take actions that have short-run costs but long-run benefits is more likely to generalize than the finding that lentils are a successful incentive for vaccination in Rajasthan (Banerjee et al. 2010). Kremer and Glennerster (2011) review more than seventy health economics RCTs and find strong similarities in consumer behavior across countries and products, including sharp reductions in take-up of nonacute care health products with small increases in price, big increases in take-up of nonacute products with small incentives (negative prices), and no evidence that paying for something makes people more likely to use it (Kremer and Miguel 2007; Ashraf, Berry, and Shapiro 2010; Cohen and Dupas 2010; Dupas 2014a).

This body of work on prices was taken up by advocates of free distribution of insecticide treated bednets (ITNs). For many years, there had been a fierce debate on the merits of free distribution, with free distribution advocates arguing that even small prices deter the poor, while others argued that small copayments were important to ensure ITNs were utilized. Armed with the evidence from RCTs, advocates of mass free distribution have successfully pushed this approach, resulting in a dramatic rise in ITN coverage across Africa from roughly 2009 to 2015. The World Health Organization reports that forty-three of forty-seven countries in sub-Saharan Africa with ITN distribution programs provide them for free (*World Malaria Report*, World Health Organization 2015). A recent article in *Nature* (Bhatt et al. 2015) examines the sharp decline in malaria infections in sub-Saharan Africa and estimates that between 2000 and 2015, malaria interventions prevented 663 million malaria cases, most of which is attributable to the sharp rise in ITN coverage: 450 million cases of malaria and roughly 4 million deaths were prevented by ITNs from 2000 to 2015.

Beyond the specific example of malaria, the policy community is coming to a more general realization that higher prices for preventive health products can sharply decrease take-up and that price elasticity of demand can be very high (Kremer and Holla 2009; Kremer and Glennerster 2011; Dupas 2014b). These results are changing the entire approach to pricing of these products.

Another area where a body of evidence from RCTs has produced both specific policy changes and given rise to more general lessons that have profoundly changed the policy debate is on attitudes toward cash transfer programs. Arguably the biggest innovation in antipoverty and social protection policies in developing countries over the past 20 years is the growth of conditional cash transfer programs (CCTs). Beginning in Mexico, these programs have now spread to more than thirty countries, and they have arguably played an important role in the decline in poverty in Latin America (Attanasio et al. 2005; Barrera-Osorio et al. 2011; Alzúa, Cruces, and Ripani 2013; Galiani and McEwan 2013). Although many factors were at play in the spread of CCTs, we and many others think that the PROGRESA experiment (Gertler 2004; Schultz 2004) and the many subsequent experiments in other contexts[2] played a significant role. These programs influenced Mexico's decision to continue and expand CCTs after the inauguration of a new administration, the active promotion of CCTs by the Inter-American Development Bank and the World Bank, and the adoption of CCTs by many countries.

More recently, additional examination of how CCTs work is further changing the policy debate. CCTs have been shown by RCTs to not only increase the behavior on which the cash is conditional but to also improve outcomes, such as height, weight, and cognitive development (Barham, Macours, and Maluccio 2013) and reduce HIV infection (Baird,

---

2. See Glewwe and Olinto (2004), Maluccio and Flores (2005), Galiani and McEwan (2013), World Bank (2013), Benhassine et al. (2015), among others, as well as the review in Fiszbein and Schady (2009).

McIntosh, and Özler 2011). No evidence indicates that poor households spend increased cash on alcohol or other temptation goods (Haushofer and Shapiro 2013; Masterson and Lehmann 2014; Evans and Popova 2014). Indeed, the evidence suggests that the income elasticity of demand for food out of cash transfers is surprisingly high (see a review in Banerjee 2016), and food transfers do not improve nutrition more than cash transfers (Cunha 2014).

This evidence is causing a movement from a situation in which policy makers would almost never consider cash transfers to one in which cash transfers, conditional or not, are becoming an accepted tool in development policy. For example, as the world struggles to cope with refugees from war, groups such as the International Rescue Committee have drawn on RCTs of cash distributions in stable environments and with refugees (Masterson and Lehmann 2014) to strongly push for cash rather than in-kind support for refugees. In an IRC press release, David Miliband, IRC president and CEO, said:

> The spate of man-made and natural disasters enveloping innocent civilians raises profound questions not just for international politics, but for NGOs and the humanitarian sector, as well. If we keep doing "business as usual," the gap between need and provision will continue to grow. Cash distribution—alongside clear humanitarian "floor" targets in the revised Millennium Development Goals, more sustainable local partnerships and better use of evidence overall—could be part of a vital renewal of the humanitarian sector.

Early in the introduction of RCTs, Lant Pritchett (2002) argued that RCTs would never become particularly popular with policy makers, because they have reason to prefer ignorance over rigorous knowledge to continue favoring their preferred program: "It pays to be ignorant." Although in some cases policy makers may have incentives to preserve ignorance, in others they are aware of the holes in their knowledge and would like to learn more. They may have a strong attachment to a favorite program, either due to inertia or a political imperative. But the experience of running the program often persuades them that they could do it better, and they are surprisingly open to ideas about how to improve their programs. The Raskin and MGN-REGS programs mentioned above, where several teams of researchers have worked with the government, are good examples: although it was clear that the programs would continue, finding ways to make them work better was of interest.

How to Assess the Policy Success (or Not) of the RCT Agenda

It is somewhat difficult to assess the causal effect of RCTs on policy adoption. Interventions subject to RCTs are not themselves randomized, and many factors influence whether and when a particular intervention is adopted. When a program is taken up after an RCT showed it has worked, it is not always because of the RCT, and it is never just because of the RCT. Nevertheless, some have argued that the influence of RCTs on policy is actually quite low, compared to the volume of RCTs. For example, Shah et al. (2015) point out that despite the 489 completed evaluations by J-PAL affiliated researchers, there were only nine scale-up or policy influence stories on J-PAL's website at the time. But this number per se is not particularly informative: for example, it is not a census of the studies that have some impact. Not all RCTs conducted by J-PAL affiliated researchers are systematically followed up. These stories are chosen precisely because of the size of their impact and because they can be documented clearly. The absolute number of lives reached by them is quite significant—the J-PAL website tells us that more than 400 million people were reached by these programs. But the main concerns with any statistic like this are conceptual:

1. The J-PAL website does not carry statistics on studies conducted by researchers outside the J-PAL network for the very good reason that, based on our experience collecting information from DIV and J-PAL, it is far from straightforward to collect information on the extent to which RCTs have influenced policy. For example, the number does not include the hundreds of millions of people who have been reached by CCTs.

2. Many RCTs are fairly recent. Taking these to the policy level requires a lot of care, especially given the external validity issues. (Would it work in government? Would it work in a different place?) The process is therefore often slow, again for good reasons. Therefore, we should not expect a lot of these to be scaled as yet.

3. Many of the most valuable RCTs are those that test popular and highly touted policies that already exist in the world on a large-scale and show that they are in fact much less effective than previously claimed or believed. Microfinance and improved cook-stoves are two obvious examples. In such cases, success would be to slow down the spread of such policies. In such cases, one would not expect something to appear on the J-PAL scale-up page, but these are two cases where the work has probably been quite influential.

4. In some cases, the primary purpose of an RCT is not to directly affect policy, but instead to investigate an underlying theoretical mechanism, which may, in turn, indirectly influence policy. However, such cases would not appear on a list of scale-ups, even though the knowledge they have provided has impacted, albeit indirectly, a large number of people. For example, the orthodoxy in development economics had long been that the poor are "poor but rational." The accumulating evidence from RCTs has undoubtedly hastened the diffusion of the idea into development economics and development policy that poor people are not always rational. This idea is reflected for example, in both the content and the number of RCTs in the *World Development Report 2016* (World Bank 2016) on psychology and poverty. In turn, publications like this and the associated discussions influence the design of policies.

5. It is not clear what the right benchmark for success should be. We suspect that if one looked at other areas of economics, one would find that research projects influenced policy at a much lower rate than RCTs have in development policy in recent years. Moreover, one would not want to say that rapid policy influence is the sole or even the major metric by which the worth of economic research should be assessed—think of the idea of congestion pricing for road use (Vickrey 1969), which is only beginning to find real world applications.

6. Perhaps most importantly, it is worth realizing that the payoff to RCTs is likely to be the average of a highly skewed distribution. Looking at the fraction of RCTs that scale, rather than the average payoff, is therefore as misleading as looking at the fraction of any research and development effort that succeeds in terms of, say, generating a successful marketed product, because the payoff to research and development in general is typically very highly skewed. As is well known, citations across scientific disciplines appear to follow a power law distribution, with a small fraction of papers accounting for the majority of citations. This peak is followed by a steep decay, as a large portion of research papers are never cited (Radicchi, Fortunato, and Castellano 2008).[3] As we mentioned, the

---

3. For instance, in the social sciences in general, papers receive on average 0.5 citations in the first 2 years after publication, including self-citations (Klamer and Dalen 2002), whereas in mathematics, medicine, and education, the number is estimated to be less than 1 (Mansilla et al. 2007). The skewed distribution implies that the median

nine policy innovations that were listed on the J-PAL website in 2015 reached more than 200 million people, and this did not include the more than 100 million people who have been reached through India's most recent round of deworming, the millions of people who have received free bed nets (since J-PAL lists it as policy influence but does not provide a count), and the 60 million people whose water and air is less polluted because of the statewide adoption of better regulation of industrial pollution in Gujarat (again, not counted).

7. For this reason, pointing out that many R&D efforts yield low payoffs does not suggest that these are bad investments ex ante. The correct analytical question to ask is whether the expected average or marginal payoff to R&D effort in RCTs is positive or greater than that in other areas of research if one takes overall research budgets as fixed. Of course, measuring the payoff to research is inherently a difficult exercise for all sorts of conceptual reasons. There is also the added statistical difficulty that a large amount of data is needed to accurately measure the mean of a fat-tailed distribution.

What Have We Learned from the DIV Experience?

Keeping all of this in mind, we now turn to one particular example, the experience of the investments made by USAID's DIV between 2010 and 2012.

DIV holds a year-round grant competition for innovative solutions to a range of development challenges, pilots and tests them using analytical methods, and scales solutions that demonstrate widespread impact and cost-effectiveness. DIV supports novel business or organizational models; operational, behavioral or production processes; and products or services that can help address development challenges. DIV's tiered-funding model provides small grants to pilot innovations in development; medium-sized grants to rigorously test for impact and cost-effectiveness (often using RCTs) or ability to pass a market test; and larger-scale grants to help transition innovations to scale that have passed a market test or that have rigorous evidence of impact and cost effectiveness.

---

paper is never cited. Similarly, most new patents have extremely low value with a small fraction of patents accounting for much of the overall value of patents.

When DIV was established, two targets were set for the program: (1) a 15 percent social rate of return on investment, and (2) a reach of at least 75 million people worldwide, through direct investment and through broader influence on the rest of USAID. Preliminary work by DIV staff suggests that the 2010–2012 portfolio easily met the first goal, even under the conservative assumptions that all innovations supported by DIV yielded no further benefits, and even looking at only a subset of innovations that yielded financial benefits or health benefits that could be valued in terms of DALYs. Although social return is a more conceptually comprehensive measure for evaluating DIV, it is difficult to measure. By considering social returns we do not seek to evaluate DIV, but rather to look at the narrower question of whether RCTs can have real world influence. We therefore focus on examining the number of people reached by innovations supported by DIV (as well as by later adapted versions of these innovations). (Note that substantial reach is a necessary but not sufficient condition for high social return because the total social benefit of an innovation equals the net benefit per person reached times the number of people reached.) This exercise is inherently limited, so readers will have to make their own judgements about the likely impact per person reached, the likely future reach of these innovations (sustainability), and the extent to which DIV funding played an important role in the reach achieved by innovations in the DIV portfolio. What we are doing here is rather the descriptive exercise of systematically tracking a portfolio. Nevertheless, following the entire 2010–2012 DIV portfolio is interesting for a paper that explores the influence of RCTs, because the premise of DIV is specifically to fund innovations in development that have the potential to cost-effectively reach a large number of people through either the public or the private sector.

In particular, whereas many other programs have a top-down approach in which program staff identify problems in advance, choose sectors on which to focus, or set strategy in sectors, DIV follows a bottom-up approach that is deliberately open across sectors: supporting innovations that will scale commercially, innovations designed to scale through the public sector, and startups and organizations proposing to change behavior within existing large organizations. Although the bulk of DIV's outreach effort has been oriented toward traditional social entrepreneurs, DIV has also made an effort to be open to proposals from development economics researchers. To balance this openness, DIV employs a staged finance approach in which innovations only receive larger-scale support after they have passed rigorous tests. DIV provides large-scale support (stage 3) only for innovations that have rigorous evidence of impact and cost effectiveness or have demonstrated market viability. At the piloting (stage 1) and testing stages (stage 2), however, DIV has historically been open to proposals that have the potential to scale based on their cost-effectiveness, for example, even if they do not necessarily already have a management team in place capable of scaling internally or written commitments from scaling partners.[4]

This combination of approaches thus helps us ask whether the engagement with the development economics research community, and the willingness to consider early-stage investments even without a fully proven capacity to scale, came at the cost of scaling success. We can shed light on these questions by comparing the scaling record across types of projects, stages of funding, and of course by looking at the scaling record of DIV.

In the online Appendices, we provide a list of all the DIV awards from this period and a description of the innovations that have, subsequent to DIV's funding, reached more than 100,000 people. Table 10. 3 shows the results of this exercise.

Here are some key insights:

1. DIV has been relatively successful in supporting innovations that scale. A relatively high fraction of DIV awards, and an even higher fraction of DIV total investment, has gone to projects that have already reached more than 100,000 people (and a smaller but still high fraction of the awards went to projects that reached more than a million people). Thirty percent of DIV awards (13/43) have so far reached more than 100,000 people within 3–5 years.[5] These awards account for 57 percent of the total value of DIV awards in this period, or $10.98 million in total funding. Fourteen percent of DIV awards (5/43) have so far reached more

---

4. Although DIV does not require a proven pathway to scale at stages 1 or 2, a promising pathway to scale through the public or private sector (or a hybrid of the two) and strong potential demand is one of its main selection criteria, particularly at stage 2.
5. Two innovations (that reached over 100,000 people) received both a stage 1 and a stage 2 award. Thus, these twelve awards support ten separate innovations.

Table 10.3

Future reach of DIV projects, by award type

Award Stage	Number of Awards	Total Awarded Value	Fraction Reaching more than 100,000 people	Fraction Reaching more than 1,000,000 people	People Reached*	DIV Expenditure per Person Reached
Stage 1 (<$100,000)	23	$2,353,136	17% (4/24)	8% (2/24)	6,723,733	$0.35
Stage 2 (<$100,000,000)	19	$9,557,926	44% (8/18)	11% (2/18)	16,931,044	$0.56
Stage 3 (<$15 million)	1	$5,516,606	100% (1/1)	100% (1/1)	1,750,000	$3.15

*Two innovations (Voter Information Report Cards and CommCare) that reached more than 100,000 people received both stage 1 and stage 2 awards. In both cases, people reached by those innovations are counted as people reached by stage 2 awards.

than 1 million people. These awards account for 33 percent of the total value of DIV awards in this period, or $6.38 million in total funding.

Why do we say that 30 percent is "relatively successful"? A rule of thumb in the venture capital world is that 10 percent of investments yield modest success, and 1 percent yield large successes. Although we have not yet identified other funders that publish data that would allow for computation of comparable statistics, our reading of the literature and our examination of websites of some other organizations suggests that these rates compare well with those achieved over a much longer time frame by other impact-investing organizations. These results are all the more striking because, although some organizations provide funding only after a certain level of scale is reached (e.g., Acumen, Skoll Foundation), DIV often supported innovations at an early stage (as well as tests to know whether they were worth scaling up), rather than waiting until innovations had already reached a certain scale and had attracted earlier support before investing.

2. Stage 1 and stage 2 awards have a particularly low DIV expenditure per person reached and account for more than 90 percent of people reached by innovations supported by DIV during this period.

One of these early stage innovations (Consumer Action and Matatu Safety) recently received a stage 3 DIV award, but in general, stage 1 and stage 2 innovations attained high levels of reach because other funders/ entities provided support based in part on the information generated from the DIV-funded project.

3. Although the estimated DIV expenditure per person is lower for earlier stage grants, it is fairly low across the board. This is because most of the reach of DIV-supported innovations was attained without the applicants returning to DIV for additional financial support.

Though many past awardees apply for additional funding, only 7 percent of DIV's 2010–2012 portfolio of grantees received follow-on funding after the initial period of performance. More than 40 percent of DIV's 2010–2012 grantees received follow-on funding from either the public or private sector after DIV's investment. DIV's capacity to be catalytic of course partly derives from the rich funding ecosystem in which it operates, where other entities (governments, NGO, private sector firms) can adopt innovations.

4. Cost was a key determinant of which innovations scaled. The largest scale was achieved by innovations with very low costs per person.

In some cases, the innovations involved the provision of information by media or phone (including voter report cards, election monitoring), or provided behavioral "nudges" in large, existing systems (e.g., Zambian community health workers). Of course, it's important to recognize that total impact depends on the benefit per person reached times the number of people reached, and some innovations with moderate cost per person (e.g., Vision Spring) and moderate reach may generate high total social benefit because the benefit per person is very high.

5. Although some innovations reached more than 100,000, or in one case, more than 1,000,000 people through the creation and growth of a new organization designed to scale the innovation, the vast majority of reach was delivered through adoption by existing large organizations, including large firms, NGOs, and governments.

Four of the DIV-supported innovations that reached 100,000 or more consumers involved the creation of new organizations that scaled from scratch. Seven involved adoption of the innovation by existing entities that already had high levels of reach.

Of the six innovations that reached more than one million people, one was scaled by an NGO that constructed and built operations around the innovation (Evidence Action in the case of chlorine dispensers), and four did so by adoption by existing organizations (an insurance company and the Kenyan National Transport and Safety Authority in the case of stickers in matatus, the Government of India in the case of biometric monitoring, political campaigns in the case of real-time efforts to send polling station outcomes to central locations by mobile phones, and newspapers in the case of voter report cards). Existing organizations with large reach that adopted DIV-supported innovations or modified versions of these innovations included private sector firms, NGOs, and governments.

6. Innovations tested with RCTs scale not only through adoption by governments, but also through adoption by private sector firms and NGOs.

Of the ten DIV awards for innovations with RCTs that have reached more than 100,000 people, there were two clear cases in which developing country governments played the lead role (scaling of an improved approach to community health worker recruitment by the government of Zambia and biometric monitoring in India). The Kenyan government seems likely to play an important role alongside the insurance industry in scaling the Kenyan matatu safety program. Donors played a key role in provision of Potential Energy's improved cookstoves in Darfur. NGO partners played a role in a number of projects. A major lesson of this analysis is that large private firms played a major role as well (e.g., an insurance company played a key role in the matatu stickers project and newspapers published the free content when an NGO provided them with voter report cards).

7. Innovations involving RCTs or developed in part by researchers (often working in close conjunction with implementers), reach 100,000 or 1,000,000 users at a particularly high rate.

Forty-three percent (10/23)[6] of awards for which an RCT was used for evaluation or development economics researchers were involved in

---

6. Projects were coded as having development economics researchers involved if the initial proposal that was funded by DIV explicitly included the efforts of researchers. Although d.light's initial proposal included an RCT on the impacts of their products, this RCT did not take place and funding strictly supported the development of a new solar home system as well as an ex post impact evaluation of these systems. Due to these circumstances, we have not included d.light in our calculation of projects

design of the innovation reached more than 100,000 people.[7] Twenty-six percent (6/23) of these awards supported innovations that had reached more than one million people in the original or adapted form (including voter report cards, election monitoring, stickers in matatus, chlorine dispensers, and biometric attendance verification). In contrast, among the innovations not including an RCT component or a strong role for development economics researchers, only 16 percent (3/19) reached 100,000 people (Vision Spring, Mera Gao, d.light), and none reached more than one million people.[8]

One could imagine multiple hypotheses for this difference in the rates of success. First, it might be easier to reach many people by persuading large organizations and governments to adopt the innovation, and in this process, the evidence from the RCTs might have played an important role. By contrast, those innovations that did not come from the academic RCT side tried to scale by directly implementing or selling their product, which may be harder, as these innovations do not have large preexisting policies, programs, or institutions as initial partners. Second, it is often argued that academic researchers mainly want to publish, and this conflicts with their incentives to get involved in projects that are socially useful but not as creative (e.g., replication, tinkering with design). But it is also argued that journals have a strong publication bias, and it is easier to publish ideas that have worked. Ergo, development economists should have strong incentives to develop and test innovations that have a reasonable chance of success.

---

developed in part by researchers in this point. If we were to include d.light, this figure would be 11/24, or 46 percent.

7. Voter information report cards (two awards), election monitoring technology, digital attendance and medical information systems in primary health care centers, mobile tools for community health care workers (two awards), consumer action on Matatu safety, bringing safe water to scale, improved cookstoves, and recruiting community health workers.

8. Twenty-four awards incorporated an RCT component or were based on an RCT. This excludes two cases in which the initial proposal included an RCT but the ultimate actual project funded by DIV did not include an RCT: Psychometric Analysis for Entrepreneurs (AID-OAA-F-13–00028) and Affordable Access to Energy for All: Innovative Financing for Solar Systems (AID-OAA-F-13–00007). Note that because there is a lot of overlap between researcher-led projects and projects with an RCT, we cannot easily separate their impact.

Moreover, perhaps economics actually gives them some useful insights into the design of projects. Third, it may also be that the recent focus on information and behavioral economics makes them particularly interested in innovations with a low cost per user ("nudges"), which seems to be a strong predictor of success. Fourth, when researchers were involved, they were typically not just evaluators: They were fully involved in the development of the innovation (e.g., voter report cards, chlorine dispensers, a monitoring project in Afghanistan), worked closely with implementing organizations, and remained closely involved in the details of the implementation. They were in fact "researcher-entrepreneurs." Many of the ideas developed by researchers drew on the latest ideas in the field, and the data suggest that the researchers who developed these ideas were then relatively successful in working with others to scale these innovations.

8. Innovations that had already been tested through RCTs and found to have impact and potential for cost effectiveness prior to applying for DIV support accounted for three of the five innovations that reached more than one million people.

   Three of the five innovations that reached more than one million people (voter report cards, Consumer Action and Matatu Safety, and Chlorine Dispensers for Safe Water) had already been subject to RCTs before applications were submitted to DIV. Although we have not yet coded the data, we believe that there were very few applications in this category, so the rate at which proposals in this category reached more than one million people was very high (possibly 100 percent).

9. Although some DIV-supported innovations have been applied in multiple countries, most have not.

   So far, DIV-supported innovations have typically not been applied much beyond the country where they have been tested. This may be an area where future work is needed.

Conclusion

The previous discussion on the role that RCTs play in policy suggests that RCTs have influenced policy both by providing evidence on individual projects and programs and by changing thinking in development more broadly.

The biotech and information technology industries routinely build on innovations developed by researchers using frontier techniques in those fields. The evidence from DIV awards is consistent with the idea that a similar approach may be effective in development, with innovations developed in part by researchers or involving RCTs reaching 100,000 or 1,000,000 users at a particularly high rate. This is absolutely not to say that work is not needed to fine tune interventions for different contexts, or that it is not important to evaluate real-world programs that have not yet been evaluated using an RCT. But the development of new ideas that are grounded in basic science actually can lead to real-life change.

One striking lesson of this analysis is that the projects that are scaled up tend to be low-cost, well-defined, and simple. Other examples, not in this list, also fit this bill (e.g., deworming, the Raskin card). There are notable counterexamples of programs that are neither particularly cheap nor simple and have scaled up: Conditional Cash Transfers and the BRAC ultra poor programs are two examples. Furthermore, those two programs were not only scaled up where they had been tested but were also implemented in many other countries as well. Interestingly, they were initially replicated as RCTs.

Well-defined interventions are also the ones that are more likely to lead to successful research projects because they can more easily pin down a specific mechanism and be construed as a test for a theory. So the reasons RCTs have been so successful as a research tool may also be what makes them successful at leading to real-world changes.

Looking forward, we don't know what the most important pathways of influence for RCTs might turn out to be. One route is that simple, clear insights, low-cost interventions, or low-cost modification to promising existing programs get adopted, as the DIV case study suggests. That these innovations are low-cost of course does not mean that they have low impact. One lesson from decades of well-identified development research is that details are incredibly important, and that the distinction between "big" and "small" questions can be very misleading (see Banerjee and Duflo 2011, chapter 10) for a more detailed discussion).

An alternative pathway is one in which more complex interventions are replicated in many contexts and then widely adopted, following the PRO-GRESA or the BRAC model. The third pathway is that rather than focusing only on the results, policy makers and other actors adopt the experimental attitude by allowing for innovations and learning perhaps inside a specialized unit (like the White House "nudge" unit) or a cross-department fund (like the Tamil Nadu innovation fund).

But to really get the full benefits of the RCT revolution, it is not enough to do more RCTs and get some of them scaled up. A range of complementary institutions are also necessary to more effectively translate research into policy. For example, we need better systems for the production of meta-analyses and review articles and for the creation of expert panels to review the evidence. Medicine has a quite involved system for this, but even setting aside the question of how well that system works in medicine (Sim et al. 2001; Kawamoto et al. 2005), the institutions that are appropriate for medicine are not necessarily appropriate for social science and development economics in particular. These institutions are just starting to be built: The American Economic Association registry of RCTs is an example of a successful effort to build a registration platform. Its popularity suggests that the development community is receptive to these efforts.

In addition to the purely scientific infrastructure for learning, the process of going from an idea to a program at scale requires appropriate institutional support. Funders are needed to finance iterative piloting before an RCT to work out the implementation details.[9] Once an RCT has been conducted, institutional support is also needed for iterating on the intervention to prepare it for transition to scale. This includes testing ways to bring unit costs down (because the first RCT often evaluates a small pilot with high unit costs); collaborate with potential implementing partners; and mitigate potential cost increases or reduced benefits that may result from institutional and personnel differences between the pilot and scaled-up versions of an innovation (due to, for example, government procurement systems with higher transaction costs or limited government capacity to implement the intervention effectively). To get to the right scaled-up version therefore involves trying them out at scale and measuring the impact at scale. Indeed, multiple iterations may be needed until something that

---

9. Development Innovation Ventures and the Global Innovation Fund—a private fund modeled after DIV and to which DIV and other bilateral donors and impact investors contribute—explicitly encompass such a piloting phase.

is appropriate for policy can work. Figuring out how best to do the scaling in each case or how to do so in additional countries takes time, specialized human capital, and additional funding.

References

Abdulkadiroglu, Atila, Joshua Angrist, and Parag Pathak. 2014. "The Elite Illusion: Achievement Effects at Boston and New York Exam Schools." *Econometrica* 82 (1): 137–196.

Alesina, Alberto, Paola Giuliano, and Nathan Nunn. 2013. "On the Origins of Gender Roles: Women and the Plough." *Quarterly Journal of Economics* 128 (2): 469–530.

Alzúa, María Laura, Guillermo Cruces, and Laura Ripani. 2013. "Welfare Programs and Labor Supply in Developing Countries: Experimental Evidence from Latin America." *Journal of Population Economics* 26 (4): 1255–1284.

Ashraf, Nava, Oriana Bandiera, and Scott S. Lee. 2015. "Do-Gooders and Go-Getters: Career Incentives, Selection, and Performance in Public Service Delivery." Working Paper, Harvard Business School, Cambridge, MA.

Ashraf, Nava, James Berry, and Jesse M. Shapiro. 2010. "Can Higher Prices Stimulate Product Use? Evidence from a Field Experiment in Zambia." *American Economic Review* 100 (5): 2383–2413.

Athey, Susan, and Guido W. Imbens. 2017. "The Econometrics of Randomized Experiments." In *Handbook of Field Experiments*, volume 1, edited by Abhijit V. Banerjee and Esther Duflo, 73–140. Amsterdam: North-Holland.

Attanasio, Orazio P., Costas Meghir, and Ana Santiago. 2012. "Education Choices in Mexico: Using a Structural Model and a Randomized Experiment to Evaluate PRO-GRESA." *Review of Economic Studies* 79 (1): 37–66.

Attanasio, Orazio P., Erich Battistin, Emla Fitzsimons, and Marcos Vera-Hernandez. 2005. "How Effective Are Conditional Cash Transfers? Evidence from Colombia." IFS Briefing Note BN54, Institute for Fiscal Studies, London.

Attanasio, Orazio P., Camila Fernández, Emla O. A. Fitzsimons, Sally M. Grantham-McGregor, Costas Meghir, and Marta Rubio-Codina. 2014. "Using the Infrastructure of a Conditional Cash Transfer Program to Deliver a Scalable Integrated Early Child Development Program in Colombia: Cluster Randomized Controlled Trial." *BMJ* 349 (September): g5785.

Attanasio, Orazio P., Arlen Guarín, Carlos Medina, and Costas Meghir. 2017. "Vocational Training for Disadvantaged Youth in Colombia: A Long-Term Follow-Up." *American Economic Journal: Applied Economics* 9 (2): 131–143.

Baird, Sarah, Craig McIntosh, and Berk Özler. 2011. "Cash or Condition? Evidence from a Cash Transfer Experiment." *Quarterly Journal of Economics* 126 (4): 1709–1753.

Bandiera, Oriana, Robin Burgess, Narayan Das, Selim Gulesci, Imran Rasul, and Munshi Sulaiman. 2013. "Can Basic Entrepreneurship Transform the Economic Lives of the Poor?" IZA Discussion Paper 7386, Institute for the Study of Labor, Bonn.

Banerjee, Abhijit V. 2008. "Big Answers for Big Questions: The Presumption of Macroeconomics." Paper presented at Brookings Global Economy and Development Conference: What Works in Development? Thinking Big and Thinking Small, Washington, DC, May.

Banerjee, Abhijit V. 2016. "Policies for a Better-Fed World." *Review of World Economics* 152 (1): 3–17.

Banerjee, Abhijit V., and Esther Duflo. 2009. "The Experimental Approach to Development Economics." *Annual Review of Economics* 1: 151–178.

Banerjee, Abhijit V., and Esther Duflo. 2011. "Policies, Politics." In *Poor Economics: A Radical Rethinking of the Way to Fight Global Poverty,* edited by Abhijit V. Banerjee and Esther Duflo, 235–265. New York: Public Affairs.

Banerjee, Abhijit V., Esther Duflo, Rachel Glennerster, and Dhruva Kothari. 2010. "Improving Immunization Coverage in Rural India: A Clustered Randomized Controlled Evaluation of Immunization Campaigns with and without Incentives." *British Medical Journal* 340: c2220.

Banerjee, Abhijit V., and Lakshmi Iyer. 2005. "History, Institutions, and Economic Performance: The Legacy of Colonial Land Tenure Systems in India." *American Economic Review* 95 (4): 1190–1213.

Banerjee, Abhijit V., Sylvain Chassang, and Erik Snowberg. 2016. "Decision Theoretic Approaches to Experiment Design and External Validity." NBER Working Paper 22167, National Bureau of Economic Research, Cambridge, MA.

Banerjee, Abhijit V., Alice H. Amsden, Robert H. Bates, Jagdish N. Bhagwati, Angus Deaton, and Nicholas Stern. 2007. *Making Aid Work.* Cambridge, MA: MIT Press.

Banerjee, Abhijit V., Raghabendra Chattopadhyay, Esther Duflo, Daniel Keniston, and Nina Singh. 2014. "Improving Police Performance in Rajasthan, India: Experimental Evidence on Incentives, Managerial Autonomy and Training." NBER Working Paper 17912, National Bureau of Economic Research, Cambridge, MA.

Banerjee, Abhijit V., Esther Duflo, Nathanael Goldberg, Dean Karlan, Robert Osei, William Parienté, Jeremy Shapiro, Bram Thuysbaert, and Christopher Udry. 2015a. "A Multifaceted Program Causes Lasting Progress for the Very Poor: Evidence from Six Countries." *Science* 348 (6236): 1260799–1260799.

Banerjee, Abhijit V., Rema Hanna, Jordan C. Kyle, Benjamin A. Olken, and Sudarno Sumarto. 2015b. "The Power of Transparency: Information, Identification Cards and

Food Subsidy Programs in Indonesia." NBER Working Paper 20923, National Bureau of Economic Research, Cambridge, MA.

Banerjee, Abhijit, Esther Duflo, Clément Imbert, Santhosh Mathew, and Rohini Pande. 2016. "Can e-Governance Reduce Capture of Public Programs? Experimental Evidence from India's Employment Guarantee." Mimeo, MIT, Cambridge, MA.

Barham, Tania, Karen Macours, and John A. Maluccio. 2013. "More Schooling and More Learning? Effects of a Three-Year Conditional Cash Transfer Program in Nicaragua after 10 Years." IDB-WP-432, Inter-American Development Bank, Washington, DC.

Barrera-Osorio, Felipe, Marianne Bertrand, Leigh L. Linden, and Francisco Perez-Calle. 2011. "Improving the Design of Conditional Transfer Programs: Evidence from a Randomized Education Experiment in Colombia." *American Economic Journal: Applied Economics* 3 (2): 167–195.

Benhassine, Najy, Florencia Devoto, Esther Duflo, Pascaline Dupas, and Victor Pouliquen. 2015. "Turning a Shove into a Nudge? A 'Labeled Cash Transfer' for Education." *American Economic Journal: Economic Policy* 7 (3): 86–125.

Bertrand, Marianne, and Esther Duflo. 2016. "Field Experiments on Discrimination." NBER Working Paper 22014, National Bureau of Economic Research, Cambridge, MA.

Bertrand, Marianne, and Sendhil Mullainathan. 2004. "Are Emily and Greg More Employable Than Lakisha and Jamal? A Field Experiment on Labor Market Discrimination." *American Economic Review* 94 (4): 991–1013.

Bertrand, Marianne, Simeon Djankov, Rema Hanna, and Sendhil Mullainathan. 2007. "Obtaining a Driver's License in India: An Experimental Approach to Studying Corruption." *Quarterly Journal of Economics* 122 (4): 1639–1676.

Bhatt, S., D. J. Weiss, E. Cameron, D. Bisanzio, B. Mappin, U. Dalrymple, K. E. Battle, et al. 2015. "The Effect of Malaria Control on *Plasmodium falciparum* in Africa between 2000 and 2015." *Nature* 526 (7572): 207–211.

Blattman, Christopher, Nathan Fiala, and Sebastian Martinez. 2014. "Generating Skilled Self-Employment in Developing Countries: Experimental Evidence from Uganda." *Quarterly Journal of Economics* 129 (2): 697–752.

Blattman, Christopher, Julian C. Jamison, and Margaret Sheridan. 2015. "Reducing Crime and Violence: Experimental Evidence from Cognitive Behavioral Therapy in Liberia." NBER Working Paper 21204, National Bureau of Economic Research, Cambridge, MA.

Bolton, Paul, Judith Bass, Theresa Betancourt, Liesbeth Speelman, Grace Onyango, Kathleen F. Clougherty, Richard Neugebauer, Laura Murray, and Helen Verdeli. 2007. "Interventions for Depression Symptoms among Adolescent Survivors of War and Displacement in Northern Uganda: A Randomized Controlled Trial." *JAMA* 298 (5): 519–527.

Bolton, Paul, Judith Bass, Richard Neugebauer, Helen Verdeli, Kathleen F. Clougherty, Priya Wickramaratne, Liesbeth Speelman, Lincoln Ndogoni, and Myrna Weissman. 2003. "Group Interpersonal Psychotherapy for Depression in Rural Uganda: A Randomized Controlled Trial." *JAMA* 289 (23): 3117–3124.

Bursztyn, Leonardo, and Lucas C. Coffman. 2012. "The Schooling Decision: Family Preferences, Intergenerational Conflict, and Moral Hazard in the Brazilian Favelas." *Journal of Political Economy* 120 (3): 359–397.

Callen, Michael, and James D. Long. 2015. "Institutional Corruption and Election Fraud: Evidence from a Field Experiment in Afghanistan." *American Economic Review* 105 (1): 354–381.

Cameron, Drew B., Anjini Mishra, and Annette N. Brown. 2016. "The Growth of Impact Evaluation for International Development: How Much Have We Learned?" *Journal of Development Effectiveness* 8 (1): 1–21.

Chassang, Sylvain, Gerard Padró i Miquel, and Erik Snowberg. 2012. "Selective Trials: A Principal-Agent Approach to Randomized Controlled Experiments." *American Economic Review* 102 (4): 1279–1309.

Clark, Damon. 2009. "The Performance and Competitive Effects of School Autonomy." *Journal of Political Economy* 117 (4): 745–783.

Cohen, Jessica, and Pascaline Dupas. 2010. "Free Distribution or Cost-Sharing? Evidence from a Randomized Malaria Prevention Experiment." *Quarterly Journal of Economics* 125 (1): 1–45.

Congdon, William J., Jeffrey R. Kling, Jens Ludwig, and Sendhil Mullainathan. 2017. "Social Policy: Mechanism Experiments and Policy Evaluations." In *Handbook of Field Experiments*, volume 2, edited by Abhijit V. Banerjee and Esther Duflo, 389–426. Amsterdam: North-Holland.

Cunha, Jesse M. 2014. "Testing Paternalism: Cash versus In-Kind Transfers." *American Economic Journal: Applied Economics* 6 (2): 195–230.

Dal Bó, Ernesto, Frederico Finan, and Martín A. Rossi. 2013. "Strengthening State Capabilities: The Role of Financial Incentives in the Call to Public Service." *Quarterly Journal of Economics* 128 (3): 1169–1218.

Deaton, Angus. 2010. "Instruments, Randomization, and Learning about Development." *Journal of Economic Literature* 48 (2): 424–455.

de Janvry, Alain, Elisabeth Sadoulet, and Tavneet Suri. 2017. "Field Experiments in Developing Country Agriculture." In *Handbook of Field Experiments*, volume 2, edited by Abhijit V. Banerjee and Esther Duflo, 427–466. Amsterdam: North-Holland.

Dell, Melissa. 2010. "The Persistent Effects of Peru's Mining Mita." *Econometrica* 78 (6): 1863–1903.

de Mel, Suresh, David McKenzie, and Christopher Woodruff. 2012. "One-Time Transfers of Cash or Capital Have Long-Lasting Effects on Microenterprises in Sri Lanka." *Science* 335 (6071): 962–966.

Dizon-Ross, Rebecca, Pascaline Dupas, and Jonathan Robinson. 2017. "Governance and the Effectiveness of Public Health Subsidies: Evidence from Ghana, Kenya and Uganda." *Journal of Public Economics* 156: 150–169.

Dobbie, Will, and Roland G. Fryer, Jr. 2014. "The Impact of Attending a School with High-Achieving Peers: Evidence from New York City Exam Schools." *American Economic Journal: Applied Economics* 6 (3): 58–75.

Duflo, Esther. 2004. "Scaling up and Evaluation." Paper presented at the Annual Bank Conference on Development Economics (ABCDE), Bangalore, May 21–22.

Duflo, Esther, and Michael Kremer. 2005. "Use of Randomization in the Evaluation of Development Effectiveness." In *Evaluating Development Effectiveness*, edited by George Keith Pitman, Osvaldo N. Feinstein, and Gregory K. Ingram, 205–230. New Brunswick, NJ: Transaction.

Duflo, Esther, Rachel Glennerster, and Michael Kremer. 2007. "Using Randomization in Development Economics Research: A Toolkit." In *Handbook of Development Economics*, volume 4, edited by T. Paul Schultz and John A. Strauss, 3895–3962. Amsterdam: Elsevier.

Duflo, Esther, Michael Kremer, and Jonathan Robinson. 2008. "How High Are Rates of Return to Fertilizer? Evidence from Field Experiments in Kenya." *American Economic Review* 98 (2): 482–488.

Duflo, Esther, Michael Greenstone, Rohini Pande, and Nicholas Ryan. 2013a. "What Does Reputation Buy? Differentiation in a Market for Third-Party Auditors." *American Economic Review* 103 (3): 314–319.

Duflo, Esther, Michael Greenstone, Rohini Pande, and Nicholas Ryan. 2013b. "Truth-Telling by Third-Party Auditors and the Response of Polluting Firms: Experimental Evidence from India." *Quarterly Journal of Economics* 128 (4): 1499–1545.

Duflo, Esther, Michael Kremer, Jonathan Robinson and Frank Schilbach. 2017. "Technology Diffusion and Appropriate Use: Evidence from Western Kenya." Working Paper, MIT, Cambridge, MA.

Dupas, Pascaline. 2014a. "Short-Run Subsidies and Long-Run Adoption of New Health Products: Evidence From a Field Experiment." *Econometrica* 82 (1): 197–228.

Dupas, Pascaline. 2014b. "Getting Essential Health Products to Their End Users: Subsidize, But How Much?" *Science* 345 (6202): 1279–1281.

Dupas, Pascaline, and Edward Miguel. 2017. "Impacts and Determinants of Health Levels in Low-Income Countries." In *Handbook of Field Experiments*, volume 2, edited by Abhijit V. Banerjee and Esther Duflo, 3–93. Amsterdam: North-Holland.

Dustan, Andrew, Alain de Janvry, and Elisabeth Sadoulet. 2015. "Flourish or Fail? The Risky Reward of Elite High School Admission in Mexico City." Department of Economics Working Paper 15–00002, Vanderbilt University, Nashville.

Evans, David K., and Anna Popova. 2014. "Cash Transfers and Temptation Goods: A Review of Global Evidence." Policy Research Working Paper 6886, World Bank, Washington, DC.

Finan, Frederico, Benjamin A. Olken, and Rohini Pande. 2015. "The Personnel Economics of the State." NBER Working Paper 21825, National Bureau of Economic Research, Cambridge, MA.

Fisher, Ronald Aylmer. 1925. *Statistical Methods for Research Workers*. Guildford, UK: Genesis.

Fiszbein, Ariel, and Norbert Schady. 2009. *Conditional Cash Transfers: Reducing Present and Future Poverty*. Washington, DC: World Bank.

Freedman, David A. 2006. "Statistical Models for Causation: What Inferential Leverage Do They Provide?" *Evaluation Review* 30 (6): 691–713.

Galiani, Sebastian, and Patrick J. McEwan. 2013. "The Heterogeneous Impact of Conditional Cash Transfers." *Journal of Public Economics* 103 (Supplement C): 85–96.

Gertler, Paul. 2004. "Do Conditional Cash Transfers Improve Child Health? Evidence from PROGRESA's Control Randomized Experiment." *American Economic Review* 94 (2): 336–341.

Glennerster, Rachel. 2017. "The Practicalities of Running Randomized Evaluations: Partnerships, Measurement, Ethics, and Transparency." In *Handbook of Field Experiments*, volume 1, edited by Abhijit V. Banerjee and Esther Duflo, 175–243. Amsterdam: North-Holland.

Glewwe, Paul, and Pedro Olinto. 2004. "Evaluating the Impact of Conditional Cash Transfers on Schooling: An Experimental Analysis of Honduras PRAF Program." Manuscript, University of Minnesota, St. Paul.

Glewwe, Paul, Michael Kremer, and Sylvie Moulin. 2009. "Many Children Left Behind? Textbooks and Test Scores in Kenya." *American Economic Journal: Applied Economics* 1 (1): 112–135.

Gueron, Judy. M. 2017. "The Politics and Practice of Social Experiments: Seeds of a Revolution." In *Handbook of Field Experiments*, volume 1, edited by Abhijit V. Banerjee and Esther Duflo, 27–69. Amsterdam: North-Holland.

Hanna, Rena, and Dean Karlan. 2017. "Designing Social Protection Programs: Using Theory and Experimentation to Understand How to Help Combat Poverty." In

Handbook of Field Experiments, volume 2, edited by Abhijit V. Banerjee and Esther Duflo, 515–553. Amsterdam: North-Holland.

Haushofer, Johannes, and Jeremy Shapiro. 2013. "Household Response to Income Changes: Evidence from an Unconditional Cash Transfer Program in Kenya." Mimeo, Massachusetts Institute of Technology, Cambridge, MA.

Heckman, James J. 1992. "Randomization and Social Policy Evaluation." In *Evaluating Welfare and Training Programs*, edited by Charles Manski and Irwin Garfinkel, 201–230. Cambridge MA: Harvard University Press.

International Rescue Committee. 2014. "IRC releases evaluation: Cash transfers work for refugees in emergencies." International Rescue Committee, New York.

Karlan, Dean S., and Jonathan Zinman. 2008. "Credit Elasticities in Less-Developed Economies: Implications for Microfinance." *American Economic Review* 98 (3): 1040–1068.

Kawamoto, Kensaku, Caitlin A. Houlihan, E. Andrew Balas, and David F. Lobach. 2005. "Improving Clinical Practice Using Clinical Decision Support Systems: A Systematic Review of Trials to Identify Features Critical to Success." *BMJ* 330 (7494): 765.

Khan, Adnan Q., Asim I. Khwaja, and Benjamin A. Olken. 2016. "Tax Farming Redux: Experimental Evidence on Performance Pay for Tax Collectors." *Quarterly Journal of Economics* 131 (1): 219–271.

Klamer, Arjo, and Hendrik P. van Dalen. 2002. "Attention and the Art of Scientific Publishing." *Journal of Economic Methodology* 9 (3): 289–315.

Kreindler, Gabriel. 2018. "The Welfare Effect of Road Congestion Pricing: Experimental Evidence and Equilibrium Implications." Job Market Paper, MIT, Cambridge, MA.

Kremer, Michael. 2003. "Randomized Evaluations of Educational Programs in Developing Countries: Some Lessons." *American Economic Review* 93 (2): 102–106.

Kremer, Michael, and Rachel Glennerster. 2011. "Improving Health in Developing Countries: Evidence from Randomized Evaluations." In *Handbook of Health Economics*, volume 2, edited by Mark V. Pauly, Thomas G. Mcguire, and Pedro P. Barros, 201–315. Amsterdam: Elsevier.

Kremer, Michael, and Alaka Holla. 2009. "Pricing and Access: Lessons from Randomized Evaluations in Education and Health." In *What Works in Development? Thinking Big and Thinking Small*, edited by William Easterly and Jessica Cohen, 91–129. Washington, DC: Brookings Institution Press.

Kremer, Michael, and Edward Miguel. 2007. "The Illusion of Sustainability." *Quarterly Journal of Economics* 122 (3): 1007–1065.

Lucas, Adrienne M., and Isaac M. Mbiti. 2014. "Effects of School Quality on Student Achievement: Discontinuity Evidence from Kenya." *American Economic Journal: Applied Economics* 6 (3): 234–263.

Maluccio, John A., and Rafael Flores. 2005. "Impact Evaluation of a Conditional Cash Transfer Program: The Nicaraguan Red de Protección Social." IFPRI Research Report 141, International Food Policy Research Institute, Washington, DC.

Mansilla, Ricardo, Elke Köppen, Germinal Cocho, and Pedro Miramontes. 2007. "On the Behavior of Journal Impact Factor Rank-Order Distribution." *Journal of Informetrics* 1 (2): 155–160.

Masterson, Daniel, and Christian Lehmann. 2014. "Emergency Economies: The Impact of Cash Assistance in Lebanon." International Rescue Committee, New York.

Meager, Rachael. 2016. "Understanding the Impact of Microcredit Expansions: A Bayesian Hierarchical Analysis of 7 Randomised Experiments." Working Paper, MIT, Cambridge, MA.

Muralidharan, Karthik, and Venkatesh Sundararaman. 2015. "The Aggregate Effect of School Choice: Evidence from a Two-Stage Experiment in India." *Quarterly Journal of Economics* 130 (3): 1011–1066.

Muralidharan, Karthik, Paul Niehaus, and Sandip Sukhtankar. 2016. "Building State Capacity: Evidence from Biometric Smartcards in India." *American Economic Review* 106 (10): 2895–2929.

Neyman, Jerzy. [1923] 1990. "On the Application of Probability Theory to Agricultural Experiments. Essay on Principles. Section 9." Translated and edited by Dorota M. Dabrowska and Terence P. Speed. *Statistical Science* 5 (4): 465–472.

Olken, Benjamin A. 2007. "Monitoring Corruption: Evidence from a Field Experiment in Indonesia." *Journal of Political Economy* 115 (2): 200–249.

Padró i Miquel, Gerard, Nancy Qian, and Yang Yao. 2014. "Social Fragmentation, Public Goods and Elections: Evidence from China." NBER Working Paper 18633, National Bureau of Economic Research, Cambridge, MA.

Patel, Vikram, Helen A. Weiss, Neerja Chowdhary, Smita Naik, Sulochana Pednekar, Sudipto Chatterjee, Mary J. De Silva, et al. 2010. "Effectiveness of an Intervention Led by Lay Health Counsellors for Depressive and Anxiety Disorders in Primary Care in Goa, India (MANAS): A Cluster Randomised Controlled Trial." *Lancet* 376 (9758): 2086–2095.

Pritchett, Lant. 2002. "It Pays to Be Ignorant: A Simple Political Economy of Rigorous Program Evaluation." *Journal of Policy Reform* 5 (4): 251–469.

Radicchi, Filippo, Santo Fortunato, and Claudio Castellano. 2008. "Universality of Citation Distributions: Toward an Objective Measure of Scientific Impact." *PNAS* 104 (45): 17268–17272.

Rao, Gautam, Frank Schilbach, and Heather Schofield. n.d. "Sleepless in Chennai: The Economic Effects of Sleep Deprivation among the Poor." Working Paper, University of Pennsylvania, Philadelphia.

Ravallion, Martin. 2012. "Fighting Poverty One Experiment at a Time: A Review of Abhijit Banerjee and Esther Duflo's 'Poor Economics: A Radical Rethinking of the Way to Fight Global Poverty.'" *Journal of Economic Literature* 50 (1): 103–114.

Rigol, Natalia, Reshmaan Hussam, and Giovanni Regianni. 2017. "Habit Formation and Rational Addiction." Harvard Business School Working Paper 18-030, Cambridge, MA.

Rubin, Donald B. 1974. "Estimating Causal Effects of Treatments in Experimental and Observational Studies." *Journal of Educational Psychology* 66 (5): 668–670.

Rubin, Donald B. 1981. "Estimation in Parallel Randomized Experiments." *Journal of Educational Statistics* 6 (4): 377–401.

Schilbach, Frank. 2015. "Alcohol and Self-Control: A Field Experiment in India." Working Paper, MIT, Cambridge, MA.

Schultz, T. Paul. 2004. "School Subsidies for the Poor: Evaluating the Mexican PROGRESA Poverty Program." *Journal of Development Economics* 74 (1): 199–250.

Shah, Neil Buddy, Paul Wang, Andrew Fraker, and Daniel Gastfriend. 2015. "Evaluations with Impact: Decision-Focused Impact Evaluation as a Practical Policymaking Tool." 3ie Working Paper 25, International Initiative for Impact Evaluation, New Delhi.

Sim, Ida, Paul Gorman, Robert A. Greenes, R. Brian Haynes, Bonnie Kaplan, Harold Lehmann, and Paul C. Tang. 2001. "Clinical Decision Support Systems for the Practice of Evidence-Based Medicine." *Journal of the American Medical Informatics Association* 8 (6): 527–534.

Todd, Petra E., and Kenneth I. Wolpin. 2006. "Assessing the Impact of a School Subsidy Program in Mexico: Using a Social Experiment to Validate a Dynamic Behavioral Model of Child Schooling and Fertility." *American Economic Review* 96 (5): 1384–1417.

Udry, Christopher. 1995. "Risk and Saving in Northern Nigeria." *American Economic Review* 85 (5): 1287–1300.

Vickrey, William S. 1969. "Congestion Theory and Transport Investment." *American Economic Review* 59 (2): 251–260.

Vivalt, Eva. 2015. "How Much Can We Generalize from Impact Evaluations? Are They Worthwhile?" Mimeo, Stanford University, Palo Alto, CA.

World Bank. 2013. *Philippines Conditional Cash Transfer Program: Impact Evaluation 2012*. Washington, DC: World Bank.

World Bank. 2016. *World Development Report 2016: Digital Dividends*. Washington, DC: World Bank.

World Health Organization. 2015. *World Malaria Report 2015*. Geneva: World Health Organization.

Comment: David McKenzie

The rise and normalization of randomized controlled trials (RCTs) as an important part of the toolkit of development economists has been rapid, with much debate as to whether this is a cause for celebration or concern. Abhijit, Esther, and Michael have been the early pioneers and proponents of the use of RCTs in development economics, and their paper represents an important stocktaking exercise, documenting this rise and attempting to draw out some of the consequences of this process for both research and policy. I group my comments around three themes: putting the rise of RCTs in perspective, considering how they have affected the practice of research, and attempting to understand how they have and have not influenced policy.

The Rise of RCTs in Perspective

Their paper documents the rapid growth in the number of RCTs published in top journals, from 0 papers in 2000 to 32 papers in 2015. In table 10.4, I extend this analysis by also considering development economics papers published in three leading general interest economics journals considered to be in the next tier below the top-five journals (*American Economic Journal: Applied Economics*, *Review of Economics and Statistics*, and *Economic Journal*), papers published in three leading development economics journals (*Journal of Development Economics*, *Economic Development and Cultural Change*, and *World Bank Economic Review*), and in *World Development*, the leading multidisciplinary journal of development. I consider papers published in 2015 and define development economics papers in the general interest journals as those with an "O" (development economics) *Journal of Economic Literature* classification code.

Table 10.4

RCTs as a share of development papers published in 2015, by journal type

	Number of Development Papers	Number that are RCTs	Percent RCT
Top five journals	32	10	31.3
Good general interest	32	14	43.8
American Economic Journal: Applied Economics	16	10	62.5
Economic Journal	8	1	12.5
Review of Economics and Statistics	8	3	37.5
Leading development journals	115	15	13.0
Journal of Development Economics	70	9	12.9
Economic Development and Cultural Change	24	5	20.8
World Bank Economic Review	21	1	4.8
World Development	275	5	1.8
All development papers	454	44	9.7

Source: Top five journals data are from Banerjee, Duflo and Kremer (2016). Data for other journals collected by author. Papers at good general interest journals classified as development if they have an "O" code in the *Journal of Economic Literature* (JEL) classification system. Counts exclude editorials, comments, rejoinders, corrigendum, the papers and proceedings issue of the *World Bank Economic Review* (WBER), and the 125th anniversary issue of the *Economic Journal* (EJ).

Several points emerge from this table that I believe are important for putting the rise of RCTs in perspective and for considering their influence on policy. First, despite the rapid growth, the majority of development economics papers published in even the top-five journals are not RCTs. Second, RCTs make up a much higher share of development papers in general interest journals than they do in development journals. Third, most published development papers are not being published in the top journals but in field journals. As a result, out of the 454 development papers published in these fourteen journals in 2015, only 44 are RCTs (9.7 percent). The consequence is that RCT studies are only a small share of all development research taking place. I believe this is evidence against the (perhaps strawman) argument that RCTs have crowded out other development research, and policy makers looking for advice on questions RCTs can't answer are missing out as a result.

Their paper also documents how RCTs have become more common among younger researchers, showing that BREAD members who graduated more recently are more likely to have done RCTs than those who graduated longer ago. This observation has led to a second caricature or strawman argument: that the "best and brightest talent of a generation of development economists have been devoted to producing rigorous impact evaluations about topics that are easy to randomize (e.g., Pritchett 2014) and that they take a "randomize or bust" attitude, whereby they turn down many interesting research questions if they can't randomize (e.g., Ravallion 2009).

To explore this, I examined the publication records of the sixty-five BREAD affiliates (this is the group of more junior members), restricting attention to the fifty-three researchers who had graduated in 2011 or earlier (to give them time to have published). The median researcher had published nine papers, and the median share of their papers which were RCTs was 13 percent. Focusing on the subset of those who have published at least one RCT, the mean (median) percentage of their published papers that are RCTs is 35 percent (30 percent), and the 10–90 range is 11–60 percent. So young researchers who publish RCTs also do write and publish papers that are not RCTs. Indeed, this is also true of Abhijit, Esther, and Michael— although known as the leaders of the "randomista" movement, the top-cited papers of all three researchers are not RCTs.

The Influence of RCTs on Development Research

Abhijit, Esther, and Michael document several important ways that RCTs have affected the way development economics research is done. I agree with their claims that RCTs have raised the bar for nonexperimental research in terms of thinking about credible identification, and that RCTs have spurred creative new ways of measurement. I want to note two other areas of influence.

The first, extremely positive, influence has been making it commonplace for researchers to actually talk to the people and firms they are studying. This is a big change from the era when most development research consisted of researchers downloading a dataset like the Penn World Tables or Living Standards Measurement Surveys, attempting to estimate some model or test some theory, and then writing the paper without ever talking to anyone in the country being studied. Indeed, this categorizes well my dissertation research: I was interested in understanding why people in Taiwan continued to save so much when their incomes had been rising rapidly for years. I carefully worked out new econometric theory and estimated and tested models of several competing consumption theories, but never asked directly any households in Taiwan "Why do you save so much?" I likewise have been on several World Bank missions where projects were being designed by talking to policy makers and perhaps a handpicked set of existing beneficiaries, and the idea of just walking into an average neighborhood and talking to some randomly selected small businesses was seen as a surprising thing to do. RCTs make this more commonplace, and they also make it much more likely that researchers actually talk to the implementers of the programs they are trying to study.

However, I also think that RCTs do affect to some extent which questions researchers work on. As noted above, there are many researchers, and most research done in development economics is still not done via RCTs. I think it is fair to say that probably some questions have been answered only because they could be answered cleanly by an experiment, and these questions would not have otherwise had researchers working on them. As I argue in the next section, it is unclear whether this is necessarily a bad thing, as it has resulted in researchers getting much more involved in the messy business of understanding how policies are implemented, which otherwise had not received much research attention.

The Influence of RCTs on Development Policy

I think it is fair to say that RCTs have had much more influence on how development economics policy is implemented rather than on what is done. Many of the questions answered by RCTs fall into the category of helping policy makers better target, or better implement, a policy they have already decided to do. For example, should grants be given conditionally or unconditionally? How can government workers be incentivized to provide the services they are meant to provide? Should mosquito nets be given out for free or offered at a price? Will people use savings products more if offered commitments or reminders? This use of RCTs is very similar to the main use of RCTs in a lot of businesses, where A-B testing is used to fine tune products and decide how to best target customers.

When it comes to what is done, I make the distinction between efforts to try to make marginal improvements in the lives of people and firms, given the economic structure they operate in, and attempts to spur the types of changes from a stagnant, largely rural, agrarian economy to a vibrant, innovative, largely urban manufacturing and services-based economy that we associate with the process of development. Much of the early RCT research was focused on the former, and many of the DIV scale-up cases profiled by Banerjee et al. also fall into this case—how can we make traffic a little less risky, water a bit cleaner, poor households get a little more electricity, and so forth. Success here is largely in terms of making poor people a little bit less poor, or making life a little easier for them. This is an important class of policies, and one where RCTs have had some policy influence.

In contrast, until recently there have been far fewer RCTs that help policy makers attempt to test policies associated with a more structural transformation—how do we get more firms innovating and growing? How do we get people to move out of poor places with few job prospects to places with better prospects? However, this is an area where RCTs are rapidly expanding, with examples like Bryan, Chowdhury, and Mobarak (2014), Atkin, Khandewal, and Osman (2017), McKenzie (2015), Beam, McKenzie, and Yang (2016), and Cusolito, Dautovic, and McKenzie (2018) showing that RCTs can also provide useful policy advice for these questions as well.

A final point I want to make is to argue against the idea that policy makers can easily substitute for RCTs by rapid, iterative learning-by-doing processes. Such an approach may be possible in some environments, but it is very difficult to learn by doing in some situations. One reason for this is that people often find it hard to generate accurate counterfactuals for themselves, even when they have gone through a program, so McKenzie (2018) finds that both treatment and control groups overestimate the effect that winning a business plan competition would have, even after the fact. Second, so many factors influence outcomes that RCTs often need hundreds or thousands of observations to detect an effect, and it is impossible for individuals to extract signal from noise to determine whether their actions are working. As an extreme example, Lewis and Rao (2015) show that firms often cannot know whether their marketing campaigns are working, even when testing on millions of customers.

References

Atkin, David, Amit Khandewal, and Adam Osman. 2017. "Exporting and Firm Performance: Evidence from a Randomized Experiment." *Quarterly Journal of Economics* 132(2): 551–615.

Banerjee, Abhijit V., Esther Duflo, and Michael Kremer. 2016. "The Influence of Randomized Controlled Trials on Development Economics Research and on Development Policy." Paper prepared for the World Bank's "The State of Economics, The State of the World" Conference, September 2016.

Beam, Emily A., David McKenzie, and Dean Yang. 2016. "Unilateral Facilitation Does Not Raise International Labor Migration from the Philippines." *Economic Development and Cultural Change* 64 (2): 323–368.

Bryan, Gharad, Shyamal Chowdhury, and Ahmed Mushfiq Mobarak. 2014. "Underinvestment in a Profitable Technology: The Case of Seasonal Migration in Bangladesh." *Econometrica* 82 (5): 1671–1748.

Cusolito, Ana Paula, Ernest Dautovic, and David McKenzie. 2018. "Can Government Intervention Make Firms More Investment-Ready? A Randomized Experiment in the Western Balkans." Policy Research Working Paper 8541, Impact Evaluation Series, World Bank, Washington, DC.

Lewis, Randall A., and Justin M. Rao. 2015. "The Unfavorable Economics of Measuring the Returns to Advertising." *Quarterly Journal of Economics* 130 (4): 1941–1973.

McKenzie, David. 2017. "Identifying and Spurring High-Growth Entrepreneurship: Experimental Evidence from a Business Plan Competition." *American Economic Review* 107(8): 2278–2307.

McKenzie, David. 2018. "Can Business Owners Form Accurate Counterfactuals? Eliciting Treatment and Control Beliefs about Their Outcomes in the Alternative Treatment Status." *Journal of Business and Economic Statistics* 36 (4): 714–722.

Pritchett, Lant. 2014. "Is Your Impact Evaluation Asking Questions That Matter? A Four Part Smell Test." *Views from the Center* (blog), November 6. http://www.cgdev.org/blog/your-impact-evaluation-asking-questions-matter-four-part-smell-test.

Ravallion, Martin. 2009. "Should the Randomistas Rule?" *Economists' Voice* 6 (2): 1–5.

Comment: Martin Ravallion

Randomized Trials and Development Policy

> Measure what is important, don't make important what you can measure.
> —Robert McNamara, president of the World Bank, 1968–1981

Randomized controlled trials (RCTs) are on the menu of options for development impact evaluation. That is not news, for it has been true for at least 40 years.[1] What has changed over the past 10–15 years is the academic popularity of RCTs. The chapter by Banerjee, Duflo, and Kremer (BDK) describes and reflects on the expanding use of RCTs in development economics. The authors have been at the forefront of this change.

In theory, the idea of an RCT is simple enough. Access to the program is randomly assigned to some units, with others set aside as a control group. The impact is then estimated by the difference in the sample mean outcomes between treated and control groups. This converges toward the true mean impact in the population as the sample sizes increase.

In practice, RCTs are rarely perfect, their internal validity is rarely assured, and their external validity is often questionable. As argued by Deaton and Cartwright (2018), these limitations do not appear to be well understood among practitioners. It does not help that prominent advocates often make unguarded claims that exaggerate the virtues of RCTs. For example, it is clearly not true that "any difference between treatment and control units reflects the impact of the treatment," as BDK say, because there is always some experimental error (including, of course, sampling error).

---

1. The earliest development RCT that I know of was done in 1978 by the World Bank and was published in 1981, namely, Jamison et al. (1981).

The concerns go deeper. Not even the theoretical rationale for randomization is as clear as advocates claim. Indeed, quite generally, there exists a deterministic (nonrandom) assignment of treatment status (based on continuous covariates) that minimizes the expected error variance, as shown by Kasy (2016). This holds for a given sample size. Comparing methods, it makes more sense to fix the budget for the evaluation than to fix the sample size. RCTs can be costly. With a given budget, RCTs will often have lower sample sizes than are possible with observational studies (OSs). An OS can then turn out to be closer to the truth in practice, even if it comes with a bias (Ravallion 2018).

Has the new popularity of RCTs in development research helped inform development policy making? That is not the only reason we might do RCTs; another is to better understand how an economy works—to identify key structural parameters. However, policy making is an important reason. BDK clearly agree. Indeed, that is explicitly the goal of the premier institution for promoting RCTs in development, namely, the Abdul Latif Jameel Poverty Action Lab (J-PAL), founded by two of the authors. On the bio page of Banerjee and Duflo (2011), it is said that "J-PAL's mission is to reduce poverty by ensuring that policy is based on scientific evidence." ("Scientific evidence" can be taken as code for RCTs.) J-PAL and other advocates of RCTs have framed their task as that of figuring out what works and what does not, to scale up the former and scale down the latter. Is that what is happening now?

To inform antipoverty policy making, researchers ideally should be filling the gaps between what we know about the effectiveness of policies and what policy makers need to know. As economists, we should first ask ourselves: Why do such gaps exist? Imperfect information plays a role. Here the problem is that development practitioners cannot easily assess the quality and expected benefits of an evaluation, to weigh against the costs. Compared to the complex econometric methods used in some OSs, the simplicity of an RCT helps practitioners understand what is being done. However (as already noted), that understanding is not always as deep as it needs to be for practitioners to properly assess the lessons from an RCT, including its limits.

There are also important externalities. The benefits of an evaluation are rarely confined to that specific project but instead spill over to future projects. These external benefits are probably greater for OSs than for RCTs, for which external validity has been a recurrent concern (see, for example, Pritchett and Sandefur 2015). In addition, current project managers cannot be expected to take proper account of the external benefits to other projects when deciding how much to spend on their own project's evaluation. Thus there may well be an underinvestment in OSs, which generate more externalities, relative to RCTs.

Knowledge gaps also stem from misalignments of evaluative effort. One aspect is that development evaluators often ignore the scope for fungibility. Recipients (governmental or not) can reallocate their own efforts in response to new funding, such as development aid. As a consequence of such fungibility, donors are often implicitly supporting something else and evaluating the wrong program from the point of view of assessing their impact. Then evaluative efforts are not aligned well with development efforts. This applies as much to RCTs as to OSs.

Methodological preferences on the part of evaluators can reinforce such misalignments, and here the emphasis on RCTs may well be hurting our progress in addressing important knowledge gaps. There are both *output* and *substitution* effects of the RCT boom. The output effect is obvious, as documented by BDK. The substitution effect relates to the methods used. There has been a marked increase in the share of journal articles on development economics that use RCTs. But that is not where a methodological substitution is worrying; instead, it is in policy evaluation. We have seen a marked switch in favor of RCTs in institutions such as the World Bank. The Bank's own Independent Evaluation Group reports that more than 80 percent of the impact evaluations starting in 2007–2010 used randomization, compared with 57 percent in 2005–2006 and only 19 percent in prior years (World Bank 2012).

A problem in overall policy evaluation stems from the fact that randomization is clearly only feasible for a nonrandom subset of policies and settings, so we lose our ability to comprehensively address our knowledge gaps (Ravallion 2009, 2018). For example, it is rarely feasible to randomize the location of medium- to large-scale infrastructure projects and sectoral and economy-wide reforms, which are core activities in almost any poor country's development strategy. Indeed, the very idea of randomized assignment is antithetical to the goals of many development programs, which typically aim to reach certain types of people or places. Governments will (hopefully) be able to do better in reaching poor people than a random assignment would. Randomization also tends to be better suited to relatively simple programs, with clearly identified participants and nonparticipants, rather short time horizons, and little scope for the costs or benefits to spill over to nonparticipants.

There are both supply and demand sides to this misalignment. On the supply side, the reality today is that graduate students and their teachers are wandering around looking for something they can randomly assign. If randomization is not feasible for the question being posed, then research-ers are often drawn to ask other questions. Governments in the developing world are having a harder time finding someone to help evaluate those public programs for which randomization is not a feasible option.

The potential biases go further. On the demand side, governments (and development agencies) are largely free to choose what gets evaluated. Even when they agree to an RCT, they can choose those programs for which they do not care what the verdict will be. Other programs will not get evaluated in equilibrium. (And, as noted, they may include what was really being funded by aid.) The risks are plain.

If we are really concerned about obtaining reliable estimates of the impact of the portfolio of development policies, we should choose a rep-resentative sample from that portfolio and then find the best method for each of the selected programs/policies, with randomization as only one of a number of options. That is not what is happening now.

References

Banerjee, Abhijit V., and Esther Duflo. 2011. *Poor Economics: A Radical Rethinking of the Way to Fight Global Poverty*. New York: Public Affairs.

Deaton, Angus, and Nancy Cartwright. 2018. "Understanding and Misunderstand-ing Randomized Controlled Trials." *Social Science and Medicine* 210: 2–21.

Jamison, Dean, Barbara Searle, Klaus Galda, and Stephen P. Heyneman. 1981. "Improving Elementary Mathematics Education in Nicaragua: An Experimental Study of the Impact of Textbooks and Radio on Achievement." *Journal of Educational Psychology* 73 (4): 556–567.

Kasy, Maximilian. 2016. "Why Experimenters Might Not Always Want to Random-ize, and What They Should Do Instead." *Political Analysis* 24: 324–338.

Pritchett, Lant, and Justin Sandefur. 2015. "Learning from Experiments When Con-text Matters." *American Economic Review: Papers and Proceedings* 105 (5): 471–475.

Ravallion, Martin. 2009. "Should the Randomistas Rule?" *Economists' Voice* 6 (2): 1–5.

Ravallion, Martin. 2018. "Should the Randomistas (Continue to) Rule?" Working Paper 492, Center for Global Development, Washington, DC.

World Bank. 2012. *World Bank Group Impact Evaluations: Relevance and Effectiveness.* Independent Evaluation Group, World Bank, Washington, DC.

Contributors

Philippe Aghion is a professor at the College de France and at the London School of Economics.

Ingela Alger is research faculty at the Toulouse School of Economics, research director at Center National de la Recherche Scientifique (CNRS), and director of the biology program at the Institute for Advanced Study (IAST) in Toulouse.

Kenneth Arrow was Joan Kenney Professor of Economics and professor of operations research, emeritus at Stanford University. He was the joint winner of the 1972 Nobel Memorial Prize in Economic Sciences.

Abhijit Vinayak Banerjee is the Ford Foundation International Professor of Economics at MIT and co-director of J-PAL.

Kaushik Basu is Carl Marks Professor of International Studies at Cornell University and former senior vice president and chief economist of the World Bank.

Lawrence E. Blume is Visiting Research Professor at the Institute for Advanced Studies, Vienna, and member of the Santa Fe Institute's external faculty.

Guillermo Calvo is professor of economics, international, and public affairs at Columbia University.

Francesco Caselli is Norman Sosnow Chair in Economics at the London School of Economics.

Aslı Demirgüç-Kunt is director of research at the World Bank.

Shantayanan Devarajan is senior director for development economics at the World Bank.

Esther Duflo is the Abdul Latif Jameel Professor of Poverty Alleviation and Development Economics at MIT and co-director of J-PAL.

Sam Fankhauser is at Grantham Research Institute on Climate and the Environment and Centre of Climate Change Economics and Policy (CCCEP) at the London School of Economics and Political Science.

James E. Foster is Oliver T. Carr Professor of International Affairs and professor of economics at the George Washington University.

Varun Gauri is senior economist in the Development Economics Vice Presidency of the World Bank. He co-leads the Mind, Behavior, and Development Unit (eMBeD), and was co-director of the World Development Report 2015: *Mind, Society, and Behavior*.

Xavier Giné is a lead economist on the Finance and Private Sector Development Team of the Development Research Group at the World Bank.

Gaël Giraud is chief economist and executive director of the Innovation, Research and Knowledge Directorate at the Agence Française de Développement (AFD).

Gita Gopinath is the economic counsellor and director of research at the International Monetary Fund (IMF) and John Zwaanstra Professor of International Studies and of Economics at Harvard University.

Robert Hockett is Edward Cornell Professor of Law and professor of public policy at Cornell University.

Karla Hoff is lead economist in the Development Research Group at the World Bank and co-director of the World Development Report 2015: *Mind, Society, and Behavior*.

Ravi Kanbur is T. H. Lee Professor of World Affairs, international professor of applied economics and management, and professor of economics at Cornell University.

Aart Kraay is senior advisor in the Macroeconomics and Growth Group of the Development Research Group at the World Bank.

Michael Kremer is Gates Professor of Developing Societies in the department of economics at Harvard University and serves as part-time scientific director of development Innovation Ventures at USAID.

David McKenzie is a lead economist on the Finance and Private Sector Development Team of the Development Research Group at the World Bank.

Célestin Monga is the chief economist and vice president, Economic Governance and Knowledge Management, African Development Bank.

Maurice Obstfeld is professor of economics at University of California, Berkeley, and a former economic counsellor and director of research at the International Monetary Fund.

Hamid Rashid is chief, Development Research, Economic Analysis and Policy Division, the United Nations Department of Economic and Social Affairs in New York.

Martin Ravallion holds the inaugural Edmond D. Villani Chair of Economics at Georgetown University. Prior to joining Georgetown he was the director of the World Bank's research department.

David Rosenblatt is manager of strategy and operations in the Development Unit at the World Bank.

Amartya Sen is Thomas W. Lamont University Professor, and professor of economics and philosophy at Harvard University. He is also a senior fellow at the Harvard Society of Fellows. He is the winner of the 1998 Nobel Prize in Economic Sciences.

Claudia Sepúlveda is a lead economist in the Development Economics Vice Presidency at the World Bank.

Luis Servén is senior advisor in the Macroeconomics and Growth Group of the Development Research Group at the World Bank.

Hyun Song Shin is economic adviser and head of research at the Bank of International Settlements.

Nicholas Stern is the IG Patel Professor of Economics and Government, London School of Economics and Political Science, and former president of the British Academy.

Joseph Stiglitz is university professor at Columbia University. He is the joint winner of the 2001 Nobel Memorial Prize in Economic Sciences.

Cass R. Sunstein is the Robert Walmsley University Professor at Harvard University.

Michael Toman is research manager of the Sustainable Development Team in the Development Research Group at the World Bank.

Jörgen W. Weibull is A. O. Wallenberg Professor of Economics at Stockholm School of Economics and visiting research fellow at Institute for Advanced Study (IAST) in Toulouse.

Index